PSEUDO-MARTYR

JOHN DONNE

PSEUDO-MARTYR

Wherein out of certaine propositions and gradations, this conclusion is evicted. That those which are of the Romane religion in this Kingdome, may and ought to take the Oath of Allegiance.

Edited,
with Introduction and Commentary by
Anthony Raspa

McGill-Queen's University Press
Montreal & Kingston • London • Buffalo

© McGill-Queen's University Press 1993

ISBN 0-7735-0994-1
Legal deposit second quarter 1993
Bibliothèque nationale du Québec

Printed in Canada on acid-free paper

This book has been published with the help of grants from the Canadian Federation for the Humanities, using funds provided by the Social Sciences and Humanities Research Council of Canada, and from the Faculté des Lettres, Université Laval.

Canadian Cataloguing in Publication Data
Donne, John, 1572–1631
Pseudo-martyr

Rev. ed.
ISBN 0-7735-0994-1

1. Donne, John, 1572–1631. Pseudo-Martyr.
2. Donne, John, 1572–1631–Religion.
3. England–Church history–17th century.
4. Catholics–England–History–17th century.
5. Church and state–England–History–17th century.
I. Raspa, Anthony.   II. Title.

BX1492.D66 1993   274.2'06   C93-090153-3

Typesetting: Carleton Production Centre, Ottawa

Pour Aurèle Thibault

CONTENTS

PREFACE — ix

ABBREVIATIONS — x

INTRODUCTION — xi

    I   The Occasion of Donne's Writing — xiii
    II The Meaning of *Pseudo-Martyr* — xxxviii
   III Copies of the Edition of 1610 — lv
   IV The Edition of 1610 — lix
    V   Biblical and Manuscript Sources — lxxi
   VI The Text — lxxviii

PSEUDO-MARTYR — 1

    The Epistle Dedicatorie — 3
    A Table of the Chapters — 5
    An Advertisement to the Reader — 8
    A Preface to the Priestes and Jesuits — 11
    The Chapters — 29

COMMENTARY — 269

FINDING LIST — 419

PREFACE

The editor must express his thanks to his former colleagues at the Université du Québec à Chicoutimi for the sabbatical year that permitted the preparation of a large part of this edition, to the Social Sciences and Humanities Research Council of Canada that supported the project with a leave fellowship grant and with a subsequent two-year research grant for its completion, to the Fondation de l'Université du Québec à Chicoutimi that generously supported the preparation of the final manuscript of the edition, to the Département des littératures at Laval that awarded a publication grant, and to the Master and Fellows of Pembroke college in Cambridge for their practical support during several research periods.

Considerable thanks are due to the librarians in the rare books room of the Cambridge University Library and to their reference librarians, and also to Father Dominique Gravel of the Grand Séminaire de Chicoutimi Library; to the librarians of York Minster Library who deposited their three copies in the C.U.L. rare books room for collation, as did the librarians of Queen's, Magdalen and Emmanuel colleges in Cambridge with their single copies; to John Sparrow and the librarians of Queen's and New colleges in Oxford who deposited their copies in the Bodleian Library for the same purpose; to Christina Thiele of the Carleton Production Centre in Ottawa who worked to develop a computer programme for this edition with the diligence and professionalism that an author-editor dreams of finding, without ever believing that he will; to Margaret Crosby of Montreal for her instruction on how to set up the manuscript of a critical edition, which has never failed me; and to my research assistants Marion Sinclair and Andrea Snadden.

Université Laval, Québec,
May, 1992

ABBREVIATIONS

The following are editions of Donne and major criticisms of his work quoted repeatedly in the Introduction and Commentary, and are referred to by short title.

I. DONNE'S WORKS:

Biathanatos. Edited by Ernest W. Sullivan. University of Delaware Press: Newark, N.J., 1984.

Devotions Upon Emergent Occasions. Edited by A. Raspa. Oxford University Press: Oxford and New York, 1987.

Ignatius His Conclave. Edited by Timothy Healy. Oxford University Press: Oxford, 1969.

Poetical Works, 2 Vols. Edited by H.J.C. Grierson. Oxford University Press: Oxford, 1912.

II. CRITICAL AND BIBLIOGRAPHICAL WORKS:

R.C. Bald. *John Donne: A Life*. Oxford University Press: Oxford, 1970.

John Carey. *John Donne: Life, Mind and Art*. Oxford University Press: New York, 1981.

Sir Geoffrey Keynes. *Bibliography of Dr. John Donne* [Fourth edition]. Oxford University Press: Oxford, 1973.

INTRODUCTION

Pseudo-Martyr is a vast, not easily read work by which one of the leading figures of English Renaissance literature made his entry into published writing. It was composed at a moment of extreme political and religious tension between Rome and London at the end of the first decade of the seventeenth century, with the ostensible object of convincing Roman Catholics in England that they could take the Oath of Allegiance to the British monarch without betraying their spiritual loyalty to Rome. The full title of the work about propositions, gradations, conclusions, the Oath of Allegiance and Roman Catholics points to its surface purpose in some detail, and Donne never wrote another work nearly as long or annotated with such complexity.

Woven into *Pseudo-Martyr*'s religio-political discussion, however, are many other interrelated issues about the Bible, Revelation, the physical world, society, the family and the written word. These issues were as profoundly interesting to Donne as the question of the Oath of Allegiance for Catholics, and they often relegate the ostensible purpose of the work to the background. The effect of this for the modern reader, who has been brought up by twentieth-century literary tradition to expect captivating wit and haunting sensibility of Donne, is that *Pseudo-Martyr* seems to move crab-like. Because Donne focuses and refocuses his attention on secondary issues that engrossed him, the complexity of the work is such that it now appears penetrable only with difficulty. Paradoxically, these issues that complicate the reading of *Pseudo-Martyr* for a modern reader are more vital today than its declared aim of reconciling Catholics to the English throne. The assumption that the world lacks models to judge its institutions often underlies the secondary issues which Donne discusses, and these secondary issues also contain a peculiarly modern ring that the individual conscience must define its path as well as follow it. As a person Donne himself is probably ultimately intelligible only with our grasp of *Pseudo-Martyr*'s supposedly secondary issues, and it is not so much the issues as his inability to resist the temptation to discuss them that distracts us. With the integration of *Pseudo-Martyr* into our appreciation of Donne, much of the unnecessary enigma about his religious conversion, his political commitments and his motives fades away.

Pseudo-Martyr is a work by an early-middle-aged ex-Catholic about loyalty to one's universal God, to one's Protestant king, and to one's interior self. If it is complex, it was made so by the enormous moral and physical effort that it took to write, and by the magnitude of the issues that Donne felt compelled to raise. *Pseudo-Martyr* examines the forms of loyalty to God, country and self, through no less than the long Christian dualistic tradition of matter and spirit, eternity and time, and their expression in church and state, in a Renaissance society which had only recently in historical terms come to disagree violently about what these meant. The work therefore tries to reorder a universe of ideas to address itself to a single current issue. Because of the magnitude of the intellectual effort involved, this need to re-order a universe of thought led Donne to raise all the major moral, literary and philosophical issues that were to concern him for the remaining brief twenty years of his life.[1] Before *Pseudo-Martyr*, Donne had destined for publication only a few short celebratory poems in the volumes of other writers like Ben Jonson.[2] Coming rapidly after these published pieces, *Pseudo-Martyr* is vast not because it is his first major published work, but because it represents the literary synthesis of the ideas of a major writer embarking comparatively late in life on a literary career which a political situation enables him to set into motion.

---

[1] As Bald writes in *Life*, p. 232, in *Pseudo-Martyr* as in *Biathanatos*, "it is clear that Donne's emotions as well as his thinking, and indeed his whole way of life, were insensibly becoming involved in the solution of such theological problems."

[2] The prefatory poem to the 1607 edition of Jonson's *Volpone*, entitled "*Amicissimo et meretissimo* Ben: Ionson;" and also "The Expiration" in Alfonso Ferrabosco's book of *Ayres* of 1609.

I
The Occasion of Donne's Writing

Donne's *Pseudo-Martyr* is a journalistic work in the sense that it addresses itself to a current political situation in a topical fashion. The situation was the martyrdom that menaced English Catholics for their refusal to take the Oath of Allegiance to James I. *Pseudo-Martyr* deals with this situation, as the serious journalistic article normally deals with its story, in the terms in which it was understood and discussed on the day in mid-January of 1610 when the work went on sale as on a newsstand at the bookseller Walter Burre's shop at the Sign of the Crane in Saint Paul's Churchyard in London.

To try to take *Pseudo-Martyr* more or less seriously than an important journalistic work is to misrepresent its purpose and the occasion which prompted Donne to write it. *Pseudo-Martyr* is not a vaulting piece of imaginative literature and it is not a failed piece of such literature either. It is, rather, part of a current affairs debate that reflected morally on all Englishmen and touched Catholics and non-Catholics alike. *Pseudo-Martyr* therefore engaged the attention of Donne's reading public as apartheid in South Africa engaged the attention of the international public in the eighties, or the so-called student revolts in the sixties, or the Nuremberg trials in the forties of the present century. Like the editorial writings on these events in Western newspapers, *Pseudo-Martyr* took a side and tried to convince English Catholics that they could take the Oath of Allegiance without betraying their Roman faith. In his detailed argument in by far the longest single work that he ever wrote, Donne supported his position with references to hundreds of authorities. These references, Keynes has written, serve to make *Pseudo-Martyr* "dull reading." Elsewhere, Evelyn Simpson quotes to even more derogatory effect an unpublished letter of Donne's biographer, Augustus Jessopp, to her. "Who but a monomaniac," Jessopp asks, "would read *Pseudo-Martyr* through?" Simpson herself is only a little kinder, and writes that "*Pseudo-Martyr* is a striking example of an almost unreadable book written by a man of genius."[3]

---

[3]Keynes, *Bibliography*, p. 4; E.M. Simpson, *A Study of the Prose Works of John Donne* (Oxford, 1948), p. 179, n. 1, and p. 2.

However, Donne's references were not overwhelming to his readers, although they may be to us. His references were as journalistic as the occasion of his writing because they practically all somehow pertained essentially to rousing new works that dealt with the Roman Catholic martyrdom on which he was commenting. The works behind his references were as well known to his readers as to him, and if they are a stumbling block to us, the reason is that as in all cases of journalism there is nothing as stale as the events behind yesterday's news. *Pseudo-Martyr* is much too long to be a tract and too annotated to correspond even vaguely to modern standards of popular reading. But Donne included hundreds of references to contemporary political works along with, and according to, the standards of humanist annotation because he wished to give his work authority as his age understood it. He thus applied an essentially scholarly system of reference to the discussion found in popular contemporary political tracts in a work that was neither a humanist treatise nor a tract. The uniqueness of *Pseudo-Martyr*, which makes it difficult reading, is that it harnesses the scholarly methods of humanist works to the written discussion of contemporary issues. This discussion, which we expect to move quickly, is repeatedly slowed down by the presence of humanist methodology.

However, Donne's gentry readers, unlike even the informed modern readers of journalistic works, lived in another social structure and had limitless time to read. The three years that it took for the first answer to be published against *Pseudo-Martyr* is testimony to the length of time over which topical contemporary political writings were absorbed by the reading public, even on issues that affected them daily in questions of, literally, life and death.[4] *Pseudo-Martyr*'s profound dimension of autobiography and philosophical concern therefore was a characteristic of the manner in which current affairs were absorbed in an age that had the press but no news media. Speed was not a priority, and there was much time in the contemplation of current affairs in Donne's day for the exploration of their philosophical dimension and of

---

[4]Thomas Fitzherbert, *A supplement to the discussion of M.D. Barlowes answere To the Iudgement of a Catholike Englishman etc. interrupted by the death of the Author F. Robert Persons of the Society of Iesus. . . And By the way is briefly censured M. John Dunnes Booke, intituled Pseudo-martyr. . . By F.T.*, 1613, pp. 80–110.

INTRODUCTION

the life of the author in relation to his ideas. Happily, literary history benefits from the slow absorption of current affairs by Donne's readers because it allowed one of the most enigmatic and fascinating writers of the English Renaissance to reveal himself intellectually in public, sometimes nobly and sometimes not. For, in doing so, Donne threw considerable light for us on recusant attitudes towards allegiance to the monarch, as he tried to convince his ex-co-religionists how to be faithfully Catholic and loyally English at the same time, in a world that for them quartered both.

The title of Donne's *Pseudo-Martyr* was itself au courant. The word was being bandied about by disputants in the current battle of martyrologies between the Catholic Church and the English reformers. The battle of martyrologies was a competition over official lists of Christian martyrs and saints. At stake was the question of whose martyrs and saints were the real ones, and no less than four of Donne's major religio-political opponents in *Pseudo-Martyr*, before the publication of his work, were using the terminology of his title against Protestants in their martyrological publications, some perhaps inspired by Burghley's description of Edmund Campion as a pseudo-martyr in *The Execution of Justice in England* in 1583. The Catholic opponents who before Donne dealt with pseudo-martyrdom were pillars of the Counter-Reformation. They were the Oratorian Cardinal Caesar Baronius, who succeeded the founder of the Oratory, Saint Philip Neri, as superior-general of the order; then, one of the major controversialists against the English Reformers, the Jesuit Robert Parsons; next, the internationally known Spanish Jesuit, historian, biographer and bibliographer, Pedro de Ribadeneira; and finally, the Franciscan controversialist Franciscus Feuardentius who in 1604 attacked the "Pseudo-martyrs of the heretics."[5]

The title of *Pseudo-Martyr* was an attempt by Donne to turn the current of the controversy over the martyrologies against the Roman disputants. For about two recent generations, the new English establishment had been officially claiming martyrdom as a mark of many of its reformers, and Donne's *Pseudo-Martyr* was an attempt to reverse the tide in its favour (pp. 128–129,

---

[5] Bald has already noted Parsons' use of the pseudomartyrial terminology, *Life*, p. 223; also William Cecil, Lord Burghley, *The Execution of Justice in England* and William Allen's *A True, Sincere and Modest Defense of English Catholics*, ed. by R.M. Kingdom (Ithaca, N.Y., 1965), p. 18; and Feuardentius, *Theomachia Calvinistica* (Paris, 1604), Book 8, Chapter 13, No. 12, p. 246.

162). The battle of martyrologies had been started in England itself, moreover, by the Protestant John Foxe with the publication in London in 1563 of the first English edition of his *Actes and Monuments* listing the persecutions of Protestants in Britain. Foxe's work, which was republished in several editions for half a century, shocked the Catholic world.[6] He proposed a new basis for sainthood rooted in the history of the English Church instead of in Roman canonization. He also provided a list of saints and martyrs conforming to his new historical norm of canonization to demonstrate that sainthood existed in the English Church before Rome appropriated it with legal canonization. In his *Actes*, Foxe sought to relocate the canonization of martyrs and other saints into the hands of the Established Church by using the pre-existing martyrologies like the Venerable Bede's list of saints as authoritative historical precedents.[7] These precedents were the norm to judge the sanctity of the suffering of current Protestant martyrs in the name of Christ.

The reply from the Continent and the persecuted underground Catholic mission in England was quick and elaborate. The polemical answer to Foxe was that his list of saints was constituted of originally Catholic saints somewhat interspersed with the names of recent Protestant pseudo-martyrs. The Roman reply, moreover, was carefully worked out over two generations, and it had just been given a new volley with a new English-Catholic martyrology only two years before *Pseudo-Martyr* appeared, and it was only to peter out towards the end of the 1620s, in 1627, with the publication of the Jesuit George Keynes' translation of Baronius' martyrology.[8] It is a measure of the deep effect of Foxe's *Actes* on the Counter-Reformation consciousness that it seems responsible, if not wholly, then at least in some significant measure for five Catholic martyrologies that appeared in Latin and English in the half

---

[6]Published in London by John Day. Other editions followed in 1570, 1583 and 1596.

[7]Foxe, *Actes*, p. 453, Col. B, and also in the 1583 edition, Vol. I, Sigs.*iiii^{r-v}. Foxe's *Commentarii Rerum in Ecclesia Gestarum* of 1554 was a short trial run of the first Latin version of 1559–1563, and of the first English version of 1563.

[8]Caesar Baronius, *Martyrologium Romanum, ad novam Kalendarii Rationem, et Ecclesiasticae Historiae veritatem restituem*, Antwerp, 1589; George Keynes, *The Roman Martyrology according to the Reformed Calendar. Faithfully translated out of Latin in English*, St. Omer, 1627.

century that followed. The underlying purpose of these Catholic martyrologies touched to some extent on the need to counter the appropriation by the English Established Church of the right to determine who could be called saint and martyr and be described as abiding venerably with the Lord.

Significantly, the battle of the martyrologies resituated the attention of both Catholics and Protestants in the matter of canonization from the past to the present. Canonization was no longer the domain of the often legendary figures who had lived and died in a faraway past, but came to be thought of internationally in terms of present martyrs. The martyrological battle refocused the attention of Christians on both political sides onto the sixteenth-century figures whose memory was still very much alive among many who had known them personally. It also drew into the contemporary self-consciousness in the early seventeenth century the question of one's own life among people who, if they managed to be still alive, nevertheless faced the prospect of an impending martyr's death with the promise of a place in a martyrology. The great relevance of *Pseudo-Martyr* therefore was that it addressed itself to minority English Catholics for whom lay waiting the uncivilized horror of execution by being hanged, drawn and quartered, and dissolved in boiling oil at the traitor's gibbet at Tyburn outside London, with the possibility of their inclusion in the Catholic calendar of martyrs as their reward. Because of its title therefore, and also because martyrdom was a looming present experience for oneself rather than the reserve of pious individuals in an abstract past, *Pseudo-Martyr* contributed to the momentum of a continuing martyrial controversy while addressing itself to the particular problem of the Catholic swearing to the Oath of Allegiance to James I. Donne's work is in fact the first major English reformed statement on martyrdom after Foxe's *Actes*.

Baronius' *Martyrologium* of 1589, the first of the four Catholic works to deal with pseudo-martyrs and to contribute to the title of Donne's book, had considerable tradition behind it. *Martyrologium* in fact reaffirmed Catholic thinking entirely. Until Foxe's *Actes*, the Catholic tradition of martyrdom had filled out exclusively the martyrial panorama of Christendom, and it claimed as its origin the decretals of the early Roman Church. For fifteen hundred years, the Church had spread its missionary martyrs throughout Europe, missionaries who answered to Rome for their sanctity and were canonized by it through a process of law. The earliest authorities of the Catholic tradition of martyrdom were Tertullian and Eusebius of Donne's marginalia (p. 35). Baronius' *Martyrologium* was a restatement of that position with the same ancient authorities and the same process of law.⁹ In addition, Baronius' *Martyrologium* was the official answer of the Counter-Reformation to the new catalogues of Protestant martyrs, it fixed a new corrected calendar for the liturgical celebration of saints and its preface introduces the word *pseudomartyris* over several folio pages of discussion to describe those who, because they were outside the church, like the Protestant martyrs of Mary Tudor's reign, could not have been martyrs even though they died for their ideas.¹⁰ *Martyrologium* made no attack on *Actes* by title, but its reassertion of the Roman origins of martyrdom was an obvious answer by Baronius to Foxe.

By contrast, Parsons' Catholic martyrology in *A Treatise of Three Conversions of England from Paganisme to Christian Religion* of 1603, which is the second work to contribute directly to the terminology of the title of Donne's work, was specifically designed to answer Foxe. Parsons repeated the charge of "pseudomartyres" against the executed, mainly Marian Reformers. In fact, two of the three thick octavo volumes of Parsons' *Conversions* are a chronological month by month examination and rebuttal of the calendar of "pseudomartyrs" of Foxe's *Actes*.¹¹ As in Baronius' martyrology, Parsons' grounds for the rebuttal were that martyrdom was impossible to the Reformers because they were outside the pale of the Church, an argument which in *Pseudo-Martyr* Donne several times takes onto himself to attack (pp. 126, 128–129, 150–151, 160–161).

Finally, the charge of *pseudomartyres* against the executed English reformers returns in Ribadeneira's *Illustrium Scriptorum . . . Societatis Iesu* of 1602 (Antwerp), of which a new Latin edition appeared early in the very same year that Donne set pen to paper for *Pseudo-Martyr*. Ribadeneira was already well known on the English religio-political scene for his *Historia Ecclesiastica del scisma del Rey de Inglaterra* of 1588, which condemned the execution of Mary Stuart as a desperate Tudor attempt to justify their illegal hold on the

---

⁹Baronius, *Martyrologium*, p. xxiv.

¹⁰Baronius, *Martyrologium*, pp. xxiii–xxiv: "Cum autem viderent haeretici Catholicam Dei ecclesiam spiritualibus charismatibus affluentem, innumerisque sanctorum Martyrum trophaeis nobilitatam: eius gloriam aemulantes, et ipsi Martyres fingere, pseudomartyres habere, et falsa Martyrologia conscribere studuerunt . . . ."

¹¹Robert Parsons, *A Treatise of Three Conversions. . . By N.D.*, 3 vols., (n.p., 1603), Part 3, Vol. III, Sig. F⁷ᵛ. Parts 1 and 2 are contained in Volume I, and Part 3 listing the martyrology is in Volumes II and III.

English throne.¹² Ribadeneira's new work, *Illustrium*, must have appeared as a continuing attack on English attempts at legal political settlement and it praises Parsons' martyrology as an attack "against the pestilence of the work of the pseudo-martyr Foxe."¹³ Within a year of the new edition of *Illustrium*, Donne's answer to Baronius', Parsons' and Ribadeneira's charges was that contemporary English Catholics by refusing to take the Oath of Allegiance were the real pseudo-martyrs, and, throughout his work, Donne refers to the points made by all four Catholic controversialists, particularly Baronius, to turn English Catholics against the sacrifice of their lives before the exigencies of James' oath (p. 123).

Therefore the background to *Pseudo-Martyr* is replete with references to the works of the Catholic martyrologists who had so far morally sustained the English Catholic objectors to the oath. In Donne's writing, there are not only references to Baronius, Parsons, Feuardentius and Ribadeneira who gave birth to the pseudo-martyrial terminology of his title, but to other lesser figures too. There is the unidentified "I.W.", the author of *The English Martyrologie*, who was probably one of two Catholic priests John Wilson or George Keynes. There is also Florimond de Raemond, the French apologist and historian, who was credited with the history of the heresy in England which was actually written by his son François. Keynes' or Wilson's *Martyrologe* contained *a Summary of the Lives of the glorious and renowned Saintes of the three Kingdomes, England, Scotland, and Ireland, collected and distributed into Moneths, after the forme of a Calendar*, and appeared in 1608 two years before *Pseudo-Martyr*. *Martyrologe* was an attempt to prove that an English tradition of martyrdom existed from primitive times, as Foxe claimed, but

---

¹²In 1588, the work appeared in Madrid with a full title explaining its purpose: *Historia Eccesiastica del scisma del Rey de Inglaterra; En la qual tratan las cosas mas notables que han sucedido en aquel Reyno, tocantes à nuestra santa Religion, desde que comenco hast a la muerte de la Reyna de Escocia.*

¹³*Illustrium Scriptorum Religionis Societatis Iesu Catalogus* (Lyons, 1609), pp. 176–177; "*Martyrologium Catholicum*, contra pestilens opus Foxi pseudomartyrium." This edition was the third, and the first edition appeared in Antwerp in 1602.

that this tradition was Roman Catholic and not Protestant.[14] Then, Raemond's translation into French of Tertullian's *Aux martyrs* (Lyons, 1595) was a prelude to his long, full *Histoire de la Naissance, Progrèz et Décadence de l'Hérésie de ce Siècle* (Paris, 1605). It is the sixth book on England of this history, written by Florimond's son François, that so provoked Donne several times in *Pseudo-Martyr*. François de Raemond described Foxe's martyrology as an attempt by the "heretics to give some lustre to the infamie of their bastard religion."[15] Two other English-Catholic martyrologies form part of *Pseudo-Martyr*'s background. They are *A Relation of sixteene martyrs: glorified in England in twelve monthes* of 1601 by an anonymous "T.W.", who could have been the Jesuit Thomas Worthington, and also *A Catalogue of martyrs in England: for profession of the Catholique faith, since the year of our Lord 1535 . . . unto this year 1608* (Douai) by an "Anonymous Priest," who could have been Lawrence Kellam or again Thomas Worthington.[16] However, Donne mentions neither of these.

In addition to the martyrologists and the commentators on martyrologies, several related biographies of saints and beatified Catholics lie prominently in *Pseudo-Martyr*'s background. Moreover, Donne often mentions the biographers themselves and their own lives. The great majority of these biographers and their holy subjects were people of the Counter-Reformation whose canonization had been obtained or was being sought even though they were only most recently dead, and Donne associated them directly with the question of martyrologies and martyrs, for and against his cause.

The biographies in question included prominently the two lives of Ignatius Loyola, the founder of the Jesuits, both by the same Ribadeneira who wrote

---

[14] The title page of *The English Martyrologe* of 1608 indicates that it was written "By a Catholicke Priest," and the work contains a prefatory "Epistle" signed "I.W."

[15] Raemond's translation of Tertullian's *Ad Martyres* under the title of *Aux Martyrs* appeared in *Erreur Populaire de la Papesse Jane* (Lyons, 1595). His *L'Histoire de la Naissance, Progrèz, et Décadence de l'Hérésie de ce Siècle* was published in eight books contained in two volumes in Paris in 1605. Book 6, in Volume II, on the English heresy was written by his son François, whose description of Foxe's *Actes* appears in Chapter 11, p. 72a.

[16] The author of *A Relation of sixteene martyrs*, which was published in Douai, was identified as "T.W." on the title page; the author of *A Catalogue of martyrs*, which also appeared in Douai, was identified even yet more simply as "Anon. Pr."

INTRODUCTION   xxi

against Protestant pseudo-martyrs. Ribadeneira's first biography was the major official life, *Vita Ignatii Loiolae*, that appeared in Spanish in Madrid as early as 1572 and that was quickly printed in several Latin editions.[17] Ribadeneira's second biography was the abbreviated life that he prefaced to his list of Loyola's writings in the first edition of his bibliography of the works of the members of the Jesuit order and published in 1602 exactly thirty years later.[18]

Donne also refers to yet two other biographies of Jesuits by Ribadeneira, those of James Layné and Francis Borgia, respectively the second and the third superiors-general of the Jesuit order, that also appeared in *Illustrium. . . Catalogus* of 1602. Donne was apparently using the later edition of 1609.[19] He also referred at considerable length to Virgilius Ceparius' life of the young Jesuit Aloysius Gonzaga, namely to the first Latin edition of 1608, two years after the original Italian edition, and equally to the derivative 1606 Latin edition of Antonio Gallanio's life of Saint Philip Neri, who founded the Congregation of the Oratory in Rome in 1585.[20] Donne also documented his arguments abundantly with references to the Franciscan Henry Sedulius' *Apologeticus adversus Alcoran Franciscorum*, which was effectively a defence of the life of Saint Francis of Assisi, and to a lesser extent with references to the life of

---

[17] The original Spanish edition of Ribadeneira's work appeared in Madrid in 1572, and was published in the same year in Naples in the first Latin edition, *Vita Ignatii Loiolae, Qui religionem Clericorum Societatis Iesu instituit*. Several other Latin editions followed in Cologne in 1602, in Mainz in 1603 and again in Cologne in 1604.

[18] *Illustrium Scriptorum. . .Catalogus* printed in Antwerp in 1602, which lists the Jesuit writers alphabetically, and precedes the writings of each Jesuit with a brief biography.

[19] In his references to the lives of the three Jesuits, Loyola, Layné and Borgia, Donne follows the pagination of the Lyons edition of 1609 rather than that of the edition of 1602. See Commentary, pp. 102, ll. 18–21.

[20] The title page of Ceparius' life of Gonzaga, published in Valencia in 1609, indicates that it is the second edition, but it must be added of the Latin edition first published in Cologne in 1608. The first edition of the work as such appeared in Italian in Rome in 1606. As Donne's references to Ceparius' *Vita* indicate, particularly in the marginalia of p. 108, he was using a copy of the Latin Cologne edition of 1608. In his references to the founder of the Oratory, Donne was using a copy of the 1606 Mainz Latin edition of Gallanio's life of Neri (see Commentary, p. 94, l. 22–p. 95, l. 2).

Saint Cajetan who, in the first wave of the Counter-Reformation, founded the order of the Theatines in Rome in 1524 to reform the non-ordered clergy.[21] There is therefore an extensive, immediate background of martyrial and hagiologic literature that gave to Donne's reader, beginning with the very title of his work, a vital sense of the issue with which he was dealing. A considerable number of Donne's notes therefore that confounded Jessopp and Keynes become quite easy to digest once we can identify their literary provenance as we read.

Similarly, a great number of *Pseudo-Martyr*'s references, in Italian, French, Spanish and Latin as well as English (for these were Donne's five languages), fall readily into the mould of current literature on spiritual and secular power. These references deal with the spiritual power of secular rulers, the secular power of spiritual rulers, and the dependence and independence of each of the two in relation to the other. The literature in which these references originated constitutes the second major backdrop to Donne's *Pseudo-Martyr* after the martyrologies and hagiologies, and one of the original characteristics of *Pseudo-Martyr* in the literature of its times is that it brought these two questions of martyrs and saints and of state authority, of both the English reformers and the counter-reformers, into the confines of a single treatise under one cover. The issue of the relations between secular and spiritual powers was perforce closely related to the question of the Oath of Allegiance, and often in *Pseudo-Martyr* appears to have interested Donne more than the oath itself.

The immediate historical background to Donne's discussion of state and church power was of course common early seventeenth-century knowledge. James I had had the Oath of Allegiance passed quickly by act of Parliament late in 1605 and early in 1606 to protect his crown against the recurrence of incidents like the recent Gunpowder Plot of early November 1605 to blow up the Houses of Parliament with everybody in them. To refuse to take the oath, if one was asked to do so, became treason. The punishment, which need not be enforced, was a martyr's death at Tyburn. The immediate precedents for the oath were the various versions of the Act of Supremacy that dated back almost three-quarters of a century to Henry VIII's break with Rome, and to Elizabeth's Protestant settlement before her excommunication by Pius V in

---

[21] Henry Sedulius, *Apologeticus adversus Alcoran Franciscorum* (Antwerp, 1607) (see Commentary, p. 58, ll. 24–30; also pp. 80–82); for Cajetan's foundation of the order of the Theatines, see Commentary, p. 102, ll. 12–17.

1570. The oath was therefore a question associated with the prickly issue of the legality of kingship as well as with the loyalty of subjects to their secular monarchs.[22] In the immediate background of *Pseudo-Martyr*, the question of the oath was being argued out in the light of two more recent papal *breves* by Paul V of 10 October 1606 and 10 September 1607. These *breves* absolved Catholics in England specifically, and everywhere in Europe generally, of loyalty to their heretical monarchs. The English case was made additionally complicated for Catholics because the monarchs of England had made themselves head of the church, so that a Catholic swearing loyalty to such a monarch as a secular ruler, was also indirectly swearing his fealty to him as head of a heretical church and apparently therefore abjuring loyalty to the papacy.

In his attempt to convince Roman Catholics that nevertheless they could take the Oath of Allegiance, Donne argued that the oath bound them in loyalty to James as temporal ruler alone. To illustrate his argument, and to render concrete and refute the numerous objections that the oath could raise in troubled Catholic minds, Donne appealed principally to three extremely important religio-political events in recent and medieval European history. All three incidents touched directly on the definition of secular and spiritual powers. They had peculiarly little direct relevance to the oath, but came nevertheless to account for a considerable number of the references in Donne's marginalia. To identify these events makes sense of a whole vast segment of Donne's apparently disconnected notes, and the first readers of Donne's *Pseudo-Martyr* were not the monomaniacs that Jessopp thought they must have been if they read the work through, but were simply familiar with the literature of their times.

The three incidents were, firstly, the conflict between Paul V and the state of Venice which had only just been resolved by diplomacy. The second was the simmering quarrel between the Spanish crown and the papacy over the

---

[22]Pius V's bull excommunicating Elizabeth was entitled "Regnans in Ecclesia," and it absolved her subjects from any oath of allegiance that they might in the past have made to her. Henry's Parliament passed the Act of Supremacy making him the head of the church in 1534, and revised versions followed under Elizabeth in 1552 and 1559. In his *Life* of Donne, Walton interestingly refers to the "Oath of Supremacy and Allegeance" with respect to Donne's composition of *Pseudo-Martyr*: John Donne, *Poetry and Prose*, prefaced by Walton's *Life* (Oxford, 1967), p. xxv.

right of the Hispanic emperors to hold a "spiritual monarchy" over the kingdom of Sicily which they owned territorially. And the third was the now historic twelfth-century quarrel between Pope Saint Gregory VII and the German Emperor Henry IV over lay investiture. The majority of Donne's political references in *Pseudo-Martyr*, extraordinarily numerous though they are, and though they now appear painfully disparate, referred Donne's readers back to the exploration of these three incidents in the context of the English Catholic having to live with a Protestant king. Notably all three incidents, Venice, Sicily and Germany, involved Catholic monarchs, and in all three the papacy had somehow finished by sharing power in the sense that some new demarcation was drawn between the rights of secular rulers and those of the popes. Donne's request to contemporary popes in *Pseudo-Martyr* was that they should be as conciliatory to England as they had been to the Venetian, to the Spanish and to the German rulers, and to free the English-Catholic conscience from having to refuse to swear fealty to James.[23]

The vast net of Donne's references to secular and spiritual authorities in *Pseudo-Martyr* has therefore much more design than a cursory, discouraging modern look at his marginalia reveals. The same sort of discouragement may also befall future generations looking at any late twentieth-century event unless they bother to find the thread running through it. The single nightmare thread of Arab terrorism and of its European supporters throughout the 1980s linked within a few months a considerable number of names of people and places that include Action Directe, the camp of Chatila, Georges Abdallah and his brothers, Ronald Reagan, Donald Regan, the White House, Whitehall, Paris, Rome, Athens, Gadhafi, Charles Ray, Libya, Jacques Vergès, Iraq and Khomeini. But who in three centuries will be able to identify the faces and the interrelated significances of the names with only a cursory look? Donne's audience would have understood the names in his marginalia with little difficulty, their authors would have been current writers and the works of these authors must have sat on their shelves if they sat on Donne's. In fact, four separate collections alone of tracts, responses and letters, all of them on the Venetian controversy and appearing in the single year of 1607, are the identifiable sources of a considerable number of names, works, notes and quotations in *Pseudo-Martyr*, which look absolutely disparate if their provenance is ignored. These four collections on the controversy between Paul and

---

[23] See Commentary for p. 15, ll. 1–4.

INTRODUCTION   xxv

the Doge and the senate of Venice are *Raccolta degli Scritti . . . co' Signori Venetiani*, published in Rome;[24] second, the *Controversiae Memorabilis Inter Paulum V Pontifex Max. et Venetos*, also printed in Rome;[25] third, the collection of *Consulta, Lettere* and *Discorsi* bound together without separate title page, probably also in 1607;[26] and, fourth, another collection, this time of *Aviso, Riposta, Dialogia* and *Avvertimenti*, in large part originally published in Bologna, and most likely issued in 1607 as well.[27]

The web of names covered by these four volumes in Donne's marginalia is extraordinary. Donne sometimes refers to both the real names and to the pseudonyms behind the faces indiscriminately as in the case of the pro-Venetian controversialist Giovanni Marsilio who wrote under the alias of Nicolas Crassus, and of the German Catholic controversialist Gaspar Schopp who sometimes signed himself Nicodemus Macrus.[28] Other names in these volumes appearing in Donne's marginalia include Lelio Medici of Piacentino, the inquisitor-general of Florence; Fra Paolo Sarpi the Venetian of the order of the Servites;[29] Matthew Tortus, which Donne did not know was the Jesuit

---

[24] *Raccolta degli Scritti usciti fuori in istampi, escritti a mano, nella causa del P. Paolo V co' Signori Venetiani. Secondo le Stampe di Venetia, di Roma, & d'altri luoghi*, Rome, 1607.

[25] *Controversiae Memorabilis Inter Paulum V Pontifex Max. et Venetos; De Excommunicatione contra eodem Venetos Romae promulgata XVII. Aprilis anno MDCVI*, Rome, 1607.

[26] *Consulta, Lettere* and *Discorsi*, by Fra Giovanni-Battista Palmerio Romito, Jacques Leschassier, Simone Sardi, Giovanni Filoteo d'Asti, Nicholas Crassus, Hieronomus Vendramenus, among others (Cambridge University Library shelf mark Acton C.7.22).

[27] *Aviso, Riposta, Dialogia, Discorso, Avvertimenti*, by Antonio Quirino, Lelio Medici of Piacentino, Teodoro Eugenio of Famagosta, Paolo Anafesto, Giovanni Bertolotti, Fra Paolo Venetiano, Matthew Tortus or Cardinal Bellarmine, and Baldassaro Nardi, among others (Cambridge University Library shelf mark Hhh. 606).

[28] See Commentary, p. 83, ll. 4–15.

[29] Donne refers to the moderate positions of both Medici and Sarpi during the Venetian controversy (see Commentary, p. 86, ll. 4–11, and p. 187). Medici's and Sarpi's tracts appeared in the collected papers of *Raccolta degli Scritti* (Rome, 1607), and in *Aviso, Riposta, Dialogia, Discorso, Avvertimenti* (mainly Bologna, ?1607).

Cardinal Robert Bellarmine's pseudonym, as well as Bellarmine writing under his own name;[30] Fra Giovanni Battista Palmerio Romito of Venice; Paul V himself, as his bull of 1606 excommunicating the Venetians was republished as a preface to *Controversiae Memorabilis*;[31] the Oratorian Cardinal Baronius who in addition to being the author of the new official Roman martyrology some twenty years earlier, was now also involved in the Venetian controversy that shook Italy; Jean Gerson, the early fifteenth-century Protestant Chancellor of the University of Paris, as though he were a contemporary political commentator because the defenders of the Venetian cause used his conciliar arguments on the restriction of papal power, in fact so effectively that it was Cardinal Bellarmine who was compelled to answer them;[32] the Venetian master of philosophy and Carmelite theologian Giovanni Antonio Bovio, and Francis Bozio the controversialist who was one of the first members of Neri's Oratory.[33]

Yet another collection of tracts, the *Monita Politica, ad Sacri Romani Imperii Principes*, again touching on the relationships between secular and spiritual rulers, though not exclusively about Venice, has the same web-like effect as the above collections of providing the cogent source of a number of Donne's seemingly disconnected notes under one cover. These notes include references to the *Monita Politica* itself, to Caesar Branchaura of Taurinus, to the letter of the Emperor Maximilian I of Germany to his counsellor, and finally to the long letter of the French diplomat, the Swiss-born Cardinal Duperron, to the French king Henry of Navarre during his role in the peace negotiations between Venice and the papacy. This letter, extraordinarily, was published in the *Monita* volume in the original French, in Latin translation

---

[30] See Commentary, p. 118, ll. 2–11; in *Controversiae Memorabilis*, p. 441, and *Aviso, Riposta, Dialogia*.

[31] See Commentary, p. 104, ll. 16–20.

[32] In *Controversiae Memorabilis*, p. 443, immediately after Gerson's *Tractus et Resolution circa volorem excommunciationum*, on p. 427; Bellarmine's *Responsio* bears the place and date of Rome, 1607; also in *Raccolta degli Scritti*, 1607, in Italian translation, pp. 292 and 309.

[33] Both Bovio and Bozio defended papal power, the former in *Riposta. . . Alle Considerationi del Padre Maestro Paolo da Venetia*, Rome and Bologna, 1606, against Paolo Sarpi; and the latter in *De Temporali Ecclesiae Monarchia et Iurisdictione* of 1602. See Commentary, p. 188, l. 28–p. 189, l. 10; p. 86, ll. 4–11; p. 16, ll. 9–11.

for international reading, and in Italian translation for maximum diffusion in Italy.[34]

Of the three controversies between the Catholic rulers of Venice, Sicily and Germany, and the papacy, that Donne used to illustrate his argument about swearing to English Catholics, the Venetian affair provided him with the most detailed parallel with the English cause. It was also precisely contemporary. The controversy had only just broken out in 1605, although it was unconnected in every conceivable way with the vigorous reapplication of the English Oath of Allegiance. On 17 April 1606, Paul V excommunicated the Doge of Venice Leonardo Dona and his senate for the specific reason of refusing to recognize the immunity of clerics from secular courts. Generally in the background of the dispute which had been brewing for several years lay a quarrel over land claims by the Church on leases to laymen.[35] The reaction of the Doge and his senate was to order all clergy to ignore the papal bull and to require it to take an oath of allegiance. With the exception of the Jesuits, Theatines and Capucines, the clergy obeyed the order.[36] The papal interdict was lifted on 21 April 1607, only after Henry IV of France's eventually successful offer to mediate in the dispute in the face of the possibility of open war. Cardinal Francisco de Castro, Spanish ambassador to Venice, and also Cardinal François Joyeuse whom Donne mentions in *Pseudo-Martyr* and whom Henry sent to negotiate, concluded the terms of peace. Rome gained cause on the two points of clerical immunity for ecclesiastics and land claims that had precipitated the conflict, but otherwise none of its orders requiring Venetian submission to papal authority was obeyed. Nevertheless as Donne points out, the pope accepted the terms of reconciliation under the instigation of both Baronius and Cardinal Duperron, to whose negotiation Donne refers.[37]

Though less used for illustration by Donne than the Venetian affair, the second controversy involving the papacy and the kings of Spain, contained many of the same parallels with the English conflict. How free was the power

---

[34] *Monita Politica, ad Sacri Romani Imperii Principes, de Immensa Curiae Romanae potentia moderanda*, Frankfurt, 1609. See Commentary, p. 45, l. 32–p. 46, l. 6; p. 53, ll. 21–30; and p. 15, ll. 11–18.

[35] Cyriac K. Pulpilly, *Caesar Baronius, Counter-Reformation Historian* (Notre-Dame, Indiana, 1975), pp. 120–121.

[36] Pulpilly, p. 125.

[37] Pulpilly, p. 132; see Commentary, p. 15, ll. 11–18.

of a secular ruler from the spiritual domination of the papacy, how much spiritual power did the secular ruler himself have over his subjects, and did this spiritual power come into his possession by right of his temporal office? Donne argued for the latter principle through a polemic based on "nature" (pp. 79, 132–133). His position was that spiritual power emerged "naturally" in a ruler with his investiture into secular power through the grouping of ordinary men beneath him into the shape of a temporal state.

But, specifically, the Sicilian controversy, in which the same figures like Baronius and Paul V appeared as in the Venetian controversy, had sprung up much further back in time. Centuries earlier in 1099, Pope Urban II had unwittingly unleashed it at Salerno when he gave Count Roger of Sicily the right to govern the Church there as a legate of the papacy, as a reward for defeating the Saracens who were threatening Rome, and the right was to pass on to Roger's descendants.[38] Throughout the sixteenth century, the Spanish crown, which now ruled Sicily, claimed to have inherited Duke Roger's right and used it liberally to resist Rome's attempt to reappropriate its power over the Sicilian church. The Spanish kings reserved the right to make ecclesiastical appointments in Sicily, and even conducted excommunications. The Council of Trent decided to put an end to this secular power over the Church on the grounds of abuses, and Popes Pius V and Clement VIII worked to effect the Council's decrees. Philip II and Philip III of Spain resisted systematically. The quarrel broke out into the open and assumed international dimensions in 1605 when the Oratorian Baronius published his treatise *Monarchia Sicilia*.[39] Baronius was an unconditional papal supporter but was also a native of Naples, which, like Sicily, was ruled by the Spanish kings so that in *Pseudo-Martyr* Donne accused Baronius of treason for supporting Rome rather than Spain (p. 17). As the international debate widened, among those to answer Baronius on the Spanish side was Cardinal Colonna of Donne's marginalia.[40] Baronius repeated his charges against the Spanish crown in the volume of his *Annales Ecclesiastici* on the history of the entire Church, for the year 1097, to which

---

[38] Pulpilly, p. 105; see Commentary, p. 17, ll. 7–17, for the marginalia "Baron. Annal."

[39] See Commentary, p. 15, ll. 1–4.

[40] See Commentary, p. 15, 11–18; and p. 17, ll. 7–17.

INTRODUCTION xxix

Donne was again to refer disparagingly several times in *Pseudo-Martyr*.[41] Baronius defended the papacy on the grounds that it had the right to retrieve the power that it had delegated to the counts of Sicily, and that the delegation of the power had in any case automatically ceased when the royal line of Roger of Sicily died out, and a different line, that of Spain, appropriated it. The question was never legally resolved until the unification of Italy in the nineteenth century with the signing of the concordat between the new Italian state and the Vatican. In Donne's hands, a whole two centuries and more earlier, the issue of the "Sicilian Monarchy" served to illustrate that Paul v had conceded the possession of spiritual power to the Catholic kings of Spain by never being able to remove from them what Urban II had given to Count Roger.

Donne's third political illustration to support James I's possession of legal spiritual and temporal power was purely historical. In 1075, Hildebrand Pope Gregory VII deposed Henry IV of Germany for refusing to allow German bishops to implement his reforms against lay investiture. Henry desired to retain the power to name ecclesiastical authorities, even if they were laymen, to their posts because of the advantage of vassalage that this gave him. In the ensuing struggle between the papacy and the German imperial crown, Gregory issued several bulls on the extent of spiritual power and on the limits of secular power, and he excommunicated Henry and liberated the German bishops from their oath of allegiance to him.[42] Henry retaliated by putting into effect an already acquired right to have a voice in naming popes, a right that had been given to the German emperors by Pope Nicholas II in 1059. He congregated the German and Italian factions hostile to Gregory in a synod of feudatory lords at Brixen in 1080, and, in the name of the right that he claimed from Nicholas II, had an anti-pope, Clement III, crowned. Henry claimed that as a secular ruler he had papally given rights over spiritual authority that no pope, including Gregory, could ignore. In turn, Gregory issued a number of decretals against Henry's actions, decretals which Renaissance popes used regularly as precedents to curtail the powers of both Protestant and Catholic monarchs. Donne found these decretals particularly odious several times in *Pseudo-Martyr*, and they inspired his repeated invective against

---

[41] See p.17, margin and ll.15–17, for Baronius, and Commentary for p. 17, ll. 7–17.

[42] See Commentary, p. 70, ll. 1–9 and p. 71, ll. 1–9.

Gregory (pp. 69, 73, 75, 214), who was a pope whom history has generally judged most favourably.

The quarrel between Gregory and Henry was never resolved in the pope's lifetime, as Gregory remained official pope and Henry stayed king and emperor. Donne's illustrative use of the incident therefore came to demonstrate what appeared to be a sharing of power by independent secular and spiritual authorities, in spite of each other, in the eleventh century. Moreover, at his own election in 1073, Gregory had failed to call on Henry to practise in an effective manner that limited consultative right which had been granted to the German rulers by Nicholas II. Gregory simply informed Henry of his election and presented him with a fait accompli to ratify, so that Donne could argue, as he does in *Pseudo-Martyr*, that the present popes were claiming a power over secular authorities that had been merely misappropriated by them by Gregory's decision to ignore a previous papal decree (pp. 68–69). Gregory was the last pope whose election had to be ratified in even the most indirect manner by a secular ruler, and so it is from this moment that, in *Pseudo-Martyr*, Donne perceives papal claims to secular power to have become voracious (pp. 40–41, 75–76, 214). In documenting this historical illustration to show how the present friction between the English king James and the papacy developed, Donne's citations and marginalia contain a considerable number of seemingly disconnected references to Gregory, Henry, Clement, Nicholas, related papal bulls and the political manoeuvres that haunted the lives of the two central papal and imperial protagonists in the dispute in the eleventh century. These references constitute a coherent body of material touching on one of the most decisive events in the history of the medieval world, and Donne considers history to be repeating itself in Rome and London in 1609.

Insofar as Donne dealt with the question of the Oath of Allegiance separately from the matter of secular and spiritual power, he wrote as a canon law lawyer. His arguments are those of a canonist. Donne wrote as a canonist because it is on the grounds of canon law, that is, on the system of law constituted of the decrees of the popes and councils of the Church, that the popes based their claims for dominion over secular rulers. In this way, Donne chose to meet the conscientious objections of his ex-co-religionists on their own grounds. Therefore a very great number of *Pseudo-Martyr*'s once more seemingly disconnected notes, quotations and citations belong in fact to a quite coherent body of literature. The body of this literature is so historically diverse, covering the events of fifteen hundred years, that the modern reader may at first not be able to encompass it. After the literature of the martyrologies and hagiologies, and after Donne's three major historical parallels for England's contemporary quarrel with the papacy, the great number of writings on canon law and the Oath of Allegiance constitute the third and final major coherent body of references in *Pseudo-Martyr*. The connection between canon law, James' oath and, for example, Caesar Baronius' seven-folio-volume history of the Church, *Annales Ecclesiastici*, published in Rome between 1601 and 1608 only brief years before *Pseudo-Martyr* appeared, may not at first sight seem evident. However, *Annales* was a chronological history pope by pope from Saint Peter onwards; it painstakingly recorded the decretals of the popes which they issued in their own names and in councils and synods, and contemporary early seventeenth-century canon law was based on the decretals of past and present popes. Donne therefore argued out the question of allegiance to secular and spiritual lords in *Pseudo-Martyr* on the basis of papal decrees.

In the prevailing context of these decrees in *Pseudo-Martyr*, and considering the great original length of *Pseudo-Martyr*'s four hundred and twenty-five quarto pages, Donne mentions the Oath of Allegiance very little. Sometimes his reader is even brought to think that he has forgotten all about it. There is also no mention of the *Constitutions and Canons* of the Established English Church that had just been translated into English, revised and republished, and canon law seems to occupy the whole forefront of his thought.[43] But Donne defended his points in the terms of Catholic canon law to prove his case to English Catholics because such was the language they understood. Moreover, he had also to resort to canon law at length to constrain its foundations themselves as a suitable basis for judging the validity of the oath. In reality, Donne writes as a canonist in order not to be a canonist. The legal significance of *Pseudo-Martyr* is that Donne attempts to shift the basis of law out of the canonical range into another range completely. This realm is the Protestant "dictate of conscience" and its associated law of nature to which Donne refers his English-Catholic reader for the truth of allegiance, and which in fact *Pseudo-Martyr* does not pursue at much length (pp. 131–132). And if Donne does not either mention the newly republished *Constitutions*

---

[43] *Constitutions and Canons Ecclesiasticall agreed upon, 1603*, of the Church of England, London, 1604.

and Canons of the Established Church, the evident reason is that he was addressing himself to Catholics. It would have been illogical of Donne to have introduced *Constitutions* into his argument when all he sought from Catholics was their loyalty to James as a temporal ruler, and not as a spiritual head.

Pseudo-Martyr is therefore not only Donne's first work in print, but it is also his first and last published work in his lifetime as a lawyer. The academic curriculum that Donne followed in his law student days at Thavies Inn and Lincoln's Inn between 1591 and 1594 plunged him deeply into canon law.[44] The continued study of this law certainly occupied him considerably between his being fired and jailed by Sir Thomas Egerton for marrying his niece Anne More secretly against her father's wishes in 1601, and his tentative return into public life at the encouragement of James I after the latter's accession to the throne in 1603. According to what *Pseudo-Martyr*'s marginal notes reveal, canon law was surely the study that filled much of his reflective time in his attempt to find out the nature of true religion. It is impossible that Donne's hundreds of references to canon law in *Pseudo-Martyr* are the fruit merely of preparation to write the work. In fact, in a prefatory note to *Biathanatos* of 1607 or 1608, a work whose composition preceded that of *Pseudo-Martyr* and which Donne never published in his lifetime, he writes that he prepared his manuscript with the help of "mine owne old notes" compiled previously during years of study, rather than with the original works themselves.[45] In that same unpublished foreword to *Biathanatos*, Donne also apologizes for the annotation errors that using such study notes may have produced.[46] As very many of the notes in *Pseudo-Martyr* come from the same sources as those for *Biathanatos*, a significant number of them and their errors as well must have originated in the same body of notes in the same period of study.

---

[44] Bald singles out Donne's legal education in the Inns of Court in *Life*, pp. 53–79.

[45] Bald discusses Donne's study of civil and canon law in *Life*, pp. 141–142, 202, and Walton in his *Life* of Donne also refers to the attention that he gave the continued study of law in this period of his life (*Donne*, p. xxiv).

[46] *Biathanatos*, p. 5.

INTRODUCTION   xxxiii

Among the sources of these notes, in Baronius' *Annales Ecclesiastici* of 1601 to 1608, there are seven folio volumes. In the German canonist Severinus Binius' *Concilia Generalia* of 1606, there are five such volumes,[47] three in the Jesuit Bellarmine's *De Controversiis Christianae Fidei* of 1590 to 1593,[48] and one immensely detailed folio volume to Gratian's *Decretum*.[49] Donne's hundreds of references to these works indicate that he was most extensively familiar, as on a daily working basis, with the entire range of Catholic canonical writings. In the forefront of these writings was the *Corpus Iuris Canonici*, "the body of canon law," which Donne knew in detail. In Donne's day, this *Corpus Iuris Canonici* consisted of Gratian's *Decretum* itself, which recorded the principal questions of Catholic faith and dogma with the related decretals of the popes up till its composition in about 1150; of the enormous gloss (the "Glosser" who haunts Donne's marginalia) added to the manuscript of *Decretum* by many authorities over the centuries, which explained the dogma and decretals and which sometimes tried to correct Gratian's errors; of the decretals of Gregory IX in 1234 called "Liber Extra"; of those of Boniface VIII in 1298 called "Liber Sextus"; of those of Clement V published by John XXII under the title of "Clementines" or "Liber Septimus" in 1317; of John XXII's own "Extravagantes," that is, the "vagantes extra *Decretum*" of Gratian, and the "extravagantes Communes" of succeeding popes, published between 1500 and 1503; and, finally, the revisions of the "Correctores Romani" ordered by Pius V in 1566 and the "Index" of the *Decretum* ordered by Gregory XIII in

---

[47] See Commentary, p. 34, l. 29–p. 35, l. 8; *Concilia Generalia et Provincialia, quaecunque reperire potuerunt; item epistolae decretales, Et Romanor. Pontific. Vitae . . . Severeni Binii*, Cologne, 1606.

[48] *Disputationum Roberti Bellarmini Politiani, Societatis Iesu De Controversiis Christianae Fidei, Adversus Huius Temporis Haereticos*, Ingolstadt, Vol. I, 1590; Vol. II, 1591; and Vol. III, 1593. The first volume of the Cologne edition of 1615 contains appendices that, though already published separately, had not previously appeared with the *De Controversiis*. The first two volumes, as Bald points out, *Life*, p. 69, appeared in 1586 and 1588, but without the indexes.

[49] Among the significant editions of Gratian's *Decretum. . . Seu Verius Decretorum Canonicorum collectanea, Ab ipso auctore Gratiano primum inscripta, Concordia Discordantium Canonum* in Donne's time, was the Antwerp edition of 1573 and the Lyons edition of 1584 which contained Gregory XIII's corrective glossary.

1582. All of the names of these popes and their collections of decretals parade through Donne's quotations and marginalia an almost limitless number of times, and yet they all referred really to a single massive volume, *Corpus Iuris Canonici*, like that of the edition of Lyons in 1591 that might contain most of the decretals and their glosses,[50] as he notes on pp. 196–197.

A work like Binius' *Concilia Generalia* or Bellarmine's *De Controversiis* which Donne also knew, it appears, by heart was meant to supplement such a *corpus*. *Concilia* was a history of Church councils, recording their decrees and the circumstances under which they were passed in an attempt to refute the attacks of the Reformers against the historical authority of the popes, while Bellarmine's voluminous *De Controversiis* was a defence of Catholic doctrine by an examination of canonical history dogma by dogma.[51] Only study over a number of years could produce the complete ease of reference with which Donne cites the many thousands of folio pages of all of these volumes several hundreds of times.

The extent of Donne's knowledge of canon law and history is also attested to by his handling of related works of moral theology and philosophy. A considerable number of moral theologians and philosophers, many of them Spanish, whom Donne cites, fall likewise into the web of his canonical references. In Catholic tradition moral philosophy and moral theology were in a practical sense the material of the manuals by which canon law was explained, understood and lived in everyday life. A selection only of Donne's references to the works of moral theologians and philosophers includes the Spanish jurist Guerrero Alvarez' *De Jure ac Potestate Romanorum Pontificorum* (Cologne, 1586), the Spanish moralist Juan Azorius' *Institutionum Moralium In quibus Universae Quaestiones Ad conscientiam recte* (Rome, 1600–1611), the Dominican Martin de Azpilcueta of Navarre's *Enchiridion sive manuale Confessionorum* (Rome, 1588), the German Jesuit Nicholas Serarius' *Minerval divinis Hollandiae* (Mainz, 1605), his *Litaneutici, seu de Litaniis* (Cologne, 1609), and his *Trihaeresium* (Mainz, 1604), the Spanish Dominican jurist Jacobus Simancha's *De Republica Recte Instituenda* (Valladolid, 1565) and his

---

[50] See Commentary, pp. 192, l. 2–p. 193, l. 8. Donne employs the term "Glosser" or "Gloss" loosely. Sometimes he uses it to refer to the actual anonymous glosses of Gratian's *Decretum* (pp. 52, 142, 195, 208, 211–212, 265), but at other times to subsequent additions to the *Decretum*, such as the "Clementines" (pp. 143, 204).

[51] See Commentary, p. 14, ll. 32–34; and p. 11, l. 30–p. 12, l. 4.

Enchiridion Iudicium (Antwerp, 1573), the German Jesuit Adam Tanner's *Ecclesiasticae Libertatis* (Ingolstadt, 1607), the Frenchman Claude Carnin's *De Vi et Potestate Legum Humanarum* (1608), the Perugian Jesuit Paolo Comitoli's *Responsa Moralia* (Lyons, 1609), and the Spanish theologian Franciscus à Victoria's *Relectiones Theologicae* (1532). Works such as these rested on the Catholic canonical tradition and, though practically unknown today, in their own day they were works of public relevance and widely read.

Donne cites these works over and over with considerable familiarity, for he knew not only the laws of the canons, but also the methods of their practical application in everyday life in the contemporary Catholic world. Many of these moralists like Navarre, Comitoli, Carnin and Victoria, Donne cites in behalf of his own case that he is presenting to English Catholics. Though the moralists appear countless in his marginalia, the great majority were his contemporaries, they quoted one another liberally and their world was actually a small one, and the influence of their works on *Pseudo-Martyr* as a treatise of moral philosophy and theology was great. Donne's extraordinarily high number of annotations was usual practice with the moralists, and his tone of arguing theology into the reaches of everyday life was theirs as well.

Against this canonical background, Donne's references in *Pseudo-Martyr* to the literature dealing directly with the Oath of Allegiance are stunningly few, but they form part of the canonical side itself of his work and are essential. This literature includes James I's defence of the oath which he originally published anonymously in Latin and English in 1607 under the title of *Triplici nodo, triplex cuneus*, and this work undoubtedly inspired Donne to write *Pseudo-Martyr*.[52] Donne claims this implicitly in his prefatory address to James (p. 3), and how *Triplici* came to form the slim but immediate context of Donne's inspiration is evident in the Catholic answers that it provoked. *Triplici* sparked a reply by the Jesuit Robert Parsons in 1608, entitled *The Judgement of a Catholicke English-man, Living in Banishment for his Religion Written to his private friend in England Concerninge A late Booke set forth, and entitled . . . An Apologie for the Oath of Allegiance. Against two Breves of Paulus V to the Catholickes of England*, to which *Pseudo-Martyr*

---

[52] Keynes discusses briefly James' role in Donne's inspiration, citing Walton's *Life of Donne*, pp. xxv–xxvi, and he also mentions Gosse's opinion that the "story is probably untrue" (*Bibliography*, p. 3; Gosse, *The Life and Letters of John Donne*, London, 1899, 2 vols., Vol. II, p. 58).

refers.⁵³ To this answer of Parsons to *Triplici*, James retorted quickly the following year, 1609, with a new edition of the work, this time only in English and acknowledging his authorship. The new edition reprinted the damning verbatim, 1607, English translation of Paul V's two Latin *breves* absolving English Catholics of loyalty to James and it introduced a long prefatory open address by James, longer than *Triplici* itself, destined for "all Christian Monarchs, free Princes, and States." James' address is reminiscent of the open letter of Caesar Branchaura of Taurinus to all rulers of Europe in the *Monita Politica* collection of documents on the friction between Venice and the papacy, which *Pseudo-Martyr* often cites, and he may have modelled his address on Branchaura's, though only months separated the publication of the two documents.⁵⁴

A year after this second edition of *Triplici*, *Pseudo-Martyr* followed with its considerable canonical annotations to distinguish its place in the series of documents on the oath. Donne pursued assiduously the details of canon law into the realm of statecraft, and the single individual, the jurist and Parliamentarian Sir Edward Coke, to whom *Pseudo-Martyr*'s "Advertisement to the *Reader*" refers, was precisely someone like Donne who in 1606 had also defended James against the arguments of canon law. Coke's defence had been entitled *The Fift Part of the Reports*. *Fift Part* developed a theory "Of the Kings Ecclesiastical Law" and challenged Catholic canonical arguments for Christian kingship on historical grounds.⁵⁵ To this historically oriented challenge, the Jesuit Parsons again immediately answered in the same year with *An Answere to the Fifth Part of the Reportes Lately set forth . . . which do apperteyne to Spirituall Power. & Jurisdiction*. Donne cites this work by

---

⁵³See Commentary, p. 217, l. 35–p. 218, l. 1.

⁵⁴James I, *Triplici nodo, triplex cuneus. Sive Apologia Pro Iuramento Fidelitatis* (London, 1607); *Triplici nod, triplex cuneus. OR An Apologie for the Oath of Allegiance, Against the two Breves of Pope Paulus Quintus* (London, 1607); and *An Apologie for the Oath of Allegiance: First set forth without a name, and now acknowledged by the Author. . . Together, with a Premonition of his Majesties to all most mightie Monarchs, Kings, free Princes and States of Christendome* (London, 1609).

⁵⁵Sir Edward Coke, *The Fift Part of the Reports*, which contains the prefatory "Of the Kings Ecclesiastical Law," London, 1607.

Parsons too, at the very beginning of *Pseudo-Martyr*.[56] It is in the light of this literature defending the Oath of Allegiance on political grounds and attacking it on canonical grounds, that *Pseudo-Martyr* must be seen as having been inspired, in a web of martyrial, political and legal crosscurrents, as the first decade of the seventeenth century drew for Donne markedly to its end.

---

[56] On p. 17. See Commentary, p. 17, ll. 7–17.

II
The Meaning of Donne's Pseudo-Martyr

Because of the complexity of the man and of the subject of his work, there are really two meanings to Donne's *Pseudo-Martyr*. The first refers us to the significance of the book in the light of his troubled life. The second meaning of the work is less biographical and refers us rather to the issues of church and state structure and to their bearing on the destiny of the individual person in the early seventeenth century.

Peculiarly, *Pseudo-Martyr*, which was intended to be a very public book, fingers on the worst sore of Donne's private life, that is, his apostasy from Roman Catholicism. Donne was not born an ordinary Roman Catholic. The picture of a man that he presented in 1610 was that of a comparatively undistinguished, awkward would-be courtier, a thirty-eight-year-old recently avowed ex-Catholic who had made no mark whatsoever in politics, religion, literature, the law or the military. He must have effectively looked like a has-been who had never been very much. To the relatively few acquaintances who could have cared to befriend him, he was known as the great-grandson of the sister of the executed Catholic Chancellor Saint Thomas More, of whom he was therefore the great-great-nephew. He was also known as the son of the aged Catholic Elizabeth Heywood who was still living in 1610, who spent the last years of her life in her son's Anglican deanery in London, and who died only three months before him.[57] If history had somehow allowed to be recorded the conversations about Catholicism that must have taken place with unspeakable delicacy between this old woman and her son, many of Donne's ideas about his religious convictions would be clearer to us. In 1610, Donne was also identified as the nephew of Elizabeth's brothers, the Jesuits Elias and Jasper Heywood. The latter of these, Jasper, had been the Society of Jesus' underground mission leader in England in 1581. Donne was known too as the brother of the young Oxford student Henry Donne, who died in prison for having got caught

---

[57]Bald describes the last days of Donne's mother in *Life*, pp. 524–525.

hiding a Catholic priest.[58] Finally, he was reputed as a man who got jailed for secretly marrying the woman he loved.[59] Consequently, Donne's début in the field of major publication, because of the personal image he presented, must have inevitably been discomforting to those who knew him.

By 1609, his reputation as a writer could not have been more reassuring to his acquaintances than the known facts of both his personal life and family history. The two short prefatory poems that were all that Donne had so far published were in volumes about courtiers, love and secular drama, namely, Ferrabosco's *Ayres* and an edition of Ben Jonson's *Volpone*. He had already written two books, one on suicide, *Biathanatos*, and the other on the despicable character of courtiers, *The Courtier's Library*, but these were unpublished and presumably Donne limited the circulation of their manuscripts, if he circulated them at all.[60] In addition, Donne had written a fair number of sexually oriented love poems in which he left the unmistakable impression, because of the often graphic nature of his descriptions, that he had enjoyed the sexual favours of many women. The details of his descriptions are not normally of the sort that are learned by theory. These poems had not been published and, perhaps worse yet, they had circulated only in manuscript, thus highlighting the risqué reputation of their author among Donne's acquaintances even more than if they had appeared in print. For Donne to plunge himself therefore into a deep religious controversy against the Roman side must have struck his acquaintances as unusual but as somehow befitting the contradictory personality of the man. His acquaintances, as it were, had already seen some of the same ambiguous conduct open to misinterpretation. Perhaps only a king like James, who had no courtier's ladder to climb and who had the ability to perceive the latent literary talent of a backbench figure of his court, would have considered Donne worthwhile befriending, and he appears to have suggested to him to write *Pseudo-Martyr*.

---

[58] The priest was William Harrington whom Donne's younger brother had hidden in his chambers at Thavies Inn in Oxford in 1593. Henry Donne was apprehended and died in the same year in prison (Bald, *Life*, pp. 58–59).

[59] Donne was at first confined to the Fleet. Bald describes Sir George More's anger at the poet's secret marriage to his daughter, and Donne's subsequent imprisonment (*Life*, p. 135, *passim*).

[60] Keynes, *Bibliography*, p. 112, and Bald, *Life*, pp. 201, 341–342, discuss the circulation of *Biathanatos*.

The picture that Donne presented to his contemporaries in 1610 was further rendered ambiguous by the nature of his lapse from Rome. In his writings that preceded his career as an Anglican priest and in those that he composed after taking holy orders, Donne does not strike his readers as having broken with Rome in the sense of contributing to a new identifiably Protestant current in the mainstream of Christianity. Rather, his eminence rests on his extraordinary capacity to convey in the written word the spiritual sensibility of an ambivalent Anglican Christianity. Under the inspiration of the Lutheran and Calvinist reformers, he shared in the desire of this Anglican Christianity to liberate itself from the domination of Rome. But at the same time, like this ambivalent Christianity, Donne shared with Counter-Reformation Catholics the desire to keep the cultural heritage of all Christianity itself historically intact in the face of the discontinuity that the break of the Reformers implied. Throughout *Pseudo-Martyr*, Donne argues for the historical persistence of Christian tradition in England rather than for its renovation. As his ideas on the subject of the historical continuity of Christianity develop, the ambiguity of his position is only sharpened by his personal history and that of his family.

Moreover, there is in *Pseudo-Martyr* an implicit suggestion that Donne is still trying to convince himself that his religious convictions are settled. The scurrilousness of some of his comments against Roman Catholicism sometimes suggests the anguish of an individual who has still not succeeded in reassuring himself that what he is saying, even though it is central to his life, is true beyond question. John Carey has already noted the bitter precision with which Donne chose in *Pseudo-Martyr* some of the most devastating vignettes in Catholic tradition and legend to demolish them.[61] There is the story of Saint Francis of Assisi's vision of eighteen thousand devils, which some Catholics had apparently come to take literally (p. 106). There may be added yet further to Carey's observation Donne's example from Gratian's *Decretum* of the accidental dropping of the word "radant" in the decree on shaving issued by the Council of Carthage in 525. The omission of the word led to the threatened excommunication for a thousand years of clerics who wore beards, when the decree really said the opposite, namely that clerics could wear beards. The comic implication was that for a millennium up to the discovery of the transcription error in the decree, clerics had been shaving religiously to avoid excommunication when none was threatened (p. 197). Donne also points out

---

[61] Carey, *Life, Mind, Art*, pp. 33–34.

that Bellarmine, in order to support the power of the popes to excommunicate secular rulers, forced the meaning of a letter by Gregory I on the general supremacy of the papacy (pp. 71–72). Donne is also quick to put his finger on the faulty transcription, once more in *Decretum*, of the word "Henry" for "heretic." Coming as it does before the word "archbishop," in reference to a thirteenth-century prelate of Ravenna, the faulty transcription turns a venerable bishop loyal to Rome into a heretic (p. 192). Elsewhere, Donne singles out that the word "hereticis" crept in, yet again, for another word, this time for "heroicis" or "heroic" in a passage dealing with poetry (p. 196). Donne writes that this error almost misled Adrian VI centuries later to consider all poetry heretical instead of heroic. In other places, Donne stresses an error in the documentation of *Decretum*, such as Gratian mistaking a quotation from Saint Paul for a quotation from Saint Peter, or another error creating a primitive pope Macharius who never existed assisting at a Church Council of Geneva that was never held, with the anxiety of an individual clutching at the most evident argument to win his point (p. 192).

The impression of Donne's over-eagerness to prove that he is convinced against Rome, moreover, does not only arise from his choice from among the painfully abundant vignettal absurdities of Catholicism. The impression also springs from his own stance as the actual writer of *Pseudo-Martyr*. Like Bellarmine, he too mistranslates and, like him, he distorts the meaning of certain events and writings. For example, Donne is quick to use the devastating criticisms of Gratian's *Decretum* by the contemporary Catholic Archbishop Augustine of Tarragona, who was a prominent participant at the Council of Trent. By quoting a prominent Catholic theologian, Donne wished to show that such an unreliable document as *Decretum* could hardly be used as historical justification by the popes to order the assassination of kings and to condemn whole races to hell with the simple issue of an edict a few pages long (pp. 192–193). But in one place in Tarragona's *De Emendatione Gratiani*, to which Donne is referring, the Catholic archbishop's references correcting Gratian's text are themselves twice wrong.[62] In *Pseudo-Martyr* (p. 193), Donne manages to correct the first of Tarragona's errors, but the second is an untraceable and perhaps unfounded citation supposedly from Gratian which

---

[62] The *De Emendatione Gratiani Dialogorum libri duo* was first published in Tarragona in 1587, a year after Augustinus' death. See Commentary, p. 199, l. 12–p. 200, l. 3.

neither Donne nor probably anybody else could correct. Nevertheless, Donne cites this untraceable reference, surely conscious of its dubiousness. Instead of referring his reader back to its source in Gratian where the citation may be non-existent, Donne dishonorably avoids the difficulty by referring his reader back to Tarragona.

Again, Donne makes great issue in *Pseudo-Martyr* of Gratian's misuse of the phrase "pro Petrum sedem," that is, "before the chair of Peter," instead of the correct, "pro Petrum fidem," that is, "for Peter's faith," in Saint Ambrose of Milan's *De Poenitentia*. Gratian was attempting to prove that by using the word "sedes" or chair, Ambrose was supporting the supremacy of the popes over secular rulers. In Donne's day, many Counter-Reformation Catholics were using Gratian's misquotation from *De Poenitentia* to the same end. Gratian's error was circulating in many editions of *Decretum*, including that of Gregory XIII's supposedly corrected texts of 1584 and 1587. However, it is difficult to believe that Donne ignored that such a pivotal text in contemporary controversies over state and church power was correctly printed in other major editions of Ambrose's works such as the Paris edition of 1529 which contains Erasmus' preface.[63] It is also hard to believe that Donne did not know that the text also appeared correctly in Ambrose's official *Opera Omnia* of as late a date as 1583, dedicated to Gregory XIII himself, and edited by no less a scholar than Donne's opponent in *Pseudo-Martyr*, Caesar Baronius, whose writings he knew authoritatively.[64] Donne gives his reader the impression that he would stop at nothing to demolish Gratian and canon law.

Though Donne's eagerness or anxiety in *Pseudo-Martyr* is often evident, it would be a serious error to attribute it merely to an ambitious desire to please James I.[65] By Donne's own admission, James' *Triplici Nodo* inspired him to set pen to paper (pp. 3–4). However, there is a personal compulsion in *Pseudo-Martyr*, given the nature of Donne's family religious background and of his adherence to the Anglican Church, that James never had. Donne would have had eventually to yield to this compulsion in his personal life, and sooner or later to give it public form. As the meeting point of the expression

---

[63] St. Ambrose, *De Poenitentia*, I, vi (Paris, 1529), p. 48^v, Col. 2.

[64] See Commentary, p. 192, l. 2–p. 193, l. 8.

[65] Bald, *Life*, pp. 201–202, Keynes, *Bibliography*, p. 3, and Carey, *Life, Mind, Art*, pp. 31–32, discuss with varying conclusions Donne's ambitions in writing *Pseudo-Martyr*.

of such private need and public form, *Pseudo-Martyr* became Donne's penultimate argument about how he could be conveniently English and peacefully Christian. Because of this, the very surface appearances of *Pseudo-Martyr* suggest its differences from *Triplici Nodo* and they emphasize the nature of the private and public challenge that Donne faced. Both documents claim to be exactly about the same subject of the Oath of Allegiance, but *Triplici* was a much shorter work than *Pseudo-Martyr* and it was also much more objective because it had no personal problem to solve. In *Triplici*, the issues were politically great for James because his life and crown were at stake. But as documents reflecting the personal destinies of their respective authors, the two works had remarkably little in common. The stakes in *Triplici* were only the king's life and crown, whereas in *Pseudo-Martyr* they were Donne's soul. In his treatise Donne gives the impression that he is still striving for his salvation and for peace of mind by trying to understand how a human being, a creature who exists in time and space, can live historically an eternal truth such as church affiliation.

As Donne argued out this affiliation for himself in *Pseudo-Martyr* and explained to his readers how he rescinded his membership in the Roman Church because of what appeared to him to be its absurdities, he left a great number of the prominent characteristics of contemporary Catholicism unattacked. Those aspects of the early seventeenth-century Roman Church that he did not denigrate are sometimes as revealing of Donne's religious convictions as those that he ridiculed. They suggest what he probably found inoffensive in contemporary Catholicism, and they give some idea of what acceptable Catholic beliefs he brought with him into the Anglican Church. For example, with the notable exceptions of Gratian's *Decretum*, of Franciscan spirituality and obedience, and of Gregory the Great's decrees against Henry IV of Germany (as though these were not enough), Donne's attacks against Catholic history are almost entirely restricted to events of the last hundred years. And, in his invective against Catholic history of the last century, his attacks are particularly noteworthy for their concentration on the new religious orders.

Moreover, some of the absences in Donne's list of dolors against Rome, like that of Saint Teresa of Avila, he could have hardly ignored. Donne cannot be expected to have known and to have read everything, and to have put everything that he both knew and read into *Pseudo-Martyr*. But he was versed in the smallest details of the Counter-Reformation and in the foundation of the new Catholic religious orders and in the reformation of the older existing orders, as both *Pseudo-Martyr* and *Ignatius His Conclave* of the following year reveal. It is impossible that he was uninformed about the greatest woman of Counter-Reformation Europe. Teresa had reformed the Carmelite order not once but twice, the second time more severely than the first, and she had successfully contested the interdiction of Gregory XIII, and suffered house arrest for two years, in order to do so.[66] Her autobiography, the *Vida*, had circulated in several editions in the original Spanish since its appearance in 1587, and its English translation of 1611 was to be published within a year of *Pseudo-Martyr*'s appearance.[67] Her spirituality does not appear to have provoked Donne as did Loyola's.

Similarly, in a work like *Pseudo-Martyr* replete with criticisms of the Franciscans, the Jesuits and the Oratorians, there is again strikingly little, in fact practically no reference to the sixth-century Saint Benedict of Nursie and his *Rule* for the Benedictines, and to the twelfth-century Saint Bernard of Clairvaux and the Cistercians whom Bernard reformed from the Benedictines. Of these monastic orders, Henry VIII had confiscated the monasteries to destroy Catholic power in England. There is criticism of these saints and their orders in *Ignatius His Conclave*, but passingly in the general sense of attacking the Catholic Church for having attempted to purge itself for over a thousand years by reforming old orders and founding new ones without ever seeming to achieve its end of self-purification (*Conclave*, p. 11). In *Pseudo-Martyr*, the two references to Benedict are asides that criticize his religious rule for its high number of administrative offices for monks and of kinds of hermits, and the one reference to Bernard is to cite him most positively as an authority in

---

[66] Teresa of Jesus (b. 1515; d. 1582) founded her first Discalced Carmelite Convent of the Primitive Rule in Avila in 1562, in the face of considerable opposition from the unreformed Calced convents. In 1575, Pope Gregory III prohibited the founding of further discalced convents. This required the intervention of Philip II of Spain, and in 1580 the constitution of the order was officially sanctioned both by Philip and by Rome. Teresa's collected works, including her *Life*, *The Interior Castle*, *The Way of Perfection*, and her letters were published in a collected edition in 1587, and rapidly translated into several languages.

[67] Saint Teresa of Avila, *Los libros de la Madre Teresa De Jesu. . . Un tratado de su Vida*, Salamanca, 1587, translated into English as *The Lyf of the Mother Teresa of Iesus, Foundresse of the Monasteries of the Descalced or Bare-footed Carmelite Nunnes and Fryers. . . By W.M. of the Society of Iesus*, Antwerp, 1611.

spirituality (pp. 109–110, 137–138). Again, *Pseudo-Martyr* contains only one reference to the Jesuit Saint Francis Xavier, called the Apostle of the Indies, and considered by Catholic tradition as more or less the co-founder of the Jesuits with Ignatius, and that reference no more than points out that Francis like Ignatius was a Navarrois, a man from Navarre (p. 104). In addition, there is deafeningly no mention of the executed Jesuit innocent, Robert Southwell,[68] and the two references to the other executed Jesuit, Edmund Campion, are only by way of criticism of Catholic apologists who praise Campion but fail to acknowledge the heroism of Protestant martyrs (pp. 119, 129).

As a convert to the Established Church therefore, the relatively few though fundamental religious elements of Roman Catholicism that Donne rejected, in fact that he could no longer live with, are suggested in *Pseudo-Martyr*. For one, he was unable to accept the spirituality of visions and their sometimes associated miracles. In this, he objected to the very spirituality that Rome encouraged to arrest the tide of the Reformation and to assure the continuity of Christian history. For it was not on the necessity of assuring Christian historical continuity that Donne diverged with the Counter-Reformation, but on the method to be used. Practically all of Donne's attacks on the Franciscans, about fifty of them, for example, are not on the order's stiff rule for poverty but on the visionary legends of Saint Francis. Secondly he rejected the Catholic tradition of clerical obedience. The other attacks on Franciscans in *Pseudo-Martyr*, by way of example once more, are most heavily concentrated on derisive instances of the excessive obedience of the friars to their superiors, such as a friar planting a plant upside down in the earth because his superior commanded him to do so in order to test his capacity to observe his vow of obedience blindly (p. 115). It was on these grounds of visions and obedience, and because of the papal interdiction against James, that Donne appears to have quit the Catholic Church.

Donne's choice of examples of Catholic spirituality from the past served to justify his defection from Catholicism before his seventeenth-century readers. These examples had the effect of explaining his vehemence against the Counter-Reformation by illustrating his fear that the contemporary Catholic

---

[68] Bald points out the importance that Southwell had as a background figure in Donne's upbringing, and suggests the possibility that the two men met (*Life*, pp. 63–65).

Church was reconstituting its ancient spirituality powerfully. Based on visionary life and obedience, this spirituality appeared to Donne to be recurrent from era to era in Catholicism, it seemed to be in the process of being reborn in the present, and the spearhead of the reborn movement seemed to be the Jesuits. As the followers of Ignatius recreated this spirituality anew, their instruments appeared to be the regulations of their founder's three little volumes of the *Rules*, the *Constitutions*, and the meditative treatise, *Spiritual Exercises*. The *Rules* and *Constitutions* stressed the military-like obedience of all Jesuits to their superiors, and the *Spiritual Exercises* put an accent on inner imaginative vicarious visions for the realization of the deepest Christian experiences, the two things which in different forms Donne held against the Franciscans. Because of the importance that Donne attached to Ignatius' three small volumes, the Jesuits share with the seminary priests one whole half of the title of his preface to *Pseudo-Martyr*. While in *Pseudo-Martyr* Donne centred his attack on the Jesuits on the *Rules* and *Constitutions*, he was to satirize the *Spiritual Exercises* frontally in *Ignatius His Conclave* in the following year of 1611,[69] and of this satire the earlier work's confrontation with Franciscan spirituality was the evident forerunner.[70]

The Jesuit vow of obedience on which *Pseudo-Martyr* concentrates was even more objectionable to Donne than the Franciscan vow. The spirit of the Franciscan vow was directed to the obedience of the friar to his superior in a monastery, but that of the Ignatian vow required the obedience of the individual Jesuit in the social world of human affairs directly and personally to the commands of the pope as well as to those of his superior in a non-cloistered house. The Franciscan vow led to forms of personal humiliation which Donne found excessive, but the Jesuit vow exceeded by its nature the moral scope of the life of the individual priest and consequently appeared far more dangerous to him. The Jesuit vow seemed to reach out beyond the individual priest and encompass the entire contemporary political world, and this explains the number and importance of the attacks on Ignatius' *Rules*

---

[69] The attacks on Jesuit spirituality underlie the mock visionary experience of the conclave in hell in *Ignatius His Conclave*, pp. 7, 31, and 63–65. The spread of Ignatius' manual, *Spiritual Exercises*, is discussed in A. Raspa, *The Emotive Image* (Fort Worth, 1983), pp. 37–50. See Commentary, p. 106, l. 30–p. 107, l. 5.

[70] In *Conclave*, p. 11, Donne describes Jesuit spirituality as an outgrowth with Franciscan mystical experience.

and *Constitutions* in *Pseudo-Martyr* (pp. 106–109, 116, 119). For, in Donne's argument, within a few years of Ignatius' death in 1556, Jesuit obedience to the papacy had been turned into a well-organized political instrument against the power of European secular rulers. A great deal of Counter-Reformation spirituality, in the forms of both religious experience and clerical obedience, therefore appeared to Donne to be now geared to the increase of political power in Rome.

The circumstances under which Jesuit obedience had been transformed into a political army would have been evident to Donne in James' English translation of *Triplici Nodo*. The 1609 signed version of *Triplici* cites and then answers each of Paul V's two *breves* of 1606 and 1607.[71] James' method of discourse was to contest the absoluteness of the authority of the popes, argument by argument, as the Jesuits tried to maintain it in England. On the Catholic side, the defence of papal power was larded with antecedents of history. Paul defended temporal papal power in his *breves* according to a tradition of government that took root in Europe with the fall of the Roman empire, and with the political void that Christianity then began to fill. This tradition developed with the fusion of Catholic biblical exegesis and ancient Graeco-Roman ideas about matter and spirit that subsequent Christian civilization produced. Paul's defence also included giving Catholics permission to assassinate their heretical kings if these required fealty of them. The very breadth of Donne's *Pseudo-Martyr* must be understood as an attempt to encompass all the major issues that such traditions and the recommended assassination of James implied. Paradoxically, the sweep of Donne's work gave birth even to his conciliatory tone to Catholics. The long letter of Cardinal Duperron to Henry of Navarre that Donne cites generously in his references to the Venetian controversy depicts Pope Paul as a man somewhat traumatized by events and frightened at the impasse between secular and religious powers into which a millennium of religio-political tradition had placed him (p. 15).[72] By such examples, showing English Catholics both sides of the question of English secular power and papal spiritual power, Donne tried to convince them to take the Oath of Allegiance. James' oath stipulated that the English king was rightfully king and that he was not a heretic for not relying on Rome for the power of his crown, and this was the point that Rome

---

[71] *An Apologie for the Oath of Allegiance*, pp. 9, 17, 31, 35.

[72] *Monita Politica*, pp. 155–156.

forbade English Catholics to concede. But Donne hoped to convince them that, the papal interdiction aside, James' position and that of the pope were not irreconcilable.

Donne's lapse from Roman Catholicism, as *Pseudo-Martyr* suggests, was at once as simple and as complicated as the impasse between the papacy and a secular ruler like James, and as the solution that he proposed to break it. And, as Donne elaborated upon how English Catholics could assuage the effects of this impasse on their lives, he revealed the logic by which he became a member of the English Church. With much courage, he engaged himself in fundamental arguments about statecraft in the long tradition of Augustine of Hippo and Gregory the Great, whom he cites abundantly. With these, he justified at once James' oath and his own position in the Anglican Church. Donne liberally evoked the argument of the City of God and the City of Man, for it was the nature of these cities that was at stake. *Pseudo-Martyr*'s long digressions into arguments of statecraft find their meaning in the tradition of the two cities, as Donne used it to attempt to reconcile English Catholics to a Protestant ruler while maintaining their allegiance to the papacy.

Moreover, Donne did not only repeat a historical argument that had already been well propounded, but developed his own small point of view towards the Cities of God and Man as well. *Pseudo-Martyr* argues the defence of James on the grounds that the organization of men into a secular state preceded the creation of a spiritual state rather than followed it. That is, secular power existed chronologically in a state before spiritual power. A pope did not therefore necessarily have precedence over a king. Although the tradition of argumentation that Donne followed is medieval, the ring of the argument itself, following in the footsteps of the French Protestants Jean Gerson, François Hottoman and Philippe Junius du Plessis de Mornay, who appear in various references in Donne's text and marginalia, is forward-looking (pp. 11, 16). For the moderns who have tended to think of Donne as an unconditional moral follower of Augustine, the break here with his Roman master is significant. Donne argued that the existence of the spiritual state originated from an already existing temporal state, and it was not the secular state, as argued by the popes, that was the emanation of the spiritual state (p. 79).

For Donne, the reason for the precedence of the secular state sprang from nothing less than the most basic history of mankind. He therefore did not hesitate to try to describe the whole history of mankind too within the confines of a single book. Donne argued that in unrecorded times, men everywhere as savages (the word that he uses) formed separate tribal states (pp. 79–80). In these tribal states originated all political power both secular and religious. These states may be thought to have resembled in Donne's mind those of the seven tribes of Israel, though he does not say so.

Unfortunately, Donne describes the secular tribal state briefly in only a few pages, but he at least tells us that it was formed in a condition of nature in primitive times. Later, if primitive men had been fortunate, destiny had somehow come to place the Bible on their shelves and they received Divine Revelation from its typological levels of meaning. With this new spiritual help in hand, primitive men then engrafted a spiritual state, based on the contents of Revelation, onto their existing natural secular state. Because Revelation came to primitive men from a typological work with levels of meaning, by a process of social sophistication the new state was marked by a typological character like the Scriptures too. That is, the state also came to possess spiritual and material levels of meaning, and it found its models in the prototypes of the Judaeo-Christian states in the Old and New Testaments. In the primitive times of human history, the ruler of such a secular state held his power from the men who accorded it to him, and if these same men so wished, they could also bestow on the secular ruler the spiritual power of the spiritual state formed when they were gifted with Revelation. Therefore in Donne's mind, by a process of social sophistication similar to that involved in the formation of the spiritual state, the holder of secular power could also wield the spiritual power that sprang from it. In this way, the two powers could be legitimately united in one ruler like James.

However, significantly in Donne's thinking, for the subject of such a ruler who held spiritual and secular powers, the two powers could remain separate. Spiritual loyalty did not follow necessarily on the secular. The subject of the ruler who held both powers was always bound by loyalty to him as a secular lord, but he was not bound to the spiritual power that other men in the state had vested in him unless he chose to do so. Spiritually, the subject remained free, without betraying the secular authority of his ruler. Versed in the law, Donne was pleading in *Pseudo-Martyr* a complicated legal case in behalf not only of James but also of his English-Catholic subjects. Therefore he argued that if secular and spiritual powers could be legitimately united in the ruler they nevertheless remained capable of being separated for his subjects, to the benefit of both (pp. 79–80).

With this separation of the powers for subjects in the forefront of his thinking, Donne argued with English Catholics in *Pseudo-Martyr* that it was quite thinkable for them to swear allegiance to their Protestant king. In the historical order of mankind, Rome and London represented for Donne separate tribes, they both sprang from antiquity, and they had both been gifted with Revelation; and it was possible for a given subject in a given country like England to swear loyalty to a secular ruler like James and yet also swear loyalty to the spiritual ruler of another state like Paul V. That is, the English Catholics could swear to both the secular authority of James and the spiritual authority of the papacy without betraying one or the other. In other words, both Rome and London were correct, because each possessed primitive legitimacy and Revelation as well. Donne writes towards the end of his work that the Oath of Allegiance "therefore containing nothing, but a *profession of a morall Truth, and a protestation that nothing can make that false*, impugnes no part of that *spirituall* power, which the Pope justly hath" (p. 253). As Donne saw it, the problem for English Catholics was not that of having to learn how to live with two conflicting powers as much as with two powers that were separate, legitimate and in different places. Consequently, in *Pseudo-Martyr* Donne appears to have made a good part of his lapse from Catholicism on the grounds that though Rome was correct as a form of spiritual power, the Established Church to which he now chose to belong was correct too.

It is in the context of this approach to international spiritual allegiances that Donne's *Pseudo-Martyr* ceases to be a personal document and becomes a difficult monument in the literature of the history of ideas. For, with his theory of international spiritual allegiances, Donne turned his personal argument with past and present history into a statement of impersonal public interest. In *Pseudo-Martyr*, Donne's main interest was to develop a working idea of the Christian Church as a temporal phenomenon touching upon not only himself but interested people in general. Consequently, *Pseudo-Martyr* was at once a personal document justifying his lapse from Rome and a public document arguing a theory of church and state for the times. Donne was interested in the structure of the church not really as an organization in the modern managerial sense of the word, but as an institution that approximated as much as possible the divine intentions of a God for his people, when, scattered over the face of the earth at different times and in different epochs, they congregated together to keep his word fully alive. *Pseudo-Martyr* was therefore an immensely public work by a profoundly private man touching on one of the central issues dominating the religio-political thought of his times. This undoubtedly explains the probability of the very large first edition of the work which its large number of eighty-two surviving copies suggests. As well as for himself, Donne sought to devise for his readers, both Catholic and Protestant, a viable idea of the church as a temporal thing. How, in time, *Pseudo-Martyr* asks, did the risen Lord take onto himself the trappings of an organization? Donne was not so much interested in the details of priesthood and clerical hierarchy as in the more fundamental question of how the Lord transferred himself out of his individual person in the realm of eternity into the likeness of a Christian collectivity in the dimension of time.

Donne's underlying object in *Pseudo-Martyr* therefore was to describe the expression of the will of the Christian God in the form of the church through the days, years and decades of its existence. For Donne, the method of the existence of things in time expressed God's manifestation of himself outside the bounds of eternity, and the appearance of the church showed God speaking directly to men. Between the two of them, God and the church created mystical and historical levels of meaning. It was this dialogue of the eternal in and with the temporal in the form of the church that concerned Donne in his otherwise out-sized, inflated political tract. Ironically, this pretentious inflation of the work outside the normal limits of political tract writing, which obscures Donne's entry as a public figure into the field of published literature, is otherwise pivotal in our understanding of his ideas as a man for the rest of his life.

Therefore as Donne argued with his principal opponents, the Jesuit Robert Bellarmine or the Oratorian Caesar Baronius, or with his hundred other lesser Catholic adversaries like Azorius, Binius, Castro and Ceparius, his answers to several questions, referring to the Bible, history and typology, all of them touching on the nature of the church, also led to enlightenment about politics. For example, typology was not only a tool for biblical exegesis. It was actually an instrument of modern political science as well.[73] Typology not only served to reveal the origin of spiritual authority in the contemporary state, but it also informed the Christian on the nature of secular state power. It thereby

---

[73]Catholic anagogy and Protestant typology are discussed in, among others, Barbara Lewalski's *Protestant Poetics and the Seventeenth-Century Religious Lyric* (Princeton, 1979), pp. 111–130; and Raspa, *The Emotive Image*, pp. 18–26.

enabled him to distinguish between the swords of spiritual and state authorities (p. 251). To the Christian whom Donne's work cumulatively describes, those unconvinced English Catholics for whom Donne's love burns between the lines of his invective against the Catholic Church, and whom he would have look at the world of Britain with his eyes, the two powers were made clear by typology. There was no need for English Catholics to be martyred uselessly for failing to apply to the present the instrument of political science that the Lord had originally given to men as a tool to understand his Scriptures in the past. It was possible, Donne told beleaguered English Catholics, to identify the just government of one nation and adhere loyally to it as its subject, and to adhere loyally to the spiritual authority that had evolved in another nation.

Donne likened this dual citizenship for heaven and earth to the union between the soul and the body in the old scholastic argument about the nature of human life. He repeatedly compared the relationship between spiritual and secular loyalties with the link between the soul and body (pp. 46, 48, 133–134, 185). In this way, he demonstrated the union of the church and state as a single vital organism and at the same time he illustrated the separation of church and state powers that their vital relationship made possible. The possible separation of the two was not a sign of weakness but of the respective strength of each. It was as though the relationship between the two powers was one of spirit and matter (pp. 131, 132, 133).

Donne's view of the church as a temporary phenomenon in *Pseudo-Martyr* was consequently fairly unique. He tried to maintain the character of the church constant by claiming a typological, mystical character for it. However, at the same time, in terms of the ancient scholastic conceptions of matter and form and of body and soul, he allowed various justifiable expressions for the structure of the church throughout human history. There was only one soul possible, namely Revelation, to all the correct churches of human history. However, that soul could inhabit as many bodies as there were kinds of Christian secular states. History could allow many valid Christian churches to exist not only chronologically throughout the past, but simultaneously in a variety of national states in the present as well. In this way, for Donne, time allowed various images of the same eternal truth to exist linearly through history and to coexist together in the present.

INTRODUCTION   liii

In the short run of things, *Pseudo-Martyr*'s help to the defence of English liberty against the papacy was undoubtedly welcomed. But Donne's international approach to the nature of the church was fraught with difficulty for the English cause. The seeds of this trouble are evident to Donne's readers quickly, and they surely account for the fact that *Pseudo-Martyr* is an unfinished work lacking the last two of the fourteen chapters that Donne originally planned for it. The titles of the originally planned chapters appear in the table of contents of the text of 1610 as though they had all been published in the book, but the last two chapters are not there. The book ends abruptly with Chapter 12. The thirteenth chapter was to have dealt with the legitimate supremacy in France of the kings of France, and the fourteenth chapter with the independence of England from the conversion of its early kings to Roman Christianity. Donne wrote in his "Advertisement to the Reader" that the titles of these chapters had circulated among his friends in a separate list with the titles of the other chapters before he wrote the book, and that they had caused dissension among those who read them (pp. 8–9). He tells us that some people thought that he should write the final chapters, and some thought that he should not. He never tells us what the objections were, but he concedes that finally he did not write them and peculiarly, perhaps even defiantly, he did not bother to remove the titles of the chapters from the table of contents for publication. However, the nature of the objections of Donne's friends to the unwritten chapters are easy to imagine. In the matter of Chapter 13, the last king of France to die, Henri de Valois, had been assassinated in a Protestant-Catholic plot, and Henri IV, de Navarre, the ruling king of France, was a convert to Catholicism, and he had submitted by his conversion to the spiritual claims of papal authority. Secondly, in the question of Chapter 14, when Ethelbert the tribal king of Kent was converted to Christianity by the Italian Augustine of Canterbury, he brought a good part of southeast England into the realm of Roman spiritual authority.

Perhaps it is not idle to consider that for the immediate English political cause at stake in *Pseudo-Martyr*, the two chapters would have been too much of a good thing. Logically, according to Donne's international approach to the nature of the church, the two chapters would have rounded off the argument of his book. They would have demonstrated by citing the contemporary example of France and the historical example of ancient Britain what he meant by the possibility of international religious allegiances. However, to have justified French secular power and papal power in France and to have justified the origins of English Christianity in the light of Ethelbert's Roman conversion may have appeared to go too far in its concessions to the papacy. Perhaps the chapters, if written, would have ended up subverting the ostensible end of defending James I for which *Pseudo-Martyr* was written. In an international political quarrel, in which assassination and military intervention were often the norms of conduct, the limit was quickly reached how much a basically maverick thinker like Donne could tell everyone that everybody could be right if they tried. In spite of the virulence of some of his comments about Catholicism, Donne's message in the final unwritten chapters of *Pseudo-Martyr* might have come perilously close to telling Christians to love one another as Christ had loved them.

Throughout its almost four hundred years of history, *Pseudo-Martyr* has left many of its readers uncomfortable, and names have been levelled against the work as against no other writing by Donne. The work has also been declared to be peculiarly unreadable. Perhaps the real reason for the negative attitudes to *Pseudo-Martyr* is that, like Donne's life itself, the work fails strangely to reinforce anyone's prejudice or presupposition. A statement elsewhere by Donne perhaps best describes the conscious motive that guided him in *Pseudo-Martyr*. "You know," Donne wrote in a letter to Sir Henry Goodyer in about 1610, "I never fretted nor imprisoned the word Religion; nor straightning it Frierly, *ad Religiones factitias*, (as the Romans call their orders of Religion) nor immuring it in a *Rome*, or a *Wittemberg*, or a *Geneva*; they are all virtuall beams of one Sun."[74] *Pseudo-Martyr* may perhaps justly be declared to be the attempted political configuration in writing of the hopeless ideal which Donne's letter to Goodyer expresses. In spite of its origin in burning political events, no one can claim *Pseudo-Martyr* comfortably for his side. And, in spite of what Jessopp, Simpson and Keynes have had to say about its unreadability, *Pseudo-Martyr* is no more unreadable than Hooker's *Laws* or Bellarmine's *De Controversiis*.

---

[74] The letter to "*Sir* H.R." or Henry Goodyer, in *Letters to Severall Persons of Honour* (1651), *Scolars' Facsimiles and Reprints* (Delmar, New York, 1977), p. 29.

III
Copies of the First Edition

The following is a list in alphabetical order of the names of the holders of the known existing eighty-two copies of the first edition of *Pseudo-Martyr*. The list, which may not be exhaustive, is markedly different from the bibliographical entries recording copies in Keynes' *Bibliography*, the *National Union Catalogue*, the Pirie *Catalogue*,[75] the Sypher list,[76] the *Short-Title Catalogue*,[77] and *A Finding-List of English Books*.[78]

For example, the copy listed for the University of Washington Library in *NUC* and the Sypher list is a 1923 photostat of the Yale copy (Y). For its part, the Trinity College, Oxford, copy, which purportedly belonged to Alexander Pope and contained his index,[79] has never been in the holdings of their library; no confirmation of the past or present existence of this copy is forthcoming. The second copies listed for Columbia University and the University of Minnesota in *NUC* do not exist, and the copy for the Washington Cathedral Library mentioned in both the *NUC* and the Sypher list, and the copy at the University of Glasgow Library indicated in *A Finding-List* are missing (and hence excluded below). The copy in the holdings of the Cosin Library mentioned in *STC* is now the second copy in the University of Durham Library as listed in Keynes; the copies of Saint Mary's Church, Warwick, and Cartmel Priory Church, mentioned in *A Finding-List*, are now respectively in the libraries of the University of Birmingham and the University of Lancaster; and

---

[75] Robert S. Pirie, *John Donne, 1572–1631, A Catalogue of the Anniversary Exhibition of First and Early Editions of his Works Held at the Grolier Club, February 15 to April 12, 1972*, New York, 1972.

[76] Francis Jacques Sypher, "Introduction," Donne, *Pseudo-Martyr* (Delmar, N.Y., 1974), p. 11.

[77] *A Short-Title Catalogue of Books printed in England, Scotland, and Ireland, and of English Books printed abroad, 1475–1640*, second edition, 2 vols. (London, Volume I, 1986; Volume II, 1976), Vol. I, entry 7048, p. 317.

[78] David Ramage (comp.), *A Finding-List of English Books to 1640 in Libraries in the British Isles* (Durham, 1958), p. 28.

[79] Keynes, *Bibliography*, p. 9.

the copy of the Hampstead Library is in Swiss Cottage Library in northwest London.

The revised *Short-Title Catalogue* also lists the presence of copies at the Westminster Abbey Library in London, at the libraries of Brasenose, Jesus and Magdalen Colleges in Oxford, in the Robert Taylor Collection at Princeton University, and in the Alexander Turnbull Library in Wellington, New Zealand.

There is the high number of eight so far unmentioned copies. Extraordinarily, three of these are in the York Minster Library,[80] a location which will eventually be published in the bibliography of the holdings of English cathedrals. Two other copies are in the Library of Trinity College, Dublin, which is listed in *A Finding-List* without reference to more than one copy,[81] when it actually has three.[82] The National Library of Scotland and Saint Paul's Cathedral Library, London, each have a second unlisted copy, in addition to the copies listed for them in Keynes' *Bibliography*.[83] McGill University Libraries in Montreal also have a fine copy in their possession.

Each of the eighty-two entries below is followed by the location code used in the revised *STC*.[84] When there is no location code for an entry in the *STC*, the present edition necessarily invents its own. For all references to the following volumes in the present edition, these codes are used:

1.	University of Aberdeen	A
2.	University of Birmingham (St. Mary's Church, Warwick, copy)	BIRM
3.	Bodleian Library, Oxford (imperfect copy)	O-1
4.	Bodleian Library, Oxford	O-2
5.	Brasenose College Library, Oxford	O^4
6.	Bristol Central Public Library	Bristol
7.	British Library, London	L-1

---

[80] York Minster Library shelf marks II.L.4/2 (YK-1); II.L.5 (YK-2); and Hackness 57 (YK-3).

[81] Ramage, *Finding-List*, p. 28.

[82] Trinity College Library, Dublin, shelf marks GG.i.20 (D-1); CC.k.29 (D-2); and G.f.29 (D-3).

[83] National Library of Scotland shelf marks Ap.2.4 (E-1), and LL.4.8/1 (E-2); Saint Paul's Cathedral Library shelf marks 14.E.7 (L^{15}-1), and 29.E.14 (L^{15}-2).

[84] *Short-Title Catalogue*, pp. xlix–liii.

INTRODUCTION

8.	British Library, London	L-2
9.	Clarke Memorial Library, University of California, Los Angeles	CAL
10.	Cambridge University Library	C-1
11.	Cambridge University Library	C-2
12.	Cambridge University Library (Peterborough Cathedral copy)	C-3
13.	Cambridge University Library (Keynes' copy)	C-4
14.	Carlisle Cathedral Library	Carlisle
15.	Chapin Library, Williams College, Williamstown, Mass.	CH
16.	Chapter Library, Windsor Castle (imperfect copy)	WIN^2
17.	Chetham's Library, Manchester	M^2
18.	Columbia University Library, New York, N.Y.	CU
19.	Cornell University Library, Ithaca, N.Y.	COR
20.	Corpus Christi College, Oxford	O^5
21.	Derry and Raphoe Diocesan Library, Londonderry	LYD
22.	Durham University Library	DUR^5-1
23.	Durham University Library (Cosin's Library copy)	DUR^5-2
24.	Edinburgh Central Library	E^8
25.	Emmanuel College, Cambridge	C^3
26.	Exeter Cathedral Library	EX
27.	Folger Shakespeare Library, Washington, D.C.	F
28.	Gonville and Caius College, Cambridge	C^9
29.	Houghton Library, Harvard University, Cambridge, Mass.	HD
30.	Hereford Cathedral Library	HER
31.	Henry E. Huntington Library, San Marino, Calif.	HN
32.	University of Illinois Library, Urbana	ILL
33.	Jesus College, Oxford	O^{18}
34.	Lambeth Palace Library	L^2
35.	University of Lancaster (Cartmel Priory Church copy)	Lancaster
36.	Lehigh University Library, Bethlehem, Pennsylvania	PBL
37.	Lincoln's Inn Library, London	L^{22}
38.	University of London (imperfect copy)	L^{30}
39.	Magdalen College, Cambridge	C^{10}
40.	Magdalen College, Oxford	O^{12}
41.	Archbishop Marsh Library, Dublin	D^2
42.	McGill University Library, Montreal	MCG
43.	Law Library, University of Michigan	MICH
44.	University of Minnesota Library, Minneapolis,	MIN
45.	National Library of Scotland (Advocates' Library first copy)	E-1
46.	National Library of Scotland (Advocates' Library second copy)	E-2
47.	New College, Oxford	O^{14}

48.	New York Public Library, New York	NY
49.	Norwich Central Library, Norwich	NOR^2
50.	Van Pelt Library, University of Pennsylvania, Philadelphia	PEN
51.	Carl H. Pforzheimer Library, New York, N.Y.	PFOR
52.	Robert S. Pirie, Hamilton, Mass.	PIR
53.	Princeton Theological Seminary, Princeton, N.J.	PN^2
54.	Queen's College, Cambridge	C^{16}
55.	Queen's College, Oxford	O^2
56.	Saint Andrews University Library	STU
57.	Saint John's College, Cambridge	C^5-1
58.	Saint John's College, Cambridge	C^5-2
59.	Saint John's College, Oxford (imperfect copy)	O^8
60.	Saint Paul's Cathedral Library	L^{15}-1
61.	Saint Paul's Cathedral Library	L^{15}-2
62.	Salisbury Cathedral Library	SAL
63.	John Sparrow, All Souls College, Oxford	SP
64.	Swiss Cottage Library, London	Swiss
65.	Ransom Humanities Research Centre, U. of Texas, Austin	TEX
66.	Robert H. Taylor Collection, Princeton U., Princeton, N.J.	PN
67.	Trinity College, Cambridge	C^2-1
68.	Trinity College, Cambridge	C^2-2
69.	Trinity College, Cambridge	C^2-3
70.	Trinity College Library, Dublin	D-1
71.	Trinity College Library, Dublin	D-2
72.	Trinity College Library, Dublin	D-3
73.	Alexander Turnbull Library, Wellington, N.Z.	WTL
74.	Burke Library, Union Theological Seminary, New York,	U
75.	Wadham College, Oxford	O^7
76.	Westminster Abbey Library	L^{13}
77.	Dr. Williams' Library, London	L^3
78.	Worcester College, Oxford	O^6
79.	Beineke Library, Yale University	Y
80.	York Minster Library	YK-1
81.	York Minster Library	YK-2
82.	York Minster Library	YK-3

IV
The Edition of 1610

The 1610 edition of *Pseudo-Martyr* is the only printed one, and therefore it awakens a considerable amount of textual and bibliographical interest for a modern critical edition. There were no other editions in Donne's lifetime, as in the case of *Devotions*, to distract the contemporary editor's attention away from it in his quest for a definitive text. Moreover, Donne left no explicit signs of his correction of the printed text elsewhere other than in his list of *errata* of the edition. No holograph or other seventeenth-century manuscript of *Pseudo-Martyr* is known to exist, and the first edition is our one source for the work. The only competition for our attention to the first edition springs from the reproduction of one of its copies, L-1, by Scolars Facsimiles and Reprints in 1974, unedited and without commentary, in quarto format, but which reduced the quarto page of the original in reproduction.[85]

Pseudo-Martyr was entered in the *Stationers' Register* on 2 December 1609 and its title page is dated 1610. Nevertheless, no dispute about the date of its completed publication is possible. The moment of the appearance of the work in print in the new year is ascertained by the existence of a letter Donne sent with a presentation copy, and also by the private papers of two seventeenth-century Englishmen recording transactions for the book, all of them dated in the last week of January.[86] *Pseudo-Martyr* therefore went through the press in December of 1609 and in the early days of 1610, and was completed by the second half of January. The book's contents are the title page, Sig. A, which does not contain Donne's name; the dedicatory address to King James, A^2–A^{3v}, which Donne signed; "A Table of the Chapters,"

---

[85] John Donne, *Pseudo-Martyr*, Intro. by Sypher.

[86] *A Transcript of the Registers of the Company of Stationers of London: 1554–1640 A.D.*, edited by Edward Arber, 5 vols. (London, 1876), Vol. III, p. 191^r; Donne's letter to Sir Robert Cotton asking him to deliver an accompanying copy of *Pseudo-Martyr* to "my Lord" (perhaps the Earl of Northampton, Bald, *Life*, p. 221) is dated 24 January (Gosse, *Life*, II, facing p. 108). Bald, *Life*, p. 222: the Earl of Rutland bought a copy on 25 January, and J. Beaulieu sent a copy to William Trumbull on 31 January (*Historical Manuscripts Commission*, Rutland MSS, IV, 1905, p. 465; Downshire MSS, II, 1936, p. 227).

A^{4rv}; "An Advertisement to the Reader," Sigs. ¶ and ¶^{2r}, and a list of *errata* by Donne, Sig. ¶^{2v}, which are quite variably placed among the surviving copies; "A Preface to the Priestes and Jesuits," B–E^{2r}; and *Pseudo-Martyr*, E^3–Hhh^{2v}. The collation thus reads A^4 ¶^{2} (variable) B–Z^4 Aa–Zz^4 Aaa–Ggg^4 Hhh^2, 216 leaves.

In the publishing context of the early seventeenth century, Donne was generally well served for his first major appearance in print. This is true in spite of his prefatory remarks in the "Advertisement" rejecting responsibility for the edition's errors. Both Donne's printer and publisher were very reputable, and the material used for the edition was highly commendable. His printer, William Stansby, was one of a group of a half dozen of the busiest and most prestigious printers in London in the long period of his publishing career from 1597 to 1639.[87] McKerrow describes Stansby as "a man of considerable position in the trade." Stansby began his career in the apprenticeship of the renowned John Windet, who was to take him into partnership in 1597, and, on Windet's death in 1615, he took over his shop.[88] Donne's good fortune was present also in his choice of the owner of rights and bookseller of *Pseudo-Martyr* in the person of Walter Burre. Burre produced Jonson's *Cynthia's Revels* in 1601[89] and, in the year after the publication of *Pseudo-Martyr*, he entered (but did not publish) yet another work by Donne, the original Latin version of *Conclave Ignatii*, in the *Stationers' Register*.[90]

The *Register*'s entry indicating that on 2 December 1609 Burre got permission to publish *Pseudo-Martyr* is straightforward as a record of licensing. As in so many of the *Register*'s notations, the entry gives little information, and it does not mention Donne's and Stansby's names. The entry reads: "Walter

---

[87] Paul G. Morrison, *Index of Printers, Publishers and Booksellers* [in *STC*] *1475–1640*, University of Virginia publications (Charlottesville, Va., 1950), p. 68. Stansby forms a group with Joseph Barnes, Nathanial Butler, Richard Jones, Felix Kingston, and Bonham Norton and, during Stansby's active years, their production is surpassed only by that of Robert Barker and John Bill (pp. 7, 16, 40, 42, 54, 5, 10).

[88] R.B. McKerrow, Gen. Ed., *A Dictionary of Printers and Booksellers in England, Scotland and Ireland, and of Foreign Printers of English Books 1557–1640* (London, 1910), p. 256.

[89] Arber, *Register*, III, p. 71^r, entered 23 May 1601; Percy Simpson, *Proofreading in the Sixteenth, Seventeenth and Eighteenth Centuries* (Oxford, 1935), pp. 11–12.

[90] Arber, *Register*, III, p. 204^r, entered on 24 January 1611.

Burre. / Entred for his Copy under th[e h]andes of master Doctor Pasfeild and master warden Waterson A booke called Pseudomartyr. . . ."[91] The Doctor Pasfeild in question was Zachariah Pashfeild, prebendary of Saint Paul's, and an official licenser for the stationer's office.[92] For his part, "Waterson" was Simon Waterson, an "Upper Warden" of the Stationers' Company in 1609, and later a Master Warden.[93] Both Waterson and Pashfeild had also in 1602 entered *Hamlet* in the *Register*, so that *Pseudo-Martyr* was channelled through the same hands for licensing as the first edition of Shakespeare's play.[94]

Both Burre and Stansby had professional interests in the field of religious controversy which made them a logical partnership for the production of *Pseudo-Martyr* in print. In 1610 Stansby also printed two other controversial religious books, Digby's translation of *A defence of the catholicke faith*, and yet another translation, *Oppositions of the word of God*.[95] For his part, the bookseller Burre's other assigned publication in 1610 was Matthew Stoneham's *A Treatise on the first psalme*. In the following year, he was also to enter John Cartwright's *The preachers travels* along with the Latin text of Donne's contentious *Conclave* in the *Stationers' Register*.[96] Once therefore Stansby and Burre had their licence for *Pseudo-Martyr* from Pashfeild and Waterson, Donne's manuscript was in the hands of a publisher and printer experienced in handling that kind of a book and its possible clientèle.

Burre's reputation spread over almost forty years, 1584 to 1622, of active life in the London publishing trade. It grew principally through his operations

---

[91] Arber, *Register*, III, p. 191^r.

[92] W.W. Greg, *Some Aspects and Problems of London Publishing Between 1550 and 1650* (Oxford, 1956), p. 53; *Licensers for the Press etc. To 1640* (Oxford, 1962), pp. 75–76; Pashfeild's name was variously spelled Pasfeyld and Pasvill.

[93] W.W. Greg and E. Boswell, Eds., *Records of the Court of the Stationers' Company 1576–1602, From Register B* (London, 1930), p. 96. Waterson became a master in 1617.

[94] Arber, *Register*, p. 84^v, entered for the bookseller James Robert on 26 July 1602.

[95] *STC* 7322, Arber, *Register*, III, p. 196^v; *STC* 7333, Arber, *Register*, III, p. 194^v. Of the nine possible entries which may be attributed to Stansby (Morrison, *Index, STC*, p. 68), four are of a religious nature and two interestingly deal with surveying (*STC* 11123 and 18640).

[96] *STC* entry 23289.

out of the last of the three of his London shops at the sign of "The Crane" in Saint Paul's Churchyard, where he established himself in 1604, and where six years later he was to put *Pseudo-Martyr* on sale.[97] In the early months of 1610, therefore, the sheets of Donne's *Pseudo-Martyr* were sold, probably loose and unbound as was the custom of the times,[98] by a knowledgeable bookseller to a clientèle of which a large part was well versed in that kind of literature. The sheets were printed on three different kinds of chained paper bearing the watermarks respectively of a pot, a small crown, and a large crown, and the initials "GH", "IC", and "IR". All three papers were fine and almost definitely imported from France.[99] According to the evidence of the end pages of C^9 and L^{15}-1, some of the copies of *Pseudo-Martyr* were inserted horizontally into the middle of a folded folio sheet as wrapper as they went into their buyers' hands.[100] The folio sheet survives in vertical position (which is

---

[97] McKerrow, *Dictionary*, pp. 56, 312.

[98] Philip Gaskell, *A New Introduction to Bibliography* (Oxford, 1974), p. 146.

[99] Gaskell discusses the use of French paper in England (*Introduction*, p. 60). In *Pseudo-Martyr*, the paper with the pot and the initials "GH", and with narrowly spaced chain marks is most likely No. 12709 in C.M. Briquet, *Les Filigranes, Dictionnaire Historique des Marques du Papier*, Vol. IV (Amsterdam, 1968); it appears in the end sheets of L^{15}-2 and C^9, and in Sig. Xx of L^{15}-2. The paper with the small crown and the initials "IC", and with more widely spaced chain marks than the first paper, is probably a predecessor of No. 1019 in *Monumentae Chartae Papyraceae*, Vol. I, *Watermarks*, by Edward Heawood (Hilversum, Holland, 1950), Plate 147; it appears clearly on pp. 35 and 167 of L^{15}-1, and Sig. B^2 of C-1. The third paper with the large crown and the initials "IR", and also with widely separated chain marks, found on pp. 151 and 195 of L^{15}-1, very strongly resembles No. 1029 on Plate 147 of Heawood's *Monumentae*, Vol. I, except that the initials are "IG", but this may indicate a sale of a papermaker's rights. The locations of the watermarks in all three kinds of paper in the centre of the separate halves of the sheets is described by Heawood as the practice predominantly of French papermakers after 1600 (*Monumentae*, Vol. I, p. 37).

[100] The chain marks in the paper of the end pages of both L^{15}-2 and C^9 are vertical rather than in the horizontal position of all the inner pages of the copies, and the watermark of the pot is upright almost in the centre of each leaf, rather than sideways in the binding. The end pages were therefore made up of folio sheets turned sideways to the order of printing, as though they had originally been folded over the spine of each quarto copy.

evident in the direction of the chain marks) in the end sheets of each of these copies. The book appears to have cost 3s 6d, according to the manuscript note of the price in the upper left hand part of the title page of L-1, and also according to the papers of one of Burre's customers, the Earl of Rutland.[101] Yet, according to the contemporary inscription on the title pages of two other copies, TEX and YK-3, *Pseudo-Martyr* cost 4s to their probable buyers, who were respectively "Peter Daniell" and "Margarett Hoby" of Hackness Hall, whose names likewise are inscribed on the title pages.[102]

The great number of eighty-two known surviving copies of the first edition of *Pseudo-Martyr* suggests that it had an extraordinarily heavy press run. Such a run would have probably eliminated the need of an immediate second edition and explain why, in fact, there was only one publication in Donne's lifetime. By contrast, there were rapidly several successive editions both of *Conclave*, which was printed in two Latin editions and in one English edition all in 1611, only one year after *Pseudo-Martyr* appeared, and of *Devotions Upon Emergent Occasions*. The first edition of *Devotions* appeared with two title pages and the work was published in yet a second edition, all in the same year of 1624. Each of these editions of *Conclave* and *Devotions* has left us comparatively few surviving copies. The *STC* lists only eight known copies of the first English edition of *Conclave*,[103] and only twenty-four copies of the first edition of *Devotions* have apparently survived.[104] Compared with these figures, the number of eighty-two known surviving copies of *Pseudo-Martyr* is strikingly high.

The publishing circumstances surrounding Donne's first major appearance in print with *Pseudo-Martyr* suggest that he had trusting relationships with his publishers and printers. The good nature of these relationships appears to have persisted throughout the publication of his work in the generation that

---

[101] Keynes, *Bibliography*, p. 9, from the *Historical Manuscripts Commission*, Rutland MSS, IV, 1905, p. 465.

[102] The University of Texas copy contains the name "Peter Daniell" written in a contemporary hand on the title page, and he appears to have been the buyer at 4s. The contemporary writing of "Margarett Hoby" of Hackness Hall appears on the title page of YK-3.

[103] *STC*, Vol. I, nos. 7026, 7027, and Keynes, *Bibliography*, pp. 15–19.

[104] According to revised *STC* pre-run proofs, nos. 7033, 7033a, p. 316, and "Introduction," *Devotions*, pp. xli–xlii.

followed. Donne's publishing career was relatively brief, beginning comparatively late for him at the age of almost thirty-eight with his solo publication of *Pseudo-Martyr*, and a short twenty-one years later he was dead of cancer. The publishing relationships in the first decade of that writing career that *Pseudo-Martyr* inaugurated are dominated by Burre's and Stansby's names, and in the second and last decade by the names of only one other printer, Augustine Matthews, and one other bookseller, Thomas Jones. Gosse, one of Donne's major biographers, has happily dwelt on these publishing relationships somewhat. Other biographers like Jessopp and Bald have unfortunately tended to ignore them.[105] Certainly, in the publication of Donne's various works between 1610 and 1620, the recurrence of Burre's and Stansby's names is significant. The repetition suggests more than a passingly accepted service rendered to an author, in spite of Donne's protest in his "Advertisement" and *errata* page of *Pseudo-Martyr* that the edition had many errors. These errors are noticeable mainly in Donne's extremely complex marginal notes, and were often not necessarily due to the printer. Moreover, Donne continued to submit his work to Burre until the latter's death in 1622, and only in that year did he change publisher to Jones.

In the decade of Donne's relationships with Burre, his contacts with Stansby also appear to have been satisfying. Stansby not only served as printer to *Pseudo-Martyr* but to Donne's secular verse and sermons as well. He saw into print Donne's three prefatory poems to Coryat's *Crudities*, and, in 1622, both issues of the first edition of his *Sermon Upon the XV Verse of the XX Chapter of the Book of Judges*.[106]

The publication of this sermon marked a watershed between the two periods of Donne's publishing career, as his good relationships with his publishers and printers continued. In 1622 Burre was only recently dead and, though for the sermon Stansby was still Donne's printer, his new publisher was Thomas Jones. Donne continued till his death to submit his material to Jones.[107] Jones was notable for both the quality and the number of his publications, and Gosse has remarked that during "Donne's lifetime, all of his occasional religous

---

[105] Bald, *Life*, p. 451, mentions the presence of the bookseller Thomas Jones' name in the *Stationers' Register* entry for *Devotions*, without discussion.

[106] *STC* entries 5808 and 7053.

[107] Jones was active in London between 1600 and 1637, and Matthews between 1619 and 1653 (McKerrow, *Dictionary*, pp. 160, 188).

INTRODUCTION   lxv

writings had been published by" him.¹⁰⁸ One notable exception which Gosse overlooked is the sermon of "Commemoration" on the death of Lady Danvers in 1627, which was published by Philomen Stevens. But with this exception, the title pages of all of Donne's other occasional writings in the period after 1622 when the majority of them were written, sixteen items in all, including the first three editions of *Devotions*, twice in 1624 and once in 1626/27, bear Jones' name.¹⁰⁹ Gosse adds that "strangely" after Donne's death "the name of this highly respectable bookseller, who must have been in close relationship with Donne for many years never appears on one of his title pages again."¹¹⁰ The printer who worked most often with Jones on Donne's work and who replaced Stansby after 1622 was Augustine Matthews. Although Matthews' name appears on Donne's title pages less frequently than Jones', it is there nevertheless eight times, including the first two editions of *Devotions* and the two editions of the same work shortly after Donne's death in 1631.¹¹¹ All the other appearances of Matthews' name on Donne's title pages in his lifetime occur with Jones' name as bookseller. However, Matthews must have seen through the press some other publications of Donne's work by Jones that did not identify the printer.¹¹² Matthews' name, like Jones', disappears from Donne's title pages after the posthumous editions of *Devotions* only, it would seem evident, because Donne's death brought the relationship to an end.¹¹³

For practically the whole of his twenty-year career as a publishing writer, Donne's professional relationships were carried out with Stansby and Burre, and then with Matthews and Jones who succeeded them. Printed in the moments of his earliest relationships with Burre and Stansby, *Pseudo-Martyr*,

¹⁰⁸Gosse, *Life and Letters*, p. 306.

¹⁰⁹*STC*, 7025, 7033, 7033a, 7034, 7035, 7039, 7040, 7041, 7042, 7050, 7051, 7052, 7053 (two issues), 7054, and 7057 (two issues). The sermon on the occasion of Lady Danvers' death is *STC* 7049.

¹¹⁰Gosse, *Life and Letters*, II, p. 306.

¹¹¹*STC* entries 7024, 7033, 7034, 7036, 7038, 7039, 7040, and 7051.

¹¹²*STC* entries 7024, 7033, 7034, 7039, 7040, and 7051.

¹¹³Matthews printed the first, second, fourth and fifth editions of *Devotions*. It may be significant of Matthews' attempted care in handling Donne's work that the fourth edition was printed from copies of the second and first editions, which he knew, rather than from a copy of the third edition that he did not know, and that also introduced many errors ("Introduction," Donne, *Devotions*, pp. liii–liv).

Donne's first major work in print, marked the beginning of a publication pattern for him that was to end only with his death a generation later. According to the early testimony of the publication of *Pseudo-Martyr*, Donne was a loyal author to his publishers and printers, and was well served by them in return.

None of this fruitful picture of Donne's publishing relationships is marred by the presence of numerous locations of the three-page-long "Advertisement to the Reader" and the one-page *errata* list among the surviving copies of *Pseudo-Martyr*. The high number of these locations raises problems but they do not compromise the relatively happy context of the early bibliographical history of the work. The positions of Sigs. ¶^{1} and ¶^{2}, which the "Advertisement" and the *errata* list occupy, vary considerably, literally from the beginning to the end of the work among surviving copies.[114] These signatures are found in different locations, among the preliminary parts of the book, after the title page but before the "Preface to the Priestes, and Jesuits," and also among the last leaves at the very end. One of these variations raises the possibility of a second issue which must be examined closely.

The first variation of the location of Sigs. ¶^{1} and ¶^{2}, first in the sense that it occurs sooner than the others in the printed text, comes immediately after the title page, that is, after Sig. A^{1v}. The "Advertisement" and the list of *errata* therefore precede the beginning of the dedicatory address to King James on Sig. A^2. There is only one copy revealing this position, and that is L-1.[115] Moving forward into the volume, there is also only one copy, O^{14}, that reveals the signature in the next location between the address to James and "The Table." The third location of the signatures is found between "The Table" and "The Preface" (between Sigs. A^4 and B^1). With some forty-nine occurrences, this location is by far the most common one among the surviving copies.[116] Less commonly, in their fourth location, Sigs. ¶^{1} and ¶^{2} come at the end of Donne's text, that is, after Sig. Hhh^{2v}. There, the "Advertisement"

---

[114] Keynes and Sypher have noted, without bibliographical comment, that Sigs. ¶^{1} and ¶^{2} have a variable location (*Bibliography*, p. 9; "Introduction," *Pseudo-Martyr* [p. 11]), while Simpson, *Prose Works*, p. 179, and Bald, *Life*, pp. 23, 201, do not mention it.

[115] Sypher has noted generally that the collation of L-1 differs from Keynes' ("Introduction," *Pseudo-Martyr* [p. 11]).

[116] The copies include D-1, D-2, YK-1, YK-2, C-1, C-3, C-4, EX, CH, LYD, Bristol, O-2, O^7, O^5, O^{18}, O^2, ILL, F, PFOR, Y, PEN, DUR^5-2, PN, WTL, PIR, COR,

and the *errata* list form a kind of appendix concluding the book before its end sheets. This location includes copies C-2, L^{30}, HER, DUR^5-1, SAL, STU, YK-3, M^2, and Lancaster. Elsewhere, in the case of two copies, O-1 and O^8, the signatures are absent and may have never been bound with Donne's text.

Finally, somewhat mysteriously, in eight copies (L-2, CU, C^{16}, Carlisle, L^{15}-1, D-3, C^2-3, and E^8), Sigs. ¶¹ and ¶² are frankly misplaced. They interrupt the continuity of Donne's text and they are also inverted. The "Advertisement" and the *errata* list are bound between the last two leaves of the work, that is, between Sigs. Hhh^1 and Hhh^2. Moreover, in their misplaced position, the last page of the "Advertisement" appears first, followed by the list of *errata*, and then come the first and second pages of the "Advertisement" (reading in this order: pages three, four, one, and two). Keynes records the existence of one of these copies, L-2. He writes that the reversion of the two leaves of Sigs. ¶¹ and ¶² between the two leaves of Sigs. Hhh^1 and Hhh^2 implies that all four signatures "were imposed together" in the printing of L-2, but not (Keynes' reader assumes) in the printing of the other copies where Sigs. ¶¹ and ¶² are located elsewhere.[117] If this were the case, now that seven other copies in L-2's state have come to light, the possibility that the reversion points to a separate issue through the "imposition" of four leaves, must be considered. More than the accidental mis-binding of a single copy can be at stake.

However, investigation shows that the existence of these eight maverick copies raises only the apparent possibility of a separate issue of *Pseudo-Martyr*'s first edition. If it was real, the issue would have been created accidentally by a press error early in the printing, during the run-off of the first sheets of the final pages of the volume. Whole signatures would have been mis-set in the printer's frame as though he had been trying to create a continuous text with a kind of appendix of the "Advertisement" and list of *errata* at the close of Donne's work. This issue would have necessarily been the first. The second issue would have been meant to correct the mis-setting of the first by creating the separate text of the "Advertisement" and *errata* list of the other surviving copies.

PBL, BIRM, MIN, TEX, CAL, L^{13}, L^2, L^{15}-2, L^{22}, L^3, HD, A, NOR^2, E-1, E-2, D^2, C^3, C^2-1, C^2-2, C^5-1, C^5-2, C^{10}, SP.

[117] Keynes, *Bibliography*, p. 9.

However, a detailed collation of the four pages of the "Advertisement" and the list of *errata* in six copies in which they are in correct order, whether they appear after the title page, or before the "Preface," or at the very end of the work (L-1; C-1, C-3, C^2-1, C^2-2; C-2), with two copies in which they are misplaced and inverted (C^2-3 and C^{16}), rules out the possibility of separate issues. There are no dissimilarities of page-setting in the printing of the "Advertisement" and the list of *errata* springing from the publication of separate issues among any of the above copies, in spite of their five different locations in the surviving texts. The blots, the slightly broken letters, and the line and word undulations in the leaves of each copy are about identical.[118] The differences of shade and spacing in the printing noticeable among them are of the order that always exists between any two copies of an early seventeenth-century edition. The same is equally to be said of Sigs. Hhh^{2rv}, and yet these signatures would also have had to be re-set in all of the above copies of the second issue.[119] Such a consistency in collation between the maverick and other copies would be impossible if there had been two issues. Moreover, the bindings of the garbled copies L^{15}-1 and C^{16} reveal Sigs. $\P^1$ and $\P^2$ to be a separate quire of two folded leaves misplaced in the quire of the folded leaves Hhh^1 and Hhh^2.

One explanation for the maverick copies is that the sheets of at least some copies of *Pseudo-Martyr*, once printed, were pre-cut for Walter Burre's customers in his shop, but not put into correct order. Someone would have evidently not been paying attention to his routine job. Not all copies of

---

[118]The blur in the "h" of "the", l. 2, and in the first "e" of "pleased", l. 12, and the off-line "er" in "over-indulgent" on l. 32 in Sig. $\P^{1r}$; the undulating "either in expecting", on l. 7, and the broken "n" in "thing" on l. 42 of Sig. $\P^{1v}$; the blot in the "A" of "Arguments" in line 11, the broken "n" in "any" on l. 19, and the slightly undulating centre page of Sig. $\P^{2r}$; and the very pale "h" in "Those" on l. 1, the pale "t" in "to" and the pale "h" in "thus" on l. 4, the two breaks in the centre page vertical line, and the broken or imperfect "2" in "244" on l. 21 of Sig. $\P^{2v}$.

[119]The imperfect or broken "g" in "Lucemburgo" on l. 2 and "a" in "lastly" on l. 4, the pale "A" in "As" on l. 17, and the undulating "Impious" on l. 24 of Sig. Hhh^{2r}; the imperfect second "e" in "sense" on l. 1, the undulating "hereticall" on l. 7, and the differently undulating "hereticall" again on l. 26 of Sig. Hhh^{1v}; the pale "i" in "their" on l. 7, and the undulating "speculation" on l. 24 of Sig. Hhh^{2r}; and the imperfect (cracked?) "n" in "in" on l. 7, the deformed "u" in "absolutely" on l. 12, and the imperfect "m" in "formerly" on l. 23 of Sig. Hhh^{2v}.

Pseudo-Martyr in sheets need have been cut and prepared for sale in this way, as the selling practices for the same book in the same shop were not always constant. The two prices of 3s 6d and 4s charged for *Pseudo-Martyr* are evidence of this. The eight copies, after sale, would have been bound as in good page order by their buyers before they checked them and discovered the error in the placing of Sigs. ¶^{1} and ¶^{2}.

Another possible explanation for the existence of the maverick copies is that the four pages of the "Advertisement" and *errata* list were printed together on one sheet with the four pages of Sigs. Hhh^1 and Hhh^2. That is, the "Advertisement" and *errata* list would have been published *recto-verso* at one end of the sheet, and the other four pages of Sigs. Hhh^1 and Hhh^2 at the other end. The sheets would have then gone to the binders in an uncut state. At this point, the various bookbinders of the maverick copies would have all made the same error of mechanically folding Sigs. ¶^{1} and ¶^{2} into Sigs. Hhh^1 and Hhh^2 once, and then twice into quarto size without verifying that what they were doing produced or did not produce a correct order in the pagination of the bound text. The printer's original intention would not have been to interlock the signatures, but to cut them apart before folding.

If the maverick copies were printed in this fashion, all other copies of the first edition of *Pseudo-Martyr* were printed in the same manner too. The difference between the correct and the maverick copies is that the majority of the bookbinders would have been looking at what they were doing, and some of them not. Indeed, there are both negative and positive kinds of evidence to suggest that Sigs. ¶ and Hhh were printed in the above fashion, one at the top *recto-verso* and the other at the bottom of a single sheet, for all copies. The bindings of copies L^{15}-1 and C^{16} reveal that Sigs. Hhh^1 and Hhh^2 which conclude the volume are a separate quire of half a folio sheet, and also that the other half of the sheet was not used for the blank end pages. The unprinted half of the sheet would have necessarily been used for the end pages if it had not been cut off. Copy L^{15}-1 also reveals that its end page is made of another paper. The end page, made from a separate sheet, was created by being cut large enough to provide a flap which was inserted under Sig. Hhh before binding to hold it in place. The flap is visible in L^{15}-1 between Sigs. Ggg^{4v} and Hhh^{1r}. On the other hand, the paper used for the leaves of Sigs. ¶^{1} and

¶² in the same volume is of the same kind as Sig. Hhh, suggesting that they could have all been printed on the same sheet.[120]

Regardless of the origin of the binding error which characterizes the eight maverick copies, it appears certain that the "Advertisement" and the *errata* list were written by Donne just as the printing was coming to its end. The fact that they are found in five different locations and that they are missing in two of the surviving copies suggests that they are a writer's afterthought to his main text. It must be assumed that Donne intended no specific place for the "Advertisement" and the *errata* list, particularly as their signatures are discontinuous with those in the rest of the work. If this is the case, Sigs. ¶¹ and ¶² would have been printed and sold separately but at the same time as, and with the main text of, Donne's work. Thence, they would have found their way into bound copies according to the instructions of Burre's customers to their respective bookbinders as to where they thought the "Advertisement" and the *errata* page should go. In the present edition, the "Advertisement" is placed after the "Table" as in the group of copies formed by C-1, EX and D-1, where it probably fits most logically, and the *errata* sheet is dropped. As far as other major variants among existing copies of 1610 are concerned, there are none — no cancelled leaves, no variant title pages, and no colophon.

A number of copies appear to retain their original, early seventeenth-century bindings. These include copies MICH (calf, rebacked), F (limp vellum), L^3 (leather), CU, D-3 (sheep, rebacked), O^2 (limp vellum), L^{15}-1 (vellum), YK-2 (limp vellum), M^2 (mottled calf), PFOR (vellum), HER (limp parchment), CH (sprinkled calf), LYD (limp vellum), and L^{13} (limp vellum).

---

[120]The end sheets are in the probably No. 12709 Briquet, *Les Filigranes*, kind of paper, with the narrowly spaced chain marks and the pot. However, the paper of Sigs. ¶¹, ² and H in copy L^{15}-1 is of the same kind (that is, with watermark Heawood No. 1029).

V
Biblical and Manuscript Sources

The examination of the surviving copies of *Pseudo-Martyr* reveals that for his biblical references, Donne used two, and perhaps three, Bibles. These were, first, the English version of the Protestant Geneva Bible; second, the official Vulgate Latin Bible of the Council of Trent sanctioned by Pope Sixtus V; and third, perhaps the Latin Bible of the Dutch reformer Francis Junius. The first two Bibles at least, one Protestant and in English, and the other Catholic and in Latin, appear incontrovertibly to have been at Donne's hand constantly during the composition of the various parts of his work. There is no visible trace of the Authorized Version, which was in preparation and which was to be published in the next year, 1611.

Several editions of the first Bible, the Geneva version, were published in English in London, including one by the king's printer, Robert Barker, in 1608.[121] Donne found this Bible greatly to his liking during the composition of *Pseudo-Martyr*, though a little more than a dozen years later, in December of 1623 during the composition of *Devotions Upon Emergent Occasions*, his preferences had transferred almost entirely to the King James version.[122] His use also of the Catholic Vulgate Latin Bible in *Pseudo-Martyr* may for its part have been due to habit and familiarity with Counter-Reformation scholarship. This Bible would have been eminently useful to him in the controversy in which he was taking part. It was the new Latin Catholic version, first officially published in Rome in 1590, and reissued in many derivative editions in several European cities.[123] Among these was an edition in Antwerp

---

[121] *The Bible. Translated according to the Ebrew and Greeke, and conferred with the best Translation in divers Languages. . . . Imprinted at London by Robert Barker. . . . 1608*. This Bible was first published in English in Geneva in 1560, hence, its name, and was subsequently published several times in London, including 1570, 1589 and 1599.

[122] "Introduction," *Devotions*, p. xlviii.

[123] *Biblia Sacra Vulgatae Editionis ad Concilii Tridentini praescriptum emendata et A Sixto V. P.M. recognita et approbata. . . . Romae [,] Ex Typographia Apostolica Vaticana [,] M.D. XC*. Another edition appeared in Rome in 1592.

in 1605, a centre for the publication of many Counter-Reformation books destined for distribution in England.¹²⁴ A copy of any edition of the Catholic Latin Vulgate Bible can be envisaged as having been available to Donne, and he also showed his familiarity with it in his writing of *Conclave* in the following year.¹²⁵ The quotations of biblical passages and their numbering in *Pseudo-Martyr* point directly to the Geneva and Vulgate versions as Donne's scriptural sources. His biblical references are either verbatim quotations, or direct vocabulary adaptations, of the Geneva and Vulgate Bibles. Compared with these Bibles, the Latin Protestant version by Junius, also printed in several cities in Reformation Europe (including London) and surely available to Donne, may have been used most sparingly, if at all, for *Pseudo-Martyr*.¹²⁶

In Donne's use of an English Protestant Bible, the natural alternative to the Geneva version was the Bishop's Bible, which was also published in London.¹²⁷ But very little evidence, if any, exists for his use of it. Donne's English quotations of Isaiah 49.23 and Deuteronomy 33.3 (p. 82), Proverbs 17.24 (p. 109), Job 2.2 (p. 110), John 10.16 (p. 222) and Jeremiah 1.10 (p. 223), in which the particularities of language are such as to make sources definite, spring from the Geneva version. The use of the word "humbled" in "the saints of God, are said to be humbled at his feete" in Deuteronomy 33.3 occurs only in the Geneva Bible and neither in the Bishop's Bible nor in the later Authorized Version; "humbled" is also the pivotal word in the correction of the garbled original printing of that note as Deuteronomy C.10 (quarto p. 89), which is an impossible reference. Similarly, the occurrence of "worship" rather than

---

¹²⁴ *Biblia Sacra Vulgatae Editionis Sixti V. Pont. Max. iussu recognita atque edita. Antwerpiae Ex officina plantiniana Apud Iannem Moretum. M.DC.V.* Other editions were published earlier in Antwerp in 1599 and 1603.

¹²⁵ Donne, *Conclave*, p. 67.

¹²⁶ *Testamenti veteris [,] Biblia Sacra, sive, Libri Canonici Priscae Iudaeorum Ecclesiae à Deo traditi, Latini Recens Ex Hebraeo facti, brevibusque Scholiis illustratiab. Immanuele Tremellio & Francisco Junio. . . . Londini. . . . R.B. . . . . 1597.* This Bible was published in Hanover in 1596 and 1602, in a very early version in London in 1580, and in Saint Gervais in France in 1607.

¹²⁷ *The Holy Bible, containing the Old Testament and the New, Authorised and appointed to be read in Churches. Imprinted at London by Robert Barker. . . . 1602.* The "Bishops' Bible" was first published in London in 1568 and passed rapidly through several editions, including 1572, 1575, 1595 and 1602, among others.

"fall before" or "bow down" in Isaiah 49.23 (quarto p. 89), and the quotation "the eies of a foole, are in the corners of the world" in Proverbs 17.24 (quarto p. 133), rather than "the eyes of fooles wander thorowout all lands" in the Bishop's Bible, and "the eyes of a foole are in the ends of the earth" in the King James Bible, speak beyond question, word for word, for the Geneva Bible as their source. Again, the numbering of the missing footnote in the list of *errata*, I Sam. 24.15, conforms to the Geneva text rather than to the 24.14 of the other two Bibles. By contrast, the Geneva numbering of this very same footnote, I Sam. 24.15, is the only one that Donne preferred to all the numberings of the King James Bible in *Devotions* in December of 1623, by which time his preferences had transferred about completely to the Authorized Version.[128] One wonders whether in the numbering of this note in *Devotions*, Donne was not unconsciously recalling by association the correction of the missing annotation in *Pseudo-Martyr* more than a decade earlier.

As far as Donne's biblical Latin quotations are concerned, several point to their provenance in the Vulgate edition. These include Deuteronomy 17.12 (p. 45), Job 26.5 (p. 51), and Exodus 22.28 (p. 55). In only one instance among all the biblical quotations of *Pseudo-Martyr*, that of Acts 10.13 (p. 84), does the Latin vocabulary appear to spring from the Protestant Junius Bible. The quotation reads "macta & manduca," rather than "occide & manduca" of the Vulgate edition, and there, ironically, Donne is citing the quotation from the Jesuit Bellarmine's *De Controversiis*. Donne probably obtained the Protestant quotation from Bellarmine rather than directly from the Junius Bible.

Two of Donne's other Latin quotations, which are also verbatim borrowings from the Vulgate, are nevertheless at the centre of textual numbering problems in spite of the certainty of their provenance. These quotations are "Super aspidem & Basiliscum ambulabis" (p. 82), and "Omnia Subiecisti sub pedibus eius" (p. 83). In both cases, the marginal references of these quotations are contradictory. The marginal note to the first quotation, "Super aspidem," points correctly to the numbering, Psalm 90.13, in the Vulgate Bible of its origin in some copies that include C-2, C-3, C^9, Y, L^2, L-2, L^{30}, C^5-1, C^5-2, O^7, O^8, O^{14}, O^{18}, and D-1 (quarto p. 89). However, the same note, for example, in copies L-1, O-1, O-2, O^5, O^2, SP, C-1, C-4, F, HD, E-1, BIRM, PN and MIN, among others, appears as Psalm 91.13, which is the numbering

---

[128] "Introduction," *Devotions*, p. xlviii.

in the English Geneva Bible. Later (on quarto p. 91), the marginal note Psalm 8.6 of the second quotation, "Omnia Subiecisti," is numerically correct in all copies if it refers to the English Geneva Bible. However, the quotation cannot possibly come from that text even as an unmotivated loose Latin rendering. The quotation is a verbatim transcription of the Vulgate Latin text where, in the Rome edition, it is numbered Psalm 8.7, and, in the Antwerp edition, 8.8. No surviving copy of *Pseudo-Martyr* exists listing a marginal note for the quotation as 8.7 or 8.8. What is to be noted in the cases of both quotations is that some attempt appears to have been made to make them concord with the Geneva Bible.

Though retaining the Latin texts of the Vulgate Bible in both quotations, Donne may have tried to make the marginal numbering conform to the Geneva version. This Bible, though not in the Latin of the quotations, was surely more available to his readers than the Counter-Reformation Bible proscribed on English soil. The text of *Pseudo-Martyr* that follows in the present edition retains the Geneva numbering that Donne probably intended. In the case of the quotation "Omnia Subiecisti," the marginal note in all surviving copies of *Pseudo-Martyr* gives the numbering of Psalm 8.6 in the Geneva Bible, so that no emendation to any printed text is needed. In the case of the other quotation, "Super aspidem," in the present edition, the Vulgate numbering of Psalm 90.13 of some copies is dropped in favour of the Geneva numbering of Psalm 91.13 of the other copies, although it is impossible to prove with finality which of the two numberings Donne intended. Donne's numbering of his biblical quotations in his marginal notes nevertheless throws light on his preparation of his manuscript, and of his interference as the manuscript was in the process of being transcribed into print.

In the present edition of *Pseudo-Martyr*, there are perforce different kinds of corrections to the biblical marginal notes as they appear in the surviving copies of 1610. Some corrections simply rectify errors of numbering according to the Bibles that Donne used. Apart from those mentioned above, these errors are wrong according to the numbering in all Bibles.[129] Another sort of correction in the present text fills out incomplete biblical references to their

---

[129] Examples are Rev. 7.15 (7.14) (quarto Sig. E^{1v}); John 1.8 (1.7) (p. 5); Deut. 17.12 (17.11) (p. 28); John 10.32 (10.30) (p. 92); Mar. 3.14 (Mat.) and Act. 9.20 (9.12) (p. 153); I Pet. 4.15, 16 (4.15) (p. 201); Acts 16.26 (16) (p. 207).

INTRODUCTION   lxxv

full numbering.[130] Donne's usual practice in his work, as in *Devotions Upon Emergent Occasions*, was to give book, chapter and verse numbers, whenever applicable. The present edition also supplies several missing biblical notes of which only a few are singled out in the *errata* list.[131] Next, a few standardizations are made of biblical references that are correct in some copies, and wrong in others.[132] This indicates that proof-reading went on as the text was being printed, or else that some characters broke during printing and were wrongly replaced. Finally, the present edition repairs the broken characters of marginal biblical notes which in surviving copies of *Pseudo-Martyr* appear never to have been repaired.[133]

The Bibles used for the collation which produced the following text are the Cambridge University Library copies of the London edition of the Geneva Bible of 1608 (shelf mark Syn. 5.60.10), the Rome edition of the Vulgate Bible of 1590 (s.m. Young 53), the Antwerp edition of the Vulgate Bible of 1605 (s.m. 1.24.19), the London edition of the Junius Bible of 1597 (s.m. Rel.b.59.2), and the London edition of the Bishops' Bible of 1602 (s.m. 2.60.4).

If our knowledge of the Bibles Donne used enlightens us considerably about his preparation of the manuscript of *Pseudo-Martyr*, so does his superficially bewildering system of annotation. The present edition therefore retains this system of annotation for diverse important historical reasons even though it does not contribute anything directly to the appearance of *Pseudo-Martyr* in modern print. Donne's discordant alphabetical reference system between the text and marginalia is found in several passages, but not in all of *Pseudo-Martyr*. That is, sometimes a little "a", "b", or "c", and so forth down the alphabet occurs slightly above line within the text, and refers to an identical letter accompanying the suitable note in the margin. This reference system,

---

[130] Examples are Mar. 10.29, 30 (10.29) (*errata*); Exod. 20.12 (20) (quarto Sig. E^2); I Cor. 15.31 (15) (p. 7); Exo. 22.28 (22) (p. 45); I Reg. 15.13 (15) (p. 79); Psal. 118.10 (118) (p. 86); Deu. 14.8 (14) (p. 173); Acts 15.1 (15) (p. 312); Gal. 5.19, 20 (5.20) (p. 383).

[131] Examples are Mar. 10.29, 30 (*errata*) (quarto p. 7); I Sam. 24.15 (*errata*) (p. 40); Numbers 29 (p. 51); Matt. 16.18, 19 (p. 71); and I Tim. 2.2 (p. 170).

[132] Examples are John 10.32 (10.30) (quarto p. 92: copies C-2, C-3, C^9, Y, L^2); John 15.13 (13.15) (p. 210: copies E-2, C-3); and Luke 22.38 (22 38) (p. 317: copies C-1, C-2, C-4, C^9, L-1, L^2, Y).

[133] For example, Numbers 35.33 (3[?].33) (Sig. C^{2v}).

which is revealing of the length and preparation of Donne's manuscript pages, is retained here.

    This system, besides being occasional, is not even necessarily continuous on a single quarto page of Donne's printed text. That is, on one page, the alphabetical numbering of the notes might begin anywhere, even though other notes precede on the same page (for example, on quarto pages 37 and 130). In such cases, moreover, the reference lettering does not even necessarily cover the notes down to the end of the page. That is, sometimes only a bunch of notes in the middle of the page is annotated (Sig. B^{1v}, quarto p. 271). The reference system also sometimes starts at the top of a page and stops part-way down and does not cover the remaining notes to the end of the page (quarto pp. 30, 81, 109). On other pages, often enough, there are two sequences, one beginning immediately at the note where the other leaves off (quarto pp. 19, 25, 248, 251), and sometimes one sequence begins on one page and ends on the next (pp. 20, 26, 35, 40, 49, 85, 130, 342), and still another sequence begins (pp. 26, 86, 131) and ends on yet the following page (pp. 87, 132). None of these sequences is ever more than about a quarto page long, that is, about approximately the length of the script that somebody like Donne writing in ink in 1609 could get onto a page of seventeenth-century paper. It is therefore highly probable that the reference system was Donne's, as the series of letters do not conform to printed quarto pages, but rather to a presentation of the text that pre-dates its composition into print. Moreover, if the reference system was Donne's, as seems certain, he tended to use it on those pages of his manuscript where the annotation in the marginalia was dense. Obviously, because Donne was preparing a manuscript for publication, he wanted the compositors to transcribe the notes correctly into the margins of his published text.

    Looking at the beginning and end of Donne's longest, densely annotated and lettered passages, the modern reader obtains a quite precise idea of the length and fullness of one of Donne's manuscript pages. All of the longest series of reference letters in Donne's printed text cover about the same number of lines. The length of each of these longest series of reference letters was obviously dictated by the length of the manuscript page. Each of these series covers about equally the same number of lines in the first edition and necessarily in the transcription of this edition into modern print here. For example, in the original quarto text, one of the manuscript pages ran from about l. 15 on p. 40 to l. 13 on p. 41, with reference letters "a" to "k"; or from about l. 20 on p. 85 to l. 24 on p. 86, with reference letters "a" to "f"; or from about l. 25 on p. 86 to l. 29 on p. 87, with letters "a" to "o"; or from about l. 16 on p. 130 to l. 19 on p. 131, with letters from "a" to "l"; or from about l. 20 on p. 131 to l. 19 on p. 132, with letters from "a" to "i"; or from about l. 10 on p. 278 to l. 20 on p. 279, with letters from "a" to "e". The length of the manuscript page may be gauged in the present edition by observing the long sequences of the reference letters in the densely annotated passages on pp. 52–53, 80–81, 81, 107–108, 108–109, and 199, corresponding to the above passages of the original quarto text. As in the sequences of the edition of 1610, the sequences in the present edition often begin on one page and finish on another, and they are never deliberately commensurate with a single page of printed text.

VI
The Text

Two copies of *Pseudo-Martyr*, C-1 (Syn. 6.61.31) and L-1 (1009.c.33), serve jointly as copy texts for the present edition. Both copies are whole, their print is clear, and their typography is generally completely accessible for examination. As in the case of all books printed in the period, the folio sheets of L-1 and C-1 were run off in piles for each eight pages, *recto* and *verso*, until the whole volume was printed. Consequently, neither L-1 nor C-1, nor any other of the surviving copies of *Pseudo-Martyr*, each of them created by the manual compilation from piles of printed sheets, appears bibliographically sounder than the others. The two copy texts share certain errors, and each has inferiorities, corrections and errors of its own. Both merit the title of copy text because of the relative success of the original printing of their sheets. They have also survived equally well the intemperies of almost four hundred years of ownership, which cannot be said of all copies by any means, particularly as their contribution to the preparation of a definitive text is concerned.

There is not so much evidence of the existence of what might be called intrinsically superior and inferior copies of the first edition of *Pseudo-Martyr*, as evidence from some leaves of certain copies that in fact all copies were subject to care. Some copies contain certain errors and corrections, but there is no pattern among them, and hence no avowedly superior or inferior copies. There is ample proof that, during printing, certain care was brought by Donne, by his compositors, and most probably by his printer Stansby, to the correction of original errors on the part of either author or printer, and of errors created during run-off by the faulty replacement of broken type or by mis-setting. This care is particularly evident in the text. There are variants among the existing copies that suggest constant editorial supervision, and there are also relatively few troubling passages in the printed text in spite of the complexity of its arguments and of its phrasing, and of the density of its allusions. The same care cannot be claimed for the marginal notes; or rather, the marginalia required several times more editorial supervision than the text, but did not receive it. The notes are often in a garbled state, or they are wrong, missing or misplaced, although their variants among existing copies also reveal much in-press correction.

Of the care brought by Donne, the evidence is significant. Indeed, the variants among the existing copies of the 1610 edition of *Pseudo-Martyr* are not without suggesting that Donne kept popping in and out of the printer's shop to cast an anxious eye on the sheets of his first book as they left the printer's frame. There are certain variants among copies of the edition that could only have come about because of the fortuitous interference of a knowledgeable author. For example, the alteration to the marginal note on quarto p. 260 from "Contr. i. Venetia." (L-1, C-1, C^{10}, YK-1, Carlisle, PIR, BIRM, TEX) to the correct "Contra. Venetia." (C-3, C^2-1, WTL, PEN, O^{18}, SP, L^2) could only have been made by someone who knew the title of the original Italian work by Lelio Medici. Medici was the Inquisitor General of Florence, and his use of the Italian article "i" in his title did not go with the noun "Venetiani" which Donne's note abbreviates, but with the other noun in the title, "fondamenti," which the note does not in any way cite (see Commentary, for p. 86, ll. 4–11). Donne it was, surely, correcting his own marginal Italian transcription. Similarly, the correction of "Ravolta" in two marginal notes (as in copies L-1, F, O^5, SP, L^{30}, C^2-1, SAL, COR, D^2, D-3, MIN) to "Raccolta" (C-1, C^5-2, O^7, PFOR, CAL, HER, E-1, E-2, E^8, C-4, C^2-2, C^2-3) on quarto p. 95 most likely originated with Donne as well. In the *errata* list Donne corrected, on Sig. C^{1r} earlier in the work, the same mis-spelling of the word. This earlier error appears to be general in all copies because Donne evidently caught it only after all sheets of the signature had been printed, and its occurrence may have prompted him to be vigilant about the word's subsequent appearances on the pages yet to be printed.

Donne also listed a number of other errors in the *errata* list that were corrected before all sheets containing them were run off. These interrupted errors, as it were, suggest his fairly constant supervision. They include the marginal annotation "pili" (C^3, L-2, PIR, PFOR, Carlisle, E-2, NOR^2, COR) for "polit" (L-1, L^{15}-1, CAL, TEX, HER, PBL, BIRM, D-2, D-3) on Sig. B^{4r}, "thereof for" (SP, CH, WTL, SAL, D^2, L^{13}, MIN, DUR^5-1, DUR^5-2, L^{13}) for "therefore" (L^{22}, L-1, E^8, PH, D-2, HER, TEX, CAL, BIRM) on quarto p. 170, and "Dominium" (MCG, C^2-3, PN, E-1, CH) for "Domicilium" (L-1, C-1, D^2, E-2, BIRM) on quarto p. 379. The correction of these errors before all the sheets containing them were run off suggests Donne's availability during printing. A compositor or printer could have signalled the presence of these errors on the already printed sheets to Donne, and could have suggested to him to put them in an *errata* list after he, the printer, had himself corrected them. However, this is unlikely because of the Latin expertise required, for example, for the first and third corrections.

A number of stylistic changes also support Donne's presence at the printing. For instance, on l. 2 of quarto p. 220, the phrase "Cuntry, as Pope Gregory the I, whom he" in some copies (such as L-1, C-2, O^8, O^2, O^{14}, O^5, O^{18}, C^5-2, D-1, D-2, D-3, E-1 and SAL) replaced, one must assume, the phrase "Country, as Pope Gregory whom hee," which lacks the words "the I" in other copies (like MCG, C-1, C-4, C^5-1, HER, WTL, PEN, E-2, and O^7). In all copies three lines later, the name of Gregory again appears with the title of "the I". In the second group of copies like C-1 and MCG in which the words "the I" appear only once, the reader is confused to have the pope named without the number on line 2, and then with the number on line 5. In *Pseudo-Martyr*, Donne deals repeatedly with about six popes called Gregory, and the reader has the impression that "Gregory the I" on line 5 is another pope than the Gregory mentioned without "the I" three lines earlier. This confusion does not exist in the first group of copies that list Gregory as "the I" on both lines. However, the repetition of "the I" on line 5 is redundant, and is dropped in the present text. The present edition assumes that the compositor's inadvertent eye inverted the identification of Gregory as "the I" from the printed line 2 to line 5, from its original appearance in the equivalent lines in Donne's manuscript. Donne can then be presumed to have corrected the error by including "the I" on line 2, but he did not bother to have the second "the I" on line 5 removed, as this would quite simply have left a gap in the printer's line of the already set page.

Similarly, among other errors producing stylistic deformations, Donne appears to have caught the compositor's misreading of "t" for "s", producing "too" for "so" in both the catchword of quarto p. 253 and in the sentence of the text on the first line of p. 254. The corrected sentence reads "receive so deepe impression of *Bellarmines* doctrine, as to pay." As catchword on quarto p. 253, the "too" does not make sense when it mistakenly also appears in some copies as the first word on the following page (for example, C-3, SP, C^{16}, L^2, C^5-1, E-2, WTL, PEN). In other copies, the correct "so" appears in both the catchword and the text (for example, C-1, L-1, C^5-2, L^{30}, O^5, HD, YK-1, O^{18}, Carlisle, CH, SAL, E-1, E-8, PIR, D^2, MIN and L^{13}). However, peculiarly, the faulty "too" continues to appear in the text of yet other copies in spite of the correction of the catchword on the preceding page to "so" (O-2, O^7, C-4, C^9, MCG, HER and PFOR). There was apparently some delay between the compositor's reaction first to Donne's probable pointing out of the error in the catchword on quarto p. 253, and then his correction of the wrong word in the text at the beginning of the next page on the other side of the sheet.

Moreover, this was not the only place where the compositor mistook Donne's "s" for "t". He made the same error in both marginal notes to Hasenmiller, "Hateum" for "Hasenm", and "Hatteum" for "Hassenm", on quarto p. 130, and the errors were apparently never corrected. The same compositor or another also mistook Donne's "l" for "t" in "Ugolini", producing "Ugotini" falsely on quarto pp. 237 and 282 apparently in all surviving copies, and on quarto p. 160 in some copies (including C-3, C-4, YK-2, C^{16} and C^2-1). The similarly erroneous "Schlussetbergius" on quarto p. 375, with its "t" for "l" in some copies (among them, D-2, Y, HD, MCG, C^5-1, C^5-2, C^3-3), was also eventually corrected to the required "Schlusselbergius" in other copies (L-1, L^{30}, C-1, C-2, C-3). Again, in the marginal note on quarto p. 192, in all copies, Donne's "t" was misread for "l" and "Romito" came out as "Romilo". However, like the "Hassenmiller" and "Ugolini" on quarto pages 86 and 281 respectively, "Romito" appears correctly on quarto p. 124 in all copies.

Donne's hand in *Pseudo-Martyr*'s press corrections is perhaps most firmly evident in the relocation of certain marginal notes to their correct positions next to the lines of his printed text. Donne warned his reader in his *errata* list that a number of notes were misplaced, that he had not corrected them, and that he was leaving their correct identification with the on-page text up to the intelligence of his readers. In reality, he located a fair number during the press run and it was he, surely, who inserted a number of missing notes. Of some thirty-one misplaced notes in some copies,[134] ten are in correct position in other copies.[135] One of these relocations on quarto page 106 involved the disentangling of the two notes, to Casaubon and to Bellarmine's *De Purgatorio*. These notes were hopelessly run into each other with faulty

---

[134] Always uncorrected, the notes on quarto Sig. B^{1v}, ll. 7, 17 and 26; C^{2v}; pp. 3 and 51; p. 52, ll. 16 and 25; p. 80, ll. 3, 5 and 8; p. 110; p. 117, ll. 10 and 13; p. 153; p. 183, ll. 11, 16 and 29; pp. 155, and 375, ll. 16 and 19.

[135] Corrected in some copies, the notes on quarto p. 6, ll. 12 and 22 (C-1, L-2, C^5-1, Y, C-2, C-3); p. 7, l. 11 (C-1, L-2, C^5-1, Y, C-2, C-3); p. 9, l. 20 (L-1, Y, F); p. 80, l. 11 (L-1, C-2, C^9, L^{22}, L^3); p. 80, l. 14 (C-1, C-4, C^5-1, C^5-2); p. 106, l. 4 (C-1, C-2, C-3, C-4, F, Y); p. 158, l. 19 (C-1, HD, MCG, L^2); p. 210, l. 8 (C-1, C-2, C-4, Y, E-1); and p. 255, l. 12 (C-1, C-2, C^3, L^{15}-1).

punctuation and missing capital letters so that they look like one note in the uncorrected copies. Conceivably, only a knowledgeable author could have disentangled them and relocated the second note to Bellarmine to its correct position. Elsewhere, the note to Alphonsus Castro on quarto page 9 (Sig. F) may be wrongly located in only three copies (C^2-2, YK-1 and HD), so that the error was certainly caught very early in the printing, but this correction could have been made by a watchful compositor as well as by Donne.

In addition, of some nine completely missing notes, Donne supplied four in the *errata* list. There are at least five other missing notes which Donne probably ignored, four of them to the Bible and one of them to Robert Parsons in which he may in fact have been working from memory (quarto p. 310). Then among the notes missing in only some copies, Donne was probably responsible for the eventual inclusion of the note to Aquinas' *Summa Contra Gentiles* on quarto p. 249 before the press run of Sig. Nn was finished, because there are about as many copies that contain the note as not.[136] Some pages later, someone, possibly Donne, noticed early in the printing of quarto p. 277 on Sig. Rr that the note "Petr. de vineis. Epist. 4. l.1" was accidentally left out, because it seems absent in many fewer copies (for example, O^2, HER, D^2, L^{13}, E-1, E-2, E^{18}, CAL, PFOR, TEX, PIR, PBL, MIN) than those that contain it (like L-1, NOR^2, D-1, CH, WTL and Carlisle).

In a very different vein of rectification in the printed text of *Pseudo-Martyr*, Donne made a correction in the *errata* list, but an attempted correction of the same error had somehow preceded his in the text. The manuscript phrase for ll. 14 and 15 on quarto p. 275 must have read, "but the panegyricke at Henry the thirds death." In the *errata* list, Donne supplied the words, "the panegyricke," which are missing between the conjunction "but" and the preposition "at" in practically all copies (among them, L-1, C-1, O-1, O^2, O^5, C-3, C-4, BIRM and D^2). But in at least five copies, O-2, PFOR, TEX, YK-2 and YK-3, the preposition "at" is also missing. The preposition was evidently added early in the printing to create the phrase, "but at Henry the thirds death," in order to make grammatical, if not logical, sense of the sentence, and in doing so the compositor turned the letter "n" in the word "concealed" into a tilde to make place for the "at" in the printed line. However, naturally,

---

[136] Among others, the following copies have the note: C-3, C-4, C^5-1, C^5-2, C^9, C^2-1, C^2-3, E-2, L^{15}-2, O^8, L^{30}, MCG, D-3, D-1, D^2, PFOR, MIN, CH, SAL, COR, BIRM, NOR^2, PIR, O^{18}, WTL, DUR^5-1, DUR^5-2 and PEN.

INTRODUCTION   lxxxiii

there was insufficient room to squeeze the words "the panegyricke" into the line as well, and they went into the *errata* list.

The 1610 text also appears to have accidently dropped a number of words here and there, creating some faulty grammatical structures which the present edition corrects. For example, on quarto p. 322, an adjective may have disappeared between the words "more" and "obligation", in the phrase "and lay a more Obligation then those other *Decretals*," or else the article "a" is a redundant word. The present edition drops the article "a" in the sentence to give it grammatical and logical sense rather than to try to guess what Donne's irretrievable adjective was, if he used one. In another case, on line 28 of quarto page 37, the verb is missing in the sentence beginning, "Nor doth the Pope improvidently, in advancing." The absence of the verb cannot simply be rhetorical, as Donne's meaning is unintelligible without it. Evidently, a small verb like "act" is missing between the noun "Pope" and the adverb "improvidently," and is supplied in square brackets in the present edition.[137] Donne's compositor may have dropped the word inadvertently when he probably interrupted briefly his normal type-setting to lop the tail off the capital letter "R" that became "P" almost, but not quite successfully, in the word "Pope" on the same line. Part of the tail is still there. Such a practice of creating the capital "P" out of the type letter "R" was fairly general in the printing of *Pseudo-Martyr*, and is evident in several places in the still visible, significant and less significant remainders of the tail of the letter "R" in a variety of words.[138]

In other places in the printed text of 1610, there are indications of the accidental dropping of small words like "and", "the" and "in". There is also a high incidence of missing punctuation at the end of lines of type, as either the compositor had no place to put it in and could not reasonably add it on in a disembodied way to the beginning of the next line, or else the punctuation

---

[137]The uses of "more" (usually spelled "mair") as a comparative adjective, and of "doth" as meaning "act" were already generally archaic by Donne's day.

[138]Part of the tail is visible in the "R" on quarto p. 251, l. 15; p. 257, l. 19; p. 267, l. 1; p. 277, ll. 18 and 25; p. 301, l. 3; and p. 315, l. 2, among other places as well.

was lost early in the printing in a poorly fit position between the text and the marginal line of the printer's frame.[139]

The suspicion also arises that a line of manuscript was lost on l. 12 of quarto p. 90, because the sentence reads, "*Baronius* his furious instigation of the Pope." As it stands, the sentence seems to suggest more than simple incitement, but factually the statement is impossible if it was intended to mean that the Oratorian Cardinal Baronius provoked Pope Paul V against him, as it appears to do. Donne could have hardly believed or mis-read, at least not under normal physical circumstances, that Baronius incited Paul against him. In the Venetian controversy to which Donne is referring, Baronius was one of Paul V's staunchest, most unconditional supporters, and never provoked criticism from him. Moreover, there is no record of Paul having ever rebuked Baronius, and, in spite of the inference of Donne's lines, no Counter-Reformation and yet anti-papal attack was ever conducted to rescue Baronius from Paul's non-existent angry rebuttal. A line of manuscript text between the proper noun "Baronius" and the personal adjective "his" may be missing. This line could refer to the Venice-based Franciscan Giovanni Marsilio who attacked both Paul and Baronius, or else to Gaspar Schopp, alias Macer, who defended both Paul and Baronius against Marsilio.[140] However, as it stands, grammatically, Donne's sentence reads perfectly well, and the present edition does not put words into Donne's mouth by changing it.

On a number of pages, the correction of one error during printing appears to have provided the occasion for proof-reading the entire contents of the signature. Hence, the corrected sheets that followed when the printing resumed produced several variants with the already printed sheets of the same signature. For example, early in the printing of Sig. S, proof-reading caught the erroneous "convenietly" instead of "conveniently" on l. 6, and "shaked" instead of "shaken" on l. 16, of quarto p. 101 (Sig. S^{1r}). Both errors are found in copies L-1, D-3, COR and O^5, and in no surviving copy of *Pseudo-Martyr* does one error ever appear corrected and not the other. But the same

---

[139]Such words are missing on Sig. C^{4r}, l. 18; p. 313, l. 8; p. 372, l. 20, and p. 377, l. 21. The apparatus of the present edition supplies several other examples. Examples of the missing end-line punctuation are in quarto p. 30, l. 2; p. 117, l. 29; p. 168, l. 15; p. 284, l. 18; and p. 387, l. 9. The apparatus records several other instances.

[140]See Commentary for p. 83, ll. 4–15, for the discussion of the problem of the possible missing line.

proof-reading failed to catch the "rhat" rather than "that" on l. 4 of p. 105 (Sig. S^{3r}), an error which seems to be present in all surviving copies.

Again, on p. 253 (Sig. Oo^{1r}), the correction of the catchword from "too" to "so" appears to have provided the occasion for separating the Latin citation "Sed iam" in the marginal note correctly into two words. It seems also to have furnished the opportunity of altering the marginalia indicating the source paragraphs for the page's last three notes, from the abbreviated word "parag." to a convenient symbol, in conformity with Donne's practice everywhere else in *Pseudo-Martyr*. All five corrections on this one page are found in each of the copies L-1, C-1, C-2, O-1, C^2-2, C-4, C^5-2, Y, HD and F, among others; none of these corrections is present in any of the incorrect copies, C^5-1, E-2, SP, C^2-1, C-3, SAL, WTL and PEN; and no copy apparently exists with only part of the corrections. Similarly, the relocation of the wrongly placed note to Maynardus to its correct place on l. 12 of quarto p. 255 (Sig. Oo^{2r}) seems to have occurred when the wrong first word "too" on l. 1 of quarto p. 254 was changed to "so". The surviving copies of *Pseudo-Martyr* have both corrections, or neither.[141]

Elsewhere, the evidences of carelessness by Donne's compositors, or, one must add, by Donne himself, are disheartening, and they are practically always in the marginal notes rather than in the text. On quarto p. 153, for example, five of the seven notes are unpardonably wrong in all copies, Nu. 119 instead of 19, Nu. 42 instead of 32, Mat. instead of Mar., Act 9.12 instead of 9.20, and I Cor. 1.13 is misplaced.

For his part, under the crushing weight of his numerous authorities, and sometimes in handling Latin, Donne was responsible for some errors. For example, he mistook three times Bellarmine's "De Purgatorio" for the "De Beatitudine et Canonizatione" (quarto pp. 196, 198 and 331), and once the chapter "De Ecclesia Militante" of Book III for the "De Notis Verae Ecclesiae" of Book IV of the controversy "De Conciliis et Ecclesia," in the Jesuit's *De Christianae Fidei* (quarto p. 251).[142] Elsewhere, Donne appears to have mistaken Peter Lombard for Saint Bonaventure, the name Sergius for Sylvius or Pius II, Pope Sixtus V twice for Pius V, and the Italian controversialist

---

[141] Other examples of the probable correction of entire signatures or pages may be found on quarto pp. 6 and 7, 210 and 255.

[142] See Commentary for p. 181, l. 29–p. 182, l. 1, for the discussion of the *De Controversiis* in relation to these errors.

Bozio for the Scottish Catholic Barclay.[143] Then, peculiarly, Donne's Latin failed him repeatedly with the feminine noun "haeresis" or heresy. He used it as either masculine or neuter four times on one page, and three times on another, before finally getting it right at the very end of *Pseudo-Martyr* (quarto pp. 120, 324, 388). However, the perception which led to the *errata* correction of "*nostram*" for "*vestram*", "our" for "your", earlier in the work, was surely Donne's (quarto p. 41, l. 8). By contrast, Donne's Italian, which he used much less during his lifetime, appears never, in *Pseudo-Martyr* at least, to have failed him.[144]

The present edition of *Pseudo-Martyr* alters the copy texts, L-1 and C-1, of the 1610 edition only when it is absolutely necessary to create a definitive modern reading. Naturally, it corrects the typographical errors of 1610, and it carries out those changes of wording that are evident deformations of Donne's sense. The present edition also follows the eccentric punctuation of the first edition, without modern standardization, as there is nothing to suggest that this punctuation, like the rest of the text, does not represent Donne's intentions. Stylistically, there is only one exception to this rule. This is the replacement of six commas by semi-colons in Donne's closing sentence of the work. This last sentence is two quarto pages long (pp. 391–392) and is unreadable without repunctuation. Donne himself, or someone close to him, apparently realized the difficult readability of the last sentence as the printing of Sig. Hhh drew to a close because, extraordinarily, one copy, YK-2, shows a change of three commas to semi-colons. Elsewhere, there is also only one exception to the present edition's rule of respecting the 1610 punctuation and capitalization, and that is the standardization of both punctuation and capitalization in Donne's marginalia. The compositors appear to have most arbitrarily and ruthlessly dropped punctuation and capitalization in the marginalia, and to have joined words together at will, to fit the notes into

---

[143]Lombard for St-Bonaventure, quarto p. 351, l. 21; Sergius for Sylvius, p. 367, l. 10; Sixtus V for Pius V, quarto pp. 33 and 279; Bozio for Barclay, p. 262, l. 2; and Commentary for the corresponding passages, on p. 243, l. 17; p. 252, l. 21; pp. 48, l. 17, and p. 199, l. 24; and p. 188, l. 28, of the present edition.

[144]In the references and translations on quarto Sig. C^{1r}, and pp. 95, 124 and 192, discussed in the Commentary for p. 16, ll. 9–11; p. 86, ll. 4–11; p. 104, ll. 16–20; and p. 145, ll. 20–26.

the margins. Without some kind of limited standardization, very many of the original notes are either unintelligible or misleading at best.

All changes to the copy texts of 1610 in the present edition are recorded in the apparatus at the bottom of each page. There are, however, three exceptions. First, the present edition drops, without mention, the period which appears at the end of many marginal notes in the first edition. The notes are already surcharged with abbreviations and punctuation without the periods, and, moreover, the appearance of the period at the end of the notes is very inconsistent. Second, the present edition corrects missing capitalization and punctuation within the marginalia, without listing the emendations below, to avoid clogging the textual apparatus uselessly. Finally, it modernizes the text typographically without mention in the apparatus. It standardizes the long "s", the "u" and the "v", the "j" and the "i", the "u" and the "w", and the "y" and the "i", and it fills out all ligatures and tildes. Therefore, "ioyned" becomes "joined", "perswade" becomes "persuade", "leaue" becomes "leave", and "comand" becomes "command" silently. However, the edition alters none of the phonetic alternatives to modern letters. For example, "relie" does not become "rely", and "neere" does not become "near". In addition, the present edition alters none of the contemporary orthography, even when there are several spellings for the same word in a single paragraph. It preserves the doubling and the elimination of letters in words because they may represent Donne's original practice, and do not necessarily suggest his printer's attempt to fill his lines out flush with his margins. Occasionally, emendations require explanations and these are given in the Commentary.

In the apparatus of the present edition, a colon and a square bracket (pointing left) are used as need be to indicate the nature of the variants. The colon occurs for emendations that depart from the copy texts, L-1 and C-1. The square bracket, on the other hand, indicates that the present edition agrees with one or both of the copy texts.

When the apparatus uses the colon, the emended text taken as the accepted reading is always the first word of the note. Often, this emended text is immediatly followed by *Ed.*, meaning that it represents an editorial change. When the emended text is not followed by *Ed.*, this indicates that it is a reading accepted from a copy or copies of *Pseudo-Martyr* (1610) other than the copy texts, and it is immediately followed by their location symbols. Then follows the colon. On the right-hand side of the colon, there always appears the unamended text as it is found in the copy texts, followed by their symbols

(L-1 or C-1). Sometimes the unamended text is also followed by the symbols of identical, rejected versions of other copies of the first edition if their identification throws light on the nature of the variants.

When the square bracket is used, the unamended text of one or both of the copy texts, which is taken as the preferred reading, appears alone on the left. The provenance of the accepted readings from the copy texts is not identified because the present edition is based upon them. The source of an accepted reading in L-1 and C-1 is automatically to be assumed. This unamended text is followed immediately by the square bracket itself and then by the rejected text. The rejected text can be from one (but never from both) of the copy texts, or from one or several other copies of the first edition, or from both. The rejected text is identified by the appropriate location symbols where it may be found. Occasionally, there are two different rejected texts for a single accepted reading, and they are identified accordingly. The number of texts that are identified as containing a rejected reading depends on the gravity of the variant in question. This rule holds true for the variants in the marginal notes as well as in the text. When the errors in the notes appear to be general in all copies, they are not identified beyond their occurrence in the copy texts. But variant correct and incorrect annotations are identified according to their occurrence in representative copies.

The eighty-two known surviving copies of the first edition of *Pseudo-Martyr* cannot be allowed to crowd the apparatus uselessly and hopelessly. Their high number necessarily confines the identification of the locations of the accepted and unaccepted readings to the copy texts and only to a selected number of other copies. The choice of these other copies must perforce be arbitrary, but the number listed is always governed by the light they throw on the accepted text and its variants.

Still in the apparatus, a page number or a signature symbol refers to the edition of 1610. The apparatus contains no page number or signature symbol of any other work. In addition, as Donne complained to his reader in his *errata* list, a great number of notes were misplaced, and these are identified in the apparatus by *note misplaced*. Similarly, *missing* means that a marginal note is absent in some or all copies. Again, a reference to a marginal note in the textual apparatus is always numbered according to the line of text to which the note refers.

The present edition also uses Roman type not only for the main body of *Pseudo-Martyr*, but also for "The Preface," "The table" and the marginal notes. In the edition of 1610, all of these appeared in Italic type. Where the Italic passages of the edition of 1610 had quotations or citations that had to be distinguished from the rest of the text, these appeared in Roman type. The present edition inverts the procedure in accordance with modern practice, and prints quotations and citations in Italic type. The edition also prints all marginalia throughout the text in Roman type rather than in the Italic type of the first edition to keep the notes as legible as possible.

PSEUDO
MARTYR,

Wherein
OUT OF CERTAINE
Propositions and Gradations, This
Conclusion is evicted.
THAT THOSE WHICH ARE
of the Romane Religion in this Kingdome,
may and ought to take the Oath of
Allegeance.

Deut. 32.15.

But he that should have beene upright, when he waxed fatte, spurned with his heele: Thou art fate, thou art grosse, thou art laden with fatnesse.

Job. 11.5.

But oh that God would speake and open his lips against thee, that he might shew thee the secrets of wisedome, how thou hast deserved double according to right.

2. Chro. 28.22.

In the time of his tribulation, did he yet trespasse more against the Lord, for he sacrificed unto the gods of Damascus, which plagued him.

London
Printed by *W. Stansby* for *Walter Burre.*
1610.

TO THE HIGH AND

Mightie Prince J<small>AMES</small>, by the Grace
of God, King of Great Britaine, France
and Ireland, defender of the
F<small>AITH</small>.

Most mightie and sacred Soveraigne.

As Temporall armies consist of Press'd men, and voluntaries, so doe they also in this warfare, in which your Majestie hath appear'd by your Bookes. And not only your strong and full Garisons, which are your Cleargie, and your Universities, but also obscure Villages can minister Souldiours. For, the equall interest, which all your Subjects have in the cause (all being equally endanger'd in your dangers) gives every one of us a Title to the Dignitie of this warfare; And so makes those, whom the Civill Lawes made opposite, all one, Paganos, Milites. Besides, since in this Battaile, your Majestie, by your Bookes, is gone in Person out of the Kingdome, who can bee exempt from waiting upon you in such an expedition? For this Oath must worke upon us all; and as it must draw from the Papists a profession, so it must from us, a Confirmation of our Obedience; They must testifie an Alleageance by the Oath, we, an Alleageance to it. For, since in providing for your Majesties securitie, the Oath defends us, it is reason, that wee defend it. The strongest Castle that is, cannot defend the Inhabitants, if they sleepe, or neglect the defence of that, which defends them; No more can this Oath, though framed with all advantagious Christianly wisedome, secure your Majestie, and us in you, if by our negligence wee should open it, either to the adversaries Batteries, or to his underminings.

The influence of those your Majesties Bookes, as the Sunne, which penetrates all corners, hath wrought uppon me, and drawen up, and exhaled from my poore Meditations, these discourses: Which, with all reverence and devotion, I present to your Majestie, who in this also have the power and office of the Sunne, that those things which you exhale,

17. expedition? *Ed.*: expedition.. L-1, C-1 **24.** with all *Ed.*: withall. L-1, C-1

you may at your pleasure dissipate, and annull; or suffer them to fall downe againe, as a wholesome and fruitfull dew, upon your Church & Commonwealth. Of my boldnesse in this addresse, I most humbly beseech your Majestie, to admit this excuse, that having observed, how much your Majestie had vouchsafed to descend to a conversation with your Subjects, by way of your Bookes, I also conceiv'd an ambition, of ascending to your presence, by the same way, and of participating, by this meanes, their happinesse, of whome, that saying of the Queene of *Sheba*, may bee usurp'd: Happie are thy men, and happie are those thy Servants, which stand before thee alwayes, and heare thy wisedome, For, in this, I make account, that I have performed a duetie, by expressing in an exterior, and (by your Majesties permission) a publicke Act, the same desire, which God heares in my daily prayers, That your Majestie may very long governe us in your Person, and ever, in your Race and Progenie.

Your Majesties most
humble and loyall
Subject:
JOHN DONNE.

A TABLE OF THE CHAPTERS
handled in this Booke.

Chap. I.

Of Martyrdome and the dignity thereof.

Chap. II.

That there may be an inordinate and corrupt affectation of Martyrdome.

Chap. III.

That the Roman Religion doth by many erroneous doctrines mis-encourage and excite men to this vitious affectation of danger: first by aviling secular Magistracy: Secondly by extolling the value of Merites, and of this worke in special, by which the treasure of the Church is so much advanced: And lastly, by the doctrin of Purgatory, which by this act is said certainly to be escaped.

Chap. IIII.

That in the Romane Church the Jesuits exceed all others, in their Constitutions and practise, in all those points, which beget or cherish this corrupt desire of false-Martyrdome.

Chap. V.

That the Missions of the Pope, under Obedience whereof they pretend that they come into this Kingdome, can be no warrant, since there are laws established to the contrary, to give them, or those which harbor them, the comfort of Martyredome.

9. aviling *Ed.*: inciting. L-1, C-1

Chap. VI.

A Comparison of the Obedience due to Princes, with the severall Obediences required and exhibited in the Romane Church: First, of that blinde Obedience and stupiditie, which Regular men vow to their Superiours: Secondly, of that usurped Obedience to which they pretend by reason of our Baptisme, wherein we are said to have made an implicite surrender of our selves, and all that we have, to the church: and thirdly, of that obedience, which the Jesuits by a fourth Supernumerary vow make to be disposed at the Popes absolute will.

Chap. VII.

That if the meere execution of the function of Priests in this Kingdome, and of giving to the Catholiques in this land, spiritual sustentation, did assure their consciences, that to die for that were martyrdome: yet the refusall of the Oath of Alleageance doth corrupt and vitiate the integrity of the whole act, and dispoile them of their former interest and Title to Martyrdome.

Chap. VIII.

That there hath beene as yet no fundamental and safe ground given, upon which those which have the faculties to heare Confessions, should informe their owne Consciences, or instruct their Penitents: that they are bound to adventure the heavy and capitall penalties of this law, for refusall of this Oath. And that if any man have received a scruple against this Oath, which he cannot depose and cast off, the Rules of their own Casuists, as this case stands, incline, and warrant them, to the taking thereof.

Chap. IX.

That the authority which is imagined to be in the Pope, as he is spiritual Prince of the monarchy of the Church, cannot lay this Obligation upon their Consciences: First because the Doctrine it selfe is not certaine, nor presented as matter of faith: Secondly because the way by which it is conveyed to them, is suspitious and dangerous, being but by Cardinall Bellarmine, who is various in himselfe, and reproved by other Catholiques of equall dignity, and estimation.

Chap. X.

That the Canons can give them no warrant, to adventure these dangers, for this refusall: And that the Reverend name of Canons, is falsly and cautelously insinuated, and stolne upon the whole body of the Canon law, with a breefe Consideration upon all the bookes thereof: and a particular survay, of all those Canons, which are ordinarily cited by those Authors, which maintaine this temporall Jurisdiction in the Pope.

Chap. XI.

That the two Breves of Paulus the fift, cannot give this assurance to there Conscience; First, for the generall infirmities, to which all Rescripts of Popes are obnoxious; And then for certaine insufficiencies in these.

Chap. XII.

That nothing requir'd in this Oath, violates the Popes spirituall Jurisdiction; And that the clauses of swearing that Doctrine to bee Hereticall, is no usurping upon his spirituall right, either by prejudicating his future definition, or offending any former Decree.

Chap. XIII.

That all which his Majesty requires by this Oath, is exhibited to the Kings of Fraunce, And not by vertue of any Indult, or Concordate, but by the inherent right of the Crowne.

Chap. XIIII.

Lastly, That no pretence, either of Conversion at first, Assistance in the Conquest, or Acceptation of any Surrender from any of our Kings, can give the Pope any more right over the Kingdome of England, then over any other free State whatsoever.

10. to there *Ed.*: to this. L-1, C-1

AN ADVERTISEMENT TO
the Reader.

Though I purposed not to speake any thing to the Reader, otherwise then by way of Epilogue in the end of the Booke, both because I esteemed that to be the fittest place, to give my Reasons, why I respited the handling of the two last Chapters, till another time, and also, because I thought not that any man might well and properly be called a Reader, till he were come to the end of the Booke: yet, because both he, and I, may suffer some disadvantages, if he should not be fore-possessed, and warned in some things, I have changed my purpose in that point.

For his owne good therefore (in which I am also interested), I must first intreat him, that he will be pleased, before hee reade, to amend with his pen, some of the most important errors, which are hereafter noted to have passed in the printing. Because in the Reading, he will not perchance suspect nor spy them, and so he may runne a danger, of being either deceived, or scandalized.

And for my selfe, (because I have already received some light, that some of the Romane profession, having onely seene the Heads and Grounds handled in this Booke, have traduced me, as an impious and profane under-valuer of Martyrdome,) I most humbly beseech him, (till the reading of the Booke, may guide his Reason) to beleeve, that I have a just and Christianly estimation, and reverence, of that devout and acceptable Sacrifice of our lifes, for the glory of our blessed Saviour. For, as my fortune hath never beene so flattering nor abundant, as should make this present life sweet and precious to me, as I am a Moral man: so, as I am a Christian, I have beene ever kept awake in a meditation of Martyrdome, by being derived from such a stocke and race, as, I beleeve, no family, (which is not of farre larger extent, and greater branches,) hath endured and suffered more in their persons and fortunes, for obeying the Teachers of Romane Doctrine, then it hath done. I did not therefore enter into this, as a carnall or over-indulgent favourer of this life, but out of such reasons, as may arise to his knowledge, who shall be pleased to read the whole worke.

In which, I have abstained from handling the two last Chapters upon divers reasons; whereof one is, that these Heads having beene caried about, many moneths, and thereby quarrelled by some, and desired by others, I was willing to give the Booke a hasty dispatch, that it might cost no man much time, either in expecting before it came, or in reading, when it was come.

5 But a more principall reason was, that since the two last Chapters depend upon one another, and have a mutuall Relation, I was not willing to undertake one, till I might persevere through both. And from the last chapter it became me to abstaine, till I might understand their purposes, who were formerly engaged in the same businesse. For the first
10 Discoverie gives some title to the place, and secludes others, without the Discoverers permission; And in men tender and jealous of their Honour, it is sometimes accounted as much injurie to assist, as to assault.

When therefore I considered, that the most Reverend and learned Sir *Edward Coke*, Lord chiefe Justice of the common Pleas (whom they
15 which are too narrow to comprehend him, may finde arguments enow to love, and admire, out of the measure and proportion of his malice who hath written against him, since wee ought to love him so much, as such men hate him) had in this point of Jurisdiction, laid so solid foundations, raised so strong walls, & perfited his house upon so sure a Rocke,
20 as the lawes of this Kingdome are. And when I saw, that as the divell himselfe is busiest to attempt them, who abound in strength of Grace, (not forbearing our Saviour himselfe) so an ordinary Instrument of his, (whose continuall libels, and Incitatorie bookes, have occasioned more afflictions, and drawne more of that bloud, which they call Catholique,
25 in this Kingdome, then all our Acts of Parliament have done,) had oppugned his Lordships Booke, and iterated and inconculcated those his oppositions, I could not know whether his Lordship reserved any farther consideration of that matter to his owne leasures, or had honoured any other man, with his commandement, or allowance to pursue it. Till
30 therefore I might know, whether any such were embarqued therein, as would either accept my Notes, and dignifie them with their style, or submit their Notes to my method, and the poore apparell of my language, or undertake it entirely, or quit it absolutely, as a body perfit already, by that forme which his Lordship hath given it, I chose to forbeare the
35 handling thereof at this time.

17. against *Ed*.: againsi. L-1, C-1   **17.** since *Ed*.: (since. L-1, C-1

One thing more I was willing the Reader should be forewarned of; which is, that when he findes in the printing of this Booke oftentimes a change of the Character, hee must not thinke that all those words or sentences so distinguished, are cited from other Authors; for I have done it sometimes, onely to draw his eye, and understanding more intensly upon that place, and so make deeper impressions thereof.

And in those places which are cited from other Authors (which hee shall know by the Margine) I doe not alwayes precisely and superstitiously binde my selfe to the words of the Authors; which was impossible to me, both because sometimes I collect their sense, and expresse their Arguments or their opinions, and the Resultance of a whole leafe, in two or three lines, and some few times, I cite some of their Catholique Authors, out of their owne fellowes, who had used the same fashion of collecting their sense, without precise binding themselves to All, or onely their words. This is the comfort which my conscience hath, and the assurance which I can give the Reader, that I have no where made any Author, speake more or lesse, in sense, then hee intended, to that purpose, for which I cite him. If any of their owne fellowes from whom I cite them, have dealt otherwise, I cannot be wounded but through their sides. So that I hope either mine Innocence, or their own fellowes guiltinesse, shall defend me, from the curious malice of those men, who in this sickly decay, and declining of their cause, can spy out falsifyings in every citation: as in a jealous, and obnoxious state, a Decipherer can pick out Plots, and Treason, in any familiar letter which is intercepted. And thus much it seemed necessary to mee, to let the Reader know, to whose charitable and favourable opinion I commit the booke, and my selfe to his Christianly and devout Prayers.

15. conscience *Ed.*: conſcience. L-1, C-1

A PREFACE TO
The PRIESTES, and JESUITS,
and to their Disciples in this
KINGDOME.

1 I am so well acquainted with the phrases of Diminution and Disparagement, and other personall aspersions, which your writers cast, and imprint upon such of your owne side, as depart from their opinions in the least dramme or scruple; as I cannot hope that any of them will spare me, who am further removed from them: For since *Cassander*, whom the two Emperours *Ferdinand* and *Maximilian* consulted, and called to them; not in any schisme betweene the Emperours and Popes, about temporall Jurisdiction: in which quarrell, whensoever it happened, the Emperours cause was ever sustained by as learned, and as Religious, and as many men, as the Popes, but in matters of Doctrine, and for a way of Reformation, when the Popes themselves confessed, that the Church was in extreame neede thereof: Since hee (I say) is called by one of them but a *Grammarian* (to which honour, if he, which cals him so in scorne, had beene arrived, he would never have translated *vindiciae contra Tyrannos*, revenge upon Tyrants, since *vindiciae* signifies a Decree or Order of the Judge, in a cause of Bondage and Liberty depending before him, by which it is ordered, that the party whose condition is in question, shall remaine either free or bond, till the matter be heard without any prejudice, if it fall out otherwise upon the hearing:) And since of *Cajetane* (when hee differs from them in the point of the Canon of scriptures) they say, *That though he were well seene in Scholastique subtilties, yet he was not so in the Fathers*: though in that very matter the same Authour confesse, that ᵃ*Cajetane* followed Saint *Hieromes* foot-steps: ᵇsince (because he denies marriage to be proved a Sacrament out of one place of Saint *Paul*) they say that he fell into grievous errors in both Testaments, *Hebraizando* and *Erasmizando*: Since, when he distasts the coursenesse of the *vulgar edition*, they say, that in three or foure pages of his Psalter, there are more Barbarismes and Solaecismes

margin notes:
P.R. Treat. of Mitiga. c.6. n.67

Idem. c.1. n.11 & c.5. n.30

Gretz. Append. I. ed. l.1. Bellar. §. Idem dictum
ᵃDefens. Bella. l.1. c.7. Quare
ᵇIbi. l.2. c.14. §. Quod Whitak.

Gretz. Tractat. de no. Translat. §. Ait Sixtus

Margin 19. Idem. *Ed.*: *note misplaced.* **Margin 25.** Append. *Ed.*: Append. L-1, C-1 **Margin 27a.** Defens. *Ed.*: *note misplaced.* **Margin 31.** Ait *Ed.*: Ait.. L-1, C-1

then in the whole vulgar Bible: Since *Erasmus* (following the opinion of *Driedo* and other Catholickes, and so denying some part of *Daniel* to be Canonicall) is called by *Bellarmine* a Halfe-Christian, these men will certainly be more rigid and severe upon me.

De Verbo Dei.
l.1. c.9

2 And if they will be content to impute to me all humane infirmities, they shall neede to faine nothing: I am, I confesse, obnoxious enough. My naturall impatience not to digge painefully in deepe, and stony, and sullen learnings: My Indulgence to my freedome and libertie, as in all other indifferent things, so in my studies also, not to betroth or enthral my selfe, to any one science, which should possesse or denominate me: My easines, to affoord a sweete and gentle Interpretation, to all professors of Christian Religion, if they shake not the Foundation, wherein I have in my ordinary Communication and familiar writings, often expressed and declared my selfe: hath opened me enough to their malice, and put me into their danger, and given them advantage to impute to me, whatsoever such degrees of lazines, of liberty, of irresolution, can produce.

3 But if either they will transferre my personall weakenesses upon the cause, or extend the faults of my person to my minde, or to her purest part, my conscience: If they will calumniate this poore and innocent worke of mine, as if it were written, either for *Ostentation* of any ability or faculty in my selfe; or for *Provocation*, to draw them to an aunswere, and so continue a Booke-warre; or for *Flattery* to the present State; which, thogh my services be by many just titles due to it, needs it not; or for *exasperation*, to draw out the civill sword in causes, which have some pretence and colour of being spirituall; or to get *Occasion* hereby to uncover the nakednes, and lay open the incommodious and undefensible sentences and opinions, of divers severall Authors in that Church; or to maintaine and further a scisme and division amongst you, in this point of the Popes pretence to temporall jurisdiction: I have no other shelter against these imputations, but an appeale to our blessed Saviour, and a protestation before his face, that my principall and direct scope and purpose herein, is the unity and peace of his Church. For as when the roofe of the Temple rent asunder, not long after followed the ruine of the foundation it selfe: So if these two principall beames and Toppe-rafters,

Margin 3. Verbo Dei *Ed.*: *note misplaced*; verbo. Dei   L-1, C-1;.   verbo Dei   O-1

the Prince and *the Priest*, rent asunder, the whole frame and Foundation of Christian Religion will be shaked. And if we distinguish not between Articles of faith & jurisdiction, but account all those super-edifications and furnitures, and ornaments which God hath affoorded to his Church, for exteriour government, to be equally the Foundation it selfe, there can bee no Church, as there could be no body of a man, if it were all eye.

4   They who have descended so lowe, as to take knowledge of me, and to admit me into their consideration, know well that I used no inordinate hast, nor precipitation in binding my conscience to any locall Religion. I had a longer worke to doe then many other men; for I was first to blot out, certaine impressions of the Romane religion, and to wrastle both against the examples and against the reasons, by which some hold was taken; and some anticipations early layde upon my conscience, both by Persons who by nature had a power and superiority over my will, and others who by their learning and good life, seem'd to me justly to claime an interest for the guiding, and rectifying of mine understanding in these matters. And although I apprehended well enough, that this irresolution not onely retarded my fortune, but also bred some scandall, and endangered my spirituall reputation, by laying me open to many mis-interpretations; yet all these respects did not transport me to any violent and sudden determination, till I had, to the measure of my poore wit and judgement, survayed and digested the whole body of Divinity, controverted betweene ours and the Romane Church. In which search and disquisition, that God, which awakened me then, and hath never forsaken me in that industry, as he is the Authour of that purpose, so is he a witnes of this protestation; that I behaved my selfe, and proceeded therein with humility, and diffidence in my selfe; and by that, which by his grace, I tooke to be the ordinary meanes, which is frequent prayer, and equall and indifferent affections.

5   And this course held in rectifying and reducing mine understanding and judgment, might justifie & excuse my forwardnes; if I shold seeme to any to have intruded and usurped the office of others, in writing of Divinity and spirituall points, having no ordinary calling to that function. For, to have alwayes abstained from this declaration of my selfe, had beene to betray, and to abandon, and prostitute my good name to their misconceivings and imputations; who thinke presently, that hee

hath no Religion, which dares not call his Religion by some newer name then *Christian*. And then, for my writing in Divinity, though no professed Divine; all Ages, all Nations; all Religions, even yours, which is the most covetous and lothest to divide, or communicate with the Laity, any of the honours reserved to the Clergie, affoord me abundantly examples, and authorities for such an undertaking.

6 But for this poore worke of mine, I need no such *Advocates*, nor *Apologizers*; for it is not of Divinity, but meerely of temporall matters, that I write. And you may as justly accuse *Vitruvius*, who writ of the fashion of building Churches, or those Authors which have written of the nature of Bees and use of Waxe, or of Painting, or of Musique, to have usurped upon the office of Divines, and to have written of Divinity, because all these are ingrediants into your propitiatory medicine, the Masse, and conduce to spirituall and divine worship: as you may impute to any, which writes of civil obedience to the Prince, that he meddles with Divinity: not that this obedience is not safely grounded in Divinity, or that it is not an act of Religion, but that it is so well engrav'd in our hearts, and naturally obvious to every understanding, that men of all conditions have a sense and apprehension, and assurednes of that obligation.

7 The cause therefore is reduced to a narrow issue, and contracted to a strict point, when the differences betweene us are brought to this; Whether a Subject may not obey his Prince, if the Turk or any other man forbid it? And as his Majestie in his Kingdomes, is Religiously and prudently watchfull, to preserve that Crowne, which his Predecessors had redeemed from the rust, and drosse, wherewith forraine usurpation had infected it; so is it easie to be observed, that all the other Princes of Christendome, beginne to shake off those fetters, which insensibly and drowsily they had admitted; and labour by all wayes, which are as yet possible to them, to returne to their naturall Supremacy and Jurisdiction: which besides many other pregnant evidences, appeares by *Baronius* his often complaining thereof; both in his Annals, when he sayes, *That the Princes of this age do exercise so much Jurisdiction over the Clergie, that the Church suffers some scandall thereby*: And in his Apologie of his owne writings, against the Cardinall *Columna*, where

To.11

Resp. Apolog.
cont. Car. Col.
nu.31

Margin 32. To.11 *Ed.*: To.II. L-1, C-1

he notes, *That the Cardinals deputed for the hearing of those causes at Rome, are tired and oppressed in these later times, with the Messengers and Appeales of Bishoppes, which in every Countrey complaine, how much the secular Princes injure them.* And this must of necessity be
5 understood of Countries, which professe the Romane Religion, because such as are Apostoliquely reformed, or are in that way, have shut up all wayes of Appellations to Rome, or remedies from thence.

8 And not to speake of the Kingdome of France at this time, because I have sepos'd and destin'd a particular Chapter for that consideration,
10 nor of the fresh Historie of the Venetians, maintaining their just Lawes for this temporall Jurisdiction: which lawes *Parsons*, without any colour of truth, or escape from malitious and grosse deceiving, sayes they have recalled, when as (not to affright you with any of those Authours which write on the Venetian part,) you may see an excellent relation of that
15 negotiation, and upon what conditions the Pope withdrew his censures, in that letter of Cardinal *Peron* to his Master the French King, about Cardinal *Joyeuse* his instructions, when the Pope sent him to Venice for that purpose; nor to looke so farre backe, as to consider what the other States of Italy and of Rome it selfe have done herein, which, as an Au-
20 thor which lived in profession of that Religion, informes us; durst always bravely and boldly defend it selfe against the Popes usurpations, though he protested, that if they would but admit him to enter againe into the towne, hee would deale no more with temporall matters; and this, at that time when England under *Henry* the second, and the remoter parts
25 trembled at him, who trembled at his owne neighbours and Subjects, as he pretended: To omit all these, the Kingdome of Spaine, which they call so super-eminently Catholicke; and of whose King, the Cardinall. which writes against *Baronius* sayes, *that he is the only Prince, who bends all the sinewes of his power, and all the thoughts of his minde, not only*
30 *to oppresse barbarous enemies of Christianity, but to containe Christian Kings in their duetie*: This Kingdome (I say) hath by all meanes, which it can, expressed how weary it is of that jurisdiction which the Pope exerciseth there, in these points which we complaine of: though the Popes

P.R.
Treat. of Mitig.
c.5. n.41

In monit. polit.
in fine

Machiavel. Hist.
Flor. l.1. f.34. Edit. Picen. An. 1587

Card. Colum.
Paris. fo.158

Margin 11. Mitig. *Ed.*: Mitig. L-1, C-1 **Margin 14.** polit. *errata*] pili.. MCG, C-3, C-4, C⁵-2, C⁹, C³, Y, C²-1, C²-3, L-2, O-2, O¹⁴, C¹⁰, C¹⁶, C⁹
Margin 27. Paris *Ed.*: paris. L-1, C-1   **30.** *Christian Ed.*: christian. L-1, C-1

have ever beene most readie to recompence these temporall detriments to those kings; as the Donations of the Indies, and of the Kingdome of Navarre, and of England, testifie at full.

9   And yet if we consider, what all sorts of persons in that Nation have done against this temporall power, wee cannot doubt, but that they travaile of the same childe, which our Kingdome and divers others have brought forth, which is their libertie from this weakning and impoverishing thraldome. For first, for Booke-men and Writers, a great Idolatrer of this temporall Jurisdiction in the Pope, Confesses, *That many of the principall Authours of the Spanish nation, concurre in this opinion, that these exemptions and immunities of the Clergie,* so much debated, are not *Iuris divini*. And it is easie to observe, what the Collection and resultanse upon this conclusion will be; Since, if they bee enjoyed by the favour of Princes, though a conveniencie, and a kind of right grounded in the law of nature, have moved Princes to graunt them: yet all graunts of Princes are mortall, and have a naturall frailtie in them, and upon just cause are subject to Revocation.

<small>Rispost. d'Anto. Bovio a P. Paulo, nella Raccolta. f.50</small>

10   And for the Sword-men, by that hostile Act upon Rome it-selfe, by *Charles Bourbon*, which was done at least by the connivencie of *Charles* the fift; and by that preparation made against the same place, by the expresse commaundement of *Philip* the second, under the Duke of Alvaes conduct, and by many other associations and Leagues against the Pope: It appeares how jealous and watchfull, they are upon this Temporall jurisdiction, and how they oppose themselves against any farther groweth thereof. For when in the differences about the Kingdome of Portugall, the Pope made offers to *Philip* the second, to interpose himselfe for the setling of all pretences to that Crowne, the King, though with sweete and dilatorie answers, refusd that offer, because (sayes the Author of that Storie) he would not by this example, acknowledge him to be the Judge of Kingdomes. And after this, when the King had proceeded farther therein, and *Antonie* was proclaimed, and that a Legate came into Spaine, and offred there, in the name of the Pope, to be a Judge betweene all pretenders, though *Philip* did not doubt the Legates inclination to his part, because he came into his Countrey to make the offer, and though he had more use of such a service then, then before,

<small>Conestaggio. l.3. fol.82</small>

Margin 8. Paulo, nella . . . . 50 *Ed*.: Paulonella . . . . 196; Raccolta *errata*:. Ravolta L-1, C-1

yet he abstaind from using him therein, because hee thought that the
Pope, under colour of doing the Office of a common father, went about
to make himselfe absolute Judge of Kingdomes; and besides the extraordinarie Authority, which he endevoured to draw to his Sea, would oblige   Idem. l.6. f.155
5 the Kings of Spaine to his house, as the same Author expresses that
Kings jealousies.

   11 And for the politique governement of that State even in that
Kingdome, which they pretend to hold of the Church, which is *Sicily*,
they exercise a stronger Jurisdiction, and more derogatorie to the Pope,
10 then this which our King claimes. And though *Parsons*, who is no longer   Answere to the
a subject, and Sonne of the Church of Rome, then as that Church is an   Reports. c.5
enemy to England (for in the differences betweene her and Spaine, he
abandons her) averre in one place, that this jurisdiction is by Indult, &
Dispensation from the Pope, yet a more credible man then he, and a   Baron. Annal.
15 native Subject to the King of Spaine, hath utterly annuld and destroyed   To.11
that opinion, that any graunt or permission of the Popes, hath enabled
the Kings of Spaine to that Authoritie, which they exercise there. And
he hath not onely told his brother Cardinall *Columna*, that the matter
it-selfe, *Is a point of the Catholicke faith*, but in his Epistle to King   Epist. Apolog.
20 *Philip* the third, hee extols and magnifies that Booke, in which he had   nu.21
delivered that Doctrine, so authentically, as if he meant to draw it into
the Canon of the Scriptures: for do these words import any lesse? *The
Booke issued from the very Chaire of S*. Peter, *by the commandement of
S*. Peter, *and is confirmed by S*. Peter, *and shal without doubt endure*   Epist. ad Philip. 3
25 *for ever*. And he addes this Commination, speaking to the King, *Let
them which resist these writings take heede, least they stumble*, In hanc
Petram, *and least they bee utterly trode in pieces, Ab ipsa, ab alto ruente
Petra*. But of *Baronius* his detestation of Monarchie, and ill behaviour
towards all Kings, as well as his owne Soveraigne, I have another occasion
30 to speake. All which I purpose to evict here, was, that if *Parsons* have
spoken so heretically, in saying, that this is done by vertue of the Popes
Indult; that remaines true, which I said before, that that Kingdome of
Spaine, endevours by all wayes it can, to redeeme it-selfe from these
usurpations, and re-invest it-selfe in her originall Supremacie.
35   12 For as in one of the Greeke States when *Nycippus* sheepe brought   Aelian. l.1. c.29

Margin 14. To.11 *Ed*.: To.II.   L-1, C-1

forth a Lion, it was justly concluded that, that portended a Tyrannie, and change of the State, from a peaceable to a bloody Governement: so since the Spirituall principalitie hath produced a Temporall, since this mild and Apostolique sheepe hath brought forth this Lion, which seekes whom he may devoure, as by his first Jurisdiction, he would make in this Kingdome a spirituall shambles of your soules, by corrupt Doctrines: so by the latter, he labours to make a Temporall shambles and market of your bodies, by selling you for nothing, and thrusting you upon the Civill sword, which is a sinne to sheath, when the Law commaunds to draw it, in so dangerous cases of polluting the Land.

<small>Numb. 35.33</small>

13 And though it be pretended by you, and for you; that the Popes have laide both a spirituall and temporall Obligation upon you: Because, besides their care for instructing your soules; they have also with some charge erected and endowed some Colledges for your Temporall sustentation, who come into those parts: yet, as the wisemen of Persia, being set to observe the first actions of their new King *Ochus*, when they marked that he reached out his hand at the Table to Bread, and to a Knife, presumed by that, that his time would be plentifull and bloody, and faild not in their conjecture: So since the Pope reaches out to you, with his small Collegiate pittance, the Doctrine of the materiall and temporall sword, howsoever hee may seeme to relieve your miserie and penurie, which you drawe upon your selves, yet it is accompanied with the presage of much blood, since either his purposes must be executed upon us by you, or our just Lawes for prevention thereof be Executed upon you.

<small>Aelian. l.2. c.17</small>

14 One of your owne Authors relates, that *Anastatius* a Monke, had a hundred Divels appointed to vexe and tempt him for foure yeares, and after hee had overcome that trouble, and tamed them, he set them on work to build him a great Monastery, & to bring Aqueducts, and other conveniencies therunto, for his temporal provision: so after the Pope hath passed over that little cost which he is at, to feede you a few yeares, you are ever after his instruments, to build up his spirituall Monarchy to the ruine of all others, and your selves must ciment and

<small>Bosquier. Concio. Quadrag. Conci. 6</small>

---

5. devoure, *catchword, Sig.* C²ʳ] devour:. L-1, C-1 **Margin 9.** 35.33 *Ed.*: 3[?].33 *note misplaced.* L-1, C-1 **11.** 13 And *new paragraph Ed.*: 13 *missing,* And *run-on line.* L-1, C-1 **30.** provision] provi sion. C⁵-2, O², YK-2, YK-3

morter the wals with your blood.

15 To let blood in some diseases, saith the eloquentest Physitian, is no new thing; but that there should scarce be any disease, in which we should not let blood, is (saith he) a strange and new fashion: So to offer our lives for defence of the Catholique faith, hath ever beene a religious custome; but to cal every pretence of the Pope, Catholique faith, and to bleede to death for it, is a sickenesse and a medicine, which the Primitive Church never understood. For the implicite faith, and blinde assent, which you were used heretofore to give to the spirituall supremacy, was put upon you, as *Annibal* [Maharabad], to entrappe and surprise his enemies, mingled their wine with *Mandrake*, whose operation is betwixt sleepe and poison: for though it brought you into a drowsie and stupid adoration of the Pope, & some dull lethargies & forgetfulnesses of your temporall dueties, yet it was not so pestilent and contagious, but that a civill state might consist with it, though in a continual languishing and consumption. But this doctrine of temporall Jurisdiction, is not onely a violent and dispatching poison, but it is of the nature of those poisons, which destroy not by heat nor cold, not corrosion, nor any other discerneable quality, but (as physitians say) out of the specifique forme, and secret malignity, and out of the whole substance. For as no Artist can finde out, how this malignant strength growes in that poison, nor how it workes, So can none of your Writers tell, how this temporall Jurisdiction got into the Pope, or how he executes it, but are anguished and tortured, when they come to talke of it, as Physitians and Naturalists are, when they speake of these specifique poisons, or of the cause and origen thereof, which is, *Antipathie*.

16 And yet we finde it reported of one woman, that she had so long accustomed her body to these poisons, by making them her ordinary foode, that shee had brought her selfe, and her whole complexion and constitution, to be of the same power as the poison was, and yet retaind so much beauty, as shee allurd Kings to her embracement, and kild and poisond them by that meanes: So hath the Romane faith beene for many yeares, so fedde and pampred with this venemous doctrine of temporall jurisdiction, that it is growne to some few of them to bee matter of faith

margin notes:
Sent. Select. ex Corn. Celso. l.2. n.10

Frontinus. Stratagem. li.2. c.5

Forestus. de Venenis. Observ. 1. Schol.

Margin 2. n.10 *Ed.*: n.12.   C-1, L-1   **Margin 10.** Frontinus. Stratagem. *Ed.*: Frontinus stratagem.   L-1, C-1   **Margin 27.** Forestus. de Venenis *Ed.*: Forestus de venenis.   L-1, C-1

it selfe; and shee is able to drawe and hold some Princes to her love, because for all this infection, she retaines some colour and probability of being the same shee was. And as that Fish which *Aelianus* speakes of, lies neere to the rocke, and because it is of the colour of the rocke, surprises many fishes which come to refresh themselves at the rocke: so doth the Romane doctrine, because it can pretend by a locall and personall succession (though both interrupted) that it is so much of the colour of the rocke, and so neare it, as *Petrus* and *Petra*, envegle and entrappe many credulous persons, who have a zealous desire to build upon the rocke it selfe.

[margin: Lib.1. c.1]

17 It is an Aphorisme of an aunceint Physitian, *that we must not purge raw humours, but such as are matur'd and concocted, except they be stirred and moved with their owne violence.* Such a patience and moderation this State used towards professors of your Religion; and onely providing some better lawes, to have them in a readinesse in occasions of much necessity; the rest of the Statutes were onely medicinall and preparatory, to lead them to Church sometimes, and so to mollifie their obduratenes, by making divine service their physicke, since they would not admit it for their ordinary diet; and so in time to draine them, and deliver them from those inundations of errours, which the Sea of Rome had degorged upon them. And though it might seeme unseasonable, by any sharper meanes to have wrastled or contended with them at the beginning, because everie sudden remove, even into a better aire, is unwholsome, and the worse, the purer the aire is; yet now it is time to worke upon you, being of better experience, since you may have observed the birth and prosperous growth of this Reformation; and seene, that though diseases affect and corrupt suddenly and violently, and the cures thereof are orderly and long in accomplishing; yet this Reformation spent lesse time then the corruption, and the Church hath recovered more health in one age, then she had lost in anie two: In so firme and constant a state of health, did the Apostles and their followers, especially the first Bishoppes of *Rome*, deliver her over, that shee was able a long time, to resist those infections, and was likely to have done it much longer, if her danger had beene onely intrinsique, by breeding *Heresies* in her

[margin: Hippocrates. l.1. Apho. 22]

---

5. themselves *Ed.*: themselves. L-1, C-1   **7.** though *Ed.*: though. L-1, C-1
22–23. at the beginning *Ed.*: at beginning. L-1, C-1   **33.** infections *Ed.*: infectious. C-1, L-1

selfe, and that shee had not received the outward poisons of *Riches* and *Honour*, and the naturall companions of those, *Avarice* and *Ambition*.

18 If you will consider the occasion of this Reformation, which Pope *Adrian* the sixt (as your *Espencaeus* relates it) ingenuously confessed in the Imperiall Parliament, *That it was occasioned chiefly by the sinnes of the Priests and Prelates, whose abuses and excesses had beene for many yeeres abominable,* And *that all things were perversly overturnd,* And *that the Disease was in the head,* And *that therefore he would provide that the Court of Rome, from whence all this corruption was derived, should be reformed, since all the world did hungerly expect it at that time:* which Reformation, sayes Espencaeus, *he died before he could performe, and his successor would not performe it*; If you consider by what instruments it tooke first hold, and that your owne Authors, even when they meane to calumniate these beginnings, say, that the desire of the French King *Francis* the first, and of his sister *Margaret*, and of the *Bishop of Meaux*, and the rest of the Lords by their example, to have about them learned and understanding persons, and such as were conversant in the holy and originall languages, gave the first entrance and way to this Reformation: If you consider with what prosperity and blessing Almightie God hath advanced it; and that in a few yeares it hath produced so many excellent authors in the Artes, and in Divinity, that neither our Schooles nor our Pulpits neede bee beholding to them, who deliver no golde without some drosse, and that for temporall blessings hee hath made us as numerous, and as potent as his adversaries, the adverse partie: If you consider the good health and sound constitution of the Reformed Religion, and that it is in all likelyhood long-lived, because it neither admits unwholesome and putrifying Traditions, and Postscripts, after the holy Ghost had perfited his writings; which Additions envenome the pure blood inwardly: nor is it outwardly in her practise deformed with the leprosies and ulcers of admitting Jewes and Stews: nor proposes and justifies any such books, as your *Taxa Camerae Apostolicae* is, in which (sayes your *Espencaeus*) *a man may learne more sinne, then in all the Summists and Casuists*: and in which the price of all sinnes are taxed; so that one may know before hand, what

In Epist. ad Tit. c.1

Florimond. Remond. Histoire de l'Heresie. l.7. c.2 & 3

In Epist. ad Tit. c.1

Margin 13. Florimond. Remond. Histoire *Ed*.: Florimond Remond Histoire .... c.2.. L-1, C-1 **23.** drosse, *Ed*.: drosse: O-1, YK-2;. drosse. L-1, C-1, MCG, C-2, C-3, C^3, C^{10}, C^2-1

an Adultery, an Incest, a Parricide, or any other enormious sinne will stand him in, before he resolve to doe it: If you consider how peaceable and compatible it is with secular Magistracy, by this experience, that more Catholique Princes admit toleration of the reformed Religion, then princes of our profession, admit yours; out of an assurance of the turbulency, and tempestuousnesse naturally venting out of the grounds of the Jesuits: you will then perceive how blinde a prognosticator that Dutch-man is, who upon two and fortie vaine and imaginary reasons, hath grownded a prophecy of the imminent ruine of this Religion; and how hasty that abortion, and precipitation was in the French-man, who hath written the history of the actuall ruine of this profession, whilst it is yet in her growing estate, and by the mercy of our Saviour, every day more and more advanced.

19 And if you will suffer these things to enter your understanding and judgement, I cannot doubt of your will to conforme your selves: For it is truely said, *Nothing is so contrarie to the will and consent, as Errour*: And whatsoever appeares true to the Judgment, seemes good to our will, and begets a desire to doe it. But if you shut up that dore, and so expose your selves, that men may possesse your Will, without entring by your Judgement, they enter like Theeves at the window, and in the night. For, though the will bee as a window, somewhat capable of light, yet your selves benight your whole house, by drawing these Curtaines upon your judgement. And in all afflictions drawne upon your selves by this will or wilfulnes, when you shal say to God, as his people did by *Esay, Wherefore have we fasted, and thou seest it not? we have punished our selves, and thou regard'st it not*: God will answer, as he did then; *Beholde, in the day of your fasts you seeke your will*: That is, you pursue your owne stubborne determinations, and have humane and corrupt respects in all your tribulations.

20 There was a law amongst some Graecians, that if a sicke man drunke wine without advise of his Physitian, though that saved his life, he should be put to death, for doing it before he was commaunded. O what bitter punishment must then attend your presumption, who in

Margin 10. Remond . . . . l'Heresie *Ed*.: Remond . . .l.Heresie. L-1, C-1
Margin 16. c.Si O-1, C-4, C^{10}, MCG; l.Si. L-1, C-1, C^9, L^2, C$^{5-1}$, C$^{5-2}$, L-2, L^{30}, O-2, O^2, O^{14}, SP, O^8, C^9 **31.** [Physi]tian, *catchword Sig*. D^{1v}: [Physi]tian;. L-1, C-1

stead of their wine, take Gall and poison, and in stead of their recovery, endanger your selves to a double perishing; and are so farre from having any direct commandement for it, that you have expresse and just inhibitions against it? O what spirituall *Calenture* possesses you, to make this hard shift to destroy your selves? If you be fishers of men, why dooth hee which sends you, first raise stormes and tempests of Treason, and scandall; and expose you to a certaine shipwracke? It is a note which one of your famous Preachers hath given; *That fish will not be taken with a bloody Nette*; and yet your Fishermen are sent with no other nets, then such as must be stained with our blood, if they can get it, or if they misse it, with yours and their owne.   Bosquier. conc. Quadrag.

21   They are content to teach in other places, *That the Pope cannot binde a man to impossible things*; and to extend the worde *Impossible* to any thing, which cannot justly, honestly, or conveniently bee done; they are content to teach, *That the Pope cannot command some things, though they be naturally good and meritorious, as to iterate a Confession after it is once made*: Onely to you they are so rigid and sowre, that a *Breve* which you are not sure was sent, and you are sure that it ought not to have beene sent, must binde you to an obedience in these Capitall dangers; and like *Pythagoras* schollers, you must suffer your selves to be slaine, rather then stirre your foote, and tread downe a Beane.   Dist. 61. Catinensis

Navar. Manual. c.23. n.38

Diog. Laertius. l.8

22   And what is your recompence? You shall bee *Martyrs*; and yet *Baronius* himselfe, who is liberall enough of Martyrdome, speakes of your case somewhat inconstantly and irresolutely, when he sayes of English and French Martyrs, *Scimus eos esse in Caelo, ut par est credere*, We know they are in heaven, as it is fit for us to beleeve. But as he which died of the bite of a Weasell, lamented because it was not a Lion: So consider, it is not the Catholicke faith, which you smart for, but an unjust usurpation, and that it is not the *Lion of Juda*, for whose service and honour your lives were well given, but it is for a Weasell, which crept in at a little hole, and since is growne so full and pamperd, that men will rather die, then beleeve that he got in at so little an entrance.   Martyrolog. c.8 Aelian. l.14. c.4

23   How hungerie of poison, how Ambitious of ruine, how pervious and penetrable to all meanes of destruction are you, upon whom your

Margin 15.   Manual. *Ed.*: Manual. L-1, C-1   **15.**   *some things Ed.*: *somethings*. L-1, C-1   **Margin 20.** Laertius. *Ed.*: Laertius. L-1, C-1

Jesuits and other *Confessors*, have not onely the force of those men, who are said to have beene able to kill men by looking upon them in anger, but of those also, which can bewitch by faire words, and can praise a man to death? For as the angrie eye of the first sort slew some: So doe the comminations and terrors of these *Breves*, thrust some of you into these dangers. And as, if the men of the second sort (whereof there were whole families in *Afrique*) did but commend Trees, Corne, Cattell, or Children, they prosperd no farther, but perish'd presently: So, after these men, with whose families *Europe* abounds, doe but tell you, that you are borne of Catholicke parents, That onely you are in the *Arke*, That you are in possession of good estates, fit sacrifices for the Catholicke Church, That you are remarkeable and examplar men, by whom your Tenants, and Servants, and Children are led and guided; That you are chosen by God for pillars to sustaine his materiall Church, as Priests are for the spirituall: That you are Martyrs apparant, and attended and staid for in the triumphant Church: you prosper no more, but wither in a Consumption, and having headlongly dissipated and scattered your estates, you runne desperately into the danger of the Law, or sustaine a wretched life by the poore Crummes of others pensions.

24 And that vicious affectation of *Priesthood*, or of *Regular Religion*, which one of your Preachers notes out of *Cassianus*, to possesse many men, whome therupon he cals, *Sacerdoturientes*, hath bewitched you with a stronger charme. And as that drawes them from their Office of societie, by a civill and Allegoricall Death, in departing from the world into a Cloister, so this throwes you into a naturall, or unnaturall and violent Death, by denying due Obedience, and by entring into Rebellious actions. *Many men*, sayes that Preacher, *are caried to this desire by humane respects, and by the spirit, either of their blood and Parents when they doe it to please them, or by the spirit of giddinesse and levitie, or by the spirit of libertie, to be delivered from the bondage and encombrances of wife and children, or else violently, by adversitie and want.* And these diseases, which hee observed in them, I know you cannot chuse but find in your selves, and in a more dangerous, and deadly measure and proportion.

Margin 1. Gellius. *Ed.*: Gellius. L-1, C-1   **Margin 21.** Conc *Ed.*: Cont. C-1, L-1   **22.** *Sacerdoturientes* errata: *Sacerdotes nonentes.* L-1, C-1

25 And if there bee not too much shame and horror in such a Meditation, but that you dare to looke backe upon all the passages betweene your Church and ours, in the time of the late *Queene*, and his *Majestie* who now governes, you shall see, that the Rocke was here, and all the stormes and tempests proceeded from you, when from you came the thunders and lightnings of Excommunications. But as in those times, when divinations and conjectures were made upon the fall of lightnings, those lightnings which fel in the Sea, or tops of Mountaines, were never brought into observation, but were cald *Bruta fulmina*: so how vaine his Excommunications against *Islanders*; and dwellers in the Sea, have proved, we and Venice have given good testimonie, as many other great Princes have done, by despising his *Bruta fulmina*, when they have beene cast upon so great and eminent Mountaines, as their *Supremacie* is.   Plini. l.2. c.43

26 From you also have come the subtill whisperings of Rebellious doctrines, the frequent and personall Traiterous practises, the intestine Commotions, and the publique and foraine Hostile attempts, in which, as we can attribute our deliverance to none but God, so we can impute the malignitie thereof originally, to none but the devill. Whose instruments the Jesuites (as we in our just warres have given over long bowes for Artillerie) being men of rounder dispatch, then the Church had before, impatient of the long Circuit and Litigiousnes of excommunications, have attempted a readier waye: and as the invention of Gun-powder is attributed to a contemplative Monke; so these practique Monkes thought it belonged to them, to put it into use and execution, to the destruction of a State and a Church; through which nimblenesse and dangerous activitie, they have corrupted the two noble Inventions of these later ages, *Printing* and *Artillery*, by filling the world with their Libels, and Massacres.

27 It becomes not me to say, that the Romane Religion begets Treason; but I may say, that within one generation it degenerates into it: for if the temporall jurisdiction (which is the immediate parent of Treason) be the childe of the Romane faith, and begot by it, treason is the Grandchilde. But as *Erasmus* said of that Church in his time, *Syllogismi nunc sustinent Ecclesiam*, wee may justlie say, that this Doctrine of temporall Jurisdiction, is sustained but by Syllogismes, and those weake, and   Annotat. in Hilarium

6. and *Ed.*: aud. C-1, L-1   27. *Artillery*,] *Artillery*. C-1, C-2, C-3, C-4, L-2, O-1, YK-3

impotent, and deceiveable. And as it cannot appeare out of all the Authors, which speake of Saint *Peters* remaining at Rome, whether his body be there, or onely his ashes: So can it not be cleare to you, that the body of Christian Religion is there, since it is oppressed with such heapes of ashes, and dead Doctrine, as this of temporall Jurisdiction; so that divers other Churches, which perchance were kindled at that, may burne more clearely and fervently, then that from which they were derived.

28   But my purpose is not to exasperate, and aggrieve you, by traducing or drawing into suspition the bodie of your Religion, otherwise then as it conduces to this vicious and inordinate affectation of danger: Yet your charitie may give me leave to note; that as *Physitians*, when to judge of a disease, they must observe *Decubitum*, that is, the time of the Patients lying downe, and yeelding himselfe to his bedde; because that is not alike in all sicke men, but that some walke longer before they yeelde, then others doe; therefore they remoove that marke, and reckon *ab Actionibus lęsis*: that is, when their appetite, and digestion, and other faculties fail'd in doing their functions and offices: so, if we will judge of the diseases of the Romane Church, though because they crept in insensiblie, and the good state of health, which her provident Nources indued her withall, made her hold out long; we cannot well pitch a certaine time of her lying downe and sickning, yet we may wel discern *Actiones laesas*, by her practise, and by her disusing her stomach from spirituall foode, and surfetting upon this temporall Jurisdiction: For then she appeared to be lame and impotent, when she tooke this staffe and crouch to sustaine her selfe, having lost the abilitie of those two legges, whereon shee should stand, The *Word* and *Censures*.

29   And if the suspicious and quarrelsome title and claime to this temporall Jurisdiction; If Gods often and strange protection of this Kingdome against it, by which he hath almost made Miracles ordinarie and familiar; If your owne just and due preservation, worke nothing upon you, yet have some pitie and compassion towards your Countrey, whose reputation is defaced and scandalized by this occasion, when one of your owne Authors, being anguished and perplexed, how to answere these of-

Examen. Edicti. Anglica. Stanislaus Christianonicus. Paris. 1607

31.   [fami]liar; *catchword Sig*. D⁴ᵛ: [fami]liar,.   L-1, C-1   **Margin 33.** Christianonicus.]   Christianoncus.   L²

ten Rebellions and Treasons, to put it off from that Religion, layes it upon the nature of an English-man, whom, in all professions he accuses to be naturally disloyall and trecherous to his Prince.

30   And have some pitie and compassion (though you neglect your particulars) upon that cause, which you call the Catholicke cause: Since, as we say of Agues, that no man dies by an Ague, nor without an Ague: So at Executions for Treasons, we may justly say, No man dies for the Romane Religion, nor without it. Such a naturall consequence, or at least unluckie concomitance they have together, that so many examples will at last build up a Rule, which a few exceptions, and instances to the contrarie will not destroy.

31   I call to witnesse against you, those whose testimonie God himselfe hath accepted. Speake then and testifie, O you glorious and triumphant Army of Martyrs, who enjoy now a permanent triumph in heaven, which knew the voice of your Shepheard, and staid till he cald, and went then with all alacritie: Is there any man received into your blessed Legion, by title of such a Death, as sedition, scandall, or any humane respect occasioned? O no, for they which are in possession of that Laurell, are such as have washed their garments, not in their owne blood onely (for so they might still remaine redde and staind) but in the *bloode of the Lambe which changes them to white*. Saint *Chrysostome* writes well, that the *Sinner* in the *Gospel bath'd and wash'd her selfe in her teares, not in her blood*: And of Saint *Peter*, hee askes this question; *When he had denied Christ, Numquid sanguinem fundit?* No, says he, but hee powrd foorth teares, and washed away his transgression. — Revel. 7.14 / Homil. 2. in Psal. 50

32   That which Christian Religion hath added to old Philosophie, which was, *To doe no wrong*, is in this point, no more but this, *To keepe our mind in an habituall preparation of suffering wrong*: but not to urge and provoke, and importune affliction so much, as to make those punishments just, which otherwise had beene wrongfully inflicted upon us. Wee are not sent into this world, to *Suffer*, but to *Doe*, and to performe the Offices of societie, required by our severall callings. The way to triumph in secular Armies, was not to be slaine in the Battell, but to have kept the station, and done all Militarie dueties. And as it was in the Romane Armies, so it ought to be taught in the Romane Church, — Vegetius. l.2. c.17

Margin 20.   7.14 *Ed.*: 7.15.   L-1, C-1

Ius legionis facile: Non sequi, non fugere. For we must neither pursue persecution so forwardly, that our naturall preservation be neglected, nor runne away from it so farre, that Gods cause be scandaliz'd, and his Honour diminished.

33 Thus much I was willing to permit, to awaken you, if it please you to heare it, to a just love of your owne safetie, of the peace of your Countrey, of the honour and reputation of your Countreymen, and of the integritie of that, which you call the Catholicke cause; and to acquaint you so farre, with my disposition and temper, as that you neede not be afraid to reade my poore writings, who joine you with mine owne Soule in my Prayers, that your Obedience here, may prepare your admission into the heavenly *Hierusalem*, and that by the same Obedience, *Your dayes may bee long in the land, which the Lord your God hath given you. Amen.*

Exod. 20.12

Margin 12. 20.12 *Ed.*: 20..   L-1, C-1

PSEUDO-
MARTYR

Chap. I.

Of Martyrdome and the dignitie thereof.

1   As a *Depositarie* to whose trust some precious thing were committed, is not onely encombred and anxious, to defend it from the violencies and subtleties of outward attempters, but feeles within himselfe some
5 interruptions of his peace, and some invasions upon his honesty, by a corrupt desire, and temptation to possess it, and to employ upon his owne pleasure or profit, that of which he is no *Proprietary*: and never returnes to his security, out of these watchfulnesses against others, and reluctations with himselfe; till he who delivered this Jewell, resume it
10 againe: So, till it please the Lord, and owner of our life to take home into his treasurie, this rich *Carbuncle* our soule, which gives us light in our night of ignorance, and our darke body of earth, we are still anguished and travelled, as well with a continuall defensive warre, to preserve our life from sickenesses, and other offensive violences; as with a divers and
15 contrary covetousnes, sometimes to enlarge our State and terme therein, somtimes to make it so much our owne, that we may unthriftily spend it upon surfets, or licentiousnes, or reputation.

2   From thence proceeded that corrupt prodigality of their lives, with examples whereof all Histories abound; honour, ease, devotion, shame,
20 want, paine, any thing served for a reason, not only to forsake themselves, or to expose themselves to un-evitable dangers, but also to be their owne executioners: yea we read of the women of a certaine town, that in a wantonnes had brought it up for a fashion to kill themselves.   Gellius. 1.15. c.10

3   Which corruption, and Ambition of beeing Lord of our selves,
25 every sort of men, which contributed their helpes to the preservation

8. others, *Ed*.: other. L-1, C-1   **9.** reluctations] reluetations. C-2   **22.** executioners: O-2, C-3, C-4: executioners·. L-1, C-1, YK-3

and tranquility of States, laboured against: as first the Philosopher, who observing that honour and ease did principally draw men into this inclination, because they were desirous to get a name of daring, and of greatnes, and to escape the miseries which every day in this life presents, and heapes upon us; did therefore teach, *That nothing was more base and cowardly, then to kill ones selfe*, so to correct that opinion of getting honour by that Act: and to overthrow the other opinion of ease, they taught *Death to be the most miserable thing which could fall upon us.*

<small>Aristot. Eth. l.3. cap.7</small>

<small>Idem. l.3. c.6</small>

<small>Matalius Metellus. prefat. in Histor. Osorii</small>

4   And when the Spaniards in the Indies found a generall inclination, and practise in the inhabitants to kill themselves, to avoide slaverie; they had no way to reduce them, but by some dissemblings and outward counterfeitings, to make them beleeve, that they also killed themselves, and so went with them into the next world, and afflicted them more then, then they did in this.

<small>Dig. l.48. Tit. 19. le.38 & Dig. l.49. Tit. 16. le.6</small>

<small>Concil.Autisi.ca.17 Conc. Bracar. 33. q.5. placuit</small>

5   The Emperors also by their lawes and civil Constitutions, have opposed remedies against this ordinary disease, by inflicting forfaitures and infamous mulctes upon them which shold do it. And the Church hath resisted it by her Canons, which denie them Christian buriall, and refuse their oblations at the Altars. And with what severe lawes, other particular States have laboured against it, appeares by the law of our nation, which esteemes it not only Man-slaughter but Murder. And by that law in the Earledome of Flanders, which reckons it amongst the heinous names of Treason, Heresie, and Sedition.

<small>Tholos. Synt. l.36. c.22. nu.13</small>

6   And yet it was observed, that this corruption was so inhaerent and rooted, and had so overgrowne our nature, or that corruption which depraves it, that neither those imperiall lawes, nor that forme of a State which *Plato* Ideated, not that Sir *Tho.* Moore did imagine and delineate, thought it possible utterly to extirpate and roote out this disposition, but onely to stoppe and retard the generall precipitation therein: And therefore in their lawes they have flattered our corruption so much, as to appoint certaine cases and reasons, and circumstances, in which it might be lawfull to kill ones selfe.

<small>De leg. 9 Utop. l.2. ca. de Servis.</small>

3. daring *errata*: during. L-1, C-1 **8.** *us. Ed.: us:.* L-1, C-1 **9.** Spaniards *Ed.*: Spaniard. L-1, C-1 **Margin 9.** Metellus. *Ed.*: Metellus, *note misplaced.* L-1, C-1 **Margin 15.** Tit. 19 . . . . Tit. 16 *Ed.*: Tit. 9 . . . . tit. 10. C-1, L-1 **Margin 18.** Autisi . . . . 33 *Ed.*: Antisi 23. C-1, L-1

7 And Almightie God himselfe, who disposes all things sweetely, hath beene so indulgent to our nature, and the frailty thereof, that he hath affoorded us a meanes, how wee may give away our life, and make him, in a pious interpretation, beholden to us for it; which is by
5 delivering our selves to Martyredome, for the testimony of his name, and advancing his glorie: for in this we restore him his Talent with profite; our owne soule, with as many more, as our example workes upon, and winnes to him. To denie him this, is not onely to steale from him, that which is his, by many deare titles; as Creating, Redeeming, and
10 Preserving; but at such a time, as his honour hath use of such a service at our handes, then to withdraw our testimony from him, is as much a betraying and crucifying of him againe, as it was in them, who by their false witnesse, occasioned his death before.

8 Saint *John* saith, that the Baptist was not that light, but (as Jo. 1.8
15 though that were the next dignity) hee came to beare witnesse of that light. And when our blessed Saviour refused to beare witnesse of him- Jo. 5.31 selfe; those, whom he reckons as his witnesses, are all of so high dignity, as no ambition can be higher, then to be admitted amongst those witnesses of Christ; for they are thus laide downe: First the *Baptist*, then
20 his *Miracles*, then his *Father*, and then the *Scriptures*.

9 How soone God beganne to call upon man for this service, by sealing his acceptation of *Abels* sacrifice, in accepting *Abel* for a Sacrifice: for so saith *Chrysostome, Abel, in the beginning, before any example,* De Martyri. *first of all Dedicated Martyredome.* And as soone as Christ came into Serm. 1
25 the world, after he received the oblations of the kings, presenting part of their temporall fortunes; the next thing wherein he would be glorified, was that *Holocaust* and *Hecatombe* of the innocent children, martyrd for his name.

10 And though wee cannot by infinite degrees, attaine to our pat-
30 terne Christ, the generall Sacrifice; yet we must exceed those *Typique* times, and Sacrifices of the old law; and be no more covetous of our selves, then they were of their beasts, when that Sacrifice is required at our hands: for when we sacrifice our concupiscences, by rooting them out, we equall them, who sacrificed their beasts; but we exceede them,
35 when we immolate our soule and body to God.

Margin 14. 1.8 *Ed.*: 1.7. L-1, C-1   **Margin 23.** Serm. 1 *Ed.*: Serm. 7. C-1, L-1, YK-1

11   The blood of the Martyres was the milke which nourished the Primitive Church, in her infancy, and shall it be too hard for our digestion now? It was the seede of the Church, out of which we sprung; and shall wee grudge to Tithe our selves to God, in any proportion that hee will accept? As *Zipporah* said to *Moses*, *vere sponsus sanguinum es mihi*; the Church may well say to Christ, who lookes for this Circumcision at her hands, and this tribute of blood, which he hath so well deserved; both by begetting the Church by his blood upon the Crosse, and feeding her still with the same blood in the Sacrament.

12   But those whom hee hath pre-ordained to this supreme Dignity of Martyrdome, God doth ordinarily bring up in a novitiate, and Apprentisage of worldly Crosses and Tribulations. And as *Justinians* great Officer *Tiberius*, when out of a reverence to the signe of the Crosse, he removed a Marble stone from the Pavement, and under it found a second stone, with the same Sculpture, and under that a third, and under all, great plenty of treasure, had not this treasure in his hope, nor purpose, nor desire beforehand, but satisfied himselfe in doing that honour to that signe, which those first times needed: So is the treasure and crowne of Martyredome seposed for them, who take up devoutly the crosses of this life, whether of poverty, or anguish'd consciences, or obedience of lawes which seeme burdenous, and distastefull to them; for all that time a man serves for his freedome, and God keeps his reckoning, from the inchoation of his Martyredome, which was from his first submission to these tribulations: which *Chrysostome* testifies thus; *That when one is executed, he is then made a Martyr* (that is, declared and accepted for a Martyre by the Church) *but from that time, when he begunne to shewe, that he would professe that Religion, he was a Martyre, though he endured not that which Martyres doe.*

13   Saint *Paul* saith of himselfe, *I die daily*; and *Chrysostome* of *David*, *He merited the Crowne of Martyrdome a thousand times in his purpose and disposition, and was slaine for God a thousand times.* And these persecutions are not onely part of the Martyredome, but they

Marginalia:
- Exod. 4.25
- Paul. Diaco. ad Eutrop. Addit.18
- Hom.1. in psal.95
- I Cor. 15.31
- Homil. de David et Saul

Margin 5. Exod. 4.25] *note misplaced.*   L-1, HD, E-1, L^{30}, O^2, O^{14}, YK-1
Margin 12. Paul] *note misplaced.*   L-1, E-1, HD, L^{30}, O^2, O^{14}, YK-1
Margin 24. Hom] *note misplaced.*   L-1, E-1, HD, L^{30}, O^2, O^{14}, YK-1
Margin 29. 15.31 *Ed.*: 15..   L-1, C-1   **Margin 30.** Homil. *errata: note missing.*   L-1, C-1

are part of the reward: for so St. *Marke* seemes to intimate, when hee Mar. 10.29, 30
expresseth Christ thus; *No man shall forsake any thing for my sake, but*
he shall receive a hundred folde now at this present, houses, Brothers,
Sisters, Mothers and Children, and land, with Persecutions. So that
5 Christ promises a reward, but not to take away the persecution; but
so to mingle and compound them, and make them both of one taste,
and indifferency, that wee shall not distinguish, which is the meate and
which is the sauce, but nourish our spirituall growth as well with the
persecution, as with the reward.

10   14   For this high degree of a consummate Martyre, is not ordinarily
attained to *per Saltum*, but we must be content to serve God first in
a lower ranke and Order: for as such Kings, as come to the possession
of a Kingdome, by a new, or a violent, or a litigious Title, doe use at
the beginning to signe their Graunts, and Edicts, and other publique
15 Acts, not onely themselves, but admit the Subscription and testimony
of their Counsellers, and Nobility, and Bishoppes; but being established
by a long succession, and entring by an indubitate Title, are confident
in their rights, and come to signe *Teste me ipso*: So doth our Saviour
Christ ordinarily in these times, when hee is in possession of the world,
20 seale his graces to us by himselfe in his word and Sacraments, and doth
not so frequently call witnesses and Martyrs, as he did in the Primitive
Church, when he induced a new Religion, and saw that, that maner of
confirmation was expedient for the credite and conveyance thereof.

And if a man should in an immature and undigested zeale, expose his
25 life for testimony of a matter, which were already beleeved, or to which
he were not called by God, he did no more honor God in that acte, then
a Subject should honour the King by subscribing his name, and giving
his Testimony to any of the Kings Graunts.

Margin 1. 10.29, 30 *Ed.*: 10.29 *errata; note missing.* L-1, C-1   **3.** houses, *Ed.*: houses. L-1, C-1

Chap. II.

That there may be an inordinate and corrupt affectation of Martyrdome.

1 The externall honours, by which the memories of the Orthodox Martyres in the Primitive Church were celebrated and enobled, (as styling their deaths *Natalitia*, observing their *Anniversaries*, commemorating them at their *Altars*, and instituting *Notaries*, to register their actions and passions) inflamed the Heretiques also to an ambition of getting the like glory. And thereupon they did not onely expose and precipitate themselves into all dangers, but also invented new wayes of Martyredome; with hunger whereof they were so much enraged and transported, that some of them taught, That upon conscience of sinne to kill ones selfe, was by this acte of Justice, a Martyrdome: upon which ground *Petilian*, against whom Saint *Augustine* writes, canonized *Judas* for a ˣMartyr. The rage and fury of the *Circumcelliones*, in extorting this imagined Martyrdome, brought them first to solicite and importune others to kill them; and if they fail'd in that suite, they did it themselves. And an other Sect prospered so farre in heaping up numbers of Martyres, that their whole sect was called *Martyriani*.

2 And a zealous scorne to be overtaken, and equal'd in this honor, provoked sometimes those who write the Actes of the Orthodoxe Martyrs, to insert into their Histories some particulars which were not true, and some which were not justifiable: for of the first sort of these insertions, which proceeded (as he saith) out of too much love to the Martyrs, *Baronius* in his *Martyrologe* complaines; and by the Canon which forbids these Histories to be reade publiquely in the Romane Church, it seems they were careful that the people should not thereby be taught and encouraged, to bring such actions into consequence and imitation, as, (if the immediate instinct of Gods spirit, did not justifie them) would seeme indiscreete and intemperate. Nor were they onely, which corrupted the stories in fault, but out of *Binius*, the last compiler of the Councels, we may perceive, that even they which were Orthodoxe professors, had

Margin notes:
Alfons. Castr. ver. Martyrium
ˣPrateolus. l.3. cap.19
Epipha. Hares. 80
Cap.2
Dist. 15. Sancta Romana

2. 1] *missing*. E-1, HD, O¹⁴, YK-1 **Margin 10.** Alfons.] *note misplaced.* YK-1, C²-2, HD **14.** Martyrdome, *Ed.*: Martyrdome;. L-1, C-1

some tincture of this over-vehement affectation of Martyredome: for he sayes, that the sixeteth Canon of the *Eliberitane* councell (by which it is enacted, *That those Christians which attempt to break the Idols of the Gentiles, and were slaine by them, should not be numbered amongst the Martyrs*) was made to deterre men from following such examples, as *Eulalia*, who being a maide of twelve years, came from her fathers house, declared her selfe to be a Christian, spit in the Judges face, and provoked him to execute her. To which they were then so inclinable, that as a Catholique Author hath observed, that state which inflicted those persecutions, sometimes made Edicts, that no more Christians should be executed, because they perceived how much contentment and satisfaction, and complacency some of them had in such dying.

<small>To.1. fo.248</small>

<small>Prudentius</small>

<small>Bodin. Daemon-um. l.4. c.3. ex Tertull.</small>

3 And although these irregular and exorbitant actes be capable of a good interpretation; that is, that the spirit of God did by secret insinuations excite and inflame them, and such as they were, to put fervor into others at that time; yet certainly God hath already made his use of them, and their examples belong no more to us, in this part and circumstance of such excesses.

4 And though this secret and inward instinct and moving of the holy Ghost, which the Church presumes, to have guided not onely these martyres, in whose forwardnesse these authors have observed some incongruity with the rules of Divinity, but also *Sampson*, and those Virgines which drowned themselves for preservation of their chastity, which are also acounted by that Church as martyres; although (I say) this instinct lie not in proofe, nor can be made evident; yet there are many other reasons, which authorize and justifie those zealous transgressions of theirs (if any such were): or make them much more excuseable, then any man can be in these times, and in these places wherein we live.

<small>Euseb. l.8. Hist. Eccles. ca.12</small>

5 For the persecutions in the Primitive Church were raised either by the *Gentiles* or the *Arrians*; either the unity of the God-head, or the Trinity of the persons was ever in question: which were the *Elements* of the Christian Religion, of which it was fram'd and complexioned; and so to shake that, was to ruine and demolish all. And they were also the *Alphabet* of our Religion, of which no infant or *Neophyte* might be

Margin 9. Daemonum. *Ed.*: Daemonom. C-1, L-1   **10.** persecutions, *Ed.*: persecutions;. L-1, C-1   **Margin 22.** 12 *Ed.*: 24. L-1, C-1

ignorant. But now the integrity of the beliefe of the Romane Church, is the onely forme of Martyrdome; for it is not allowed for a Martyrdome to witnes by our blood, the unity of God against the *Gentiles*, nor the Trinity of persons against the *Turke* or *Jew*, except we be ready to seale with our blood contradictorie things, and incompatible for the time past: (since evidently the Popes have taught contradictorie things) and for the time present, obscure and irrevealed thinges, and entangling perplexities of Schoolemen; for in these, yea in future contingencies, we must seale with our blood, that part which that Church shall hereafter declare to be true.

_{Feuardentius. Theom. Calvin. l.8. c.13. n.13}

6 This constant defence of the foundation, and this undisputable evidence of the truth, was their warrant: And they had another double reason, of making them extremely tender, and fearefull of slipping from their profession; which was first the subtilties and Artifices of their adversaries, to get them to doe some acte, which might imply a transgressing and dereliction of their Religion, though it were not directly so; and so draw a scandall upon their cause, and make their simplicity seeme infirmity, and impiety: and secondly, the severity which the Church used towards them, who had done any such acte, and her bitternesse and aversenes, from re-assuming them, even after long penances, into her bosome. For by the third Canon of the *Eliberitane* Councel, which I mentioned before, it appeares, that even they whom they called *Libellaticos*, because they had for money bargained and contracted with the State, to spare them from sacrificing to Idolles (though this were done but to redeeme their vexation and trouble) were seperated from the holy Communion. But none of these reasons can advantage or relieve those of the Romane persuasion in these times, because no point of Catholique faith, either primary and radicall or issuing from thence by necessary deduction and consequence, is impugned by us; nor their faith in those points, wherein it abounds above ours, explicated to them by any evidence, which is not subject to just quarrell and exception; nor are our Magistrates laborious or active to withdrawe them by any snares from their profession, but only by the open and direct way of the word of God, if they would heare it: nor is the Church so soure and tetricall, but that she admits with ease and joy, those, which after long straying, not only into that Religion, but into such treasons and disobediences, as that Religion produces, returne to her againe.

Chap. III.

That the Romane Religion doth by many erroneous doctrines misencourage and excite men to this vicious affectation of danger: first by aviling secular Magistracy: secondly by extolling the value of merites, and of this worke in special, by which the treasure of the Church is
5 *so much advanced: and lastly, by the doctrine of Purgatory, which by this acte is said certainely to be escaped.*

The first part of Principallity and Priest-hood.

1   Having laide this foundation, that the greatest Dignitie, wherewith
10 God hath enriched mans nature, (next to his owne assuming thereof) may suffer some infirmitie: yea, putrefaction, by admixture of humane and passionate respects, if when we are admitted to bee witnesses of Gods honour, we love our owne glory too much, or the Authoritie by which this benefit is deriv'd upon us, too little, which is the function of
15 secular Magistracie: We are next to consider, by what inducements, and provocations, the Doctrine and practise of the *Romane* Church doth put forward, and precipitate our slipperie disposition into this vicious and inordinate affection, and dangerous selfe-flatterie.

2   In three things especially they seeme to me, to advance and foment
20 this corrupt inclination. *First*, by abasing, and aviling the Dignitie and persons of secular Magistrates, by extolling Ecclesiasticke immunities and priviledges: *Secondly*, by dignifying and over-valewing our merits and satisfactions, and teaching that the treasure of the Church, is by this expence of our blood increased. And thirdly, by the Doctrine of
25 *Purgatorie*, the torments whereof are by this suffering said to be escaped and avoided.

3   And in the first point, which is a dis-estimation of Magistracie, they offend two wayes: *Comparatively*, when they compare together

3. *aviling errata: inciting.*   L-1, C-1   **9.** 1] *missing* .   C⁵-1, SP, C¹⁶ that and Priest-hood, and *Positively*, when not bringing the Priestly function into the ballance, or disputation, they give the Pope authority as *Supreame spirituall Prince*, over all Princes.

4 When the first is in question of Priesthood and Magistracy, then enters the Sea, yea Deluge of *Canonists*, and overflowes all, and carries up their *Arke* (that is the Romane Church, that is the Pope) fifteene cubites above the highest hils, whether Kings or Emperours. And this makes the Glosser upon that *Canon*, where Priesthood is said to exceede the Layetie, as much as the Sunne, the Moone, so diligent to calculate those proportions, and to repent his first account as too low, and reforme it by later calculations, and after much perplexity to say, That since he cannot attaine to it, he will leave it to the *Astronomers*; so that they must tell us, how much the Pope exceedes a Prince: which were a fit work for their *Jesuite Clavius*, who hath expressed in one summe, how many granes of Sand would fill all the place within the concave of the firmament, if that number will seeme to them enough for this comparison. But to all these Rhapsoders, and fragmentary compilers of *Canons*, which have onely amass'd and shoveld together, whatsoever the Popes themselves or their creatures have testified in their owne cause; *Amandus Polanus* applies a round, and pregnant, and proportionall answere, by presenting against them the Edicts and Rescripts of Emperours to the contrary, as an equivalent proofe at least.

5 And for the matter it selfe, wherein the Ecclesiastique and Civill estate are under and above one another, with us it is evident and liquid enough, since no Prince was ever more indulgent to the Clergie, by encouragements and reall advancing, nor more frequent in accepting the foode of the worde and Sacrament at their hands, in which he acknowledges their superiority, nor the Clergy of any Church more inclinable to preserve their just limits; which are, to attribute to the king so much, as the good kings of *Israel*, and the Emperours in the Primitive Church had.

6 It is intire man that God hath care of, and not the soule alone; therefore his first worke was the body, and the last worke shall bee the glorification thereof. He hath not delivered us over to a Prince onely, as to a Physitian, and to a Lawyer, to looke to our bodies and estates;

Margin: Extra de maior. & Obed. Solitae. Quinquagesies septies & Centies quadragesies septies & medium, & septies medies & septingesies, quadragesies, quater & medium Comment. in Sacro. Bosc. fol.219

Simphon. c.24. Thes. 9

3. *Prince errata: Princesse.* C-1, L-1   **Margin 8.** medies *Ed.*: mesies. C-1, L-1

and to the Priest onely, as to a Confessor, to looke to, and examine our soules, but the Priest must aswel endevour, that we live vertuously and innocently in this life for society here, as the Prince, by his lawes keepes us in the way to heaven: for thus they accomplish a *Regale Sacerdotium*; when both doe both; for we are sheepe to them both, and they in divers relations sheepe to one another.

7 Accordingly they say, that the subject of the Canon law is *Homo dirigibilis in Deum, & Bonum Commune*; so that that Court which is *forum spirituale*, considers the publique tranquility. And on the other side *Charles* the great, to establish a meane course between those two extreame *Councels*, of which ᵃone had utterly destroyed the use of Images in Churches: the ᵇother had induced their adoration, takes it to belong to his care and function, not onely to call a ᶜ*Synode* to determine herein, but to write the booke of that important and intricate point, to *Adrian* then Pope; which ᵈ*Steuchius* saith, remaines yet to be seene in *Bibliotheca Palatina*, and urges and presses that booke for the Popes advantage. And in the preface of that booke, the Emperour hath these wordes: ᵉ*In sinu Regni Ecclesiae gubernacula suscepimus*; and so proceedes, that not only he, to whom the Church is committed, *ad regendum*, in those stormy times, but they also which are *Enutriti ab uberibus* must joine with him in that care: and therefore he addes, That he undertooke this worke, *Cum Conhibentia Sacerdotum in regno suo*; neither would this Emperour (of so pious affections towards that Sea, expressed in profuse liberalities) have usurped any part of Jurisdiction, which had not orderly devolved to him, and which he had not knowne to have beene duely executed by his predecessors.

8 Whose authoritie, in disposing of Church matters, and direction in matters of Doctrine, together with the Bishops, appeares abundantly and evidently out of their owne Lawes, and out of their Rescripts to Popes, and the Epistles of the Popes to them. For we see, by the Imperial Law, the Authoritie of the Prince and the Priest made equall, when it is decreed, ᵃ*That no man may remove a body out of a Monument in the Church, without a Decree of the Priest, or Commandement of the Prince.*

Margin notes:
Reg. Iu. Possessor. in 6. Glos.
ᵃConstantin. Ann. 754
ᵇNicenum 2. Anno 787
ᶜFrancofur. Anno 794
ᵈDonat. Constant. l.2. nu.60
ᵉHaimiusfeldius. Decretu. Impp. de Imaginibus. fo.91
ᵃDig. li.xi. Tit. 7. l.8. Ossa

Margin 7. Iu.] Iu. L-1, C-2, O², O¹⁴ **Margin 7.** Possessor. *errata*: Possore,. L-1, C-1 **Margin 18e.** Haimiusfeldius *Ed*.: Haimius Feldius. C-1, L-1 **19.** so proceedes *errata*: to proceede. L-1, C-1

And yet there appears much difference, in degrees of absolutenesse of power, betweene these limitations of a *Decree* and a *Commandement*. And *Leo* the first, writing to the Emperour *Martianus*, rejoises, that he found ^b*In Christianismo Principe Sacerdotalem affectum*. And in his ^cEpistle to *Leo* the Emperour, using this preface for feare least hee should seeme to diminish him in that comparison (*Christiana utor libertate*) he saith, *I exhort you to a fellowshippe with the Prophets and Apostles, because you are to be numbered, inter Christi praedicatores*: Hee addes, that kings are instituted, not onely *ad mundi regimen*, but chiefly *ad Ecclesiae presidium*: and therefore he prayes God to keepe in him still, *Animum eius Apostolicum & Sacerdotalem*.

^bLeo I. Martia. Epist. 70
^cEpist. 75

9 So for his diligence in the Church-governement, *Simplicius*, the Pope salutes the Emperour *Zeno*: *Exultamus vobis in esse animum Sacerdotis & principis*: For which respect his successor ^a*Felix* the third, writing to the same Emperour, salutes him with this style: *Dilectissimo fratri Zenoni*, which is a style so peculiar to those, which are constituted in the highest Ecclesiastique dignities as Bishoppes and Patriarches, ^bthat if the Pope should write to any of them by the name of Sons, which is his ordinary style to secular princes, it vitiates the whole Diplome, and makes it false.

Simplicius Papa. An. 479. Epist. 14
^aAnn. 488. Epist. 8

^bExtra. de Rescript. Ad audientiam. glos. verb. manifestum

10 And a ^cSynodicall letter from a whole Councell to a King of *France*, acknowledges this Priestly care in the king, thus, *Quia Sacerdotali mentis affectu, you have commaunded your Priests to gather together, &c.* which right of general superintendencie over the whole Church, ^d*Anastasius* the Emperour dissembled not, when writing to the Senate of Rome to compose dissentions there, hee called *Hormisda* the pope, *Papam Almae urbis Romae*, but in the Inscription of the Letter, amongst his owne Titles, he writes *Pontifex inclitus*.

^cConc. Aurelian. I. Clodu. regi. c.2

^dHabetur in Binio. To.2. f.320. Anno. 516

11 ^e*Gregory* himselfe (though his times to some tastes, seeme a little brackish, and deflected from upright obedience to princes) saith of the Emperours *That no man can rightly governe earthly matters, except he know also how to handle Divine*. And in the weakest estate, and most dangerous fitt that ever secular Magistrate suffered and endured, *Gre-*

^eLi.4. Epist. 32

Greg. 7. Duci Sueviae. l.1. Epist. 19

Margin 5c. ^c*Epist Ed.*: Epist.. C-1, L-1 **Margin 12.** 479 *Ed.*: 471. C-1, L-1 **Margin 14a.** 488. Epist. 8 *Ed.*: 486. Epist 14. L-1, C-1 **Margin 33.** Sueviae *Ed.*: Sue viae. C-1, L-1

gory the seventh denied not, that these two dignities were *as the two eyes of the body, which governd the bodie of the Church in spirituall light*; which is more, then the Comparisons of *Soule* and *Body*, and of *Golde* and *Leade*, as they are now usurped and detorted, can affoord. And the evidence of this truth hath extorted from *Binius* (a severe and heavie depresser of kings,) thus much (though but in a marginall note) *Imperatores Sacra & secularia ex aequo curant*. And so much did pope *John* the eight willingly acknowledge to *Lodovic* the sonne of *Charles*, *That he was Cooperator sui certaminis*. And as *Balsamo* saith upon the fourth generall Councell of *Chalcedon*, that it belongs to the Emperour to designe the limits of Dioceses, and to erect a Bishopricke into a Metropolitane seate, and to appoint who shall possesse them. So to that Canon in the Councell of *Trullo* which forbidding all Lay persons to come within a certaine distance of the Altar, doth not extend to the Emperours, *Si quidem voluerit Creatori dona offerre ex antiquissima consuetudine*: And to Balsamoes Notes thereupon, *that Orthodoxe Emperours, because they are Christi Domini, have also Pontificall Graces from God, and by Invocation of the holy Trinity, they create Patriarchs, they come unto the Altar, Et sufficiunt sicut & Antistites*: *Binius* opposes no more, but that the Canon was made in flatterie of the Emperour, which is not enough to defeate the Canon, nor enervate the credite thereof, since that Canon was not *introductory*, then, but *Declaratorie* of an aunceint custome, as the words thereof doe fully evict and prove.

12 And not onely Councels submitted their Decrees to the Emperours for Authoritie, and supplement of defects, but the Popes themselves consulted the Emperours before hand, by their Letters, in matters of greatest difficultie and importance: So *Leo* the first writes to *Martianus* the Emperour, about the establishing of *Easter*, in which point the Church suffered more stormes & schismes, then almost in any other, that did not concerne the Trinitie, and at this time nothing was certainely determined and decreed therein. Thus then he writes to him, *Cupio vestrae Clementiae studiis adiuvari*, *That so no error may be committed in the observation thereof*. And *John* the eight, exhorts the Sonnes of *Charles*, as partners in his Pastorall care to imploy *Baculos redargutio-*

Margin notes:
Binius. To.5. fol.831.A
Ioan. 8. Papa. Ann. 873. Epist. 87
Balsamo. in Conc. Chalced. can.17
Concil. Quinisex. in Trullo. ca.69. Anno 692
Notae in hunc can. To.3. par.1. fo.156.A
Leo. Martiano. Epist. 64
John 8. Epist. 87

Margin 13. Quinisex *Ed*.: Quinosen.. C-1, L-1 **Margin 19.** Notae] Notes. L-1, C-2 **Margin 33.** John *Ed*.: Leo. C-1, L-1 **33.** John *Ed*.: Leo. C-1, L-1

nis. And concerning some spiritual matters, then to be determined, he ends his Epistle thus, *The penne must first be dipped in the fountaine of your heart, and then my Hand shall frame the Characters*. And so when a Bishop of *Constantinople* stood out in some things against the Emperor, the Bishop of *Rome*, who at that time had justly acquir'd a great reputation in the Catholicke Church, writes to the Emperour, *That if that Bishop persever in such courses, as displease God, and the Emperour, Salva Mansuetudinis vestrae Reverentia, utar in eum liberiori Constantia*. So that having first asked the Emperour leave, he offers him his assistance.

<small>Leo I. ad Martian. Epist. 70</small>

13 And though *Gregorie* the first (whom wee may justly call a border-pope, because though hee made no deepe roades into the jurisdiction of Princes, yet he extended his owne to the uttermost inch, and sometimes transgressed a little beyond) though he, I say, suspended one, to whome Orders were given by the Emperours commandement, yet hee doeth not this absolutely, but because he knew (as he said) the Emperours minde therein, and that particular parties unworthinesse; he suspended him, untill he might understand from his *Responsall* with the Emperor, whether that pretended Commandement from the Emperour were not subreptitious.

<small>Grego. I. li.3. Epist. 20</small>

14 And when this correspondence was intermitted, as it appeares often to have beene, to the prejudice of the whole Church, the Emperours were ever forwardest to labour a re-union and concurrence of their powers, to the benefit and peace thereof; as *Anastasius* testifies thoroughly in a Letter to *Hormisda*, in these words; *Before this time, the hardnesse of them, to whom the care of this Bishopricke, which you now governe, was committed, made us abstaine from sending any Letters; but now, since their runnes a sweete opinion of you, it hath brought backe to our memorie, the goodnesse of a fatherly affection, that we should require those things*, and so foorth. By which, all these circumstances appeare, That the Emperours did use to write, and that the fault which induced a discontinuance thereof, proceeded from the Pope; and that the Emperour pretermitted no opportunitie of resuming that custome; and that when he writ, he did it out of a fatherly care, and by the way of requiring. And how much joy *Hormisda* conceived by this Letter, ap-

<small>Anastas. Imp. Hormisdae Papae. Binius. To.2. fo.315.A</small>

<small>Hormisda. Epist. 2</small>

34. when C²-2, L²², D-1, D-3, O², O¹⁴: where. L-1, C-1, MCG, C-2, C⁹

peares by his phrase of expressing it, *Sacros affatus congrua veneratione accepimus.*

15 With like care *Justinus* the Emperour exhorts the same Pope, to a Peace and Union with the Easterne Church, by his Letters which hee cals *Divinos Apices.* And scarse by any one thing doth this care of Princes, and obsequiousnesse of Popes appeare more, then by the Letter of *Pelagius* the first (who was little above 550. yeares from Christ) to *Childebert* King of *France*, in these words. *We must endevour, for the taking away of all scandall of suspition, to present the obsequiousnesse of our Confession, unto Kings, to whom the holy Scriptures command even us to bee subject. For* Ruffinus, *your Excellencies Ambassadour, asked from us confidently, as became him, that either we should signifie to you, that we did observe in all points the Faith, which* Leo *had described, or send a Confession of our Faith in our owne words.* And so accordingly he performes both, as well binding himselfe to the Faith of his predecessours, as exhibiting to the King another forme of the same Faith, compos'd and digested by himselfe; which, if the Bishops of that Sea would accept now, I doe not perceive wherein there could be any Schisme.

16 And as the Emperours were carefull assistants of the Popes, that that mother Church, at whose breast most of the Westerne Churches sucked their spirituall nourishment, should be infected with no poison, because it might easily be derived from thence to the other members; so did they not attend the leisure of that Churches resolution, nor the incommodity of Generall Councels, but used their owne power to governe their Churches, by constitutions of their owne; for so [a]*Justinian* the Emperour says of his owne lawe, by which he priviledges certain religious houses; *We offer up this Divine law as a faire and convenient sacrifice to Christ.* So that either that attribute *Divinum* was then affoorded to civill Constitutions, or the Emperour made Ecclesiastique lawes, if that word belong onely to such. [b]The Emperours tooke it into their care, to dispose of their estates which entred into Monasteries; [c]And of theirs also which dyed in Monasteries; so that neither the purpose of entring, nor the acte, nor the habite, and perseverance devested the Emperour of his right, or hindred the working of the Law. [a]The Emperours also

Binius. To.2. fo.335.B

Pelagius I. Epist. 16. Satagendum

[a]Cod. l.1. Tit. 3. l.ultim. in fine

[b]Cod. l.1. Tit. 2. le.13
[c]Cod. l.1. Tit. 3. l.20

[a]Cod. l.1. Tit. 3. l.4 & 27

Margin 8. 16. *Ed.*: 16. & 25. q.1.   C-1, L-1

by their lawes appointed which of their subjects might not take. Orders,
^band at what age Orders might be confer'd; and that no woman after
a second marriage might be ^cDiaconissa; which was, to make a law of
Bigamy.

17 Yea they commanded and instructed in matter of Faith; for so
^dJustinian sayes of himselfe, we are forward to teach, what is the right
faith of Christians, and we *Anathematize Apollinarius*. ^eSo also, *Honorius* and *Theodosius* inflict the punishment of death upon any Catholique Minister (for then neither that name was abhorred by Priests, nor they exempt from criminall lawes) which shold re-baptize any man; and yet this was a meere spirituall offence. And so ^fValentinian and his Co-emperours pronounce marriage betweene *Jewes* and *Christians* to be adultery. And ^gJustinian interprets how a Testator shall bee understood, when he appoints Christ, or an Angell, or a Saint to be his heire.

18 Nor deale they onely with temporall punishments upon Ecclesiastique persons, which is farder than is affoorded them now, but they inflict also spirituall censures: for *Gratian* and his Co-emperours pronounce against Heretiques, (that is, Impugners of the Nicene councell) *That they shall be utterly secluded from the threshold of the Church*: And in the next law, which is against *Nestorians*, they say, *If the offenders be Laymen, Anathematizentur, if Clergie men, Eijciantur ab Ecclesiis*. ^aAnd another of their lawes doth not only inflict temporal & ignominious punishment upon Clergy men, but Ecclesiastique censures also in these words: *If a Clergy man be guilty of fals witnes in a pecuniary cause, let him be suspended three yeares, and in a criminall, let him be deprived*. ^bAnd another susspends for three yeares, even *Sanctissimos & venerabiles Episcopos*; if they doe but looke upon players at Tables: and that law authorizes him, under whose power that offender is, if he appeare penitent, to abbreviate his punishment; ^cand of Bishoppes which will not forsake women, it pronounces thus; *Abiiciantur Episcopatibus*. And in the matter of establishing and ordering *Sanctuaries*, ^done of the writers of the Romane parte hath presented civill constitutions enow, to teach us that, that was within the care and Jurisdiction of secular Princes.

Margin notes:
^bIbid. le.9
^cIbid. §. Diaconissa
^dCod. li.1. Tit. 1. l.6
^eCod. lib.1. Tit. 6. l.2
^fCod. l.1. Tit. 9. lib.6
^gCod. l.1. Tit. 2. l.ult.
Cod. l.1. Tit. 1. l.2
^aCod. l.1. Tit. 3. l.7. §. Presbiteri.
^bIbid. le.17. §. Interdicimus
^cIbid. l.19
^dSimancha. de Repub. l.8. c.40

3. ^cDiaconissa *Ed.*: Diaconissa. C-1, L-1   7. Apollinarius. ^eSo *Ed.*: Apollinarius^e. So. C-1, L-1

19 ᵉAnd when an Emperour had created a Bishop of *Antioch*, contrary to the forme prescrib'd in the Nicene Councell, of an intire observation, whereof the Christian Church was extremly zealous, the Pope proceedes not by anullings and vociferations, but writes thus to the Emperour: *We may not dissallow that which you have done holily and religiously out of a love to peace and quietnes*; by which we see that Canons of Councels, though they were *Directions*, yet they were not *Obligations* upon Princes for their governement. By all which it appeares, that those Christian and Orthodoxe Emperors, justifying their inherent right, by these frequent and un-interrupted matters of fact, apprehended not this vast and incomprehensible distance betweene secular and ecclesiastique power, but that they were compatible enough, and conduced, and concurred to one perfection, and harmony of the whole state.

ᵉSimplicius Zenoni. Ep. 14

20 And it is related by ᵃan Author of great estimation in the Romane profession, that *Gregory* the seventh was author of a new scisme, dividing and tearing priesthood and principality. ᵇAnd it is evident that *Bertram* a priest under *Carolus Calvus*, almost eight hundred yeares since, writing of that Divine and abstruse mysterie, *De corpore Domini*, submits his opinion to the judgement of the King and his Counsaile, as competent Judges of that question: and ᶜCochlaeus saith, that *Luthers* doctrine was condemned for hereticall by an edict of the Emperours, with the common assent of the Princes and the States. And the holy Ghost had well intimated the concurrence of their two powers in ᵈDeuter. if those wordes which are in the Text, *Nolens obedire sacerdotis Imperio, & Decreto Iudicis, moriatur*; were not chaunged by the vulgate edition, into *Ex Decreto*; and thereby only the priest made Judge of the controversies, and the Magistrate onely executioner of his Sentences.

ᵃEspencaeus. Com. in Tim. l.2. pag.275
ᵇIndex Expur. Belg. fo.15
ᶜPrefatio in Histor. de Act. & Script. Lutheri
ᵈDeut. 17.12

21 For certainely these two functions are not in their nature so distinct, and Diametrically opposed, but that they may meete in one matter, yea sometimes in one man, and one man may doe both: for amongst the Gentiles, it was so for the most part: and sometimes amongst the Israelites. And in late times ᵃ*Maximilian* the first, a Catholique Emperour, thought it belonged to the *Empire*, to have also the *Papacy* united

ᵃEpist. Maximili. ad Baro. Leichtensteni. Habetur in Monit. polit. edit. Franct. Ann. 1609. fo.33

3. Christian *Ed.*: christian. L-1, C-1 **Margin 23d.** 17.12 *Ed.*: 17.11. L-1, C-1 **25.** *Iudicis*, C³, YK-2, F, HD, Y, L³⁰, C⁵-2, O², O¹⁴: *Iudici,,*. L-1, C-1, MCG, L², L-2, SP, C¹⁰, C¹⁶, YK-1

to it: and therefore when *Julius* the second lay desperately sicke, he endevoured to bring to execution, that which he had often meditated, and consulted, and received as approved from some great persons of dignity in that Church, which was to bee elected Pope in the next Conclave, and to restore the Papacy (as he thought or pretended) to the Emperiall Crowne.

22 [b]And if a Lay-man be elected Pope, he need not presently be made Priest, but he may, if hee will, stay in *Subdiaconatu*. And to that degree they seeme to admit the Emperour, when he comes to be crowned at *Rome*; [c]for at the Communion he administers to the Pope in the place of Subdeacon. And this in the Primitive Church was not (as [d]themselves confesse) *Ordo Sacer*: though of late it be growne to be such a perplexed case, whether it were or no, that of those commissioners, which two Popes made to survay the *Decretals*, one company expunged, the other re-assumed [e]one place in that book, which denies this to have beene amongst holy Orders.

23 The Emperour also puts on a Surplis, and is admitted as a Canonick not only of Saint *Peters* Church, but of Saint *John Laterane*; to which particular Church (of which the Pope is Parson, as he is Bishoppe of *Rome*, Metropolitane of *Italy*, patriarch of the West, and pope of the world,) all those blessings and priviledges which are ordinarily spoken of the Catholique Church are said by [a]some to bee irremoveably annexed and appropriate: hereupon some of their owne lawyers say, [b]That all kings are clergie men; and that therefore it is sacriledge to dispute of the authority of a King.

24 But howsoever these two functions, since the establishing of Christianity, have for the most part beene preserved distinct, and ought so to be; yet they are at most, but so distinct as our *Body* and *Soule*: and though our Soule can contemplate God of herself, yet she can produce no exterior act without the body. Nothing in the world is more spirituall and delicate, and tender then the conscience of a man; yet by good consent of Divines, otherwise diversly persuaded in Religion, the civill lawes of Princes doe binde our consciences: and shall the persons of any men, or their temporal goods, be thought to be of so sublime, and spiri-

[b]Ceremoniae Sacrae. Cap. de Ordinatione

[c]Idem. ca. de Coronat.

[d]Alfon. Alvares. Specul. utriusque. Dig. c.10. nu.3

[e]Extra de Digam. non Ordin. Super eis. glos. verbo Sacros

[a]Alvares. Specu. utri. Digni. ca.1. nu.40

[b]Cassanaeus. par.5. consid.24. art.59 & 181

Margin 15e. Digam. *Ed.*: bigam.. C-1, L-1 **19.** Church *errata*: Churches. L-1, C-1 **21.** world,) *Ed.*: world,. L-1, C-1 **26.** establishing *errata*: establing. L-1, C-1

tuall a nature, that the civill constitutions of Princes cannot worke upon them? Nor doe we therfore decline the comparison, so much urged by the Romanes, that the Clergie exceede the Laiety as much as the *body* the *soule*, when it is so conditioned and qualified, as the authors thereof intended it; That is, that the seales and instruments of Gods grace, the Sacraments, are in the dispensing of the Clergy, as temporall blessings are in the Prince and his lawes, strictly and properly, though concurrently both in both, (for the execution of the most spirituall function of the priest, as it is circumstanced with time and place; and such, is ordinarily from the Prince): But we are a little affraid, that by a literall and punctuall acceptation of this comparison, we may give way to that Supremacy, which they affect over Princes; because their *Sepulveda* saith, *That the soule doth exercise over the body, Herile Imperium, ut Dominus in servum*: and so by the insinuation should the pope doe over the prince.

25 Howsoever in their first institution Popes were meere Soules, and purely spirituall, yet as the purest Soule becomes stain'd and corrupt with sinne, assoone as it touches the body: so have they by entring into secular businesse, contracted all the corruptions and deformities thereof, and now transferre this originall disease into their successours. And as in the second *Nicene* Councell, when the Bishop of *Thessalonica* averr'd it to be the opinion of *Basil*, *Athanasius*, and *Methodius*, and the Universall Church, that *Angels*, and *Soules* were not meerely incorporeall, but had bodies: The Councell in a prudent connivencie, forbore to oppose any thing against that asservation, because it facilitated their purpose then, of making Pictures and representations of Spirits (though *Binius* now upon that place, say, his Assertion was false and injurious to the Church:) So though in true Divinitie the Pope is meerely spiritual, yet to enable him to depose Princes, they will invest and organize him with bodily and secular Jurisdiction, and averre that all the Fathers, and all the Catholicke Church were ever of that opinion. For the Pope will not now be a meere Soule and Spirit, but *Spiritualis homo, qui iudicat omnia, & a nemine iudicatur*. For so a late writer styles him, and by that place of Scripture enables him to depose Princes. Nor will this serve, but

Bellar. de Pont. Ro. l.5. c.6. §. Est igitur. Ex Nazianz.

Sepulveda. de Regn. & Reg. Offi. l.1

Concil. Nice. 2. Actio 5

To.3. par.1. fol.399

I Cor. 2.15
Maynardus. de Privileg. Eccles. Art.9. n.1

5. and instruments *Ed.*: instruments. C-1, L-1; and *catchword* p.30 **Margin 12.** Offi. *errata*: Hu.. L-1, C-1

he must be also *spiritualis Princeps*; of which we shall hereafter have occasion to speake.

26 And as a cunning Artificer can produce greater effects, upon matter conveniently dispos'd thereunto, then nature could have done, (as a Statuarie can make an Image, which the Timber and the Axe could never have effected without him: And as the *Magicians* in *Egypt* could make living Creatures, by applying and suggesting Passive things to Active, which would never have met, but by their mediation:) So, after this *Soule* is entred into this *Body*, this spirituall Jurisdiction into this temporall, it produces such effects, as neither power alone could worke, nor they naturally would unite and combine themselves to that end, if they were not thus compressed, and throng'd together like wind in a Cave. Such are the thunders of unjust Excommunications, and the great Earthquakes of transferring Kingdomes.

27 And these usurpations of your Priests have deserv'd, that that stigmaticall note should still lie upon them, which your Canons retaine, [a] *That all evill proceedes from Priests.* For though [b] *Manriqe* whom *Pius* the fift employ'd, had remooved that glosse, yet *Faber* to whom *Gregorie* the thirteenth committed the survey of the Canons, retaines it still. And (if the Text be of better credit then the glosse) the Text hath averred Saint *Hieromes* words, *That searching ancient Histories, he cannot find, that any did rent the Church, and seduce the people from the house of God, but those which were placed by God, as Priests, and Prophets, that is, Overseers; for these are turned into winding Snares, and lay scandals in every place.*

28 Even the Name of King, presents us an argument of pure, and absolute, and independant Authoritie; for it expresses immediatly, and radically his Office of governing, wheras the name of *Bishop* hath a metaphoricall, and similitudinarie derivation, and being before Christianitie applied to Officers, which had the overseeing of others, but yet with relation to Superiours, to whom they were to give an account, devolv'd conveniently upon such Prelates, as had the overseeing of the inferiour Clergie, but yet gave them no acquitance and discharge of their dueties to the Prince.

[a] Dist. 50. Et Purgabit. glos.verb.Domo
[b] Index. Expur. Belg. fol.306
24. q.3. Transferunt

17. *Pius Ed.*: *Sixtus.* C-1, L-1   **Margin 20.** Transferunt *Ed.*: Trans.ferunt. L-1, C-1

CHAPTER THREE 49

29   And God hath dignified many races of Kings, with many markes and impressions of his power. For by such an influence, and infusion, our kings cure a disease by touch, and so doe the French Kings worke upon the same infirmitie. And it is said that the kings of *Spaine* cure all Daemoniaque and possessed persons. And if it bee thought greater, that the Pope cures spirituall Leprosies, and lamenesses of sinne, his Office therein is but accessorie and subsequent; and after an Angel hath troubled our waters, and put us into the Poole, that is, after we are troubled and anguished for our sinnes, and after we have washed our selves often in the river Jordan, in our teares, and in our Saviours blood upon the Crosse, and in the Sacrament, then is his Office to distinguish betweene Leaper and Leaper, and pronounce who is clensed: which all his Priests could doe as well as he, if he did not Monopolize our sinnes by reservations.

30   And this is as much as seemes to me needfull to bee said of their aviling Magistracy, in respect of Priesthood: for, for us private men it must content us, to be set one staire higher then dogges; for so they say in their Missall cases, that *if any of the consecrated wine fall downe, the Priest or his assistant ought to licke it up; but if they be not prepar'd, any Lay-man may be admitted to licke it, least the dogge should*. And of the comparison of these two great functions, Principality and Priesthood, I will say no more, least the malignity of any mis-interpreter might throw these aspersions, which I lay upon persons, upon the Order. And therefore since we have sufficiently observed, how neare approaches to Priest-hood the Christian Emperours have justly made, and thereby seene the injustice of the Romane Church, in dejecting Princes so farre under it: we will now descend to the second way, by which they debase Princes, and derogate from their authority.

31   For it is not onely in comparisons with Priesthood, that the Romane writers diminish secular dignity, but simply and absolutely, when they make the Title and Jurisdiction of a king so smoakie a thing, that it must evaporate and vanish away by any lightning of the popes *Breves* or censures, except they will all yeeld to build up his Monarchy, and make him heire to every kingdome, as he pretends to be to the Empire:

[margin: Valdesius. de Dignitate regum Hispa. c.16]

[margin: Ioan. de Lapide. Casus missal. cap.6. Ar.5. §. Quocunque]

Margin 17. Lapide. *Ed.*: Lapide·.   L-1, C-1   **Margin 17.**   5.   C³, O², O¹⁴, SP, YK-2:   5.   L-1, C-1, O-2

for ^a*of that* (saith a Jesuite) *now there is no more controversie.* ^b*And if the electors dissagree in their election, then the election belongs to him.* And whether they agree or no, ^c*this forme of Election is to continue but so long, as the Church shall thinke it expedient.* And if he had such title to all the rest, that Monarchie might in a vaster proportion extend it selfe, as farre as one limme thereof, the *Jacobins*, do in *Paris*: ^dto whom *Philip le longe*, gave a Charter for their dwelling in that Citie, in these wordes: *A porta eorum, ad portam Inferni, inclusive.*

[marginalia: ^aAzor. par.2. l.10. c.9: §. Caeterum / ^bAlvares. Spec. utr. Dign. ca.56. nu.12 / ^cIdem. ca.16. nu.15 / ^dRen. Choppinus. de Iure Monast. l.1. Tit. 1. nu.15]

32 And how easily and slipperily Princes incurre these censures, may be collected by *Navarrus*, who sayes, *It is the Catholique faith, without firm beleefe whereof, no man can be saved; that no Prince can erect or extinguish a benefice without the Pope; and to thinke the contrary* (saith he) *doth taste of the English Heresie.*

[marginalia: Navar. Manual. c.27. nu.13]

33 Scarce any amongst themselves can escape that excommunication Dormant, which they call *Bullam Coenae*; in which *Navarrus* reckons up so many hooks, with which it takes hold, that every honest man, and good subject with us now, ought to be affraide, least he have not incurred it, since all they are within the danger thereof, that adhere to any, who hath but offended a Cardinall: of whose safety the popes are growne so carefull, that in the later *Decretals* it is made *treason*, even in a stranger and no subject; *If he have any kind of knowledge, or conjecture of any harme, intended to any of them.* And *the Emperour himselfe if he abett, or receive, or favour, or countenance any that doth, or intends personall harme to a Cardinall, becomes a traitor.* For *they are the eldest sonnes of the Church, and partake of the Majesty of their father.* Nor are they brethren to any of lesse ranke, but to such, their style is but *vester uti frater*, as *Baronius* writes to *Schultingius* his abbreviator. And though *Bishops* and the *Emperour* swear fidelity to the pope; yet, sayes *Gigas*, *the Cardinals doe not take that oath, because they are parts of his body, and his owne Bowels.*

[marginalia: In septimo. Tit. 4. c.3 / Hiero. Gigas. de laesa ma. l.1. Rubr.4. q.5. nu.10 / Ibid. nu.2 / Ante. librum Schultingii. To.1 / Ubi supra. c.6]

34 And not onely all princes are bound to a reverend respect of them, but ^ain solemne processions, the *Image of Christ must looke backward, if a Cardinall follow*; and God himselfe in the Host, must give them place: for at the Coronation of the *pope*, ^bwhen they provide twelve horses for the *Pope*, and one gentle one for the Host, the dignity of the place being measured by the nearenesse to the *Popes* person; the Cardinals place is, to ride betweene the Host and the *Pope*. And in their mysterious

[marginalia: ^aParis Crassus. De ceremo. Episcop. li.2. ca.42 / ^bCerem. Sacrae. cap. de consecrat. fo.36]

CHAPTER THREE   51

passages upon Ash-wednesday, ^cwhen the *Pope* layes the ashes upon a   ^cPar. Crass. l.2. c.43
Cardinall, he sayes not to him, as to all others, *Memento homo, quia
Cinis es*, but *quia pulvis es*: Intimating perchance, that they are never
so burnt to ashes, but that the fires of lust or ambition are still alive
5 in them. To which, I thinke there was some regard had, when it was
so wisely provided, ^dthat when a Cardinall did celebrate masse, there   ^dIdem. l.1. c.27
might enter no woman, nor man without a beard.

   35 Nor doth the Pope [act] improvidently, in advancing them with
these dignities and priviledges, nor in multiplying their number, so di-
10 rectly against the Councell of *Basil*, ^ewhich limits them to twentie foure   ^eConc. Basil. Sess.
(except, upon uniting the Greek Church, it might be thought fit to add   23. cap. de nume.
two more) and forbids expresly any Nephues of the Popes to be admitted.   et qualit. Card.
For no excesse in number, ^f(though they were returned to two hundred   ^fAlvares' Spec. Utr.
and thirty at once, as they are said to have beene in *Pontianus* his time;   Dig. ca.24. n.15
15 and though he should pile them up, and throw them downe, as fast as
those Popes which created sixe and twenty in one day, and executed sixe   Theod. a Niem. de
in another) could disadvantage that Sea of Rome, if they might be pro-   scism. l.1. cap.12
vided out of the states of other Princes (as in a great measure they are)   & 57
since the Church is their heire, and they are all but stewards for her. Of
20 which the Pope gave a dangerous instance, when he put in his claime for   Conestaggio. della
the kingdome of *Portugall*, because the last king was a Cardinall. These   Unione di Port. et
princes, no secular prince may dare to offend, nor subject adhere to him,   Castig. l.3. in prin-
if he doe, upon danger of that Bull: and yet they are made Judges of the   cip.
actions of all Princes, as *Baronius* sayes; and so oppressed with infinit   Resp. ad Card.
25 suits against Princes, that it may be fitly said of them, which *Job* sayes,   Colum. nu.31
Ecce gemunt gigantes sub aquis, & qui habitant cum eis: which wordes   Job. 26, 5
the Cardinals will not thanke *Baronius* for applying to them, if they
consider that *Lyra* interprets this *place* of Giants drowned in the flood,
and now damn'd and lamenting in hell. But now, a Cardinall cannot
30 chuse but bee a person of great holinesse and integritie, since there is a
Decretall in a generall Councell, and a Bull of *Leo* the tenth, which doe   In septimo. Tit. 4.
not only *Hortari*, and *Movere*, but *Statuere*, and *Ordinare*, that every   ca.4
Cardinal shall be of good life.

Margin 1c. Crass. l.2 *Ed.*: crass. ¹.2 L-1, HD, L³⁰, O², SP; crass 1.2 C-1,
C-3, C-4, O-2;.   crass . .2 C⁵-2, C¹⁶   **8.** Pope [act] *Ed.*: Pope. L-1, C-1
Margin 13f. Spec. Utr. *Ed.*: specutr. L-1, C-1   **Margin 20.** et Castig
Ed.: Et custig. L-1, C-1   **26.** *gemunt errata: genuit.* L-1, C-1

36   And as these censures and Excommunications of the Pope, involve all causes, so doe they all persons, except the Pope himselfe, and such companie, as the Canons have appointed him in this exemption, which are, *Locusts, Infidels, and the Divell*. For these, and the Pope, sayes *Navarrus*, cannot be Excommunicated: Yet as in their exorcismes of persons possessed, it is familiar to them, when the Divell is stubborne, to call him [a]*Heretique*, and [b]*Excommunicate*, so some Popes have kept him companie in both those titles. And as they cal their *Hermits locusts* (because as it is in *Salomon*, *They have no Kings, yet they goe forth by bands*) and accordingly the *Hermits* are subject to no *Superiour*, and in that sense *Locusts*, as their owne *Glosser* styles them: so may they prodigally extend the name and priviledge of Inexcommunicable *Locusts*, to many in the other Orders, since as the *Hermits* have no kings, so many of the others wish, that none else had any King, and doe their best endevour by aviling them, to bring them into contempt, and to annihilate their dignitie and them.

37   He that should compare the style of *Thomas Becket* to his King (*Olim servus, nunc in Christo Dominus*) with that of *David*, after he knew *Saule* to be reproved by God, and himselfe anointed, (*After whom is the King of Israel come out? After a dead Dogge, and after a Flea?*) would suspect that this difference of style, was not from one Author. Saint *Chrysostome* notes, that even to *Nabuchonozor*, who persecuted them for their faith, they which were condemned, said: *Notum sit tibi Rex*; and would not offer to the Tyrant, that contumelious name. And to prophane and irreligious Princes, God himselfe in his Bookes, affoords one of his owne names, Christ.

38   What high styles did many Christian and Orthodoxe Emperours assume to themselves? The Law styles the Emperour, [a]*Sanctissimum Imperatorem*: And his priviledges, [b]*Divinas Indulgentias*. So *Gratian* and his Colleagues in the Empire, in the first Law of the Code, call their [c]*Motus animi, Caeleste arbitrium*. And *Theodosius* and *Valentinian* making a Law with a *non obstante*, preclude all dispensations, which the Emperours themselves might graunt, in these words, [d]*Si Caeleste proferatur Oraculum, aut Divina pragmatica Sanctio*. So also *Theodosius*

Margin sidenotes:
Navar. Manu. ca.27. n.13
[a]Menghi. Flagel. Daemo. fo.42
[b]Fo.79 Prov. 30.27
16. q.1. qui vere. glos. verbo. vero
In Epist. eius ms.
I Sam. 24.15
Chrisost. ad Pop. Antioch. Ho.23
[a]Dig. li.31. Ti. 1. L.87. §. Imperator
[b]Dig. l.1. Tit. 4. Le.3
[c]Cod. l.1. Tit. 1. L.1
[d]Cod. l.1. Tit. 1. Le.10

Margin 17. ms. *Ed.*: m.s. C-1, L-1   **Margin 19.** I Sam. 24.15 *errata*: note missing . L-1, C-1   **21.** would *Ed.*: Would. L-1, C-1

CHAPTER THREE 53

and *Arcadius*, when they make a Law for dispatch of Suites, begin thus, ^e*Nemo deinceps tardiores affatus nostrae Perennitatis expectet.* And *Justinian* in the inscription of one of his owne Lawes, inserts amongst his owne Titles, ^f*Semper Adorandus Augustus.* And in a Lawe of *Monas-*
5 *teriall*, and *Matrimoniall* causes, (which are now onely of spirituall jurisdiction) he threatens, that if any *Bishop* infringe that Law, ^g*Quam nostra sanxit Aeternitas, Capitis supplicio ferienter.* In which style also *Theodosius* and *Arcadius* joine, ^h*Adoraturus aeternitatem nostram dirigatur.* And another proceedes somewhat further, ⁱ*Beneficio numinis*
10 *nostri.* And *Theodosius*, and *Valentinian* deliver it more plainely, ^k*Ut sciant omnes, quantum nostra Divinitas aversatur Nestorium*; and so in favour of the puritie and integritie of Christian Religion, in contemplation whereof, it seemes they were Religiously exercised, even at that time, when hee assum'd these high styles, they proceed in the same
15 Law, *We anathematize all Nestorius followers, according to those things which are already constituted A Divinitate nostra.* And *Constantius*, and *Irene* write themselves *Divos*; and their owne Acts, *Divalia*. And this, Pope *Adrian*, to whom they writ, reprehended not; but the Emperour *Charles* did, and another phrase of as much exorbitance, which
20 was, *Deus qui nobis conregnat.*

39   The highest that I have observed any of our Kings to have used, is in *Edward* the fourth, who in his creation of *Marques Dorset*, speakes thus of himselfe; *Cum nostra Majestas, ad Regium Culmen sublimata existat*; and after, *Tantum splendoris nostri nomen.* But a little before
25 his time *Baldus* gave as much to the king of France, as ever any had; for he said he was in his kingdome, *Quidam Corporalis Deus.* And in our present age, a Roman Author in a Dedication of his booke, thus salutes our Queene *Mary*: *because your Highnesse is the strongest bul-warke of the Faith, Tua Numina supplex posco*; which is also attributed to the
30 Emperour in a late Oration to him, and to other Princes. And in some Funerall Monuments of Queene *Maries* time, I have read this inscription; *Divis Philippo & Maria Regibus*, which word *Divus*, *Bellarmine* values

^eCod. l.1. Tit. 4. L.3

^fCod. l.1. Tit. 17. Le.3

^gCod. l.1. Tit. 3. L.56. §. His ita

^hCod. l.11. Tit. 9. L.2
ⁱCod. l.1. Tit. 2. Leg.8
^kCod. l.1. Tit. 1. L.3

Carol. Mag. l.1. c.1 & 3

Glover. de Nobilit. fol.75

Cassanaeus. Catal. Glor. par.5. consid. 30
Alvares. Specul. utri. Dign. Epist. ad Mariam
Oratio Caesarii a Branchedoro. in subscriptione

Bell. Recogn. fo.2

2. ^e*Nemo Ed.*: *Nemo.* C-1, L-1   **Margin 4f.** Tit. 17. *Ed.*: Tit. 15. C-1, L-1   **Margin 4f.** Le.3] L.e.3. F   **Margin 6g.** L.56 *Ed.*: L.55. C-1, L-1
7. *ferienter Ed.*: *ferieter.* C-1, L-1   **Margin 8h.** 11 *Ed.*: II. C-1, L-1
8. *nostram errata*: *vestram.* L-1, C-1   **Margin 29.** Branchedoro *Ed.*: Branhedoro. L-1, C-1

at so high a rate, that he repents to have bestowed it upon any of the Saints; and therefore in his late Recognition blots it out: which tendernesse in him, another *Jesuite* since disallowes, and justifies the use of the worde against *Bellarmines* squeamish abstinence; because the worde, sayes *Serarius*, may be used aswel as *temple* or as *fortune*, which are also Ethnique wordes. But by his leave he is too hasty with the Cardinall, who doth not refuse the word, because the Ethniques used it, but because they appointed it onely to their Gods; *Bellarmine* insimulates al them, which allow that worde to Saints, of making Saints Gods.

<small>Serarius. Litaneuticus. l.2. q.6</small>

40   And though in some of these Titles of great excesse, which these Emperours assum'd to themselves, we may easily discerne some impressions of Gentilisme, which they retain'd sometimes, after Christian Religion had received roote amongst them; as they did also their Gladiatorie spectacles, and other wastefull prodigalities of mens lives; and Bondage and servility, and some other such: yet neither in them, nor in other Princes, is the danger so great, if they should continue in them, as it is in the Bishoppes of Rome. For Princes, by assuming these Titles, do but draw men to a just reverence, and estimation of that power, which subjects naturally know to be in them: but the other, by these Titles seeke to build up, and establish a power, which was ever litigious and controverted, either by other Patriarchs, or by the Emperours: for *Bellarmine* having undertaken to prove the Pope, to be *Peters* successor in the Ecclesiastique Monarchy (which Monarchy it selfe is denied, and not onely the popes right to it) labors to prove this assumption, by the fifteene great names, which are attributed to the Popes.

<small>De Pont. Ro. li. 2. c.12</small>

<small>Ibid. ca.32</small>

41   And the farthest mischiefe, which by this excesse Princes could stray into, or subjects suffer, is a deviation into Tyranny, and an ordinary use of an extraordinary power and prerogative, and so making subjects slaves, and (as the *Lawyers* say) *Personas Res*. But by the magnifying of the Bishoppe of Rome with these Titles, our religion degenerates into superstition; which is a worse danger: and besides our temporall fortunes suffer as much danger and detriment, as in the other; for Princes by their lawes worke onely upon the faculties and powers of the soule, and by reward and punishment, they encline or avert our dispositions to a love

12. Emperours *Ed*.: Emperous.   C-1, L-1

or feare. But those Bishopps pretend a power upon the substance of our soules, which must be in their disposition, for her condition and state in the next life. And therefore to such as claime such a power, it is more dangerous to allow and countenance any such Titles, as participate in any signification of Divinity.

42 For since they make their Tribunall and Consistory the same with Christ, since they say [a]*It is Heresie and Treason to decline the Popes judgement, per ludibria frivolarum Appellationum, ad futurum Concilium*, as one Pope sayes; since they teach, [b]*that one may not appeale from the Pope to God himselfe*: [c]since they direct us *to bow at the name of Jesus, and at the name of the Pope, but not at the name of Christ*; for that being the name of Annointed, it might induce a reverence to Princes (who partake that name) if they should bow to that name; since they esteeme their lawes Divine, not as Princes doe, by reason of the power of God inherent in all just lawes, and by reason of the common matter and subject of all such lawes (which is publique utility and generall good) but because their lawes are in particular dictated by the holy Ghost, and therefore it is *Blasphemy and sinne against the holy Ghost to violate any of them*; since themselves make this difference betweene the name of God, as it is given to Princes, and as it is given to them: that *Princes are called Dii laicorum, and they Dii principum*; since to prove this, they assume a power above God, to put a new sense into his word, which they doe, when they prove this assertion out of these words in Exodus; *Diis non detrahes, & principi populi non maledices*, for by the first, they say, the popes are understood, and by the second princes; when as Saint *Paul* himselfe applies the latter part to the high priest, and their expositor *Lyra*, and the *Jesuite Sà*, interpret the first part of this Scripture of *Judges*: Since, I say, they entend worse ends then Princes doe, in accepting or assuming like Titles; and since they worke upon a more dangerous and corruptible subject, which is the Conscience and Religion; since they require a stronger assurance in us by faith; since they threaten greater penalties to any which doubt thereof, which is damnation; the popes cannot be so excuseable in this excesse as princes may be. And yet princes never went so farre as the

[a]Epist. Pii 2. ad Norinbergenses

[b]Maynardus. de Privileg. Eccles. art.27. n.15

[c]Par. Crassus. de Ceremo. Episcop. & Card. l.1. c.5 & cap.22

25. q.1. violatores

Maynard. de Privileg. Eccles. ar.14. nu.1

Exo. 22.28

Act. 23.5

Lyra. in hunc locum, & Eman. Sà

18. *Blasphemy Ed.*: *Blaspemy.* C-1, L-1 **Margin 21.** Maynard. *Ed.*: Maynard'. L-1, C-1 **Margin 24.** 22.28 *Ed.*: 22. L-1, C-1 **32.** to *errata*: in. L-1, C-1

popes have done, as we shall see, when we come to consider the title and power of spirituall prince.

All this I say, not to encourage princes to returne to those styles, which Christian humilitie hath made them dis-accustome, and leave off, and which could not be reassum'd without much scandall, but to shew the iniquitie and perversenesse of those men, who thinke great Titles belong to Kings, not as Kings, but as Papisticall Kings.

43   For so at a Consultation of *Jesuites* in the *Tower*, in the late Queenes time, I saw it resolved, that in a Petition to bee exhibited to her, shee might not be styled *Sacred*. Though one of their owne Order have observed that attribute to bee so cheape, that it was usuall to say, *Sancti Patres conscripti*, and *Sacratissimi Quirites*, and *Sanctissimi Milites*. And our English *Jesuites* use to aggravate her defection much, by that circumstance, that shee had beene Consecrated, and pontifically Anointed, and invested at her Coronation, and therefore was Sacred.

44   How great a detestation they had of her Honour, and of all Princes which professe the same Religion that shee did, appeares in no one such thing more, then in *Quirogaes expurgatorie Index*, where admitting all the reprochfull calumnies of *Eunapius* against Martyrs, whose reliques he cals *Salita Capita*, with other opprobrious contumelies, they have onely expunged an Epistle of *Junius* to her, in which there was no word concerning Religion, but onely a gratulation of her Peace, and of her Learning; which also they have done in *Serranus* his Edition of *Plato*. And as God hath continued his favours showen to her, upon her successour, so have they their malice: For in the second Tome of that worke, they have taken away an Epistle Dedicatorie to his Majestie, that now is.

45   And as in many of their Rules, for that Dissection and Anatomising of Authours, they have provided that all Religion, and all prophane knowledge shall depend upon their will: So have they made a good offer, that all cariage of State businesse shall bee open to them, by expunging all such sentences, as instruct or remember Princes, in that learning, which those Rules call *Rationem status*, and which (because *Italians* have beene most conversant therein) is vulgarly called *Ragion di stato*.

Margin notes:
Serarius. Litaneutic. l.2. q.4. n.4
Index Expurg. Hispan. fo.92
Ibid. fol.150
Ibid. fol.150
Instruct. circa lib. corrig. 2

2. prince *errata*: princes. L-1, C-1   **22.** word *Ed.*: words. L-1, C-1   **Margin 23.** fol.150 *Ed.*: fol.151. L-1, C-1   **Margin 31.** 2 *Ed.*: 10. C-1, L-1   **33.** call *errata*: cals. L-1, C-1

For this *Ragion di stato*, is, as the Lawyers call it, *Ius Dominationis*; And as others call it, *Arcana Imperii*. And it pretends no farther, but to teach, by what meanes a Prince, or any Soveraigne state, may best exercise that power which is in them, and give least offence to the Subjects, and yet preserve the right and dignitie of that power.

46 For it is impossible, that any Prince should proceede in all causes & occurrences, by a downright Execution of his Lawes: And he shall certainly be frustrated of many just and lawfull ends, if he discover the way by which he goes to them. And therefore these disguisings, and averting of others from discerning them, are so necessarie, that though, *In Genere rei*, they seeme to be within the compasse of deceite and falshood, yet the end, which is, maintenance of lawfull Authoritie, for the publike good, justifies them so well, that the Lawyers abhorre not to give them the same definition (with that Addition of publike good) which they doe to deceit it selfe. For they define *Ragion di stato* to be, *Cum aliud agitur, aliud simulatur, bono publico.*

47 And the Romane Authors doe not onely teach, that deceit is not *Intrinsicè malum*, but upon that ground and foundation, they build Equivocation, which is like a Tower of *Babel*, both because thereby they get above all earthly Magistracie, and because therein no men can understand one another. Nor can there be a better example given of the use of this *Ragion di stato*, then their forbidding it: Because nothing conduces more to the advancing of their strength, then that Princes should not know, or not use their owne, or proceede by any wayes remov'd from their discernings. Indeed those bookes of Expurgation, are nothing else but *Ragion di stato*: That is, a disguised and dissembled way, of preferring their double Monarchie. And they that forbid Princes the lawfull use of these *Arcana Imperii*, practise for their owne ends, even *Flagitia Imperii*, which are the same things, when they exceede their true endes (which are just authority, and the publique good) or their lawfull wayes to those ends, which should ever be within the compasse of vertue, and religion.

_{Soto. de teg. secret. memb.3. q.3. Ad tertium}

48 Of which sort are all those enormous dispensations from Rome, which no interpretation nor pretence can justifie: as (to omit some sacrilegious and too immodest licenses) that of *Gregory* the third is one, who

32. religion. *Ed.*: religion:. L-1, C-1

writ to *Boniface* his Legate in *Germany*, *that they, whose wives being overtaken with any infirmity, would not reddere Debitum, might marry other wives*: which *Binius* hath wisely left out.

49   But they are in these expurgations injurious also to the memorie of dead princes: ᵃfor they will not admit our k. *Edward* the sixt, to be said to be *Admirandae indolis*, nor the Duke of ᵇ*Wittenberg praeclarus*. They will not allow ᶜ*Ulrichus Huttenus* to be called *A learned Knight*: no, ᵈneither him, nor *Oebanus Hessus* to be so much as *good poets*. But with the same circumspection, that the ᵉ*Belgique Index* could add to *Borrhaeus* writing uppon *Aristotles* politiques, in this sentence, *Religionis cura semper pertinuit ad principes*, this clause, *& Sacerdotes*; the ᶠ*Spanish Index* dooth mutilate *Velcurio* upon *Livy*, and from this sentence (*the fift age was decrepite under the Popes and Emperours*) takes out the Popes, and leaves the Emperours obnoxious to the whole imputation. And as with extreame curious malignity, they have watched that none of our side be celebrated, so have they spied some invisible dangers, which the Popes honor might incurre: and therefore as the ᵍ*Spanish Copie*, hath before *Luthers* name expunged the letter *D*, least it might intimate *Doctor*, or *Divus*; so the ʰ*Dutch Copie*, having found nothing to quarrel at in *Schonerus* the Mathematician, expunges in many places a great *D.* at beginning of Divisions, because in it (as ordinarily those great initiall letters, have some figure) there is imprinted the popes head, and by it the divell, presenting him a Bull.

50   But this inhumanity of theirs hath not deterr'd *Thuanus* from his ingenuity, in giving to all those learned men, whom he hath occasion to mention, the attributes and epithetes due to their vertues, though they be of a divers persuasion in Religion from himselfe: But those other men, who in a proude humility will say *brother Thiefe*, and *brother Wolfe*, and *brother Asse*, (as Saint *Francis* (perchance not un-prophetically) is said to have done) will admit no fraternity nor fellowshippe with Princes.

51   And though the *Jesuites* by the advantage of their fourth Supernumerary vow, of sustaining the Papacy, by obeying the Popes will, seeme to have gone further herein then the rest, yet the last Order

Margin:
Carranza. Sum. Concil. fo.353
ᵃHispanic. Ind. fo.148
ᵇIbidem
ᶜIdem. fo.93
ᵈId. fo.148
ᵉInd. Belg. fo.146
ᶠInd. Hisp. fo.158
ᵍFol.93
ʰInd. Belg. fo.154
Sedulius. Apol. pro lib. Conform. l.1. c.9 & l.3. c.29
Congregatio Oratorii

5.   ᵃfor *Ed.*: for. C-1, L-1   11. *Sacerdotes Ed.*: *Sacerdotem*. C-1, L-1   **Margin 19h.** Ind. Belg. fo.154 *Ed.*: fo.154. L-1, C-1   19. Dutch *Ed.*: Duch. C-1, L-1   **Margin 28.** c.9 . . . . c.29 *Ed.*: c.12 . . . . c.28. C-1, L-1   32. will, *Ed.*: will;. L-1, C-1

CHAPTER THREE

erected by *Philip Nerius*, which was saide to have been purposed to enervate the Jesuites; and by a continual preaching the lives of Saints, and the Ecclesiastique story, to counterpoise with devotion, the Jesuites secular and active learning, though they set out late, have aemulously
5 endevoured to overtake the *Jesuites* themselves in this doctrine of aviling Princes: For *Bozius* hath made all Princes Tributary or Feudatary to the Pope, if not of worse condition. And *Gallonius* seemes to have undertaken the History of the persecutions in the Primitive Church, onely to have occasion by comparison thereof, to defame and reproach the lawes,
10 and Governement of our late Queene. Bozius
Gallonius. de Cruciat. Martyrum

52 But *Baronius* more then any other exceeds in this point, for obeying his owne scope and first purpose to advance the Sea of Rome, he spares not the most obedient childe of that mother, the Catholique King of *Spaine*: for, speaking of the Title which that King hath to the
15 Kingdome of *Sicily*, he imputes thus much to *Charles* the fift, that *being possessed with employments of the fielde, hee gave way to an Edict, by which, Grande piaculum perpetratur against the Apostolique authority and al Ecclesiastique lawes were utterly dissipated*: And that *hee joined together temporall and spirituall jurisdiction, and pretended a power to*
20 *excommunicate and to absolve even Cardinals, and the Popes Nuncioes; and so*, says he, *hath raised another Head of the Church, pro monstro, & ostento*. He addes with extreame intemperance, that this claime to that Kingdome *was buried a while, but revived againe by Tyrannicall force, by violent grassation, and by the robbery of Princes, who commaunded that*
25 *to be obeyed as reasonable, which they had extorted by Tyranny*. And least hee should not seeme to extend his bitternes to the present time, he sayes, *those Princes which hold Sicily by the same reasons, doe imitate those tyrants*. And so he imputes upon all the later kings of Spaine, as much usurpation of Ecclesiastique Jurisdiction, and as monstrous a
30 Title of head of the Church, as ever their malice degorged upon our king *Henrie* the eight. Baron. Annal. To.11. Ann. 1097. n.18

Nu.28
Nu.29

Nu.87

Nu.88

53 And though in some passages of that history, he hath left some wayes to escape, by laying those imputations rather upon the kings of-

---

Margin 17. Nu.28 *Ed.: note misplaced.* L-1, C-1   **18.** *Ecclesiastique Ed.: Ecclestiastqiue.* C-1, L-1   **Margin 18.** Nu.29 *Ed.: note missing.* L-1, C-1   **29.** usurpation *Ed.: usupation.* C-1, L-1

_{Card. Colum. fo.158. Paris}

ficers then upon the king, yet that Cardinall who hath censured that part of his worke, espies his workemanshippe and arte of deceiving, and therefore tels him, *that he hath invayd against Monarchy it selfe, and all defenders thereof*; and that *as many, and as great things might be spoken against him*: Nor doth *Baronius* repent that, which hee hath spoken of those kings, but in his answere to this Cardinall; he says, *that if the King were impeccable, if he were an Angell, if he were God himselfe, yet he is subject to just reproofe.* And in his Epistle to *Phil.* 3. in excuse of himselfe, though hee seeme to spare the present king, yet it is (as he professes) because he hopes that he will relinquish that Jurisdiction in *Sicily*; els he is subject to all those reproofs & reproches, which *Baro.* hath laid upon his father and Grandfather.

_{Nu.19}

54 And though this were a great excesse in *Baronius*, to lay such aspersions upon those Princes, yet his malice appeares to bee more generall; for the reason why he makes this pretence so intollerable, is, *because thereby* (sayes he) *that King becomes a Monarch; and there can be no other Monarch in the world, then the Pope; and therefore that name must be cutte off, least by this example it should propagate, and a whole wood of monarchs should grow up, to the perpetuall infamy of the Primacy of the Church.* And so this care of his, that no Monarches be admitted, implies his confession, that they which are Monarches have right in their Dominions, to all that which those kings claime in Sicily, which is as much as our kings exercise in England, (if *Baronius* do not exceede in his imputation.)

_{Nu.29}

_{Nu.31}

55 But because there is nothing more tender then honour, which as God will give to none from himselfe, being a jealous God, so neither ought his *Vicegerents* to doe; it shall not be an unseasonable and impertinent, at most, an excuseable and pardonable diversion, to observe onely by such impressions, as remaine in the letters betweene the Emperours and Popes, at what times, and upon what occasions the Clergie of that Sea insulted upon secular Magistracy; and by what either dilatory circumventions, or violent irruptions, they are arrived to this enormous contempt of Principality, as of a subordinate instrument of theirs.

Margin 1. Card. *Ed.*: *note misplaced.* L-1, C-1 **Margin 1.** Paris *Ed.*: paris. C-1, L-1 **Margin 5.** Nu.19 *Ed.*: *note misplaced.* C-1, L-1 **10.** relinquish *Ed.*: relinguish. C-1, L-1 **Margin 15.** 29 *Ed.*: 28. L-1, C-1

56 Before they had much to doe with Emperours, (for they were a long time religiously, and victoriously exercised with suffering) we may observe in *Cyprians* time, that he durst speake brotherly and fellowly to that Sea, and intimate the resolutions of his Church to that, without asking approbation and strength from thence: for to Pope *Stephen*, he writes, *Stephano fratri*; and then *Nos qui gubernandae Ecclesiae libram tenemus*: and after, *Hoc facere te oportet*: with many like impressions of equality: But in *Firmilianus* his Epistle to *Cyprian*, written in opposition to *Stephanus* his Epistle; who was growne into some bitternesse against *Cyprian*, there appeares more liberty: for thus he sayes; *Though by the inhumanity of Stephen, we have the better triall of Cyprians wisedome, we are no more beholden to him for that, then we are to Judas for our salvation.* He addes after, *That that Church doth in vaine pretend the authority of the Apostles; since in many sacraments Divinae rei, it differs from the beginning, and from the Church of Hierusalem, and defames Peter and Paul as Authors thereof*. And therefore (sayes he) *I doe justly disdaine the open and manifest foolishnesse of Stephen, by whom the truth of the Christian Rocke is abolished*. So roundly and constantly were their first attempts and intrusions resisted, and this not onely by this Advocate of *Cyprian*, but even by himselfe also, in as sharpe words as these, in his Epistle to *Pompeius*.

57 And for their behaviour to the Emperors, as long as *Zeale* and *Povertie* restrain'd them, it cannot be doubted, but that they were respective enough. The preambulatorie Letters before the Councell of *Chalcedon*, testifie it well: Where the Letters of the Emperours, yea, of their Wives, are accepted by the name of *Divales*, and *Sacrae literae*, and *Divinae syllabae*. And about the same time, *Leo* the Pope writing to *Leo* the Emperour, he sayes; *Hanc Paginam necessariae supplicationis adieci*; And in the next Epistle but one, *Literas Clementiae tuae veneranter accepi, quibus cuperem obedire*. So also *Felix* the third, to *Zeno* the Emperour, cals himselfe *Famulum vestrum*, and such demissions as these; *Liceat, venerabilis Imperator, exponere*; And, *Per mei Ordinis parvitatem audias*, are frequent in him. And in *Justinians* time, which was presently after, that Church sensible of the use and neede,

Circa. 249

Cypr. Epist. 1. ad Steph.

Binius. To.1. fo.191

Anno 451
Binius. To.2. in Princip.
Epist. 73 Anno 457

Epist. 2. Circa 482

Anno 530

Margin 3. 249 *Ed.*: 240. C-1, L-1 **Margin 27.** Epist. 73] Epist 73. L-1, MCG, C-2, L-2, C⁵-2, O-2, YK-1 **Margin 30.** 482 *Ed.*: 527. C-1, L-1

which it had of his favour, so hee would be content to extend to their benefit, prescription, which before was limited in thirtie yeares, to a hundred, never grudged at the phrase and language of his Law, by which he affoorded the Church that priviledge, though it were very high; *Being willing to illustrate Rome*, Lege speciali nostri Numinis, *That that Church may eternally by this, remember the providence of our Governement, we graunt, &c.*

Autent. Coll.2. prefatio Iustiniani

58   And *Gregorie* the first was, out of his wisedome at least, if not Devotion, as temperate as the rest, when he writ to the Emperour *Maurice*, to sweeten and modifie that Law, which forbad some persons to enter into Monasteries; For there he cals himselfe *Famulum*, and *Servum*: And addes this, *Whiles I speake thus with my Lords, What am I, but dust and wormes?* And though *Binius* is loth to pardon him this duetifulnesse, and respect to his Princes, and therefore sayes, *That he protested in the begining of that Letter, that hee spoke not as a Bishop*, but *Iure privato*, And so out of *Baronius*, he sayes, *That he playde another part, as upon a stage*: Yet, if he wore this maske and disguise cleane through the Epistle, then he spoke personately, and dissemblingly, as well with Christ, as with the Emperour, when he sayes: *I, the meanest of Christs servants and yours.* Nor do I thinke that *Binius* or *Baronius* would say, that he spoke personately of the Execution of the Emperours Law, but that hee had truely done as he said: *I have done all which I ought to doe; for I have both performed my obedience to the Emperor, and I have uttered that which I thought fit concerning God.* And he was wisely carefull that his Letter to the Emperour, concerning his opinion of the iniquitie of that Law, should not come to the Emperour inopportunely, nor as from a person of equall ranke to him; and therefore he forbids his own *Responsall* (for the dignitie of a *Nuncio*, was not yet in use) to deliver it, but sends it to the Emperours Physitian, because saith he, *Vestra Gloria*, may secretly, at some convenient time, offer him this suggestion; And that this Physitian might be confident in this employment, he assures him of his affection and Allegeance to his Prince, by this Confession, *God hath appointed the Emperour to rule, not onely Souldiours* (which were the persons forbid in that Law) *but also Priests*

Margins:
L.2. Epist. 62
To.2. fo.770.B
An. 593. n.18
L.2. Epist. 65. Theodo. Medico.

Margin 16. n.18 *Ed.*: n.17. L-1, C-1   **26.** Emperour *errata*: Emperours. C-1, L-1   **30.** *convenient Ed.*: conveniet. C-1, L-1

CHAPTER THREE

(whose privileges seem'd to be impair'd thereby.)

59 With like respect doth one of his successors *Vitalian*, write to *Vaanus*, who was *Cubicularius, et Chartularius Imperialis*, to mediate & provide, that a Bishoppe unjustly deposed, might be restored. And to him the Pope affoords this style, *Celsitudo vestra*, and addresses the depos'd Bishop, *Ad vestra ambulaturum vestigia*, and promises that they both shall all the dayes of their lives, pray to God for the prosperity, and long-living *Suae excellentissimae Charitatis* Epist. 2. Anno. 655

60 And in all this course of time, the Popes, some out of a just contemplation of their duety, some out of the neede, which they had of the Emperours, from whom they received daily some additions to their immunities and exemptions, were agreeable and appliable enough to them. And when *Italy* suffered a dereliction, by the absence of the Emperours in the East, and thereby was prostituted and exposed to barbarous Invaders, the Bishoppes of this Citie, which was the fairest marke to invite the *Lumbards* and the rest, solicited those Easterne Emperours to their succour, with all sweetnesse and humility; but at last, desperate of such reliefe, casting their eyes upon the mightiest kingdome of the West, they invited the French to their succour.

61 And at this time came from them those lamentable supplications, which *Stephen* the third sent to *Pipin* and *Carloman*: In the first whereof, he urges them with their promise of certaine lands, by them vowed to the Church: And having called them, *Dominos excellentissimos*, and *spiritualem Compatrem*, and prepared them with wordes of much sweetenesse, *Mellifluam bonitatem, Mellifluos obtutus*, and such, hee comes to the point: *That which you have offered to Peter by promise, you ought to deliver him in possession, least when the Porter of heaven, the Prince of the Apostles, at the daye of judgement shall shew your hand-writing, you be put to make a more strict account with him.* So therefore he felt and lamented their slackenes in endowing the Church; yet at that time he would not undertake to be the Judge, nor make the *Camera Apostolica* the Court; but he referres it to Saint *Peter*, and to the last day, and onely remembers them, That *Dominus per meam humilitatem, mediante B. Petro, vos unxit in reges.* Epist. 2

62 The next letter written in the person of the Pope, and all the

---

27. *possession errata: profession.*   C-1, L-1

Romane people, and Romane armie, *et omnium in afflictione positorum*, is an earnest and violent conjuration; *per Deum vivum vos coniuro, Save us, most Christian Princes before we perish; the soules of all the Romans hang upon you, and so forth.* And when all this did not effectually stirre them to come, as the letter solicited, *Cum nimia festinatione*; then came a third letter in the name and person of Saint *Peter* himselfe, in this style: *I Peter the Apostle, and by me all the Catholique Romane Church, Head of all the Churches of God, vobis viris excellentissimis. I Peter, exhort you, my adopted Sonnes, to defend that house, where I rest in my flesh: and with me Marie, with great Obligations, Advises, and Protests, and so forth. And whatsoever you shall aske of me, I will give you. If you doe not performe this, know ye, that by the authoritie of the Apostleshippe given me by Christ, you are alienated from the Kingdome of God, and from life everlasting.*

<small>Epist. 4</small>

63 And when *Stephen* the fourth came to that Sea, and that the sonnes of these Princes beganne to incline to ally themselves by marriage with the *Lombards*; the Pope seeing then his whole temporal fortune at the stake, neglects no way of withdrawing them, from that inclination: hee sayes therefore, Saint *Peter, by our unhappines, beseecheth your Excellence*: and then, *vouchsafe to bend your eares, inspired by God, to our Petition, and to him whom we have sent, ad Regale vestrum Culmen.* And then, in an inconstant distemper, he threatens, and he promises in St. *Peters* name, as bitterly, and as liberally, as his predecessor had bid S. *Peter* himselfe to doe, in the former Epistle.

<small>Epist. Steph. 4. ad Carol. et Carlom. An. 768</small>

64 And when these Princes after much entreaty, had delivered Italy from the infestation of the Lombards, and devided the profite and spoile with the Church, and that that Sea had recovered some breath and heart, then their Bishopps began to reprehend with some bitternesse, the Easterne Emperours: And then came that notorious letter of *Nicholas* to *Michael* the Emperour; In which though he style him, *Superatorem Gentium, piissimum filium, Dulcissimum, Tranquillissimum* (for as yet hee doubted that he might be necessary to him) yet he cals him also *Golias*, and himselfe *Hymnidicum Davidem*. And part of the quarrell was, because the Emperour had written *Insolentia quaedam*, certaine unusuall phrases: which were, *Iussimus, ut quosdam ad nos mitteretis*: for,

<small>Nichol. Epist. circa 874</small>

Margin 19. 768 *Ed.*: 831. C-1, L-1

sayes *Nicholas, Honorius* said to *Boniface, Petimus*; and other Emperours, *Invitamus,* and *Rogamus,* and *Constantine* and *Irene, Rogamus, magis quidem Dominus Deus rogat*: which phrase, though *Charles* the great, at that time, when it was written, reprehended, and allowed a whole Chapter in his booke for the reproofe thereof, yet not onely that Pope dissembled it, but this draws it into example and precedent. Li.1. c.4

65 And in this letter the Pope gives the Emperour some light, that hee is not long to enjoy the style of Romane Emperour; for he having despised the Romane tongue as Barbarous, (as every Prince loves to be saluted in his owne, or in an equall language) the Pope replies: *That if hee call the Romane tongue barbarous, because hee understands it not, it is a ridiculous thing, to call himselfe Romane Emperour.*

66 And thus having at once received and recompensed a benefite, by concurring in the advancement of the French to the Empire, they kept good hold upon that Kingdome, by continuall correspondencies, and by interceding with those Kings, for pardons and favours, when any delinquents fled over to them, and by advising them in all emergent causes, and by doing them many services in *Italy*, and so establishing the Empire in that family, upon good conditions to them both. For so *John* Epist. 216
the eight writes to *Charles*, as well to refresh his benefite in his memorie, as the reasons that moved him to conferre it. *Well knowes your Kingly Highnesse, that I was desirous a long time, for the profit and exaltation of the Apostolicke Sea, to bring you* Ad Culmen Imperii. *And as we with all our endevour, have desired to give perfection to your Honour and glorie, you also must performe those things, which are profitable to the utilitie and exaltation of that Seate.* And there he addes, That *for Conference about that, he came to meete him at Ravenna, leaving his owne Church in the cruell hands of enemies.* And in the next Epistle, he sends to the Epist. 217
same purpose his Nephew *Farulfus, Deliciosum consiliarium nostrum;* Because, sayes he in another place, *We desire greedily to accomplish this.* Epist. 230
And yet at this very time, for his better indemnitie, hee practis'd with the *Esterne* Emperour, and kept faire quarter with him also, as appeares by his Letter to him. Epist. 251

67 Having thus establish'd a stronger reputation, and laide earnest Obligations upon *France*, and by example and authoritie thereof, in

Margin 3. Li. O-2, YK-2: Li. C-1, L-1   **4.** allowed *Ed.*: al-allowed. C-1, L-1

other places also, they beganne to feele their strength, and to draw their swords as farre as they would goe, which was to excommunication, even in France it selfe.

68 But because in the excommunications issuing in these times, and in the times betweene this, and *Gregory* the seventh, and perchance in some before this time, there is found often mention of punishment after excommunication, which hath occasioned some to erre in an opinion, that besides spirituall censures, temporall penalties were also inflicted upon private persons, and consequently eradication upon Princes, we will arrest, and stay a little upon the style and phrase of some of those excommunications, by which it wil appeare, that they intended nothing but spirituall punishment.

<small>Epist. 30</small>

69 The first which I have observed, is a letter of *Innocent* the first, to *Arcadius* the Emperour, whom he thought guilty of the ejecting & of the death of *Chrysostome*: His words are; *Ego minimus & peccator, segrego te a perceptione mysteriorum Christi*. This then went no farther then to deprive him of spirituall foode, and the Pope (if that Epistle be genuine) was very hasty in it; for the Emperour discharged himselfe presently, by pleading ignorance of the fact; which that Bishoppe ought to have tried, before hee had proceeded to excommunication. *Chrysostome* himselfe, whose quarrell it was, had taught sufficiently the limits of that jurisdiction; for he said, *When the Priest had reprehended Ozias, De spreto Sacerdotio, he could doe no more; for it is his part onely to reproove, and to persuade, not to stirre warre*: and he addes, *that God himselfe* (to whom onely it belongs to punish so) *inflicted a leprosie upon the King, in which* (sayes he) *we see Humanitatem Divinae ultionis, who sent not lightning, nor shaked the earth, nor moved the Heavens*: So farre was *Chrysostome* from counsayling any such punishment, as should be accompanied with tumult.

<small>De verb. Esaiae. Hom. 4. To.1. fo.207</small>

70 And to a just estimation, and true understanding of their liberties, in Ecclesiastique causes, were the Fathers in the Councell at *Ephesus* arrived, when in that *Synodicall* Letter to the Emperour, which they call, *Libellum supplicem*, they make this protestation, *The scope of our profession provides, that we be obedient to all Princes and Potentates, as long as that obedience brings no detriment to our Soules health*;

<small>Binius. To.1. fol.803</small>

6. punishment] pnnishment. L-2, C⁵-1, SP, O-1, C³, C¹⁰, YK-1, YK-2, YK-3

but if it come to that, we must dare to use our libertie, Adversus Regium fastigium. And how farre, may this courage and libertie carie us, if the Prince command any thing in detriment of our soule? As farre, as those Fathers durst adventure upon that ground, which they expressed thus
5 to the Emperour, *If you approve the banishment of Cyrill and Memnon, which were banished by persons Excommunicate, then know you, that we are ready, with that alacritie which becomes Christians, to undergoe any danger with them, that is,* to suffer as they doe.

71   But about this time of *John* 8. it was very frequent, that Ex-
10 communications had a farther comminatorie clause. For so, against a *Bastard of Lotharius*, who had broke an Oath made to a French King,   Epist. 123
he says, *We deprive him of all Christian Comunion, and if he persever, let him know, that Anathematis vinculis innodabitur.* So to an
Earle and his *Lady*, which had seduced a Nunne from her profession, he   Epist. 165. Luid-
15 says, *We seperate them from the body and blood, and all fellowship with*   tefrido
Christians, and if they neglect to restore her, Anathemate innodamus.
So in the next Epistle he threatens a *Bishop*, that refus'd to come to   Epist. 166. Wi-
him, *Know that you are to be Excommunicate, and if you persever, A*   berto
Communione alienandus. And against another *Bishop*, and his whole
20 charge he pronounces *Privation from the Communion, seperation from the Church, and except they convert, Maioris damnationis sententiam,* and with such as these, his time abounds.

72   And his predecessour *Adrian* the second, had gone thus farre to-   Epist. 18
wards the King of *France*, when hee attempted to invade his Brothers
25 Dominion, *We admonish you, by our Apostolique Authoritie, and by all spirituall meanes, which we may use, we persuade you, and in a Fatherly affection command you to forbeare; else, we will performe that which belongs to our Ministerie.* But in another letter to his Nobles, he threatens   Epist. 24
them, That if they aide the Father to warre against the Sonne, who was
30 then in his displeasure, *They shall not onely be enwrapp'd in the bands of Excommunication, but cast into hell, Vinculis Anathematis.* And this
John the eight, at the same time when he alowes him all due attributes,   Epist. 28
& desires him *to incline his sacred eares to him,* threatens *Charles* him-   Epist. 42
self, that if he restore not certain things, taken from a Nunnerie, by a

Margin 14. Luidtefrido *Ed.*: L idtefrido.   C-1, L-1   **Margin 17.** Wiberto *Ed.*: Ubiberto.   C-1, L-1 certaine day, *He should bee Excommunicate till restitution, and if, being thus lightly touched, he repented not, Durioribus verberibus erudiendus erat.*

73   So that whether this farther punishment were no other, then that which is now called *excommunicatio Maior*, or that which is called in the Canons *Anathema maranatha*, the denouncing of which, and the absolving from it, was acted with many formalities, and solemnities, and had many ingredients, of burning tapers, and divers others, to which none could be subjected without the knowledge of the Arch-Bishoppe, it appears that it nowhere extends to temporall punishment, or forfaitures and confiscations.

74   Of which there appears to me no evidence, no discernable impression, no just suspition, till *Gregory* the sevenths time: And then, as it may well be said of *Phalaris* his letters, that they were al *writs for execution*, and of *Brutus* his letters, that they were all *Privy Seales* for money: so may wee say of *Gregories* judging, by the frequency thereof, that they were all cholerique excommunications; and that with *Postscripts* worse then the body of the letter; which were Confiscations, never found in his predecessors, which should have beene his precedents.

75   And for this large and new addition of *Eradication*, hee first threatned it to the French King, and then practised it effectually upon the *Emperour*. To the Bishoppes of France he writes, *That their King Philip is not to be called King, but a Tyrant, which by persuasion of the Divel is become the cause and the head of all mischiefe :* Therefore (sayes he) *all you must endeavour to bow him*, (And thus farre his Pastorall care might binde him) *And to shew him, that he cannot escape the sword of Apostolique animadversion* (and thus farre his jealousie of his spiritual Primacy might excuse him.) But when he adds, *Depart from communion with him, and obedience to him, forbid Divine Service throughout all France, and if he repent not, we will attempt to take the Kingdome from his possession*: they are wordes of *Babel*, which no man at that time understood: yet he writes in the same tenour to the *Earle of Poictou*,

Margin notes: 11. q.3. cum aliquis; 11. q.3. Nemo; Anno 1073; Li.2. Ep. 5; L.2. Ep. 18

Margin 5. 11 *Ed.*: 21.   C-1, L-1   **10.** nowhere *errata*: now here.   L-1, C-1
Margin 13. 1073 *Ed.*: 1063.   C-1, L-1   **14.** writs *errata*: writ.   L-1, C-1
21. French *Ed.*: Fench.   L-1, C-1   **25.** him, (*Ed.*: him. (.   L-1, C-1
32. *Poictou*   F, Y: *Poicton*,.   L-1, C-1, MCG, L-2, SP, O-1, O-2, O^2, O^{14}

That if the king persevere, both he and all which give any obedience to him, shall be sequestred from the communion of the Church, by a Councell to be held at Rome. So assuredly, and confidently could hee pronounce before hand of a future determination in a Councell there.

76 And of his owne severity, used towards the Emperour, whom upon severe penances hee had resumed into the Church, he blushes not to make an Historical Narration, to the Bishops and Princes of Germany, thus: *He stood three dayes before the gate, despoiled of all Kingly ornaments, miserable and barefoote; till all men wondred at the unaccustomed hardnesse of our minds. And some cried out, that this was not the gravity of Apostolique severity, but almost the cruelty of Tyrannique savagenesse.* Li.4. Ep. 12

77 And when *Rodulphus* whom he had set up against the Emperour, was dead, seeing now, as himselfe confesses, *almost all the Italians* enclin'd to admit the Emperour *Henry*, even they whom he trusted most (for so he sayes, *Pene omnes nostri fideles*) he protesteth that *Rodolphus* was made without his consent, *Ab ultramontanis*, and that he meant to depose him, and to call those Bishops to account which adhered to him: And then he writes to certaine Prelates, *to slacken the Election of a new Emperour*, and gives instruction what kind of person hee would have to bee elected; *One which should be obedient, humbly devout, and profitable to the Church: and that would take an oath to doe any thing which the Pope would commaund him, in these wordes: Per veram obedientiam;* and that hee would be made a Knight of Saint Peter, and of the Pope. Lib.9. Ep. 3
Li.9. Ep. 28
L.9. Ep. 3

78 But although many watchfull and curious men of our Church, and many ingenuous of the Romane, have observed many enormous usurpations, and odious intemperances in this tempestuous Pope *Gregory* the seventh, and amongst them, almost anatomiz'd every limme of his Story; yet it may bee lawfull for mee, to draw into observation, and short discourse, two points thereof, perchance not altogether for their unworthines, pretermitted by others: Of which the first shall be the forme of the excommunication against *Henry*, because by that it will appeare what authority hee claimed over Princes: And the other shall be his letter to a *Bishop*, who desired to draw from him, some reasons by which he might defend that which the Pope had done; because by

---

17. meant *errata*: went. L-1, C-1   **26.** ingenuous *errata*: ingenious. L-1, C-1

that it will appeare, upon what foundations he grounded this pretence and authority.

<small>Binius. To.3. fo.1282.A</small>

79 The excommunication is thus delivered; *Contradico ei, I denie him the government of al the kingdom of Germany, & of Italy: and I absolve all Christians, from the band of the oth, which they have made to him, or shall make: and I forbid any man to serve him as his king: for it is fit, that he which endevors to diminish the honor of the Church should loose his owne honour. And because he hath contemned to obey as a Christian, participating with excommunicated persons, and despising my admonitions, and seperating himselfe from the Church, I tie him, in vinculo Anathematis.*

By which we see, that he beginnes with *Confiscation*: And because it had never beene heard, that the Popes authority extended beyond *Excommunication*, therefore hee makes Deposition a lesse punishment then that, and naturally to precede it: for he makes this to bee reason enough, why he should forfait his dignity, *because he attempted to diminish the Dignity of the Church*: But for his *Disobedience* to the Church and him, he inflicts *Excommunication* as the greater, and greatest punishment which he could lay upon him. And it is of dangerous consequence, if *Excommunication* be of so high a nature, and of so vast an extent, that wheresoever it is justly inflicted, that presupposes *Confiscation* and *Deposition*.

80 And another dangerous prejudice to the safetie of all Princes, ariseth out of this precedent, which is, that hee absolves the Subjects of all Oathes of Alleageance, which they *shall* make after that Denunciation: For if his successor that now governes, shall be pleased to doe the same in *England* at this time, and so give his partie here such leave to take the *Oath of Alleageance*; doth he not thereby utterly frustrate and annihilate all that, which the indulgence of a mercifull Prince, and the watchfulnesse of a diligent Parliament, have done for the Princes safety, and for distinction between traiterous and obedient subjects? Yet both this *Deposition*, and this *Absolution* of subjects and this *Interdiction* were all heaped, and amass'd upon a Catholique Prince, before the *excommunication* it selfe, or any other fault intimated then *diminishing of the honour of that Church, and participating with excommunicated persons*.

34. then *errata*: the.   L-1, C-1

CHAPTER THREE

81   And now we may discend to the survay of that letter, which he writes to a Bishoppe, who desired to have something written by him, wherby he might be help'd and arm'd against such as denied that by the authority of that Sea, he could excommunicate that Prince, or
5 absolve his subjects. First therefore he says, That there are manie, and most certaine Documents in the Scriptures to that purpose, of which hee cites; those which are ordinarily offered, as *Tu es Petrus*, and *Tibi dabo Claves*, and *Quodcunque ligaveris*: and then he askes, *Whether Kings be excepted?* But, Kings are not excepted; but this proceeding against
10 Kings is excepted: That is, it is not included in that Commission, as hath beene enough and enough proved by many.

82   Then followes that testimony of *Gelasius* a Pope, *That Priesthood is above Principality, and that the Bishoppe of Rome is the chiefe Priest*. If wee allow both *Testem, & Testimonium*, yet the cause is safe;
15 he may be above all, in some functions, yet not in *temporall*.

83   His next authority, is *Julius*, another Pope, who expounding the wordes, *Tibi dabo Claves*, to certaine Easterne Bishoppes, sayes, *Shall not he that opens heaven, judge of the earth?* But this dooth as much destroy all *Judicature* and all *Magistracy*, as justifie the deposing of
20 Kings.

84   After this, he cites (though not as *Gregories* words are) a priviledge graunted by *Gregory* the first, to a Monasterie and *deprivation* from secular dignity, and *excommunications* to any that infringe that priviledge. And this priviledge *Bellarmine* also produces, to prove the
25 Popes soveraignty in temporall matters. It is the priviledge of the Monastery of S. *Medard*, which is in *Gregories* Epistle: and as it is cited by this other *Gregory*, it makes *deposition* the lesser punishment, and to precede *excommunication*, for he sayes; *That Gregory though a milde Doctor, did not onely depose, but excommunicate the transgres-*
30 *sors*: But both this Pope that cites it, deceives us, by putting in the word *Decrevit*, as though this had the solemnities of a Popes *Decree*, which presumes an *infallibility*, and *Bellarmine* deceives us, by mutilat-

margin notes:
Li.8. Ep. 21. Episco. Metenti
Matt. 16.18, 19
De Pontif. l.5. c.8. §. Quartum
L.2. post Ep.38

Margin 2. Li.8. *Ed.*: *note misplaced*. L-1, C-1   **6.** Scriptures] -tures, *catchword* p.70 . L-1, C-1   **Margin 7.** Matt. 16.18, 19 *Ed.*: *note missing*. L-1, C-1   **22.** first *Ed.*: fi st. L-1, C-1   **Margin 24.** c.8 *Ed.*: c.7. L-1, C-1   **26.** and as it *errata*: and it. L-1, C-1

ing the sentence, and ending at that word *Honore privatur*: for he that reads the whole sentence, shall see, that all this Decree of *Deposition* and *Excommunication*, was no more than a *comminatory imprecation*, to testifie earnestly the Founders affection to have those priviledges observed, and deterre men from violating thereof; as the vehemence and insolent phrase of the *Instrument* do intimate, by a bitternes unusuall in medicinall excommunications: *For all the curses due to Heretiques*; and *all the torments which Judas endures* are imprecated upon him; & it is subscribed not only by *Gregory*, with 30. *Bishops*, but by a *King* and a *Queene*, no competent Judges (in this *Gregories* opinion) of faults punishable by *excommunication*.

85 And the same Pope in erecting of an Hospitall, and endowing it with some immunities, uses the same language, that *the infringers thereof, should loose all their power, and honour, and dignity, and after be excommunicate*; and yet this is never produced, nor understood to confirme his *temporall soveraignty*.

_{Li.11. Ep. 10}

86 The *Donation of Constantine*, which was not much lesse then 300. yeare before this, ends in like words: *If any man violate this Donation, let him be eternally condemned, let him finde Peter and Paul in this life, and in the next his enemies, and let him perish with the Divell and al the reprobate, burning in Inferno inferiore*. And wil they from this argue in *Constantine* a power, to open and shut hel gates? And will they endanger al those Catholique authors to this eternall damnation, which have violated this *Donation of Constantine* by publique bookes?

_{Dist. 96. Constantinus}

87 And such a *Commination* as this of *Gregory* appears in a *Canon* of the first Councell at *Paris*, not long before his, where it is threatned, *that whosoever shall receive a person suspended from the Communion, himself shal be seperated A concordia fratrum, and (as we hope, or trust) shall sustaine the wrath of the eternall Judge for ever*. And (not to insist long upon examples of such imprecations) about 160 yeare after *Gregory*, *Paulus* I. erecting a Monastery in his owne house, makes this Constitution; *If any of the Popes, our successors, or any mighty or Inferiour person, of what dignity soever, alien any of these things, let him know, that he is anathematiz'd by Christ and Peter, and estranged*

_{An. 553. ca.5. Summa. Carranza}

_{Baron. Annal. To.9. fo.319. Anno 761}

---

1. *privatur errata faults*: privetur. L-1, C-1   **18.** ends *errata*: end. L-1, C-1   **Margin 25.** Carranza *Ed*.: Carranze. C-1, L-1

CHAPTER THREE 73

from the Kingdome of God: and that he shall give an account thereof to the Saints, in the day of judgement: For (sayeth hee) *I desire the Judge himselfe, that hee will cast uppon them the wrath of his power, that their life may bee laborious and mournefull, and they may die consuming, and may bee burnt eternally with Judas, in hell fire, in voragine chaos, And that they that observe this Constitution, may enjoy all blessednes at the right hand of God.*

88   And when in the behalfe of the Kings of Spaine, the same argument is made for them; that because there are many *Diplomes* extant in Sicily, by which the Kings Anathematise infringers of their Constitutions, that therefore they exercised *Spirituall Jurisdiction: Baronius* sayes, *that this argument is ridiculous, because it is hard to finde any instrument of Donations from Princes, or from private men, or from women; in which these bitter formes of excommunication are not: Which* (sayes he) *do not containe any sentence of excommunication, but Imprecations to deterre others, as every man was at libertie to doe, when he made any such graunts.* So that *Baronius* hath laughed out of countenance this argument upon *Medardus* priviledge, which hath beene so often, and so solemnly offered and iterated. And it appeares hereby that the punishments mentioned in these Constitutions, were not such as the makers thereof could inflict, but onely such as they wished to fall upon them that offended: and such I doubt not, was *Gregories* Imprecation, in his successors interpretations, that is, that hee wished all Kings to be deprived.

Ubi supra

89   His next reason why Princes may be deposed by Priests, is the diversity of their *Beginning* and *first Institution*: for, as before he had said to another *Bishop* of the same place, *Regall Dignity was found out and invented by humane pride, but Priests were instituted by the Divine pietie,* So here he repeates it with more contumely; *Who knowes not that Kings had their beginnings from those men, who being ignorant of God, and provoked by the prince of the world the Divell, through Pride, Rapine, Perfidiousnesse, Murder, and all wickednesse, affected a government over their equalls, by a blind Ambition, and intolerable presumption.*

L.4. Ep. 2

---

5. chaos, Ed.: chaos. C-1, L-1   **16.** others errata: other. L-1, C-1   **28.** instituted errata: intituled. L-1, C-1   **29.** repeates] repeares. O²

90   Then he proceeds to the examples, of *Innocent* who excomunicated *Arcadius*, and of *Zachary* who deposed *Childerique*. The first of which is not to the purpose, Except *Excommunication* presume *Deposing* which *Innocent* intended not. And the second hath beene abundantly, and satisfactorily spoken to, by very many of ours, and of their owne authors, who determine it roundly, *Deposuit, id est, Deponentibus consensit.*

91   And therefore insisting little upon these, hee makes hast to that wherein he excels, which is, to reproach and debase the *State* and *Order* of Kings. For he says, *That even Exorcists* (which is no sacred order) *are superiour to Princes.* Nor is his intemperance therefore excessive, because hee subjects men to such as are in the way going towards Priesthood, for that will bee still upon the old ground, that priesthood is in an incomprehensible distance and proportion above principalitie, but his reasons why *Exorcists* are above Princes, discovers more malignitie to Princes absolutely; which is, *That since they are above the Divell himselfe, much more are they Superiour to those which are subject to the devill, and members of the devill.* Nor could his argument have any life or force here, except he presum'd Kings to be poisoned & corrupted by the very place, & by the order it selfe; for otherwise, if he meant it onely of vicious Kings, why should he institute this comparison of *Exorcists* and Kings, since it ought to bee of Exorcists and vicious men? And therefore (as he sayes after in this Epistle,) *That he finds in his owne experience, that the Papacie either finds good men, or makes them good, and that if they want goodnesse of their owne, they are supplied by their predecessours, and so, Aut Clari eriguntur, aut Erecti illustrantur:* So he thinkes either, that onely members of the devill come to be Kings, or that kings grow to be such, when they are kings. For so much he intimates even in this place, when hee sayes, *In Regall dignitie very few are saved, and from the beginning of the world til now, we find not one King equal in sanctitie to innumerable Religious men. What King hath done any miracles? To what King have Churches or Altars beene erected? How many Kings are Saints? Whereas, onely in our Sea there are almost a hundred.*

92   And thus I thought it fit to runne over this Letter, because here

15. q.6. Alius. glo. ver. Deposuit

Margin 6.   15. q.6.   *Ed.*: 15.9.b.   C-1, L-1

seemes the first fire to have beene given, and the first drop of poison to
have beene instil'd of all those virulencies and combustions, with which
the later Authours in that Church, are inflam'd and swollen up, in this
point of aviling Princes. Of which ranke, this Pope had respect to none,
but those who were really profitable to him: Nor have I observed any
words of sweetenesse in him towards any of them, but onely to our King
the *Conquerour*, and to one King of *Spaine*. To ours he sayes, *We*   L.1. Epist. 70
account you the onely man amongst Kings, that performes his duetie,
and this he sayes, because *he should graunt more to God, and Saint*
Peter, and Saint Stephen, and be vigilant upon Saint Peters estate in
England, that he might find him a propitious debter. And to the king
of *Spaine* he sayes, *The present which you sent me, is so ample, and so*   L.9. Epist. 2
magnificent, as became a King to give, and Saint Peter to receive; and
you show by your present, how much you esteeme him.

    93 And such Princes as these he was loath to loose: For he accounted
that a losse, which now they call the onely perfection, that is, to enter
into a Religious and regular Order. For this *Gregorie* chides an *Abbot*   L.6. Epist. 17.
bitterly, for admitting a *Prince*, who might have beene profitable to his   Abbati Cluniae
state, into the Cloister. For he sayes: *To doe so, is but to seeke their*
owne ease; and now, not onely the Shepheards depart from the care of the
Church, but the Dogges also; which he speakes of Princes. He tels him,
That he hath done against the Canons, in admitting him: and that he
is therein an occasion, that a hundred thousand persons doe lacke their
guide. And therefore sayes he, *Since there are scarce any good Princes*
to bee found, I am griev'd that so good a Prince, is taken away from his
mother That is from the Church, as it must necessarily be intended in
this Epistle. So pliant and serviceable to his uses, would *Gregorie* make
Regall dignitie, or else breake it in peeces.

    94 And where could our later men find better light in this mis-
cheivous and darke way, then in this *Gregories Dictates*, of which, these   Binius. To.3. pa.2.
are some, *That onely the Pope may use Imperiall Ornaments; That all*   fol.1196
Princes must kisse his feete: That onely his Name must be rehearsed in
the Church; That there is no other Name in the world, with many such
transcendencies. And accordingly he is wel seconded by others, which   Cassanae. Catal.
say, that he is *Superillustris; and may not be cald so neither, because*   Glor. pa.4. Con-
he is so much above all Dignitie, that our thought cannot extend to his   sid. 7
Majestie: And to prevent all opposition against it, *Baldus* in a choler

sayes, *That he that sayes the contrarie, Lies.*

95 And upon what place of Scripture may they not build this supremacy, and this obedience to it, after a Pope, who is heire to an *Active* and *Passive infallibility*, and can neither deceive nor be deceived, hath extorted from *Samuel*, so long before the *Apostolique* Sea was established, a testimony, *That not to obey the Apostolique Sea, was the sinne of Idolatrie, teste Samuele*: which he iterates againe, and againe in divers other Epistles.

96 From this example and from this libertie proceedes that malignity, wherewith the later writers wrest every thing to the disgrace of *Principality*. By this authority *Simancha* drawes into consequence, and urges as a precedent to be imitated, the example of the *Scythians*, who killed their king for admitting some new rites in divine worshippe; *Which (sayes Simancha) was justly done; for the Subjects of hereticall Princes are delivered from their Jurisdiction.* And in like maner, *Schultingius* an Epitomizer of *Baronius*, finding in him out of *Strabo*, that in Egypt *the Priests had so much authority over the Kings, that sometimes by a bare message they would put one King to death, and erect another*: and repeating the same gloriously and triumphantly a second time; at last in a Marginall note hee claimes the same authority for the Pope, when he notes, and sayes thereupon, *The supreame authority of the Clergy, is proved against the Calvinists*: So that we may easily discerne, by these examples which they propose for imitation, what authority they aime at. But *Schultingius* might also have observed, as a prophecy of the ruine of their usurpation, that as soone as a learned and understanding king *Ergamenes*, came amongst them, he tooke away that custome.

97 From this libertie, *Bellarmine* also, to the danger of any Prince, differing in any point from the integrity of the Romane profession, hath pronounced, *That Heretiques are deprived of all Jurisdiction, even before excommunication.* And that therefore an Emperour cannot call a Councell, because that must be done in *Nomine Christi*: and that Princes

Margins:
L. 4. Epist. 2
I Reg. 15.13
Enchirid. Iud. Tit. 21. n.9
Schultingius. Thesaur. Antiq. Eccles. To.1. c.8 & 243
Diod. Sicul. Bibliot. l.4. ca.1
Bell. de Pont. l.2. c.30. §. Nec valet
Ide. de Concil. et Eccles. l.1. c.12. §. Esse autem
Ide. de laicis. l.3. c.17. §. In quem

Margin 7. 15.13 *Ed.*: 15.. C-1, L-1 **Margin 11.** Enchirid. Iud. *Ed.*: Enchird. Ind.. C-1, L-1 **11.** drawes] dr awes. C-1, C-2, C-4, O-1 **12.** precedent *Ed.*: preeedent. L-1, C-1 **Margin 27.** Pont. l.2. c.30. §. Nec valet *Ed.*: *note misplaced* Pont. l.2. c.2. §. Nec valet L-1;. Pnt. l.2. C.2. § Necvalet C-1, C-4, O-1 **Margin 29.** Concil. . . . 12 *Ed.*: Concil. . . . 2 *note misplaced*. C-1, L-1 **Margin 31.** laicis. *Ed.*: *note misplaced* . C-1, L-1

have not their precedencies, as they are members of the Church, for so Ecclesiastique Ministers are above them.

98 And this hath made a Contry-man of ours deliver as mischevous doctrine, *that the power of excommunication, is got by prescription*; And so sayes another great Patron of that greatnesse, *the Priests obeyed the Kings of Israel, but contrarily our Priests doe prescribe over the temporall power.* And *Sayr* proceedes further, and sayes, *that though Panormitane be of opinion, That one can prescribe in no more then that which he hath put in practise, yet if hee have so exercised any one act of Jurisdiction* (as excommunication is) *as that he had a will to doe all, he prescribes in all.* And there is no doubt, but that when *Pius* the fift *excommunicated*, he had a good will to *Depose* also.

Sayr.Thesaur.Cas. Consc. l.1. c.6. nu.30

Stephan. De Osculat. ped. pont. ca.16. §. quare

99 From this also have proceeded all those enormous dejections of Princes, which they cast and derive upon al *Kings*, when they speake them of the Emperour: for though the later writers, are broder with the Emperour, and chose rather to exemplify in him, then in any other Soveraigne Prince; upon this advantage, that they can more easily prove a Supremacy over him, by reason of the pretended translation of the Empire, yet it is a slippery way and conveyance of that power over all other *Princes*; since in common intendment and ordinary acceptation, no man can be exempt from that, to which the Emperour is subject. And of the Emperour they say, [a]*That not onely he may be guilty of Treason to the Pope,* [b]*but if a subject of the Pope offend the Emperour, the treason is done to the Pope.* Yea, [c]*if it be the Emperours subject, and the injury done to the Emperour, yet this is treason to the Pope*: So that the Emperour doth but beare his person; for in his presence hee must descend: and in [d]*a Councell his seate must be no higher, then the Popes footstoole, nor any State be hunge over his head.*

[a]Hiero. Gigas. de laesa mai. l.1. Rubr. 4. q.2. n.5
[b]Ibid. q.4. n.2
[c]Ib. q.1. n.6

[d]Ceremo. Sacr. Ca. de Concil.

100 And from hence also hath growne that Distinction, Superstitious on one part, & Seditious on the other, of *Mediate* and *Immediate* institution of the two powers: for Ecclesiastique authority is not so *immediate* from God, that he hath appointed any such certaine *Hierarchy*,

---

Margin 3. Consc. l.1 *Ed.*: Consc. par.1, l.1 C-1, L-1;. *note misplaced* C-1, MCG, C-4, C²-3, O-1 **Margin 5.** Stephan *Ed.*: Stephan' L-1, C-1; *note misplaced.* L-1, C-2, C-3, L-2, L³⁰, O-2, SP, YK-1, YK-2 **16.** exemplify *errata*: exemply. L-1, C-1 **Margin 24c.** n.6 *Ed.*: n.8. C-1, L-1

which may upon no occasion suffer any alteration or interruption: Nor is secular authority so *mediate*, or dependant upon men, as that it may at any time be extinguished, but must ever reside in some forme or other.

^{De translat. Imp. l.1. c.8. in princip.}

And *Bellarmine* himselfe confesses, That *as Aaron was made Priest over the Jewes, and Peter over the Christian Church, immediately from God, so also some Kings have beene made so immediately without humane election, or any such concurrence*: So that *Regal Dignity* hath had as great a dignification in this point from God, as *Sacerdotall*; and to neither hath God given any necessary obligation of perpetuall enduring in that certaine forme. So that, that which *Bellarmine* in another place

^{De Pont. l.2. c.17. §. Observandum}

says to be a *speciall observation*, wee acknowledge to bee so: which is, *That in the Pope are three things; His place, his person, and the union of them: the first is onely from Christ, the second, from those that elect him, and the third from Christ, by mediation of a humane act.*

And as wee confesse all this in the Pope, so hath he no reason to denie it to be also in kings: he addes further, That *the Cardinals are truly said, To create the Pope, and to be the cause why such a man is Pope, and why he hath that power; but yet they doe not give him that power: as in generation, a father is a cause of the union of the body and soule, which yet is infused onely from God.* And in all this we agree with *Bellarmine*; and we adde, that all this is common to all supreame, secular, or Ecclesiastique Magistrates.

101 And yet in *Hereditary* kings, there is lesse concurrence, or assistance of humane meanes, then either in elected kings, or in the Pope himselfe: for in such secular states, as are provided by election, without all controversie the supreame power, in every *vacancy*, resides in some subject, and inheres in some body, which as a Bridge, unites the defunct, and the succeeding Prince. And how can this be denied to be in

^{aTheod. a Niem. de Schism. l.3. c.1}
^{bSayr. Thes. Cas. consci. l.2. c.20. nu.20}

the Colledge of Cardinals, If (as one sayes) ^a*the dominion temporall be then in them, and* ^b*that they in such a vacancy, may absolve any, whom the Pope might absolve*. If therefore in all the cases reserved to himselfe, as namely in *deposing* Princes, and absoluing subjects, he proceed not

^{De Pont. l.5. ca.6}

as he is Pope, but as he is spiritual Prince, as *Bellarmine* sayes, and wee shall have occasion hereafter to examine; If that Colledge may absolve

---

Margin 29a. Theod.] T heod. L-1; Th eod. L², O-2   **29.** ^a*the Ed.*: the. C-1, L-1   **Margin 30b.** l.2 *Ed.*: par.1, l.2. L-1, C-1

CHAPTER THREE 79

subjects as he might, this supreamacy and spirituall Principality resides in them, and is transfer'd from them to the Successor.

102   Certainely all power is from God; And as if a companie of *Savages*, should consent and concurre to a civill maner of living, Magistracie, & Superioritie, would necessarily, and naturally, and Divinely grow out of this consent (for Magistracie and Superioritie is so naturall and so immediate from God, that *Adam* was created a Magistrate, and he deriv'd Magistracie by generation upon the eldest Children, and (as the Schoolemen say) if the world had continued in the first Innocency, yet there should have beene Magistracie.) And into what maner and forme soever they had digested and concocted this Magistracie, yet the power it-selfe was *Immediately* from God: So also, if this Companie, thus growen to a *Commonwealth*, should receive further light, and passe, through understanding the Law written in all hearts, and in the Booke of creatures, and by relation of some instructers, arrive to a saving knowledge, and Faith in our blessed Saviours Passion, they should also bee a *Church*, and amongst themselves would arise up, lawfull Ministers for Ecclesiastique function, though not derived from any other mother Church, & though different from all the divers Hierarchies established in other Churches: and in this State, both Authorities might bee truely said to bee from God. To which purpose *Aquinas* sayes expressely and truely, *That Priesthood* (that is all Church function) *before the Law given by Moses, was, as it pleasd men, and that by such determination of men, it was ever derived upon the eldest Sonne*; And we have also in the same point *Bellarmines* voice and confession, That in that place of S. Paul to the Ephesians, which is thought by many to be so pregnant for the proofe of a certaine Hierarchie, *The Apostle did not so delineate a certaine and constant Hierarchie, but onely reckoned up those gifts, which Christ gave diversly, for the building up of the body of the Church.*

103   To conclude therefore this point of the distinction of *Mediate* and *Immediate* Authoritie, a Councell of *Paris* under *Gregorie* the fourth, and *Lodovicke* and *Lotharius* Emperours, which were times and persons obnoxious enough to that Sea, hath one expresse Chapter, *Quod*

margin: 1.2.ae. q.103. art.3

margin: De Pont. l.1. c.9. §. Potest etiam Ephe. 4.11

margin: An. 829. Binius. To.3. par.1. fo.562. ca.5

Margin 21. 1.2.ae. . . . art. *Ed.*: 1.2. . . . ad   C-1;. 1.2ae. . . . ad   L-1, L², C⁹, Y, L³⁰, C⁵-1, SP, O-2, O¹⁴, O²   **Margin 25.** l.1. c.9] l.c.9.   C-1, C-4, MCG, O-1   **Margin 31.** 829] 822. C-1, C-4, MCG, O-1   **Margin 31.** Binius *Ed.*: Binnius. L-1, C-1

Regnum non ab hominibus, sed a Deo detur. There it is said, *Let no King thinke that the Kingdome was preserv'd for him, by his Progenitors, but he must beleeve that it was given him by God. For he which is King of men, had not this Kingdome from men, but from God*: And so hee proceedes to apply many places of Scripture to this purpose, to the shame and confusion of them, who to overthrow, or subject secular principalitie, extort Scriptures for the advancement of Ecclesiastique immunities: As in the *Septimes*, that new limme of the body of the Canon Law, those priviledges are proved to be *Iure Divino*, out of the word of the *Psalme*, *Nolite tangere Christos meos*, which was spoken of all the Children of *Israel*, as they were protected in their passage to the land of Canaan, and cannot be appropriated to Priests onely.

In 7. 1.2. Tit. 1. De for. comp. ca.1. glos. verbo, eo ipso

104   And from this libertie which men of this Religion, have taken to speake slightly, and malignantly of the Person and dignitie of *Kings*, a long and inveterate custome hath so wrought upon them, that it hath caried them farther, and made them as bold with the word of God himselfe. Out of which they can deduce principall and direct Prophecies for every passage in Saint *Francis* his storie. For ^athe Dreame of *Pharoes* officer (*A vine was before me, and in the Vine were three branches*) signifies Saint *Francis*, and the three Orders derived from him, says the *Booke of Conformities*, and *Sedulius* the fresh Apologer thereof. So he sayes, ^b*Christ prophecied of this Order; and it is fulfilled in this Order which hee said, Feare not little flocke, for it is your Fathers pleasure, to give you the Kingdome*. And ^c *of these it is spoken*, sayes hee, *The sound of them is gone into all Nations*. Of these prophanations the examples are too frequent; for as they have fitted all other things spoken of Christ, to Saint *Francis* in the *Booke of Conformities*, so doth ^d*Sedulius* maintaine the giving to him, the title of *Jesus of Nazareth, King of the Jewes*.

^aSedulius. Apol. cont. Alcora. Francisca. l.2. c.1 Gen. 40.10

^bSedul. l.2. c.1. Luc. 12.32

^cSedul. l.3. c.13. Psal. 118.10

^dL.1. ca.18

105   So also must the Scriptures afoord prophesies for every ragge and inch of the *Sindon*, which wrapped our Saviour in the Sepulchre. For in ^ethat *Liturgie* or *Office*, (as they call it) which is appointed by the Pope to be said in the Chappell where this *Sindon* is preserved; all those places of Scripture, which speake of *Christs body sprinkled with blood*, are

^eMallonii. Notae in Paleotum de Syndone. l.1. c.1. nu.18

Margin 9. 7. 1.2] 7. 1 2. C^5-1, SP, C^{10} **Margin 24c.** 118.10 *Ed*.: 118. L-1, C-1   **31.** *Sindon* C-2, C-3, C^9, L^2, L-2, Y, O^2, HD, O^{14}: *S ndon.* L-1, C-1, MCG, C-4, L^3, F, O-2, YK-3

CHAPTER THREE   81

referred and saide to bee intended of this *Sindon*. And therefore sayes the Author thereof, *Since the Pope hath so applied them, this exposition thereof cannot be reprehended.*

106   By this license they give all the names of Christ to the ^fPope; yea *the name of God himselfe*; And *of* ^a*Goddesse to our Lady.* And by this license did ^bCrusius the Jesuit, *call Ignatius Constitutions the Decalogue*: because sayes *Gretzer*, his fellow Jesuite, *Metaphorically any instruction of our life, is call'd the Decalogue.*

^fExtrava. Jo. 22. Cum inter. glos. in fine
^aLiter. Leo. 10. per Benchum. l.8. Ep. 1.17
^bGretzer. Cont. Hassenmiller. fo.141

107   Nor can these blasphemous detorsions, & bold mis-applications, be salved, by *Sedulius* his guiltie excuse, that they ^c*are somewhat too freely written, according to the simplicitie of the age,* And ^d*such as some men would rather wish unwritten*, and ^e*Circumspect men wish'd unsaid*; And *some things too* ^f*rawly, somethings too couragiously uttered.* And these which he so tenderly, and calmely passes over, with light animadversion, are such sayings as these, *That S. Francis was* ^g*deified; That* ^h*was made one spirit with God: That* ⁱ*hee saw the secrets of hearts: And* ^k*that he was more then* John Baptist, *and better then the Apostles: And* ^l*that God did obay him at a beck in every thing.*

^cSedul. Apol. prefat.
^dL.1. c.9
^eL.1. c.18
^fIbid. & c.20
^gL.1. c.20
^hL.1. c.13 ⁱL.1. c.15
^kL.1. c.18
^lL.2. c.6

108   Nor will *Serarius* his elegant evasion serve them in this, ^m*That some men too indulgent and carefull of their verse, or the delicacie of the Latine language, may have gone into these excesses.* For the first place, where the Pope is called *the Lord our God*, is in a place barbarous and loose inough, which is the glosse upon an Extravagant. And though *Bembus*, in whose letters written for *Leo* the 10 our Lady is called *Goddesse*, doe often stray into prophane elegancies (as ⁿin another place, when he would express an inspiration of the Holy ghost in one, he sayes, he was *afflatus Zephiri caelestis auram*, And ^ocalls Excommunication, *Interdictionem aquae & ignis*) yet this will neither excuse that Pope which sign'd those Letters, nor those to whose care the expurgation of bookes, hath beene committed. So that none of their *piae fraudes*, with which they emplaster this venemous & contagious wounding the scriptures of God, & the phrase of his spirit, will acquit or excuse them.

^mSerar. Litaneuti. l.2. c.13
ⁿEpist. Leo. 10. l.2. Ep. 21
^oL.4. Ep. 15

109   And if their mis-applying of Scriptures carried them no further, then to simple and childish actions (as Saint *Francis* commanded *Mas-*

Margin 5a. 1.17 *Ed.*: l.17.   C-1, L-1   **Margin 16h.** ⁱL.1 .... ^kL.1 *Ed.*: ⁱL.b .... ^kL.b.   C-1, L-1   **Margin 19m.** l.2 *Ed.*: l..   L-1, C-1

Apolog. l.3. c.1. nu.3	*saeus* to tumble round like a childe; because, sayes *Sedulius*, it is written, *Nisi Conversi fueritis, & efficiamini sicut parvuli, non intrabitis*): Or if
Idem. l.3. c.13. nu.3	it carried them but to stupid actions (as the penitent which confessed to S. *Anthony*, that he had kicked his mother, receiving this answere: *If thy foote offend thee, cut it off*, went, and cut off his foote, (but S. *Anthony* honestly set it on againe,) Or if it carried them but to bolde and con-
Idem. l.3. c.28. nu.31	fident actions (as Saint *Anthony*, when his *Host* set him a Toade upon the Table, and tolde him that it was written in the Gospell, *De omni quod tibi apponitur, comedes*, he with the signe of the Crosse, made it a Capon ready rosted) sillinesse or some such disease might lessen the fault.
	110 But then is there extreame horrour and abominations therein, when God and his Lieuetenants are at once injur'd, which is, when places of Scripture are malitiously or ridiculously detorted to the aviling of Princes: With what soule then could Pope *Alexander* say, treading
Psal. 91.13	upon *Fredericke*, *Super aspidem & Basiliscum ambulabis*: of which Acte,
Jos. Stepha. de Osculat. ped. Pont. cap.11. §. Ex quo	a Bishoppe in that Church sayes, *that it ought to be commended, and that it was lawfully and worthily done.*
	And with what conscience could the same servile Bishoppe of *Six-tus* the fift, prove the kissing of the popes feete, out of those wordes
Esa. 49.23	of *Esay*, *Kings and Queenes shall worshippe thee, with their faces to-*
Jos. Steph. c.5	*wards the Earth, and licke up the dust of thy feete*? how durst hee say,
Luc. 7	that this kissing of the popes feete, was established in saint *Luke, when*
Idem. ca.7.38	*the sinner kissed Christs feete? Because* (sayes he) *if it were affoorded Christ, belongs it not to his Church, which is bone of his bone?* And out
Deut. c.33	of Deuteronomy hee thinkes this reverence is evidently enough demon-
Idem. c.33.3	strated, because it is saide of God, *the saints of God, are said to be humbled at his feete.*
	So that whatsoever is applied to the Church, or to God, by this detorsion is given to the pope: But this Bishoppe is so transported with this rage of detorting scriptures, that rather then not mis-applie them, hee will apply them to his owne Condemnation: For thus hee concludes
Epist. lecto.	his Epistle with the wordes of the Apostle: *Gaudeo sive per veritatem,*

Margin 3. 13. C[16]: 13. L-1, C-1 **Margin 16.** 91.13] 90.13. C-2, C-3, C[9], L[2], Y, L-2, L[30], C[5]-1, C[5]-2, SP, O[14], O[8], C[3], C[10], C[2]-1 **Margin 24.** 7.38 *Ed.*: 7.. L-1, C-1 **Margin 26.** c.33 *Ed.*: c.1.3. L-1, C-1 **Margin 27.** c.33.3 *Ed.*: c.10. L-1, C-1

sive per occasionem, Romanae Ecclesiae dignitatem extolli: so that it is all one to him, whether scriptures bee faithfully applied or no, so it be to the profit and advantage of that Church.

111   And though *Bellarmine* seeme to deplore and lament that unworthy manner of handling serious Controversies, of which hee accus'd that Authour, which called his booke *Aviso Piacevole*, because he cites some of the *Italian Poets* against the Church of Rome, yet is this fashion still in so much use amongst them, that in their last busines with the state of Venice, one authour, though in a disguised name, that undertooke the defence of *Baronius* his furious instigation of the Pope, doth not onely wound and staine the memory of our late Queene, with impious calumniations, and wrest the Scriptures, to defame our present King; but he protests that hee chuses this way of doing it, to imitate *Socrates*, who was (sayes he) *Derisor hominum, maxime potentum*, and exhibites his booke *as a sacrifice, Risui, & Lubentiae*.

[margin: Append. ad lib. de Pont. respons. ad lib. Aviso Piacevole. ca.2]

[margin: Nicod. Macer. de Paren. Baro. ad lecto.]

112   Where then shall we hope, that these men will stoppe or limit their blasphemies? when in the licentious fury thereof, having made it habituall to them, and an *Idolisme* of that Religion, they set (in their account) God against God; that is the word of God against the Pope, and defame him in their owne Pasquils by the phrase of Scripture. In which kind of prophane libelling, I had thought their malignity, and irreligion had beene at the highest, when they called *Lucretiaes* bastard, by Pope *Alexander*, and his sonne, the *holy Ghost*: till of late we see one of our owne nation hath drunke so deepe of that cuppe, that he hath swallowed the dregges also; and in a childish and traiterous itch of witte, at once wounded the Majestie, both of his God, and of his King, by imputing false faults to the one, that hee might misuse the word of the other.

And by this meanes, as when they determined to kill the Emperor *Henry* the seventh, that they might poison him, they forbore not to poison their owne God in the Sacrament first: so when they purposed to teare and deface the name and honour, and lawes of the King, they first offer the same violence to the word of God himselfe.

113   Thus the scriptures serve them for *Panegyriques*, to advance the Pope; [a]*Omnia Subiecisti sub pedibus eius*: which being spoken of beasts subjection to men, [b]they make it of men to the Pope. Thus the

[margin: [a]Psal. 8.6]
[margin: [b]Maynardus. de Privil. Eccl. Art.2. n.22]

18. *Idolisme Ed.: Idiolisme.* L-1, C-1   **Margin 35b.** Art.2. n.22 *Ed.:* Art.2 n.21.   C-1, L-1

scriptures serve them to devest and disarme Princes; ^c*Ecce duo gladii*, which being (if we ^dbeleeve the Jesuite *Sà*) no other then those knifes, with which they had cutte up the paschal Lambe, ^ea pope applies to the spirituall and temporall Jurisdiction.

And thus the scripture serves them for provocation, and incitements to warre, and devastation: ^f*Macta & Manduca*: which being spoken of baptizing the Gentiles, ^g*Baronius* detorts to the excommunication of Christians. Onely they are content to spare scriptures, when they come to defend their late-borne *Heresies*; for, for the *necessity* of beleeving *Purgatory*, *Invocation*, *Transubstantiation*, and some others of the same age, they offer no scripture; but they thinke it victory enough that *Galatine* can prove all these out of the *Talmud*, and *Cusanus* out of the *Alcoran*: For, for the olde and new Testaments, they finde other employment. They must serve them against the *office* and *dignity* of Princes, to exhibit them as a prey to their neighbours, and a scorne to their owne Subjects.

114 As Christ asked of the *Jewes, for which of his good workes they would stone him*: Princes may aske of the Romane Church, for which of their benefites they are so injurious to them? Is it for having established a Primacy upon that Bishoppe, above his fellow Patriarches, which was so long litigious? Or for withdrawing him from the jawes of the Barbarous devourers of *Italy*? Or for enriching him with a *Patrimony*, and *Priviledges* almost equall to their owne? Is it for any of these, that you say, *A Clergy man cannot be a traitor, though he rebell; because he is no subject*? By which you cut off so great and so good a part, as in your opinion the state without it, is but a meere Carcasse, for the Clergie is the soule.

And you extend those immunities, not onely to your boyes which light your Candles, and locke the Church doores, but to every sullen fellow, that will retire himselfe into a wood, without either assuming Orders, or subjecting himself to any Religious Rule, or despoiling himselfe of his temporall possessions, as you say of your *Ermits*: Yea to *Nunnes*, who though they be not of the Clergie, yet are *Ecclesiastique persons*, and

yet they are so prophane, as *they may not be admitted to touch any thing*   Dist. 23. Sancti-
which belongs to the Altar. And not onely the Nunnes within profession,   monialis
have these priviledges, but also their Novices, who are under no vow:
yea they enjoy them, whom you call *Canonicas Saeculares*, which may
5 travell, traffique, marry, and do any civill, or uncivil function: (for of
the continency of *Regular Nunnes* I am of a better persuasion, for this
reason especially; that the *Jesuites* by a Constitution, are forbid to have   Regula. 47
the care of them: and those secular women, which I mentioned, are
Ecclesiastici fori (by a late *Decision* in the *Rota*) because though they   D'Alvin. de Pot.
10 be not *Ecclesiasticae*, yet they are *Personae Miserabiles*, and *weare an*   Episco. ca.3. nu.13
uniforme habite: and to raise the number, you say, *If an injury be done*   Paris de Puteo.
to any kinsman of an Ecclesiastique person, it is done to him. And that   de Synd. ca. de
                                                                                                                                     exces. reg. nu.29
if any *offence bee committed by divers persons, amongst whome there*   Maynardus. de
is one Clergie man, none of the offenders can bee subject to Temporall   Privileg. Eccles.
                                                                                                                                     Art.17. nu.9, 10
15 *Jurisdiction*.

    115   And not onely all these persons, but all which appertaines to
them, becomes spirituall: and by a new *Alchimy*, they doe not onely
extract spirit out of every thing, but transmute it all into spirit, and by
their possessing them, *Houses*, *Horses*, and *Concubines* are spirituall.
20 But as every thing returnes to his first state, and being; and so Rome
which was at first built, and governed by *Shepheards*, is returned to the
same forme after the decay of the Empire: and as the name of *Bishopp*,   Tholosa. synt.
which was at first given to *Clerkes of the Market*, and Overseers of things   l.15. c.2. nu.4
to be bought and solde, agrees still with these Simoniaque Bishoppes of
25 Rome: so many of these pretious Jewels, which are employed about
the Images and Reliques, which were at first *temporall*, and then by this
tincture growne to be *spirituall*, returne againe to their temporall nature,
when any of the Popes taken occasion to serve their pleasure, or foment
dissensions amongst other Princes, and schisme amongst themselves, by   Theod. a Niem. de
30 coining the Images, as *Urbanus* did, in such a case.   Schism. l.1. ca.22

    116   But the greatest injury that is done to Princes in this matter of
Exemption, is, that they will not be beholden to Princes for it: but plead
their *Ius Divinum*, not onely the positive Divine Law, by which, they
say, that the Popes if they had not found these men naturally exempted,

Margin 13. Privileg .... nu.9, 10 *Ed*.: privileg nu.10. C-1, L-1
28. occasion *Ed*.: ocsion. C-1, L-1

and if Princes had not granted these exemptions, might by their Constitutions, have exempted them, without asking leave of Princes, but they pretend the text of Scripture, though detorted and misus'd, to prove this Exemption. And for the Persons they pretend many; but with no more directnes, then that by which they prove exemption of their goods, from secular charges and burdens, which is, *Domini est terra, & plenitudo eius*, and since it is the Lords, it is theirs.

117 But all Princes grow weary and jealous of that claime; and a *Catholique* Writer hath observed, that many of the Writers of the Spanish Nation in these later times, have resisted that opinion, of which he names *Medina, Victoria, Soto, Ledesma*, and *Bannes*.

And if that Nation grow into jealousies, and feele her right, as *France* hath done before, all the *Italian* Writers, will be but weake evidence, to prove this exemption to bee *Iure Divino*. But as though all this were not enough, and that the states of Princes were not enough infirm'd by withdrawing of all these, they teach, *That a Subject by removing into another Province hath devested his allegeance and subjection: And that every man is free concerning his owne person: And that the band is stronger between a Creditor and a Debtor, then between a Prince and subject*. Upon all which, what mischievous conclusions will follow, is evident and obvious enough.

118 To conclude therefore this point, this Ecclesiastique immunity which they claime, is the debasing of Princes; And the defence of this immunity, and consequently of this debasing of Princes, is so just a cause of Martyredome, that *Baronius* says; *The Students in the English Colledge, have good title to two Crownes of Martyrdome, because they return into England, both to defend the Catholique faith, and the immunity of the Church*. Where we will content our selves, till wee come to a further exagitation of that point, with this confession from *Baronius*, that they are by your doctrin received in that Colledge, incited to Martyredome, for the *Immunities* of the Churche, which himselfe in the same place distinguishes from the Catholique faith. And thus farre I was willing to extend this point, That the Romane Doctrine by extolling Church Priviledges above Princes, and by an absolute and direct aviling

---

3. the text of Scripture *Ed.*: text of Scriture. C-1, L-1 **Margin 3.** Raccolta] Ravolta. L-1, F, L30, C5-1, SP, O14, O8, O5, YK-1, YK-3

Margins:
Laelio Medico. contra. Venet. fo.196. Nella Raccolta

Risposta di Ant. Bovio al. Paulo. Nella Raccolta. fo.50

Bell. de Clericis. l.1. c.ult.

Martyrolog. Ro. 29. Decemb.

them, doth mis-provoke her disciples to a vicious affectation of imaginarie Martyrdome. In the two other points of *Merite* and *Purgatory*, which produce the same effect, I may have leave to contract my selfe, into a shorter roome, because of those, many others have spoken more abundantly, then of this last point which I undertooke.

THE SECOND PART
OF MERIT.

1   The next Doctrine which I noted to mis-incite men to an imagined Martyrdome, is the Doctrine of Merites. [a]*In every good worke*, you say, *there is somewhat of merite, and somewhat of satisfaction.* The first is said to belong to our selves, and that by it we establish our salvation: So that the passion of our Saviour is but as *Baptisme* to us, and our owne workes, as *Confirmation*: [b]*Which Sacrament you say, confers more grace then baptisme dooth, for strengthning us against the Divell*: [c]*And that the holy Ghost is given more fully therein.*

And accordingly you teach, that justice of workes doth give the forme and life to faith. And the second, which is *Satisfaction*, is reserved in the common stocke, the treasury of the Church, and husbanded and dispensed by the generall steward thereof the Bishoppe of Rome.

2   But for that Merite, which you teach, to say *That our workes of their owne nature, without considering any Covenant or Contract with* GOD, *deserve Heaven*, dooth not onely diminish CHRISTS Passion, by associating an Assistant to it, and determine his Priesthood, which is everlasting, by usurping that office our selves, but it preferres our worke before his, because if wee could consider the passion of Christ, without the eternall *Decree*, and *Covenant*, and *Contract* with his father, his worke (saving the dignity which it had by Acceptation, by which the least step of his humiliation might worthily have redeemed tenne thousand worlds) had not naturally merited our salvation.

3   Now betwixt God and us there is no such Covenant; our best plea is, The sinner must repent, and God will blotte out his sinnes. If a Prince should so farre prostitute his mercie, as to proclaime a veniall Pardon,

[a] Bell. de Indul. l.1. c.2. propos.1

[b] Idem. de Confirmatione. c.11. §. Duplex
[c] Ibid. ca.2. §. Sed respond.

Bell. de Iustif. l.5. c.17. §. Nobis

by which for certaine money, any Malefactor might be pardoned, no such Malefactor as by the nature of his fault, had at that instant forfaited and confiscated all his estate, should have benefite by that pardon, because he had nothing to give. All these dis-advantages and infirmities oppresse us; no good worke is naturally large enough to reach heaven; no promise nor acceptation of God hath changed the nature of a good worke: And lastly, we can do no perfit good work; for originall sin hath poisoned the fountaines, our hearts: and those degrees and approaches, which we seeme to make towards good workes, are as if a condemned man would make a large will, to charitable uses. For, as that which hee gives is not his owne, so the goodnesse of good workes is not ours; and as it is in the Princes pleasure and allowance, whether his will shall take any effect, or no; so is it in the pleasure of God, whether any workes of ours shal be accepted.

4   Yet there is more Devotion in our Doctrine of good works, then in that of the Romane Church, because wee teach as much necessity of them, as they doe, and yet tie no reward to them. And we acknowledge, that God doth not onely make our faith, to fructifie and produce good workes as fruits thereof, but sometimes beginnes at our workes: and in a mans hart morally enclined to doe good, dooth build up faith: for if an Angell could transport *Abacuc*, for Gods service, by onely taking hold of his haire, God can take such holde of our workes, and carrie us further by them. And further then this I see not that moderate men may goe: and they startle too easilie that dare not come so farre. And if it had beene expedient for *Bellarmine*, to have spoken plaine, I thinke he would have come to that, when hee was so neere towards it, as to say, *That it is the safest way to place all our confidence in the onely mercy of God, by reason of the incertainety of our owne righteousnesse, and the danger of vaine-glory*: for he seemes else where to be so farre from doubting, that a man may not be sure of his owne righteousnesse, that himselfe had such an assurance of righteousnesse in another man, that upon his Oath before a publique Notarie he affirmes, *That hee verily beleeves that Gonzaga*, (who left the dignitie and inheritance of a Marquisate) *never committed mortall sin, and that from his age of seven yeares, he is certaine of it.*

De Iustificat. l.5. c.7. proposit.3

Ceparius. de vit. Gonzag. l.3. c.2

35. *it.* YK-1, C⁵-2: *it:.* L-1, C-1, L³⁰, L², L-2, C-3

5 The Doctrine of good workes in the Reformed Churches, is uniforme and consonant. For though *Luther*, to relieve and succour the doctrine of faith, which then languish'd desperately in the *Romane* Church, for just dignification thereof, sometimes omitted, sometimes spoke remissely of good workes, yet betweene those, who severely adhere to him, & other Churches, which in some other things depart a little from them, in this point, I have observed no dissention.

6 But the Romane Church at this present is tempested with a violent storme in this matter: that is, *by what way and meanes, man can be enabled to doe any meritorious worke*. In which Controversies, after the *Dominicans* and the *Jesuites*, had with much earnestnesse provoked, and with much bitternes replied upon one another, *Benius* in a booke as moderate and elegant, as any these later ages have afforded, projecting a way, in his Epistle to *Clement* the eight, how these dissentions might be re-united, and reconciled, observes that all the Controversies betweene them, arise out of presuming a false ground and foundation to be true, which is the famous Distinction of *Sufficient* and *Efficient* Grace. And so he dooth not onely demolish all that they had diversly built thereupon, but defeats and destroyes that foundation, which *Bellarmine* himselfe was most confident in, and evicts, that *that distinction, which that Church hath used of late yeares against all opposition, is neither contain'd, nor conveniently derived, either from Scriptures, Councels or Fathers, but is refeld & resisted by the Councell of Trent it selfe*. Nor can they extenuate this matter, as though it were of small consequence; since neither small matters should produce amongst Religious men, so much and so bitter Argumentation: nor can it bee in it selfe esteemed a small matter: upon which *Benius* says, *the questions of Predestination, Justification, Merite, Perseverance, Glorification, and many more depend, and that all Divinitie is shaken therein*.

7 And if they thinke, howsoever they suffer an intestine war, to make us beleeve that all is *peace*, and that this variety is onely *De modo*, they must remember, that that for which they burne and damne men, which is *Transubstantiation*, is but a question *De modo*, which may be sometimes

---

Margin: Benius. de Controversia. de lib. Arb. & Dei auxil. inter Catholicos. Epist. ad Cle.8

Li.I. de grat. & lib. arb. ca.III
Fo.4
Fo.91

Fo.2

---

16. arise *errata*: ariseth. L-1, C-1 **Margin 20.** III *Ed*.: II. L-1, C-1 **22.** conveniently] convenietly. L-1, O⁵ **29.** shaken C³, C¹⁰, C¹⁶, YK-1, YK-2, YK-3, C-1, C-2, C-3, C-4] shaked. L-1, O⁵

so essentiall, That if the *Arrians* had agreed with the *Orthodox*, of the maner of the generation of the son, or the *Greeke* Church would agree yet with the western, of the maner of the proceeding of the *Holy Ghost*, there could be no diffrence in these points and therfore these diffrences & controversies, & irresolutions in the *Romane* Church cannot be excus'd or diminished by this, that they are *De modo*, since they are not *De modo probationis*, which is when a certaine truth is illustrated by divers wayes of proofe, but they are *De modo essendi*, or *existendi*; So, as if you remove these wayes, by which they are said to be, they are not at all.

^{Willoti. Athenae Oxthodox.}

8   And howsoever those Doctors, whome they style *Seraphicos*, and *Illustratos*, and *Irrefragabiles, & Fontes vitae*, with which transcendent Titles, they enamell so many of the writers in the *Franciscan Families*, so are in so high a pitch as dazles us, or dive so low, as we cannot discerne what they hold in this matter of *Merit*; yet what the vulgar doctrine is in this point, the *Expurgatory Indices* shall sufficiently informe us: for no opinion of any Father, or Doctor, or of any university, can be of so much credite, and authority, as those books; since they are compiled by a commission issuing from the Pope himselfe, who was either authorized or entreated to that office, by a generall Councell. So that in these books there are all these approaches to an *infallibility*, that they were determined and provided by a Councel, executed by a Popes Buls, and justified by him, when they were perfited and accomplished.

^{Ex Conc. Trid. Bull. Pii 4. de Ind. libro.}

9   And those bookes have not bestowed so much diligence, upon any point, as this, that nothing remaine in any Authour, which may preferre Christs passion before our merits. And therfore, to omit innumerable instances to this purpose, in that ^aCatholique booke, ^bimprinted in a Catholique state, which is styled, *Ordo Baptizandi, cum Modus Visitandi*, they have expunged these wordes: *Doost thou beleeve to come to glory, not by thine owne merites, but by the vertue and passion of our Lord Jesus Christ?* And a little after they have cut off this question; *Dost thou beleeve that our Lord Jesus Christ died for our salvation, and that no man can be saved by his owne merits, or any other way, but in the merite of the passion of Christ?* And though they might have excuse

^aIndex Hispan. fo.149
^bVenet. 1575

8. are *De errata*: are so *De*. L-1, C-1   **27.** purpose, *Ed.*: purpose). L-1, C-1   **27.** ^aCatholique *Ed.*: Catholique. L-1, C-1   **28.** cum Modus *Ed.*: & Modus.   C-1, L-1

to extoll our merites, yet they might have spared the first part of the sentence, and given us leave to beleeve, *That our Lord Jesus Christ died for our salvation.*

10   Amongst these great works, pregnant both of Merite for our selves, and satisfaction for others, Martyrdome is in their Doctrine, that *Opus privilegiatum*, which takes away al sinnes; by occasion of which wordes, *To take away*, I cannot forbeare to warne you in this place, of one ordinarie indirect dealing in *Bellarmine*; which is, that in his *Indices*, and *Tables*, he presents wordes, verie farre from the sense of the place to which they relate: As in this point of merite, where his Index says, *Martyrium tollit peccata, S. Hierome*, out of whom the Text, to which he relates, is drawne; says only *per martyrium peccata non imputantur*; which is nothing to the naturall condignitie of the worke it selfe. And I should have neglected to have noted *Bellarmines Index*, but that I observe that they are so severe upon the *Indices*, made by some of their owne Church, that pretending still to have rased nothing in the body of the fathers, they expunge in the *Indices* many sentences, though the very wordes be in the Text it selfe: as in this point of Merite, *Junius* hath noted, that these wordes, *Meritum nullum, nisi quod a Christo confertur*, are cut out of the Index to *Chrysostome*, though the same wordes be in the text.

11   To proceede then, for the dignity of this worke, *Bellarmine* against *Soto*, and *Ledesmo* maintaines, that *martyrdome doth save a man, ex opere operato*. And that *there is required in the martyre, no further disposition, nor other preparation, then in one who is to be baptized. For (sayes he) though Charity be required, it is not precedent Charity, but it is, because a Martyr cannot depart without Charity, because by a covenant from God, Grace is infus'd, and so Charity: and therefore it abolishes originall sinne, and actuall sinne, and both eternall and temporall punishment belonging thereunto.* And in another place *Bellarmine* says, *That it is evident that martyredome is so full a satisfaction, that it expiates all guiltinesse, contracted by all sinnes, how huge soever the number, or haynousnes thereof be*: and if any milder man of that Church would say otherwise (as *Ferus* doth directly, *the Passions in this life,*

Bell. de Iustifi. l.2. c.9. §. Sanctus Hieronimus

Epist. ante Ind. Belg.

De baptism. l.1. c.6

De Indulg. l.1. c.2. §. Et tamen

L.3. Com. in Mat. 20. c.18

29–30. temporall *Ed.*: temporoll. C-1, L-1   **Margin 30.** Et tamen *Ed.*: Quinto. L-1, C-1   **Margin 34.** c.18 *Ed.*: c.8. C-1, L-1

are not worthy of future glorie) hee must be detorted to the other sense, (as *Senensis* says of this place, *I am of opinion, that Ferus his wordes might bee deflected to the other sense:*) Or if the wordes will not confesse uppon that racke, they must bee utterly expunged, as wee noted of others before.

_{Sext. Sen. Bibliot. Sanct. l.6. Annot. 99}

12 And upon this superabundant value of the merite of Martyredome, *Bellarmine* builds that conclusion, which wee now condemne; which is, *That because many martyres have but fewe sinnes of their owne, and their passion is of a large and rich satisfaction, a mightie heape of Satisfaction superabounds from martyrs.* And so they being sent hither, as Factors to encrease that banke and Treasurie, it appears, I thinke, sufficiently, that the doctrine of merites, dooth misprovoke and inordinatly put forward inconsiderate men, to this vitious affectation of Martyrdome. To which also the Doctrine of *Purgatory* contributes as much persuasion.

_{De Indulg. l.1. c.2. §. Et tamen}

THE THIRD PART
OF PURGATORY.

1 As *Morbizan* the Turke, being mooved by a Bul of *Pius* 2. by which he granted Indulgences to all them, that would take Armes against him, by a Letter to the Pope; required him to call in his *Epigrammes* againe: And as a great learned man of this time calls *Paulus* the fifts Excommunication against the Venetians, *Dirum Carmen*: And as *Bellarmine* sayes of *Prudentius*, when he appoints certain *Holydayes* in Hell, *Paenarum celebres sub styge feriae,* That he did but play *More poetico*: So all discourse of Purgatorie seemes to me to bee but the *Mythologie* of the Romane Church, and a morall application of pious and useful fables.

_{Historia & alia impressa. ante Alcoran. fo.99}

_{Casabonus. prefatio de liber. Eccl. De purgato. l.2. c.18. §. Ad quintum. Hymno de nova lumine pasch. Sabba.}

2 To which opinion *Canus* expresses himselfe to have an inclination, when he sayes, *That men otherwise very grave, have gathered up*

_{L.11. c.6}

Margin 2. 99 *Ed.*: 89. L-1, C-1 **4.** that *Ed.*: rhat. L-1, C-1, MCG, C-2, C-3 **5.** before. *Ed.*: before:. L-1, C-1 **Margin 7.** Et tamen *Ed.*: Quinto. L-1, C-1 **Margin 22.** De purgato . . . . Sabba.] *note misplaced* . L-1, MCG, L³⁰, C⁵-1, SP, O¹⁴ **Margin 28.** 11. *Ed.*: II. L-1, C-1

rumours, and transmitted them to posterity, either too indulgent to themselves, or to the people: and that Noble Authors have beene content to thinke, that that was the true law of History, to write those things which the common people thought to be true: And this censure he forbears not
5 to lay upon *Gregory*, and *Bede*, by which two, so many fabulous things were convaied to posterity. To which ingenuity in *Canus*, *Lypsius his Champion* says, *That he preferres Gregory and Bede before Canus, for opinion and judgement*: But in this, onely their discretion, and an abstinence from a slippery and inconsiderate credulitie is in question: and
10 even in matter of judgement, in as good judgement as this Authour hath, *Canus* will justly enough in that Church have a good roome. And if this Authour, as hee pretends in that place, accept none of these fables, but *such as the authoritie and judgement of the Church hath approved*, either many of the Stories must loose their credit, or els the Popes that
15 approved them.

   3 Who have beene wisely and providently most liberall, and carefull to affoord most of that sustentation of Approving, to those things that were of themselves most weake and indeffensible: for so S. *Brigids* Revelations are not onely approved by *Boniface* the ninth, but confirmed by
20 *Martin* the fift: Both which having concurred to her canonization, one reason why it was done, on her part, is, *because at her marriage, being at thirteene yeares of age, and her husband eighteene, she vowed one yeares continency*; and the reason on the Popes part was: *That there might some goodnesse proceed out of the North*, for she was of Swethland.
25 According to which superstition, in their Mysterious ceremonies, when the *Gospell* is song, all other parts being done towards the East, hee must turne to the *North*, from whence all evill is derived, and where the Divels dwell.

   But for all their barbarous and prophane despite and contumelies,
30 which they impute (not to the Divell) but to Princes, and all sorte of people beyond their Hilles, their Stories are full of the memorie of Benefites which that Sea hath received from Northern Princes, and *Binius* confesses, that the remote and *Northerne*, people, did so much honour the *Romane* Church, *that whomsoever they heard to sit in that Chaire,*
35 *and to be Pope, though but in name, without any discussion of his en-*

Palestrita Honoris. Anastas. Cochelet. fo.285

Paleotus. de Syndone, par.1. Ep. lectori
Revel. Brigid. Bull Canone. Bonif. 9

Par. Crassus. de cerem. Epis. & Cardin. l.1. c.39

To.3. par.2. fo.1052.B

32. that Sea *errata*: Sea. L-1, C-1   **34.** *heard errata*: heaved. L-1, C-1

trance, they reverenced him as S. Peter himselfe, which (sayes he) *is a wonderfull thing to be spoken.* Which imputation since *Binius* layes upon Northerne Catholiques, they are fairely warned to bee more circumspect in their obsequiousnesse to that Church, without discussing the persons, and the matter which is commaunded them.

<small>Epist. Ruthalo. Reg. Secret. ante Dial. Luciani</small>

4 But to returne to this *Comique-Tragicall* doctrine of *Purgatory*, if *Canus* weigh nothing with them: Sir *Thomas Moore,* of whose firmenesse to the integrity of the Romane faith, that Church neede not be ashamed, intimates as much, when he sayes, *That hee therefore undertooke to translate Lucianus Dialogue Philopseudes, to deliver the world from superstition, which was crept in under Religion: For* (sayes he) *superstitious lies have beene tolde with so much authority, that a Cosoner was able to persuade S. Augustine, thogh a grave man, & a vehement enemy of lies, that a tale which Lucian had before derided in this Dialogue, was then newly done in his dayes. Some therefore thinke* (sayes he) *that they have made Christ beholden to them for ever, if they invent a fable of some Saint, or some Tragedie of hell, to make an olde woman weepe or tremble. So that scarce the life of any Martyr or virgine hath escaped their lies, which makes me suspect, that a great part of those fables, hath beene inserted by Heretiques, by mingling therof to withdraw the credite due to Christian Histories.*

<small>[a]Vita eius. fo.17 & 24 & 57
[b]Fo.33
[c]Fo.383</small>

5 And in our dayes, *Philip Nerius* the Institutor of the last *Order* amongst them, who was so familiar in heaven, whilst hee lived upon earth, that [a]*he was faine to intreat God to depart further from him, And* [b]*to draw back his minde from heavenly matters, and turne them upon earthly, before he was able to say Masse, And* [c]*could heare the Musique and Symphonie of the Angels, And could distinguish any vertue, or any vice, by his smelling,* This man I say was ever an enemie to these

<small>Fo.107</small>

Apparitions: and used to say, *That God would not take it ill, not to be beleeved, though he should truly appeare to us in any shape.* And to a Scholler that tolde him that our *Lady* appeared to him in the night, he

<small>Fo.108
Fo.229</small>

said, *next time she comes, spit in her face, which he did, and found it to be the divell.* Nor did hee easily beleeve possessions, but referred it commonly to the indispositions of the body: and suspecting justly the

---

6. *Comique-Tragicall*] Comique Tragicall. L-1 **11–12.** *superstitious*] superstiiious. L-1, O⁵

same diffidence in others, which he found in himselfe, hee prayed to God, *that he would worke no miracles by him.*   Fo.488

    6   So that not onely for feare of illusions, and mistaking bad spirits for good, (for that, their greatest Authors which have writ of that sub-
5 ject, even in these cleare & curious times, are still confident, that *An evill spirit, what shape so ever hee appeare in, may be knowne by his feete or hands, And that he is ever notoriously deformed either by a Taile, or by Hornes, And that hee will vanish, if one use him, as Friar Ruffin did,* who when the divell appeared to him ordinarily in the forme of Christ
10 crucified, by S. Francis his counsaile, said to him: *Open thy mouth, & implebo stercore,* and thereupon was delivered from that apparition. And some of their saddest Divines, have eased them thus much in any such perplexitie, that *to worship the divell himselfe in such a forme, with opinion that it were God, is not Idolatry,*) not onely for these in-
15 conveniences, but even for a generall infamy and suspition, that these apparitions which begot *Purgatorie* have in them, the more moderate sort of *Catholiques* have declined from any great approving of them.

    7   Yea *Serarius,* though of that order that hath lost all ingenuity, confesses from *Baronius* and *Villa Vincentius,* that in these legends, in
20 their Histories there are vaine and vitious relations, and that the pictures of those Saints, are but Symbolicall. And *Sedulius* acknowledges, that, *that storie in the booke of Conformities, that S. Francis was seene to goe out of the wound in Christs side with a banner, and a great Armie, is but figurative.* Of which, says he, *there are many so highly mysterious,*
25 *that it is not fit to discover and explicate them to the wicked.* So that these *Mirabilarii & Mythologistes* of that Church, wil solemnly reserve these their *Arcana Ecclesiae* to themselves, and shall without any envie from us.

    8   And yet I denie not, but that in sober antiquitie, and in the gravest
30 Fathers, there are some impressions, which occasioned this error, of purifying soules after this life, As *Bellarmine* says truly, *that for the most part, lies have their foundation upon some truth*; For it was very long in the Church of God, before the state of the soule after our death, was cleare, and constant and uniforme: the Fathers being divided in their

Margin notes:
Binsfeldius. de Confes. Sagar. fo.67 & 68
Menghi. fust. Daemo. c.8
Ibidem

Vasques. de Adorati.

Litan. l.2. ca.20. n.3
Ibid. n.4
Sedul. Apol. pro libro. Confor. l.1. c.20. n.7

De Pont. l.4. c.8. §. Quia

---

4. for that *Ed.*: for for that. L-1, C-1   **Margin 18.** ca.20 *Ed.*: ca.2. L-1, C-1   **Margin 21.** Sedul. . . . 7 *Ed.*: *note misplaced* . L-1, C-1

opinions, whether our soules enjoyed perfect happinesse presently, or expected and attended it till the generall judgement. And the phrase and language, in which sometimes they spoke of the last consummation of our happinesse, in the re-union of the body and soule, being obscure, and various, gave occasion of doubting, that they reserved and adjourn'd all our happinesse till that time. And that which they meant of that perfect and consummate happinesse, not to bee enjoyed till then, hath beene mis-understood, or detorted to the soule alone. And by such irresolution in some, and perplexity in collating their opinions, and misapplying their words, have been imprinted indelible characters of *Purgatorie*, and of prayer for the dead, of whose condition in the next worlde, they were not throughly assured.

9 If any of the Fathers have strayed farther then so, to speak doubtfully of some such thing as *Purgatorie*: Wee will not say, as you doe, [a]*Let us excuse it, or extenuate it, or denie it by some devise, or faine some other convenient sense, when it is opposed in Disputation.* Nor dare we obtrude a contrarie exposition, as you doe, when you make *Pope Telesphorus* instituting the *Quinquagesima* for the Clergy, by his worde *Statuimus*, to meane *Abrogamus*; Or when Pope *Innocent* writes to *Decentius* a Bishop, *that it is not reade, that in all Italie, France, Spaine, Affrique, and the Ilands, there was Alius Apostolus praeter Petrum*, to make him meane by *Alius Contrarius*; which the *glosse* upon the *glosse* in the Margine mis-likes, because no *Apostle* was contrarie to *Peter*, and therefore makes the Pope to meane; *that there was no other Apostle in those places, then Peter, or such as he sent.* We dare not correct so boldly as to make *Bertram*, who for 800. yeares together had said *Visibiliter*, now to say *Invisibiliter*. Wee dare not hope to scape with such a small insertion, as *Non*, which you have intruded to the destruction of *Didacus Stellaes* sense, in his *Commentarie* uppon Saint *Luke*, and in *Eucherius* his *Commentarie* uppon *Genesis*.

Wee dare not steale out that little particle, to alter the whole intention of him that hath it; as *Bellarmine* hath done, out of a sentence cited by *Gratian*, out of *Leo*, by which Mariage is no *Sacrament*, if, *Non*, be admitted. Wee will not be so unnaturall to the Fathers, as *Bellarmine* makes the Pope to be, when being pressed by *Nilus*, to followe in the question of the *Primacie*, the opinion of the Fathers, sayes, *that the Pope hath no Fathers in the Church, but that they are all his Sonnes.*

[a]Ind. Expurg. Belg. fo.12

Dist.4. statuimus. gloss.

Dist.12. quis nesciat glos.

Ind. Expur. Belg. fo.18

Index. Hisp. fo.66

Idem. fo.92

De Matrimo. l.1. c.5. §. ubi tamen 27. q.2. Cum societas
De pont. l.2. c.27. §. respondeo istas

CHAPTER THREE

Nor can wee exceede *Bellarmine* in dis-esteeming the Fathers, who hath called in question some bookes of almost everie one of them, as *Clement, Anicetus, Cyprian, Tertullian, Ambrose, Augustine, Hierome, Damasus, Damascen, Basil, Justine, Nyssene, Honorius, Eusebius, Chrysostome* and others.

And when *Damascene* cites out of *Palladius, That a dead scull beeing asked, whether our Prayers did them any good in hell, aunswered, that it brought them some ease and relaxation,* Bellarmine sayes, *This is false, and Apocryphall, and that there is no such thing in Paladius*: So ill a Patrone is hee, of *Damascenes* credite heerein. Nor doth hee onely indefinitely say of the Fathers, *That it is evident that some of the chiefest of them have grievously erred*, but as of *Tertullian*, who imputes Montanisme to Pope *Zephirine*, hee sayes, *There is no faith at all to be given to him*, And in another place somewhat more sharply; *Wee doe not reckon* Tertullian *amongst the Catholiques*, So doth he to very many of the other Fathers, boldly impute such errours, as would vitiate any Author now to have but observed them, and for touching whereof the *Centuriators* are by him accounted prophane and blasphemous. So also doth *Medina* say, That *Hierome, Ambrose, Augustine, Sedulius, Primasius, Chrysostome, Theodoret, Oecumenius, Theophilact*, and others, were of the same opinion as *Aerius* was, and the *Waldenses*, and *Wickliffe*.

10 But as *Gratian* preferred *Hierome* before a *Councell*, because hee had *Scripture* on his side, And as your *Expurgatorie Index* (which I cite so often, because no booke of equall authoritie, doth shew so well your corrupt doctrine, that is, what you cannot endure to heare, and your indirect practise, to make Authors speake your words) addes to one Author in the Margine, *Wee must give no credit to these words of Eusebius*, and after; *This opinion of Justin, and of Epiphanius, is not true*: So, if for the defence of *Purgatorie*, in the full sense of the *Trent Councell*, you obtrude any Father (which yet I professe that I have never seene) if that Father be destitute of the support of Scripture, you must allow us, some of that libertie which you take, since we are more modest in the use thereof then you are.

Margins:
De Purgat. l.2. c.18. §. preterea & §. Ad quartum

De verbo Dei. l.3. c.10. §. dices

De Pont. l.4. c.8. §. respondeo
De penitent. l.1. c.1. §. igitur

De Sacro. homin. Orig. & contin. l.1. ca.5

36. q.2. placuit
Ind. Hispa. fo.146

Fo.147

Margin 11. dices *Ed*.: dicens. L-1, C-1 **17.** now *errata*: not. L-1, C-1

11   For we need not (even by your frequent examples,) binde our selves to that servility, which your *Azorius* subjects himselfe unto: who disputing of the immolation of *Jepthes* daughter, confessing, *That it is not evident, that she was killed, nor likely; nor that she could be comprehended in that vow, any more then any uncleane thing which might have met him, and That the contrarie is more Analogall to the other places of Scripture, and that the Rabbines, Lyra, and some other Catholiques, denie her death, yet*, sayes he, *because we are bound* (that is, by the oath of the Trent Councell) *to expound Scriptures according to the sense of the Fathers, I thinke we ought to adhere to the opinion that she was slaine. But if the sense of the Fathers did not stand in my way, to confesse the truth, I should approve the other opinion, because that delivers so great a person as Jephthe was, both from rashnesse and foolishnesse in making the vow, and from impietie and cruelty in keeping it.*

12   This bondage and yoake we need not cast upon our selves, but may lawfully take *Chrysostomes* libertie, (since our cause is better then his, for hee dis-approved all Oathes) *Never produce to me*, sayes that Father, *this Saint or this chaste man, or this milde man, or this Priest; for if you tell mee of Peter, and Paul, or of an Angell from Heaven, you shall not thereby terrifie me with the dignitie of the persons.*

13   The Fathers which must governe in these points, must not be the Fathers of the Societie; but they must be *Patres Patrati*; Fathers which have Fathers; that is, whose words are propagated from the Apostles. Of which sort of Fathers, in my poore reading, I never found any that consented with the Doctrine of *Purgatorie* now established.

14   In which, that which we principally complaine of at this time, is, that it incites to this false martyrdome. Not but that they confesse, that there are also some other wayes besides martyrdome to escape *Purgatorie*; else how got *Lypsius* so soone to heaven? for as soone as his Champian *Cochelet* calls him, *Lypsius* aunswers, *Wee that are receaved into heaven, doe not despise our fellowes*: And that powerfull Indulgence (which, though Saint *Francis* obtained immediately from *Christ*, yet *Christ* sent him to aske it againe, at the Popes hands, because, sayes

---

Margin notes:
Moral. Instit. par.1. l.xi, c.14. §. Secundo quaeritur
Ad Populum Antiochum. Ho.4. To.5. fo.209
Palestrita Honoris. fo.1
Sedulius. Apolo. contr. Alcora. l.1. c.16. n.4 & 6

---

14. *and from Ed.*: aud from. L-1, C-1   **Margin 17.** Ad Populum Antiochum. Ho.4 *Ed.*: De militia spirituali Ho.4. C-1, L-1

Sedulius, hee would not derogate from the power, which he had delivered to his Vicar) delivers as many *as doe but come to a certaine place, from all sinne, and danger of Purgatorie. All which die in that Order, are saved; yea, All which love that Order hartily, how great a sinner soever*   L.2. c.9. n.1

L.2. c.11. n.4
5 *he be, shall have mercie. And yearely on his birthday, all which are in*   L.1. c.19. n.3
purgatory, especially of his Order, flie up to heaven. And hee himselfe carried above 1000. *away with him from thence, when he went.* At one   Ibidem
Masse, at the Commemoration of the Dead, *a Friar saw soules flie from*   L.3. c.21. n.4
Purgatorie as thicke as sparks from a furnace: and this Masse he cele-
10 brated every day, and so did infinite others. If then that Friar made a   Ibid. n.7
true *relation* of the state of *Purgatorie* in his time, *That of* 5000 *which died in the world since his comming thether, there came but three to that place*, there is no great use of heaping so much treasure, for that imployment, since by these computations, neither the Number can bee
15 great, nor the stay long.

15   And if the authoritie of this *Sedulius* seeme light, (yet his booke   In fine libri
is dignified with this Approbation, *That the impudency of Heretiques, may bee beat backe, with most firme arguments, and with most cleare reasons*) *Soto* might weigh more; who considering the intensnes of the   4. Sent. dist. 19. q.3. ar.2
20 fire of Purgatory, thinkes none shall remaine there above tenne yeares.
But for all this *Bellarmine* says, *That by most certaine apparitions it is*   De purgat. l.2. c.9. §. Preterea
evident, that some soules already there, shall remaine there till the day of judgement: And though hee make an impertinent doubt, *Whether*   De Indulg. l.2. c.2. §. Sed primum
ever any Popes have graunted Indulgences for many thousand yeares,
25 yet in another place he assignes certain reasons, why conveniently the
Popes may do so; *because the penitentiall Canons inflict many yeares*   De Indulg. l.1. c.9. §. Responsio
punishment, for divers sinnes which many men commit often every day.

16   But of this the Popes are so liberal (though it is impossible they should keepe any just *Audit*, or account, since they neither know what
30 they receive, nor what they lay out) that they will put in 1000. yeares
more rather then remit that six pence, which you must paye, not for
the pardon, but for the paper. And therefore *Martin* 5. had a just and   Turselinus Iesuit. Histor. Lauret. l.1. ca.22

16. (yet *Ed*.: yet. L-1, C-1   **Margin 23.** De . . . . primum *Ed*.: *note misplaced*. L-1, C-1   **Margin 26.** De . . . . Responsio *Ed*.: De . . . . Respontio *note misplaced*. L-1, C-1   **28.** 16 But *new paragraph Ed*.: 16 *missing*, But *run-on*. L-1, C-1   **29.** account, *Ed*.: account. C-1, L-1   **Margin 32.** Lauret. *Ed*.: laurel.. C-1, L-1

proportionall respect to the nature of this ware, when he appointed a yearly *Faire*, and yearely *Indulgence*, both of three moneths continuance, to be kept together at *Loretta*; and that the *Priests* and *Merchants* should open and shut up shoppes together.

17 But Martyrdome is of much more value, then these Indulgences, because it is infallible; for, some incapacity, and indisposition in the partie, may hinder the working of an Indulgence, but Martyredome cannot faile of the effect, to worke our deliverance, as appeared by that which we cited out of *Bellarmine* in the end of the last part of *Merite*. And therfore that doctrine, which teaches such a *Purgatory* as you speak of, incites to such a *Martyrdome*, as we speake of, & disapprove.

18 Having therefore proceeded thus farre, That the purest and acceptablest Sacrifice which we can offer to God, which is our lives, may be corrupted and envenomed with distastefull mixtures, and that even in the devotedst and safest times, it fell out, not seldome to be so; And that our corruption now is more obnoxious and apter to admitte and invite such poisonous ingredients, and temporall respects, then in those purer times, especially in the Romane Church, which misinflames the minde to false Martyredome, both by depressing and trampling uppon the dignity of Princes, and maintaining every litigious clause of *Ecclesiastique immunity* with our blood; And also by extolling our owne Merites, and encouraging us thereby, to trafique, though with losse of our life, for the benefit and advancement of the treasury of that Church; And lastly by the certainety, severenesse, and length of *Purgatory*, which are infallibly hereby avoided: the next thing which I present to your discourse, and consideration, is, That the Jesuites more then any other Order, claim to themselves a greater forwardnesse, and alacrity to this, and are therefore busier and apter to provoke severe lawes, against themselves, and to incurre the dangers thereof.

6. infallible; *Ed*.: infallible. L-1, C-1

Chap. IIII.

That in the Romane Church the Jesuites exceed all others, in their Constitutions and practise, in all those points, which beget or cherish this corrupt desire of false-Martyrdome.

1   Till the *Jesuites* have a Pope of their owne, it will be (I hope) no Heresie, to doubt, or call in question their sanctity: they may be content yet to afford us (since our cause is safer) the same excuse which is allowed for *Origen, Chrysostome, Hierome,* and *Cassianus,* even for maintaining a lawfulnesse in lying, *That the Church had not then determined the contrary.* They may favour our weakenesse with the same helpe, which they apply to a Pope himselfe, *That it was then lawfull, without danger of Heresie, for him to beleeve in earnest, that our soules should not see God, till the resurrection, because there was no Definition of the Church in that point.*

_{Observationes in Cassianum. fo.739. Ex Collat.17 Bell. de Pont. l.4. c.14. §. Respondeo De Ioan.22}

Their Charity may relieve us with the same Indulgence, which they afford to *Senensis,* who rejects some part of the Canonicall Scripture, after the determination of the *Trent Councel, Because he did not reach and attaine to the force of that Canon,* sayes *Gretzer,* who allowes him all these escapes, *That he did it either by negligence, inconsideration, a foreconceiv'd persuasion, or some other cause,* which is large enough.

_{Gretzer. Defens. Bellar. To.1. fo.362. §. Nam quod}

2   But if ever a Jesuite come to be the Church, that is, the Pope, we shall soone be precluded by the Churches Definitions. And as now to doubt whether the Pope without a Councell, may teach an Heresie, is *Haeresis proxima,* and so is *Semi-haeretica,* when a *Jesuite* is Pope, it will be *Hyper-haeretica,* and *Sesqui-haeretica*: for we have beene already taught, that something may be more then heresie, when by a new *Decretall of Paul the fourth,* they say, *That any great person falling into Heresie or Schisme, shall for the first offence be esteemed relapsed, and be in the same desperate state, as if he had formerly juridically abjurd*

_{Bell. de Pont. l.4. c.2. §. Ex his}

_{In septimo. l.5. Tit.3. c.9}

Margin 8. Collat.17 *Ed.*: Collat.19.   C-1, L-1   **Margin 22.** l.4. c.2. *Ed.*: l.1. c.2.   L-1, C-1   **23.** *Haeresis proxima Ed.*: *Haeresi proximum.*   L-1, C-1   **23.** *Semi-haeretica Ed.*: *Semi-haereticum.*   L-1, C-1   **24.** *Hyper-haeretica Ed.*: *Hyper-haereticum.*   L-1, C-1   **24.** *Sesqui-haeretica Ed.*: *Sesqui-haereticum.*   L-1, C-1

the same heresie. At least, when a Jesuite comes to that Throne, as in this last volume of the Canon law, we have a new title presented, *De Cardinalibus*, which was in none of the rest, where they are call'd, *The principall members of the Church, constituted by the holy Ghost,* And the most noble part of the Popes body, And *the clearest lights, and most speciall children of the Church;* where, *to take any thing from them is called Sacrilege,* and to favour any which hath dis-favoured them, or hurt them, is made Treason, so without doubt the *Jesuites* will be as indulgent to their owne Order, and we shall have at the next croppe, when there is a new Harvest of ripe *Decretals,* a title, *De patribus Societatis Iesu.*

In septimo Tit.4
Ibid. ca.3
Ibid. c.2
Ibid. c.3

3   As at their first institution they were thus neere the Papacy, that the Order of the *Theatines,* of which *Paulus* the fourth (who was at that time Pope) was either the authour, or a principall man, desired to be united to them, by which meanes they might have compassed the Papacy in their Cradle, so have they of late made suspicious approaches thereunto, by admitting Cardinalshippes, and other Dignities.

Histor. Ordi. Jesuit. refut. a Gretzero. fo.45

4   Those of their Order, who heretofore refused offers of that Dignity (as you say *Laynez* did from *Paulus* the fourth, and *Borgia* from *Julius* the third) did it *Constantissimè*: and, I beleeve with such constancy in resistance, *Tolet* and *Bellarmine* might have prevailed. Hee which gives rules for the institution of Monkes, forbiddes not onely Bishopprickes, but all acquaintance with Bishoppes: *By all meanes* (saith hee) *let a Monke avoide women and Bishops, because both hinder Divine Contemplation*; which Rule when Jesuites broke, and came to live in secular and Ecclesiasticall Courts, they shewed that they were not stubborne and inexorable against these preferments.

Ribadeneira. de Scripto. Jesuit. fo.100 & fo.60

Cassianus. l.11. c.17

5   And if ever they attaine the Papacy, they have already laide good foundations for the entailing thereof upon their owne Family, by *Azorius* his disputation, what the authority of the Pope is in *designing a Successor*: for he delivers it, as the common opinion, *that the forme of electing the Pope being founded upon the Canons, it may at his pleasure be changed.* So that the Pope may establish the *Provincials of the Jesuites* to be the Electors.

Instit. Moral. To.2. l.4. c.5. §. Secundo

18. their *Ed.*: theit.   L-1, C-1   **19.** *Paulus Ed.*: Raulus.   L-1, C-1   **20.** beleeve *Ed.*: beleeeve.   L-1, C-1

And then descending to another question, *whether the Pope himselfe may designe his Successor*, hee says, *that the Canons against it cannot prejudice him, because he is above them, and that it is not forbid Iure Divino; and that for matter of fact, he beleeves S. Peter did chuse*
5 *Clement*: but least the Popes should have nothing to avert them from this course, before any Jesuite were Pope, and so worke an exclusion, he says, *It is not lawfull, Iure Naturae: that is*, says he, *because natural reason informes, that it were inconvenient for the Church*: And, *but for that inconvenience*, he says, *they might cast lots for the papacy*: But
10 this inconvenience depends upon such reasons, and circumstances, as are alterable, and when they cease, this law of nature ceases too.

    6 And though *Laynez* in the vacancy after *Paulus* the fourth, is said by you to have had twelve of the best voices for the Papacy, though he were out of the Colledge of Cardinals; And in one Conclave, *Bellarmine*
15 also is said, to have had some, yet if any Jesuite had voices enow, would his Superiour allow him the Religion of his vow, by which he ought to refuse it, or his naturall liberty, by which, any man that is chosen Pope may, if he will, refuse it?

    7 If it were once come to that, as you are content yet, to seeme
20 as modest as the *Carthusian*, who says, *that he beleeves it to be a singular blessing of God, that no Carthusian hath beene Pope*: you would make good hast, to reckon with the forwardest Orders, how many Popes you had had: And quickly in these accounts overgoe the Franciscans themselves, who reckon of their Order, not onely Popes and Martyres,
25 and such possible things, but are so precipitate and transported with this fury, that they reckon, how many of the *Apostles*, *Prophets*, and *Patriarches* they have had of their Order; So, as I thought, whilst I reade it, they would never have stopped, till they had tolde us, how many *Adams* and *Eves* had beene of their Order, and how many *Jesus*
30 *Christs* besides S. *Francis*: For I understand not by what other figure they use this anticipation, and call these aunicents Franciscans then that by which *Serarius* the Jesuit sayes *Herod* was a great Machiavellian: and *Gregorie de Valentia*, that *Plato* might learne the doctrine of Purgatory out of the booke of the Machabees, which was written after his death.

Margin 12. Ribadeneira *Ed*.: Ribadency. C-1, L-1 **Margin 16.** Cerem. *Ed*.: Cerem:. C-1, L-1 **17–18.** Pope . . . will, *Ed*.: Pope, . . . will. L-1, C-1 **Margin 20.** Biblioth *Ed*.: Biolioth. C-1, L-1

Margin notes:
- Ibid. §. Tertio
- Ibid. §. Exploratum
- Ribadeneira. ubi supra
- Cerem. Sacr. Cap. De elect. pont.
- Petrei. Biblioth. Carthusia. fo.304
- Sedulius. Apolog. cont. Alcora. l.2. c.11. §. Innocentius
- Serarius. Trihaeres. l.2. cap.24 Grego. de Valent. De purgat. c.8

8   But besides that the Jesuites decay in the hearts of Princes (which *Philip* the second of *Spaine* testified well, because though he had great use of their service, hee never did any thing for them) this also makes me doubt that they will never have Pope, because it is already reveil'd by *Christ* to S. *Francis*: that *Antichrist shall come out of the family of the Franciscans.*

9   This also encreases my suspicion, that they could never compasse, that which is much lesse then a Pope, which is a *Saint*, in their family. For *the Authority of the Pope is greater, then of a Saint*, sayes *Cassanaeus*: And in his Indulgences he doth as familiarly command Angels, as the yonger Prentizes, the *Exorcists*, do devils: To whom they use this language, when any spirit possesses a body, *I command Lucifer, and all the Furies in hell, to precipitate you into hell fire presently, indispensably and eternally, till the day of judgement: And I forbid the Aire to have any power to receive you.*

10   And though *Tortus* say, *That the time of the Canonizing of the founder of that Order is not yet pass'd*, and therefore hee may bee Canonized in good time (which is a poore comfort, since I never found any such limitation, nor that a Saint apparant, as *Ignatius* is, may be superannated, and grow too old to bee Canoniz'd) yet since those two great Princes, *Philip* the second of *Spaine*, and *Henry* the fourth of *France*, either out of devotion to the Order, or for their owne ends, have both pretended the solicitation of *Ignatius* his canonizing to belong to them, and both affected the honour of procuring it, the pursuite and effecting thereof hath beene intermitted and retarded. And howsoever for *Ignatius* and for *Xaverius*, who was also a *Navarrois* as well as *Ignatius*, it might please those Princes, for respect to one another to forbeare any solicitation in their behalfes, yet the King of Spaine had very many subjects in that Order, to whom no other Prince pretended any such precontract or interest: and yet he procur'd the canonization of *D'Alcala a Franciscane*, and *Pennafort a Jacobin*, and neglected the *Jesuites*. And though the present Pope *Paulus* the fift, have beene much solicited for the Canonizing of *Gonzaga* the Jesuite by the Princes of that Family (the memory of his exempler life being yet fresh, and his worthinesse certified (as the custome is in preparing Canonization) by Cardinals which had

Margins:
Pierre Mathieu. Histoire de France. l.1. Narrat.4

Sedulius. Apol. l.2. c.12. n.8

Catalog. Glor. par.4. Consid.7

Menghi. Flagell. Daemon. fo.9 Ide. fol.105

Mat. Tortus. sopra la Lettera di Palmieri Romito. Raccolta. fol.126

Pierre Mathieu. Histoire de Fran. l.1. Nar.4

Ceparius. de Vita Gonzag. Epist. Dedic.

Margin 16. sopra *Ed.*: supra.   L-1, C-1

CHAPTER FOUR 105

commission to search therinto) yet he hath allowed him no other title
then *Beatus*: which might have beene given him without that Rescript
of the Pope, as *Ignatius* and many other have it: since, as *Serarius*   Litaneut. l.2. q.7
sayes, *Custome gives that Title to those, of whose salvation there is a*
5 *strong opinion, and yet are not adorned with the publique testimony of*
the Church.

    11 Nor doe I perceive that they are in any great forwardnesse, to
get a *Saint*, since in canonizings after the consideration of the truth
of the miracles, they fall in the Consistory to another consideration,
10 of the sufficiency of them. And besides that, your own *Acosta* makes   De procurand.
us doubt of the truth of those miracles, which are related, because he   Indo. Salut. l.2.
spends a Chapter in giving reasons, why in our age, in preaching the   c.9
Gospell in the *Indies*, there is not that strength of miracles, which was
in the primitive Church, since, as he says there, *It would prevaile very*
15 *much, if it might be*, those which are said to be done by you, are for
the most part so poore and beggerly, and silly things in respect of the
Franciscans, as betweene yours and theirs there is as much difference,
as betweene Jugling and Conjuring.

    12 Methinks you should offer no more to play at that game, af-
20 ter you have beleeved (as I hope you doe, since so fresh, and so well
approoved an author as *Sedulius* gives new life to these miracles) That   Sedul. Apol. l.3.
S. *Anthony when the heretiques refused to heare him preach, went to the*   c.13. nu.8
Sea side, called the fish, which came of all sorts, stayde in peace, put
their heads above water to hearken, and at the end of the Sermon, some
25 *spoke, and some did but bow their heads, and so the Heretiques were*
converted: or that Frier *Andrew* to correct his appetite of eating birds,   Idem. l.3. c.28.
at the Table, *by the signe of the Crosse, commanded them to flye away,*   nu.30
though they were rosted.

    13 And how much more luxuriant of Miracles would their Historie
30 be, if they had not commanded Friar *Conrade* to doe no more Miracles   Id. l.3. c.24.
after his death, because he was buried out of their Colledge: And if Saint   n.25.26.27
Francis had not enjoin'd Friar *Peter*, upon his Grave, *Per sanctam*
obedientiam, that he should doe no more Miracles, *because they were*
thereby disquieted with concurse of people. Of which kinds there are
35 many Commaundements, which lessons their number of Miracles.

    14 And this *Philip Nerius*, founder of the last Order, fear'd in him-

selfe, and therefore hee told *Baronius*, that he had intreated God that he might doe no Miracles.

<small>Vita. Nerii. fol.488</small>

15 You can therefore in nothing equall that order of *Franciscanes*; for if you thinke to overtake them in number, you will be farre short. Saint *Francis* saw at the first Chapter or meeting, sixe thousand *Friers*, and eighteene thousand *Devils*, which *Ignatius* could never get neere, except hee made it out in *Devils*. For the whole number of his societie, doeth not much exceede ten thousand yet.

<small>Sedul. Apol. l.2. c.2. n.3</small>

<small>An. 1608. they were 10501. Ribad. Scrip. Iesuit. in fin.</small>

16 But that which is truly proper and peculiar to you, you doe earnestly and intensly, and you excell in it; which is, in kindling and blowing, begetting and nourishing jelousies in Princes, and contempt in Subjects, dissention in families, wrangling in Schooles, and mutinies in Armies; ruines of Noble houses, corruption of blood, confiscation of States, torturing of bodies, an anxious entangling and perplexing of consciences. And to facilitate your way to these effects, you are in your institution mixt and complexioned of all Elements, and you hange betweene Heaven and Earth, like *Meteors* of an ominous and incendiarie presaging. You pretend to forsake the world, and to looke all upward; But, saith *Cassianus*, *Such renunciation is threefold; Of all temporall fortunes, and of our maners and conditions, and of our minds from all present things*. But all your labour is to understand the present state of Kingdomes, and where any overture is given for the Popes advantage, and where any interposition or hinderance is interjected against his purposes. And therefore that saying of Saint *Basil* to a *Senatour*, that seem'd to renounce the world, and yet retain'd part of his state, *Thou hast spoiled a Senatour, and hast not made a Monke*, belongs almost to all of this Order. For you are but as *Eunuches*; you have lost your apprehension and capacitie of worldly Estates, yet the lust, and itche, and concupiscence, to be conversant therein, remaines with you still.

<small>Cassian. l.7. c.19</small>

17 For this purpose you have care in admissions, *That none be received whose Parents bee poore*, (which your *Examiner* hath in charge) least that should divert them from the integritie of this service. For this purpose it is, *That the Superiour himselfe cannot dispence to admit any deformed person*, because you will have men sociable, acceptable, and agreeable to companie. For this purpose *your Superiours and Rectors*

<small>Iesuitar. Regula. Commu. Cap. Examinator</small>

<small>Regulae Provincial. 36</small>

<small>Cap. de formula scribendi</small>

Margin 7. 10501 *Ed.*: 10581. C-1, L-1 **Margin 33.** 36 *Ed.*: 56. C-1, L-1

CHAPTER FOUR

must write every weeke to the Provinciall, not onely of their owne state, but of all things done amongst strangers, by the service of this societie. For this purpose *you must have a Proctor generall at Rome, who must buy and studie all the Rules of that Chancerie, and all the Breves, and* 5 *Buls, which the Popes send forth.* And to this purpose was that attempt of the Jesuite, who (if a Catholicke Historiographer relate truely) published at *Rome, That Confession by letters was Sacramentall and effectuall.* Into which opinion though [a]some before had strayed, yet it had received no such strength and authority as at that time, when it 10 was so hotly pursued, that *Clement* 8. was forced to oppose a direct Decree against it, and *to condemne it as false, rash, and scandalous at least.* For if this opinion had beene beleeved and authorized, the secrets of all states, and passages of all Courts, had had no other Register then the breasts of Jesuites; who are so wise Apothecaries of penances, and 15 have so plentifull shops of those druggs of Indulgencies, that all those Princes, to whom any of them had beene Confessor, would neither open their disease, nor seeke their physicke at any other place: when they might be delivered of the painefullest part of Confession, which is the personall shame of accusing ones selfe.

20   18 And that they may attend this service of *Intelligencers*: First, they have one Rule of State, which is, *That they let no stranger understand their Rules and Priviledges*, And their Superiours have the prerogative to interpret and extend, and limit the constitutions; whereas, for the Rule of the *Franciscans*, Christ himselfe was heard in the aire, 25 saying to S. *Francis, This Rule is mine, not thine, and I will have it observed, Ad literam, ad literam, sine glossa, sine glossa.*

   19 And then by one *Bull* they are enabled (for at their first institution they were not so) to *heare Confessions, and to change vowes*; And by another *Bull*, they have priviledge *to absolve from all censures, except* 30 *those of Bulla Caenae*. And by [a]another, they are licenced *to practise Physique*, which doth not onely give them access to Death-beds, which is one of their chiefest *Scenes*, but excludes all others, because they are competent for all offices. And I wonder that they have not procured a *Bull*, that they might be *Midwifes*.

Cap. procurator Gener.

Pier. Mathieu. Histoire de Fran. To.2. l.7. Nar.4
[a]Vide Soto. de teg. Secret. memb.3. q.4. Dub.4. & Zambran. Cas. Consci. cap.4. de poenit. Dub.2. Sect.5. ubi etiam est hoc Decretum Clem. 8. nu.31

Reg. Commu. 38

Sedul. Apolo. l.2. c.3. n.2

Bulla tertia. Gretzer. in Hasenm. fo.168
D'Avila. de Censur. par.2. ca.7. Disp.3. Dub.8
[a]Bulla 18. Gretzer. in Hassenm. fo.211

Margin 27. Hasenm. *Ed.*: Hateum.   L-1, C-1   **Margin 30a.** Hassenm. fo. *Ed.*: Hatteum l.fo..   C-1, L-1

20 To this purpose also of *spying*, [b]their constitution bindes them *to no ordinary penances*, nor disciplinary macerations of the bodie: yea, that which they are content to call *Indiscretam castigationem*, which others magnifie so much, is so much forbid amongst them, [c]*that they are bound to deliver it in confession, if ever they transgresse into it.* And the *Rector* is to provide, not onely against these *Mortifications*, but [d]against too much *Devotion, as Impediments which call them from their studies.* And the charge which is given to him who is president over their spirituall matters, is to see, [e]*That whilst they have too much desire of Devotion, they doe not impaire their strength*: and therefore that *Gonzaga* of whom it is often [f]said in his life, that *hee shortned his life with such discipline,* [g]*laying sharpe chips betweene his sheetes,* [h]*whipping himselfe with Iron chaines, and* [i]*putting spurres betweene his Dublet and his flesh*, before he came into the Rules of the *Jesuites*; wonne, and overcame his Father and Mother, to encline to his purpose of entring this Order, because they sawe, [k]*That this Order would be wholsome for his body, and not allow him such severity.*

21 For priviledges of *Addition*, they have by [l]one *Bull*; all the *immunities of the Mendicants*, which are very many and advantageous, because thereby they must be received, as they travell into any religious house: And by [a]another *Bull*, at one liberalitie, *the priviledges of all Orders, are extended to them.*

22 And for *Exemptions*, they are delivered by [b]one *Bull from keeping their houres in the Chappell*; and by [c]another *from attending at Procession*: and by [d]another *dispenced from fastes, and forbidden meates*: and by their [e]*Rule* bound *to no habite*: and by [f]another Bull, *licensed to read all bookes*; which is so great a libertie in that Church, that in the *Septims*, there is [g]a Decree of *Gregory* the thirteenth *forbidding even Arch-Bishops, and Kings, and all persons, but the Inquisitors, to read Hereticall bookes, uppon paine of Heresie.*

23 If therefore, as in their [h]*Constitutions* they call themselves, they be but *Cadavera*, they are either such corrupt and putrified carcasses as infect and envenome all places where they reside, or such Carcasses, as

[b]Iesuit. Constitut. spirit.4

[c]Reg.48

[d]Reg. Com. ca. Rector. reg.38

[e]Cap. prefect. Rer. spirit.

[f]Cepari. Iesuit. de vita Gonzag. fo.58 & saepe
[g]Fo.84 [h]Fo.83
[i]Fo.84

[k]Fo.154

[l]Bulla.13. Gretz. fo.195

[a]Bull.17. Gretz. fo.207

[b]Bull.15. fo.197
[c]Bull.19. f.213
[d]Bull.7. fo.186
[e]Regula. Provincial. 84
[f]Bull.16. fo.198
[g]In septimo. 1.5. Tit.4. c.6

[h]Constitut. spirit.36

Margin 7d. reg.38 *Ed.*: reg.8. C-1, L-1 **Margin 11f.** Cepari. *Ed.*: Cepari'. L-1, C-1 **Margin 24c.** f.213 *Ed.*: f.217. L-1, C-1 **Margin 26e.** Regula. Provincial *Ed.*: Regu[?]vincial. L-1, C-1

evill spirits have assumed to walk about in: and if they be (as they say there) but *Baculasenis*, This old man is the pope, whom they cannot put off, and they are such staves, as have swords sheathed in them, and such as wound and bruise, even the inwardest marow of Kingdomes.

24 For this purpose is that obedience to their Superiours, wherein *Ignatius* wils his Disciples to exceed (*Let* [i]*us, says he, suffer our selves to be exceeded by others, in fastings, and in watchings, and such; but let our marke be an abdication of the will, and judgement.*) And so he gives them good blinde Counsaile, for their beleefe, and for their actions: *As to beleeve what the Catholique faith teacheth, so be you carried with a blinde violence of obeying, whatsoever your Superiour commands.* And though their Superiour command nothing expresly, yet they are bound once in a weeke, to say one Masse, *to the Intention of the Generall*, though they know not what it is. And of this generall intention the Center, and Basis is, the advancement of that Sea, about which these planetary Monkes, have their course and revolutions.

[i]Epist. Ignatii ad fratr. in Lusita.

Reg. Commu. ca. Missa

25 Olde Monkes were used heretofore to be but *Coasters*, hovering about their owne *Cloister*; further then the Contemplation of Heaven, which was the *Bible*, and of the starres, which were the devout interpreters therof, guided them, they did not easily venter: except some storme of disputation or passion transported them: But the *Jesuites* in this later age have found the use of the *Compasse*; which is the Popes will, and now they have not the patience to be *Fishers of men*, but they are *Merchants of Kingdomes*, and *Pirates* both of spirituall and temporall treasure. But *the eyes of a foole, are in the corners of the world*, saith *Salomon*. And even the desire of going to the *Indies* (which is their best pretence) if we beleeve the life of *Nerius*, was corrected in him, by an apparition of S. *John the Evang.* who tolde him, *That Rome was his Indies, for there was matter enough for his instruction, and his example to worke upon.*

Pro. 17.24

Vita Phil. Nerii. fo.110

26 And of foure sorts into which they use to divide Monks, which are *Caenobites*, who keepe their Cloister, *Eremites* who adventure into a Solitude, *Sarabaits*, who by their workes keeping still their contract with the world, have dissembled with God, *per tonsuram*, and lastly, *Gy-*

Regula Benedict. c.1

---

2. whom *Ed.*: whon. L-1, C-1 **Margin 6i.** fratr. C[5]-2, O[14]: fratr. L-1, C-1, C-2, C[3], C[10], YK-1 **8.** judgement.)] judgement). C-1, L[30], C[3]

rovagi, who all their lives wander through divers Provinces, the *Jesuites* seeme guilty of transgressing in both the last wayes. For, besides the Pallaces, and abundant possessions, which they have as they are Corporations, Onely *They* of all sorts, *are not in their particular incapable of inheritances which devolve upon them, by their triple vow made before the Governour of that Convent, till they confirme it againe in a generall Chapter. Quod ita iudicatum*, (sayes a French Lawyer) *Mirabundus accepi.*

<small>Ren. Choppinus. de iure Coenobit. l.2. Tit.3. n.9</small>

27 The *Franciscane* Friar *Giles*, did so much abhorre all temporall provisions, that hee told *Saint Francis*, hee did not like the *Antes*, because *they tooke such paines to provide victuals for Winter*. And when a Friar told Saint *Francis*, that hee came, *A Cella Tuâ*, when he heard the word *Tuâ*, he would lie no more there. But the *Jesuites* have not so much devested themselves of *Proprietie*, but that they may have proprietie in temporall possession: Yea, they will have *Proprietie* in *Treason*; and will have proper and singular Plots of their owne, and not joine with your Priests, *Watson* and *Clarke*, in their Plot, nor bee Traitors in common with them.

<small>Seduli. Apolo. l.2. c.6. n.7</small>

<small>Ibid. n.14</small>

28 This is their arrand; and for this, like him, who imployes them, *They compasse the Earth, too and fro.* Nor are they more like the *Circuitores*, and *Circumcelliones*, a limme of the *Donatists*, in this their uncertaine running about, then in that other qualitie of theirs, to urge and importune, and force men to kill them, and if they could not extort this from others, then to kill themselves, and call all this Martyrdome. For onely of this vicious inclination of *Jesuits* to an imaginarie Martyrdome, I purpos'd to speake in this Chapter; but that being occasioned by the way, to deale with men of a various uncertaine Constitution and Nature, I have taken part of their fault, and as a *Physitian* comming to cure, sometimes receives some of the Patients infection, so speaking of their running and wandring, I have strayed somewhat from the directnesse, and strictnesse of my purpose.

<small>Job 2.2</small>

<small>Danaeus. in Aug. de Haeresib. c.69; Prateolus. verbo Circuitores; Alf. Castro. verbo Ecclesia. & Martyrium</small>

29 Therefore to pursue it now, they are so much more intemperate and importunate upon this *Pseudo-Martyrdome*, then any others; by how much they are more severe maintainers and encreasers of those

---

Margin 7. Coenobit. 1.2 *Ed.*: Coenobit. .2. C-1, L-1 **20–21.** *Circuitores Ed.*: *Circulatores.* C-1, L-1

Doctrins of the Roman Church, which we noted to beget this inclination. For when the spirit of God awaked certaine Reformers of his Catholicke Church, of which the Romane Church had long time beene the head, that is, the *Principall* and *most eminent*, and *exemplar member* (for I am ever loth, to seeme to abhorre, or abstaine from giving to that Church, any such Styles and Titles, as shee is pleas'd and delighted in, as long as by a pious interpretation thereof, her desire may thereby be satisfied in some measure, our Churches not injur'd nor prejudiced, and the free spirit of God, which blowes where it pleaseth, not tied nor imprison'd to any place, or person) at that time, I say, these servants of God, and of his Church, had no purpose to runne away from her, and leave her diseases to putrifie and fester within her bowels. Nor did they uncover her nakednesse, out of any petulancie of their owne, nor proclaime her filthinesse to defame or diminish her dignitie. But with the libertie of a Midwife, or Physician, or Confessor, they survey'd her secretest infirmities, they drew to the outward and visible parts, that is into consideration, her inwardest corruptions, and so out of that duetie, were enforced to looke into and bee conversant about her Ordures, and other foulenesses, and could not dissemble nor forbeare, earnest, and bitter informing her of her owne distemper and danger, which was a worke of more zeale and humilitie, then those childish obediences, which you so much extoll in your Disciples, of sweeping Cobwebs and washing dishes.

30   And they proceeded so wisely, and temperately, and blessedly herein, that in a short time many of her swellings were allay'd, and her indurations somewhat mollified, as appears by the Colloquies, and consultations in many places, for a moderate and manerly way of purging her corruptions. For certainely her diseases were not then so much in question or doubt, as whether it were for her honour, to be beholden to so meane Persons for health, as these beginners were: Or for her safetie to trust her selfe in such Physicians hands; for now divers secular Princes were come to give their assistance. And as some diseases produce so violent and desperate Symptomes, as the Physician must sometime neglect the maine originall Disease, and attend onely to cure the Accidents: So, though the Doctrine of *Purgatorie*, were at that time no member of the body: That is, no part of the Catholicke faith, but serv'd that body onely for Nailes to scrape and scratche together, Those spirituall Physi-

cians busied themselves much, to paire those Nailes which defaced the beautie and integritie of the whole body, and so to slacken that griping hold, which they had taken upon mens estates and Consciences, by the terrour of *Purgatorie*, and vertue of their *Indulgences*.

31 And as to both sides, there appear'd evidently in the Doctrine of *Merits*, as the *Schoolemen* (which then Govern'd in the Church, by reason of the discontinuance of *Councels*) had sauced and disguis'd it, many abominations, derogatorie to the Passion of our *Blessed Saviour*: So did they all confesse, in the Doctrine of *Purgatory* so many mixtures of conjecturall, incredible, impossible fables, as might have scandaliz'd and discredited any certaine trueth by their Addition. But when on the one side, the Reformers encouraged by this entrance, thought they might proceede further, and so offered to dissect and anatomize the whole Church, and thought to fill every veine, and restore and rectifie every Sprane and dislocation, and to take off every Mole, and paire away every Wemme, and to alter even the fashion of her clothes, so that all, both substance and ceremony came in question: And the Romane Church on the other side, foresaw her precipitation, that if they stop'd not at the toppe, they could not at the middle of the hill, thought it better not to beginne, then not to know where to end, and so mistaking the medicine to be worse then the disease, departed from further consultation, justified their corruptions, and by excommunications put away those servants, which had done them these offices, and whom now they call *Schismatiques* and *Heretiques*, for departing from that Church, which would affoord them, not onely no wages, but no other roome, then a fire.

32 And then, as all recidivations and relapses, are worse then the disease, upon this relapse, came the Councell of *Trent*, which did cover and palliate some of these ulcers, and promised the cure of the rest, though they never went about it yet; And then the *Jesuites*, who crye that all there is health and soundnesse, and that there is none any where else, yea that the Church was borne thus, and that she is as well, as she was in her Cradle, and that whatsoever she thinkes, or sayes, or does is by a divine power, inherent in her; as though there had beene sowed in her at first certaine seedes of *Iure Divino*, which now in our age, by the cultivating, and watering, and industry of the *Jesuites* must fructifie and produce in her, all these effects. For they will abate nothing; their

consciences are as tender and delicate, as the ground at *Coleyne*, where some of S. *Ursulaes* eleven thousand Virgines are buried, *which will cast up againe in the night, any that is enterred there, except shee were of that company, though it be a childe newly baptized*: So the *Jesuites* stomaches
5 cannot indure this, that the Popes should be great by Priviledges of Princes, or Canons of Councels: but all must be *Iure Divino*. So that that note, which the law casts upon some Advocates, will lie heavie upon the *Jesuites, They are too carefull of their cause, and therfore they are presum'd to invent falshood.*

Baron. Martyrolo. 21. Oct. ex Lindano

Par. de Puteo. De Syndic. c. de excess. Advocator. nu.15

10   33 For though it be hard for any man to goe further on the left hand, then the Councell of *Trent* hath done, in these two doctrines of *Merite* and *Purgatory*, and every Catholique be bound to that Councell, yet as in most other Doctrines, so in these also, *Pelargus* hath noted the *Jesuite* to have gone beyond others, and therefore more then others,
15 they incite, in these points, to a false Martyrdome.

Pelargus. de Novo Iesuitismo

   34 But as the late invention of Artillery and Gunpowder, though it have much horrour and affrightment in it, yet hath not done so much harme, as it threatned, because the fury and violence thereof, hath occasioned men to study more wayes of defence and avoidance, so that
20 wee see the warres devoure fewer men now, then before this invention came: so hath the impetuous rage and pertinacy of the Jesuits, in oppugning everie thing which they find not to be at Rome, encouraged other Churches to oppose strong defences against them, and superstition swallowes fewer men now, then before these new Engineers laboured
25 to promote and advance her: And as those instruments of battery which the aunciencts used in the warres, were more able to ruine and demolish, then any which are made out of this new invention, but were left off, and dis-accustomed only because they were not so maniable and tractable, and apt for transportation, as these are; So certainly the Arguments
30 and bookes of the Friars, and *Schoolemen* of the Romane Church, which is the *Arsenall* from whence the *Jesuites* provide and furnish themselves, have as much force against the truth, as the subtilties of the *Jesuites*,

9. *falshood. Ed.: falshood:.* L-1, C-1   **12.** *Purgatory Ed.: Purgatrry.* L-1, C-1, O², O¹⁴, SP, O-1, O-2, O⁵   **15.** *in Ed.:* tn. L-1, C-1, C-2, C-3, C-4   **22.** *Rome,* YK-2, C²-2: Rome. L-1, C-1, C³, C¹⁰, C¹⁶, YK-1, YK-3   **28.** *dis-accustomed* YK-2, C-2: dis accustomed. L-1, C-1, C-3, C-4, L-2, L³⁰, O-1, O-2, SP

but that these men are by their Rule and Constitutions, apter for conveyance and insinuation, then the dull cloisterall Monkes can be.

35   For there are divers poisons which cannot work, except they be ejaculated from the creature it selfe that possesseth it, and that his personall and present lively malignity concurre to it, and give it vigour; for which these *ubiquitary Monks* have the advantage of all others.

36   *Nimietates sunt aequalitates*, sayes *Cassianus*. And so, two extreamities, have made the *Schoolemen* and the *Jesuites* equally valiant: for the *Schoolemen* out of an ignorance of danger, having never come to hand-blowes, would venter upon any peece of service, and any employment, and pierce through and spye, even into Gods secret Cabinet of his *Essence*, and of his *Counsails*, as a fresh Souldier will goe with alacrity to any breach. And then because these sublime and airie meditations must have some body to inhere in, they used to incorporate their speculations of God, in the Pope; as it were to arrest and conserve them the better, being else too spirituall and transitorie. And so they have so much exemplified them, one in the other, that they have made them so like, and equall in their writings, as though they were but one.

37   And the *Jesuites* out of a desperate necessity must maintain their station, because if they yeeld one steppe, they will be the lesse able to stand in the next; but after they have confessed that the Church hath erred in one thing, thinking that will subject her in all, no place of Scripture is so abundantly and evidently pregnant, no reason or consequence so directly and necessarily deduced, and concluded, no History nor matter of fact so faithfully presented, and so certainly and religiously testified, but they will stand stubbornly, and desperately to oppugne and infirme it.

38   What wound so ever they receive in this battaile, they disguise and hide from their Disciples, by forbidding our bookes. And as *Ribadeneira* sayes of their Father *Ignatius*, *That he halted of the wound which he receaved at Pampelune, but so little, that the most curious could scarse discerne that he halted*, So by some evasions, or supplements, or concealings, they ever dissemble their maimes and deformities.

L.4. c.18

39   To which purpose they have one round and dispatching way, which is, not onely to neglect, but to bragge of all which we impute to them: for so one of them sayes, *That it is the greatest Argument of Innocence, to be accused by us: And that he cannot be guilty of error in*

Spongia. pro Jesuitis. cont. Equit. Polon. fo.20

CHAPTER FOUR 115

Religion, whom an Heretique condemnes. For, as it was part of the Oath of the *Grecians*, against *Xerxes*, that *those Temples which the barbarous Armie had demolished, they would not reedifie, that thereby there might bee a continuall testimonie remaining of the impiety,* So I thinke the
5 *Jesuites* flatter themselves with some such resolution, by leaving unanswered the books and arguments of so many reverent persons, which have spoken plentifully and prosperously, of these points of *Merit* and *Purgatorie*.

    40 But of their other Doctrine, by which more then others, they
10 provoke to this lavish, and contemptuous expence of life, which is, *The aviling of the dignitie of Princes*, there can never enough be said. For all other Orders may consist, and execute and performe all their vowes, without any injurie to Princes: They may be as poore as they will, till they come to that state, if they desire it, which *Nerius* begd of God, *That*
15 *he might lacke a pennie, and no body might give it him,* They may be as chaste, as that *Jesuite* which *Gretzer* says hee knew, *who being not able to scape from a woman which tempted him, and held him, anointed his owne face, retrimentis suis, that thereby she might abhor him,* They may be as obedient as *Cassianus* says the *Tabennentiotes* were, *who*
20 *durst not presume, without leave of their Superiour, Naturali necessitati satisfacere*; Or as that Friar *John,* who at his *Abbats commaund,* planted *a dry withered sticke, and twice a day, for a whole yeare, fetched water two miles of, to water it, sparing no festivall day, nor apprehending any impossibility in it*; Or as Saint *Francis* his Novice, *who at his bidding*
25 *set plants, with the head downward.* These things they may doe, and yet be good subjects. But the Supernumerary Vow of the *Jesuites*, by which they doe especially oblige themselves to the Popes will, doth in the nature, and Essence, and scope thereof, make them enemies to the dignitie of all Princes, because their *Soveraigntie* cannot consist, with
30 that temporall *Supremacie* which the *Jesuites* must maintaine, by the obligation of that vow, by which they are bound, with expence of their lives, to penetrate any Kingdome, and instill Sedition into their Disciples, and followers.

    41 How fast this infection works in them, as by many other Demon-
35 strations, so by this also it appeares evidently, that there are extant more

Margin notes:
Muretus. Variar. Lection. l.3. c.10
Vita eius. fo.491
Gretz. in Hasenmill. fo.118
De Institut. Renuntiant. l.4. c.10
Idem. l.4. c.24
Sedul. Apolo. l.2. c.5. n.5

Margin 14. 491 *Ed.*: 591. C-1, L-1

Authors of that one Order, that have written of Secular businesses, and of Jurisdiction of Princes, then of all the rest, since their beginning. For, their *Casuists*, which handle *Morall Divinitie*, and waigh and measure sinne (which for all that perplexitie and entangling, we may not condemne too hastily, since in purest Antiquitie there are lively impressions of such a custome in the Church, to examine with some curiositie the circumstances, by which sinnes were aggravated or diminished) doe not onely, abound in Number, especially of the *Spanish* Nation, but have filled their bookes with such questions as these, *How Princes have their jurisdiction, How they may become Tyrants, What is lawfull to a private man in such a case*, and of like seditious nature. So that they have abandoned the stale, and obsolete names, of *positive Divinity*, or *Controverted*, or *Schoole Divinitie*; and have reduced all to *Crowne Divinity*.

42   And yet they account the handling of these points, to bee but a dull and obvious learning in their Colledges, as though any man were able to resolve questions against Princes; for they have a Rule, *that they which are unapt for greater studies, shall study cases of conscience.*

43   So also of the *Immunitie of the Church*, out of which, if it be denied to be by the Indulgence of the Prince, issues and results presently the diminution of the Prince, they have written abundantly, and desperately. So have they of the *Institution of a Prince*; of which, one of them writing and presuming and taking it as vulgarlie knowne, that it is lawfull in some cases to kill a King, is carefull to provide, least when you goe about to kill him, by putting poison in his meat or drink, you make him, though ignorantly, kill himselfe. So have they also of Militarie institution many Authors; and of as many sciences as concurre to publique affaires.

44   And with such bookes as these they allure and catch ambitious wits; which having had a lower and darker breeding in schooles and universities, have some hunger of reading state learning, in any forme, much more, where they shall finde it more freely debated upon, then if they had had place at twentie Councell Tables, or Conspiracies. And as *Averroes* is saide to have killed *Avicen*, by anointing the booke which hee

---

Reg. provincial. 56

Mariana. de Rege. l.1. c.7

Binsfeld. de Confess. Sagarum. fo.216

20. diminution *Ed.*: dimunition. C-1, L-1   **Margin 33.** Confess. . . . fo. C-3, C⁵-2, YK-2, O¹⁴: Confess. . . . fo   C-1, L-1, C³, L-2;.   Confess . . . fo. C-4, O-2, O²

knew the other would read, with certaine poison: and as it is said, that   Pet. Galatin. de
whatsoever flew over the *Jewes Targum*, whilst the authour thereof was   verit. Christ. l.1.
compiling it, was scorched with the beames therof, so doe these bookes   c.3
of theirs envenome and catch hold of all such, as bring in themselves
5 anye desire to come within too neere a distance of them.

    45 And of all these kindes of bookes, without doubt we should have
had many more, but that, as the gatherer of all the writers of the *Carthu-*
sian Order, not daring to slippe and leave out the present Generall   Petrei. Bibliothe.
Bruno, and finding no books of his making, says, *That since he hath*   Carthus. fo.35
10 *an excellent wit, and singular learning, he could write many bookes if*
he had leisure, and in the meane time, hee tooke care that the missall
should be printed in a faire character and delicate paper: So the *Jesuites*,
since they have a vow to binde them to it, and a naturall disposition to
incline them, could write more bookes to this purpose, but that they are
15 continually exercised in disposing actuall plots: And yet in the meane
time they take care, that the Popes *Breves* be procur'd, promulged, con-
ceal'd, interpreted, or burnt, as the cause may be most benefited and
advanced.

    46 And I do not remember, that I have found in the Approbation of
20 any *Jesuits* booke, this clause which is so ordinary, in most of the workes
of other men, *Nihil fidei contrarium, aut bonis Moribus, aut Principibus*:
And yet they say, that in printing their bookes, *there is great caution and*   Spongia. contr.
diligence used, and that they passe the hands of men most intelligent, and   Equit. polon. f.78
of mature judgement: but, as it seems by this remarqueable omission,
25 no good subjects nor favourers of Princes.

    47 If they doe thus much when they are *Servi papae*, what will they
doe when they are *famuli*? which diffrence I learned out of the *Missal*;   Missal. Roma, ex
where a *Bishoppe* must pray, *una cum me indigno Servo tuo*; but the   Decret. Con. Trid.
Pope, *Famulo*: For he may well be said to be *in Ordinary* with God,   restitut.
30 since he is one *Ordinary* with him; for so sayes *Alvares*, *God and the*   Specul. utriusque
Pope have one Consistorie: and in an other place, *All cases reserved to*   Dignit. c.1. n.35
God, are reserved to his Vicar: so that by that Rule, what ever God   Idem. c.18. n.7
can do, in disposing the matters of this world, the Pope also can do:
for there he sayes, out of *Hostiensis*, that that direction, *Dic Ecclesiae*,
35 if the Pope sinne, who cannot be complain'd of, is ment, *Dic Deo, ut*

    1. [poi]son:] -son, *catchword quarto p.145.* L-1, C-1

convertat eum, aut Dic Ecclesiae Triumphanti, ut oret pro eo.

48 So when *Bellarmine* who had done sufficiently for the Pope, whilst he was but a *Servant*, that is an Ordinarie *Jesuite*, came to his familiarity, and housholde service, by being a *Cardinall* in the Consistorie, and so grew more sensible of the Papacy, being now himselfe, as they speake, *Papabilis*, he takes al new occasions, to extoll his Master, and his Throne and Sea: And having manie yeares neglected his owne defence, and answered such great men as opposed him, onely with such Proctors as *Gretzer* and *Eudaemo-Ioannes*, unprovoked he rises up in the *Venetian*, and in the *English* cause, to establish by new bookes, the new Article of *Temporall authority* in the Pope. And since that, as *Aeneas Sylvius*, retracted all which he had written before for the *Basil Councell*, when he came to be Pope: so *Bellarmine* when perchance hee would be Pope, hath made a new survay and Recognition of all his workes; in which, as though he had beene too moderate before, in al those places, which concerne this question, he hath expressed a supple and variable conscience, a deject slaverie to that Sea, and a venemous malignity against Princes; of which it seemes to me expedient to present a few examples.

<small>Binius. To.4. fo.512</small>

49 I allow not now, sayes *Bellarmine*, that which I said before, *That Infidell Princes may not be deprived by the Church, of that Jurisdiction which they have over Christians: for though Durandus doe probably teach so, against Saint Thomas, and I then followed his opinion, yet now the authority of S. Thomas prevailes more with me.* Yet he had seene and considered both their reasons before.

<small>De pont. l.5. c.7. §. probatur</small>

50 In another place he sayes, *Now I allow not that which I said before, that Paul appealed to Caesar, as to his Judge.* And after, *Whereas I said, that Popes used to be chosen by Emperours, the word Emperour, potest & forte debet deleri: For* (sayes he) *I followed Gratians Canons, which, as I learned since, are not approved.* And againe, *when I said That the Pope was subject to the Emperour, as to his temporall Lord, I meant De facto, not De iure*: and this course he holdes in that booke of Recognitions.

<small>De pont. l.2. c.29. §. secundo. De Clericis. l.1. c.16. §. postea</small>

<small>De Concil. l.1. c.13. §. Quarta</small>

51 And here we may conveniently conclude this Chapter, of the *Jesuites* speciall advancing all those doctrines, which incite to this Mar-

12. *Aeneas Ed.*: *AEneas.* L-1, C-1 **Margin 20.** pont. l.5. c.7 *Ed.*: pont. l.4. c.8. L-1, C-1

tyrdome, after we have produced some of their owne testimonies of their inordinate hunger thereunto, and of the causes for which they affect it.

52   One of their spirituall Constitutions is, *That every one of that Order must thinke that Christ spoke to him when he said, he that doth not hate his owne life, &c.* And so they make an obligatorie precept, to binde at all times, of that which was but a direction for our preparation and readinesse to suffer for his sake.   Constit.40

53   *Ribadeneira* names two *Jesuites* in the *Indies, which being sicke in bedde, when they might have escaped, came forth halfe naked, and voluntarily offring their throates, were slaine.* And hee sayes that *Simon Acosta* (one of the five brothers, who were all of this Order) *declared himselfe to bee a Jesuite, when he was not knowne, that he might be put to death.* And so *Aquaviva, being pursued, refused a horse, by which hee might have scaped, and chose rather to die, then ride.* And yet this was amongst Infidels, where the Harvest was great, and the worke-men few: which kind of intemperance hath beene formerly condemned out of their owne authors.   Catalog. Scrip. Iesuit. fo.190

Fo.196

54   But of this point it is enough to relate the wordes of him, who speakes in the person of all the *Jesuites*; who cals himselfe *Clarus Bonarscius*, but is unmask'd and disanagrammatiz'd by his fellow, who calls him, *Carolus Scribanius* he sayes, *That the Scaevolaes, the Catoes, the Porciaes, and the Cleopatraes, are nothing to the Jesuites: For they* (sayes he) *lacked courage, Ad multas mortes, And in a fewe yeares*, he sayes, *they have had three hundred Martyres*: Therefore he sayes, *that they of that Order doe violently teare out Martyrdome, rapiunt spontanea irruptione*; and, *Crederes Morbo adesos*: and for what causes do they this? *Least the rest of their life should be barren of merites, and passe away emptie of glorie*: and then hee passes to them who have died in *England*; and as in these men, this hunger of false-Martyrdome, goes ever together with blasphemy against Princes, there he heapes Eulogies upon *Campian*, and reproaches upon that sacred Prince, for treason to whom he perished, whom this wretch dares call *Anglicanam Lupam*, and after, *Saevientem Calvinianam lupam*: and after this he sayes, *That when they come to this Order, they bargain upon this condition, ut liceat prodigere animas, hostili ferro*. In which, I thinke, he relates to that Oath, which   Ribadeneir. Catal. Script. Jesuit.

Amphitheatrum Honoris. l.1. c.4. §. Primo Fo.41

Fo.44

Margin 3.   40 *Ed.:* 4.   C-1, L-1   **Margin 11.**   Fo.196 *Ed.: note misplaced.* C-1, L-1

they take in the Colledge at Rome, by a Constitution of the Pope; *that they shall returne into England, to preach the Catholique faith publiquely there*: which Oath *Navarrus* sayes *bindes them so strictly, that they are disabled to enter into any rule of stricter religion, though that were a further degree of perfection, but must necessarily returne into England*: Of which oath we will say no more, but onely repeat *Baronius* his *Panegyrique*, and incitatorie encouragement, speaking thereof: *The holy societie in her safe sheep-folds hath fatted you, as innocent lambes for this Martyrdome, and she sends you forth to triumphes, and advances you to Crownes. Be therefore couragious and valiant, you who have vowed and betrothed your blood by an Oath: for my part, I envie you, that are design'd and apparant martyres, and wish that my end may be like yours.* And what he assignes for one cause of this Martyrdome, to which he provokes them, and congratulates their interest therein, we declared out of his words before in the shutting up of the last Chapter, which was *Defence of Ecclesiastique immunity*; that is debasing, and diminishing of Princes.

And thus we have gone one steppe further: and to the former, which were, That the desire of Martyrdome might be vicious, & that, as the Roman authors observe in the first times, it had beene so; and, That by the Romane doctrine it must of necessity be so, we have added now, that the *Jesuites* more then any, inflame thereunto.

[margin: Baron. Martyrolog. Decemb.29]
[margin: Navar. De Regular. I]

Margin 3. Regular. I *Ed.*: Regular. Consil. I.   C-1, L-1

Chap. V

That the Missions of the Pope, under Obedience whereof they pretend that they come into this Kingdome, can be no warrant, since lawes established to the contrarie, to give them, or those which harbour them, the comfort of Martyrdome.

1   In the end of the second Chapter, I mentioned a Canon of the *Eliberitane Councell*; And as in that place it had this use and office, to shew that the intemperate and inopportune affectation of Martyrdome, needed a restraint in some, too aemulous thereof, by *Eulalias* Example, So may it very properly and needfully have a place here, because it showes the reasons, why certaine men were not receiv'd for Martyrs, by the Church.

2   And the Authoritie of this Councell is of great force, as well by reason of the puritie of the time, in which it was celebrated, which was about three hundred and five yeeres after Christ, and twentie yeeres before the *Nicene* Councell, as especially, in this point of Martyrdome, because it was held in continuing Persecution, and when the danger was imminent in those parts, in which the people needed direction and instruction: And also, because now there is no doubt of the genuine integritie of this Councell. For, though *Bellarmine* imputed some errours to it, as being too severe against such as had slipp'd in time of Persecution, and *Baronius* spoke sometime of it, *Somewhat freely and sharpely*, sayes *Binius*, yet after that, he changed his opinion, and hee, and *Binius*, have now redeem'd all the Canons of that Councell from any imputation.

    De Imagin. l.2. c.9

    Ann. 55. nu.19
    Ann. 305. nu.32

3   Of which Canons, this is the sixtieth: *That they which breake the Idols of the Gentiles, and are slaine by them, shall not be received into the number of Martyrs. Because, this is not written in the Gospell, nor found that it was ever done by the Apostles.* So that by the opinion of that Councell, that onely is a sufficient cause to intitle and interest a man in the Crowne of Martyrdome, *Which was found written in the*

---

5. 1 *Ed.: missing* . L-1, C-1   **8.** *Eulalias errata: Eulalines.* L-1, C-1
Margin 21. nu.19 *Ed.:* nu.119. L-1, C-1   **Margin 22.** nu.32 *Ed.:* nu.42. L-1, C-1

Gospell, or practised by the Apostles. And is there any thing found in either of them, which may be a precedent to this mission? *Christ appointed twelve,* whom hee might send to Preach; but what? *The Kingdome of God.* And assoone as *Saule* had an inward mission, the Text sayes, *Straightwayes he Preached even in the Synagogue.* But what? *Hee Preached Christ*; And what did hee Preach of him? *That he was the Sonne of God*; And *that it was hee that was ordain'd of God, a judge of quicke and dead:* And, as himselfe sayes, of his practise after, *We preach Christ crucified.* But this mission from *Rome*, is not to Preach *Christ,* but his *Vicar*: Not his kingdome of *Grace,* or *Glorie,* but his title to Temporall kingdomes: Not how hee shall judge quicke and dead at his second comming, but how his Vicar shall inquire, Examine, Syndicate, Sentence, Depose: yea, Murder Princes on earth: Not Christ crucified, languishing for us under Thorns, Nailes, Whippes & Speares, but his Vicar enthron'd, and wantonly groning under the waight of his Keyes, and Swords, and Crownes.

4 *Christ* said to those whom he sent, *What I tell you in darkenesse, that speake you in light, and what you heare in the eare, that Preach you on houses, and feare not them that kill the body.* And if no other thing were told you in darkenesse, and whisper'd into your ears, at your missions hither, then those which our Saviour deliver'd to them, you might be as confident in your publicke Preachings, and have as much comfort of Martyrdome, if you died for executing such a Commission. But what your instructions delivered in darkenesse, and told in your eares, are, appeares now enough, by *Inspection,* by *Confession,* by *Testimonie,* by *Practise,* by *Analogie of your doctrine,* and by *Baronius* words, *That you are sent hither to defend the immunities of the Church,* which delivers you from all subjection to the King, and from being Traitors whatsoever you attempt: as also to defend the *Catholicke* Faith, which first makes it heresie to depart from the subjection to Rome, and then makes it a forfeiture of all Jurisdiction to incurre that heresie. Except this be *written in the Gospell, or practised by the Apostles,* you cannot be Martyres for this.

Margin 2. Mar. 3.14 *Ed.*: Mat. 3.14. L-1, C-1   **Margin 5.** 9.20 *Ed.*: 9.12. L-1, C-1   **Margin 8.** I Cor. 1.23 *Ed.*: note misplaced. L-1, C-1   **Margin 17.** 10.27, 28 *Ed.*: 10.27. L-1, C-1

CHAPTER FIVE 123

 5 But to descend to reasons of a lower nature, of the law of Nations, and conveniency and decency; since all those which maintaine the *Spanish* Expeditions, and proceedings in the *Indies*, by the strength of the Popes *Donation*, concurre in this, *That into what place soever the Pope,* [5] *or any Princes may send Priests, they may also send Armies for the security of those Priests, and them whom they have reduced*: and since it is evident by all your Writers, that *the Pope hath more Jurisdiction over Christian Princes relapsed from Rome, then over Infidels*, might hee not for safe-guard of his *Apostles*, sende Fleetes and armies hither? and [10] is it not the common and received opinion, which *Maynardus* delivers, *that in all cases where the Pope may enjoine, or commaund any thing, he may lawfully proceede by way of warre, against any that hinder the execution thereof*. If then such armies and Fleets were sent to conduct you, and were resisted in their landing, or defeated in battell; had not [15] they as good title to Martyrdome as you? and may not the Pope as well Canonize the whole *Spanish* Fleete, which perished in 88. for your Catholique faith, and Ecclesiastique immunitie? since in many cases, as in the *Innocent children* (of whom *Hilary* says, that *they were exalted to eternity, by Martyrdome*) one may bee an implicite Martyre, though [20] he know not why he died, so he have no actuall reluctation against it.

 6 And it is very probable, that their title was better then yours, for this point of *sending*, because they were under the obedience of them which sent them: but for you, (not to dispute now whether the cause be enough for Martyrdome, or whether your obedience can give it that [25] forme, and life, and vigour) you are so farre from being sent, or from exercising any obedience in this act, that your first step, which is going out of the kingdome, is absolutely and evidently disobedience to your Prince, before you have any colour of having submitted your selfe to any other superiour; and then you enter into the *Colledge*, upon condition [30] that you may returne, and you take an *Oath* before hand that you will returne: So that you returne not hither in obedience of your *Superiour*, but in performance of your owne unjust, and indiscreete *Vowes*: both which, in all Vowes, are *Annulling or vitiating* circumstances. Neither dooth this Oath so farre binde you to returne, (though *Navarrus* say so) [35] but that one of the learnedst of the *Jesuites*, thinkes, *If that be forborne*,

margin notes:
Alf. Alvares. Spec. utri. Dig. c.31. n.1, 2, 3, & 12, 16, 17. & ca.41.12

Azor. Mor.. Just par.2. l.4. c.18 & par.1. l.8. ca.24

De privileg. Eccles. Ar.10. n.25

Commen. in Mat. 1. in fine

Azor. par.1. l.11. c.5. §. Animadvertum

Margin 7. Azor. *Ed.*: *note misplaced* . L-1, C-1

and some Order of Religion embraced in stead thereof, the oath is better performed.

7   And, if these lawes which take holde of you, when you returne hither, had been made betweene the time of your vowe, and your returning: and if they had beene made directly to that end, to interrupt and preclude the performance of this Vow, yet naturally they would worke the same effect upon this Vow of yours, and make it voide, because something was now interpos'd, which may justly, yea ought to change your purpose: For if that law had beene made before, your Vowe had beene unjust from the beginning; which is the case of as many of you, as have gone since the making of those prohibitory lawes. For *a law which forbidds upon paine of losse of goods, death, banishment, or such, bindes a man upon paine of mortall sinne*; and therfore no Vow can justifie the breach thereof.

<small>Sayr. Thesau. Cas. Consc. l.3. c.7. nu.25</small>

8   All this, if the lawes be just, is evident and without question, and how could it be evident to all those yong Schollers which went over, and made this vowe, that these lawes were unjust? What infallible assurance could they have of this, to excuse them of *disobedience* in going, or *indiscretion* in swearing?

9   Their owne men teach, that *the lawes of Princes are not therefore necessarily unjust and voide, because the Prince had an ill intention in making them*. As if the Prince propose and purpose particular gaine, by exacting the penalty of the law, or revenge upon certaine persons, by executing thereof; this makes not the law voide, so that it be profitable to the bodie of the Common-wealth: much lesse were our lawes in this case, subject to that frailty, and defeseablenesse, because they were made (to omit in this place the principall inducement, for the glorie of God, and preserving his *Gospell* in purity and integrity) in such necessities, as without such defence, the person of the Prince, and the civill and Ecclesiastique state, must have suffered daily, and dangerous fluctuations, and perils of shipwracke; which dangers continue upon us yet; and therefore the same physick must be continued.

<small>Alf. Castro. de Potest. Legis. l.1. c.5. Docum.1</small>

10   For *Lawyers* teach us, that the word *Potest, doth often signifie Actum*: And what the Pope *may* do, their bookes threaten in every leafe:

<small>Bartol. Dig. Iudi. Sol. le.3. §. Si rebus</small>

---

2. *performed Ed.*: performde. L-1, C-1 **24.** the law *errata*: your law. L-1, C-1   **Margin 33.** Iudi. . . . 3 *Ed.*: Indi. . . . 4. C-1, L-1

and then *against such a man as useth to doe as much as hee threatens: the Lawyers* tell us, *any defence is lawfull, even to the taking away of the threatners life: For hee which hath injured one, hath threatned many*; And against such all wayes of defence are just, when any danger (to use
5 the extent of Lawyers) are *Meditated, Prepared, Likely,* or *Possible,* for it is a beggerly thing, rather to be beholden to others modestie and abstinence, then to our owne Counsaile and strength for our securitie. So that, as when the three Emperours, *Valentinian, Valens* and *Gratian,* had made a lawe, *that no Ecclesiastique person should have any capacity*
10 *to receive from noble women;* who were then observed to bee profuse in these liberalities, to the detriment of their own estates, and of the publique, Saint *Hierome* says, *Hee did not grieve that such a law was made, but that the covetousnesse of the Clergy had occasioned these most religious Princes to make that law*: So you ought rather to lament, that
15 the *Doctrine* and *practise* of some of your principall men, hath raised these jealousies and suspitions in a Prince, out of the conscience of his owne equalitie, naturally confident, then murmure at the law, or discouncell the obedience to it.

11 For in these cases of *naturall preservation*, it is not onely law-
20 full to make new lawes, but to breake any other, which are not directly Divine. And if you impute the worst condition of these lawes, which malignitie can object to them, which is, that those Catholiques, which are innocent, which meerely out of conscience, abstaine from communicating with us, in the Word and Sacraments, shall be utterly starved
25 and deprived of all spirituall sustentation, if the lawes which forbid all Priests to enter, should be still executed; yet that inconvenience will not annull and make voide a law, so farre, as that to doe against it shall be a just cause of *Martyrdome*: for in making of lawes, *those evils which doe occasionally or consequently arise from the execution thereof, must not*
30 *be considered, but what the principall intention of the law-maker was*: Which, in our case was, the preservation of the publique.

12 And yet the Catholiques in England shall for all this be in as good condition here, as they should be in any Catholique Countrie,

Alvares. spec. utr. Dignit. c.41. n.10. ex multis aliis

Gent. de Iure belli. l.1. c.14

Cod. Theodos. de Ep. & cler. le.20

Epist. ad Nepotia

Alvares. spec. utr. digni. c.41. n.7

Margin 5. Gent.] *note misplaced*. L-1, C⁹, E-1, L-2, L³⁰, O², O¹⁴, YK-1
Margin 5. l.1. C¹⁰: l.1. L-1, C-1   **17.** equalitie, *Ed*.: equalitie. L-1, C-1
22. Catholiques *Ed*.: Catholiqnes. L-1, C-1   **24.** starved SP, O-2, C⁵-1, C⁵-2, C²-1, C²-3, C⁹: sterved.   L-1, C-1, O-1, O², O¹⁴, O⁵, YK-1, C²-2

which were by the Popes displeasure under a *locall Interdict*; which the Popes doe often impose, with small respect to the Innocents: for in the late businesse betweene the *Church* and the State of *Venice* by the Popes *Breves, the whole Dominion was Interdicted*, because the *Senate*, which onely was excommunicated, did not within three dayes do all those acts, which were so derogatory to the Soveraignty of that State. And so, that punishment, which is so severe, by the *Canons*, that as *Boniface* the eight observed, *It occasions many Heresies, and indevotion, and many dangers to the soule*: And, as the *Glosse* says there, by experience it appeared, that *when a place had lien long under an Interdict, the people laughed at the Priests, when they came to say Masse againe*; was inflicted upon many Millions of innocent persons: all which, if that State had not provided for their spirituall food by staying the priests, had bin in as ill case by that *Interdict*, and evocation of the Clergie, as the Catholiques in *England* were by those lawes of interdicting their entrance, considering with how much lenitie in respect of their extreame provocations, they were executed. And if that reliefe which *Ugolini* gives to comfort the *Venetians* consciences, be of any strength, which is; *that that which they loose in spirituall sustenance, they gaine in the Merite of obedience*, it may as effectually worke upon English Consciences, as it could upon theirs.

13 Nor is it so harsh and strange, as you use to make it, that Princes should make it *Treason*, to advance some Doctrines, though they be obtruded as points of Religion, if they involve *Sedition*, and ruine or danger to the State; for the Law sayes, *That is Maiestatis crimen, which is committed against the securitie of the State*; and in that place, it cals *Securitie*, *Tranquilitie*: And whether our *Securitie* and *Tranquilitie* have not beene interrupted by your doctrine, your selves can judge, and must confesse.

14 These Lawes against which you complaine, drewe not in your Priests which were made in Queene *Maries* time, though they were *Catholicke* Priests, and exercis'd their Priestly function; and though they had better meanes to raise a partie in *England*, because they were acquainted with the state, and knew where the seedes of that Religion

17. *Ugolini*] *Ugotini*. C-3, C-4, YK-2, C¹⁶, C⁵-1, C²-1, C²-3, C⁹ **Margin**
17. Inter. Ven. cap.1. nu.1, 11 *Ed*.: Intend. Ver. §. 1, nu.11. C-1, L-1

remain'd: But in that *Catholicke* Religion of which they were Priests, they found not this Article of *Tumult* and *Sedition*, and withdrawing Subjects from their obedience.

15 Is there not a *Decretall* amongst you, by which it *Is made Treason to offend a Cardinall?* which is a *Spirituall* offence; For it is also *Sacriledge*. And is there not another by which *All practisers by Simoney in a conclave, though they be Ambassadours of other Princes, are punished as Traitors? And if their Masters seise not their goods, confiscate by this Treason, within a certaine time, the Church may.* Doeth not one of your owne Sect urge a Statute in *Poland*, against a Gentleman of that Nation, *That whosoever shall be infected or suspected of heresie, shall be apprehended as a Traitor, by any man though he bee no Officer?* And we Dispute not now whether your Doctrine be *Heresie*, but whether such points of Religion, as are no Articles of Faith, nor derived from them, if they be *Seditious*, may not be punished as *Treason*, and properly enough call'd *Treason*. In which *Pius* the second hath clear'd us and given us satisfaction, who says, That *to appeale to a future Councell, is not onely Heresie, but Treason*. And *Simancha* concurres to that purpose, when hee says, That *they which have beene teachers of Heresie, cannot be received though they recant in Judgement, because it is enough to forgive one fault, but such are guiltie of two deaths, and must bee punished, as enemies to the State; And that therefore he which attempts to corrupt the King or his Queene, or his Children with Heresie, is guiltie of Treason.*

16 And that there is a *Civill* trespasse in *Heresie*, as well as a *Spirituall*, appeares by confiscation of their goods in your Courts; which goods and temporall detriments, though the offenders bee pardoned, and receiv'd into the bosome of the Church, and so the *Spirituall* offence be remitted, are never to be restored, nor repaird. If therefore the *Canon* Lawe can extend to create *Treason* in a *Spirituall* cause: If amongst you, as it is *Heresie* to beleeve, so it is Treason to teach, that there is no Purgatorie, shall it not be lawfull to a Soveraigne and independent State, to say by a Law; That he which shall teach, *That a Priest cannot be a Traitor though he kill the King: and except a King professe intirely the Romane Faith, he hath lost all title and Jurisdiction,* and shall corrupt the Subjects with such seditious instillations as these, shall be guiltie of Treason?

17 The *Parliament of Paris* in that Arrest and sentence, by which

In 7°. Tit.4. c.3

Ibid. Tit.3. c.3

Spongia. Contra. Eq. Polon. fo.29

Epist. ad Norimbergens.

Enchirid. Jud. Tit.56. nu.5

it condemn'd the *Jesuites* Scholler *Chastel*, who attempted to murder the King, makes it Treason to utter those scandalous and seditious words, which hee had spoken, and which he had receiv'd from *False and damnable instructions* (wherein it intimates the *Jesuites*, whom the sentence in other places, names directly:) which words are expressed or implied almost in all the *Jesuits* Bookes of State matters: That sentence also pronounces all the Jesuites *Corrupters of youth, troublers of the Peace, enemies of the King and State, And if they depart not within certaine dayes, Guiltie of Treason*. And this sentence pronounces, *That if any of the Kings Subjects, should send his Sonne out of the Realme, to a Jesuites Colledge, hee should incurre treason*.

18   And though your *Expurgatorie Index* can reach into all Libraries, and eate and corrupt there more then all the Moathes and Wormes, though you have beene able to expunge, yea evert, and demolish the *Pyramis* erected in detestation of you by this Arrest, yet your *Deleatur* will never stretch to the scarre in the Kings face, nor your *Inseratur* restore his Toothe, not your expunctions arrive to the *Recordes* which preserve this sentence.

19   And came it (thinke you) ever into the opinion of the *Catholickes* of *France*, that if a man by vertue or example and precedent of this Arrest, had beene Executed as a Traitor, for speaking those forbidden words, or for sending his Sonne to the Jesuits, he should have beene by the *Catholicke* Church reputed a *Martyr*?

20   When the *Jesuits* were lately expell'd from *Venice*, and when other Priests which stay'd there, were commanded by Lawes to doe their functions, did either the *Jesuites* apprehend this opportunitie of *Martyrdome*, and come backe, or did the Priests find such spirituall comfort in transgressing this Law, that they offred to goe out?

21   And in all our differences, which fell out in this Kingdome betweene our Kings, and the Popes, when so many capitall Lawes were made against *Provisions* and *Appeales*, (not to dispute yet whether *de Iure* or *de facto* only, or whether by way of *Introduction*, or *Declaration*) doe you finde that the Catholiques then used the benefite of those lawes, to the procurement of *Martyrdome*? or hath the blood of any men executed by those lawes, died your *Martyrologes* with any *Rubriques*?

5. directly:) HD, F: directly).   C-1, L-1

And yet those times were apt enough to countenance any defender of *Ecclesiastique immunity*, though with diminution of Civill and Secular Magistracie, as appeares by their celebrating of *Becket*: yet I find not that they affoorded the title of *Martyre* to any against whom the State proceeded by the Ordinary way and course of law.

22 Why therefore shall not the *French*, and *Italian*, and olde *English* lawes give occasion of *Martyrdome* in the same cases, as these new lawes shall? At least why should *Campian*, and those which were executed before these new statutes, be any better *Martyres* then they? since they were as good Catholiques as these, and offended the common law of England in the same point, as these. But if the Breach and violating of the later statutes, be the onely or liveliest cause of *Martyrdome*, then, of *Parsons*, who every day of his life doth some act to the breaking thereof, it is verie properly said by one of his owne sect, *That hee is per totam vitam martyr*. Ribaden. Catal. scrip.Jesuit.fo.175

23 And this may suffice to remember you, that you *intrude* into this employment, and are not *sent*, and that our Lawes ought to worke upon your Oath, returning to the annihilation thereof, because both the necessitie of the making and continuing thereof, and the precedents of our owne, and other Catholicke Kingdomes, give us warrant to make seditious Doctrine *Treason*, and your owne *Canons* and *Judicature* give us example, and (if we needed it) Authoritie to proceede in that maner.

Margin 14. 175 *Ed.*: 109. C-1, L-1 **18.** returning to the Y: returning to of the. L-1, F, HD

Chap. VI.

A comparison of the Obedience due to Princes, with the severall obediences requir'd and exhibited in the Romane Church; First, of that blind Obedience, and stupiditie, which Regular men vowe to their Superiours: Secondly, of that usurped Obedience to which they pretend by reason of our Baptisme, wherein we ar said to have made an implicite surrender of our selves and all that we have, to the Church; And thirdly of that Obedience, which the Jesuits by a fourth Supernumerarie vowe, make to be dispos'd at the Popes absolute will.

1   There hath not beene a busier disquisition, nor subject to more perplexitie, then to finde out the first originall roote, and Source, which they call *Primogenium subiectum*, that may be so capable of *Power* and *Jurisdiction*, and so invested with it immediately from God, that it can transferre and propagate it, or let it passe and naturally derive it-selfe into those formes of Governement, by which mankind is continued and preserved; For at the resolution of this, all Questions of *Subjection* attend their dispatch. And because the *Clergie* of the *Roman* Church, hath with so much fierce earnestnesse and apparance of probablenesse, pursued this Assertion, That *that Monarchall forme, and that Hierarchie, which they have, was instituted immediately from God*; Many wise and jealous *Advocates* of *Secular Authoritie*, fearing least otherwise they should diminish that Dignitie, and so prevaricate and betray the cause, have said the same of *Regall* power and Jurisdiction. And even in the Romane Church a great Doctor of eminent reputation there, agrees (as he sayes) *Cum omnibus sapientibus*, That *this Regall Jurisdiction and Monarchie* (which word is so odious and detestable to *Baronius*) *proceedes from God, and by Divine and naturall Law, and not from the State or altogether from man*. And as we have it in *Evidence*, so we have it in *Confession* from them, that *God hath as immediately created some Kings, as any Priests*. And *Cassanaeus* thinkes this is the highest *Secular Authoritie* that ever God induced: For he denies *That old or new Testament have any mention of Emperour*.

Fra. a Victor. Relect. de Pot. Civi. nu.8

Catal. Glor. pa.5. Consid. 28

9. 1 *Ed.*: missing.   L-1, C-1

CHAPTER SIX 131

2 But to mine understanding we injure and endanger this cause more, if wee confesse that that *Hierarchie* is so *Immediately* from God as they obtrude it, then we get by offering to drawe *Regall* power within the same Priviledge. I had rather thus farre abstaine from saying so of either, that I would pronounce no farther therein, then this, That *God* hath *Immediately* imprinted in mans Nature and Reason, to be subject to a power immediately infus'd from him; and that hee hath enlightned our Nature and Reason, to digest and prepare such a forme, as may bee aptest to doe those things, for which that *Power* is infus'd; which are, to conserve us in *Peace* and in *Religion*: And that since the establishing of the Christian Church, he hath testified abundantly, that *Regall Authoritie*, by subordination of *Bishops*, is that best and fittest way to those ends.

3 So that, that which a *Jesuite* said of the Pope, That *the Election doth onely present him to God*, wee say also of a King; That whatsoever it be, that prepares him, and makes his Person capable of *Regall Jurisdiction*, that onely presents him to *God*, who then inanimates him with this Supremacy immediately from himselfe, according to a secret and tacite covenant, which he hath made with mankinde, That when they out of rectified Reason, which is the Law of Nature, have begot such a forme of Governement, he will infuse this *Soule* of power into it.

_{Tannerus. de libert. Eccles. l.2. cap.5}

4 The way therefore to finde, what Obedience is due to a King, is not to seeke out, how they which are presum'd to have transferr'd this power into him, had their Authoritie, and how much they gave, and how much they retain'd; For in this *Discoverie* none of them ever went farther, then to *Families*; In which, they say, *Parents* and *Masters* had Jurisdiction over Children, and Servants; and these *Families* concurr'd to the making of *Townes*, and transferr'd their power into some *Governour* over them all.

5 But, besides that this will not hold, because such *Savadges* as never rais'd *Families*, or such men as an overburdned kingdom should by lot throw out, which were peeces of divers families, must have also a power to frame a forme of Governement, wheresoever they shall reside, which could not bee if the onely roote of Jurisdiction were in *parents*

12. *Bishops*, Ed.: *Bishops*. L-1, C-1 **Margin 14.** Tannerus. C-3, C-4: Tannerus. L-1, C-1, C-2, L-2 **22.** Obedience] [Obe]dience, *catchword quarto*. p.168

& *masters*; This also will infirme and overthrow that Assertion, that if *parents* and *masters* had not this *supreme Soveraignty*, which is requisite in Kings, they could not transferre it into Kings, and so Kings have it not from them: And if they were Soveraignes they could not transfer it, for no *Soveraigne* can devest himselfe of his Supremacie.

6 *Regall* authority is not therefore derived from men, so, as that certaine men have lighted a King at their Candle, or transferr'd certaine *Degrees of Jurisdiction* into him: and therefore it is a cloudie and muddie search, to offer to trace to the first roote of *Jurisdiction*, since it growes not in man. For, though wee may goe a steppe higher then they have done which rest and determine in *Families*, which is, that in every particular man considered alone, there is found a double *Jurisdiction* of the *soule* over the *body*, and of the *reason* over the *appetite*, yet those will be but examples and illustrations, not Rootes and Fountaines, from which *Regall* power doth essentially proceede. *Sepulveda*, whom I cited before, sayes well to this purpose; *That the soule doth exercise, Herile Imperium upon the body*: and this can be no example to Kings, who cannot animate and informe their Subjects as the soule doth the body. But the power of our *reason* upon our *appetite*, is, as he sayes pertinently, *Regale Imperium*; and Kings rule subjects so as reason rules that.

7 To that forme of Governement therefore, which rectified reason, which is Nature, common to all wise men, dooth justly chuse, as aptest to worke their end, God instils such a power as we wish to be in that person, and which wee beleeve to be infused by him, and therefore obey it as a beame derived from him, without having departed with any thing from our selves.

8 And as the end of this power, is always one and the same, *To live peaceably and religiously*, so is the power it self, though it be diversly complexioned, and of different stature; for that naturall light and reason, which acknowledges a *necessity* of a *Superiour*, that we may enjoy *peace*, and *worshippe God*, did consent in the common wish and tacite prayer to God, and doth rest in the common faith and beliefe, that God hath powred into that person all such authority as is needefull for that

De regn. & reg. offi. l.1

I Tim. 2.2

---

3. could *Ed.*: cold. L-1, C-1 **6.** as that *errata*: as at that. L-1, C-1
21. therefore *errata*: thereof for. MCG, C-2, C-3, L³, SP, Y, O-2, O², O¹⁴, YK-3, L³⁰, D-1, D-3 **Margin 27.** I Tim. 2.2 *Ed.*: *missing*. L-1, C-1

use; Therefore of what complexion soever the forme of governement be, or of what stature soever it seeme, yet the same authority is in every *Soveraigne* State: thus farre, That there are no Civill men, which out of *rectified Reason* have provided for their *Peaceable* and *religious* Tran-
5 quility, but are subject to this *regall* authority, which is, *a power to use all those meanes, which conduce to those endes.*

    9 For those diffrences which appeare to us in the divers formes, are not in the essence of the *Soveraignty*, which hath no degrees, nor additions, nor diminutions, but they are onely in those *instruments*, by
10 which this Soveraignty is exercised, which are ordinarily called *Arcana*, and *Ragion di stato*, as I noted before: and as the soule it selfe, hath as good understanding in an *Idiote*, and as good a *memory* in a *Lethargique* person, as in the wisest and liveliest man; So hath this *Soveraignty* in every state equall vigour, though the *Organes* by which it workes be not
15 in all alike disposed. And therefore the governement amongst the *Jewes* before *Saule*, was fully a *Kingdome* in this acceptation: nor did they attend any new addition to this power, in their solicitation for a *King*: but, because they were a people accustomed to warre, they wished such   Sepulved. de regn. a *Soveraigne* as might lead their *Armies*; which office their *Priestes* did   & reg. offi. l.2.
   fo.91
20 not; and they grudged that their enemies should be conducted by better persons then they were.

    10 And so, though some ancient *Greeke* states, which are called *Regna Laconica*, because they were shortned and limited to certaine lawes, and some States in our time seeme, to have *Conditionall* and
25 *Provisionall* Princes, betweene whom and Subjects, there are mutuall and reciprocall obligations; which if one side breake, they fall on the other, yet that *soveraignty*, which is a power to doe all things availeable to the maine endes, resides somewhere: which, if it be in the hands of one man, erects and perfects that *Pambasilia* of which we speake.

30   11 For God inanimates every State with one power, as every man with one soule: when therefore people concurre in the desire of such a *King*, they cannot contract, nor limitte his power: no more then parents can condition with God, or preclude or withdraw any facultie from that Soule, which God hath infused into the body, which they prepared, and
35 presented to him. For, if such a company of Savadges, or men whom an

    20. conducted *errata*: conduced. L-1, C-1

overloaded kingdome had avoided, as we spake off before, should create a *King*, and reserve to themselves a libertie to revenge their owne wrongs, upon one another, or to doe any act necessary to that end, for which a King hath his authority, this liberty were swallowed in their first acte, and onely the creation of the King were the worke of rectified reason, to which God had concurr'd, and that *reservation* a voide and impotent act of their appetite.

12   If then this give us light, what and whence the Kings Jurisdiction is; we may also discerne by this, what our obedience must be: for *power* and *subjection* are so *Relative*, as since the King commaunds in all things conducing to our *Peaceable* and *Religious* being, wee must obey in all those. This therefore is our first Originary, naturall, and Congenite obedience, *to obey the Prince*: This belongs to us as we are *men*; and is no more changed in us, by being *Christians*, then our *Humanity* is changed: yet hath the *Romane* Church extolled and magnified three sorts of *Obedience*, to the prejudice of this.

13   The first is, that which they call *Caecam obedientiam*: which is an inconsiderate & undiscoursed, and (to use their owne word) an *Indiscreete* surrendring of themselves, which professe any of the *rules* of Religion, to the command of their Prelate and Superior; by which, like the uncleane beasts, *They swallow, and never chaw the cudde*: But this obedience proceeding out of the *will* and *election* of them, who applie themselves to that course of life, cannot be of so great authority and obligations, as the other which is *naturall*, and borne in us; and therefore, farther then it agrees with that, it is not out of rectified reason.

14   And though it seeme scarce worthy of any further discourse, yet I cannot deny my selfe the recreation of survaying some examples of this blinde and stupid obedience, and false humility, nor forbeare to shew, that by their magnifying thereof, and their illations thereupon, not only the offices of mutuall society are uncharitably pretermitted, but the obedience to Princes prejudic'd and maimed, and the lively and active, and vigorous contemplation of God clouded and retarded.

15   For when a distressed Passenger intreated a Monke to come forth, and helpe his Oxe out of the Ditch, was it a charitable answere to tell him, *That he had bin twentie years dead, & in his grave, and could not*

Margin 21. Deu. 14.8 *Ed.*: Deu. 4.. L-1, C-1   **25.** that, *Ed.*: that;. L-1, C-1

Deu. 14.8

Cassian. Collat.24. c.9

CHAPTER SIX 135

now come forth? Yet it may seeme excusable in them to neglect others, if this obedience make them forget themselves; as certaine youthes whom their *Abbot* sent with Figges to an *Ermit*, loosing their way, sterved in the Desart, rather then they would eate the Figges, which they were 5 commanded to deliver. Is it likely that when *Mucius* a Monke, at the commaund of his *Abbot*, who bid him *cast his crying sonne into the river and drowne him*, did in the fervor of obedience obey it, God should reveale, *That in that acte, he accomplished Abrahams worke?* Idem. de Instit. Renunc. c.40. l.5
Ibid. l.4. c.27 & 28
Idem. Collat.4. c.20

16 Are these wholsome instructions, *That it is a greater pride to* 10 *doe a good worke against the Superiours commaund, then a bad, because they are vices under pretence of vertue?* or this, *That it is better to sinne against God, then our spirituall Father, because he can reconcile us to God, but no body to him?* Which doctrine it seemes *Heli* had not accepted, when he said, *If one man sinne against another, the Judge* 15 *shall judge it, but if a man sinne against the Lord, who will pleade for him?* How many greater matters must they of necessity leave undiscussed, that professe such tendernesse and scrupulosity of conscience, as the late *Jesuit Gonzaga*, who doubted that when hee had said he would goe, *Ad Domum professorum*, he had sinned in an *idle word*, since he 20 might have beene understood well enough though he had left out the last worde? or that he had *sinned* in answering *affirmatively* to his Superiours question, *whether he would go to a certaine place*, because he ought to have left it all to his Superiours will, without any affirmation? Was it due and necessary obedience, when desirous to be instructed in 25 that point of *Predestination*, and his *Superiour* turning to a place in *S. Augustine*, and bidding him *read there*, being come to the end of the page, but not of the sentence, he durst not turne over the leafe, because he was bid to *read there*? Climachus. Scala. parad. Grad.4

I Sam. 2.25

Cepari. de eius vita. fo.196
Fo.242

Fo.244

17 *Sedulius* seemes glad that he had examples enough to furnish a 30 Chapter, *De simplicitate Minoridarum*; and hee seemes to have much comfort that he is of the same order, as *Friar Ruffin* was, who out of simplicity *cut off a living Hogges foote, to dresse for a sicke bodie, and* Apol. l.3. c.1

Margin 2. 40. l.5 *Ed.*: 40. l.4. C-1, L-1   **Margin 9.** Climachus.] Climachus. MCG, C-2, C-3, L³⁰, SP, C¹⁶   **15.** but *Ed.*: bu. L-1, C-1   **Margin 18.** Cepari. *Ed.*: Cepari'. L-1, C-1   **21.** worde *errata*: wordes. L-1, C-1   **30.** Minoridarum *Ed.*: Minoritarum. L-1, C-1

sodde his Birds in the feathers: who also out of his humility, *desired that he might stinke when he was dead, and that he might be eaten with dogges.* And he sayes that *Friar Juniper* was so simple, that a *Daemoniaque* possessed man, ranne seven miles from him, because the divell could not abide *Patientiam Iuniperi*.

18   Was it not *Prodigium Obedientiae*, as *Sedulius* justly calles it, in *Friar Ruffin to go preach naked*? And were there not some degrees of *spirituall pride* in *Gonzaga*, who is praised because *he had a paire of patched hose in Deliciis*? and that he refused to put on a paire of old bootes, *because a worshipfull man had worne them*? and that when his handes did cleave with colde, *he would put on no gloves*? Was there not some measure of *stupid insensiblenesse* in him, when he durst not *spit* in any necessity at his prayers; and that he knew not *how many brothers he had*? And of *desperate provocation*, when he heard of a plague likely to be in those parts, to *make a vow to visit those which were infected*? And of *murmuring*, when he grudged and grieved, *That he could find out no veniall sinne in himselfe*? And of *Inhumanity*, when *he was sorry, if any body loved him*? And of a fear'd and shamelesse *Stubornenesse*, when *he therefore desir'd to speake in publicke, because hee had an ungracious and ridiculous imperfection in pronouncing the letter R*. And ask'd leave, *E suggestu dicere*, (which, I thinke, is to Preach) *in Spanish, because he was sure to be laugh'd at by that meanes, being imperfect in that language*? And doeth it not taste of an unnaturall *Indolencie* in him, to say no more at the newes of his Fathers death, but that nowe nothing hindered him from saying, OUR FATHER WHICH ART IN HEAVEN; As if it had troubled his conscience, to say so before?

19   Who would not have beene glad, that such a Preacher should give over, as when Friar *Giles* a Lay man, call'd to him, *Hold your peace Master, for now I will Preach*, gave him his place? Who would wish S. *Henrie* the *Dane* any health, that had seene him, *When wormes crawled out of a corrupted Ulcer in his Knee, put them in againe*? Or who would have consented to the *Christian* buriall of that Monke, which *Dorotheus* speakes off, if he had died of that *Poison*, which hee saw his Servant mistake for *Honie*, and put it into his Brothe, and never

Margins:
Idem. l.3. c.2. n.2
Ide. l.3. c.14. n.2
L.2. c.5. n.7
Vita eius. fo.100
Fo.306
Fo.326
Fo.225
Fo.191
Fo.360
Fo.220
Fo.346
Fol.335
Fol.288
Fol.187
Sedul. Apolo. l.3. c.6. n.1
Engl. Martyro. Janua.16
B. Dorotheus. Doctrina.7ª

Margin 1. 3. c.2 *Ed.*: 2. c.2. L-1, C-1   **Margin 6.** 2. c.5. *Ed.*: 2, c 5,. L-1, C-1   **Margin 17.** Fo.346] Fo 346. L-1, Y, L-2

reprehended him, before nor after he had eaten the Soppes: But when his Servant apprehended it, and was much mooved, the master pacified him with this, *If God would have had me eate Honie, either thou shouldest have taken the Honie, or hee would have changed the Poison into Honie.*

5 Who would ever have kept companie with the *Jesuite Barcena*, after he had told him, as he told another *Jesuite, That when the divell appeard to him one night, out of his profound humilitie, hee rose to meete him, and prayd him to sit in his Chaire, because he was more worthy to sit there then he?* Who would wish Father *Peter* alive againe, since being 10 dead, he is so afraid of disquieting his fellowes, that he will give over doing of Miracles, for their ease? Or who would not wish them all dead, who possessing and filling all good places in their life, will bee content to give some roome after their death; as Friar *Raynold*, who having beene three yeres dead, when another Holy man was brought to be buried in 15 the same Vault, rose up and went to the Wall, and stood upright there, that the other might have roome enough.

20 This is that Obedience by which they say, *If a man were dignified so much as to talke with Angels, if his Superiour call'd him, he must come away*; Yea, one of them *Being in discourse with our Lady,* 20 *when an inferiour Friar call'd him, unmannerly quitted her.* And of this Obedience is *Ignatius* himselfe especially carefull, *Least* (sayes he) *that famous simplicitie of blind Obedience should decay*. But this Obedience, and all other, are subordinate to that naturall Obedience to your Prince, as Soveraigne controller of all: For in all Obligations the Authoritie of 25 the Superiour is ever excepted.

21 And this Obedience must not be so blind, but that it may both looke upward, what *God*, in his *Lieuetenant* appoints to bee done, and also round about to see, wherein they may relieve others, and receive from them. They may be circumspect, though they must not be curious. 30 For *Abbayes*, at first institution, were not all *Chappell* but *Schooles* of Sciences, and *Shops* of manufactures. Now they are come to that, that they cannot worke, *Quia Officia longa*. They have indeede so many Offices, and so many Officers, that they neede not worke. But this

Relatione di Diego Torrez. Edit. Venet. 1604. fo.52
This Jesuite died in Cusco. An. 1598

Sedul. Apolo. l.3. c.24. n.26

Id. l.3. c.25. n.18

Id. l.2 .c.5. n.8

Epist. ad fratres in Lusitan.

Extra. de Jur. Iur. sufficiat. Glo.

Regul. Benedict. c.48. Declaram.

Margin 5. fo.52 *Ed.*: fo.5. C-1, L-1 **Margin 21.** Epist. *Ed.*: Epist,. L-1, C-1 **Margin 23.** Jur. Iur. *Ed.*: Jur; Iur.. C-1, L-1 **30.** *Chappell errata*: Chappels. L-1, C-1 **Margin 32.** Declaram *Ed.*: Declarat. C-1, L-1

strict obedience was impos'd upon them then, because they were great confluences of men of divers *Nations*, *Dispositions*, *Breedings*, *Ages*, and *Employments*, and they could be tied together in no knot so strongly, nor meete in any one Center so concurrently, and uniformely, as in the Obedience to one Superiour; And what this Obedience was, and how farre it extended: *Aquinas*, who understood it well, hath well express'd, *That they are bound to Obey only in those things which may belong to their Regular conversation.* And this use and office, that obedience which is exhibited in our *Colledges*, fulfils and satisfies, without any of these unnatural, childish, stupid, mimique, often scandalous, and sometimes rebellious singularities.

2.2.ae. q.104. Ar.5. ad 3^{m}

22 Any resolution which is but new borne in us, must bee abandon'd and forsaken, when that obedience which is borne with us, is requir'd at our hands. In expressing of which trueth, Saint *Bernard* goes so exceeding farre, as to say, That *Christ gave over his purpose of Preaching, at the increpation, Mulieris unius, & fabri pauperis: And because his Mother chid him, when shee found him in the Temple, from twelve yeeres to thirtie, we find not*, sayes hee, *That hee taught or wrought any thing, though this abstinence were contrarie to his determination.* So earnest is that devoute father, to illustrate our *Blessed Saviours* obedience, to a jurisdiction which was *Naturally* Superiour to him. And therefore this submission, by our owne *Election*, to another Superiour, cannot derogate from the Prince, nor infirme his Title to our Alleageance or obedience.

Ser.3. de Resurr. Domini

23 Another obedience derogatorie to Princes, they have imagined, connaturall, and congenite with our *Christianitie*, as this is with our *Humanitie*, and conducing to our *Wel-being*, and our everlastingnesse, as this doeth to our *Being* and temporall tranquilitie; which is, An obedience to the *Romane* Church, and to him, who must bee esteem'd certainely the *Head* thereof, [a]though sometimes *he be no member thereof*.

[a]Azor. Mor. Instit. To.2. l.4. c.7. §. Deinde

24 Certainely the inestimable benefits which wee receive from the *Church*, who feedes us with the *Word* and *Sacraments*, deserves from us an humble acknowledgement, and obedient confidence in her: yea, it is *spirituall Treason*, not to obey her. And as in temporall Monarchies, the light of nature instructs every man generally, what is *Treason*, that is, what violates or wounds or impeaches the Majestie of the State, and yet he submits himselfe willingly to the *Declaration* and *Constititions*,

by which some things are made to his understanding *Treason*, which by the generall light he apprehended not to be so dangerous before; So in this case of *spirituall Treason*, which is *Heresie*, or *Schisme*, though originarily, and fundamentally, the *Scriptures* of God informe us, what our subjection to the Church ought to be, yet we are also willing to submit our selves to the lawes and decrees of the Catholique Church her selfe, what obedience is due to her. He therefore that can produce out of either of these *Authentique* sorts of *Records*, *Scripture*, or *Church*, that is, *Text* or *Glosse*, any law, by which it is made either *High Treason*, *Heresie*, not to beleeve, that in my baptisme I have implied a confession, That the Bishop of Rome is so monarch of the Church, that he may depose Princes; or *petit Treason*, that is *Schisme*, to adhere to my naturall Soveraigne against a Bull of that Bishop, shall drawe me into his mercy, and I will aske Pardon, where none is graunted, at the *Inquisition*.

25 Else it is most reasonable (and that is ever most religious) to relie upon this, That obedience to Princes is taught by Nature, and affirm'd and illustrated by Scriptures. If the question be, how much this obedience must be, I must say, all, till it be proved, either that *Peaceable* and *religious* being be not all the ends, for which we are placed in this world, or that the authority of Kings, exercised by the Kings of *Israell* and the *Christian Emperours*, is not enough to performe these endes. For, to say that a King cannot provide for meanes of salvation of soules, because he cannot preach, nor administer the Sacraments, hath as much weakenesse, as to say, hee cannot provide for the health of a City, because he cannot give physicke.

26 Till then, I shal be deterr'd from declining to this second obedience, by the contemplation of many inconveniencies, and impieties resulting from thence; first, by the *vastnes* of that Jurisdiction: For since they have taught us to say so, we may say, *Dominus non esset discretus, ut cum reverentia eius loquar*, if he had laid the cure of the whole Church and the judgement of all matters emergent, of *fact* and *faith*, upon one man; which he hath done, if *Pesantius* say true, That *the Pope is, Iure Divino, directly Lord of all the World*: which booke is dedicated to the present Pope, who by allowing it may justly be thought to favour that opinion.

Extrav. Com. de Maior. & Obed. unam sanctam. Addit.

Bertr. §. Respondeo & dico Alex. Pesant. de immunit. Eccles. & potest. pont. pag.44

1. some things *Ed*.: somethings. L-1, C-1   **Margin 28.** sanctam. O²: sanctam. L-1, C-1

27   How much it is, that they would entitle him to, appeares by their expunction of a Sentence in *Roselli a Catholique*, though a Lawyer, *That it is hereticall to say, that the universall temporall administration is, or may be in the Pope*: upon which booke mine eye fals often, because you have beene so lavish and prodigall in those *expunctions*, that a man might well make a good *Catechisme*, and an *Orthodox Institution of Religion*, out of those places, which you have cast away. And by this one place we see what you would have, For if the universall administration of temporall matters be in the Pope, what neede is there of Kings? You would soone forget kings, or remember them to their ruine; and looke that kings should do to you, as condemned men are said to have done to the kings of *Persia*, to thanke them that they were pleased to remember them. And *Azorius* will not pardon their modesty, that say, *that the Pope in dealing with temporall matters uses but a spirituall power* (though this in effect worke as dangerously) *but he useth* (sayes he) *Absolutely and simply a temporall Jurisdiction*.

[margin: Ind. Belg. fo.86]
[margin: Simancha. de Rep. l.3. c.7. ex Strabao]
[margin: Azor. To.2. l.4. c.19. §. Mihi]

28   And what can impeach this *Universall Jurisdiction*, since al matter and subject of Jurisdiction, that is, all men, may by their Rules be under him, by another way, that is, by entring into Religion: for first, *Tannerus* the *Jesuit* says, *If Princes had their authority immediately from God, yet the Pope might restraine that authority of theirs, that it should fall onely upon Lay-men*: For, sayes another, *He may take from the Emperour, all his Jurisdiction, therefore any part thereof*. And as many as will (sayes Bellarmine) *may without the consent of their Prince, yea though he resist it, thus devest their Allegeance, as they might resist their parents if they should hinder them*.

[margin: De libert. Eccles. l.2. c.1]
[margin: Maynardus. de Privileg. Eccles. Ar.16. nu.2]
[margin: Bell. de Cler. l.1. c.ult.]

29   And in contemplation of this *Universall Jurisdiction*, which might be, if it be not, in the Pope; the Jesuite whom we first named, breakes out into this congratulation: *If at this instant all the Princes and all their subjects, would enter into Religion, and transferre all that they had into the Church, would it not bee a most acceptable spectacle to God, and Angels, and Men?* Or (as he sayes before) *if their estates were so transferr'd to the Church, though not their persons, could not Ec-*

[margin: Tannerus. l.2. c.12. in fine]

Margin 2. fo. *Ed.*: fo:. L-1, C-1   **Margin 11.** Simancha. *Ed.*: note misplaced . L-1, C-1   **Margin 13.** Azor. *Ed.*: note misplaced . C-1, L-1   **Margin 20.** 1.2. c.1 *Ed.*: l,2: c:1. L-1, C-1   **Margin 28.** 12. *Ed.*: 12,. C-1, L-1

clesiastique Princes rule and governe all these lay men, as well as they doe some others already? But because, as hee doubts in that place, *Hoc in aeternum nunquam fiet*, that all Laymen will come under them, they have provided that all Clergie men which be under them, shall be
5 safe enough, as well by way of *Counsell* (for so *Mariana* modefies his Doctrine, that the Prince should not execute any Clergy man, though hee deserve it) as by positive way of *Aphorismes*, as *Emanuel Sâ* doth, That *they are not subjects, nor can doe treason*: and by way of *Fact*, and publique troubling the peace of al Christendome, as appeared by
10 their late attempt uppon *Venice* for this Exemption.

    30 And as the immensnesse of this power averts me from beleeving it to bee just, so doeth this also decline me, that they will not bee brought to tell us, *How he hath it*, nor *How hee get it*. For as yet they doe but stammer, and the Word stickes in their jawes, and wee know not
15 whether, when it comes, it wil be *Directly*, or *Indirectly*. And they are as yet but surveying their *Evidence*; they have join'd no issue; nor know we whether they will pleade *Divine Law*, that is, places of Scripture, or *Sub-divine Law*, which is interpretation of Fathers, or *super-divine* law, which is Decretals of Popes. But Kings insist confidently, and openly,
20 and constantly upon the law of Nature, and of nations, & of God, by all which they are appointed what to do, and enabled to do it.

    31 Lastly, this infames and makes this Jurisdiction suspicious to me, to observe what use in their *Doctrine* and *Practise* they make of this power. For when they have proceeded to the execution of this *Tempo-
25 rall* power, it hath beene either for their owne reall and direct profit and advantage, as in their proceeding with the *Easterne Emperours*: And drawing the *French* Armies into *Italy*, and promoving and strengthning the change of the family and race of the Kings in *France*, or else the benefit hath come to them by whose advancement that *Church* growes
30 and encreases, as in the disposing of the Kingdome of *Navarre*; Or at least, the example and terrour thereof magnifies the dignitie, and reputation of that Church, and facilitates her other enterprises, for a good time after, as a Shippe that hath made good way before a strong winde,

De Institut. l.1. c.10

Aphor. confes. verb. clericus

Margin 5. *1.1. c.10 Ed.*: l:1: c:10. L-1, C-1   **18.** *Sub-divine Ed.*: Sub divine. L-1, C-1   **18.** *super-divine Ed.*: super divine. L-1, C-1   **21.** *it. Ed.*: it,. L-1, C-1

and under a full Saile, will runne a great while of her selfe, after shee hath stricken saile.

15. q.6. Alius

32 When any of these reasons invite them, how small causes are sufficient to awake and call up this temporall Authoritie? The cause why *Childerique* was deposed, was not, sayes the *Canon*, for his *Iniquities*; but because he was *Inutilis*. And this was not, sayes the *Glosse*, because hee was *Insufficient, for then hee should have an assistant, and coadjutor*; but because hee was *Effeminate*. So that the Pope may depose upon lesse cause, then hee can give an *assistant*. For to bee *Insuficient* for the Governement, is more directly against the office of a King, then to bee subject to an infirmitie, which concernes his humanitie, not his office.

Paris de Puteo. de syndic. Ca. de Excess. Regum

Dist.86. qui venatoribus

Par. de Put. ca. Rex autem

33 And when the officers and Commissioners of the Romane Court, come to *Syndicate* Kings, they have already declar'd, what they will call *Enormities* and *Excesses*, by involving almost all faults, whether by *Committing* or *Omitting* in generall words; As, *When he doeth not that for which he is instituted; when he useth his prerogative without just cause, when he vexes his Subjects; when he permits Priests to kisse his hands; when he proceeds indiscreetly, and without just reason*; And lastly, *For any such hunting as they will call intemperate*. To which purpose they cite against Kings generally those *Canons* which limit certaine men, and times, and maners: And which, as the *Glosse* sayes of some of them, are meant *De venatione arenaria, When men out of vaine-glorie, or for gaine, fought in the Theaters with wild beasts*. And least any small errour in a King might escape them, they make account that they have enwrapp'd and pack'd up all in this, *That it is all one, whether a King bee a Tyrant, or a Foole, or Sacrilegious, or Excommunicate, or an Hereticke*.

In Io. l.12. c.56

34 This obedience therfore which we neither find written in the tables of our *Hearts*, nor in the *Scriptures*, nor in any other such *Record*, as either our adversary wil be tried by, or can bind us, must not destroy nor shake that obedience which is *Naturall* and *Certaine*. *Cyril* hath made this sentence his owne, by saying it with such allowance, *It is wisely said, That hee is an impious man, which sayes to the King, thou dost unjustly*. Much more may wee say it of any, that affirmes a King to bee naturally impotent, to doe those things for which he is instituted; as he is, if he cannot preserve his Subjects in *Peace* and *Religion*, which the

Heathen kings could doe; whose Subjects had a *Religion*, and *Ministers* thereof, who wrought upon men to incline them to Morall goodnesse here, and to the expectation of future blessednesse after death, though not by so cleare nor so direct wayes as *Christian* Religion doth.

35 The king therefore defends the *Liberties* of the Church, as the nature of his office, which he hath acknowledged, and Declar'd, and seal'd to his Subjects by an Oath, binds him to do, if he defend the Church of England from foraine usurpation. And a most learned and equall man hath observed well, That *in the differences betweene Gregorie the seventh, and the Emperours, the defence of the liberties of the Church, was the title and pretence on both sides*. And since a *Jesuite* hath affoorded us this confession, That *the Prince hath this Authoritie over Bishops, that hee may call them as Peeres of his Realme*, And since their *Clementines*, or the *Glosser*, yeeldes to us, That *a Church Prelate may bee a Traitor, because hee holdes some temporalities*: how can they escape from being subject in all other cases; since their *naturall* and *native* obedience is of a stronger obligation, then the accepting or possessing of these *Temporalities*: for, if *Iure Divino*, the Character of *Order*, did obliterate and wash out the Character of *civill Obedience*, and subjection, the conferring of any temporall dignity or possession, could not restore it; for under color of a benefit, it should endammage and diminish them, when a little Temporall honour or profit shall draw their spirituall estate and person to secular Jurisdiction: for, as *Azorius* will prove to us, the king may call a *Bishoppe* as a *Baron* to the Parliament, and as the *Canonist* will proove to us, he may call him to the *Barre* as a *Traitor*.

36 To recollect therefore now, and to determine & end this point, the title which the Prince hath to us by *Generation*, and which the Church hath by *Regeneration*, is all one now. For we are not onely Subjects to a Prince, but *Christian* Subjects to a *Christian* Prince, and members as well of the Church as of the Common-wealth, in which the Church is. And as by being borne in his Dominions, and of parents in his alleageance, we have by birth-right interest in his lawes and protection: So by the *Covenant* of Almighty God to the faithful and their *Seede*, by being born of Christian Parents, we have title to the *Sacraments*; which

Casub. de lib. Eccles. fol.46

Azor. Instit. Moral. To.1. l.5. c.14. in fine

De sent. & re iudic. Pastoralis Glossa

Margin 14. iudic] *Ed.*: indic. C-1, L-1 **30.** a Prince *Ed.*: a Prinee. L-1, C-1

the king (to whom, as all the kingdome is his house, so al the Clergy are chaplaines) takes care, that they duly administer to us which are his sonnes, and servants.

37   Nor dooth the king and the Church direct us to divers ends, one to *Tranquility*, the other to *Salvation*, but *both* concurre in *both*: For wee cannot ordinarily be saved (which seemes to be the function of the *Clergy*) without the exercise of morall vertue here in this life, nor can *Christians* do those morall vertues (which seeme to bee the Princes businesse) without faith, and keeping the right way to salvation, because a *Christian* must doe them *Christianly*.

38   For though *Theologall* vertues, *Faith*, *Hope*, and *Charity*, are infus'd from God, yet all religious worshippe of God is morall vertue. As therefore the office of all *Heathen* Princes, was to conserve their subjects in the practise of morall vertue, so farre as it was revealed to their understanding; So is it now the office of *Christian* Princes to doe the same. For God hath now so farre enlightned us to the understanding of morall vertue, that we see thereby, that after God hath infused *Faith*, wee make sure our salvation, by a morall obedience to the kings Governement, and to their Ministery whom his providence appoints over us for our instruction. So that *Christian* subjects need no higher power then kings are naturally indued and qualified withall, to direct them to *Salvation*; but, because morall vertue is now extended, not in it selfe, but to our understanding, or perchance perfited (for the Fathers denie often, that the *Philosophers* had any true morall vertues) *Christian* kings must now provide lawes, which may reach as far in their direction, as morall vertue reaches now; and Ministers, that may teach us how farr that is, and to conserve us in the observation therof: For as, when all things are in such sort wel composed and established, and every subordinate Wheele set in good order, we are guilty of our owne damnation, if wee obey not the Minister, and the Minister is guilty of it, if hee neglect to instruct us, so is the Prince guilty of our spirituall ruine, and eternall perishing, if hee doe not both provide able men to give us spirituall foode, and punish both their negligence and our transgressions: So that hee is to account to GOD for our soules, and therefore must have naturall meanes to discharge that duety well, or else could not be subject to such a reckoning for his transgressions therein.

23. to our] o our.   C-4, YK-2

39   The last Obedience which I intimated, as prejudiciall to this of kings, is that which the *Jesuites* vowe to the Pope; which is not the same blind Obedience, which I spoke of before, for the *Jesuits* sweare that also to their *Superiours*, before they come to the perfection of this: But, as that is blinde out of *darkenesse*, so this is blinde out of *dazeling*. For they must be instruments in matters of State, and disposing kingdomes.

40   When some Priests in England were examined, what they would thinke of the *Oath of Alleageance*, if the pope should pronounce that it were to be held *De fide*, that hee might depose Princes, they desired to be spared, because they could not pronounce *De futuris Contingentibus*. But these votaries, the Jesuites are not so scrupulous; They can resolve to execute whatsoever he shall commaund: perchance they thinke the Pope so much God, (for Jesuites must exceede in everything) that in him, as in GOD, there can bee no *Contingency*. And therefore vowing their travell and labour, to the corrupting and aliening of subjects, to the combustion or translation of Kingdomes, to the aviling and eradication of Princes, they do not vow *De futuris Contingentibus*, but of things ever constantly resolved in the Decree, and Counsell, and purpose of the Bishop of Rome.

41   Though therefore *Mat. Tortus* be no *Jesuite* himselfe, yet in respect of his Master, who was one, I wonder he durst say, *That the Jesuites made no other vow of obedience to the Pope, then other religious Orders did*; which is such an excuse in their behalf, as no accusation could offend them so much; since their ambition is to serve the Pope by a neerer Obligation then the rest: which appeares evidently enough, in the *Bul* of *Paul* the third, where this fourth vow is repeated. Sopra la lettera de Palmieri Romito. Nella Raccolta. fo.126

42   And is it not a strange precipitation to vow their helpe to all his errours? of which they confesse he may commit many in matter of *Fact*, by mis-information. So that they sweare to execute that, which they are not bound to beleeve to be well commaunded: yea they are not bound to beleeve, that he which commaunds them, is that person whose commaundements by their vow they are bound to doe, and yet they must do them. For though they bee bound to obey the Pope, Yet Simancha. Enchir. Iud. Tit.5. nu.3

18. resolved] tesolved. L-1   **Margin 20.** Sopra la lettera de Palmieri Romito. Nella Raccolta. fo.126 *Ed.*: Sopra. la. lettera de palmieri Romilo. Nella Roccolta. fo.183. L-1, C-1   **27.** strange *Ed.*: stange. C-1, L-1   **30.** are not *errata*: are. L-1, C-1

they are not bound to beleeve that Paul the fift is Pope: because those Elections have many vitiating circumstances, which annuls them. For if they could be certaine, that the *Election* were free from all other corruptions, yet that *Decretall* in the *Septimes*, of *Simoniacall Election*, must of necessitie keepe all indifferent men in continuall anxietie and perplexitie. For, *if any thing by any Cardinall, were given, or promis'd before, though the Election be by way of Assumption and Adoration, when all concurre in it*, which they call, *Viam spiritus Sancti*, and therefore not subject to errour, Yet *there is a Nullitie in this Election*, and the holy Ghosts confirmation workes nothing upon it, And *the Person elected, hath neither spirituall nor temporall Jurisdiction, but looses all the dignities which he had before, and becomes incapable ever after; And no subsequent Act, of Inthroning, Oathes of Obedience by the Cardinalls, nor possession, though of long time, can make it good*: And *even those Cardinals, which were parties to the Simony, may at any time after, depart from his obedience, & all the rest of the Cardinals, which do not, forfeit their dignities*.

Li.1. Ti.3. c.1

43 It is scarce possible to bee hoped, that in Elections there should be no degrees of that corruption, which this Decree labors to preclude, & which, it takes knowledge, to be so clandestine, and secretly caried, that comming to the point of annulling all those promises which were so made, your Law expresses it thus, *Cum quamvis Inexcogitabili solennitate & formâ iurata*. And if ever it should breake forth, that any such thing were committed at *Paul* the fift his Election, then hee was never Pope: Which, though perchance it will not make voide all his Acts, for some civill and convenient reasons, doth yet show the injustice, and indiscretion of such a vowe, as binds the Votarie to doe some acts, which were not lawfull for him to doe, except an assured Authoritie of the commander did warrant it.

44 And if that measure which *Aquinas* gave before of *Blind obedience*, must also serve in this, which is; That *they must obey in all things, which belong to their Regular conversations*, that is, In all things to which their Rule, and Vowe obliges them, then as no Sea can wall any kingdome against their entrance: So no watchfulnesse can arme any

2.2.ae. q.104. Art.5. ad 3^m

Margin 4. Ti. *Ed.*: To.. C-1, L-1 **7.** Assumption *Ed.*: Assumtion. L-1, C-1 **22.** quamvis *Ed.*: quavis. C-1, L-1

CHAPTER SIX 147

brest against their violence, since the increasing of that *Monarchie* which they must advance, growes from the decay of others.

45   But I forbeare *Exasperation*; and will here ende this Chapter; by which, I hope, it appeares, that no latter band of Obedience, can slacken this first, which was borne with us. For, though amongst Lawyers, *To commit my selfe or my cause,* [a]*Liberae voluntati hominis*, or to bee used by him, [b]*Prout voluerit*, amount very farre, and create a large power in him, yet they conclude, That, [c]*In nullo arbitrio, How large so ever, any thing is included which was formerly prohibited.* And of these three Obediences which we have handled, though all the three essentiall properties of all Oathes and Vowes be wanting in them all, yet the *blinde obedience* to your spirituall Superiour, doth especially want *discretion*, and the *implicite Obedience*, imagin'd to bee vowed to the Church in Baptisme, doeth lacke *Trueth*, and that *seditious* and *servile Obedience* vowed by the *Jesuites* to the Popes wil, doeth want *Justice*.

Par. de Put. de Synd. fo.[a]179. [b]192. [c]193

Margin 5.   Put. . . .   [b]192.   [c]193   *Ed*.: put. . . .   b.192.   c.193.   C-1, L-1
15.   the Popes *errata*: your Popes.   L-1, C-1

Chap. VII.

That if the meere execution of the function of Priests in this Kingdome, and of giving to the Catholickes in this Land, spirituall sustentation, did assure their consciences, that to die for that, were Martyrdome; yet the refusall of the Oath of Alleageance doeth corrupt and vitiate the integritie of the whole Act, and dispoile them of their former Interest and Title to Martyrdome.

<small>2.2.ae. q.124. Ar.4</small>

1 We speake of *Martyrdome* now, in the proper and restrain'd sense and acceptation, that is, of *Consummate Martyrdome*, and so, as *Aquinas* takes it, when he sayes, *Mors est de ratione Martyrii*. I know the Primitive Church denied it not to them, whom the latter Church hath call'd *Confessors*; So ^a*Ignatius* writes himselfe Martyr; and so doeth ^bSaint *Paul* say, that hee dies daily. And sometimes, when the Church enjoyed her ease, and was pamper'd with securitie and rest, to excite men to a publicke confession of their Faith, if there arose any case wherein it was needfull, the *Ministers* of that Church, which was ever apter and forwarder to suffer *Martyrdome*, when any long persecution had accustom'd her to the expectation and patience and glorie thereof, then in the times of dull abundance and tranquilitie, would affoord the Title of *Martyrs*, to any persons who suffred any persecution for the testimonie of *Christ*, though they died not: As the Church celebrates the Martyrdome of Pope *Marcellus*, who died in Prison. So also sometimes their indulgence alowed that Name, for some *abstinencies* and *forbearings*, if they conduced to the depressing of *Idolatrie*. For so Saint *Chrysostome* sayes, *If thou refuse to be cured by Magique, and die of that sickeness, thou art a Martyr.*

<small>^aEpist.8. ad Polycarpum
^bI Cor. 15.31</small>

<small>Aquin. ibid.</small>

<small>Advers. Iudaeos. Orat.5</small>

<small>De Sanc. Beat. l.1. c.7. §. Quinto</small>

2 Devotion is apt to overvalew other mens actions; And *Bellarmine* confesses out of *Sulpitius*, *That the people did long time devoutely celebrate one for a Martyr, who after appear'd, and told them that he was damn'd*. So also were those men inclin'd, whom *Alexander* the third reprehendes, *For giving the honour of a Martyr to one that died drunke.*

<small>Extrav. de Reliquii. Audivimus</small>

---

7. 1 *Ed.*: missing . L-1, C-1 **Margin 8.** 2.2. *Ed.*: 22.. C-1, L-1 **15.** Church *Ed.*: Chnrch. L-1, C-1 **25.** Martyr. *Ed.*: Martyr. L-1, C-1 **Margin 26.** De Sanc. Beat. *Ed.*: De Purgat.. L-1, C-1

So doeth another *Jesuite* proove *Hyrcanus* to bee an *Hereticke*, whom *Albertus Magnus* hath put into his *Litany*, and so drawne into continuall Invocation ever since. And when *Gregory* the thirteenth made Commissioners to survay the *Martyrologe*, they found the Histories of Pope *Felix* the second, so various and repugnant, that they were determined to expunge his name, but that opportunely there was a Marble Coffin found, with such an Inscription as alterd them, and relieved the Popes fame. And one principall inducement to the Pope, to come to these solemne *Canonizations*, is, *because before the people did often mistake*.

3 And this medicine, as it was very late applied (for *Bellarmine* cannot finde, *that the Popes canonizd any in eight hundred yeares after Christ*:) So neither hath it, nor can it naturally extinguish the disease. The most that it can worke, is an Assurance, that they which are publiquely canonized are true Saints: for *Bellarmine* sayes, *That it is the opinion of Heretiques, that the Pope can erre in such Canonizations*: and yet, to prove it, he argues but thus: *If we beleeve that there was such a man as Caesar, why should we not beleeve that which God testifies by miracles?* But how shall wee beleeve that these miracles are from God, or that he doth them in testimony of that mans sanctity? For that miracles are done, is not enough to constitute a Saint, for wicked men may doe them, say your Authors: And in this case they can proceed no farther, then to an *Historicall* beleefe, that Miracles are done. And I had thought that *Bellarmine* had required a better faith at our hands, then *Historicall*, and such as assures us, that *Caesar* was, to ground Invocation of Saints, and to constitute an *Heresie*.

4 And though not in *Bellarmine*, yet in the Pope himselfe, there appeare some scruples of diffidence, and frailty, and fallibility in this acte of *Canonizing*, because, after all his severall *Inquisitions* and searches, which depend upon matter of *Fact*, and after his divers iteration of prayers, *That hee may not erre*, and That *hee may not be permitted to erre*, hee makes at last a publique protestation, *That he intends not by that act, to do any thing against Faith.*

5 But if this can be certaine, That those, and none but those, which are so Canonized, may be publiquely Honoured as *Saints*, yet that disease, of which we spoke before, is not cured hereby. For it is still lawfull

Margin 3. Bini. *Ed.*: Bini'. C-1, L-1   **Margin 16.** l.1. c.9 *Ed.*: c.9. §. 1. C-1, L-1

Serarius. Trihaeres. l.2. c.28

Bini. To.1. f.490

Bellar. ubi supra

Ibid. c.8. §. Dices

Ibid. l.1. c.9. §. Tertio

Extra. de Reliq. gloss. verb. miraculis

Ceremon. Sacrae. Cap. de Canoniz.

privately to worshippe any, of whose sanctity I have an opinion. Nor is this *private* worship, so private in *Bellarmines* account, that it may not bee exhibited before others; but onely so private as it may not be done, *In the name of the Church, and as though it were instituted by the Church.* So that whole Multitudes, and Congregations may erre still: and this, by the authority of the *Canon* it selfe. For thus *Bellarmine* reasons, with more detortion and weakenesse then becomes the cause of his gravity: *In the two Canons,* sayes he, *Audivimus, and Cum ex eo, the Pope forbiddes publique worshippe; and therefore, a Contrario, permits private.* If then, that worshippe which in those two *Canons* he forbiddes to be *publiquely* exhibited, may *privately* be given, and this *privatenesse* exclude not whole Congregations, then whole Congregations may lawfully worshippe as a *Saint*, a man slaine in drunkennesse, which is the case of the first *Canon*, and lawfully worshippe venall and uncertaine *Reliques*, which is in the second *Canon*; since the forbidding of this in *publique*, hath permitted it in this large and open *private*, by *Bellarmines* fashion of arguing; who sayes also for this, *That the Doctors doe commonly affirme it.*

6   And whatsoever is said heere of *Saints*, holdes as well in *Martyres*, for with the same faith, that I beleeve a man to be a *martyre*, I beleeve him to be a *Saint*: And so, it seemes, doth that Catholique Priest, who hath lately published a History of English *Martyres*: For that which in the Title he calls *Martyrologe*, in his Advertisement he calles *Sanctiloge*. And therefore it becomes both our *Religion* and *Discretion*, to consider thoroughly the circumstances of their *History*, whom we admit to the honour of Martyrdome.

7   All Titles to *martyrdome* seeme to me to be grounded upon one of these three pretences, and claimes. The first is, to seale with our bloode the profession of some *morall Truth*, which though it be not directly of the body of the Christian faith, nor expressed in the *Articles* thereof, yet it is some of those workes, which a Christian man is bound to doe. The second is, to have maintained with losse of life, the *Integrity* of the Christian faith, and not to suffer any part thereof to perish or corrupt. The third is, to endevour by the same meanes to preserve the *liberties* and *immunities* of the Church.

margin: De Sanc. Beat. l.1. c.10

margin: Extra. de Reliq. c.1 & 2

Margin 2. De Sanc. Beat. l.1. c.10 *Ed.*: De Purgat. c.10, §. 1.

8   By the first way they entitle *S. John Baptist* because he died for reprehending a fault against a *morall Truth*: and that truth being resisted, the *Authour* of truth is despised: And therefore all truth is not matter convenient for the exercise of this vertue, as the conclusions of *Artes* and *Sciences*, though perfectly and demonstratively true, are not; but it must be such a truth, as is conversant about *Christian piety*, and by which *God may be glorified*: which cannot be, except he might be injured by the denying thereof. So, the *Evangelist* when our *Saviour* spake of *S. Peters* Martyrdome says, *He signified by what death hee should glorifie God*: For all Martyredome workes to that end. And this first occasion of *martyrdome* seldome fals out in *Christian* Countries, because in *Christ*, the great Mirrour of all these truthes, we see them *distinctly* and evidently. But sometimes with *Heathen* Princes, before they arrive to this rich and pregnant knowledge, men which labour their conversion, begin, or touch by the way, some of these *Morall dueties*; and if they grow odious, and suffer for that, they are perfect *Martyrs*, dying for a *morall Trueth*, and in the way to Christ.   Joh. 21.19

9   By the second claime, which is the *Integritie* of Catholicke Religion, the professors of any *Christian* Church, will make a specious, and apparant Title, if they suffer persecution in any other Christian Church. For the Church of *Rome* will call the whole totall body and bulke of the points of their profession, *Integritie* of Religion, and the *Reformed* Churches call, soundnesse, puritie, and incorruptnesse, integritie. The Roman thinkes *Integritie* hurt by nothing but *Maimes*, and we, by *Diseases*. And one will proove by his death, that too little is professed, and the other, that too much. But this advantage we have, that by confession of our adversaries, all that wee affirme, is *True*, and *Necessarie*: and upon good ground we assure our selves, that nothing else is so, and we thinke that, a propensenesse to die, for profession of those points, which are not necessarie, will not constitute a Martyrdome, in such a person especially as is of necessarie use.

10   Amongst other things which our *Blessed Saviour* warnes his followers, this is one, *That none of them suffer as a busie body in other mens matters, but if he suffer as a Christian, let him not be ashamed, but glorifie God*. And in another place, hee cals them blessed: *If oth-*   I Pet. 4.15, 16

Matth. 5.11

Margin 33. 4.15, 16 *Ed.*: 4.15..   L-1, C-1

ers say all maner of evill of them, falsely, and for his sake. So that the *prohibition* forbids us, to suffer for those things which doe not certainely appertaine to us; And the *instruction* ties the reward to these conditions, That the imputations be *false*, That they be imputed *for Christs sake*, that is, to dishonour him, and that we suffer *because we are Christians*.

11   Since therefore some of you, at your *Executions*, and in other *conferences*, have added this to your comfort, and glory of Martyrdome, *That because the Kings mercie hath beene offred you, if you would take the Oath, therefore you died for refusing the same*, (Though your Assertion cannot lay that upon the State, who hath two discharges; One, that you were condemn'd for other *Treasons*, before that offer; The other, that the Oath hath no such *Capitall* clause in it) yet since, as I said, you take it upon your Consciences to bee so; Let us Examine, whether your refusall of the Oath, bee a just cause to Die, upon this point of *Integritie of Faith*, by that measure which our Saviour gave in his *Prohibition*, and in his *Instruction*.

12   Is it then *any of your matters*, or doeth it belong to you, by your *Doctrine*, and by your *Example*, in refusing the Oath, to determine against Princes Titles, or Subjects Alleageance? If this be *any of your matters*, then you are not sent onely to doe Priestly functions; And if it be not, then you suffer as *busie bodies in other mens matters*, if you suffer for the Oath.

13   And then, what is imputed to you, which is *false* (which is another condition required by *Christ*) if you be called traitors then, when after apparant transgressing of such lawes as make you Traitors, you confirme to us a perseverance in that Traiterous disposition, by refusing to sweare Temporall Alleageance? Wherein are you lesse subject to that name, then those *Priestes* which were in *Actuall* plots, since *mentall Treason* denominates a man as well as *mentall heresie*? You neither can nor will condemne any thing in them, but that they did their treason, before any Resolution of the *Church*: and have you any resolution of the *Church*, for this, *That the King may be deposed, when he is excommunicated*? if you have, you are in a better forwardnesse then they, and you may undertake any thing, as soone as you will, that is, as soone as you can. For you have as good opinions already, and as strong authorities, *That a King of another Religion then Romane, is*

CHAPTER SEVEN 153

in the state of an excommunicate person, before Sentence, as you have for this, *That an Excommunicate King may be deposed*; And would you thinke it a just cause of Martyrdome, to averre, *that the King is already under excommunication?*

5   14   And (to proceede farther in *Christs Instruction*) are these things said of you for *Christs* sake? Are you (if you be called Traitors for refusing the Oath) reproved for anie part of his Commandements? If it were for exercising your Priestlie functions, you might have some colour, since all your Catholique Religion, must bee the onely Christian Religion. But can that *state* which labours watchfullie and zealouslie for the promoving of *Christs* glorie in all other things, bee saide to oppose *Christ*, or persecute him in his Members, for imputing traiterous inclinations to them, who abhorre to confirme their Alleageance by a just Oath?

15   Lastly, can you say, *you suffer as Christians*, that is (as *Christ* there intended) for *Christian* faith, which is principally the matter of Martyrdome? *Aquinas* cites this, out of *Maximus, The Catholique faith is the mother of martyrdome*. And he explicates it thus, *That though martyrdome be an act of fortitude, and not of faith, yet as a civill man will be valiant to defend Justice, as the Object of his valour, so doth a Martyr, faith*. If then to refuse this Oath, be an object for a Martyrs fortitude, it must be because it opposes some point of faith, and *faith is that, which hath beene beleeved ever, and every where*; And how can that be so matter of faith, which is under disputation, and perplexitie with them, and the contrarie whereof we make account, that we see by the light of Nature and Scriptures, and all meanes conducing to a divine and morall certitude?   2.2.ae. q.124. Art.2. ad 1m

16   *Leo* the first, in an Epistle to the Emperour, by telling what hath beene, informes summarilie and soundly, what should be a just cause of Martyrdome. *None of the Martyrs*, says he, *had any other cause of their suffering, but the confession of the true Divinitie, and true humanitie in Christ*. And this was then the *Integritie* of faith, in both acceptations; *All*, and *sound*. Which is neither impaired in the extent, nor corrupted in the puritie, by any thing proposed in the Oath.   Epist.24

17   But as *Chrysostome* expounding that place of *Jeremie, Domus Dei facta est spelunca Hyaenae*, applies it to the *Priests* of the Jewes,   In Marc. Hom.13. To.2. fo.270

Margin 16. 2.2.ae *Ed.*: 22ae. C-1, L-1

as hardest of all, to be converted, so may we apply it to the *Priests* of the *Romanes*, who abhor the Oath, and deter their Schollers. For, *the Hyena,* sayes *Chrysostome, hath but one backe bone, and cannot turne except it turne all at once.* So have these men, one back bone, the Church; (for so sayes *Bellarmine, if we were agreed of that, we should soone be at an end:*) and this Church is the Pope; And they cannot turne, but all at once, when he turnes; and this is the *Integritie* of the faith they talke of. And, as that Father, addes of the *Hyena, Delectantur cadaveribus*; they are delighted with impious provocations to the effusion of bloud, by suggesting a false and imaginarie martyrdome.

18 The third and last just ground of martyrdome, of those which we mentioned, is *Ecclesiastique Immunitie*, which is of two sorts; one *inhaerent*, and *Native*, and *connaturall* to the Church, and the other, *Accessory*, and such, as for the furtherance and advancement of the worship of God, Christian Princes, in performing a religious dutie, have afforded and established. Of the first sort are, *preaching the word, administring the Sacraments, and applying the Medicinall censures.* And if any, to whose charge God hath committed these, by an ordinarie calling, loose his life in the execution thereof, with *Relation* to the cause, we may justly esteeme him a martyr. And so in the second kinde, if onely for a pious and dutifull admonition to the Prince, to continue those *Liberties* to the Church, without which she cannot wel doe her offices, hee should incurre a deadly displeasure, he were also a *Martyr*.

19 And if the Romane Priests could transferre upon themselves this title to Martyrdome, due to defenders of either of these Immunities, yet by refusall of this Oath, which is an implied affirming of some doctrine contrarie to it, they forfait that interest, by obtruding, as matter of Christian faith, that which is not so: For *Baronius* himselfe (as once before wee had occasion to say) distinguishes the defence of the liberties of the Church, from the Catholique faith; and yet he and many others, make the defence of these immunities the object of Martyrdome: so various and uncertaine is the doctrine of defending those priviledges, whose ground and foundation they cannot agree upon.

20 And as all right to the crowne of Martyredome, growing from any of these three titles, perishes by their refusal, for the reasons before

---

31. make *Ed.*: makes. L-1, C-1

expressed: so doth it also upon this ground, that hee which refuses to defend his life by a lawfull acte, and entertaines not those overtures of escape, which God presents him, destroyes himselfe, especially if his life might be of use and advantage to others. For when the Prison was opened to *Paul* and *Silas*, the learned Expositors excuse his stay there, by no other way, then that it appeares, that he had a revelation of Gods purpose, that he should convert the Keeper; for otherwise not to have hastened his escape, had beene to abuse Gods mercie by not using it. Acts 16.26

21   Those lawes from which these conclusions are deduced, *that if a man receive a Corporall injurie, and remit the offence, yet the state may pursue it against the trespasser, because no man is Lord of himselfe*: and that *a covenant from a man, that if you finde him in your ground you may beate him, is voide upon the same reason*, Intimate thus much to this purpose, That no man by lawe of nature may deliver himselfe into a danger which he might avoide. Par. Put. Syndic. fol.484

22   How many actes of good and meritorious nature, if they had all due circumstances, have beene vitiated by *Indiscretion*, and changed from nourishment to poison? of which *Cassianus* hath amass'd many usefull examples, and made all his second *collation* of them. Of which I will remember one hapning about his own time: *Heron* which had lived fiftie yeares austerely in a Desart, trusting indiscreetely an illusion of an evill spirit, threw himselfe downe into a Well; and when he was taken out, and in such torment with those bruses, as killed him within three dayes, yet he beleeved that he had done well, though the rest beleeved him to be as *Cassianus* sayes, *Biothanatum*, a selfe-murderer. Collat.2. ca.5

23   How deeply, and how irremediably doth this indiscretion possesse many others, whom themselves only, and a few illuders of their weaknesses, esteeme to be *Martyres*, for provoking the execution of just lawes against them? For what greater *Indiscretion* can there be, or what more treacherous betraying of himselfe, then to die in despite of such a Princes mercie, as at once directs him to understand his duety to himselfe, and to his Prince: and shewes him, that his owne preservation is a naturall duety; and that hee may not neglect it in any cause, but where it appeares evidently, Catholiquely, and indisputably (amongst them to whose instruction he ought to submitte himselfe) that God may

Margin 4.   16.26 *Ed.*: 16..   L-1, C-1

bee glorified in it; And that his obedience to the King was borne in him, and therfore was once, without all question, due, & could not be taken away, with out his consent, who is damnified by the losse of a Subject; at least by such a litigious Authoritie, as is yet in Disputation, *What it is, whence it comes*, and *how it resides in him*, and *how it is executed*.

24 For as a man may be *felo de se*, by destroying himselfe by our Law; And *fur de se*, by departing, and stealing himselfe away, from him to whom his service is due, by Imperial law: so he may be *proditor de se*, by the law of Nature, if hee descend from the Dignitie of humanitie, & submit himselfe to an usurpation, which he ought to resist, which is; All violence and danger which hee might avoide.

25 And since, if the King would pardon him, upon doing of any act, which depended upon his owne will, he were guiltie of his death, if hee refused it, he is so also in this case; since he can propose to himselfe no such restraint as binds his wil; For *scruples*, and things in *Opinion* and *Disputation*, do not binde in this case, Of which we shall have proper occasion to speake in the next Chapter.

26 Let us then proceede further, to that which gives the *forme*, and *measure*, and *merit*, even to Martyrdome it-selfe, which is *Charitie*. And this is not meant onely of Charitie, as it is a *Theologall* vertue, and unites us in an earnest love to God, which is, *Charitas patriae*, but also as from that fountaine is derived upon all his creatures, which is *Charitas viae*: For so Saint *John* says, of this charitable act of which wee speake, *Greater love then this no man hath, when hee bestoweth his life for his friend*: Which also appeares out of that History recorded of *Nicephorus*: [a]who being brought to the place where he was to receive the Crowne of Martyrdome, and seeing *Sapritius*, betweene whome and him, there had before some bitternesses and enmitie broke foorth, fall downe before him, and begge a Pardon and reconcilement, was so much elated with this glory of *Martyrdom*, that uncharitably he disdain'd to admit any reconciliation. In punishment of which uncharitablenesse, he lost his whole hope and victorie: For the spirit of God forsooke him, and he Apostated from his Faith: So that Charitie is justly esteem'd the forme of Martyrdome.

Jo. 15.13

[a]Metaphrast. in Nicepho. Mar.

Margin 23. 15.13] 13.15. C-3, E-2, MCG, C^5-1 **Margin 26a.** Metaphrast.] note misplaced . C-3, E-2, MCG, C^5-1, SP

27   And is there any Charitie in this Doctrine, or in this act of *Refusall*? Is there any to your self? (For, at least *in spiritualibus, Charitie begins at home*) when at once you divorce that body which your Parents prepar'd, from that Soule which God infused and married to it: and so leave, not onely to be *men*, and to be *Subjects*, but to be *Priests*, and benefactors to that cause, which you hinder by this pretence of loving it. How much opportunitie of Merit, even in advancing the Catholique cause, which to you is so certaine, doe you loose, by exposing your selfe to *certaine* ruine, upon *uncertaine* foundations? Is there any charitie to the Church, or partie, or faction, which you have in this Kingdom? towards whom the King brought with him so much tendernesse, that hee cast in a dead sleepe all *bloudy* lawes, and in a slumber all *pecuniarie* lawes which might offend, & aggrieve them. Is it charitably done towards them, that by your unnecessarie act, their peace be interrupted, his Majesties sweetnesse distasted, his softnesse indured, and those faire impressions which hee had admitted, That civill obedience might consist with your Religion, defaced and obliterated? And that to all these should succeede, jealousies in him, imputations upon them, and dutifull solicitations from his Parliament, & Counsaile, and Subjects of all rankes, to awaken his lawes against these suspitious men?

28   Was it charitably done of that *Priest*, who apprehending a generall inclination of taking the Oath, advanced it so farre, as to make a Declaration that it was lawfull, and never retracting that opinion, yet would die in the refusall thereof, *because it seemed not expedient to him, to take it then*; and so to cast snares and tortures upon their consciences, who were before in possession of a peaceable, & (by his own testimony) a just resolution?   [Jervase]

29   When S. *Paul* uses that phrase, he expounds the word *Expedient*, by *Profitable* and by *Edifying*: And hath the example of his death profited and edified that Church as much, as the perplexities certainely growne in Catholique consciences thereby, and those exasperations, and bitternesses occasioned, by all probabilitie in the state, by that perverse and peevish behaviour, may shake and tempest it?   [I Cor. 6.12 & 10.23]

30   I doe not thinke that they would have denied him to have beene a *Martyr*, if he had beene executed upon the *Statute* against *Priests*, though he had before taken the oath. If therefore the taking of the oath

cannot vitiate and annull martyrdome, the refusing it cannot constitute martyrdome.

31 And if you will make the difference onely by reason of the Popes *Breve*, which perchance came betweene his first resolution, and his last, then you reduce your Martyrdome to a more slipperie and more dangerous distresse then before: For as before you quitted all your benefite and interest to martyrdome, for having exercised *Priestly* functions, and proclaimed and solaced your selfe with this, that you died for refusing the oath; so now you waive that, and sticke to a worse title, which is, obedience to an uncertaine and suspicious Breve; For, for your first title, which is preaching of the Catholique faith, you have the intire and unanime consent and concurrence of the whole Christian Church; which alwayes confesses, that the profession of the Catholique faith, is, a true and just cause of Martyrdome; though she doe not confesse, that that which you teach, is that Catholique Faith, but for that Title you had also the consonance and agreement of all the Romane Church. And for your second claim, which is, the defence of the Popes *temporall Jurisdiction*, by refusing this oath, you had some voices of great authority in that Church, to encourage you, though farr too weak, either to blot out a naturall truth, or to make an indifferent, or perplex'd point so necessary to you, as to dy for it. But for this third title to martyrdome, which arises from obedience to the *Breves*, which are *matters of fact*, & subject to a thousand infirmities & nullities, who ever justly grounded a necessity of dying, upon them, or added the comfort of martyrdome to such a precipitation?

32 Thus dooth *Aquinas* argue against a farre better Title to martyrdome, then this is: *Though virginity be more pretious then life, yet if a virgine shold be condemned to be deflowred, Occasione fidei Christianae, because she was a Christian, though all those conditions, which we noted in our Saviors prohibition, and instruction, concurred in her case, That she were no busie body in provoking, That she were persecuted, and that unjustly, And with relation and despite to Christ, and so she suffered as a Christian, yet, sayes he, this were no Martyrdome.* Yet he assignes not the reason to be, because she died not, but because *Martyrdome is a testimony, by which it is made evident to all, that the Martyres love*

2.2.ae. q.124. ar.4. ad. 2

9. waive *errata*: waine. L-1, C-1 **Margin 27.** 2.2. *Ed.*: 22.. C-1, L-1

CHAPTER SEVEN 159

Christian faith above all things, and it cannot appeare by this act of hers, whether she suffered this for the love of Christian faith, or for contempt of chastitie. But in this acte of dying for obedience to the Breves, there is by many degrees lesse manifestation, that they die for Christian Faith, which is not in question; and there appeare evident impressions of humane respects, which would vitiate a better title to martyrdome, and of such unnaturall dereliction of themselves, as I doe not see how they could escape being *selfe-murderers*, but that their other Treasons, and condemnations for them, make their executions just.

33 And besides that, *Bellarmine* makes this hard shift, and earnest propensenesse to die, no good signe of a good cause, or of a true martyrdome (for thus he makes his gradations, That *the Anabaptists are forwardest, and the Calvinists next, and the Lutherans very slacke*: So that he makes the vehemency of the professors, in this kind, some testimony of the ilnesse of the Religion) we may also observe, that all circumstances (except the maine point, with which we intercharge one another, which is *Heresie*) by which they labour to deface and infirme the zeale of our side in this point, and to take from them, all comfort of martyrdome, doe appeare in them directly or implicitly, in this denying of civill obedience. _{De Not. Eccles. l.4. c.2. §. Item}

34 And because we may boldly trust his malice in gathering them, that he will omit none, we will take them as they are objected against us in *Feuardentius* the Minorite: A man of such dexterity and happines in converting to the Romane Faith, that all *Turquy* and the *Indies* would not bee matter enough for him to worke upon one yeare, if he should proceed with them in the same pace, as he doth with the *Minister of Geneva*: For meeting him once upon a time by chaunce, and falling into talke with him, in the person of a Catholique *Doctor*, he dispatches a *Dialogue* of some eight hundred great leaves, and reduces the poore Minister, who scarce ever stands him two blows, from *one thousand foure hundred Heresies*: And as though he had but drawne a Curtaine, or opened a boxe, and shewed him catholique Religion, he leaves him as sound, as the *Councell of Trent*.

35 First therefore in this matter of *Martyrdome*, he takes a promise

---

2. *suffered* Ed.: *suffer*. L-1, C-1   **19.** appeare Ed.: -peare L-1, C-1; ap- catchword quarto p.214. L-1, C-1

of the *Minister, That he will be diligent hereafter, from being amazed at the outward behaviour of men which suffer death.* By which direction & good counsell, the confident fashion and manner of any *Jesuite* at his execution, shall make no such impression in us, as to produce arguments of his innocency. After this, he says, that our men are not martyres, *Because they have departed from the Church, in which they were baptized, and have not kept their promise made in Baptisme, but are therefore Apostats and Antichrists.* Another reason he assignes against them, *because they have beene put to death for conspiracies, rebellions, tumults, and civill Warres against lawfull Princes,* and that therefore *they have beene proceeded against in Ordinary forme of Justice, as Traitors.* And againe, hee sayes, *They have beene justly executed for making, and divulging libells against Princes. And for Acts against a Canon of the Eliberitane Councell,* of which I spoke before. And lastly, this despoiles us of the benefite of Martyrdome in his account, *Because we offer our selves to dangers, and punishments, seeking for honour out of misery, and blowen up with ambition and greedinesse of vaine glorie.* Thus farre *Feuardentius* charges us.

36   And is it not your case also, to forfait your Martyrdome upon the same circumstances? Are not many of you departed from your promise in *baptisme* to our Church? or did those which undertooke for you, ever intend this forsaking? and this *act* of departing is by *Feuardentius*, made an Essential circumstance, abstract, and independent and incohaerent with that of the *Catholique* Church, for that is another alone by it selfe.

37   And have not you beene proceeded with, *in Ordinarie course of Justice, as Traitors, for Rebellions, and Conspiracies, and Tumults?* And after so many protestations so religiously delivered, so vehemently iterated, so prodigally sealed with bloud, and engaging your Martyrdome upon that issue, that you never intermedled with matters of state, nor had any other scope or marke of all your desires and endevours, but the replantation of Catholique Religion, hath not the *Recorder* and mouth of all the English *Jesuites*, confessed, (upon a mistaking, that the evennesse of his Majesties disposition might be shaked by this insinuation,) ᵃ*That in the Sentence of Excommunication against Queene Elizabeth, the Popes relating to a statute in England, respected the Actuall right of*

Margin side notes:
Theomachia. Calvinist. l.8. c.13. nu.1
Ibid. nu.3
Nu.4
Nu.6
Nu.10
ᵃJudgement of a Catholique. of the Apologie of the Oath. Pag.91

Margin 1. c.13. *Ed.*: c.18. C-1, L-1   **Margin 8.** 4] 1. C-4, SP

his Majesties mother, and of him, and proceeded for the removall of that Queene, whom they held an usurper, in favour of the true inheritours oppressed by her, not only by spirituall, but temporall armes, also, as against a publique Malefactor, and Intruder. And having thus like an indiscrete *Advocate*, prevaricated for the Pope, doth hee not as much betray all his owne complices, when he addes, *This doth greatly justifie the endevours and desires of all good Catholique people, both at home, and abroad, against her, their principall meaning being ever knowne to have beene, the deliverance and preferment of the true heire, most wrongfully kept out, and unjustly persecuted for righteousnes sake.* Did you *intend* nothing else, but Catholique *Religion*, and yet was the *desire*, and *endevour* of all good Catholiques at home, and abroad, to *remove* her, and *plant* another, and that by vertue of a *statute* in *England*? Did the Popes in their *Bulls*, intimate any *illegitimation*, or *usurpation*, or touch upon any such statute? Or did they goe about to advance the *right Heire* in the *Spanish Invasion*? or was the way of the *right Heire* Catholiquely prepared by *Dolemans* booke? Or was the Author thereof no good Catholicke?

38   For these Conspiracies, and for the same Authors monethly Libels, which cast foule aspersions upon the whole cause, in defence wherof they are undertaken, and published, are your pretences to Martyrdome unjust and invalid, if your *Feuardentius* gives us good rules. So are they also because you seeke it against the *Eliberitane* Councell; That is, *By wayes not found in Scriptures, nor practised by the Apostles*: And last of all, because you seeke it with such intemperate hunger, and vaine-glorie, *Cultum ex Miseria quaerentes* (as your Friar accuses our Churches) and hunting and pursuing your owne death; First, over the tops of mountaines, the Popes *Spirituall power*, then through thicke and entangling woods, without wayes in or out, that is his *Temporall power*, and then through darke caves and dens of his Chamber Epistles, his *Breves*, ready, rather then not die, to defend his personall defects, and humane infirmities. And all these circumstances, are virtually and radically enwrapt in this one refusall of the Oath, which therefore alone doeth defeate all your pretences to Martyrdome.

17–19. 38 For these *errata*: 38 *misplaced at* Or was. L-1, C-1

39 And though it may perchance truely bee said by you, that all those persons which the *Reformed* Churches have Enregistred in their *Martyrologies*, are not certainely and truely *Martyrs*, by those Rules to which we binde the signification of the word in this Chapter, and in which you account, all which die by way of Justice, for advancing the Romane *Doctrine* or *Dignitie*, by what seditious way so ever, to be true Martyrs, yet none of them hath ever transgressed so farre, as your Example would warrant them. For, not to speake of *Baronius* his *Martyrologe*, where verie many are enrolled, which lived their Naturall time, and without any externall persecution for their faith, and where verie many of the olde Testament are recorded, besides those which are canonized in the Epistle to the Hebrewes, and manie which are mentioned in that Epistle are left out by him, not onely *Enoch*, *Noe*, and such other as suffered not death in their bodies, as *Martyrs*, but even *Abel* whom he might have beene bolde to call a *Martyr*; to omit him, I say, why doth our *Countryman* amongst you, which hath lately compiled an *English Martyrologe*, present a *Calendar*, in which of almost 500 whom he names, scarse 60 are *Martyrs*; and of the rest, some were not of our Nation, as *Constantine* the Emperour, whose festivall hee appoints 21 of May; And some never saw this Cuntry, as Pope *Gregory* the I, whom he celebrates 25 December. And of those which did suffer death, the credit and estimation of as many as died, within 200 yeares of *Gregory*, are much impaired by one to whom I thinke, hee will subscribe, who sayes, *That in that 200 yeares, our Nation had no Martyrs, that commonly are knowne*. And those whom hee reckons, must of necessitie be knowne to them, whom that knowledge concernes, as it did *Parsons*, when hee writ that booke, since the knowledge thereof was so obvious & easie, that this Author professes, *that all their Histories are in Authors approved or permitted by the Sea Apostolique, & that he cites no Apocryphall legend, nor fabulous Historie, that may be suspected of the least Note of falsitie, or errour whatsoever*. But he which shall survay his *Catalogue* of Authors, will finde it safer not to beleeve him,

Ca.11

3. Conversions.
par.3. chap.1.
nu.16

20–21. Cuntry, as Pope *Gregory* the I, whom he] Country, as Pope *Gregory*, whom hee. C-1, MCG, C-3, C-4, C⁵-1, SP, O-1, O-2, O⁷, C¹⁶, C²-1, C²-3, C⁹ **22.** death, *Ed.*: death. L-1, C-1 **23.** *Gregory*, are much *Ed.*: *Gregory* the I. is much. L-1, C-1 **Margin 23.** nu.16 *Ed.*: Nu.19. L-1, C-1

CHAPTER SEVEN 163

then to bee bound by him, to beleeve all them to be free from the least note of falsitie or error. For we shall be somwhat hard to beleeve this extreme innocence, and integritie in *Surius*, and in *Saunders*, or in *Cornelius Tacitus*. And many of his owne profession will hardly beleeve
5 that *Gregory*, and *Bede* were free from all falsitie or error, And himselfe, I beleeve, would not stand to this, if we should presse him with some places, out of *Parisiensis*, and *Westmonasteriensis*, and *Walsingham*, and *Polidore Virgil*: all which have beene tried in the furnace of this *Divine Critique*, & are pronounced by him free from the least *note*
10 *of falsitie, or errour whatsoever*. But if these Authors were knowne to *Parsons*, and that hee pronounced truely, that *that 200 yeares was without Martyrs*, then, not onely the *Abbesse of Elies* heardsman, *S. Alnoth*, slaine about 670 in *hatred of Christian Religion*, and celebrated 27 Febru. but the first Christian King of the *Northumbers*, *S. Edwyn*, slaine
15 also in *hatred of our Religion Anno 634.* and observed 4. Octob. with divers other after that time, must be expunged out over this new *Martyrologe*. So also must that Author confesse himselfe to have been too forward, in canonizing *S. Hugh* for a *Martyr, whom at 10 yeares of age,*   July 27 *the Jewes crucified at Lincolne, Anno 1255.* since *Parsons* had told him
20 before, *that after Becket, which was An. 1171. our Church had no more*   Ibid. nu.21 *Martyrs in 400 yeares.*

   40 But for all this, it is not your errour, and vicious example which shall excuse us, if at any time wee have inserted such, as *Martyrs*, which were not precisely so. For if we have committed any such slip in storie
25 and matter of fact, there is not that danger in our transgression, which is in you, because you, by giving them that title, assure the world of a certaine and infallible present salvation, by *vertue* of that suffering, and that they have title thereby to our *Adoration*, and are in present possession of the office of *Advocation* for us. Out of which confidence, I
30 have seene at some Executions of Traiterous *Priests*, some bystanders, leaving all old Saints, pray to him whose body lay there dead; as if hee had more respect, and better accesse in heaven, because he was a stranger, then those which were familiar, had.

7. *Parisiensis Ed.*: Parsiensis. L-1, C-1   **22.** 40 *Ed.*: 30. L-1, C-1

Chap. VIII.

That there hath beene as yet no fundamentall and safe ground given, upon which, those which have the faculties to heare Confessions, should informe their owne Consciences, or instruct their penitents; That they are bound to adventure the heavie and Capitall penalties of this Lawe, for refusall of this Oath. And that if any Man have received a scruple against this Oath, which he cannot depose and cast off, the Rules of their own Casuists, as this case stands, incline, and warrant them, to the taking thereof.

1 Since by refusall of this Oath, which his Majestie hath rather made an *Indulgence* then a *Vexation,* by withdrawing some clauses of bitternesse, and of strict inquisition into the whole Catholicke partie, which the fresh contemplation of the Powder-Treason, had justly urged the Lower-house of Parliament to insert therein: And studying to find a way by which he might discharge both dueties to God and his Kingdome, would in his Princely and Pastorall care, provide a triall, by which those which were corrupted with the poison which broke out in those Treasons, might be distinguish'd from Catholickes of better temper and more duetifull affections towardes him, and our Peace, from which sort of Catholickes, after so many provocations, by persons of the same persuasion in Religion, he seem'd loth to withdraw those favours and graces, which he had ever since his comming expressed towards them: Since, I say, by refusall thereof, both the Catholickes lay a heavie scandal, and dangerous aspersions upon the cause, and declare themselves more slavish to the Pope, and consequently apter to defection from the Prince, then the Subjects of forraine States now are, or the Subjects of this Kingdome were heretofore, And also his Majestie, and all those which affect his safetie, which not only involves but procures and causes theirs, may justly encline at last to thinke, that the very ground, and principles of that Religion nourish these rebellious humours, and so finde it necessarie for preservation of the whole bodie, to apply Medicines more corrosive and sharpe to that member which appeares so corrupt and

2. heare C-3, C⁵-2, O²: hears. L-1, C-1, C-4, L-2, O-1   9. 1 *Ed.: missing.* L-1, C-1

dangerous, And everie Catholique in particular, to whom this Oath is offered, by refusall forfaits his libertie, & by pertinacie therein, incurres other mulcts and penalties, It is therefore the dutie of everie Catholique, out of his religious zeale to the cause, drawne into suspition thereby, and out of his Naturall obligation for preserving his life, fame, and fortune, all which are endangered by this refusall, not to adventure the losse of these, but upon Evidence of much clearenesse, and grounds of strong assurednesse, and constancie.

2   And as it is certaine, that at the first promulging of this oath, they had no such ground, nor Evidence (for them, that light must have beene upon them all, and so many good and earnest maintainers of that Religion, would not have enclined to the Oath, if they had had such Evidence against it) so also after some scruples were injected, and the tendernesse of some consciences vitiated and distracted with some doubts, and that it had beene submitted to Disputation, and consulting amongst themselves, and so passed all those furnaces of Examination, it was held lawfull, and accordingly many tooke it. So that neither by the Evident and undeniable authoritie of Nature, or Scripture, nor by Deductions and conclusions necessarily derived and issuing from thence, any Conscience had sufficient assurance, to incurre these dangers.

3   If since, by some arguments of probabilitie, and of Conveniencie, or by some propositions propagated & deduced from those first principles of Nature, and Scripture, by so many descents and Generations, that it is hard to trie whether they doe truly come from that roote, or no, any Conscience have slackned it selfe, and so be strayed, and dissolved, and scattered, by this remissnesse, and vacillation, it ought rather to recollect it selfe, and returne to those first ingraffed principles, then in this dissolute and loose distraction, to suffer an anxious perplexitie, or desperately to arrest it selfe upon that part, which their owne Rules given to reduce men in such deviations, and settle them in such waverings, cannot assure him to be well chosen, nor deliver and extricate him, in those laborinths.

4   For, let the first roote and parent of all propositions in this matter of Obedience, be, that which we know by nature, *That we must obay such a power, as can preserve us in Peace and Religion*, and that which wee

30. such waverings *Ed*.: sueh waverings.   L-1, C-1

find in Scriptures, *Let every Soule be subject unto the higher powers*; And let us drawe downe a Pedigree, and Genealogie of reasons and conclusions derived from this. The eldest, and that to which most reverence will belong, will be the *Interpretation of the Fathers* upon this place, which is (as your owne men confesse,) *That the Apostle speakes rather of Regall and Secular power, then of that which you call Ecclesiasticke.*

5 Let us then pursue the line, of which the first end is; Kings must be obeyed. It followes, Therefore they must be able to commaund justly; therfore they must have some to enable and instruct them; therefore they must doe according to their instruction; therefore if they doe not, they are subject to their corrections; therefore if they be incorrigible, they are no longer Kings; and therefore no subject can sweare perpetuall Obedience, to his person, who by his owne fault, and his superiours Declaration, may growe to be no King.

6 Now, as no man can beleeve the last of these propositions, as roundly and constantly, as the first, because though it seeme to be the childe of the first, yet in it self, or in some of the meane parents by the way, there may be fallacies which may corrupt and abastard it; so is there no other certaine rule to trie it, but to returne to the first principles, and see if it consist with them. For if it destroy the first, it degenerates and rebels, and we may not adhere to it. And if the first may still consist without it, though this may seeme orderly and naturally deduced from thence, yet it imposes not so much necessity upon us, as the first doth; for that bindes us peremptorily; this, as it is circumstanced and conditioned.

7 And though these circumstances give it all the life it hath, so that to make it obligatory, or not so, depends upon them, yet it is impossible to discerne those circumstances, or unentangle our consciences by any of those Rules, which their *Casuists* use to give, who to strengthen the possession of the *Romane* Church, have bestowed more paines, to teach how strongly a conscience is bound to doe according to a *Scruple*, or a *Doubt*, or an *Opinion*, or an *Errour*, which it hath conceived, then how it might depose that *Scruple*, or cleare that *Doubt*, or better that *Opinion*, or rectifie that *Errour*.

---

1. *the higher* errata: *your higher.* L-1, C-1   **29.** strengthen *Ed.*: stengthen. C-1, L-1

CHAPTER EIGHT 167

8   For, That we may at once lay open the infirmity, and insufficiency of their *Rules*, and apply the same to our present purpose; What use and profite, can those *Catholiques*, which doubt whether they may take that *Oath*, make of that Rule, *that they must follow in doubtfull points,* *that opinion which is most common and generall*? For, though this be understood of the opinion of such men, as are intelligent and understanding, and conversant in the matter in question, yet oftentimes, amongst them, both sides say, *This is the common opinion*; and who can judge it? Yea many circumstances change *the common opinion: For* (sayes *Azorius*) *it fals out often, that that which was not the common opinion a few yeares since, now is*; And that *that which is the common opinion of Divines in one Countrie, is not so in another*; As in *Spaine* and *Italy*, it is the common opinion, *That Latreia is due to the Crosse*, which in *France* and *Germany* is not so. And *Navarrus* says, *That at Rome, no man may say, that the Councell is above the Pope; nor at Paris, that the Pope is above the Councell*. Which devision also there is amongst them, in a maine point which shakes their *Doctrine*, of the Popes being immediately from God, since they cannot agree, *Whether at the Popes death, his power remaine upon the earth, or flie up to heaven*. He is a Catholique, and a temperate discreete Authour, which notes, *That the writings of Catholique men, have something in them which must be allowed to the times when they writ, which being more diligently examined by them which follow, are found exorbitant from the soundnesse of faith*: which hee speakes of those that denie, *that the lawes of civill Magistrates doe binde the conscience*. And after, speaking against them which thinke, *That if we undergoe the penaltie of the law, we do not sinne in the breach therof*, he says, *it was the opinion of some Schoolemen, who thought it a glorious matter, and fit to raise them a name, to leave the common and beaten wayes; having perchance a delight saucily to provoke, to gnaw, to calumniate, & to draw into hatred those powers and authorities which made those lawes*.

9   And if of late dayes, The opinion of refusing the Oath, bee become

[margin: Instit. Mora. To.1. lib.2. c.12. §. quando]

[margin: De Judiciis. Ca. Novit.]

[margin: Ibid.]

[margin: Carninus. de Potest. Leg. Hum. par.1. c.6]

[margin: Idem. par.2. c.2]

Margin 10. lib.2] fo.2.   L-1, L-2, O², O¹⁴, YK-1   **Margin 10.** quando *Ed.*: Si quando.   L-1, C-1   **15.** *Pope; nor* YK-2: *Pope, nor*.   L-1, C-1   **27.** *therof*, he says, *Ed.*: *therof·(he sayes)*.   C-1, L-1   **32.** 9 *Ed.*: 8.   L-1, C-1 **32.** bee become *errata*: become.   L-1, C-1

the more *common opinion*, it is upon some of these circumstances, that at these times, when *Catholiques* are called to professe civill obedience, in this place, where *Jesuites* are in possession of most hearts, to get reputation, or to avile secular Magistracy, they have suddenly made it the more *common*: for they can raise the *Exchange* in an houre, and advance and crie downe an opinion at their pleasure.

But to determine of *mortall sinne* (as the taking of this Oath must be, if it be matter enough to adventure these dangers for it) the same Authour says well, doth not so much appertaine, *Ad pulpita Canonistarum*, as it doth *ad Cathedras Theologorum*: and therefore it ought to be tried by the principles of *Divinity*, not by the circumstanciall ragges of *Casuists*.

<small>Par.1. c.5</small>

But, to goe forward with them, if this *Common Opinion* were certaine, and if it were possible to discerne it, yet it doth not so binde us, but that we may depart from it, when another opinion is *safer*: And from that opinion which is *safer*, wee may also in many cases depart. For which, those examples, which *Carbo* a good *Summist* alleages, may give us satisfaction, which are, *If I doubt of my title to land, I am not bound to restore it (though that were the safest way) because in doubtfull matters, Melior est Conditio possidentis*. And, but for this helpe, I wonder with what conscience, the *Catholiques* keepe the possession of such landes as belonged to the *Church*; for they cannot be without some scruples of an unjust title, and it were safest to restore them. Another example in *Carbo* is, *If my superior command a difficult thing, and I doubt whether he command lawfully or no, though it were safer to obey, yet I am not bound to doe so*. And he gives a *Rule*, which will include a thousand example, That *that Rule, That the safest part is to be embraced, is then onely true, when by following this safer part, there ensues no notorious detriment*. And *Soto* extends this *Doctrine* farther, for he says, *Though you beleeve the precept of your Superior to be just* (which creates *Conscientiam Opinantem*) *yet you may doe against it: Because* (sayes he) *it is then onely sinne to doe against your conscience, when to do according to your conscience, is safe, and that no danger to the*

<small>Summa Summarum. To.1. par.1. lib.5. c.14. §. Tertium</small>

<small>De Ratio. Teg. Secret. Memb.3. q.2. §. Sed contra</small>

1. circumstances *Ed.*: circumstanees. L-1, C-1 **Margin 9.** c.5 *Ed.*: c.6. C-1, L-1 **Margin 17.** par.1. lib.5. c.14 *Ed.*: par.1. c.14. L-1, C-1 **22.** belonged *errata*: belong. L-1, C-1 **Margin 30.** Ratio. Teg. . . . Memb *Ed.*: ratio. teg. . . . memb. L-1, C-1

state, or to a third person, appears therein. So that *Tutius* in a spirituall sense, that is, *in a doubtfull matter rather to beleeve a thing to be sinne, then not,* must yeelde to *Tutius* in a temporall sense, that is, *when it may be done without notorious detriment*; For when it comes to that, we shall finde it to be the *common* opinion of *Casuists*, which the same *Summist* delivers, *That there is no matter so waighty, wherein it is not lawfull for me, to follow an opinion that is probable, though I leave the opinion which is more probable; yea though it concerne the right of another person*: as in our case of obedience to the *King* or the *Pope*. And then, wheresoever I may lawfully follow an opinion to mine advantage, if I will leave that opinion with danger of my life or notorious losse, I am guilty of all the damage I suffer. For these circumstances make that Necessary to me then, which was *indifferent* before: the reasons uppon which *Carbo* builds this Doctrine of following a *probable* opinion, and leaving a more *probable*, which are, *That no man is bound, Ad melius & perfectius, by necessity, but as by Counsell*: And that this Doctrine hath this commoditie, *that it delivers godly men, from the care and solicitude, of searching out, which is the more probable opinion*, shew evidently, that these Rules give no infallible direction to the conscience, and yet in this matter of Obedience, considering the first native certaintie of subjection to the King, and then the damages by the refusall to sweare it, they encline much more to strengthen that civill obedience, then that other obedience which is plainly enough claimed, by this forbidding of the Oath.

So that in these perplexities, the *Casuists* are indeede, *Nubes Testium*: but not in that sense as the holy Ghost used the Metaphore. For they are such *clouds* of witnesses, as their testimonie obscures the whole matter. And they use to deliver no more, then may beget farther doubts, that so every man may from the *Oracle* of his *Confessors* resolution, receive such direction, as shall be fit at that time, when hee gives the aunswere. Which *Navarrus* expresses fully, when he confesses, *That having beene consulted fiftie yeares before, whether they who defrauded Princes in their customes, were bound to restitution, he once gave an aunswere in writing: but having recovered that writing backe againe, he studied twentie yeares for his owne satisfaction, and found no ground*

Heb. 12.1

Ca. Confraternitas. 12. q.2

34. *againe* Ed.: *a-againe.* C-1, L-1

whereupon he might rest: And all that while he counsailed Confessors, to absolve their penitents, upon this condition: That they should retaine a purpose to doe so, as they should understand hereafter to be just.

These *spirituall Physitians* are therefore like those *Physitians*, which use to erect a *figure*, by that Minute in which the patients Messenger comes to them, and thereby give their judgment. For the *Confessours* in *England*, in such resolutions as these, consider first the *Aspects*, and *Relations*, and diverse *predominancies* of *Superiours* at that time, and so make their determinations seasonable, and appropriate.

_{Enchirid. Iudi. Tit.35. n.41}

But to insist more closely upon this point in hand, your *Simancha* speaking out of the law, sayes; *That that witnesse which deposes any thing upon his knowledge, must also declare and make it appeare, how he comes to that knowledge. And if it bee of a thing belonging to the understanding, hee must make it appeare by what means, and instrument his understanding was instructed. And that which he assignes for the reason, must be of that nature, that it must certainely, and necessarily conclude and proove it.* If then you will subscribe with your blood, or testifie by incurring equivalent dangers, this Doctrine upon your *Knowledge*, you must bee able to tell the *Christian* world, how you arriv'd to this *Knowledge*. If you will say, you have it *Ex Iure Divino*, and meane by that, out of the *Scriptures*, you must remember that you are bound by *Oath*, never to accept nor interprete Scriptures, but according to the unanime consent of the Fathers. And can you produce such a consent, for the establishing this Doctrine, in interpreting those places of Scripture, which are offred for this matter? If you extend this *Ius Divinum*, as *Bellarmine* doeth, not onely to Scriptures, but to *Naturall light and reason, and the Law of Nature,* (in which he is no longer a *Divine,* as he uses to professe himselfe, but a *Canonist*, who gives this large interpretation of *Ius Divinum*, whereas *Divines* carie it no further, then to that *which God hath commanded or forbidden, as* Azorius *tels us*) this cannot bee so strong and constant, and inflexible a Rule, but that the divers objects of *sense*, and images of the *fancie*, and wayes of *discourse*, will alter and vary it. For though the first notions which wee have by the light of nature are certaine, yet late conclusions deduced from thence are not so.

Bull. Pii.4. de Form. Iur.

Responsio ad Docto. Venet. proposit.5ª. §. ad rationes

To.2. 1.4. c.18. §. Deinde

Margin 20. Form *Ed.*: form. L-1, C-1   **28.** gives *Ed.*: give *errata,* gave. L-1, C-1

If you pretend *common consent* for your ground, and *Criterium*, by which you know this truth, and so give it the name of *Catholicke Doctrine*, and say that *Faith* is to be bound to that, and Martyrdome to be indur'd for Faith, you must also remember, that that which is so call'd *Catholicke*, is not onely a common consent of all persons at one time, but of the Catholicke Church ever. For, *Quod ubique, quod semper*, is the measure of *Catholicke Doctrine*. And can you produce Authours of any elder times, then within six hundred yeares, to have concurr'd in this?

And in these later times, is not that *Squadron* in which *Navarrus* is, of persons and voices enow, to infringe all reasons which are grounded upon this *universall consent*? He proclaimes confidently, *That the Pope, take him despoiled and naked, from all that which Princes have bestowed upon him, hath no temporall power, Neque supremam, neque mediam, neque infimam*. Doe not some *Catholiques* confesse, that *they are readie to sweare to the integrity of the Romane faith, according to the Oath of the Councell of Trent*, and yet protest against this temporall jurisdiction? And doth not another *Catholique* say, *That when a lay man sweares Obedience to the Pope, according to that Oath of Pius the fourth, it must be restrained, in his understanding, onely to his spirituall power?* Herein therefore is no *universall consent*.

And are not they which seeme to maintaine this *temporall power*, so divided amongst themselves, that in a *mutinie*, and *civill* dissention, they rather wound one another, then any third *enemie*, when they labour more, to overthrow the way, by which this *temporall* jurisdiction is claimed, then to establish the certaintie of the matter it selfe? And though such things as appeare to us, *evidently*, and *presently* out of the *Scriptures*, binde our assent, and beleefe, though wee may dispute about the way and manner, (as no man denies the *conception* of our blessed *Lady*, though it be disputed, whether shee were conceived with original sinne, or without it) And though those things which appeare to us out of the first *intrinsique light of Nature* and reason, claime the same authoritie in us (as no man doubts whether he have a soule or no, though many dispute whether we have it by *infusion* from God, or by *propagation* from our parents) yet in things further removed, and which

Novit. de Iudic. nu.41

Marsilius. Contr. Respons. Bellarm. Ad Gener. Inquisitor. Venet.

Barclaius. de Potest. Pont. ca.2. in princip.

Margin 12. Iudic *Ed.*: Indic. C-1, L-1 **20.** spirituall *Ed.*: spiriuall. C-1, L-1

are directed by more wheeles, and suggestions, and deducements, we cannot know certainely enough (for so great a use, as to testifie them in this fashion, as we speake of) that they are, except we know first *how*, and in *what manner* they are. As if a man be convented before a *Judge*, (especially when he is bound in conscience not to answer, except he be his competent Judge, as you teach, when *Ecclesiastique* persons are called to *Secular* tribunals) he cannot be sure that man is his competent Judge except he know first, whether he have that authority, as *Ordinary*, or by *speciall Commission*. Though therefore in this point in question, for a pious credulity, and generall intention to advance the dignity of the Church of *Rome*, a *Catholique* may have an indigested and raw opinion, that this power is in the Pope, yet when he examines himselfe, and calls himselfe to account, he must first know how it is, before he can resolve, that it is. And though he may erre in the manner, by which he beleeves it to be in him, yet certainely he must arest himselfe upon some one of those wayes, by which the Pope is said to have that Jurisdiction, or else hee doth not answere his conscience, that askes him how he knowes it? and if his conscience doe not aske him, he is in too drowsie and stupid a fit to be a Martyr.

Since therefore all his authority must be *Direct* or *Indirect*: *Ordinary* or *Extradordinary*: as he is *Pope* or not as he is *Pope*, whosoever will seale with his blood the averment of this Jurisdiction, averres one of these wayes, how it comes to him: Which being so, he cannot justly be called a *Martyr*, since he only is a Martyr, whom *all the Church* esteemes to be so. And he which should die, for maintenance of *Direct* power, should never be admitted into such a *Martyrologe*, as the favourers of *Indirect* power should compile; nor these, into the other. And if two should come to execution together, upon *occasion* of denying this *Oath*, of which one refused it, because hee thought the Pope *Direct* Lorde, the other *Indirect*, if they forbore hard words to one another at that time, doubtlesse in their consciences they would impute to one another, the same errours, and the same falshoods, of which they inter-accuse one another in their bookes, and neither would beleeve the other to be a true *Martyr*. And might not a dispassioned and equal spectator apply to them both severally, that Rule of the law, *That to that, which is*

14. beleeves *Ed.*: beleeeves. L-1, C-1 **24.** called a *Martyr*, *Ed.*: called a *Martyr*;. L-1, C-1

forbidden to be had by one way, one may not be admitted by another? Especially since a *Lawyer* which hath written on that side, takes the advantage of this Rule, against Princes, when he sayes, *That they have no Jurisdiction upon Clergie mens goods, because this were indirectly, to* 5 *have jurisdiction upon their persons, which being*, sayes he, *forbidden to be had one way, may not be permitted another*. It was saide to *Pompey*, when hee wore such a *scarfe* about his legge, as Princes wore about their head, *That it was all one in which place he wore the Diademe*, and that his *Ambition* appeared equally in either. And so ought this *indirect* 10 power, though it pretend more tamenesse, and modestie, avert men, as much as the other: for *Bellarmine* can finde as good an Argument for *Peters Supremacie*, out of *Christs washing his feete*, as his appointing him *to kill and eate, which is*, sayes hee, *the office of the Head*. So that from *head* to *foote*, all arguments serve his turne.

15 But to turne a little back to this point of *knowledge*, since the *conscience* is by *Aquinas* his definition, *Ordo scientiae ad aliquid*, and *an Act by which wee apply our knowledge to some particular thing*, the *Conscience* ever presumes *Knowledge*: and we may not, (especially in so great dangers as these) doe any thing upon *Conscience*, if we doe it 20 not upon *Knowledge*. For *it is not the Conscience it selfe that bindes us, but that law which the Conscience takes knowledge of, and presents to our understanding*. And as no *Ignorance* excuses us if it be of a thing which wee *ought* to know, and *may* attaine to: so no misconceived knowledge bindes our conscience in these dangers, if it be of a matter not 25 *pertinent* to us, or to which wee have no such certaine way of attaining, that we can justly presume our *Knowledge* to be certaine.

For though in the questions raised by *Schoolemen* of the *Essence* and *Counsailes* of God, and of the Creation, and fall, and Ministerie of *Angels*, and such other removed matters, to the knowledge whereof, God 30 hath affoorded us no way of attaining, a man may have some such knowledge, or opinion, as may sway him in an indifferent action, by reasons of conveniencie, and with an apparant *Analogie*, with other points of more evident certainty: yet no man may *suffer* any thing for these points, as

Ugolini. de Validit. Censura. ca.3

De Pont. l.1. c.21. §. Decima, et cap.22. §. Decima septi.

1. q.79. Ar.13. Conclus.

Carbo. Summa Summar. To.1. par.1. lib.5. c.12. Secundum

Margin 2. Ugolini *Ed*.: Ugotini.   C-1, L-1   **Margin 11.** Pont.... c.21.... Decima, et cap.... Decima septi *Ed*.: pont.... C.2.... Decima et cap... Decimasepti.   L-1, C-1   **Margin 20.** par.1. lib.5. c.12 *Ed*.: par.1. C.12.   C-1, L-1

for his *Conscience*, because, though he have lighted upon the truth, yet it was not by any certaine way, which God appointed for a constant and Ordinarie meanes to finde out that truth.

And if this *refusall* of the Oath, and *implication* of a power to depose the King, be a matter pertinent to us, that we are bound to know it, (*As all men in generall are bound to know the principles and elements of the Christian faith, and the generall precepts of the law, And every particular man is bound to know, those things which pertaine to his state and office*) Then every Subject which doth not know this, is in an inexcusable and damnable ignorance; which was the case of as many, as did at first, or do yet, allow the taking of the oath. Or if it be not so immediat to us, as those principles of faith, or as the duties of every particular man (for though we know naturally that Princes must be obeyed, yet, you wil say, som cases may occur, in which we may not obey) then there must be some certaine way for us to attaine to the knowledge therof by discourse & industrie, if we may adventure these dangers for it, and we may not adventure them, till we have by that industrie sought it out. For, if we shall say, that some things are to be held by a man, *De fide*, of which he shall still be under an invincible ignorance, though he bestow and employ all possible diligence, (as it is said of *Cyprian, that hee did erre in matter of faith, after he had used all possible industrie*) then contrarie opinions in matter of faith may be just causes of *Martyrdome*, and yet one of these opinions must of necessitie bee *Hereticall*. For if *Cyprian* were under an *invincible ignorance*, he was bound to doe according to his *erroneous conscience*, since he had no way to rectifie it. So that he must have died for his *Conscience* in that case, that is, for such an opinion, as all his *Adversaries* were bound to die for the contrarie.

But since this seemes incongruous and absurd, the other opinion will stand safe and uncontrouled, that our *Conscience*, whose office is to apply our *knowledge* to something, and to present to us some law that bindes us in that case, cannot binde us to these heavy incommodities, for any matter, but that, which wee therefore beleeve that wee know, because there are certainely some meanes naturally and ordinarily provided for the knowledge thereof; and that wee have used those meanes.

Margin side notes:
Carbo. Summa Summar. To.2. par.1. lib.4. c.2. §. Tertium

Ibid. c.3. §. Tertium

Margin 6. par.1. lib.4. c.2 *Ed.*: par.1. c.2. C-1, L-1   **Margin 18.** c.3. *Ed.*: C.3:. L-1, C-1

CHAPTER EIGHT 175

Now, in a man, in whom there are all these just *prejudices* and *prescriptions*, That *Nature* teaches him to obey him that can preserve him, That the *Scriptures* provoke him to this obedience, That the *Fathers* interpret these Scriptures of *Regall power*, That subsequent acts, and
5 *Experience* teaches, Regall power to be sufficient for that end; what can arise, strong enough to defeate all these, or plant a *knowledge* contrary to this, by any evidence so neere the first *Principles*, as this is grounded upon?

If it were possible that any thing could be produced at last, by which
10 all these reasons should be destroyed, yet, till that were done (which is not yet done) both the priority and birthright of the reasons and rules of nature, which are on that side (for Rules are elder then the exception) and the dangers which would overtake, and entrap, and depresse such as refused the Oath, must prevaile against any thing yet appearing on
15 this part: for thus farr the *Casuists* agree, as in the better opinion, That although that which they cal *Metum iustum*, which is, *such a feare as may fall upon a constant man, and yet not remove his habite of Constancy*, doth not excuse a man from doing any *Evil*, yet that is meant of such an *Evill*, as is *Evill* naturally, and accompanied with
20 all his circumstances: for, though no such feare can excuse me in an absolute deniall to restore any thing, which was committed to my trust, yet I may be excused from delivering a sword committed to me, if I have such a just feare, that the owner will therewith offend me or another. And they account not onely the feare of death, to be this *just feare*,
25 which may excuse in transgressions, in any thing which is not *naturally evill*, but the feare of *Torture, Imprisonment, Exile, Bondage, Losse of temporall goods, or the greater part thereof, or infamy, and dishonour*. And not onely when these are imminent uppon our selves, but upon our wives and children: And not onely when a law hath directly pronounced
30 them, but when the State threatens them, that is, is exasperated and likely to proceed to these inflictions. And though *Canonists* are more severe and rigid in the observation of their lawe, yet the common opinion of Divines is, *That this just feare excuses a man from the breaking of any humane lawe, whether Civill or Ecclesiastique*: and that none of those
35 lawes bindes us to the observation therof, in *danger of death, or these*

2. obey *errata*: bey. L-1, C-1   **22.** may be *Ed*.: maybe. L-1, C-1   **35.** bindes *Ed*.: binde. L-1, C-1

distresses, except in this case, that *these punishments are threatned to us, because we will not breake the law in contempt and despite of that authority, which made the law*: for then no feare can excuse us, because the obedience to Superiour authority in general, is *morall* and *naturall*; and therefore the power it selfe may not be contemned; though in case of this *just feare*, I may lawfully thinke, that that power which made the law, meant not to binde me in particular, in these heavy inconveniences.

To apply this to our present purpose, since this *Oath* is not Naturally Evill, so as no circumstance can make it good (for then, it would have appeared so at first, and the Pope himselfe could by no *Indult* or *Dispensation* tolerate it, which, I thinke, they will not say), nor offered in *contempt* of the Church of Rome, or in such sort as it should be *a signe of returning to our Religion*, or abandoning the Romane profession, but onely for the Princes security, certainely though the refusall thereof were commanded by any law of humane constitution, and so it became Evill, because it was Forbidden, yet in these afflictions, certainely to be endured by the letter of an expresse law, by every Refuser, and in this bitternesse and exasperation of the whole State, against that whole Partie, and the cause of Catholiques, the taking of the Oath were so excusable, as the refusing thereof could not be excused. For in such *a just Feare*, even *Divine Positive Law* looses her hold and obligation, of which sort *Integrity of Confession* is by all helde to be; and yet such sinnes may be omitted in confession, as would either *Scandalize* the Confessor, *Endanger* the penitent, or *Defame* a third person. In which the Casuists are so generally concurrent, that wee neede no particular authorities.

^{Tractat.7. Theol. de Interd. Pauli 5. propos.5^a}

And in the matter of the greatest importance, which can be in that Church, which is the Election of the Pope, and an assurance, that he whom they acknowledge for Pope, is true Pope, which *Comitolius* (a *Jesuite* as much more peremptorie then the rest of the Jesuites, as they are above all other Friars) sayes, ^a*To be an Article of Faith, and that we are bound to beleeve the present Pope to bee Christs Vicar, with a Divine and with a Catholicke Faith, and that all Decrees of Popes, which annull all Elections, if they appeare after, to have beene made by Simonie, intend no more, but to declare that GOD will never suffer that to bee done, or discover it presently* (in which opinion, *that matter of*

^aComitol. Respons. Moral. l.1. q.99

11. say), *Ed.*: say). L-1, C-1 **Margin 30a.** Moral *Ed.*: Mo[?]al. L-1, C-1

fact, should so binde our Faith, hee is (for any thing which I remember to have read) singular, and I had occasion before to name [b]one great Doctor of his owne Religion, directly contrarie to him in the very point.) In these *Elections*, I say, which induce (by his Doctrine) a *Divine* faith,
5 and necessarily, such a probable, and morall certitude, that it were sinne in them, who are under the obedience of that *Church*, not to obey the just *Decrees* of the present *Pope*, or quarrell at his *Election*: The Councell of *Constance*, (as [c]another *Jesuite* urges it) hath decreed that this just feare of which we speake, *Doth make voide any such Election of*
10 *the Pope*. And that, *If after the Cardinals are delivered of that feare, which possessed them at the Election, they then ratifie and confirme that Pope, yet he is no Pope, but the Election voide*: So farre doeth this *just feare* (which cannot be denied to bee in your case) extend, and upon so solemne, and solid Acts, and Decrees is it able to worke, and provide us
15 a just excuse for transgressing thereof.

And in a matter little different from our case, *Azorius* gives this resolution; That *if an hereticall Prince commaunds his Catholicke Subjectes to goe to Church, upon paine of death or losse of goods, if hee doe this onely because he will have his Lawes obeyed, and not to make*
20 *it Symbolum Hereticae pravitatis, nor have a purpose to discerne therby Catholickes from Hereticks, they may obey it*. And the case in question fals directly and fully within the rule: For this Oath is not offred as a *Symbole* or token of our Religion, nor to distinguish *Papists* from *Protestants*, but onely for a *Declaration* and *Preservation* of such as are well
25 affected in *Civill Obedience*, from others which either have a rebellious and treacherous disposition already, or may decline and sinke into it, if they bee not uphelde and arrested with such a helpe, as an Oath to the contrary. And therfore by all the former Rules of *just feare*, & this last of *Azorius*, though there were an evident prohibitory act, against the tak-
30 ing of the Oath, yet it might, yea it ought to be taken: For, agreeable to this, *Tolet* cites *Caietans* opinion, with allowance and commendations, *That the Declaration of the Church, that subjects may not adhere to their King, if he be excommunicated, extends not to them, if thereby they be*

[b]Simancha. Enchirid. Judic. Tit.5. nu.3

[c]Azor. Instit. Moral. par.2. l.4. c.2. §. Sexto

Defence of English Cathol. ca.4

Margin 2b. Enchirid *Ed*.: Enchird. C-1, L-1 **7.** *Election*: C-2, F, HD, L-2, L³⁰, C⁵-2: *Election*. L-1, C-1, MCG, Y, O-2, O², C¹⁶ **Margin 8c.** par.2 L³⁰, F, HD, Y: [?]ar. L-1, C-1, C-2, O-1, SP, YK-3, C³ **16.** this *errata*: the. L-1, C-1

brought into feare of their lives, or losse of their goods. For in *Capitall* matters, sayes your great *Syndicator, it is lawfull to redeeme the life, per fas & nefas.* which must not have a wicked interpretation; and therefore must be meant, whether with, or against any humane lawes; which he speakes out of the strength and resultance of many lawes and Canons there alleadged. And therfore it can never come to be *matter of Faith*, that subjects may depart from their Prince, if this *just feare* may excuse us from obeying, as these Authors teach; for that never delivers us in matters of so strong obligation as matter of Faith, from which no feare can excuse our departing.

<small>Par. de Puteo. fo.327 & fo.778</small>

To conclude therefore this *Chapter*, since later propositions, either Adulterine, or Suspicious, cannot have equall authority, and credite, with the first, and radicall trueth, much lesse blot out those certaine and evident Anticipations imprinted by nature, and illustrated by Scriptures, for civill obedience, since the Rules of the *Casuists* for electing opinions in cases of *Doubt*, and *perplexity* are uncertaine and flexible, to both sides, since that *Conscience*, which we must defend with our lives, must be grounded upon such things, as wee may, and doe not onely know, but know *how* we know them, since these *just feares* of drawing scandall upon the whole cause, and afflictions upon every particular Refuser, might excuse the transgression of a direct law, which had all her formalities, much more any opinions of *Doctors* or *Canonists*, I hope we may now pronounce, That it is the *safest*, in both acceptations, both of *spirituall safety*, and *Temporall*, and in both *Tribunals*, as well of conscience, as of civill Justice, to take the Oath.

Chap. IX.

*That the authority which is imagined to be in the Pope, as he is spiritu-
all Prince, of the Monarchy of the Church, cannot lay this Obligation
upon their Consciences: first because the Doctrine it selfe is not certaine, nor presented as matter of faith: Secondly because the way by
which it is conveyed to them, is suspitious and dangerous, being put
by Cardinall Bellarmine, who is various in himselfe, and reproved by
other Catholiques of equall dignity, and estimation.*

1   Wee may bee bolde to say, that there is much iniquity, and many degrees of Tyranny, in establishing so absolute and transcendent a spiritual *Monarchy*, by them, who abhorre *Monarchy* so much, that though one of their greatest Doctors, to the danger of all Kings, says, ᵃ*That the Pope might, if hee thought it expedient, constraine all Christians to create one temporall Monarch over all the world*: yet they allow no other Christian *Monarchy* upon Earth, so pure and absolute, but that it must confesse some subjection and dependencie. *The contrarie to which* ᵇ*Bellarmine* says, is *Hereticall*; And yet there is no *Definition* of the Church, which should make it so. And hereby they make *Baptisme* in respect of *Soveraintie*, to bee no better then the bodie in respect of the soule. For, as the body by inhaerent corruption vitiates the pure and innocent soule, so they accuse *Baptisme* to cast an Originall servitude and frailtie upon *Soveraintie*: which, having beene strong and able to doe all Kingly offices before, contracts by this *Baptisme* a debilitie and imperfection, and makes Kings, which before had their Lieutenancie and Vicariate from God, but Magistrates and Vicars to his Vicar, and so makes their *Patents* the worse by *renewing & confirming*.

2   Nor doe they only denie *Monarchie* to Kings of the Earth, but they change the state and forme of government in *heaven* it selfe; and joine in *Commission* with God, some such persons, as they are so farre from beeing sure that they are there, that they are not sure, that ever they were heere. For their excuse, that none of those invocations which are used in that Church, are so directly intended upon the Saints, but

ᵃFran. a Victor. Relect. de Potest. Civili. nu.14

ᵇRespons. ad Doct. Venet. propos.1. §. Prima haec

---

5. *put Ed.*: but. L-1, C-1   **8.** 1 *Ed.*: missing. L-1, C-1   **11.** says *Ed.*: say. L-1, C-1

that they *may* have a lawfull interpretation, is not sufficient. For words appointed for such uses, must not only be so conditioned, that they *may* have a good sense, but so, that they may have no ill. So that to say, *That God hath reserved to himselfe the Court of Justice, but given to his Mother, the Court of Mercie*, And that a ^a*desperate sicke person was cured by our Lady, when he had no hope in Physitians, nor much in God*, howsoever subtill men may distill out of them a wholesome sense, yet vulgarly and ordinarily they beget a beliefe, or at least a blinde practise derogatorie to the Majestie, and Monarchie of God.

^aSwertius. in Epitaph. Patavi. Nulla erat in Medico spes, neque multa Deo

3 But for this *spirituall Monarchie* which they have fansied, I thinke, that as some men have imagined, and produced into writing, divers *Idaeas*, and so sought what a *King*, a *Generall*, an *Oratour*, a *Courtier* should be, So these men have only Idaeated what a *Pope* would be. For if he could come to a true and reall exercise of all that power which they attribute to him, I doubt not, but that *Angell*, which hath so long served in the place of being the particular *Assistant* in the *Conclave*, (for, since they affoord a particular *Tutelar Angell* to everie *Colledge* and *Corporation*, And ^a*to the race of Flyes and of Fleas, and of Ants*, since they allowe such an *Angell* ^b*to every Infidell Kingdome*, ^c*yea to Antichrist*, ^d*yea to Hell it selfe*, it were verie unequall to denie one to this place,) This *Angell*, I say, would be glad of the roome, and become a Suiter to the *holy Ghost*, to name him in the next *Conclave*. For he should not onely enlarge his *Diocesse*, and have all the lower world under him, but hee shall have those two principall *Seraphins* which ever attend the *Pope*, *Michael*, and *Gabriel*; (for, that *Gabriel* is the second, *Victorellus* produces two very equall witnesses, *The Romane Litanie*, and *Tassoes Hierusalem*.) And all the particular *Angels* of all spirituall *Societies*; And (because also (as he sayes) he is *Temporall Lord*) all the *Archangels*, and *Principalities*, which governe particular estates, shall concur to his Guard and assistance.

Victorellus. de Custodia Angelorum

^aFol.16
^bFol.133   ^cFol.121
^dFol.17

Fo.104

Fo.105

Fo.106

4 As *Nero* had an officer *A voluptatibus*, So, it seemes, have the Popes, *A titulis*. And flatterers have alwayes a Complacencie and Delight in themselves, if they can bestow a style and Title upon a great Prince, because therein they think they contribute somthing to his greatnesse; since Ceremonie is a maine part of Greatnesse, and Title, a great part of that. And now they had observed, that all the chiefe Titles of the Pope had been attributed to others, and were in their Nature and use

communicable; For *all the Apostles, and all the Disciples of Christ, are called Vicarii Christi*; And this name will not serve his turne, if it were peculiar to himselfe. For, as his *Victoria teaches us,* ᵃ*This Vicariate doth not enable him to doe all thinges which are not expresly forbidden*
5 *him (as some doe thinke) but onely such things as are expresly graunted unto him*, and therefore his claime by that Title will be too strict. And the name of *Universall Bishop*, was given to *Cyprian*, when hee was styled, *Totius orbis Praeses*. And in that sense it may justly bee given; For as a *Physician* or *Chirurgion*, which hath taken into his Cure any
10 one part of a mans body, either corrupted, or in danger of being so, may justly be said to looke to, and preserve the body of such a man; So that *Bishop* which governes well one Church, is therein a *Bishop* of the whole Church, & benefits the whole mystical body therof, by reason of the strong relation, & indissoluble connexion of all the parts, with one
15 another, and to the head.

  5 And for that style of *Pontifex Maximus*, which either is not due to the Pope, or else is so sublime and transcendant a name, as *Bellarmine* could bring it within no *Rule* nor *Predicament*, when hee makes up the *Canon* of the Popes *fifteene Titles, by all and every one of which*, hee
20 sayes, *his Primacie is evidently collected*; They saw it given to *Athanasius*, in *Ruffinus*. And the name of *Pope* was so communciated, that not onely every *Bishop* was called a *Pope*, but *Cyprian, The Pope. Quem Christiani suum Papam vocant*. In the estimation of which name, they have often fluctuated and wavered. For, almost for nine hundred yeeres,
25 they affoorded it to all: Then they restrain'd it to the *Bishop of Rome*, to which purpose ᵃ*Biel* upon the *Canon of the Masse*, cites divers Canons, though farre from the matter.

  6 And ever since the *Reformation* of the Church was couragiously begun, and prosperously and blessedly prosecuted, they having beene
30 call'd *Papists* for their implicite relying upon the *Pope*, lest their owne Argument against us, *That to bee denominate from any person, is a*

Margin notes:
Aquin. contr. Gent. cap.20
ᵃFranc. a Victor. de Potest. Papae et Concil. §. Ad Quintum
Hiero. de locis Hebrae.
De Pont. l.2. c.31. §. Argumentum
L.2. c.16
Hiero. Epist. ad Chromat. par.2. l.4
Azor. Instit. Mor. par.2. l.4. c.4. §. Porro
ᵃLect. 23. Dist.96. In Scripturis, & c.6. q.1. Sacerdotes, &c.
Bellar. de Notis Eccles. l.4. c.4

Margin 1. Aquin. contr. Gent. cap.20 C⁵-1, O⁸, E-2, MCG, L³⁰, L¹⁵: *missing*. C-1, L-1, YK-1, O⁵, L²², L³ **12.** Church,] Church: F, Church. O¹⁴, YK-2 **Margin 20.** 16 *Ed*.: 26. L-1, C-1 **Margin 25.** Instit. Mor. par.2. l.4. c.4 *Ed*.: Mor. Instit. c.4. L-1, C-1 **25.** *Bishop catchword quarto p.250* L-1, C-1: *Bishops.* L-1, C-1 **Margin 31.** de Notis Eccles. *Ed*.: de Eccles. milit.. L-1, C-1

marke of Heresie, should be retorted upon themselves, they have in all Dedications and publike Acts, as much as they can, forborne, and declin'd that name *Pope*, and still usurped, *Summus Pontifex*, and *Pontifex Maximus*. And yet being stil urged and followed, and having no escape, but that the name of *Papists*, stickes to them, and by their Rules imprints some markes of *Heresie*; though *Bellarmine*, a little ashamed of the name Papist, say; *That onely the Lutherans, and a few neighbour Countreyes call them so*: Yet that late *Carmelite* that hath defended *Lypsius*, sayes confidently: [a]*We are Papists; we confesse it; and* [b]*we glory in that Name*.

7 And this name of Pope, they are the rather content to take to him againe, because they thinke that we grudge him that name. For so that *Councellour* of the *Parliament* of *Burdeaux*, which in his *Historie of the progresse and decay of Heresie*, hath taken occasion to speake of the affaires of *England*, in which, because no man should doubt of the trueth therof, he professes to follow *Sanders*, and *Ribadeneira*, (by whome a Morall man may as well be instructed for matter of Fact, as a Christian might be by *Arrius* or *Mahomet*, for his Faith) sayes, *That Henrie the eight, made it Felonie to call the holy Father Pope, or to reade that name in any Booke, and not to blot it out*.

8 Having therefore found such easinesse, and flexbility in all olde Names, they have provided him now of this name *spirituall Prince*; in a larger sense, then that great Prince, whom they call *Praeste-gian* assumes it (for that name signifies *Apostolique*, and *Christs Vicegerent*, in his owne kingdomes) or then *Christ* himself ever assumed, or the *Holy Ghost*, by the Prophet *Esay*, reckoning up his most glorious titles, ever attributed to him; and yet in that place of *Esay*, both his eternall Kingdome by his filiation, and his everlasting Kingdome of glory, inchoated in his resurrection, and his Kingdome of grace in our consciences, are evidently to bee discerned: For, though there be mention of *Principality*, yet it is said, *Principatus super humerum eius*, which your *Doctor* expounds of *carying the Crosse*; and that he shall be *Princeps pacis*, which is *Intrinsicall*, sayes the same *Expositor*, & belonges to the Conscience.

Margin notes:
Ibidem. §. At inquiunt
[a]Anastas. Cochelet. Palestrit. hono. f.9
[b]Fo.6
Florimond. de Remond. l.6
Branchedoro. Orati. ad Imp. de mutat. Imper. fo.18
Esay 9.6
Lyra

5. *Papists Ed.: Rapists.* L-1, C-1 9. confidently: *Ed.:* confidently.. L-1, C-1 **Margin 9a.** hono *Ed.:* bono. C-1, L-1 12. For *Ed.:* Por. L-1, C-1 **Margin 23.** Branchedoro. *Ed.:* Brancheda. L-1, C-1

But this *Doctrine* which must so settle and affirme a Catholique conscience, that it must binde him to die, and entitle him to *Martyrdome*, hath no touch, nor tincture of either of these Principalities, of *Patience*, or of *Peace*; but all therein is *Anger* and *Warre*, not onely with that sword of two edges, of the *Word* and *Censures*, which is his, but with two swords; which now we shall see how he claimes.

9   *The Pope represents Christ to us (sayes Bellarmine) as he was, whilst he lived amongst men: nor can we attribute to the Pope any other office, then Christ had, as he was a mortall man.* And in this Capacitie, sayes he, *Christ neither had the execution, nor the power of any temporall Kingdome.* And that therefore, *if the Pope, as a King, can take from any King the execution of his place, he is greater then Christ; and if he cannot, then he hath no Regall power.* Thus hee disputes against those which entitle the Pope to a Direct, and Ordinary Jurisdiction over Princes.

10   And the same reasons and groundes, by which he destroyes that opinion, will destroy his; which is, *That as Christ was, so the Pope is, spirituall prince, over all men, and that by vertue of that power, he may dispose of all temporall things, as hee shall judge it expedient to his spirituall ends.*

11   For first, against that opinion of *Ordinarie* Jurisdiction, hee argues thus; *If it were so, it would appeare out of the Scriptures, or from the Tradition of the Apostles: but in the Scriptures, there is mention of the keyes of Heaven, but none of the Kingdomes of the earth; nor doe our Adversaries offer any Apostolique Tradition.* Will not you then, before you receive so deepe impression of *Bellarmines* doctrine, as to pay your lives for maintenance thereof, tell him, That if his opinion were true, it would appeare in *Scripture*, or *Apostolique tradition*? And shal poore and lame, and slacke arguments conjecturally and unnecessarily deduced from similitudes and comparisons, and decency, and conveniency binde

De Pont. l.5. c.4. §. Superest

Ibid. §. Sed iam §. Caeterum

Ca.3. §. Gregorius

Ca.4. §. ut igitur

Ca.3. §. Eadem

Margin 10. Sed iam] Sediam. C-3, C⁵-1, SP, C¹⁶   **Margin 13.** §. Gregorius] parag. Gregorius. C-3, C²-1, E-2, C⁵-1, SP, C¹⁶   **15.** Princes *Ed.*: Prinees. L-1, C-1   **Margin 17.** §. ut] parag. ut. C-3, C²-1, E-2, C⁵-1, SP, C¹⁶   **21.** Jurisdiction, YK-3: Jurisdiction. L-1, C-1   **Margin 21.** 3. §. Eadem *Ed.*: 3 parag. Eadem. C-3, C²-1, E-2, C⁵-1, SP, C¹⁶   **26.** so *catchword quarto* p.253] too *catchword*. C-3, L², C⁵-1, SP, C¹⁶   **26.** so *text quarto* p.254] too *text*. C-3, L², C⁹, C-4, MCG, C⁵-1, O⁷, O-2, C¹⁶

your judgements, and your lives, for reverence of him, who by his example counsels you, to cal for better proof? wil you so, in obeying him, disobey him, & swallow his conclusions, & yet accuse his fashion of proving them? which you do, if when he cals for scriptures against others, you accept his positions for his sake, without scriptures.

12   Another of *Bellarmines* reasons against *Ordinary* Jurisdiction, is, *That Regall authority was not necessary nor of use in Christ to worke his end, but superfluous and unprofitable.* And what greater use, or necessity can the Pope have of this *Extraordinarie* authority (which is a power to work the same effects, though not by the same way) then *Christ* had, if his ends be the same which Christs were? and it appeares that *Christ* neither had, not forsaw use of either, because he neither exercised nor instituted either. For, that is not to the purpose, which *Bellarmine* says, *that Christ might have exercised that power if he would,* since the Popes authority is grounded upon *Christs example*; and limited to that: For *Christ* might have done many thinges which the Pope cannot do; as converting all the world at once, instituting more sacraments, and many such: and therefore *Bellarmine* argued well before, *that it is enough for him to prove, that Christ did not exercise Regall power, nor declare himselfe to have it*, which *Declaration* only, and practise, must be drawen into Consequence, and be the precedent for the Pope to follow.

13   The light of which Argument, *that the Pope hath no power, but such as Christ exercised*, hath brought so many of them to thinke it necessarie to prove *That both Christ did exercise Regall authority in accepting Regall reverence upon Palme-Sunday, and in his corrections in the temple, And his judgement in the womans case which was taken in Adulterie. And that S. Peter used also the like power, in condemning Ananias and Saphira, and Simon Magus.*

14   In another place *Bellarmine* says, That *S. Paul appealed to Caesar, as to his Superiour Judge,* not onely *de facto,* but *de Iure*; and that *the Apostles were subjects to the Ethnique Emperours, in all temporall causes, and that the law of Christ, deprives no man of his right, which he*

---

20. *it, Ed.: it.* L-1, C-1 **20.** *Declaration Declarion onely.* MCG, C-3, C⁵-1, SP, O-2, C¹⁶, C²-3 **Margin 25.** Maynardus] *note misplaced .* C-3, C-4, C⁹, C²-1, L², MCG, C⁵-1, SP, O-2, C¹⁶ **Margin 28.** n.3.4 *Ed.*: n.3.5. L-1, C-1

CHAPTER NINE

had before. And lately in his *Recognitions* he departs from this opinion, and denies that he was his Judge, *de Iure*. If his first opinion be true, can these consist together, that he which is subject in temporal causes, can at the same time and in the same causes be superiour? Or that
5 he over whom the Emperour had supreame temporall authority, should have authority over the Emperour in temporall causes? and what is there in the second opinion, that should induce so strong an Obligation upon a conscience, as to die for it; Since the first was better grounded (for, for that he produced Scriptures) and the second is destitute of
10 that helpe, and without further search into it, tels us, that neither the Doctrine, nor the Doctor are constant enough to build a Martyredome upon.

15 Thus also *Bellarmine* argues, to our advantage (though he doe it to prove a necessity of this power in the Church) *that every Common-*   L.5. ca.7. §. Se-
15 *wealth is sufficiently provided in it selfe, to attaine the end, for which it*   cunda ratio
is instituted. And, as we said before, the end of a Christian Commonwealth, is not onely Tranquility (for that sometimes may be maintained by unchristianly meanes) but is the practice of all morall vertue, now explicated to us, and observed by us, in the exercise of Christian Re-
20 ligion; and therfore such a Common-wealth hath of it selfe, all meanes necessary to those ends, without new additions: as a man consisting of bodie and soule, if he come from Infidelity to the Christian Religion, hath no new third essential part added to him, to governe that body, and soule, but onely hath the same soule enlightned with a more explicite
25 knowledge of her duety.

16 *Bellarmine* also tels us, *That in the Apostles time, these two*   Ca.6. §. Ita
powers were seperated, and so all the Temporall was in the *Emperour*, as   prorsus
all the Ecclesiasticke in the *Apostles* and that *Hierarchie*. By what way then, and at what time came this Authoritie into them, if it were once
30 out? For, to say, that it sprong out of Spirituall Authoritie, when there was any use of it, were to say, that that Authoritie at *Christs* institution had not all her perfections and maturity, and to say, that it is no other but the highest act, and a kinde of *prerogative* of the spirituall power, will not reach home. For you must beleeve and die in this, that the
35 Pope as spirituall Prince, may not onely dispose of temporall matters,

Margin 14. L.5. ca.7. *Ed.*: Ca.7. L-1, C-1

but that herein hee uses the *temporall sword*, and temporall jurisdiction.

<small>L.5. c.6</small>

17 But when *Bellarmine* says, That *this supreme authority resides in the Pope, yet not as he is Pope, And that the Pope, and none but he, can depose Kings, and transfer Kingdomes, and yet, not as Pope*, I professe that I know not, how to speake thereof with so much earnestnesse, as becomes a matter of so great waight. For other Princes, when they exercise their extraordinarie and Absolute power, and *prerogative*, and for the publique good put in practise sometimes some of those parts of

<small>I Sam. 8.11</small>

their power, which are spoken of in *Samuel*, (which to many men seeme to exceede *Regall power*) yet they professe to doe these things as they are *Kings*, and not by any other authoritie then that.

18 And if there be some things which the *Pope* cannot doe as *Pope*, but as *chiefe spirituall Prince*, this implies that there are other *inferiour spirituall Princes*, which are *Bishops*: (for so *Bellarmine* says,

<small>De Pont. l.4. c.15. §. At in</small>

That Bishops in their Diocesses are Ecclesiastique Princes.) And have *Bishops* any such measure of this spirituall *principality*, that they may do somthings by that, which they cannot doe, as they are *Bishops*?

19 All *Principalities* maintaine their being by these two, *reward*, & *punishment*. How lame then and unperfect in this spirituall *principality*, which can affoord but one halfe? For it is onely then of use, when the *Pope* will punish, and correct a King, by Deposing him: for all *Rewards & Indulgences* in this life, and in the next, hee conferres and bestowes, as hee is *Pope*, and needes not this Title, to doe any good which is in his power. And for corrections and punishments, all which we are sure he can lawfully doe, which is, to inflict Church censures, upon those who are under his spirituall obedience, he doth as he is *Pope*, and needes not this *principalitie* for that use neither.

20 But for irregular actions, and such as occasion tumult and sedition, he must be a *spirituall Prince*. For, sayes *Bellarmine*, *Though the*

<small>De Concil. l.1. c.18. §. Dico</small>

Pope as he is president of a generall Councell, (and he is that, as he is *Pope*) *ought to follow the greatest number of voices in making Decrees, yet as he is chiefe Prince, hee is not bound to doe so, but may follow the lesser number.* And yet scarse constant to himselfe, he says, That *this libertie belongs to the Pope, because he hath the assistance of the holy*

Margin 14. 1.4 C-3, C-4, C⁵-2: 1.[?].   L-1, C-1, L², C⁹, F, L-2, O-1, YK-2
Margin 29. c.18] c.18.   C-1, C-2, C⁹, F, HD, O-2, YK-1

CHAPTER NINE

Ghost. Now the Pope, as Pope, hath the assistance of the holy Ghost, (for else his Determination in Cathedra, in matters of faith, were not by his Ordinarie, and Direct power,) and therefore as Pope hee may follow the fewer voices in a Councell, and as Pope (or no way) he may depose
5 Princes.

21 For as, though they seeme to place more power, or dignitie, in *Pontificatu*, then in *Apostolatu*, because the Popes date their *Rescripts*, from the time of their *Election* to their *Coronation*, thus, *Anno Apostolatus primo, &c. and seale but with halfe the seale*, but after their
10 Coronation, they begin to call their government *Pontificatum*: yet all the authority which they have, is certainly in them from their *Election*, because sayes the *glosse*, that conferres *praesulatum*: so they have fancied & imagined a *Principatum* above all these, yet certainly all the authoritie they have, is as they are *Popes*. Which served them to doe
15 mischiefe enough, before this new title was invented. And to say, that they have authoritie, as they are *Popes*, to do some acts, as they are not *Popes*, is such a darke, and mistie, and drowsie Doctrine, as it is the fittest and most proportionall *Martyrdome* in this businesse, for a man to dreame that he died for it.

20 22 For it is strange that these men can discerne and distinguish in the same *office*, betweene the Pope, and a spirituall Prince, when as *Philip* the last King of Spaine, could not distinguish betweene the *Person* and the *Office* of the Pope: for being in so much forwardnesse, that he had given the *D. of Alva* an Order to besiege *Rome*, because
25 *Paul* the fourth had brought into *Italy* an Armie of *French*, to infest the Kingdome of *Naples*, and being solicited by the *Venetians*, to desist from offending the Pope, though hee aunswered, *That his preparations were not against the Pope, but against Peter Caraffa his subject, and a Rebell*, yet when the *Venetians* replied, *that if he could seperate Caraffa*
30 *from the Pope, they would intercede no farther, else they would give the Pope their assistance*, the King, sayes a Catholique writer, gave over, *because he saw it impossible to distinguish them*.

23 And as the *Doctrine* it selfe is too inexplicable, for any man to adventure thereupon his life, or such dangers as the lawe esteemes

Reg. Juris in 6. c. fin. glos. verb. Pontificatus

Lelio Medici. Contr. Venetia. Sopra il fonda 2. fo.194

24. an Order *Ed*.: Order. L-1, C-1 **Margin 27.** Medici. Contr. Venetia *Ed*.: medici contr. Venetia SP, C²-1, L², C⁵-1, C¹⁶,. medici contr. i. Venetia L-1, C¹⁰, C-1, L²², L³, L¹⁵-1, O⁸, O⁷, O-1

equivalent to this purpose, which are, *all such damages as induce a just feare*: So is the Channell and way by which it is derived to us, so various, and muddy, as that also should retard any man, from such a Prejudice, and such an Anticipation of the resolution of the Church herein as it is, to seale with life, that which no man yet knowes, how the Church will determine. For, in *Bellarmine*, who hath got the reputation to be the principall of this faction (though I confesse he founds the foundation of it, and his best Arguments for it, in our Countriman *Sanders*, out of whom and *Stapleton* and a few more, that Church hath received more strength, then from the late writers of all other Nations,) his authority and credit is not onely infirmed and impaired, in that, *Baronius*, a man of as much merit of the Church, and rewarded by her, with the same *Dignitie*, is of a contrarie opinion, but also, because averring, *that his opinion is the opinion of the Divines, and the other onely of Canonists, Divines* themselves, (for such *Baronius* and *Bozius* are) have more then others oppugned it.

24 And so that new *Order* of the *Congregation*, of which both they are, beeing (as I said before) laid for a stumbling block, that the world, which in such a rage of Devotion ranne towards the *Jesuites*, might be arrested a little upon the contemplation of an Order which professed *Church-knowledge*, as the other did *state-knowledge*, hath exceeded the *Jesuites* in their owne Art, of flattering and magnifying the Pope. For they have maintained his *Direct* and *Ordinarie* power, whereas the other have but provided him a new and specious Title. And so not only such as *Carerius* layes the imputation of *Impious Politician* upon *Bellarmine* and all his followers in this point, And bitterly *Anathematises Bellarmine* by name, and maintaines *this power to be in the Pope, either as Pope, or not as Christs Vicar*, But *Bozius* [*Barclay*] also calls these men *novos Theologos*, and sayes, *They teach doctrine evidently false, and such as fights against all Truth*. And another *Catholique* writer, though hee impugne both these opinions, of *Bellarmine*, and *Baronius*, yet he protests, that the opinion which *Bellarmine* calls the *Canonists* opinion, is the more probable, and defensible: *because*, sayes hee, *that opinion is not against the order of Nature, that the Pope should exercise such a power,*

Margin notes:
Titulo libri
De Pont. l.2. c.8
L.2. c.11
L.5. c.Ulti.
Barclaius. de Pot. Pap. c.1. §. mihi

---

7. founds *Ed*.: found. L-1, C-1 **26.** Anathematises *Ed*.: Anathmatises. C-1, L-1 **28.** Bozius [*Barclay*] *Ed*.: Bozius. L-1, C-1

which they maintaine to be directly granted to him: but that opinion, which they call the Divines opinion, is against Nature, since it admits the exercise of such an Authority, as is neither by name granted, nor necessarie to the ends of the Church: And therefore, says this Catholique, though the Divines overthrow the Canonists, yet they prove not their owne opinion. And in another place he says, That *though Bellarmine have given as much to the Pope, as honestly he could, and more then he should have done, yet he was so farre from satisfying the Pope herein, that for this opinion the Pope was very neere condemning all his workes, as*, says he, *the Jesuites themselves, have tolde mee.* Cap.3. in Princ. et ca.40

25 Which disposition of enclining to the *Canonists* opinion, appeares still in the Popes, who accept so well the bookes of that purpose, that the greatest part of those Authors, which I have cited in this booke, of that matter, are dedicated to the late Popes. So that, that Doctrine, which is so much denied in the *substance* and *Essence* therof, that all wayes of the *existence* thereof are peremptorily denied, hath not yet receaved concoxions enow from the Church, to nourish a conscience to such a strength, as *Martyrdome* requires. For that, which their great Doctor *Franciscus à Victoria* pronounces against his *direct Authoritie*, we may as safely say against that & the *indirect*, This is the strongest proofe that can be against him, *This Authority is not proved to be in the Pope, by any meanes, and therefore he hath it not.* To which purpose he had directly said before, of the direct Authoritie, *It is manifestly false, although they say that it is manifestly true; And I beleeve it to be a meere devise, only to flatter the Popes. And it is altogether fained, without probability, Reason, Witnesse, Scripture, Father, or Divine. Onely some Glossers of the law, poore in fortune and learning, have bestowed this authority upon them.* And therefore, as that *Ermit* which was fed in the Desert by an Angell, receaved from the Angell withered grapes, when hee said his prayers, after the due time, and ripe grapes when he observed the just time, but wilde sower grapes when he prevented the time, so must that hasty and unseasonable obedience to the Church, to die for her Doctrine, before she her selfe knowes what it is, have but a sower and unpleasant reward.

De potest. Eccles. Sect.6. nu.4
Ibid. nu.2. et 3

Alvarez. Specul. ultri. Dignit. ca.33. nu.4

Chap. X.

That the Canons can give them no warrant, to adventure these dangers, for this refusall: And that the reverend name of Canons, is falsly, and cautelously insinuated, and stolne upon the whole body of the Canon law, with a briefe Consideration upon all the bookes thereof; and a particular survay, of all those Canons, which are ordinarily cited by those Authours, which maintaine this temporall Jurisdiction in the Pope.

1   To this *spirituall Prince*, of whom we spoke in the former Chapter, the huge and vast bookes of the *Canon law*, serve for his *Guarde*. For they are great bodies loaded with divers weapons of *Excommunications*, *Anathems*, and *Interdicts*, but are seldome drawen to any presse or close fight. And as with *temporall Princes*, the danger is come very neere his person, if the remedie lie in his *guard*, so is also this *spirituall Prince* brought to a neere exigent, if his title to depose Princes must be defended by the *Canons*. For, in this *spirituall* warre which the *Reformed Churches* under the conduct of the *Holy Ghost*, have undertaken against *Rome*, not to destroy her, but to reduce her to that obedience, from which at first she unadvisedly strayed, but now stubbornly rebels against it, the *Canon* law serves rather to stoppe a breach, into which men use to cast as wel straw and Feathers, as Timber and Stone, then to maintaine a fight and battell.

2   This I speake not to diminish the Reverence or slacken the obligation which belongs to the ancient *Canons* and *Decrees* of the Church; but that the name may not deceive us; For, as the heretiques *Ursalius*, and *Valens*, got together a company at *Nice*, because they would establish their Heresies, under the name of a *Nicene* Councell, (which had ever so much reputation, that all was readily received, which was truely offered under that name) so is most pestilent and infectious doctrine, convayed to us, under the reverend name of *Ecclesiastique Canons*.

3   The body of the *Canon law*, which was called *Codex Canonum*, which contained the Decrees of certaine aunchient Councels, was usually

Carranza. Sum. Concil. fo.92

5. *all those* Ed.: *allt hose*. L-1, C-1   8. *1* Ed.: *missing* .   L-1, C-1

CHAPTER TEN 191

produced in after-*Councels* for their direction, and by the intreaty of popes, admitted and incorporated into the body of the Romane and Imperiall law; and ever in all causes, wherein they had given any *Decision*, it was— judg'd according to them, after the Emperours had by such admittance given them that strength.

4 And if the body of that law, were but growen and not swelled, if this were a *Gravidnes*, & *Pregnancy* which she had conceived of *General Councels* lawfully called, and lawfully proceeded in, and so she had brought forth children loving and profitable to the *publique*, and not onely to the *Mother*, (for how many *Canons* are made onely in favour of the *Canons*?) all Christian Princes would be as inclinable to give her strength, and dignity, by incorporating her into their lawes, and authorising her thereby, as some of the *Emperours* were. And had the *Bishops* of *Rome* maintained that purity, and integrity of Doctrine, and that compatiblenesse with Princes, which gave them authority at first, when the Emperours conceived so well of that Church, as they bound their faith to the faith thereof (which they might boldly doe at that time) perchance Princes would not have refused, that the adjections of those later Popes should have beene admitted as parts of the *Canon law*: nor should the Church have beene pestred, and poisoned with these tumors, & excrescences, with which it abounds at this time, and swelles daily with new additions.

Cod. de Sum. Trinit. le.1. Conctos

5 In which, if there bee any thinge which bindes our faith, and derives upon us a *Title to Martyrdome*, if we die in defence thereof (as there are many things derived from *Scriptures* and Obligatory *Councels*) the strength of that band rises so much from the nature of the thing, or from the goodnesse of the soile, from which it was transplanted to that place, that though we might be *Martyrs*, if we defended it in that respect, yet wee should loose that benefit, though it be an evident and Christian truth, if we defend it upon that reason, *That it is by approbation of the Pope inserted into the body of the Canon law*; which is a *Satyr*, and *Miscellany* of divers and ill digested Ingredients.

6 The first part whereof, which is the *Decretum* compiled by *Gratian*, which hath beene in use above foure hundred yeares, is so diseased

---

6. not swelled *errata*: swelled. L-1, C-1, MCG **21.** excrescences] excrescenges. L-1, C-3, L^{30}, O-1, O^{14}, O^2, YK-1, C^2-2

and corrupt a member thereof, that all the Medicines, which the learned *Archbishop Augustinus*, applied to it, and all that the severall *Commissioners*, first by *Pius the fift*, then by *Gregory the thirteenth*, have practised upon it, have not brought it to any state of perfect health, nor any degree of convalescence.

De Emendat. Grat. l.1. Dial.1
Ibid.

7 But though that *Bishop* say, *That Gratian is not worthy of many words*, though in his dispraise, yet because he tels us, *That the ignorant admire him, though the Learned laugh at him*; And because hee is accounted so great a part of the *Canon Law*, as even the *Decretall Epistles* of the Popes are call'd *Extra*, in respect of him, as being out of the *Canon Law*, it shall not be amisse to make some deeper impressions of him.

L.2. Dial.8

8 Thus farre therefore the *Catholicke Archbishop* charges him, *To have beene so indiscreete and precipitate, that he never stood upon Authoritie of Bookes, but tooke all, as if they had beene written with the finger of God, as certainely as Moses Tables*; And hee is so well con-

L.1. Dial.4

firm'd in the opinion of his negligence, that he sayes, *He did not onely never Judge and waigh, but never see the Councels nor the Registers of*

L.1. Dial.19

Popes, nor the workes of the Fathers: And therefore sayes hee, *There is*

L.1. Dial.16

onely one remedy left, which is, Una litura. And in another place, *That there can bee no use at all made of this Collection, but that a better must be attended, out of the Originals*.

L.1. Dial.3

9 But if his errour were onely in *Chronologies*, as to give Pope *Nicholas* a place in the Councell of *Carthage*, who was dead before;

Ibid.

Or in *Arithmeticke*, as when purposely he enumerates all the *Councels*, to make the number lesse by foure. If this weakenesse had onely beene, that he was not able to spell, and so in a place of much importance,

Ibid.
1. Dial.4

to Read *Ephesus* for *Erphesfurd*, *Hierome* for *Jeremie*, and *Hereticke* for *Henrie*, and a hundred such; If he had stopp'd, either at mistaking

1. Dial.5

of true Authors, as to cite out of Saint *Peter*, that which Saint *Paul* sayes (which libertie his *Glosser* extends farther, and therefore cites a

Dist.54. c.12.
Hoc tunc

whole sentence, for *Scripture*, which is no where) Or if he had stay'd at

L.1. Dial.4

imagining words out of false Authors, as to cite the *Councell* of *Geneva*, and *Macharius* the Pope, which never were, (as he and the *Palea* doe)

28. *Hierome Ed.*: *Hierome*,. L-1, C-1 **Margin 30.** 1. Dial.5 *Ed.*: Ibid.. C-1, L-1 **Margin 31.** Dist.54. c.12. Hoc tunc *Ed.*: Dist.43. si quis. verb. postulat.. C-1, L-1

CHAPTER TEN

there were an open way for him, as it is said in that *Dialogue*, to say with the Apostle, *Quia ignorans feci*.

10 But we also finde malignitie and danger to our cause, in his *Falsifications*. For, to dignifie the Sea of Rome, hee cites *Ambroses* wordes thus, *Non habent Petri haereditatem, qui non habent Petri sedem*; which in *Ambrose* is observ'd to be, *Petri fidem*. And to establish the exemption of Clergie men from secular Justice, hee cites this out of a *Councell* now a thousand yeeres past, *Clericum nullus presumat pulsare apud Iudicem Saecularem*; Whereas the words of the Councel are *Clericus nullus presumat*. And so the Councell layes a Commandement upon the Clergie, but *Gratian* layes it upon the Layetie.

11 Which falsitie, *Binius*, citing the Councell aright, and *Gratians* words also right in the Margine, forbeares to observe or reprehend, and dissembles the injurie done to the world therein. But *Bellarmine* hath delt herein with more obnoxiousnesse, and lesse excuse, then *Binius*, because having no reference at all to *Gratian*, hee cites the words out of the Councell it-selfe; and having said, *That Counsell pronounces in this point more clearly, in these words*; He cites the words, falsely, and corruptly as *Gratian* did before.

12 And as for such iniquities as these, we have reason to decline *Gratian*, as injurious to us: So also in Charitie towards them, which are caried with an implicite Faith in *Canons*, in which name *Gratian* is enwrapped, we are bound to tell you how unworthy he is, to bee relied upon by you. For in the point of the *Emperours* Electing the *Pope*, hee hath spoken so dangerously, that *Baronius* is forced to give this censure upon him, *Gratian, out of too much credulitie, improvidently writ out a most manifest imposture, and inserted that, as a most strong Decree, all which, with the Author thereof, should rather have beene hissed away, and pursued with execrations*, which also he sayes of another place in *Gratian*, to the same purpose; and accuses him *of mutilating the famous lawes of Charles the Great, called Capitularia*.

13 With like danger to the *Romane* Sea, hee cites a *Canon* of a *Greeke* Councell, whose sense he apprehended not, in the matter of

Margin 14. Tertio *Ed.*: Tertia. L-1, C-1 *Margin 26.* Dist.63. Cap.22. Hadrianus. Et Idem. Cap.23. In Synodo *Ed.*: Dist.65 Hadrianus. Et Dist.63 In Synodo.. C-1, L-1 *Margin 29.* 622. n.12 *Ed.*: 622.. C-1, L-1 *Margin 30.* 11.q. *Ed.*: note misplaced . C-1, L-1

Margin notes:

L.2. Dial.8
I Tim. 1.13

De Penit. Doct.1. potest fieri

11.q.1. Clericum. Ex Conc. Agath. Can.32

Tom.2. fo.306

De Clericis. l.1. c.28. §. Tertio

Baron. To.9. Ann. 774. n.13
Dist.63. Cap.22. Hadrianus. Et Idem. Cap.23. In Synodo
To.9. Anno 801. fo.622. n.12
11.q.1. Volumnus

Dist.31. quoniam

mariage of Priests; for he sayes, *that that Canon was grounded upon the Apostles Canons*; and yet it is contrarie to the Canons of the Romane Church. So that of this place, that *Archbishop* of whom I spoke before, exclaimes, *who can endure this?* and that *by no meanes it may be receaved.*

14 And not onely in matters of fact (though that be the right legge upon which the Romane Religion, (especially in Crowne Divinitie) doth stand) doth *Gratian* deceave you, but even in such things as are *matters of faith*: both naturally, and so, common to all men; As when he allowes *that there may be perplexities in evill*, and so in some cases a necessitie of sinning, and then, sayes he, *the remedie is to choose the lesse evill*; as also of that which is matter of faith, especially to the professors of your Religion, which is the necessitie of *Orall Confession*: for, having produced authorities on both sides, whether it be *necessarie* or no, he leaves it as indifferent to the Reader, to allow & choose which opinion he likes best.

15 And because the *Glosse* is now by some thought, to be of equal authoritie with the *Text*, it is not an inconvenient way to enervate both, by presenting some of the vanities and illusions of that. And though I will not in so serious a businesse, insist upon such thinges, as might make sport and move laughter, yet these few I may be excusable to let fall in this place. When *Gratian* speakes of that *Parable* of the *lost sheepe*, and sayes, out of the Gospell, that the 99 were left in *Deserto, id est*, sayes the Glosse, *In Caelo, quod Diabolus per peccatum deseruit*. Which besides the detortion, destroyes utterly the purpose of our *Saviour*, in that *Parable*. And so when *Gratian*, out of a *Councell* cites an Act to be done, *In Ecclesia Romanorum, id est*, sayes the Glosse, *Constantinopolitanorum*.

16 In many places *Gratian* sayes, that [a]*Dioscorus had not erred, in fide*; which being evidently false, for [b]he followed and defended *Eutyches* his Heresie, the glosse remedies it thus, *Non in fide, id est, non in fide tantum*. And out of his favour to *Priests*, where *Gratian* sayes out of *Bede*, *That Priests must alwayes abstain from their wives*, the

Margin notes:
Li.1. Dial.8
Dist.13. Duo Mala. And Nerui
De Penitent. Dist.1. Quamvis in fine
Luc. 15.4
Dist.50. Quia sanctitas. verb. In Deserto
24.q.2. Sane profectur. Verb. Item
[a]Dist.21. in tantum. in fine; 24.q.2. Sane profectur
[b]Dist.15. Canones. et glos. ver. Defensorem
Dist.31. Sacerdotibus. ver. semper

Margin 24. Dist.50 *Ed.*: Dist.5. C-1, L-1 **Margin 29a.** Dist.21 *Ed.*: Dist.22. C-1, L-1 **Margin 30b.** Canones C-3, C^9, L^2, O-2, L^{30}, MCG, Y, F: Cansnes. L-1, C-1, HD, L-2, O-1, C^3

glosse sayes, *Semper, id est, Horis debitis*. And when out of the *Nicene* Councell it was produced, *That a Prelate might have in his house no women, except his mother, or sister; or such fit persons, as might avoid suspition*, that is, sayes the glosse, *His mens wives*. And when *Lanfred* a young lusty *Bishop*, and a great huntsman, was defamed also for immoderate familiarity with his owne daughter, the glosse sayes, *It was not for any evill, for they were too neere in blood, but because he kissed her so much openly, and put his hand in her bosome*. Dist.32. Interdix-
it. verb. Idoneas

Dist.34. Quorun-
dam. ver. fama

17 And lastly, to stay you no longer, in this ill aire, where the text sayes, *Meretrix est, quae multorum libidini patet*, the glosse brings this indefinite number to a certaine, and sayes, that that name belongs to her, *when she hath lyen with* 23000. *men*. Ibid. Vidua. ver.
multorum

18 And as these Authors in whom there are these aspersions, and such weedes as these, are therefore unworthy, that either the Popes approbation should fall upon them, or that any obligation should be throwne upon our consciences, from their authoritie: so is it impossible, that any such approbation should include them both; for the *glosse* doth sometimes (when no reconciliation can serve him) depart from *Gratian* with some disdaine; as when he sayes, *Superficialis est Argumentatio Magistri*: and sometimes in choler; as one notes him to say, *Fateor plane te mentitum, Gratiane*: And sometimes hee doth positively teach the just contrarie to *Gratian*, in matter of faith; as in the Doctrine of *perplexities*, which wee noted before. Dist.68. Sicut.
ver. sicut

Alb. Gent. de Lib.
Jur. c.2

Dist.13. Duo mala

19 How dangerous therfore it is to confide in *Gratian*, we see already, & may have further light, by observing, That *Bellarmine* sayes, that in a main point of Canonicall Scriptures, *Gratian was deceived by trusting a false copie of Saint Augustines workes*: And as *Bellarmine* sayes here, that *Gratian* was deceived, so *Gratian* deceived him; for in that Canon which we cited before, of the exemption of Clergy men, either *Bellarmine* was a direct falsifier of the *Councel*, or an indiscreet & credulous swallower of *Gratians* errours; which in his Recognition he refuseth not to confesse in another matter, when he retracts some things which he spoke upon the credit of *Gratian*, & there repents & recants them. De Concil. Au-
tor. l.2. c.12.
§. Sed obiiciunt

Dist.19. In
Canonicis

Margin 2. Dist.32 *Ed*.: Dist.33. C-1, L-1 **Margin 25.** Autor. . . . 12 *Ed*.: autor. . . . 13. L-1, C-1

20   But you and *Bellarmine* may easily be misled by him, since even a Pope himselfe was brought into a false persuasion by his errour. For, till of late, all the copies of the *Decretum*, in that famous *Canon*, *Sancta Romana*, which distinguishes *Canonicall* from *Apocryphall* writings, in stead of the wordes, *Sedulii opus, Heroicis versibus descriptum*, had these wordes, *Hereticis versibus*; Which sayes a Catholique authour, *induced not onely many wise men, but even pope Adrian 6. to a persuasion, that al Poetry was Hereticall*; since *Gelasius* a Pope, and Author of that *Canon*, though he praised *Sedulius* his worke, in that place, yet because it was writ in verse, he cals them *Hereticos versus*.

_{margin:} Dist.15

_{margin:} Pierius. de Barb. Sacerdo. §. At videte

21   Of them therfore which will binde their faith to the *Canons*, and adventure these dangers for that faith (as the *Canonists* say, *that Saterday and Sunday is all one, fictione Canonica*) so wee may say, that they are but Martyres *fictione Canonica*; and that not onely a *Martyr*, and a *Selfe-murderer*, but a *Martyr* and a *Traitor*, may be all one, *Fictione Canonica*. And by such fiction, that English Priest *Bridgewater*, which cals himselfe *Aquipontanus*, overturning and renversing his name with his conscience, may be beleeved, when he sayes, *That those Priests which were executed under Queene Elizabeth, died pro inficiatione pontificatus faeminei*: But their malice was not because she would have bin a *Priest*, but because she would not be a *Sacrifice* to their *Idolatry*, nor *Ambition*; nor open her heart to their inchantments, nor her throate and sides to their poisons and swords.

_{margin:} Dist.75. Quod a Patribus. gloss. ver. sabbati

_{margin:} Respo. ad Georg. Sohn. de Antichrist. Thes.15

22   The next limme in this great body of the *Canon* law, after the *Decretum*, is the *Decretall*; set out by *Gregory* the ninth, who was Pope about the yeare one thousand two hundred thirty. And as the *Decretum* pretends to bring to all purposes, sentences of Fathers, and Canons of Counsells, So this pretends principally the *Rescripts* and *Decretall* letters of Popes. So also, doe all the other bookes, which were set out after, in supplement of this: as that, which is called *Sextus*, set forth by *Boniface* the eight, who was Pope, *Anº*. one thousand three hundred: and the *Clementines*, which *Clement* the fift set out, who was Pope within six yeares after: and those *Extravagants*, which beare the name

4. from *Ed*.: fcom. L-1, C-1 **6.** *Hereticis versibus*; *Ed*.: *Hereticis versibus*.. L-1, C-1 **13.** *Canonica*) so *Ed*.: *Canonica* so. C-1, L-1 **17.** renversing errata: re-enversing L-1, C-1, O-2;. re enversing O^2, O^{14}

of *John* the two and twenty, within ten yeares of *Clement*: and those which are called *common Extravagants* because they come from divers Popes: and to these is added not long since the booke called *Septimus Decretalium*.

23   And thus this fat law (for so *Civilians* say of it, that it is *Crassa aequitas*; which is a praise beyond desert, though they speake it in diminution & scorn) grows daily so fast, that as any corruption can get entertainment in a grosse body, so I doubt not but this, or the next age, shall see in their *Octaves* and future *Volumes*, not onely many of their letters, yet for shame concealed, but the panegyricke at *Henry* the thirds death, canonized in the body of this law. For though they have denied it with some earnestnesse, yet they have also confest, that if it were such as it is said to be, it admits a good interpretation.

24   But for these bookes, though they have more credit with them then the *Decretum* hath, I will ease my selfe of that labour, which I tooke in that booke, in presenting particular defects and infirmities, both because we have *Bellarmines* confession, *That there are many things in the Decretall Epistles, which doe not make a matter to be De fide, but onely doe declare, what the opinions of the Popes were in those causes*, and because a Catholique authour of whom we spake before, hath observed, that the compiler of the Decretals, by leaving out a word, in a Canon of a Councell of *Carthage*, hath occasion'd the Church ever since, to doe directly against the purpose of that Councell, in shaving the beards of *Priests*. For whereas the Councell is cited by him, *Clerici nec Comam Nutriant nec barbam*, by occasion whereof, many subsequent orders were brought in, for *Shaving*, and transgressors severely punish'd, it appeares that he left out in the end, the word *Radant*, which utterly changes the precept into the contrary. These Canons therefore, of so sickely and weake a constitution, that any thing dejects them, cannot prevaile so much upon our consciences, as to imprint and worke such a confidence in them, and irremoveablenesse from them, as to maintaine them with

De Pont. l.4. c.14. §. Respond. nec

Pierius. de Barba Sacerd. §. Hoc in genere

De Vit. & Hon. Cleri. Clericus

---

5. of it *errata*: of that. L-1, C-1   **6.** they *Ed.*: rhey. L-1, C-1   **10.** concealed O-2, YK-2, YK-3, C⁹: cõcealed.   L-1, C-1, O-1, O², O¹⁴, SP, O⁵, YK-1, C³, C¹⁰, C¹⁶   **10.** but the panegyricke at *Henry errata*: but at *Henry* L-1, C-1, O-1, O², O¹⁴, SP, O⁵, YK-1, C³, C¹⁰, C¹⁶;. but *Henry*   O-2, YK-2, YK-3, C⁹   **23.** beards *errata*: heads. L-1, C-1

the same maner of testimonie, as we would doe the words of God himselfe.

25 For, howsoever they depart from them, and seeme somewhat negligent of the *Canons*, when we make use of them to our advantage against them, yet they affright and enthrall the tender consciences of their owne *Disciples*, with nothing more, then the name of *Canons*, to which promiscuously they ascribe all reverence and assent, without distinguishing to them, which are *Gratians*, and which are *opinionate*, and which *Decretall*, for all together are approved and confirmed. And therefore the *Canons* themselves not only inflict an *Anatheme* uppon any Lay-man, which shall so much as dispute upon, the text, or any one *Iod* of the Epistle of Pope *Leo*, which is in the *Canons*, but also pronounce it *blasphemy against the holy Ghost, to violate a Canon willingly*, because they are made by the holy Ghost. And *Bellarmine* also, writing against a *Doctor* which had defended the *Venetian* cause, against the Popes Censures, says, *That it is a grievous rashnesse, not to be left unpunished, that he should say, The Canons, as being but Humane lawes, cannot have equall authority with Divine*. For this (sayes *Bellarmine*) *is a contempt of the Canons, as though they were not made by the direction of the holy Ghost*. And yet these Canons which that *Doctor* intimated, were but two, and cited but by *Gratian*, and concerned onely Exemption of Clergie men from secular Judges.

26 And so *Parsons* when he is to make his advantage of any Sentence in *Gratian*, uses to dignifie it thus, *That it is translated by the Popes into the Corps of the Canon law*, and so not onely *allowed* and *admitted*, and *approved*, but *commended*, and *commanded*; and as he addes after, *Canonized and determined for Canonicall law, and authorized and set forth for Sacred and Authenticall, by all Popes whatsoever*: For they continue still that practise which *Frederic* the *Emperour* observed in his time, when they interdicted his Kingdome of *Sicily*, *offundunt bibulis auribus Canones*.

27 And when they list to urge a *Canon*, any litle rag torn or fallen off from thence, must bind the Church *de fide*, as a cathedrall, and Dec-

---

Margin notes:
- Dist.15. Sancta Romana
- 25.q.1. Violatores
- Respons. ad Docto. Theolo. proposit. tertia. §. Tertia haec
- Marsilii. Defens. Docto. ca.5, §. Errat.XI
- Treat. of Mitig. ca.7. n.42
- Nu.43
- Nu.45.
- Petr. de Vineis. Epist.4. l.1

---

14. are made] arem ade   C-4; ar emade.   L-1, HD, C⁵-2, O-1, C³, C¹⁰, C¹⁶, YK-1 14. holy *errata*: hyol. L-1, C-1 14. Ghost. *Ed.*: Ghost. L-1, C-1 23. *Parsons Ed.*: Rarsons. L-1, C-1 **Margin 27.** 45 *Ed.*: 43. L-1, C-1 **Margin 28.** Petr.] *note missing* . O²

CHAPTER TEN

retall resolution: for so sayes he, that made the Notes upon *Cassianus*, excusing *Origen, Chrysostome*, & some other Fathers, for inclining to *Platoes* opinion of *allowing some use of lies, in wise men, That it was lawfull till the Church had defined the contrary:* But now, sayes he, *the Pope hath decreed it.* And how hath he decreed it? In a letter upon a question of *Usurie*, the Pope sayes, [a]*Since the Scriptures forbid lies, even for defense of any mans life, much lesse may usury be permitted.* But, if in this question of lying, the band did not arise out of the evidence and truth of the matter it selfe, but relied uppon the authority of the Popes *declaration,* and *decision,* can such a ragge casualy and incidentally fallen into a letter of another purpose, by way of comparison, binde the whole Church, *De fide?* when as, though *Sixtus* 4. had so much declared himselfe to favour the opinion of our *Ladies conception* without originall sinne, that he had by [b]one Canon instituted a particular *Festivall* thereof, and appointed a particular *Office* for that day, with many Indulgences to the observers thereof; yet the favourers of the contrary opinion, forbore not for reverence of that Canon, to preach publiquely against that Doctrine, till some yeares after, he forbad it under paine of Excommunication, by another Canon, [c]*that any should affirme that she was conceaved in originall sinne*; and yet, [d]this is not esteemed as yet for all this, *to be decreed as a matter of faith* in that Church: yea, it is so farre from it, that after all these solemnities and prejudices of that Pope, yet the *Commissioners* of *Pius the fift, and Gregory the thirteenth (appointed to expunge all dangerous passages in the Canons)* in the Glosse upon that [e]*Canon,* which reckons all the festivall dayes which are to be observed, have left these words untouched, *The Conception of our Lady is not named, because it ought not to be kept, though in England, and some other places it be; And the reason is, because she was conceaved in originall sinne, as all but Christ, were.* And after, *the Jesuite,* of whom I spoke before, had refreshed that Doctrine, *That a Confession of a person absent, made by letters, was Sacramentall,* and Clement the eight, was so vehement against it, that by a solemne decree he condemned it, for false, rash, and scandalous at least, and commaunded, that no man should speake of it but by way of condemning it, and

[a] De Usuris. super eo

Cassianus. Lugduni. Ann. 1606. fo.740

[b] Extrav. Com. De reliqui. cum preexcelsa

[c] Ibid. Grave

[d] Victorell. de Custod. Angelo. fo.99

[e] De Consecra. Dist.3. Pronunciandam. Glos. ver. Nativitas

---

4. he, the] he the. L-1, HD, L-2, O[14]   **11.** fallen *errata*: fall. L-1, C-1
23. *Pius* Ed.: *Sixtus.* C-1, L-1

excluded even dumbe men from this benefit, yet another Jesuite since, a great Doctor perplexorum, findes escapes to defend that Doctrine from beeing Hereticall.

<small>Comitolus. Resp. Mor. Lib.1.q.16</small>

28 So that though in trueth there goe verie many Essentiall formalities to such a *Decree* as bindes the conscience, *De fide*, yet these men when they need the Majestie of a Canon, will ever have fetters in all corners, to holde all consciences which offer to slip or breake from them, and still oppresse them with waights, and with Mountaines of *Canons.* Which way, the *Canonists* doe not only approve as the most convenient to hold men in that *Religion*, because the *Canons* are more easily varied, and flexible, and appliable to occasions, then the *Scriptures* are, but also (because ordinarily the *Canonists* have no other learning) they think the way by Canons, to be the fittest means, to reduce them whom they call *Heretiques*. For so sayes one of them, in his booke to the present *Pope*, (with much acutenesse, (certainely), and subtilty,) *The Canons may well be alleadged against Heretiques; because they alleadge Scriptures, and they cannot know Scriptures, by any other way then Canons.*

<small>Maynardus. de Privil. Eccl. Ar.11. n.8.9</small>

29 But besides, that I have given you sufficient light, to look into the deformity and corruption of the *Canons*, (which, GOD forbid any should understand me to meane of *Canons*, in that sense and acceptation, that the Ancients receaved it, which is, of the Constitutions of Orthodox Councels, for I take it here, as your *Doctors* do, & as your *Confessors* doe, for the whole body of the *Canon law*, extant) before I enter into the survay of those particular *Canons*, which usually are obtruded in this point of the Popes *temporall Supremacie*, I will remember you briefly, of some of those reasons and occasions, (such as may be fittest to unentangle your consciences, and deliver them from perplexities) in which the *Canons* doe not binde us to their observation.

30 Of which, one of the most principall and important is, That *Canons doe never binde, though they be published and knowledge taken of them, except they bee receaved, and practised in that Country.* So sayes *Gratian, Lawes are instituted, when they are published, but confirmed, when they are put in practise.* And therefore, sayes he, *none are guilty of transgressing Telesphorus Decree, that the Clergie should fast fiftie dayes, because it was never approved by practise.* No more doth the

<small>Dist.4. In istis</small>

---

15. (certainely) *errata:* certainty. L-1, C-1

CHAPTER TEN 201

Decree of *Alexander* the third, though under excommunication, *That in Armies there should bee abstinence, for reverence of certaine dayes*, binde any man, because it was not practised: which opinion *Navarre* also followes; and a late *Canonist* writing to this Pope, calls it, *Singularem,*
5 *et Magistralem, et a toto mundo allegatum.* And upon this reason the Councell of *Trent* bindes not yet in some Countries, in neither Tribunall of conscience, or the outward censures of the Church, because it is not receaved.

De Tregua et Pace. c.1. Tregua. glos. ver. frangere
Manual. c.23. nu.41
Ugolini. Resp. ad 7. Theolo. Cap.I. §. 1. nu.9

31 And can you finde that any such *Canons*, as enable the Pope
10 to depose a Prince, have beene admitted by our Princes, and practised as ordinarie and currant law? Or can you finde any *Canon* to this purpose, with the face and countenance of a law, made by the Popes in reposed & peaceable rimes, and delivered quietly as a matter of Doctrine and conscience, and so accepted by the Church and state? For if in
15 *temporall Scismes*, and differences, for *temporall* matters, betweene the *Popes* and other Princes, the Popes to raise or maintaine a party against their enemies, have suffered seditious *Bulls*, and *Rescripts* to passe from them, to facilitate and effect their enterprises then in hand, this is farre from the nature of a law, and from being accepted and *practised*, and
20 so justified, as it may be drawne into consequence, and have power and strength to binde the conscience.

32 And as *acceptation* gives life to law, so doth *disuse*, or *custome* to the contrarie abrogate it. And howsoever a superstition toward the *Canons*, may still be preserved in some of you, yet the generall state,
25 that is, the same authority, by which those Canons were receaved before, which ever had anie strength here, hath disused them, & pronounced against so many of them, as can fall within this question, that is, *Such as bee derogatorie to the Crowne*. For, if these lawes bee not borne alive, but have their quickning by others *acceptation*, the same power
30 that gives them life, may by *desertion* withdraw their strength, and leave them invalid.

Azor. To.2. l.7. c.3. §. Quaeres
Ugolini. ubi supra

33 And thus much seemed needfull to be said in the first part of this chapter, that you might see how putrid and corrupt a thing it is, which is offered to you under the reverend name of *Canons*; And that

Margin 4. Resp. . . . Cap.I. §. 1. *Ed.*: resp. . . . §. I.. C-1, L-1 **Margin 22.** Ugolini *Ed.*: Ugotini. C-1, L-1

though this *Canon law* be declined, and extenuated when we urge it, yet every Sentence thereof is equall'd to *Divine Scripture*; and produced as a *definition* of the Church, when it may worke their ends upon your consciences, which, for divers reasons issuing out of their owne rules, should now be delivered from that yoake.

THE SECOND PART.

1 For the second place in this Chapter, I reserved the consideration and survay of those *Canons* which are Ordinarily usurped for defence of this *temporall Jurisdiction*: In which my purpose is not, to amasse all those *Canons* which incline toward that point, of which condition those which exempt the Clergy from secular Jurisdiction, and very many other, are, but onely such as belong more directly to this point, to which the *Oath* stretches, That is, whether the Pope may depose a Soveraine Prince, and so we shall discern whether your consciences may so safely relie upon any resolution to be had out of the *Canons*, that you may incurre the dangers of the law, for refusall thereof.

2 Of which Canons, though I will pretermit none, which I have found to have beene urged, in any of their Authours, I will first present those *Fower*, which are always produced with much confidence and triumph: Though one *Catholique* Author, which might be alive at the making of the *Clementines* (for he lived and flourished about 1350, and *Clement* the fift died not much before 1320.) have drawen these foure *Canons* into just suspition: for thus he sayes of them, *The Pastors of the Church putting their Hooke into another mans Harvest, have made foure Decretals, which, God knowes, whether they be just or no: But I doe not beleeve (yet I recall it if it be erroneous) that any of them is agreeable to Law, but I rather beleeve that they were put forth against the libertie of the empire.*

3 The first is a letter of *Innocent* the third, who was Pope about 1199. to the *Duke of Caringia*, the occasion of which Letter, was this;

Albericus. in Dictionar. ver. Electio

De Electio & Elect. Potest. Venerabilem

8. 1 *Ed.*: missing. L-1, C-1   **12.** exempt *Ed.*: ex-exempt. C-1, L-1   **31.** Caringia, *Ed.*: Caringia. L-1, C-1

Henry the son of *Frederic* the first, of the house of *Suevia*, succeeding his Father in the *Empire*, had obtained of the Princes of *Germany*, to whom the Election belonged, to chuse as Successor to him, his sonne *Frederic*: but hee being too young to governe, when his father died, they tooke thereby occasion, though against their Oath, to leave him; being also desirous to change the stocke, and chuse an Emperour of some other race; By this meanes was Duke *Bertholdus*, by some of the Princes elected; but resign'd againe to *Philip* brother to the dead Emperour, in whom the greatest number consented. But some of the other Princes had called home out of *England*, *Otho* of the house of *Saxony*, and elected him. Hereupon arose such a *schisme*, as rent that country into very many parts: And then *Innocent* the third, an active and busie Pope (for it was he which so much infested our King *John*) sent his *Legate* into those parts, upon pretence of composing those differences. And being in displeasure with the house of *Suevia* for the Kingdome of *Sicily*, which was in their possession, but pretended to by the Church, his Legate disallowed the election of *Philip*, and confirmed *Otho*. But some of the Princes ill satisfied with the Legates proceeding herein, complained thereof to the Pope; in aunswere whereof the Pope writes to one of them, this Letter. In which, handling his Right of *confirming* the elected Emperor, though he speake divers things derogatorie to the dignity of *Princes*, discoursively, and occasionally, yet is not this letter such a *Decree*, as being pronounced *Cathedrally* in a matter of faith, after due consultation, should binde posteritie, but onely a direction to that person, how he ought to behave himselfe in that businesse.

4 The Letter may be thus abridged; *We acknowledge the right of the Election to be in the Princes, especially because they have it from the Apostolicke Sea, which transferred the Empire unto them: But, because we must consecrate the Person elected, we must also examine his fitnesse. Our Legate therefore did not Acte concerning the Election, but the person elected. Wee therefore repute OTHO Emperour; For, if the Electors would never agree, should the Apostolicke Sea alwayes be without a defender? We have therfore thought it fit, to warne the Princes, to adhere to him. For there are notorious impediments against the other:*

---

4. *Frederic* Ed.: *Henry.*   C-1, L-1   **4.** governe,] governe.   C-1, C-4, MCG, SP, YK-2   **30.** *not* Ed.: *no.*   L-1, C-1

as publicke Excommunication, persecuting the Church, and manifest perjurie. Therefore wee commaund you to depart from him, notwithstanding any Oath made to him, as Emperour.

5   And is there any matter of Faith in this Decretall? Or any part thereof? Is it not all grounded upon matter of fact, which is, the Translation of the Empire which is yet under disputation? Doe not many Catholicke writers denie the verie act of *Transferring* by the Pope; And saye, That the people being now abandoned and forsaken by the *Easterne Emperours*, had by the law of Nature and Nations, a power in themselves to choose a King? And doe not those which are more liberall in confessing the *Translation*, denie that the Popes *Consecration*, or *Coronation*, or *Unction*, infuses any power into the Emperor, or works any farther, then when a Bishop doeth the same ceremonies to a King? Is it not justly said, that if the Emperour must stay for his Authoritie, till the Pope doe these acts, he is in worse condition, by this increase of his Dominions then he was before. For, before he was *Emperour*, and had a little of *Italy* added to him, there was no doubt but that he had full jurisdiction, in his owne *Dominions* before these Ceremonies, and now hee must stay for them.

6   And may not the Popes question in this letter, be well retorted thus, *If the Pope will not crowne the Emperour at all, shall the Empire ever lacke a head?* For the Pope may well be presumed to be slacke in that office, because he pretends to be *Emperour* during the *vacancie*. But besides that an over earnest maintaining of this *that the Emperour had no jurisdiction in Italy, before these Ceremonies*, would diminish and mutilate the patrimonie of the Church, of which a great part was conferred and given by *Pipin*, before any of these ceremonies were given by the pope, the glosser upon the *Clementines*, is liquid & round in this point, when he sayes, *That these ceremonies, and the taking of an Oath, are nothing*; and that now, *Resipiscente mundo*, the world being growne wiser, *there must be no longer striving for both swords*.

7   For those *notorious impediments*, which the Pope objects in this letter, against *Philip*, if they were such as made him *Incapable* of Election, then there was a *Nullity* in the choise, and the Pope did nothing but declare that; which may often fall out in states, which elect their

De Iure Iurando

Margin 28. Iure Iurando *Ed.*: Iureiurando.   L-1, C-1

CHAPTER TEN 205

Princes, because there are many limitations, but in *Successorie* princes, it cannot hold: but if these were not such impediments, by the lawes which governed the Electors, they became not such, by this Declaration. For one of them, which is *manifest perjurie*, the pope himselfe was some
5 cause of his continuing therein. For the oath was made to his brother, in the behalfe of his young Nephew, who should have been *Emperour*. And now the Pope had not onely disabled him, but all the other Princes, from keeping that oath, by electing or confirming another Emperour.

8 But if all which the Pope sayes in that letter, shall not onely bee
10 strong enough to binde the Election, but to binde the consciences of posterity, as matter of faith, his last reason against *Philips* election, must have equall strength with the rest, which would bee of dangerous consequence; for it is, *That if after his Father had beene Emperour, and his Brother, he also should succeede, the Empire would passe from*
15 *Election to succession, and none should be assumed but of one house*; Either then it is matter of faith, *that three of one family may not succeed in an Elective state*, or, as this is, so all the rest are but arguments of inconveniencie & unfitnes.

9 And this absolving this *Duke*, to whom he writes, of his Oath, is
20 but of an Oath made *Ratione Regni*, to him who never had the Kingdome: and therefore that power of absolving, cannot by this *Decretall* be extended to such *Oathes*, which are acknowledged to have beene just, when they were made, as being made to lawfull and indubitable Princes. And certainly (for though you dare not heare, yet wee dare
25 speake trueth,) the whole purpose in that act, of the Pope, was corrupt, and farre from intention of making peace. Of whose profit by reason of that dissention one of your owne *Abbats*, sayes, *That there was scarse*   Urspergens.
any Bishoprick, or Parish Church, which was not litigious, and the Suite   fo.1198
brought to Rome, Sed non vacua Manu, And so he proceedes, *Gaude,*
30 *Mater nostra Roma*, because all flowes to thee, *aperiuntur Cataractae thesaurorum. Rejoice for the iniquitie of the Sonnes of men; Jocundare de Adiutrice tua Discordia. Thou hast now that which thou didst alwayes thirst. Sing thy song, because thou hast overcome the world, not by thy Religion, but the wickednesse of men, for men are not drawne to thee*
35 *by their owne Devotion, or by a pure Conscience, but by the doing of*

Margin 27. Urspergens *Ed.*: Uspergens. C-1, L-1

manifolde wickednesses, and by buying the Decision of their Suites and Causes.

10   The second *Canon* usually produced, and noted by *Albericus* (as I said) to be against *Justice*, issued upon this occasion. When *Otho* whom the former Pope had established against *Philip*, became unthankfull to the Pope, hee also was excommunicate: and *Frederick*, the Sonne of the first *Frederick*, to whom the Princes had sworne in his Cradle, was elected and crowned; with whom also, because hee would not goe into the holy land, and expose the Kingdome of *Sicily* to their Ambition, the Popes fell out, and excommunicated him thrice. And when a generall Councell was gathered by *Innocent* the fourth, for the reliefe of the holy land, the Pope himselfe proposed Articles against the *Emperour*. Whose Advocate *Thaddaeus* promised all, which might conduce to peace and Reformation on his Maisters behalfe. This satisfied not the Pope, but he asked for *Sureties*: and when the Kings of *England* and *France*, were offered, the pope refused them, upon pretence, that if the Emperor should remaine incorrigible, the Church should by this means raise more heavy enemies to it selfe. Then *Thaddaeus* proceeded to excuse his Maister, in all the particular objections, and desired that hee might be personally heard, but to that the pope replied, *If he come I will depart, for I doe not yet finde my selfe fit and ready for martyrdome.* Yet the *English* which were there, extorted a fortnights leasure for the *Emperours* comming: but he not daring or disdaining to come, the pope proceeded to this sentence of *Deprivation*; which, says the Relater thereof, *He thundred out terribly, not without the amazement and horrour of all the hearers and by-standers.* And *Thaddaeus* protested upon it, *This day is a day of wrath, and of calamity and miserie.*

11   So this Bull proceeded from a distempered Pope, and at a time when hee was not assisted with the *Holy Ghost*, for he was not in a readines to suffer *Martyrdome* for him. And where the *Inscription* sayes, it was *Presenti Concilio*; the Margin notes, that it is not said *approbante Concilio*, though it assigne this for the reason, least the Pope should seeme to neede the Councell.

12   So that, though it reach full as farre as *Pius* the fift his Bull against our late *Queene* (for it *deprives*, it *absolves* Subjects, and it *excommunicates* all adherents) yet it hath nothing by which it should be called a *Canon*, or lawe to direct and governe posterity; for there

---

De Sent. et Re
Iudic. in 6. Ad
Apostolicae

Binius. To.3.
par.2. fo.1482

might be as much infirmity in this act of *Depriving*, as in the former of *Excommunicating*; yea it was subject to much more errour then that acte of spirituall jurisdiction, which hath beene lesse questioned: yet in the preamble of this sentence, the pope sayes of those former sentences, *If the Church have injured him in any thing, she is ready to correct her selfe, to revoke, and to make satisfaction.* So that it may be, the pope erred in both these acts.

13 Nor doe those wordes which are in the Inscription, *Ad perpetuam rei Memoriam*, give it the strength of a precedent, and obligatorie *Canon*, but rather declare out of what shoppe it came, since that is the ordinary style of the *Romane Court*, and not of the *Canons* of Councels. Nor can it ever be deduced by any consequence, out of this *Sentence*, That the Pope hath the same power over other *Soveraigne Princes*, as he exercised there against the *Emperour*; because hee proceeded against him (though vitiously and injuriously, and tyrannically) by colour of a *Superiority* claimed by him, and then not denied by the Emperour, but testified by divers *Oathes of Fidelity* to him, which cannot be extended against those princes, which admit no dependency upon him, by any reason conteined in this Sentence.

14 By the third of these foure principall *Rescripts*, *Clement* the fift annuls a *Judgement* made by the Emperour *Henry* the seventh, against *Robert* king of *Sicily*, whom as a subject of the *Empire*, the *Emperour* had declared a Rebell, and deprived him of his Kingdome and absolved his subjects of their obedience. And the reasons why the Pope interposes himselfe herein, are not grounded upon his power, as he is *Pope*, or as he is *spirituall Prince*, but meerely as he is a *temporall Prince*. For first he sayes, *The King of Sicily held that Kingdome of the Church; and the Pope, who was thereby his ordinary judge, ought to have beene called to the judgement*; And that the *Emperour could not take knowledge of faults committed at Rome*, as those, with which that King was charged, were laid to be: *Nor his Jurisdiction and power of citation extend into the territory of the Church where that King was then residing: nor he bee bound upon any Citation, to come to a place of so certaine danger.*

Clement. de Sentent. & Re Iudic. Pastoralis. Anno 1306

15 It is not therefore for this part of the *Decretall*, that either they alleadge it so frequently, or that *Albericus* laid that marke upon it, that it betrayed the authority of the Emperours; for in this particular

case, it should not bee difficult to confesse, some degrees of *Justice*, in providing that the *Sentence* of the *Emperor* should not prevaile, where naturally and justly it could not worke; especially the pope proceeding so mannerly, as to revoke it after the *Emperors* death; and as the Glosse says, *Ad tollendum murmur Populi*, who grudged that the *Emperour* should dispose of them, who were the subjects of the Church.

16 But the danger is in the last clause, which is, *We out of the Superiority, which without doubt we have over the Empire, and out of that power, by which we succeed therein, in a vacancy, and by that power which Christ gave us in Peter, declare that judgement to bee voide, and revoke all which hath beene done thereupon*. For the first part of which Clause, touching his *Superiority* over the *Emperor*, if he had any (which, as many good authors denie, as affirme it) he had it by contract betweene the *Emperour* and the *Church*; and he neither can, nor doth claime that, at least not all that which hee pretended in the Empire, in other princes dominions; for where doth he pretend to succeede in a *Vacancy*, but in the *Empire*? And if he had that right, *Iure Divino*, it would stretch to all other places: And if it be by *Contract*, that cannot be but conditionall and variable in it selfe, and not to be drawen into example to the prejudice of any other prince. And for his last title, which is the power derived by *S. Peter* to him, because in this place he extends it no further, but to a defence of *S. Peters patrimony*, and onely by declaring a *Sentence* to be void, which otherwise might scandalize some of his subjects, we have no reason to exagitate it in this place, nor have you any reason to assure your consciences, by the instruction or light of this *Canon*, that that power extends to any such case, as should make you, in these substantiall circumstances, of great detriment, refuse this Oath.

<small>Clement. de Iure Iurando Unica</small>

17 The fourth *Canon*, which is, the *Clementine* of the divers Oathes sworne by the *Emperours* to the Popes, though it be ever cited, and be by *Albericus* justly accused of injustice: yet it can by no extension worke upon your conscience. For the purpose thereof is but this; That differences continuing betweene the *Emperour* and the King of *Sicily*, and the Pope writing to reconcile them, he useth this as one induction, *That they had both sworne Fidelity and Alleageance to him*. The Emperor answered, *That he understood not that Oath, which he had taken, to be an*

---

1. it should *Ed*.: I should. L-1, C-1

CHAPTER TEN 209

Oath of Alleageance: And therfore the Pope, after the *Emperours* death, in this *Decretall* pronounces, That *they are Oathes of fidelities and Alleageance, and that whosoever shall be created Emperour, shall take those Oathes, as such*. But, to leave it to the Lawyers, (whose tongues, and
5 pennes are not silenced by this *Decretall*,) to argue whether they be oathes of *Alleageance*, or no, and imposed by the Pope essentially, so as the Emperour had no jurisdiction without them (the first being a *Constitution* of the Emperour *Otho*, and not of the Pope, (if it be rightly cited by *Gratian*) The second but an oath of *Protection* of the Church,
10 and the Pope, And the third, only of a pure and intire observing of the *Catholique* faith), who can presse an argument out of this *Canon*, though it were wholy confessed and accepted as it lies, that the Pope may depose a king of *England*? For *Bellarmine* informes your consciences, better then any of those Confessors, who avert you from the oath, by
15 this, and such *Canons*, That *the Empire not depending absolutely upon the Pope, but since Charlemains time, this Oath of Alleageance is taken of the Emperour, because the Pope translated the Empire upon him*. And whether this be true or false, in the latter part of translation, yet his reason and argument discharges all other supreme Princes, over whom
20 the Pope hath no such pretence.

    18 Having passed through these foure, wee will consider those *Canons*, which are in *Gratian*, to this purpose. The first whereof may justly be the *Donation* of *Constantine*. Which though it be not *Gratians*, but inserted, by the name of *Palea* (of whom, whether hee were a man of
25 that name, a Scholler of *Gratian*, or whether he called his Addition to *Gratian*, *Paleas* in humility, the *Canonists* are like to wrangle, as long as any body will read them) yet it is in the body and credit of *Canon* law.

    19 Towards the credit of this *Donation*, there lackes but thus much,
30 to make it possible, That the *Emperour* had not power, to give away halfe his Empire, and that that *Bishop* had not capacitie to receive it, And but thus much of making it likely, That the Church had no possession thereof, but that it remained still with the Successors of the Emperours: for if it had these degrees of *possibility* or *credibility*, & did

Marginalia:
Dist.63. Tibi Domino
De Pontif. l.5. c.8. §. septimum
Dist.96. Constantinus

---

11. faith), *Ed.*: faith). L-1, C-1   **14.** better] beeter. C-2, C-3, O², O¹⁴, C³, C¹⁰, YK-1, YK-2, YK-3, C²-2

not speake in barbarous language discording from that time, nor in false Latine unworthy of an Emperours Secretarie, nor gave the pope leave to confer orders upon whom he would, nor spoke of the Patriarchate of *Constantinople*, before it had either that *Dignity*, or that *Name*, I should be content, as I would in other fables, to study what the Allegory thereof should be. But since the Pope can live without it, And *Azorius* tells us, that though the Donation bee false, yet the Pope hath other just titles to his estates, (though, by his leave, he hath no such title, as will authorize him to depose Princes, as Soveraigne Lord over all the Westerne Kings, as they pretend by this, if it were justifiable) I will leave it as they doe, as a thing too suspicious and doubtfull, to possesse any roome, but that which it doth in *Gratian*. Onely, this I will adde, that if the power of the Emperour were in the Pope, by vertue of this Donation, yet wee might safely take this Oath, because this Kingdome hath no dependance upon the Empire.

20 The next that I finde alleadged, (to keepe this Order, as they lie in *Gratian*) is a sentence taken out of *S. Augustine*, by which you may see how infinite a power, they place in the Pope: His words are: *If the King must bee obeyed, though hee commaund contra Societatem, yea, it is contra Societatem, if he be not obeyed, because there is a generall contract in humane Societies, that Kings must be obeyed; how much more must we obey God, the Governour of all Creatures?*

And do they which alleadge this for the Popes Supremacy over Princes, intend the Pope to be Governour of all Creatures? Doth he governe Sea, and Elements? or doe they thinke that the will and commandements of God are derived to us onely by the way of the Pope? or why should not wee thanke them, for producing this *Canon*, since it is direct, and very strong for Kings, and for the Popes, it is but common with all other Magistrates, who must be obeyed, when God speaks in them, or when they speake not against God?

21 In the tenth *Distinction*, one Pope by the testimony of two other Popes, sayes, *That the Ecclesiastique Constitutions must be preferred before the Emperours lawes*: And the cases mentioned there, are, the constituting of a Metropolitane, & the dissolving of a Mariage, upon entring into Religion; to which, I say, that these cases, by consent of the

Marginalia: To.2. l.4. c.19 et 20 · Dist.9. Quae contra · Dist.10. lege

23. alleadge this *errata*: alleadge. L-1, C-1

CHAPTER TEN 211

Emperours, were under their jurisdiction. And if you gather a generall rule by this, of the force of *Canons* above *Civill* lawes, you proceede indirectly, accepting the same persons, for *Parties*, *Judges*, and *Witnesses*: and besides it is not safe arguing from the Emperour to another absolute
5 Prince, nor from the authority, which Canons have in his Dominions, to what they should have in all.

22 In the 22. *Distinction*, A Pope writing to a Bishoppe of *Milan*, Dist.22. Omnes telles him, That the dignities and preheminences of Churches, must be as the Bishoppe of Rome shall ordaine, because Christ committed to
10 *Peter*, which hath the keyes of eternall life, *Iura terreni simul & Caelestis Imperii*. But if he meane by his *Terrenum Imperii*, the disposing of the dignities and preheminencies of Churches one above another in this world: Or if he meane by it, That he hath this *Terrenum Imperii*, as he hath the keyes of heaven, that is to binde and loose sinnes, by spirituall
15 censures and Indulgences of absolution, in which capacity he may have authority over the highest secular Princes; for any thing conteined in this Oath, this *Canon* wil do us no harme. But if hee meane that Christ gave him both these authorities together, and that thereby he hath them as *Ordinary Judge*, then *Bellarmine* and all which follow the
20 Divines opinion of indirect power, will forsake him; and so may you by their example.

23 After, another Pope, *Gelasius* writes to *Anastasius* the Emperour, comparing Secular and Ecclesiastique dignity: And he sayes, *You know that you depend upon their judgement*: but this is, sayes the Glosse,
25 *in spirituall matters*. And because this *Canon* comes no neerer our question, then to justifie in the Pope a power of excommunicating Princes, (for it assumes no more then *Ambrose* exercised upon *Theodosius*) I will stand no longer upon it. Dist.96. Duo sunt

24 And these be the *Canons*, which out of the Distinctions, I have
30 observed to be scattered amongst their Authours, when they teach this doctrine: for any that preferres *Priest-hood* before *Principality*, seemes to them to conduce to that point. Now I will follow *Gratian* in his other parts, where the first is, the Canon *Nos si incompetenter*, which is very 2.q.7. Nos si often urged; but it is so farre from including this power of *Deposing*,

7. 22. *Ed.*: 21.. C-1, L-1 **Margin 7.** 22. *Ed.*: 21.. C-1, L-1 **Margin 33.** 2.q.7 C-2, C⁵-2, C³, YK-1: 2[?]7. L-1, C-1, YK-3

that it excludes it; for, allowing the *Priest* power to *Reprehend*, and remembring former examples of *Excommunication*, hee addes, *Nathan in reprooving the King, executed that office, in which he was Superiour to him, but he usurped not the Kings office, in which he was inferiour; nor gave judgement of death upon him as Adulterer, or murderer.*

25 In the second *Question* of the ninth *Cause*, from the Canon *Episcopo*, to the end of that *Question*, there are many sayings, which advance the dignity of the *Romane* Seate, and forbidde al men to hinder *Appeals* thither, or to judge of the popes *Decrees*: But all these were in *spirituall causes*, and directed to *spirituall persons*, and under *spirituall* punishments. Onely, in the Canon *Fratres* the king of *Spaine* seemes to be threatned, but it is with *Excommunication* onely. And all these *Canons* together, are delivered by one *Pope* of another, In whome, says the Glosse, *It is a familiar kinde of proofe, for one Pope to produce another for witnesse, as God did prove the sinnes of Sodome, by Angels.*

And as there is much injustice in this manner of the *Popes* proceeding, so is there some tincture of blasphemy, in the maner of justifying it, by this Comparison.

26 The Canon *Alius*, which droppes out of every penne, which hath written of this Subject, is the first wherein I marked any Pope to speake of *Deposing*; In this, *Gelasius* writes to *Anastasius*; a Pope to an Emperour, that Pope *Zachary* his predecessor, *had deposed the King of France, because he was unfit for so great a power.* But the Glosser doth the Pope good service, and keepes him to within such a convenient sense, as may make him say true; For, says he, He deposed, that is, *Hee gave consent to them which did depose*, which were the States of that Kingdome; which he sayes, out of the Evidence of the history; for he is so farre from coarcting the Popes power, that wee may easily deprehend in the *Glosse*, more fraud and iniquity, then arrogance and tyrannie in the Pope. For, says he, *the unfitnesse of the French King, was licentiousnesse, not insufficiency to governe, for then the Pope ought to have given him an assistant.* To prove which, he cites two other Canons; In which places it appeares, That to Bishoppes unable by reason of age, to discharge their functions, the Pope assigns *Coadjutores*, and by this

---

6. second *Ed*.: seventh. C-1, L-1 **Margin 6.** 9.q.2 *Ed*.: 9.q.7. C-1, L-1
17. blasphemy *Ed*.: blaspemy. L-1, C-1 **24.** Pope *Ed*.: Rope. L-1, C-1

CHAPTER TEN 213

the *Glosser* might evict, that he hath the same Ordinary authority to dispose of *Kingdomes*, as of— *Bishoprickes*. This *Canon* therefore doth onely unfaithfully relate the act of another *Pope*, and not determine nor decree any thing, nor binde the conscience.

27 In the same *Question*, there is a *Canon* or two, in which our case is thus farre concern'd; that they handle the Popes authority in *Absolving* and *Dispensing* from Oathes: And the first is cited often and with great courage; because besides the word *Ab omnibus Iuramentis, & cuiuscunquemodi obligationibus absolvimus*, there followes, *pursue them with the spirituall and materiall sword*. But when we consider the case and the History, this power will not extend to our cause. For the Pope thereby doth give liberty to some *Bishops*, to recover by just violence, such parts of the *Church Patrimonie*, as were taken away from them, and doth dispence with such oathes as they had beene forced to take, by those which injuriously infested the Church. Yet I denie not but that the *glosser* upon this *Canon* is liberall enough to the Pope, for he says, *hee hath power to dispence against the law of Nature, & against the Apostle*. [15.q.6. Authoritatem &c.]

28 After this, followes that solemne and famous *Canon* of *Gregory* the seventh, *Nos sanctorum*. Of whom, since he had made a new rent in the body of the Church, (as Authors of his own Religion (if he had any) professe,) it is no marvaile that he patched it, with a new ragge in the body of the Canon law. Thus therefore he says, *Insisting upon the statutes of our predecessors, by our Apostolique authority, We absolve from their Oath of Alleageance, all which are bound to persons excommunicate; And we utterly forbid them, to beare any Alleageance to such, till they come to satisfaction*. But to whom shall these men be subject in the meane time? To such a one as will be content to resigne, when so ever the other will aske forgivenesse? Ambition is not an ague; it hath no fits, nor accesses, and remittings; nor can any power extinguish it upon a sodaine warning. And if the purpose of Popes in these depositions, were but to punish with temporarie punishment, why are the Kingdomes, which have been transferred by that colour, from *Hereticall* Princes, still with-held from their *Catholique* Heires? [Ibid.]

29 But who these predecessors, of whom the Pope speaks in this letter, were, I could never find. And it appears by this, that this was an *Innovation*, and that he used *Excommunication* to serve his own

ends, because in another *Canon* he sayes, *That many perished by reason of Excommunications; and that therefore he being now overcome with compassion, did temper that sentence for a time, and withdraw from that band, all such as communicated with the excommunicate person, except those by whose Counsaile, the fault was perpetrated, which in- duced the Excommunication.* And this, sayes the glosse, he did, *because he saw them contemne excommunication, and never seek Absolution*; for all those whom he exempts by this Canon, were exempt before his time by the law it selfe. So that where he sayes *Temperamus*, it is but *Temperatum esse ostendimus*; and hee did but make them afraid, who were in no danger, and make them beholden to him, whom the law it selfe delivered. And of this Canon in speciall words [a]one of their great men sayes, *That it binds not, where it may not be done, without great damage of the subject.*

30 Of his Successor, almost immediate, (for *Victor* the third lasted but a little) I finde another *Canon*, almost to the same purpose; for he writes to a *Bishop*, to forbid the Souldiers of an *Earle*, who was excommunicate, to serve him, though they were sworne to him. For, sayes he, *They are not tied by any authority to keepe that alleageance, which they have sworne to a Christian Prince, which resists God and his Saints, and treads their precepts under his feete.* But in this man, as *Gregories* spirit wrought in him, whilst he lived, for he was his Messenger to publish the Excommunication against the *Emperour* in *Germany*, so *Gregories* ghost speakes now; for all this was done to revenge *Gregories* quarrell; though in his owne particular hee had some interest, and reason of bitternesse, for he had beene taken and ill used by *Henry* in *Germany*.

31 In the 25 *Cause* there is a *Canon* which tasts of much boldnesse; *What King soever, or Bishop, or great person, shall suffer the Decrees of Popes to be violated, Execrandum Anathema sit.* But these (for in this *Cause* there are divers *Canons*, for the observing of the *Canons*) are for the most part such imprecations, as I noted before, *Gregory* the first to have made for preservation of the priviledges of *Medardus* Monastery, and some other of the same nature (of which kinde also *Villagut*, hath gathered some other examples;) And at farthest, they extend but to

Margins:
11.q.3. Quoniam
Ver. Quoniam
Ver. Temperamus
[a]D'Avila. par.2. ca.6. Disp.11. Dub.9
15.q.6. Iuratos
Binius. To.3. par.2. fo.1293
q.1. Generali
De Rebus Eccles. Restitu. par.2. l.3. c.5. n.17

Margin 12a. Dub.9 *Ed.*: Dub.90. C-1, L-1 **Margin 16.** Iuratos *Ed.*: Iuratis. C-1, L-1 **33.** nature *errata*: name. L-1, C-1

CHAPTER TEN 215

excommunication; and are pronounced by the *Popes* themselves, and are intended of such *Canons*, as are of matters of faith, that is, such as even the Popes themselves are bound to observe; as appeares here, by *Leo* the fourths *Canon, Ideo permittente*. And here I will relieve
5 you from *Gratian*, and leade you into the *Decretals*, whom they justly esteeme a little better company.

32 To prove the Popes generall right, to interpose in all causes (which seemes to conduce to the Question in hand) they cite often this case falling out in *England*; which is, upon severall occasions three or
10 foure times intimated in the *Decretals*. It was thus: *Alexander* the third, writes to certaine Bishoppes in *England*, to judge, as his *Delegates*, in a *Matrimoniall* cause. And because the person whose legitimation was thereby in question, was an heire, and the Mother dead, and the Pope thought it not fit, that after her death, her marriage should bee so nar-
15 rowly looked into, since it was not in her life, therefore he appoints, *That possession of the land should bee given first, and then the principall point of the marriage proceeded in*. And by this they evict for him a title in *temporall* matters *Accessorily*, and *Consequently*. But if they consider the times, they may justly suspect unjust proceeding; For
20 it was when *Alexander* the third did so much infest our King *Henry* the second. And it seemes he did but trie by this, how much the King would endure at his hands; for when he understood that the king tooke it ill, then came another Letter, related also in the *Canons*, wherein hee confesseth, that *that matter appertaines to the King, and not to the*
25 *Church*, And therefore commaundes them to proceede in the matter of the marriage, without dealing with the possession of the land.

33 Another *Canon*, not much urged by the defenders of *direct* Authoritie, but by the other faction, is a Letter of *Innocent* the third. In which Letter, I beleeve the Pope meant to lay downe, purposely and
30 determinately, how farre his power in *Temporall* matters extended. For it is not likely, that upon a Petition of a private Gentleman, for Legitimation of his Children, who doubted not of his power to doe it, the Pope would descend to a long discourse and proofe out of both testaments, and reasons of conveniencie, that he might doe it, and then in the
35 end, tell him, hee would not, except hee meant, that this Letter should

[margin: Qui filii sunt legit. Causam quae. c.4 & c.7 & De offic. Deleg. ca.17]

[margin: Tit. eod. per venerabilem]

---

4. relieve *errata*: receive. L-1, C-1

remaine as evidence to posteritie, what the Popes power in *Temporall* causes was. Let us see therefore what that is which he claimes.

34 A Subject of the King of *France*, who had put away his Wife, desires the Pope to legitimate certaine Children which he had by a second wife. And, it seemes, he was encouraged thereunto, because the Pope had done that favour to the King of *France* before: The Pope answers thus, *By this, it seemes, that I may graunt your request, because I may certainely Legitimate to all spirituall capacities, and therefore it is Verisimilius, & probabilius, that I may doe it in Temporall*. And, says he, *It seemes that this may be prooved by a similitude, because hee which is assumed to bee a Bishop, is exempted thereby from his fathers jurisdiction; and a slave delivered from bondage, by being made a Priest*: And, hee addes, *In the patrimonie I may freely doe it, where I am supreme Prince: But your case, is not the same as the Kings was, not only for spirituall considerations, which are, That he was lawfully seperated, and pretended neerenesse of blood, and was not forbid to marrie againe, and your proceeding hath beene without colour, and in contempt of the Church. But the King, who had no Superiour in Temporall matters, might without doing wrong to any other, submit himselfe to our jurisdiction; But you are knowen to be subject to another*. Thus farre hee proceeded, waveringly, and comparatively, and with conditions and limitations.

35 And least this should not stretch farre enough, he addes; *Out of the Patrimonie in certaine causes, wee doe exercise Temporall jurisdiction casually*, which the *Glosse* interpets thus, *That is when wee are requested*: And the Pope hath said before, *That he which makes this request, must be one that hath no Superiour*: And in this place he says, *That this may not be done, to prejudice anothers right*. But after this, upon a false foundation, that is, an errour in their Translation (where in *Deuteronomie*, Death being threatned to the transgressour of the sentence, *Of the Priest and Judge*, they have left out the *Judge*) he makes that state of the Jewes, so falsely understood, to be a Type of *Rome*, and so *Rome* at this time to be Judge of all *difficulties*, because it is the seate of the high Priest. But he must be thought more constant, then to depart from his first ground and therefore must meane, *When superiour Princes, which have no other Judges, are in such doubtes, as none else can determine, Recurrendum est, ad sedem Apostolicam*; that

Ver. Certis

17.12

CHAPTER TEN 217

is, *they ought to do it*, rather then to go to the onely ordinary Arbitrator betweene Soveraigne Princes, the sword.

36 And when such Princes doe submit their causes to him, in such cases hee declares himselfe by this *Canon*, to be a *competent* Judge, though the matter be a civill businesse, and he an Ecclesiasticall person: and though he seeme to goe somewhat farther, and stretch that typicall place in *Deuteron.* to agree with *Rome* so farre, that as there, so here, he which disobeyes, must die, yet hee explanes this death thus, *Let him as a dead man, be seperated from the Communion, by Excommunication.* So that this *Canon* purposely enacted to declare *temporall* authority, by a Pope, whom none exceeded in a stiffe and earnest promoving the dignity of that Sea, procedes onely by *probabilities*, and *verisimilitudes*, and *equivalencies*, and endes at last with *Excommunication*; and therefore can imprint in you no reason to refuse this Oath. For out of this Canon, doth *Victoria* frame a strong argument, *That this most learned Pope doeth openly confesse, by this Canon, that he hath no power over the King of France in Temporall matters.* De Potest. Eccles. §. 6. nu.2

37 Another *Canon* of the same Pope is often cited, by which, when the King of *England* complain'd, that the King of *France* had broken the Peace, which was confirm'd by Oath, the Pope writes to the Bishops of *France*, That *though he intende not to judge of that Title in question, which appertaines not to him, yet the perjurie belongs to his cognisance: and so, he may reproove, and in cases of Contumacie, constraine, Per districtionem Ecclesiasticam, without exception of the persons of Kings*: And therefore, says he, *If the King refuse to performe the Articles, and to suffer my Delegates to heare the cause, I have appointed my Legate, to proceede as I have directed him.* What his *Instructions* were, I know not by this; but beyond *Excommunication*, you see by the Text, he pretends not: Whatsoever they were, this is certaine, That the Princes of those times, to advantage themselves against their enemies, with the Popes helpe, did often admit him, to doe some acts against other Princes, which after, when the Pope became their enemie, themselves felt with much bitternesse. But in this *Canon*, hee disclaimes any Jurisdiction to *judge of Titles*; which those Popes tooke to themselves, who Excommunicated our late *Queene* (if *Parsons* say true, *That they had respect to the* De iudiciis novit.

Margin 15. De Potest. Eccles. §. 6. nu.2 *errata* Ed.: note missing, L-1, C-1; Nn.. *errata*

injustice of her Title, by reason of a Statute) and all those Popes must doe, which shall doe any act, which might make this Oath unlawfull to you.

<small>Noverit. Gravem</small>

38   In the title *De Sent. Excom.* there are two *Canons*, which concerne onely *Excommunication* of *Hereticks*, and infringers of *Ecclesiasticke Immunitie*, and are directed but to one particular place. Which, though they can impose nothing upon your conscience against this Oath, may yet teach you not to grudge, that a State which provides for her securitie by Lawes and Oathes, expresse it in such words, as may certainely reach to the principall purpose thereof, and admit no evasions. For so these Canons doe, when they Excommunicate, *All, of all Sexe*, of *any Name, Favourers, Receivers, Defenders, Lawmakers, Writers, Governours, Consuls, Rulers, Councellours, Judges*, and *Registers of any statutes, made in that place against Church liberties.*

<small>De prescriptionibus</small>

39   That the *Canons* have power to abrogate *Civill* lawes of Princes, they use to cite the Canon *Quoniam omne*, made by *Innocent* the third, who hath made more *Canons* then halfe of the Popes before him. And if this doe not batter downe, yet it undermines all secular power. For they may easily pretend, that any Lawe, may in some case *occasion sinne*.

<small>De Pont. l.5. c.6. §. Itaque. Ex Cod. De prescriptionibus</small>

This *Canon* hath also more then Ordinary authority, because it is made in a generall *Councell*: thus it sayes, *Absque bona fide, nulla valeat praescriptio, tam Canonica, quam civilis*: And *this*, sayes *Bellarmine*, *doth abrogate an Imperiall lawe*, by which prescription would serve, so that it begann *Bona fide*, though at some time after, he which was in possession, came to know, that his title was ill; but the *Canon* law requires that he esteeme in his conscience, his title to be good, all the time, by which he prescribes. But by this *Canon*, that particular *Imperiall* lawe is no more abrogated, then such other lawes as cannot be observed without danger of sinne, which includes not onely some *Civill* Constitutions, but also some *other* Canons; For your Glosser sayes, *That the Canon derogates from all Constitutions, Civill and Ecclesiastique, which cannot be observed without deadly sin*: that is, it makes them guilty *In foro interiori*. He addes, *That he doth not beleeve, that the Pope did purpose by this Canon, to prejudice the civill lawes, nor that the wordes are intended of civill and secular law, but that by those wordes, Tam*

<small>Ver. Nota quod</small>

<small>Ver. Tam Canonica</small>

Margin 4. Noverit *Ed.*: Nonerit. C-1, L-1   **4–5.** concerne *Ed.*: concernes. L-1, C-1

CHAPTER TEN 219

civilis, quam Canonica, the Pope meanes, that a prescriber *Malae fidei,* is guilty in conscience, whether it be of a matter Secular or Ecclesiastique. For (sayes hee) though some say, the Pope meant to correct the law herein, yet this correction is not observed in *Iudicio Seculari.* And
5 therefore (sayes hee) *I doe not beleeve, that the Pope himselfe is bound to judge according to this Canon, where he hath temporall jurisdiction, because hee hath that Jurisdiction from the Emperour*: therefore the Imperiall law standes still, and is not abrogated by this *Canon,* though of a generall Councell.

10   40 This Pope also by a *Canon* in the title *de Voto,* hath gone the farthest of any, which have fallen within my observation: for a King of *Hungary,* which had made a vowe to undertake a warre for *Hierusalem,* prevented by death, imposed the execution thereof upon his yonger sonne, who binding himselfe to performe it, with the armie which he
15 levied for that purpose, in pretence, troubled his brother in his Kingdome: To him therefore *Innocentius* writes, *That except he doe forthwith performe the vow, he shall be excommunicate and deprived of all right to that Kingdome; and that the kingdome, if his elder brother die without issue, shall devolve to his younger brother.* But all these threatnings,
20 except that one of Excommunication, were not thundered by the Pope, as though hee could inflict them, out of his authority, but he remembers this ill-advised Prince, that *except he performe the will of his father, he looses his inheritance by the law*: Which the Glosse in this place, endevours to prove, and to that *purpose* cites, and disputes some of the
25 lawes in that point.

    41 The Canon *Solitae,* though it be every where alleadged, and therefore it importunes me to mention it, reaches not to our question, for it is onely a *Reprehension* made by a Pope, to a *Greeke Emperour,* because hee did not afford his Patriarch of Constantinople dignity
30 enough in his place. And he tels him, that he mistakes *S. Peters* meaning, in his *Epistle,* where he teaches obedience to Emperours; For, sayes he, *he writ but to those which were under him,* and not to al; and *he did provoke them to a meritorious humility,* and not informe them of a necessary Duety; For, sayes he, if that place shall be understood of
35 Priests, and literally, then Priests must bee subject to Slaves, because it

Cap. licet

Verb. privandum

De Maior. & Obedient.

I Pet. 2.13

33. *humility,* and *Ed.*: *humility,.* L-1, C-1

is *Omni Creaturae*, neither (sayes he) is it said, *To the King*, absolutely *Precellenti*, but *tanquam precellenti, which was not added without cause.* For (sayes the Glosse) *this word, Tanquam, is Similitudinarium, non expressivum veritatis*; So that S. *Peter* doth not call the king Superiour in truth, but as it were Superiour; as I noted the Cardinals to subscribe Letters to persons of lower ranke, *Vester uti frater*. And that which followes, *of the punishment of evill doers, and praise of the good*, is not (sayes he) *that the King hath power of the sword over good and evill, but onely over them, which because they use the sword, are under his jurisdiction*. Then proceedes he to magnifie Priesthood, because *Jeremie, to whom Commission was given over Nations was descended of Priests*: and because *the Sunne which designes Priesthod, is so much bigger then the Moone*: with so many more impertinencies, and barbarismes, and inconsequences, that I wonder why he, who summ'd it, should so specially say of this Canon, that *it is Multum Allegabile*.

42 In the Canon *Gravem, Honorius* the third writes to certaine Prelates, whose Church had received much detriment by a Noble-man, *That since he hath continued contemptuously under Excommunication two yeares, if upon this last monition he refuse to conforme himselfe, they should discharge those Churches from their obedience to him, and denounce those which ought him alleageance, to be discharged therof, as long as he remained Excommunicate.* But it appeares not here, whether hee were a *Subject* of the Romane Church or no; And yet appeares plainely that he was no *Soveraigne*, and therefore no precedent in our case, in which there could not easily be restitution given to any, after another were in possession.

43 In the next volume of the law, which they call *Sextus*, I have noted in their Authours but one *Canon*, which comes within any convenient distance of this point, which is a Letter of *Innocent* the fourth to the Nobility of *Portugall*, by which, under paine of *Excommunication* hee commaunds them, to receive the kings brother, as *coadjutor* to that king, *Notwithstanding any Oath of Alleageance, or resistance of the King*; So that they preserved the right in the King, and in his children,

---

2. *Precellenti*] Precellent i. MCG, C⁵-2, C-4, SP, C³, C¹⁰, YK-2 **Margin 3.** Tanquam] Tanqu am] L-1, L-2, C-2, HD, L³⁰, F, C⁵-1, O-2, O², O¹⁴, YK-1, YK-2; T anquam. Y, C¹⁶ **7.** the good errata: God. L-1, C-1 **Margin 10.** Jer. 1.10 *Ed.*: note missing. L-1, C-1

if he shall have any: Which, being but matter of fact, doth not constitute a rule, nor binde consciences, especially when for the fact it selfe, the note sayes in that place, *That the Pope ought not to have interposed himselfe in that businesse*.

_{Litera, b. in Margine}

44 In the *Extravagants* of Pope *John* the two and twentieth, there is one *Canon* which would take great hold of consciences obliged to that Sea, but that it proceeds from a Pope infam'd for heresie, and claimes that *Jurisdiction*, which it there inculcates, in the right of being *Emperour*, at that time, when the throne, by the death of *Henrie* the seventh, was vacant. Thus it says, *Since it is cleare in law, and constantly observed of olde, that in a vacancy of the Empire, because then there can be no recourse to any Secular Judge, the Jurisdiction, Government, and Disposition of the Empire devolve to the Pope, who is knowne to have exercised all these therein by himselfe, or others: whereas divers continue the offices of the Empire, without our Confirmation, we admonish all under Excommunication, even Kings, to leave off those titles; and if they doe not so, within two monethes* (how could hee prophesie so long a vacancie?) *Wee will Excommunicate the persons, and interdict the Dominions of them all, Etiam superiores et inferiores Reges, and proceede with them, spiritually and temporally, as we shall farther see to be expedient. And wee absolve all men, of all Oathes, by which they were bound to them*. But, as I said before, this right of inflicting temporall punishment hee claimes as *Emperour*; and the spirituall punishments are threatned to no other, nor in any other Capacity, then as they are *officers of the Empire*, of which then hee imagines himselfe *supreme Prince*, and so he is enabled to doe all those acts, upon any Prince which depends upon the *Empire*, which he might doe *Ordinarily* in the *Patrimony*; and all, which the Pope and the Emperour together might doe upon any Prince, which usurped the titles and dignities of the *Empire*, without the Emperours approbation.

_{Si fratrum}

45 In the *Common Extravagants*, that which they call *unam Sanctam*, made by *Boniface* the eight, Anno 1302. hath the greatest force of all: both because it intends to *prove* and to *Decree* a certaine proposition, *That it is of the necessitie of Salvation to be subject to the Pope*, and also because it determines it with Essentiall and formall words, belong-

---

13. devolve Ed.: devolves. L-1, C-1

ing to a *Decree, Declaramus, Definimus, Pronunciamus*. And though in the body and passage of the *Decree*, there are sometimes arrogations of Secular *Jurisdiction*, by way of *argument*, and *conveniencie*, and *Probable consequence*; yet is there nothing drawne into the *definition*, and *Decree*, and thereby obligatorily cast upon our Consciences, but onely this, *That a Subjection to the Pope is, of the necessitie of Salvation*.

Ver. ponatur For, sayes the glosse, *it was the intention of the Pope in this Decretall, to bring reasons, examples, and authorities, to prove that Conclusion*. So that, as if it pleased him to have said so *definitively*, without arguing the case, the *Decretall* had beene as perfit and binding, as it is after all his reasons, and argumentation: so doe not his Reasons bind our reason, or our faith, being no part of the *Definition*, but leave to us our liberty, for all but the *Definition* it selfe.

46 And a *Catholique* which beleeves by force of this Decretall, That he cannot be saved except he obay the Pope, is not bound to beleeve therefore, that these words of *S. John, There shall be one sheepe-folde, and one sheepheard*, are meant of a Subjection of all *Christian* Princes to the Pope, as this *Decretall*, by way of Argument, sayes; but he may be bold, for all this, to beleeve an elder Pope, that *this is spoken of joining Jewes and Gentiles in one faith*; or *Theophilact, That this proves one God to be the sheepheard of the olde and new Testament, against the Maniches*. Nor is he bound, because this *Decretall* sayes it by the way, to beleeve that the words in Saint *Luke, Behold here are two swords, to which Christ did not answere, It is too much, but it is enough*, doe prove the *spirituall* and *temporall* swords to bee in the disposition of the Church; but he is at liberty for all this, to beleeve *Chrysostome, That Christ by mentioning two swords in that place, did not meane, that they should possesse swords, (for what good (sayes he) could two swords doe?) but he forwarned them of such persecutions, as in humane judgement would neede the defence of swords*. Or he may beleeve *Ambrose, That these two swords, are the sword of the Worde, and the sword of Martyrdome*: of which there is mention in *S. Luke, A sword shall passe thorow thy soule*. So that these swords arme them to *seeke* the truth, and to *defend* it with their lives: or hee may beleeve *S. Basil*, who

Marginalia:
- 10.16
- Grego. Homil. 14
- Citat. Ema. Sâ
- 22.38
- Sâ
- L.10. Com. in Lucam
- Luc. 2.35

Margin 23. 22.38] 22 38. C-1, C-2, C⁹, L², C³, L-2, C⁵-2, O-2, O¹⁴, YK-1
33. *thy soule* Ed.: *my soule.* L-1, C-1

sayes, *That Christ spoke Prophetically, that they would encline to use swordes, though indeede they should not doe so.* Both which expositions of *Chrysostome* and *Basil*, a *Jesuite* remembers, and addes for his owne opinion; *That Christ did not confirme two Swords to the Church, by Saying, It is enough, but onely, because they could not understand him, he broke off further talke with them, as we use when we are troubled with one, who understands us not, to say, Tis well, Tis enough.* — Ema. Sâ

47 For *Bellarmine* is our warrant in this case, who sayes, *That those wordes intimate no more, but that the Apostles, when persecution came, would be in as much feare, as they who would sell all to buy swords: and that Pope Boniface did but mystically interpret this place.* — De Pont. l.5. c.5. Secundo

48 And as the exposition of other places there cited by *Boniface*, and his divers reasons scattered in the *Decretall*, fal not within the *Definition* therof, nor binde our faith; so doth it not, that those wordes spoken by God to *Jeremy*, *I have set thee over the nations, and over the Kingdomes, and to plucke up, and roote out, to destroy and to throw downe, to build and to plant*, are verified of the Ecclesiastique power, though he say it. But any *Catholique* may boldly beleeve that they were spoken only to *Jeremy*, who had no further Commission by them, but to *denounce*, and not to *inflict* those punishments. For it were hard, if this Popes Mysticall expositions should binde any man (contrary to this oath appointed by the *Trent Councell*) to leave the *unanime consent of the Fathers in expounding these Scriptures*: and so an obedience to one Pope should make him perjured to another. The last *Definition* therefore of this *Decretall*, which was first and principally in the purpose and intention of this Pope, which is, *Subjection to him*, is matter of faith to all them, in whom the Popes *Decrees* beget faith, but *temporall Jurisdiction* is not hereby imposed upon the conscience, as matter of faith. — Jer. 1.10

49 But because this *Canon* was suspiciously penn'd, and perchance misinterpretable, and bent against the kingdome of *France*, betweene which state and the Pope there was then much contention, so that therefore it kept a jealous watch upon the proceeding of that Church, *Clement* the fift, who came to be pope within foure yeares after the making of this *Canon*, made another *Decree*, *That by this Definition or Declaration of Boniface, that Kingdome was not prejudiced, nor any more subject to Rome, then it was before the making of that Decree.* And — Extrav. Com. De Privileg. Meruit

though it was not *Clements* pleasure to deale cleerely, but to leave the *Canon* of *Boniface*, as a stumbling blocke still to others, yet out of the whole *History* this will result, to us, that if this *temporall Jurisdiction*, which some gather out of this *Canon*, were in the Pope, *Iure Divino*, hee could not exempt the kingdome of *Fraunce*; and if it were not so, no Canons can create it. But even this exemption of *Clement* proves *Bonifaces* acte to be *Introductory*, and new, for what benefite hath any man by being exempted from a *Declaratorie* law, when for all that exemption, hee remaines still under the former law, which that declares: So that nothing concerning *temporall Jurisdiction* is defined in that *Canon*; but it is newly thereby made an *Article of faith, that all men must upon paine of damnation be subject to the Church in spirituall causes*; from which Article it was necessary to exempt France, because that kingdome was never brought to be of that opinion.

50   And in the last Volume of the *Canon* law, lately set out in the Title, *De Rescrip. & Mand. Apost.* there is one *Canon* of *Leo* the tenth, and another of *Clement* the seventh, which *annull all Statutes and civill constitutions, which stoppe Appeales to Rome, or hinder the execution of the Popes bulles; and inflicts Excommunication, and Interdicts the Dominions of any, which shall make or favor such Statutes*. But because these *Canons* doe not define this, as *matter of faith*, I doubt not but the Catholiques of England would bee loath to adventure the daungers which our Lawes inflict, upon such as seeke Justice at Rome, which may be had here: And they doe, though contrarie to these *Canons*, in continuall practise, bring all their causes into the Courtes of Justice here, which, if the *Canons* might prevaile, belong'd to Rome.

51   And these be all the *Canons*, which I have mark'd either in mine owne reading of them, or from other *Authors* which write of these questions; to bee cited to this purpose. Those which concerne *Ecclesiasticke immunitie*, or the Popes *spirituall* power, I omitted purposely: And of this kind which I have dealt withall, I doubt not but some have escaped me. But I may rather be ashamed of having read so much of this learning, then not to have read all.

52   Heere therefore I will conclude, that though to the whole body of the *Canon Law*, there belong'd as much faith and reverence, as to the

Margin: Licet faelici. Rescriptorum

6. it. O-1, O², O¹⁴, YK-2: it.   L-1, C-1, SP, O-2, C-2, C⁵-1

Canons of the old Councels, yet out of them, you can finde nothing to assure your consciences, that you may incurre these dangers for refusall of the Oath. Nor may the Pope bee presum'd to imagine, that he shal re-establish himself in any place, which hath escaped, and delivered it selfe from his usurpations, by any *Canon Law*, except he be able to use that *Droict du Canon*, which *Montmorencie* the French Constable, persuaded his King to use against a Towne which held out against him.

Chap. XI.

That the two Breves of Paulus the fift, cannot give this assurance to there Conscience; First, for the generall infirmities, to which all Rescripts of Popes are obnoxious: And then for certaine insufficiencies in these.

1 Though that which hath beene said in the former Chapter of the *Decretall* Letters of Popes, extend also to these *Breves*, since they are all of the same elements and complexion, and subject to the same diseases and infirmities: Yet because these two *Breves*, may bee said to have beene addressed directly and purposely to give satisfaction in this particular businesse, they may challendge more obedience, and lay more Obligation then those other *Decretals*, which issuing upon other occasions, doe not otherwise concerne the question in hand, then by a certaine relation, and consequence, and comparison of the circumstances which produced them, with the circumstances which begot these Breves.

2 It seemes that the Pope when hee would restraine the subjects of Princes, and keepe them short, when he would cut off there naturall and profitable libertie of obeying *Civill* Lawes, when he would fetter and manacle them in perplexities, and make them doe lesse then they should, to the losse of life, and liberties, he is content to send his *Breves*; But when he will swell and blow up Subjects with Rebellion, when he will fill them with opinions, that they may resist the entrances, or interrupt the possessions of Princes, when hee will have them doe more then they should doe, then come forth his *Buls*. For they say their *Buls* are so called out of the tumor, and swelling of the *Seale*; And the other, because they are dispatch'd under a lesse Seale, *Sub Annulo piscatoris*, are therefore called *Breves*; For, in temporall businesses of forraigne Princes, his Letters are ever defective, or abundant; they command too much, or too little.

3 And as the Popes have ever beene abstinent in declaring and expressing in certaine and evident tearmes, *how they have this temporall Jurisdiction*, least having once joined issue upon some one way, all men

Anto. August. de Emend. Grat. l.2. Dial. 2
Tholoza. Syntag. l.15. c.24. n.10

1. there errata faults: this. L-1, C-1, errata correct. 4. 1 *Ed*.: missing. L-1, C-1 9. lay more *Ed*.: lay a more. L-1, C-1 **Margin 23.** c.24 *Ed*.: c.4. L-1, C-1 30. joined *Ed*.: joinde. L-1, C-1

should bende their proofes against that, and being once defeated, they could be admitted to no other plea, then themselves had chosen to adhere to, and relie upon: So have they abstained as much from giving any binding resolution, in the question, *how farre the civill lawes of Princes doe binde the subjects conscience.* For *Navarrus* testifies of himselfe, and of *Cajetane*, and others, that it was much desired of the Councell of Trent [Third General Lateran Council]; *that it would have defined something certainely in that point*: for the want of this *definition* brought him to contradict himselfe, and to hang in a perplexed suspence, and various change of opinions, fiftie yeares; and at last to resolve, *That Civill lawes doe not binde the consciences, ad Mortale, in some such cases*, as *Carninus*, his *Catholique* Adversarie, sayes, It is *Haeresi proxima, and Temeraria, and sometimes Haeretica to say so.*

    4 If therefore we shall follow in this point *Carninus* his opinion, who delivers as the most common and most probable, yea, necessarie Doctrine, That *because Civill lawes are no more to be called Humane lawes, then Ecclesiastique are*, (for so also *Navarrus* confounds the names) and that *in power of binding, Humane lawes, that is, Civill, and Ecclesiastique, are equall to Divine law, because in every just law the power of God is infused*, And therfore, *Divinitas ista* (as he calls it) *inheres in all lawes*, & to transgresse them is sin, And not only because the Majestie of God, who quickens and inanimates this law, by a power derived upon his Lieutenant, is violated thereby, but even *in respect of the matter and Subject, which is in every law,* that is, *The common good, and tranquility*, and to offend against that, is to offend against rectified Reason, and therefore sinne; This opinion, I say, being received as true, and so this law which commaunds this oath, made by a *lawfull power*, and *for the publique Good*, and *generall tranquility*, being in possession of the Subjects Consciences, and binding them under danger of Mortall sinne, whatsoever can warrant any man to transgresse this law, must have both *Authority*, and *Evidence* enough, to assure the Conscience, which till then is bound thereby, that either for some *Substantiall*, or for some *formall* Defect, this was never any law, or that it is *Abrogated*, or that the persons of Catholiques are *exempted* from it.

Manual. c.23. nu.48

De Vi et Pot. Leg. human.

Ca.8

Par.1. c.1
C.3

12–13. *proxima . . . Temeraria . . . Haeretica Ed.: proximum . . . Temerarium . . . Haereticum.* L-1, C-1   **26.** sinne *errata*: since. L-1, C-1

5   And have these *Breves* of the Popes gone about to give your Consciences, as good reasons against the oath, as you were possessed withall before, for it? Are you as sure that these *Breves*, or that any *Breves* can binde your Conscience in this Case, as you were before, that the law could? And are you as sure that there are *Breves*, as that there is a law?

6   If the *statute* which enacts a *Subsidie*, which by the Kings acceptation becomes a law, and so bindes the Conscience, should so esteeme the refusall of the payment of his taxation in any person, to bee an argument of disloyalty, as to make it capitall to refuse it, would you thinke that if such a *Breve* as these are, should tell you, that you might not pay it, without detriment of Christian faith, you might die as *Martyrs* for refusall thereof?

7   If such a *Breve* should forbid you to suffer your children to bee wards, to deliver land escheated, or confiscate, to disobey the Kings emprest when hee levies an Armie, or any such act due by conscience to his lawes, should this worke so upon you, as to make you incurre the penalties of lawes, or suspicion of ill affected subjects? Nor can you say, that these are meere temporall matters, and therefore removed from his Jurisdiction; *for all sinne is spirituall, and hee is Judge what is sinne.*

8   How weake a ground for *Martyredome*, and how unsufficient to devest a conscience of an obedience, imposed in generall by nature, and fastned with a new knot by an expresse law, are such sickly and fraile *Breves*, as the smallest and most undiscernable errour, even in matter of forme doth annihilate? for first, in the Title of *Constitutions and Rescripts* of Popes (which is always the next Title to that of the *Trinity and Catholique Faith*, in all the bookes of the *Canon law*, except those bookes which have no Title of the *Trinity & Catholique faith*) there appeares very many Reasons by which a *Breve* may bee of no force.

Extra. de Rescript. ex parte

9   *Alexander* the third, writing to an *Archbishop of Canturbury*, gives a rule of large extent; That in these kinde of letters (that is, such as proceede upon information, as our case is) *this condition; If the request be upon true grounds, is ever understood, though it be not expressed.*

Ibid. Si quando

And writing to the *Archbishoppe of Ravenna*, he sayes, *If at any time we write such things to you, as exasperate your minde, you must not bee troubled; but diligently considering the quality of the businesse, whereof*

---

15. hee] he he. L-1, MCG, L-2, O², O¹⁴, C²-2

we write, either reverently fulfill our command, or pretend by your Letters a reasonable cause why you cannot: for we will endure patiently, if you forbear to performe that, which was suggested to us, by evill information. And so doth that title abound with *Interpretations, Limitations,* and *Revocations* of such *Breves.*

10 And not onely *Delegate Judges*, and such persons as have an inward knowledge, of errour in the cause which mooved the Pope to write, have power to judge these *Breves*, to bee invalid, and of no force, but every *Schoole master*. For *Lucius* the third, by a *Rescript* of his, forbids *any credit to be given to any Rescript, in which there is false Latin:* to which also the *Glosser* adds, *That it vitiates a Breve, if the Pope speake to any one man in the plurall number; or call a Patriarch or a Bishop sonne.*

_{Ibid. ad Audientiam}

_{Ver. Manifestum}

11 And, as many *Omissions*, and many *Adjections* in the body of the *Breve*, either in matter, or in forme, doth annull it, So would it make any considerate conscience to doubt, whether such a *Breve* can warrant the expence of blood, or incurring other Capitall dangers, that observes how often the *Breves* which have issued upon best consideration, and assistance of Counsell, have beene revoked; not upon new emergent matter, but upon better knowledge of the former. Of which it seemes to me to be of good use, to present one illustrous and remarqueable example.

12 *Eugenius* the fourth, having first by one *Bull* dissolved the Councell held at *Basil*, and transfered it to another place; the Councell for all that proceeding, the Pope by a second *Bull* annuls all which that Councell had yet, or should after Decree; and this, *by the Councell, and Assent of the Cardinals*. After this, the Councell cites him, and all his *Cardinals*, upon whom it inflicts *confiscation*, and other penalties, if they forbeare to come. And then the Pope by a third *Bull* annuls that *decree* of Citation, and excommunicates al persons, even *Kings* and the *Emperour*, if they execute upon any, that Decree of the Councell. And then he publishes a fourth *Bull*, by which he answeres all objections made against him by the Councel, and having so established his owne innocence, he annuls all acts made in prejudice thereof, and this also *with assent and subscription of the Cardinals*. And at last he sends out a fift *Bull*, in which hee takes knowledge, that his first *Bull* of dissolving

9. his, *Ed.*: his. L-1, C-1

the Councell, had occasioned many grievous dissensions, and was like to occasion more, and therefore now, he *Decrees* and *Declares* (*by the Councell and Assent of his Cardinals still*) not only that the Councell of *Basil* should *from thenceforth be good and lawfull*, but that it *was so, when that Bull came, and that it had beene so from the time of the beginning thereof*. And so in expresse wordes, hee annuls his annulling of it: and he revokes two former *Buls*, and pronounces them *Irritas, Annullatas, Cassatas*; by the first whereof he had disabled the Councell, and by the second had excommunicated *Princes*, which should execute that, which he pronounces now to be just: and of the other *Bull* he sayes, *It proceeded not from him, nor by his knowledge*, though it were testified by the *Cardinals*, and endorsed formally by his *Secretary*. And even this last *Bull* of so many *Revocations, Annihilations, and Tergiversations* was not thought strong, nor out of the danger of being revoked againe, till the Councell accepted it, and ratified it by applying the BULL and Seale of the Councell to it.

13   So is it familiar in the Popes, not for the variety of just occasion, but for personall hate to their predecessors, to annull the acts of one another. So *Stephen the sixth or seventh, abrogated Omnes ordinationes, of Pope Formosus, and digged him up, and cut of some of his fingers, and cast him into the Tiber, and made all to whom he had given Orders, take new Orders againe*. And next yeare Pope *Romanus abrogated all Stephens Acts*; and within seven yeare after, came *Sergius*, who refreshed the hate against *Formosus*, and *beheaded his body*; which I wonder how he found, since Pope *Stephen* had so long before cast it into *Tiber*.

Caranza. fo.414
Binius. To.3. par.2. fo.1047
Carran. Ibid.

Id. fo.415

14   And in a matter so mainly concerning faith, as amongst them, an Autentique translation of the Bible, is, betweene the Edition of *Sixtus* the fift, and the Edition of *Clement* the eight, there is so much difference, even in absolute and direct *Contradictions*, as he which reades the severall *Breves*, by which those two Editions are authorised; both having equall justifications of the present Editions, equal absolutions from oathes for admitting any other, equall imprecations and curses, for omitting these, may well thinke that that is a weake and litigious title to *Martyrdome*, which is grounded upon the Popes *Breves*, which he himselfe, when he sends them, knowes not whether they be just or no.

15   For, as they have forbidden many lawfull things, and offered to destroy the lawes themselves, so have they allowed and authorized

manie things, which our owne Reason, and discourse, and Experience, can convince of falshood.

16   It is the common opinion that *Eugenius* the third, confirmed *Gratian*. Of whom, we may be bolde, out of that learned *Bishop* which hath made animadversions upon him, to say, That he knew neither *things* nor *words*, mistooke *matters* and *names*, erred in *places*, and *times*, and had neither seene Fathers, Councels, nor Rolls. And though this *Bishop* seeme not to beleeve that *Eugenius* did confirme him, yet hee confesses, *That hee which doth beleeve such a confirmation, is bound thereby to beleeve as many errours, as are in Gratian.* For, it seemes we have no longer liberty to doubt, after such a confirmation: as it will follow evidently out of *Bellarmines* fashion of arguing, when he sayes, *We are bound to obay the Pope, when hee institutes a festivall of a Saint; yet wee are never bound to doe against our conscience*; and therefore we may no longer doubt it; but wee must make his Decree our conscience. So that if either *Eugenius* confirmed it before, or *Gregory* the thirteenth since, our liberty is precluded, and we must credulously, and faithfully swallow, not onely all the unwholsome, and insipid negligences, ignorances, and barbarismes of *Gratian*, but all the bitter and venemous mixtures to *Christs* merit, and all the blasphemies and diminutions of his Majestie, which *Boniface* the ninth, and *Martin* the fift, have obtruded to us, by approving and confirming by their *Bulls*, the *Revelations of Saint Brigid*; for so sayes *Paleotus* they have done.

Dialo. 3

De Sanc. Beat. l.1. c.9. Altera

Histor. de Sacr. Sindone. par.1. Epist. lector.

17   These heavie inconveniencies, and dangerous precipitations into errours, being foreseene by some of the ancient Schoolemen, out of their Christian libertie, and prudent estimation of the Popes Authoritie, they have pronounced this infallibilitie of judgement, to bee onely then in the Pope, *When he doeth applie all Morall meanes to come to the knowledge of the trueth*; As, hearing both parties, and waighing the pressures and afflictions, which he shal induce upon them whom he inflames against their Prince, and proceeding mildly and dispassionately, and not like an interested person, and to the edification, not destruction of them, whom onely he esteemes to be his Catholicke Church.

18   And this seemes so reasonable, that though the *Jesuite Tannerus* at first cast it away, as the opinion onely, *Quorundam ex Antiquioribus*

De libert. Eccles. l.2. c.9

Margin 12. De Sanc. Beat. *Ed.*: De purg.. L-1, C-1   **29.** and waighing *Ed.*: aud waighing. L-1, C-1

Scholasticis, yet afterwards hee affoords an interpretation to it; but such a one, as I think any *Catholique* would be loth to venter his *Martyrdome* thereupon, if he were to die for obedience to a *Breve*. For thus he sayes, *In every matter, when a Hypotheticall proposition is made, of the condition whereof we are certaine, then the whole proposition must not be said to be Hypothetically and Conditionally true, but absolutely.* And this he exemplifies by this Proposition: *If Christ doe come to judgement, there shall be a resurrection; which proposition is absolutely and not conditionally true, because we are certaine that Christ will come to Judgement*: And so he sayes, *That it is the meaning of all them who affirme that the Pope may erre, except he use ordinarie meanes, onely to inferre, that hee dooth ever use those meanes, without all doubt and question.* But with what conscience can this *Jesuite* say, *That this was the meaning of these Schoolemen*, when in the same place it appeares, that the purpose of those Schoolemen, was to bring the Pope to a custome of calling Councels, in determining waighty causes; for when they say, *He may erre except hee use Ordinarie meanes*, and they intended generall Councels for this ordinary meanes, can they bee intended in saying so, to meane that the Pope did ever in such cases use *Generall Councels*, when they reprehended his neglecting that ordinary meanes, and laboured to reduce him to the practise thereof?

19 And though most of these infirmities incident to *Breves* in generall, doe so reflect upon these two *Breves* in question, that any man may apply them, yet it may doe some good to come to a neerer exagitation and trial, of the necessary obligation which they are imagined to impose. It is good *Doctrine* which one of your men teaches; *That even in lawes, every particular man hath power to interprete the same to his advantage, and to dispence with himselfe therein, if there occurre a sudden case of necessity, and there be no open way and recourse to the Superiour.* The first part of which *Rule* would have justified them, who tooke the oath before the *Breves* (though they had had some scruples in their conscience) by reason of the great scandall to the cause, and personall detriment, which the refusall was likely to draw on.

20 Nor can the *Catholiques* be said, to have had as yet *recourse to their Superiour*, when neither their reasons have beene aunswered or heard, which thinke the oath *naturally* and *morally* lawfull, nor theirs who thinke, that in these times of imminent pressures and afflictions, all

[margin: Carnin. de Vi et Pot. Leg. Huma. c.10]

inhibitions ought to have beene forborne, and that any thing which is not ill in it selfe, ought to have been permitted for the sweetning and mollifying of the state towards them.

21   Their immediate *Superiours* here in *England* have beene in different opinions, and therefore a recourse to them cannot determine of the matter: And for recourse to the *Pope*, the partie of Secular Priests have long since complained, that all wayes have beene precluded against them. And if they had just, or excusable reasons to doubt, that the first *Breve* issued by *Subreption*, they had more reasons to suspect as many infirmities in the second, because one of the reasons of suspecting the first, being, *That their Reasons were not heard*, but that the Pope was mis-informed, and so misledde by hearking to one partie onely, the second *Breve* came before any remedy or redresse was given, or any knowledge taken of the complaint against the first.

22   Certainely I thinke that if he had had true information, and a sensible apprehension, that the suffering of his party in this Kingdome, was like to be so heavie, as the lawes threatned, and a pertinacy in this refusall, was likely to extort, hee had beene a lavish and prodigall steward of their lives, and husbanded their bloods unthriftily, if he had not reserved them to better services heereafter, by forbearing all *inhibitions* for the present, and confiding and relying upon his power of absolving them againe; when any occasion should present it selfe to his advantage, rather then thus to declare his ambitions, and expose his servants and instruments to such dangers, when by this violence of his, the state shall be awakened to a jealous watchfulnes over them.

23   It is not therefore such a disobedience as contracts, or induces sinne (which it must be, if it be matter enough for *Martyrdome*) not to obey these *Breves*, though thus iterated; for it is not the adding of more *Cyphars* after, when there is no *figure* before, that gives any valew, or encrease to a number. *Navarrus* upon good grounds, gives   Man. c.23. n.38
this as the Resultance of many *Canons* there by him alleadged, *That it is not sinne in a man not to obey his Superiour, when hee hath probable reasons to thinke, that his Superiour was deceived in so commaunding, or that he would not have given such a command, if he had knowne the truth.* And can any *Catholique* beleeve so profanely of the Pope,

13. came *Ed.*: came,. L-1, C-1

as to thinke, that if hee had seene the effects of the *powder treason*, every Church filled with devout and thankfull commemorations of the escape, every Pulpit justly drawing into suspition, the *Maisters* which procured it, and the Doctrine wherewith they were imbued, every vulgar mouth extended with execrations of the fact, and imprecations uppon such as had like intentions, every member of the *Parliament* studying, what clauses might be inserted for the Kings security, into new lawes, and the King himselfe to have so much moderated this common just distemper, by taking out all the bitternesse and sting of the law, and contenting himselfe, with an oath of such obedience as they were borne under, which if they should refuse, there could be no hope of farther easinesse, or of such as his Majestie had ever shewed to them before, Might any *Catholique*, I say, beleeve, that the Pope if he had seene this, would have accelerated these afflictions upon them, by forbidding an Act, which was no more but an attestation of a morall truth, that is, civill obedience, and a profession, that no man had power, to absolve them, against that which they justly averred to be such a Morall & indelible truth? Might he not reasonably and justly have applied to the Pope, that which *Anselmus* is said to have pronounced of God himselfe, *Minimum inconveniens est Deo impossibile*, and concluded thereupon, that it was impossible for the Pope to be Author of so great inconveniences?

<small>Citat. Theod. Niem. Nem. unio. Tract.4. ca.9</small>

24 And if the Popes *Breves* were not naturally conditioned so, that in cases of *enormous detriment* and inconvenience, to the cause and persons, the rigour thereof might be remitted, since in such occurrences, the reason of those *Breves* doth evidently cease, which is ever understood to be the advancement of the Romane Church; And if in all cases, all *Breves* must have their full execution under the paines and penalties inflicted therein, the *Catholiques* of *England* are in worse condition by some former *Breves* of the Popes, then the offending and violating these two later, can draw them into. For (to omit many of like, and worse danger) That generall *Rescript* of *Clement* the seventh, which I mentioned before, pronounces, *That not onely by the Bulla Coenae, all such are excommunicated though they be Princes, as hinder the execution of the Apostolique letters, or such as give such hinderers any Counsaile, helpe,*

---

1. effects] effect.   C-3   **Margin 19.** Citat. *Ed.*: *note misplaced.*   C-1, L-1
20. *impossibile Ed.*: impossible.   C-1, L-1   **25.** ever *Ed.*: ever,.   L-1, C-1

or favours directly, or indirectly, publiquely, or secretly, or by any colour or pretence, (which words will reach to all those, who have refused, or doubted and disputed these *Breves*) *but also that the Kingdomes and places, where those offenders are remaining, are interdicted*; And then
5 in the rigour of this *Breve*, how can the *Priests* exercise their functions heere in *England*, if the *Bulla Coenae*, and a *locall interdict* oppresse it.

25   And by such servile obedience to *Breves*, as this is all such Catholickes as have reliev'd & succor'd themselves, with that weake distinction of the *Court of Rome*, and the *Church of Rome*, shall loose
10 and forfeit all the advantage which that affoorded them; For, when they shall bee pressed with numbers of *Veniall Indulgences*, and of ambitious *Buls*, and usurpations upon the right of other Princes, they shall not bee able to finde this ease, to dischardge all upon the *Court of Rome*, if the *Church of Rome* make it matter of Faith to obey the *Rescripts* of
15 the *Court of Rome*, which produce these enormities. For since the *Pope* is the *Church*, how can you divide the *Church* from the *Court*? Since, either as the *Court* is *Aula* or *Curia*, the Pope is the Prince, and as it is *Forum*, he is the Judge, and the Ordinarie. And since all those *Buls*, which are loaded with censures, or with Indulgences, proceede from him
20 as he is the *Church*, (for those powers are onely in the Church) how can you impute to his act any errour of the *Court*?

26   It was whilst *Nero* continued within the limits of a good and just Prince, that *Tacitus* said of him, *Discreta fuit domus a Repub*. but when   Annal.13
hee stray'd into *Tyrannie*, it was not so. Nor is the *Court of Rome*, any
25 longer distinguished from the *Church of Rome*, if the *Church* justifie the errours of the *Court*, and pronounce, that hee which obeyes not that *Court*, is not in that *Church*, as it doeth in Excommunicating all them, which obey not the *Rescripts* and *Breves* of Popes.

27   So that when *Bellarmine* undertooke to aunswere all, which had   Append. ad Lib.
30 been objected out of *Dante*, and *Bocace*, and *Petrarche*, against *Rome*, it   de Pont.
was but a lasie escape, and a round and Summarie dispatch upon wearinesse, to say, that all that was meant of the *Court of Rome*, not of the *Church*; and therefore it was a wise abstinence in him, not to repeate *Petrarchs* words, but to recompense them by citing other places of *Petrarch*
35 in favour of the *Romane Church*. For though *Petrarch* might meane the *Court*, by the name of *Babilon*, and by imputing to it *Covetousnesse* and *Licentiousnesse*, yet when he charges *Rome* with *Idolatrie*, and cals

it the *Temple of Heresie*, can this be intended of the *Court of Rome*?

28   The disobedience to Popes (in whome no moderate men ever denied some degrees of the leaven and corruption, of such passions and respects as vitiate all mens actions) was not always esteem'd thus hainous, though in matters neerer to the foundations of Faith, then these which are now in question.   The famous dissention betweene Pope *Stephen* and *Cyprian*, is good evidence thereof. For though now they say, *That the Pope did not pronounce, De fide, against rebaptization, but onely say, that it might not bee used: And that he did not Excommunicate Cyprian, but onely say, that he ought to be excommunicate*; yet this is as farre as the Pope hath proceeded with you: and after he had done thus much, *Bellarmine* sayes, *it was lawfull for Cyprian to differ from him: because hee thought that the Pope was in a pernitious errour*. And though *Cyprian* is never found to have retracted either his *Doctrine* of rebaptization, or his *behaviour* to the Pope, yet the severest Idolaters of that Sea, have never denied him a roome amongst the blessed *Saints* of the purest times.

29   And though they are for their advantage content to say now, that *Cyprian was never excommunicated*, yet it is not denied by *Baronius*, but that *Ignatius* the *Patriarch* of *Constantinople* was, and that he died excommunicate; and resisted to the end of his life, the Popes *Rescripts*, by which hee was commaunded to leave all the Countrie of *Bulgaria* to the jurisdiction of the Church of Rome. But this (sayes *Baronius*) *he did not out of any displeasure to the Pope, but to defend the jurisdiction of his Church, as he was bound by oath, under the danger of damnation: for his purpose was not to take away anothers right, but to keepe his owne.*

30   And was not this your case, before the *Breves* came? Is not civill obedience either really or by intention and implication sworne by every subject to the King in his birth, and after? and do you not by this last oath defend, not onely the Kings right, as you are bound, under danger of damnation, but your owne libertie, who otherwise must bee under the obedience of two Masters? and have these two *Breves* made your case to differ so much from his, that that which was lawfull to him, may not be so to you? when as to you the *Breves* have onely brought a naked and

Margin notes:
Bell. de Pont. l.4. c.7. §. tertia ratio
Ibid. §. & per hoc
To.10. Anno 878. n.42

Margin 19. 42 *Ed.*: 41. L-1, C-1

bare commandement, without taking knowledge of your allegations: but the Pope gave *Ignatius* three severall *warnings*; and disputed the case with him: and tolde him *that by the records at Rome, it was evident, and that no man was ignorant, that that region belong'd to the Romane Church, and that Ignatius his pretences to it, because the enemy had interrupted the Romane possession were of no force; which he proves by a Decree of Pope Leo, and divers other wayes*: Yet for all this, *Ignatius* held out, endured the excommunication, and died under that burden, and yet God hath testifed by many miracles, the holinesse and sanctitie of this reverent man.

31 *Dioscorus* the Bishop of *Alexandria*, exceeded al these passive disobediences and contempts of the Popes, and proceeded to an *Active* excommunication of the Pope himselfe: and yet for all this, it is said of him, *Non erravit in fide*. And what opinion was held of our Bishoppe *Grosthead*, that his disobedience to the Pope despoiled him not of the name of *Catholique*, a late *Neophite* of your Church hath observed.

<small>Dist.21. In tantum & 24.q.2. Sane profectur</small>

<small>Higgons. fo.32</small>

32 For the Pope is subject to humane errors, and impotencies; and when a great sword is put into a weake hand, it cannot always be well governed; And therefore when *Bartholinus* an advocate in the Court of *Rome*, a bolde and wittie man, had adventured to convay secretly certaine questions, in which he declared his owne opinion affirmatively; amongst which, one was, *That if the Pope were negligent, or insufficient, or head-strong to the danger of the Church, the Cardinals might appoint him a Curator and Guardian, by whom hee should dispatch the affaires of the Church*, his reasons are said to have *prevailed with excellent Masters in Theology, and Doctors in both lawes, and that many Cardinals adhered thereunto, till the Pope comming to the knowledge thereof, imprisoned six of the Cardinals, and confiscated their estates.*

<small>Theodor. à Niem. de Schis. l.1. c.42</small>

33 But if, as it is forbidden under Excommunication, *to make any Comment upon one Canon which concernes the privileges of the Franciscans*, (which were the best labourers in the Popes Vineyard, til the *Jesuits* came) so it were forbidden upon like penaltie, to interpret the Popes *Breves*, yet no such law can take away our natural libertie, nor silence in us these dictats which nature inculcates, *That against the end*

<small>Navar. Manual. c.27. n.147. Clem. Exivi. Tit. de verb. signif.</small>

Margin 19. Schis. *Ed*.: Scrip.. C-1, L-1 **Margin 29.** 27 *Ed*.: 21. C-1, L-1 **Margin 29.** signif] signtf. L-1, MCG, C-2, C-4, L-2, O-1, C^3, C^{16}, YK-1

for which it was instituted, no power can be admitted to worke. For from your *Sylvester* wee learne, *That the Popes precepts binde not, where there is vehement likelyhood of trouble or scandall.* And so he puts the justifying and making valid the Popes Breves, to the judgement of considerate men, though parties.

34   So also is it said there, *That it is not the purpose nor intention of the Church to bee obeyed in such dangers*; For avoidance of scandall, is *Divine law*, and to be preferred before any commaund of a Pope, which is but *Humane* law: for *Divine positive* law yeeldes to this precept of avoiding *scandall*, as I noted before, in the integrity of confession, where some sinnes may be omitted, rather then any scandall admitted. And therfore their great *Victoria* complaines justly of great inconveniences, ^a*If all matters should be left to the will of one man, who is not confirmed in grace, but subject to error: of which*, says he, *I would it were lawfull for us to doubt*, meaning that daily experience made it evident; for so hee addes in the point of Dispensations, *We see daily so large and dissolute dispensations, as the world cannot beare it.* And not long after, in the same *Lecture* he sayes, ^b*We may philosophy, and we may imagine, that the Popes might be most wise men, and most holy men, and that they would never dispense without lawfull cause, but experience cries out to the contrary, and we see that no man which seekes a Dispensation misses it. And therefore we must dispaire if it be left, Arbitrio humano: For* (sayes he) *the Pope must trust others, and they may deceive him, if hee were Saint Gregory himselfe.* And he addes further, ^c*We talke as though wee needed great Engines to extort a Dispensaton, as though there were not men expecting at Rome, when any man wil come and ask a dispensation of all those things, which are provided against by the lawes*: and though hee confesse, that former Popes were not so limited, as he desires the Popes in these times, might be, *it was*, sayes hee, ^d*because they did not presume, so easily to dispence against Councels. Da mihi Clementes, provide me, sayes he, such Popes as Clement, Linus and Sylvester were, and I will allow all things to be done, as they list.*

35   And then since *de facto*, it may bee, and often is so, whether

---

Ver. Obedientia

^aDe Pot. Pap. & Conc. §. Sed quia

^bIbid. §. preterea

^cIbid. §. & preterea

^dIbid. si quis

---

7.   dangers;] dangers. catchword quarto p.342. L-1, C-1   **29.**   desiers catchword quarto p.343] desiers. L-1, C-1   **Margin 29d.**   ^dIbid. si quis *Ed*.: Ibid. 87 si quis. C-1, L-1   **29.**   ^d*because Ed*.: because. C-1, L-1

a Precept of the Popes, doe worke to that end for which the Church government was committed to him, or no, *Naturall Reason*, sayes a [e]learned *Jesuite, will instruct us.* Who thereupon makes a free and ingenuous conclusion, in a question of the Popes power in making a Law, of *Electing a Successour, That the Pope might make such a Law, if hee would, but the Church would never receive it.* Which how could *Azorius* pronounce, or know, but by the insinuation of naturall reason, and conveniencie; which Counsailer and Instructer, every other temperate and intelligent, and dispassioned man, hath as well as he?

[e]Azor. To.2. l.4. c.5. §. Tertio

36   And so also sayes *Fran. a Victor.* and as manie as speake ingenuously, *That where the Mandates of the Pope, are in Destructionem Ecclesiae, they may be hindred and resisted.* For in the greatest effect which can be attributed to the Popes *Bulls*, in these temporall affaires, which is, discharging of Subjects from their obedience, that peremptorie Canon, *Nos Sanctorum, bindes not, except it may be done without grievous damage to the Subject*, and though by the vertue of that Canon, they may forbeare their obedience if they will, yet *they are not bound thereby to doe it.* Yea, it were unlawfull, to denie that obedience, *in cases of scandall or tumult.* For so also, sayes another of your great men, *It is often expedient to obey even an unjust law, to avoid scandall.* [a]And the late un-entangler of perplexities, *Comitolus* the Jesuite, who undertakes to cleare so many cases, which *Navarrus* and many others left in suspence, when he comes to handle the question, *whether a Professor of the Romane faith, being sent into those parts where the Greeke Church observes other rites, may goe to their service*; in such cases as he allowes it, he builds upon this Reason, *That by the law of God, and of Nature, it is lawfull, and the Precepts of the Church,* (which forbid this) *doe not binde Christians, in cases of great detriment to the life, or soule, or honor, or fame, or outward things.*

Ibid. §. Decimaseptima

D'Avila. de Censuris. par.2. c.6. Disp.11. Dub.9

Alf. Castr. de Potest. Leg. l.1. c.5. Docum.1

[a]Comitolus. Resp. Moral. li.1. q.47

37   Since therefore a *civill constitution*, which in power of binding, and all validities, except immutablenesse, is by your owne Authors equall to *Divine*, had possessed your conscience, and so refreshed by a new solicitation your naturall & native *Alleageances*, so that no *Breve* could create in you a new conscience, in this case, no more then if it had forbidden Obedience to the common law, or any other statute, because

Margin 19. Docum.1 *Ed.*: Docum.. L-1, C-1

it belongs not to you to judge what is sinne, and what conduces to
spirituall ends, since by the testimonie of the Popes owne *Breves*, his
Breves are subject to many infirmities, and open to the interpretation
of meane men, since they are often revoked, and pronounced to have
beene voide from the beginning, uppon such reasons as it is impossible
for you to suspect or spie in them, when you admit them, since these
Breves have contributed their strength, and given authority, to *vaine*,
and to *suspitious*, and to *false*, and to *blasphemous* legends, since the
Pope is allowed, to neglect all wayes of informing himselfe of the truth,
in the most generall & most important matters, since recourse to your
Superiours is not affoorded, which you know both by the practises of
one partie and faction at Rome, and also by effects thereof, because by
the second *Breve*, the complaints against the first were not remedied,
And since in such cases, the interpretation and dispensation of *Breves*,
when necessitie oppresses you, belongs to your selfe, who cannot bee
esteemed disobedient, for abstaining from doing such a commaund, as
you doe justly thinke to be erroneous, and that your *Superiour* would not
importune it, if hee knew perfitly your condition, and estate: since their
rigorous observation of *Breves*, might cast you under a *locall interdict*,
and sterve you for *spirituall* food, And makes you justifie all the errours
of the *Court of Rome*, by making the *Court*, & the *Church*, all one:
since *Cyprian*, *Ignatius* and others, have beene justly reputed holy men,
& Saints, though they disobeyed the precepts of Popes, made upon more
reasons, and stronger comminations, and broken with lesse excuse, then
these *Breves* may be by you: since lastly the Pope cannot by pretence
of advauncing the *Church* serve his owne ambitions to your destruction,
you may as well flatter your selfe, with specious Titles, for not swimming
if you were cast into a River, or for not running out of a house, if it were
ready to fall uppon you, as you may thinke your selves Confessors (in
your sense) for suffering the penalties of this law, or they may thinke
themselves *Martyrs*, whose execution for other treasons, this Refusall
may hasten.

19. under *Ed.*: un.der. L-1, C-1

Chap. XII.

That nothing requir'd in this Oath, violates the Popes spirituall Jurisdiction; And that the clauses of swearing that Doctrine to bee Hereticall, is no usurping upon his spirituall right, either by prejudicating his future definition, or offending any former Decree.

5   1   The same office which our suerties performe for us, at our *Baptisme* and Regeneration, the Lawe undertakes at our *Civill* birth; For the Law is *Communis sponsio Reip*. And as they which were our stipulators at the Font, take care when we come to abilitie of Discretion, that we doe by some open declaration, as frequenting Divine Service, and so communicating with the Church in the worde and Sacraments, testifye that wee acknowledge our selves incorporated and matriculated into that Christian warfare, wherein they entred our Names, So hath Law provided, that when we grow to be capable of *Good* and *Evill*, wee should make some publicke protestations of that Obedience to the Prince, which by our birth in his *Dominions*, and of his *Subjects*, wee had at first contracted. Thereupon hath it proceeded that by our Lawes at sixteene yeares of age, an Oath hath beene requir'd of every Subject. And besides this generall Oath, it hath in all well govern'd Estates, beene thought necessary, that they which were assum'd to any publicke function in the State, should also by another Oath, appropriated to that calling, be bound to a just execution of that place; And therfore it seemes reasonable which a *Lawyer* says, *That he which undertakes to exercise any Office, before he have taken the Oath, belonging thereunto, Tenetur Maiestatis*, because he seemes to doe it by his owne Authoritie. Nor might a *Souldier*, though hee were in the Tents at the time of Battell, be admitted to fight against the enemie, if he had not taken the Oath. And the *Notaries* in the *Courts* of *Rome*, if they delay to dispatch them, who would by *Appeale*, or otherwise bring causes into those *Courts*, are by a late *Decretall* guilty of *perjury*, because being sworne *to advance the profit of that place, and the Apostolique Authority*, this is accounted an interpretative perjury.

Dig. Tit.3. Le.1

Par. de Put. de Syndic. fo.481

Mar. Donatus. in Sueto. c.16

In septimo. Tit.2. c.1

5. 1 *Ed.: missing.*   L-1, C-1   **Margin 7.** 3 *Ed.:* 5.   C-1, L-1

2 So also hath it beene a wise and religious custome, in matters newly emergent, and fresh occurrences, if either forraigne pretences, or inward discontentments, threatned any commotions in the State, to minister new Oathes, to all whom it might concerne; not as newe obligations, but as voluntary and publique confessions, that all the former oathes sworne in *Nature* and in *Law*, doe reach and extend to that case then in question, and that they were bound by them, to the maintenance of the peace and tranquility of the present State.

3 And at no time, and to no persons, can such *Oathes* be more necessary, then to us now, who have beene awakened with such drummes as these, *There is no warre in the world so just and honourable, be it civill or forraigne, as that which is waged for the Romane Religion.* And especially in this consideration are *Oathes* a fit and proper wall and Rampart, to oppose against these men, because they say, *That to the obedience of this Romane Religion, all Princes and people have yeelded themselves, either by Oath, vow, or Sacraments, or every one of them.* For against this their imaginary oath, it is best, that a true, reall, and lawfull oath be administred by us.

4 The *Jesuites* which in their Vowe to the Popes will, have sworne out all their obedience at once, in a *Hyperbolicall* detestation of oaths, doe almost say true, when they professe, *That they avoide an Oath worse then perjury*: But though they have borrowed this protestation of the *Esseni*, who were in so much estimation amongst the Jewes, yet this declining of *Oathes* wrought not uppon them, as it doth upon the *Jesuites*; for the *Esseni* did willingly take *Oathes*, that they would attempt nothing against the Magistrate; out of this reason, that *they beleeved it hapned to no man, to be a governour without the pleasure of God*: Since therefore the Jesuites abhorre such oaths, & it is a good presumption, *that Schollers are guilty if their Masters were,* and *sonnes are punished, because they are justly suspected to inherit their fathers malignity, and ill disposition*; It was necessary to present such an oath, as might discover how much of their *Masters* poison, and of their *Fathers* ill affections to this State, the *Jesuites* disciples, and spirituall sonnes had swallowed and digested.

Margin 11. Jesuits *Ed.*: Jesuit,. C-1, L-1 27. *God*: C-2, L-2, O-2, O²: *God·*. L-1, C-1, MCG, Y, YK-1

Apolog. of Jesuits. c.5

Ibid.

Spongia. pro Iesuit. fo.79
Serarius. Trihaeres. l.3. c.4. Ar.34

Ar.37

Par. de Put. de Syndic. fo.990
Hier. Gigas. de Laes. Ma. l.3. rubr.1.q.5. nu.2

CHAPTER TWELVE

5   And when an *Oath* is to bee conceived and framed, which hath some certaine scope and purpose; it were a great impotencie or slackenes in the State, if it should not be able, or not dare to expresse it in such tearmes, as might reach home to that purpose, and accomplish fully all that which was intended therein; especially in these times of subtile evasions and licentious equivocations.

6   When *Paulus* 4. had a purpose to take in, and binde more sorts of men, by that oath which was framed according to the *Trent Councell*, for them onely who were admitted to spirituall dignities, and some few others, and so to swear all those men fast to the Doctrine of that Councel, and to the obedience of the Church of Rome, it is expressed in so exquisite and so safe wordes, as can admit no escape. For, how ignorant soever he be in controverted *Divinity*, every one which takes that oath, must sweare, *That there are seven Sacraments instituted by Christ*; which any of their Doctors might have doubted and impugn'd an houre before; as it appeares by *Azorius*, that *Alensis* and *Bonaventure* did *of Confirmation*, *Hugo Victor* and *Bonaventure* of *extreame unction*, *Hostiensis* and *Durandus* of *Matrimony*, and others of others: and he must sweare, *That he beleeves Purgatory, Indulgences, and veneration of Reliques*: and hee must sweare, *That all things contrary to that Councell are hereticall*. And this oath is not onely *Canonized* (as their phrase is) by being inserted into the body of the *Canon* law, but it is allowed a roome in the Title, *De Summa Trinitate, & fide Catholica*, and so made of equall credite with that. And that [a]oath by which the *Cardinals* are bound to the maintenance of the Church privileges is conceived in so strong and forcible wordes, that *Baronius* calls it *Terribile Iuramentum*, & sayes, *that the only remembring of it inflicts a horror upon his minde, and a trembling upon his body.*

7   And with equall diligence are those oathes framed which are given to the *Emperours*, when they come to be Crowned by the Pope. For before he enters the land of the *Church*, he takes one oath, *Domino Papae iuro, that I will exalt him with all my power.* And before he enters Rome, he sweares, *that he will alter nothing in that Governement*, And

Azori' Instit. Mor. To.1. l.2. ca.9. praecep. prima. §. quotiescunque

In septimo. Tit.1. ca.4

[a]*Baron. Resp. ad Card. Colum. nu.31*

Cerem. Sacr. Ca. de Coron. Imp.

Margin 16. quotiescunque YK-3, O-1: quoti[?]scunque. L-1, C-1, O², O¹⁴, C¹⁵-1, L³⁰   **17.** *Bonaventure of Ed.*: Lombard of. L-1, C-1 **Margin 29.** Cerem. Sacr *Ed.*: Cerem sacr L-1, C-1, HD, F, Y, O-2;. Cerem. sacr MCG, C-2, C⁵-2, O-1, O², YK-3

before he receives the Crowne, he sweares, *that he will protect the Popes person and the Church*. And in the creation of a *Duke*, because hee might have some dependance upon another Prince, the Pope exhibites to him this oath; *I vow my reverence and obedience to you, though I be bound to any other*.

Ibid. ca. de Creat. Duc.

8 So did *Gregory* the seventh exact a curious oath of the Prince of *Capua, that he would sweare Alleageance to the Emperour, when the Pope or his Successors should admonish him thereto, and that when hee did it, he would doe it, with reservation of his Alleageance to the Pope*. And so when the Emperour *Henrie* the seventh, though he confessed that he had sworne to the Pope, yet denied *that hee understood that Oath to be an Oath of Alleageance or Fidelity*, the Popes have tooken order, not onely to insert the oath into the body of the *Canon Lawe*, but to enact thereby, That *whosoever tooke that Oath after, should account and esteeme it to bee an Oath of Alleageance*.

Binius. To.3. par. 2. fo.1161

Clem. de Iure Iurand.

9 With how much curiositie and unescapablenesse their formes of *Abjuration* under oath are exhibited? They thought they had not given words enow to *Berengarius*, till they made him sweare, *That the body in the Sacrament, was sensibly handled, broken, and ground with the teeth*; which he was bound to sweare, *Per Homousion trinitatem*. And they dressed and prepard *Hierome* of *Prage*, an oath, in the Councell of *Constance*, by which he must sweare, *freely, voluntarily,* (or else bee burned) and *simplie*, and *without condition, To assent to that Church, in all things, but especially in the Doctrines of the Keyes, and Ecclesiastick immunities and reliques, and all the ceremonies*, which were the most obnoxious matters.

De Consecrat. Dist.2. Ego

Sess.19

10 But yet this seem'd not enough; And therefore, though *Castrensis* say, That *there is no Law, by which he which abjures, should bee bound to abjure any other Heresie, then that of which he was infamed, yet* hee sayes that *it stands with reason, that he should abjure all*. And accordingly the *Inquisition* give an oath, in which, sayes hee, *Nulla manet rimula elabendi*; For he must sweare, *That he abjures all Heresies, and will alwayes keepe the faith of Rome; And that he hath told all, of others, and of himselfe, and ever will doe so; And that if he*

De Iusta Haereti. Punitio. l.1. c.3

Margin 28. Punitio. l.1. c.3 *Ed.*: Punitio. l.1. c.III.   **33.** he] hee catchword quarto p.353.

CHAPTER TWELVE 245

doe not, he renounces the benefit of this Absolution, and will trouble the Court with no more dayes of hearing; but sayes he, *Ego me iudico*.

11   And if wee doe but consider the exacte formes, and the advantagious words and clauses, which are in their *Exorcismes*, to cast out,
5 and to keepe out *Divels*, they may be good inducements, and precedents to us, how diligent we should be, in the phrase of our Lawes, to expell and keepe out *Jesuites*, and their *Legion*, which are as craftie, and as dangerous.

12   When therefore it was observed, that not onely most of the *Je-*
10 *suites* Bookes which tooke occasion to speake either of matter of *State*, or *Morall Divinitie*, abounded with traiterous and seditious *Aphorismes*, and derogatorie from the dignitie of Princes in generall; but that their Rules were also exemplified, and their speculations drawne into practise in this Kingdome, by more then one Treason; and by one, which
15 included and exceeded all degrees of irreligion and inhumanity, then was it thought fit to conceive an oath, whose end, and purpose, and scope was, to try & finde out, who maintained the integrity of their naturall and civill obedience so perfectly, as to sweare, that nothing should alter it, but that he would ever do his best endevour to the preservation of
20 the Prince, *what enemie so ever* should rise against him.

13   And if any of the materiall words, or any clause of the Oath, had beene pretermitted, then had not the purpose and intent of the Oath beene fulfilled; That is, no man had averr'd by that oath, that he thought himselfe bound to preserve the King against *All* enemies,
25 which to doe, is meere Civill obedience. For though the generall word of *Enemie*, or *Usurper*, would have encluded and enwrapped as wel the *Pope*, as the *Turke*, when either of them should attempt any thing upon this Kingdome; yet, as it hath ever beene the wisdom of all States, in all *Associations* and leagues, to ordaine Oathes proper to the busines then
30 in hand, and to the imminent dangers: So now it was most necessarie to doe so, because the malignitie of men of that persuasion in Religion, had so violently broke foorth, and declar'd it-selfe; Which happie diligence, the effect praises and justifies enough, since it appeares, that if these particular clauses had not beene inserted, they would have swallowed any
35 Oath, which had beene presented in generall termes, and have kept their

35. termes,] termes.   L-1, MCG, Y, C-4, C^5-2, O^2, C^{10}

Consciences at large to have done any thing, which this Oath purpos'd to prevent.

14 He therefore that should desire to bee admitted to Sweare, that hee would preserve the King against all his enemies, *Except* the Pope, or those whom he should encourage or imploy; Or that he would ever beare true Allegeance, *Untill* the Pope had discharged him, or that hee would discover any conspiracie which did happen *before* the Pope did authorize it; Or that he would keepe this Oath, *Untill* the Pope gave him leave to breake it: this man should be farre from performing the intent and scope of an Oath, which should be made for a new attestation, that hee would according to his naturall duetie, and inborne obedience, absolutely defend the King from *All* his enemies.

15 I make no doubt but the *Jesuites* would have given way to the Oath, if it had beene conceiv'd in generall words, of *All obedience*, against all *Persons*; for it were stupiditie to denie that to be the dutie of all Subjects. Nor would they have exclaim'd, that spirituall Jurisdiction had beene infringed, if in such times as their Religion govern'd here, this clause had beene added to defend the King, *Though the Metropolitane of England should Excommunicate him*. And yet by there *Doctors* it is averr'd, that *Iure Divino*, and *Iure Communi Antiquo, A Bishop may Excommunicate a King*, as *Ambrose* did *Theodosius*, and that *excepting onely infallibilitie of judgement, in matter of Faith, a Bishop might, Iure Divino, doe all those things in his Diocesse, which the Pope might doe in the whole Church*. For, so *Bellarmine* himselfe concludes, arguing from the Popes Authoritie in all the world, to a Bishop in his Diocesse. If therefore an Oath had beene lawfull, for defending the King against *All* enemies, though a *Bishop* Excommunicate him, And the Pope have onely by *positive* lawes, withdrawne from the Bishops some of the exercise of their jurisdiction, and reserved to himselfe the power of excommunicating Princes, it is as lawfull to defend him after a *Popes* excommunication now, as it was after a *Bishops*, when a *Bishop* might excommunicate: and no man ever said, that a Bishop might have deposed a King.

16 All which they quarrell at in the oath, is, that any thing should be pronounced, or any limits set, to which the Popes power might not extend: but they might as well say that his *spirituall* power were limited

Margin notes:
D'Avila. de Censu. par.2. c.4. Disp.1. Dub.4
Ibidem
De Pont. l.5. c.3. §. Item

Margin 18. Censu *Ed.*: Censa. C-1, L-1

CHAPTER TWELVE 247

or shortned, and so the Catholique faith impugned, if one should denie him to have power over the winde and sea; since to tame and commaund these, *in ordine ad spiritualia*, would advance the conversion of the *Indies*, and impaire the *Turks* greatnesse, and have furthered his fatherly
5 & spirituall care of this Kingdome in 88.

17   All the substance of the *oath* is virtually comprehended in the first proposition, *That king James is lawfull King of all these Dominions*; The rest are but declarations, and branches naturally and necessarily proceeding from that roote. And as that *Catholique* which hath sworne,
10 or assented, that *Paul the fift*, is Pope canonically elected, hath implicitly confessed, that no man can devest or despoile him of that spirituall jurisdiction, which God hath deposed in him, nor of those temporall estates, which by just title his predecessours possessed or pretended too: so that Subject which sweares king *James* to bee his true and lawfull
15 King, obliges himselfe therein to all obedience, by which hee may still preserve him in that state; which is to resist *all* which shall upon any occasion be his enemies.

18   For if a king be a king upon this condition, that the Pope may upon such cause as seemes just to him, depose him, the king is no more
20 a *Soveraigne*, then if his people might depose him, or if a Neighbour king might depose him: For though it may seeme more reasonable and convenient, that the Pope, who may bee presumed more equall, and dispassioned then the people, and more disinteressed then the neighbour Princes, should be the Judge and Magistrate to depose a Prince
25 enormously transgressing the wayes, in which his duety bounde him to walke, though, I say, the king might hope for better Justice at his hand, then anothers, yet he is no *Soveraigne*, if any person whatsoever may make him none. For it is as much against the nature of *Soveraignty*, that it may at any time be justly taken away, as that it shall certainly
30 bee taken away. And therefore a King whom the Pope may depose, is but a *Depositarie*, and *Guardian* of the *Soverainty*; to whose trust it is committed upon condition: as the *Dictators* were *Depositaries* of it, for a certaine time. And Princes in this case shall bee so much worse then *Dictators*, as Tenants at will are worse then they which have certaine
35 leases.

19   And therefore that suspition and doubt, which a learned *Lawyer* conceived, *that the Kings of France and Spaine lacked somewhat of*   Alb. Gent. de Legatio. l.4

Soverainty, because they had a dependance, and relation to the Pope, would have had much reason and probability in it, (though he meant this onely of *spirituall* matters concerning religion) if that authority which those Kings seeme to be subject to, were any other, then such, as by assenting to the Ecclesiastique Canons, or confirming the immunities of the Ecclesiastique state, they had voluntarily brought upon themselves, and the better to discharge their dueties to their Church; and to their civill state, had chosen this way as fittest to governe their Church, as other wayes, by Judges and other Magistrates to administer civill Justice.

20 So therefore *his Majesties* predecessors in this Kingdome were not the lesse *Soveraigne* and absolute, by those acts of Jurisdiction which the Popes exercised here. For though some kings in a mis-devout zeale, and contemplation of the next life, neglected the office of governement to which God had called them, by attending which function duely, they might more have advanced their salvation, then by Monastique retirings (of which publique care, and preserving those which were committed to their charge, and preferring them before their owne happinesse, *Moses*, and St. *Paul* were couragious examples) Though, I say, they spent all their time upon their owne future happinesse, and so making themselves almost *Clergy* men, and doing their duties, gave the Clergie men way and opportunity, to enter upon their office, and deale with matter of State; And though some other of our kings, oppressed with temporall and personall necessities, have seemed to diminish themselves, by accepting conditions at the Popes hands, or of his Legates, And some others, out of their wisedome avoiding dangers of raw and immature innovations, have digested some indignities and usurpations, and by the examples of some kingdomes about them, have continued that forme of Church Government, which they could not resist without tumult at home, and scandall abroad; yet all this extinguished no part of their Soverainty; which Soverainty without all question they had, before the other entred into the kingdome, intirely: and Soverainty can neither be divested nor devided.

21 As therefore Saint *Paul* suffered *Circumcision* as long as toleration thereof, advancd the propagation and growth of the Church, when

[margin: Exod. 32.32 / Ro. 9.3]

23. kings, *Ed*.: kings. L-1, C-1   **35.** [pr̂opa]gation] -gaton *catchword quarto* p.360. L-1, L²

CHAPTER TWELVE 249

a severe and rigid inhibition thereof would have averted many tender and scrupulous consciences, which could not so instantly passe from a commandement of a necessity in taking Circumcision, to a necessity in leaving it; But when as *certaine men came downe and taught, that* Act. 15.1
5 *circumcision was necessary to salvation*, and so overthrewe the whole Gospell, because the necessity of both could not consist together, then Circumcision was utterly abolished: So, as long as the *Romane* Religion, though it were corrupted with many sicknesses, was not in this point become so infectious and contagious, as that it would utterly destroy and
10 abolish the *Soverainty* of Princes, the kings of *England* succourd, relieved, and cherished it, and attended an opportunity, when God would enable them to medecine and recover her; but to be so indulgent to her now, is impossible to them, because as every thing is jealous of his owne being, so are kings most of any: and kings can have no assurance of
15 being so, if they admit professors of that Religion, which teaches, that the Pope may at any time Depose them.

22 We doe not therefore by this oath exempt the King from any *spirituall* Jurisdiction; Neither from often incitations to continue in all his dueties, by Preaching the word; nor from confirming him in grace,
20 by the blessed Sacrament; Nor from discreet reprehension if hee should transgresse. We doe neither, by this oath, priviledge him from the *Censures* of the Church, nor denie, by this oath, that the Pope hath justly ingrossed and reserved to himselfe the power to inflict those censures upon Princes. We pronounce therein against no power which pretendes
25 to make Kings *better* Kings, but onely against that, which threatens to make them *no* kings.

23 For if such a power as this, of deposing and annihilating Kings, bee necessarie, and certaine in the Church, and the Hierarchie thereof be not well established, nor our salvation well provided for, without this
30 power, as they teach, why was the Primitive Church destitute thereof? For if you allow the answere of *Bellarmine, That the Church did not de-* De Pont. l.5. c.7.
pose Kings then because it lacked strength, you returne to the beginning §. Quod si
againe, and goe round in a circle. For the wisedome of our Saviour is as much impeached, and the frame of the Church is as lame, and im-
35 potent, and our salvation as ill provided for, if *Christ* doe not alwayes

Margin 4. 15.1 *Ed.*: 15.. L-1, C-1 **34.** as lame *Ed.*: aslame. L-1, C-1

give strength and abilitie to extirpate wicked kings, if that be necessarie to salvation, as he were if he did not give them Title and Authoritie to doe it. Yea, all these defects would still remaine in the Church, though *Christ* had given *Authoritie* enough, and *Strength* enough, if he did not alwayes infuse in the Pope, a *Will* to doe it.

24 And where this power of deposing Princes may be lawfully exercised, as in States where Princes are *Conditionall*, and not absolute and Soveraigne, as if at *Venice* the State should depose the *Duke*, for attempting to alter that Religion, and induce *Greeke* errours, or *Turcisme*, or if other States, which might lawfully doe so, should depart from the obedience, and resist the force of their Princes, which should offer to bring into that State, the *Inquisition*, or any other violence to their Conscience, if the people in these States should depose the Prince, did they doe this by any *Spirituall* Authoritie, or Jurisdiction? Or were this done by such a *Temporall* Authoritie, as were *indirect*, or *casuall*, or *incident*, or springing out of the spirituall authoritie, as the Popes ridler makes his authoritie to bee? Or must they stay, to aske and obtaine leave of their *Clergie*, to depose such a transgressor? If therefore such a particular state, in whom the *Soveraignty* resides, have a *direct temporall* power, which enables it sufficiently to maintaine, and conserve it selfe; such a *supreme spirituall* power, as they talk of in the Pope, is not necessarie for our salvation, nor for the perfection of the Church government.

25 Nor is there any thing more monstrous, and unnaturall and disproportioned, then that *spirituall* power should conceive or beget *temporall*: or to rise downwards, as the more degrees of heigth, and Supremacie, and perfection it hath, the more it should decline and stoope to the consideration of secular and temporall matters. It may well have some congruity with your Rules, that the Popes of Rome, in whom the fulnesse of spirituall power is said to be, should have more jurisdiction in *spirituall* matters, then other Prelates. They may be better trusted with the *spirituall food* and physicke of the Church, and so prepare and present, the *word*, and the *Sacraments*, to us, in such outward sort and manner, as wee may best digest, and convert them to nouriture. They may be better trusted with the *spirituall Justice* of the Church, and make the *censures* thereof profitable to the delinquent, and others by his example. They may be better trusted with the *spirituall treasure*

CHAPTER TWELVE 251

of the Church, and apply and dispence the graces, of which they have the *stewardship*, at their discretion. They may be better credited with *canonizing* of Saints, and such acts of *spirituall power*, then others: and these are many, and great offices, to be put into one bodies hands. But that out of this power, and then onely when this power is at her fulnesse and perfection, in the Pope, there should arise and growe a *temporall* power, which in their estimation, is so poore and wretched a thing, that a boy which doth but shave his head, and light a candle in the Church, is above it, (for so they say, even of the *lesser Orders*) is either impossible, or so prodigious, as if (to insist upon their owne comparisons of *spirituall* and *temporall* power) the *Sunne* at his highest glory, should be said to produce a *Moone-light*, or *golde*, after all trials and purifyings, should bring forth *Lead*.

26 Nor doe they for this *Timpany*, or *false conception*, by which *spirituall* power is blowne up, and swelled with *temporall*, pretend any place of *Scripture*, or make it so much as the putative father thereof. For they doe not say, that any place of *Scripture* doth by the literall sense thereof, immediatly beget in us, this knowledge, *That the Pope may depose a Prince*; but all their arguments are drawne, from *naturall reason*, and *discourse*, and *conveniencie*. So that, if either the springe which moves the first wheele, or any wheele by the way be disordered, the whole Engine is defeated, and made of no use.

27 And in this wee will joine and concurre with *Azorius*, the *Jesuite*, *That though there be somethings which neither the Scriptures doe in expresse words forbid the Pope to doe, nor the Canons can disable him, because hee is above them, yet the very law of Nature inhibits them, and provides that by no meanes they may be done; and that if the Pope should doe such a thing, there were a Nullity in the action, and the Church would never permit it, but doe some act in opposition against it,* And all this out of this respect, *That naturall Reason would teach them, that the generall peace and tranquility of the Christian Common-wealth would be disturbed thereby.* To.2. l.4. c.5. §. Tertio

28 If therefore in the point in question, wee must be directed by *naturall reason*, and dispute which is most profitable and convenient for the peace of *Christian* states, though it may bee long uncertaine on both sides, where the victorie will fall, yet, during the suite, *Melior est conditio possidentis*. And since it is confessed, that Princes before

they accepted Christianitie, had no *Superiour*, and nothing appeares why Princes should not be as well able to governe Subjects in *Christian* Religion, as in *Morall vertue*, or wherein they neede an equall *Assistant*, or *Superiour*, now, more then before, or by what authoritie the Pope is that *Officer*, it is a precipitate and hastie prejudice for any man, before judgement, to set to the seale of his bloud, and a licentious and desperate extending of the *Catholique* faith, to intrude into the body thereof, and charge upon our consciences, under paine of *damnation*, such an *article*, as none but the thirteenth Apostle *Judas* would have made, and in which their owne greatest Doctors, are yet but *Catechumeni*, and have no explicite beliefe thereof: for they neither bring to that purpose, *Scripture, Tradition, consent of Fathers, generall Counsaile, nor Decree of any Pope.*

29 And, I thinke, I may safely averre, that it will not constitute a *Martyrdome*, to seale with your bloud any such point heere, as the affirming of the contrary, would not draw you into the fire at Rome. Except you should be burned for an Opinion there, you cannot be reputed *Martyrs*, for holding the contrarie here. As therefore it were no *Heresie* at *Rome*, to denie the Popes *direct* power, nor his *indirect*, (for if it were, *Bellarmine* and *Baronius* had made up an *Heresie* betweene them, as *Sergius* and *Mahomet* did) so is the affirmation thereof no *article of faith* in *England*.

30 This then being so farre from being an *Article of faith*, by what power the Pope may depose a Prince, as that it is even amongst them which affect an *Ignorance*, but *Dubium speculativum*, a man may safely, and ought to take the Oath: For so a man of much authority amongst themselves doth say, *That in a doubt which consists in speculation, we doe not sinne, if we doe against it*: and himselfe chuses this example, *If a Souldier doubt whether the warre which his Prince undertakes be just or no, yet in the practique parte, hee may resolve to fight at his Princes command, though he be not able to explicate the speculative doubt.* And he ads this in confirmation; *That where one part is certaine, and the other doubtful, we may not leave the sure side, and adhere to the other.* In his example that which hee presumes for certaine, is this, *That every*

Carbo. Summa Summarum. To.1. par.1. lib.5. c.14. §. prima

---

12. nor Ed.: no nor. L-1, C-1 **Margin 26.** lib.5. c.14 Ed.: c.14. C-1, L-1
30. practique] pract que. C-4, L-2, O-1, O², C¹⁶, YK-3

man ought to defend his Prince, and the speculative doubt is, *Whether the warre be just or no*. If this be applied to our case, every man will finde this certaine impression in himselfe, that hee ought to sweare civill obedience to his Prince, and this will be so evident to him, that no doubt can arise, so strong, or so well commended to him, by any pretence of Reason, and deducements, as may make him abstaine from a practique duety, for a speculative doubt. For so, *Fran. a Victoria*, maintaining the same opinion, gives these reasons for it, *That not onely in defensive warre, but in offensive* (which is further then our case, in any probability, is like to extend to) *the Prince is not bound to give an account to the subject of the justice of the cause: And therefore (sayes hee) in doubtfull cases, the safer part is to be followed: And if he should not fight for his Prince, he should expose the State to the enemy, which is a much more grievous offence, then to fight against the enemy, though he doubt of the cause.* For if their opinion were an *evident Truth*, both their *Doctors* would be able to explicate it, and their *Disciples* would neede no explication.

_{Franc. a Victor. Relect.6. De Iure Belli. §. Tertium Dubium}

31   This Oath therefore containing nothing, but a *profession of a morall Truth, and a protestation that nothing can make that false*, impugnes no part of that *spirituall* power, which the Pope justly hath, nor of that which he is charged to usurpe. That which hath seemed to many of them, to come neerest to his *spirituall* power is, that the Deponent doth sweare, *That the Pope hath no power to absolve him of this Oath.* But besides, that it hath beene strongly and uncontroulably prooved already by divers, that no absolution of the Popes can worke upon the matter of this Oath, because it is *a morall Truth*, I doe not perceive, that *to absolve a man from an Oath, belongs to spirituall Jurisdiction.*

32   For Dispensations against a law, and absolutions from Oathes and Vowes worke onely as *Declarations*, not as *Introductions*. And that power which gives me a priviledge, with a *Non obstante* upon a law, or an absolution from an oath, doth not enable mee to breake that lawe, or that Oath, but onely declares, *That that law and Oath, shall not extend to me in that case*, and that if this particular case could have beene foreseene, at the making of the law, or the Oath, neither the Oath, nor the law ought to have beene so generall.

33   So therefore these Absolutions, are but *interpretations*, and it belongs to him who made the law, to interpret it. For without any use

of *spirituall* Jurisdiction, the Emperour *Henry* the seventh, absolved all the Subjects of *Robert* king of *Sicily* of their oathes of Alleageance, when he rebelled against the Empire, of which hee was a *feudatarie* Prince. And though the Pope annulled this sentence, it was not because the *Emperour* might not doe this, but because the king of *Sicily* held also of the Church, and this absolving of Subjects made by the *Emperour*, extended to the Subjects of the Church.

Clem. de Sen. et Re Iud. Pastoralis

34 So also the Emperours *Antoninus* and *Verus*, when one had made an oath, that *he would never come into the Senate*, creating him such an *Officer*, as his personall attendance was necessary in the Senate house, by an expresse *Rescript*, absolved him of his oath. Of which kinde there are divers other examples.

Dig. li.50. Tit.1. Ad Munic. le.fin.

35 And your *Canons* doe not require this *spirituall* Jurisdiction, alwayes in this Act of absolving an oath. For if I have bound my selfe to another by an unjust oath, in many cases I may pronounce my selfe absolved; and in others I may complaine to the Judge, that hee may force him, to whom I swore, to absolve me of this oath. And in such cases as we are directed to goe to the Church, and the governour thereof, it is not for absolution of the oath, but it is for judgement, *whether there were any sinne in making that oath, or no*. For when that appeares, out of the Nature of the matter, arises and results a Declaration sufficient, whether wee are bound or absolved. If therefore the matter of this oath be so evident, as being Morall, & therefore constant and ever the same, that it can never neede his judgement, because it can in no case be sinne, the scruple which some have had, that by denying this power of absolving, his spirituall power is endamaged, is vaine and frivolous.

15.q.6. Authoritatem. gloss.

The Second Part.

36 From this imputation, of impairing his *spirituall* power, every limme and part of the oath, hath beene fully acquited, by great, and reverend persons, so, as it were boldnesse in me, to add to that which they have perfited; since additions doe as much deforme, as defects. Onely, because perchance they did not suspect, that any would stumble

at that clause, which in the oath hath these words, *I abjure as impious, and Hereticall, that position, &c.* I have not observed that any of them, have thought it worthy of their defence; But because I have found in some *Catholiques*, when I have importuned them to instance, in what part of
5 the oath *spirituall* Jurisdiction was oppugned, or what deterr'd them from taking the same, that they insisted upon this, That it belonged onely to the *Pope*, to pronounce a *Doctrine* to be *Hereticall*, and that, since there was a *Canon* of a generall *Councell* pretended for the contrary opinion, and that it was followed by many learned men, it were too much
10 boldnesse for a private man, to averre it to be *Hereticall*, I am willing to deliver them of that scruple.

37 It is no strange nor insolent thing with their Authors, to lay the Note of *Heresie* upon *Articles*, which can neither be condemned out of the word of God, nor are repugnant to any Article of faith; for *Cas-*
15 *trensis*, that he might thereby make roome for *traditions*, liberally confesses, *That there are many Doctrines of the Heretiques, which cannot be refelled by the testimonie of the Scriptures.* And the *Jesuite Tannerus* is not squeamish in this, when hee allowes thus much, *That in the communion under one kinde, and in fasts, and in feasts, and in other*
20 *Decrees of Popes, there is nothing established properly concerning faith.* So that with you, a man may be subject to the *penalties*, & so to the *infamie*, & so to the *damnation* belonging to an *Heretique*, though hee hold nothing against the Christian faith.

Adver. Haere. l.1. c.5. in princ.

De Liber. Eccles. l.2. c.9. §. Secundus

38 But wee lay not the Name of *Heresie* (in that bitter sense in
25 which the Canons accept it) upon any opinion which is not against the Catholique faith. Which faith wee beleeve *Leo* to have described well, when hee sayes, *That it is singular, and true, to which nothing can be added, nor detracted:* and we accept S. *Augustines* signification of the word *Catholique*; *wee interpret the name Catholique, by the Communion*
30 *with the whole world; which is so Essentiall & so truly deduced out of the Scriptures, that a man which will speake of another Church, then the Communion of all Nations, which is the name Catholique, is as much Anathematized, as if he denie, the Death and Resurrection of Christ.* And what is this *Essentiall* truth so evident out of *Scripture*, which
35 designes the *Catholique Church*? Because, sayes *Augustine*, the same

Ad Leo. Aug. Epist.97. in princi.
Epist.48. Cont. Rogat. et Donat.

4. *Catholiques Ed.*: *Catholiqus.* L-1, C-1   **24–25.** in which *Ed.*: which. L-1, C-1

Evangelicall truth which tells us the Death and Resurrection, tells us also, That Repentance, and Remission of sinnes shall be preached in his Name, through all Nations.

39 That therefore is *Catholique* faith, which hath beene alwayes and every where taught; and *Repentance*, and *Remission* of sinnes, by the *Death* and *Resurrection* of *Christ*, and such truthes as the *Gospell* teaches, are that *Doctrine*, which coagulates and gathers the Church into a body, and makes it *Catholique*; of which opinion *Bellarmine* himselfe is sometime, as when he argues thus, *whatsoever is Heresie, the contrarie thereof is veritas fidei*; for then it must be matter of faith, And an errour with pertinacie in those points onely, should bee called *Heresie*, in that heavie sense, which it hath in a Papists mouth.

40 *Castrensis* foresaw this Danger of *Recrimination*, and retorting upon themselves, this opprobrious name of *Heretique*, if they were so forward to impute it, in matters which belonged not to faith, for accordingly he sayes, *They amongst us, which doe so easily pronounce a thing to be Heresie, are often striken with their own arrow, & fall into the pit which they digged for others.* And certainly as the *Greeke* Church by using the same stifnesse and rigour towards the *Romane*, as the *Romane* uses towards the other *Westerne* Churches, (which is, not onely to justifie their opinions, but to pronounce the contrarie to be *Heresie*,) hath tamed the *Romane* writers so farre, as to confesse that they condemne nothing else in their opinion and practise of consecrating in a different bread, but that they impose it, as *a necessitie upon all other Churches*, and hath extorted a *Decretall* from Pope *Eugenius*, *That Priests in Consecrating* (not onely may) *but ought to follow, the custome of that Church where they are*, whether in leavened, or unleavened bread, and *Innocent* the third, required no more of them, in this point, but *that they would not shewe so much detestation of the Romane use therein, as to wash and expiate their Altars, after a Romane Priest had consecrated*, So if it should stand with the wisedome and charity of the *Reformed Church*, Juridically to call, all the Additions which the Romanes have made to the Catholique faith, and for which, wee are departed from them, *absolute and formall Heresie*, though perchance it would not make them

---

De Euchar. l.3. c.8. §. Ac primum

Adver. Heres. l.1. c.7

Bovosius

In 7º. Tit.1. c.2

Azor. To.2. l.4. c.15. §. Item eo

---

4. 39 That *new parag. Ed.*: 39 *in margin*, That *run-on.* L-1, C-1 15. forward *Ed.*: for ward. C-1, L-1 20. (which *Ed.*: which. L-1, C-1 21. Heresie,) *Ed.*: Heresie,. L-1, C-1

abandon their opinions, yet I thinke it would reduce them to a more humane and civill indifferencie, & to let us, without imposing their *traditions*, enjoy our own Religion, which is, of it self, in their confession, so free from *Heresie*, that they are forced to make this all our *Heresie*, that we will not admit theirs.

41 Yet some things have so necessary a consequence, and so immediate a dependance upon the Articles of faith, that a man may be bolde to call the contrary *Hereticall*, though no *Definition* of any Councell have pronounced it so; yea some *Notions* doe so precede the *Articles* of our faith, that the *Articles* may be said to depend upon them so farre, as they were frustrate, if those *prenotions* were not certaine. Of that sort is the *Immortality* of the soule, without which the worke of *redemption* were vaine. And therefore it had beene a vitious tendernesse, and irreligious modesty, if a man durst not have called it *Hereticall*, to say, that the soule was mortall, till *Leo* the tenth, in the *Laterane Councell* Decreed it to bee *Heresie*. For though *Bellarmine* in one place require it as *Essentiall* in an *Heresie*, That it have beene condemned in a *Councell of Bishoppes*, yet he says in another place, That the Popes alone without Councels, have condemned many Heresies.

In septimo. l.5.
Tit.3. c.8
De Euchar. l.3. c.8.
§. Ac primum

De Pont. l.4. c.3.
§. Alterum

42 And this liberty hath beene used as well by *Epiphanius*, and S. *Augustine* in the purer times, as by *Castrensis* and *Prateolus*, in the later *Romane* Church, and of late yeares (of those which adhere to *Calvins* Doctrine) by *Danaeus*, and of *Luthers* followers, by *Schlusselbergius*; all which in composing *Catalogues* of *Heretiques*, have mentioned divers, which as yet no generall Councel hath condemned. So did the *Emperours* in their constitutions pronounce against some *Heresies* of which no Councell had determined. So did the *Parliament* of *Paris* in their sentence against *Chastell* for the assassinate uppon the person of this King of France, pronounce certaine words, which he had sucked from the *Jesuits*, and uttered in derogation of Kings, to bee *Seditious, Scandalous, and Hereticall*.

12. *Immortality* C-2, C-3, C-4: *Immortal ty.* L-1, C-1, L-2, O¹⁴, YK-3 **Margin 15.** In septimo. *Ed.*: In septimo *note misplaced.* L-1, C-1 **Margin 16.** De Euchar. *Ed.*: *note misplaced.* L-1, C-1 **Margin 18.** De Pont. *Ed.*: *note misplaced.* L-1, C-1 **23.** Doctrine) *Ed.*: Doctrine,. L-1, C-1 **23–24.** *Schlusselbergius*] Schlussetbergius. MCG, Y, HD, C⁵-1, C⁵-2, O-2, C³-3

And if the Oath framed by order of the Councell of *Trent*, and ratified and enjoined by the Popes *Bull*, be to be given to all persons, then must many men sweare some things to be of the *Catholique faith*, and some other things to be *Hereticall*, in which he is so farre remooved from the knowledge of the things, that he doth not onely not understand the signification of the wordes, but is not able to sound, nor utter, nor spell them.

43 And hee must sweare many things determinately, and precisely, which even after that *Councell* some learned men still doubt, As, that *a license to heare confessions, in every Priest not beneficed, is so necessarie, necessitate Sacramenti, that except hee have such a license, the penitent, though never so contrite and particular in enumeration of his sinnes, and exact in satisfactions, and performing all penances, is utterly frustrate of any benefite by vertue of this Sacrament.* So therefore a certaine and naturall evidence of a morall truth, such as arises to every man, *That to a King is due perpetuall obedience*, is better authority to induce an assurance, and to produce an oath, that the contrary is *Hereticall*, then an implicite credite rashly given to a litigious Councell, not beleeved by all Catholiques, and not understood by al that sweare to beleeve it.

44 For the other obstacle and hinderance which retards them, from pronouncing that this position is *hereticall*, which is, *the Canon of the Laterane Councell*, enough hath beene said of the infirmity and invalidity of that Councell by others. Thus much I may be bolde to adde, that the *Emperour* under whome that Councell was held, never accepted it for a *Canon*, neither in those wordes, nor in that sense, as it is presented in the *Canon law*; from whence it is transplanted into the body of the *Councels*. And the Church was so farre from impugning the *Emperours* sense and acceptation thereof, that *Innocent* the fourth, and divers other Popes being to make use thereof, cite the *Constitution of the Emperour*, and not any *Canon of a Councell*, in their Directions to the *Inquisitors*, how to proceede against Heretiques. They therefore either knew no such Canon, or suspected and discredited it.

D'Alvin. de Pot. Epis. c.23. n.5. ex Suares

Ann. 1215. ca.3

Extra. de Heresi. c.13

Direct. Inqui. Lit. Apostol. pag.13, 27, 51

1. And *Ed*.: 42 And. L-1, C-1   3. some things *Ed*.: somethings. L-1, C-1 **Margin 29.** Direct. . . . Lit *Ed*.: Direct . . . lit L-1, C-1;. Direct . . . l t YK-2   **31.** and not *Ed*.: not. L-1, C-1

CHAPTER TWELVE 259

45   Thus therefore that pretended Canon sayes, *If a temporall Lord warned by the Church, do not purge his land of Heretiques, let him be excommunicate by the Metropolitane and Conprovinciall bishopps; if he satisfie not within a yeere, let it be signified to the Pope, that he may denounce his subjects to be absolved from their Alleageance, and expose his Land to Catholickes, which may without contradiction possesse it, the right of the principall Lord* (which we call Lord Paramount) *being reserved, if hee give no furtherance thereunto*. And thus farre without doubt the *Canon* did not include *Principall* and *Soveraigne Lords*, because it speakes of such, as had *Lords* above them. And where it concludes with this clause, *The same Law being to be observ'd toward them, Qui non habent Dominos principales*, The *Imperiall* Constitution hath it thus, *Qui non habent Domos principales*.

Cod. l.1. Tit.5. l.4. §. Si vero

46   And certainly the most naturall and proper acceptation of *Domos Principales* in this place, in the *Emperours* Lawe, is the same as the word, *Domicilium Principale*, hath in the *Canons*; which is a *Mans chiefe abiding and Residence*, though upon occasion he may be in another place, or have some relation and dependance upon a Prince out of that Territorie. And it may give us much clearenesse to the understanding of this Lawe, if wee compare with it, the great and solemne *Clementine Pastoralis*.

De Sent. & Re Iud.

47   For then *Robert* being King of *Sicily*, that is, such a *Principall Lord*, as this pretended *Canon* speakes of, but yet no *Soveraigne* (for he depended both upon the *Empire* and upon the *Church*) was condemned as a *Rebell* by the *Emperour Henrie* the seventh. And *Clement* the fift, annull'd and abrogated that *Sentence*, of the Emperours, upon this reason; That *though the King of Sicily held some Lands of the Empire, yet Domicilium suum fovebat in Sicilia*, which belong'd to the Church, and therefore the Emperors Jurisdiction could not extend to him, because he had not *Domicilium in Imperio*. Hereupon the *Glosse* enters into Disputation, how farre a man which hath goods in one *Dominion*, shall be subject to the Lawes of that place, though his *Principale Domicilium* (as he still cals it) be in another. So that it seemes the *Emperour* had

19.   give us *errata*: give as   L-1, C-1;.   g ve   C¹⁶, YK-1, YK-3   **Margin**
20.   Re Iud. *Ed*.: reiud.   L-1, C-1   **32.**   *Domicilium* L², C⁵-1, L-2, L¹⁵-2, L²², O⁵, D-2, C⁹, O⁷, YK-1, F, C¹⁶, C³] *Dominium*.   MCG, C²-3, L³, HD, Y, C⁵-2, C¹⁰, O-2

this purpose in this *Constitution*, that those *Domini Principales*, which were under the *Jurisdiction* and *Dependance* of the *Empire*, should indure the penaltie of this Law, if they transgressed it, though they had not there *Domos Principales* within the limits of the Empire. For at the time, when this *Constitution* was made, the Emperours thought it lawfull for them to doe so, though a hundred yeere after, *Clement* the fift, denied by this *Canon*, that they had so large a power. But this Constitution inferres nothing against *Soveraigne Lords*, whom the *Emperour* could not binde by any *Constitution* of his, because they had no dependance upon him.

48   And as the *Constitution* differs from the *Canon* in such materiall words as overthrowes that sense which they would extort out of it, which is, *That Soveraignes are included therein*, so doeth it in the sense, and in the appointing of the *Officer*, who shall expel these favourers of *heretiques*. For where the *Canon* says, *Let it be tolde to the Pope, who may absolve the Subjects, and expose the land*, the *Emperour* speakes of himselfe, *we do expose the land*. So that he takes the authority out of the Popes hand; which he would not have done, nor the Pope have cited as to his advantage, that lawe by which it was done, if either *Iure Divino* such a power had resided in him, or a *Canon* of a generall Councell had so freshly invested him therewith.

49   And as it is neither likely that the *Emperour* would include himselfe in this law, nor possible that he should include others as *Soveraine* as himselfe, at least: so doth it appeare, by the *Ordinary Glosse* upon that constitution (which hath more authority, then all other *Expositors*) that that law is made against such Lords and Subjects, as have relation to one another by feudall law; for so it interpretes *Dominum temporalem*, and *Dominum principalem* to be, *when some Earle holdes something of a King; which King also must have a dependency upon the Empire*, because otherwise the *Imperiall* law could not extend to him. And yet even against those *principal Lords*, the law seemes so severe, that the Glosse sayes, *Non legitur in Scholis*. So that so many proofes having beene formerly produced, *That this Councell made no Canons*, but that those which are usually offered now, are but ragges torne out of one booke, and put into another, out of the *Extravagants* into the *Councels*, and this *Imperiall* constitution, which to the Pope himselfe seemed of more force, then his Predecessors *Decretall*, neither

concerning *Soveraine Lords*, nor acknowledging this power of absolving Subjects, to be in the Pope, but in himselfe, no sufficient reason arises out of this imaginary Canon, which should make a man affraid to call that *Hereticall*, which is against his naturall reason, and against that
5 maine part of *Religion*, which is, civill obedience.

50   For the *Romans* dealing more severely, and more injuriously with us, then the *Greeke* Church did with them, when they presented to the *Emperour*, upon a commission to make an Inquisition to that purpose, 99. *errours and deviations in matter of faith, in the Romane Church*: of
10 which some were *Orthodoxall* truths, some, no matter of faith, but circumstantiall indifferencies, though they called them all errours in faith; the *Romane* Church, I say, traducing our doctrine, with as much intemperance and sower language, gives us example to call all their errours *Hereticall*. And so, when *Drusius* in his owne defence against a *Jesuite*
15 who had called him Heretique, says, That *Heresie must be in fundamentis fidei*; the *Jesuite* replies, that *even that assertion of Drusius is Heresie*.

51   And this doctrine and position, which this Oath condemnes, will lacke nothing of *formall and absolute Heresie*, if those notes bee true,
20 by which *Bellarmine* designes *Heresie*, and sayes, *that if that be not Heresie to which those Notes agree, there is no heresie in the world*. For, (as he requires to constitute an *heresie*) we can note the *Author*, to have beene *Gregory* the seventh; the *place* to have been *Rome*, the *time* betweene five and 600 yeares past, And that *it began with a few*
25 *followers*, for [a]*sometimes but fifteene, sometimes but thirteene Bishops adherd to Gregory, when even the Bishops of Italy favoured the other part*: And that *it appeared with the admiration of the faithfull*; for so it is noted to have beene, *Novium scisma*: And that contradiction and *opposition was made* by all the *Imperiall Clergy*, and much of *Italy* it
30 selfe. And, for that which is the last note proposed by *Bellarmine*, *that it bee condemned by a Councell of Bishops, and all faithfull people*, though that have not yet beene done, because God for our sinnes, hath punished us with a Dearth of Councels, and suffered us in a hunger, and rage of glory, and false constancie, to eate and gnaw upon one another,
35 with malignant disputations, and reproachfull virulencies, yet when his

Azor. par.2. l.4. c.15. §. Item eo

Serar. Trihae. l.3. c.20

De Euchar. l.3. c.8. §. Ac primum

[a]Vercellus. De Unitat. Eccles. conserv.

Margin 25a. conserv *Ed.*: c[?]nserv.   L-1, C-1   **26.** *Gregory, Ed.*: Gregory,).   L-1, C-1

gracious pleasure shall affoord the Church, that reliefe, wee doe justly hope it will have that condemnation, and so be a *consummate heresie*, because no *Pseudo-Councels* as yet have beene able to establish the contrarie.

52 And though these markes and certaine notes of *Heresie* be tyrannically, and cautelously put by *Bellarmine* (because it is easie to name manie *Heresies*, in which many of these markes are wanting, of which wee know neither Parents, Country, nor age, and which insinuated themselves, and got deepe roote in the Church, before they made any noise or trouble in the state thereof, and at the first breaking out, were countenanced with many and mighty favourers, and which no generall Councell hath yet condemned) yet, as I said, we refuse not these marks, but submit this opinion, to that triall, whether it be properly *Hereticall*, or no. For it will as well abide this triall, as an other, proposed long before by S. *Augustine*, *That hee is an Heretique, which for any Temporall advantage, and advancement of his Supremacie, doth either beget, or follow false and new opinions*, Which seemes directly spoken of this Temporall Supremacie: to which also, S. *Paul* may justly bee thought to have had some relation, when he reckons *Heresie, amongst the workes of the flesh and worldly matters.*

53 But leaving this exact and subtill appellation of *Heresie*, let him whom that scruple deterrs from the oath, *That hee must sweare the doctrine to be Hereticall*, consider in what sense our law understands the word in that place.

54 The *Imperiall* Law layes an imputation upon that man, *Qui Saeva verborum praerogativa fraudulenter contra Iuris sententiam abutitur*; that *he is as guilty as he, which breakes the law.* For hee which picks a quarrell with a law, by pretence of an ambiguous word, declares that hee would faine escape the obligation thereof. But, saith the same law, *A Law-maker hath done enough, when he hath forbidden that which he would not have to be done; the rest must bee gathered out of the purpose of the law, as if it had beene exprest.* And no man can doubt, but that the law-maker in this law, hath forbidden *Defection* from the Prince; and the purpose of the law, was to provide onely against that. Out of

Marginal notes: 14.q.31. Haeretic. ex Lib. de Util. Credendi; Gal. 5.19, 20; Cod. l.1. Tit.14. le.5; Ibid.

Margin 15. 14.q.31. *Ed*: 24.q.3. C-1, L-1 **Margin 18.** 19, 20 *Ed*.: 20. L-1, C-1 **Margin 25.** Tit.14 *Ed*.: tit.1. C-1, L-1

which purpose no man can justly collect, that the Deponent should pronounce the contrarie Doctrine, so *Hereticall*, as that he which held it, or relapsed into it, might be burnt; but that it was apparently *erroneus*, and *impious*, and *fit to bee abjured*; And how little *erroneous* lackes of 5 *Hereticall*, and wherein they differ, *Divines are not agreed*, sayes your *Simancha*, and it is yet undetermined.

Enchirid. Iud. Tit.24. n.20

55 Nor is there required in this *Deponent*, such an assurance in Faith, as belongs to the making of an Article, *Formall Heresie*, but such an assurance in Morall reason, and Humane discourse, as *Bartholus* 10 requires in him which takes an Oath, when he sayes, *He which sweares the trueth of any thing, understands not his Oath to be of such a trueth, as is subject to sense, Sed iurat de vehementi opinione*.

In Dig. l.39. de Dam. Infe. le.13. nu.14

56 And the word *Hereticall* in this Oath, hath so much force, as the word to *Anathematize*, hath in many *Councels*. As, for example, 15 in that place of the Councell of *Constantinople*, where it is said, *Let him be Anathematiz'd, which doeth not Anathematize Origen*. Which is meant of a detestation and abhorring som of his opinions, not of pronouncing him, a formall and consummate Hereticke. For you may well allow a *Civill* and convenient sense to this word, in this Oath, that 20 it meanes onely *Impious*, and *inducing of Heresie*, since you have bound all the world upon paine of *Damnation* to beleeve, *That S. Paul call'd* Concupiscence *sinne, not because it was sinne, but because it proceeded from sinne, and induced to sinne*.

Ca.11

Conc. Trid. Sess.5. de Peccat. Orig.

57 A great *Casuist*, and our *Countreyman*, delivers safe Rules which 25 may undeceive them in these suspicions, if they will not be extremely negligent; and *Negligentia dissoluta Dolus est*. For thus hee sayes, *Though a law should provide expresly, that the words of the law should bee understood as they lie, yet they must receive their interpretation from the common use of speach; which is, that which the most part in that* 30 *Country doe use. And if both significations may be found in common use, that must be followed, which out of likelihood and reason, seemes to have beene the meaning of the lawmaker, though it be improper: And his meaning appeares, when the word taken in the other sense, would create some absurd, or unjust matter. And as amongst us, those with*

Sayr. Thes. Cas. Consc. l.3. c.8. n.6 & 7

Margin 3. Enchirid. Iud *Ed*.: Enchird. Ind.   C-1, L-1   **Margin 9.** 14 *Ed*.: 18.   C-1, L-1   **Margin 20.** 5 *Ed*.: 4.   C-1, L-1

whom this word *Hereticall* is in most use, which are *Divines*, use the word promiscuously, and indifferently, against all *impious* opinions: so especially did the Lawmaker at this time use it, because otherwise, it had beene both *absurd*, to decree a point to be properly *hereticall*, which was not brought into debatement, as matter of faith, and it had beene *unjust*, under colour of requiring civill obedience, to have drawn the deponent, to such a confession, as if he had relapsed and fallen from it, after hee might have beene burned.

58 And the words of the oath agree precisely to *Sayrs* rule; for the deponent must sweare, *according to the expresse wordes, and the plaine and common sense, and understanding of the same.* And *Sayr* says, *That if we must sweare to a Law, according to the proper signification of the words, then there is no place for such discretion, and for admitting a divers sense*: but the wordes of our Oath, which are, *According to the plaine, and common sense*, fall directly within his first Rule.

59 And the law hath good warrant and precedent to assume the word, *hereticall*, in such a moderate signification; for so the *Scriptures* use the word, when S. *Paul* says, *oportet hereses esse*, which *Gretzer* confesses, when to excuse the *vulgate Edition*, which hath in that place, left out the wordes, *In Vobis*; he sayes, *It would do no harme to their cause to admit those wordes, because it is not spoken, De haeresi propriè dicta*.

I Cor. 11.19

Defensio. Bell. l.2. c.14

60 And so the generall Councell of *Constantinople* within the first foure hundred yeares, calles some *Heretiques*, though they be not *Anathematized* by the Church, *because they make Conventicles against bishopps, and accuse them unorderly, and against the forme of Canons*. So also doth another Councell say of *Simony*, that it is not onely *Sacrilegious*, but *hereticall*.

Can.6

Turon. 2. ca.ult.

And accordingly to these, a late Pope, *Leo* 10., in a formall *Decree* and *Bull*, uses the worde in a like sense. For he condemnes the Articles imputed to *Luther, Tanquam respective haereticos, because out of some of them it would follow, that the Church had erred*. But that proposition, out of which the next deducted Conclusion, might bee Heresie, is not it selfe necessarily Heresie, properly understood.

Binius. To.4. fo.654

7–8. it, after *Ed*.: it after,. L-1, C-1   **29.** 10., *Ed*.: 10.. L-1, C-1

CHAPTER TWELVE 265

61   And as these do, so also doe the *Canons* in the law, speake in a moderate phrase: For in one place, wher the text says, that a thing is done, *Contra fidem Catholicam*, the Glosse explicates it, *Contra bonos Mores*: and in another place, it interprets the same wordes so, because
5 it dooth *Sapere heresim*; and yet it is not *heresie*: and so we finde a late *Decretall*, to call Simony, *True and undoubted heresy*; where *Gregory* is produced, to give this reason why *Simony* is called *heresy*, because *whosoever is ordained by Simony, is therfore ordained that he may be an heretique*. So that we see, such acts as beget or accompany *heresy*, are
10 called *heresy* in this milde acceptation, which our law gives it.

Dist.12. consuetudinem. ver. fidem

De Consecrat. Dist.4. Si non. ver. catholicum

In septimo. Tit.3. c.1

62   From which sense the *Fathers* did not abstaine in using that worde; for *Tertullian* sayes, *That no man will doubt to call Adams transgression heresie, since by his owne election, he adhered rather to his owne will, then to Gods*. And in another booke he sayes, *Not so much newnes,*
15 *as truth doth convict things to be heresies, for whatsoever tastes against truth, is an heresie, though it be an ancient custome*. And so sayes S. *August*. (if their owne men cite him truely) That Schisme is called Heresie, *not that it is heresie, but that it disposes to heresie*.

L.2. Adver. Marci. c.2

De Veland. Virg. c.1

Alf. Castr. Adv. Her. l.1. c.9

63   And the *Jesuits* themselves, who are the preciseest and severest
20 accepters of this word, come thus neere, *That some things tolerated by the Church, though they be not propriè haeretica, yet they are haeresi proxima*. For so sayes *Bellarmine*; and hee might justly make this position which wee speake of, his example. And his defender *Gretzer* sayes, that *some opinions are so framed, that though no Decree of the Church have*
25 *yet condemned them, yet they are enormous, Scandalous, and haeresi proximae*.

De Pont. l.4. c.2. §. Ex his Append. ad Lib.1. Bell. §. Haec

64   And thus also do the *Schoolemen* somtimes take it; For so, sayes *Aquinas* out of S. *Jerome*, that *he which expounds the Scriptures against the sense of the holy Ghost may be called an heretique, though he depart*
30 *not from the Church*. And so have divers compilers of the Ecclesiastique history done; for *Epiphanius* reckons divers sects of the *Jewes* and *Gentile* Philosophers, amongst *Heretiques*. And *Bernardus de Lucemburgo*

2.2.ae.q.11. ar.2. Ad.2

De Haeresib.
Alf. Castr. Adv. Heres. l.1. c.9

Margin 2. 12 *Ed*.: 11.   C-1, L-1   **Margin 17.** Her *Ed*.: Ham.   L-1, C-1
Margin 22. Pont. . . . 2 *Ed*.: pont. . . . 5. L-1, C-1   **Margin 23.** Haec *Ed*.: Interim.   L-1, C-1   **Margin 28.** 2.2.ae.q.11 *Ed*: 22.ae.q.II.   C-1, L-1
31–32. [Gen]tile] -tiles catchword quarto p.388.

inserts into his Catalogue of *heretiques*, *Averros* and *Avicen*, though they were not *Christians*. And lastly that the word was vulgarly so used, as by many other observations, so is it evident by a Story in [a]*Math. Paris*, where one upon his death-bed cals the Friers *heretiques for not reprehending the Prelates*, & the Prelates *heretiques, for conferring Benefices upon unworthy persons*: yea, in this very case, which we have in hand [b]an authour, of your owne Religion, pronounces thus of those fifteene Bishops, which adhered to *Gregory* the sevenths party, against the Emperor, *It is great heresie to resist the Ordinance of God, who onely hath power to give Empire, which heresie it appears that those fifteene false Bishops have committed.*

[a]Catalog. Test. ex Mat. Paris. Anno 1253

[b]Vercell. de Unitat. Eccles.

65 As therefore all sorts of men, into whose mouthes upon any occasion this word was like to come, have used the word for *Erroneous*: and *Impious*, and *Corrupting* good manners, and disposing & preparing absolute and proper Heresie, so doth the law accept it in this oath, where it makes it equivalent, and Synonimous, to the wordes which are joined with it, which are *Impious* and *Damnable*: and therefore it is but a Calumny cast upon the law, and a tergiversation picked out for their escape, if any pretend for that word, to decline the Oath.

66 But if this word in this place, were to be understood in the strictest and severest sense, that a *Jesuite* could use it against us, yet hee that shall take the Oath, doth not thereby pronounce, *that any Position, which attributes any power to the Pope, is hereticall*. Nor, that hee may excommunicate a King; no, nor that he may deprive him: but it is thus conceived, *That this position is hereticall, That Princes which be excommunicate, or deprived by the Pope, may be deposed or murdred by their subjects or any other.* So that it cast no Manicles upon the Popes hands; if he will *excommunicate*, let him; if he will *deprive*, let him. Onely them, who by his act, (of the goodnes or badnes whereof this Proposition pronounces nothing) may be mis-led to an unchristian & undutifull desperatenes, it forewarnes, and advises, to a due and just consideration of such proceedings. For, as when men were content to heare *heresies*, *Leo* said wisely, in reprehension of that easinesse, *They which can hearken to such things, can beleeve them*, So since it is too

Epist.39. Turibio. in fine

Margin 3a. [a]*Catalog Ed.*: catalog. C-1, L-1 **3.** [a]*Math Ed.*: Math. L-1, C-1 **6.** yea, *Ed.*: yea. L-1, C-1

late to forbid hearing of this *heresie*, of deposing Princes, since out of *Jesuites* bookes, which speak of state-learning, scarce any thing is to be sucked, but it, or such preparatives, as worke and conduce to it, it was necessary to begin a step higher then *Leo* did, and pronounce it
5 *hereticall*, that so none might beleeve it, since hee that can beleeve it, can be content to affoord his helpe to the doing thereof.

67 And having thus gone as far as I purposed in both parts of this Chapter, in the first whereof I shewed, that in speciall cases *new oathes* were necessary, and that the forme of them ought to bee such, as might
10 reach home to the *intent* thereof, and not be eluded, which had beene, if any part of this oath had been omitted; and that their writers, which never teach, that upon a Bishops excommunication a Prince may be deposed, denie implicitly this power in the Pope, because onely that power which was in the Bishops, in this matter, is transferd by Reser-
15 vation into the Pope; and that where such Depositions are needefull, the state is provided naturally with a temporall power to effect it, and therefore it is not necessarie to place it in the spirituall, which were monstrous and unperfect, if it should produce, as the most excelent issue therof, a power so base in their estimation; And that this possibility
20 of being Deposed, is as contrary to *Soverainety*, as a certaine limitation, when he shall be removed; And that those writers, which limit the Popes power by *Naturall Reason*, and which teach, that in doubts of speculation, we may for all that proceede to practise, as farre, as wee doe in this Oath; And having in the second part declared, That though
25 the *Papists* make proper, and absolute *Heresie*, to be without matter of faith, yet we doe not so, and yet in points necessarily and immediately issuing out of these principles, a generall Councell needs not be attended to informe a mans understanding what is *Hereticall*, because the *Emperors* and other Princes, and divers *Authors*, and registers of
30 *heresies*, have pronounced therin before any Decision of Councells; and that the Canon which is obtruded, in the name of the *Laterane Councell*, for divers reasons, cannot impeach this proposition, *That the Doctrine is hereticall*, which proposition, though if it were tried by *Bellarmine*,

11. omitted; *Ed.*: omitted,. L-1, C-1 **15.** Pope; *Ed.*: Pope,. L-1, C-1
19. estimation; *Ed.*: estimation,. L-1, C-1 **21.** removed; *Ed.*: removed,.
L-1, C-1 **24.** Oath; *Ed.*: Oath,. L-1, C-1 **30.** Councells; *Ed.*: Councells,.
L-1, C-1

and by Saint *Augustines* description of heresie, it would appeare absolutely *hereticall*; yet this law gives it that name in a vulgar and common sense, as *Scriptures, Councels, Buls of Popes, Fathers, Schoolemen, Historians, Jesuits*, and the *Common* sort hath used and accepted it; and that if it be taken in the sharpest sense, the Oath may neverthelesse be taken without prejudice, or limitation of any power which the Pope himselfe claimes; I make account that I have discharged my promise and undertaking in this Chapter, and delivered as much as, without inculcating that which hath beene formerly said by others (which I purposely avoided) in this point of the oath, neede to be said to any, of indifferency or equall inclination.

FINIS.

---

2. hereticall; YK-2: hereticall,. L-1, C-1 **4.** it; YK-2: it,. L-1, C-1 **7.** claimes; YK-2: claimes,. L-1, C-1 **8.** much as, *Ed.*: much, as. L-1, C-1 **9.** others *Ed.*: others,. L-1, C-1 **10.** oath, *Ed.*: oath. L-1, C-1

COMMENTARY

Preface
Page 3.

7   *Press'd men, and voluntaries*:   Conscripted soldiers and volunteer military.

15–16   *your Books . . . Kingdome*:   *Triplici Nodo, triplex cuneus*, London, 1607, followed by the English translations in 1607 and 1609.

Page 7.

4   *cautelously*:   deceitfully or artfully.

10–11   *to there Conscience*:   See Commentary for p. 226, l. 1.

20   *Indult*:   A special privilege granted by the authority of the Pope which is otherwise denied by the common law of the Roman Catholic Church.

Page 9.

14–26   *Sir Edward Coke . . . his Lordships Booke*:   Sir Edward Coke (b. Mileham, Norfolk, 1552; d. Stoke Pogis, 1634) was named Chief Justice of the Common Pleas (the position to which Donne alludes) in 1606. As an outstanding legal figure of James' reign, he undertook one of the most famous works of English common law writings, his *Reports* of current cases in English courts. The reports recorded in a detailed explanatory fashion, suitable for use in the education of lawyers, the cases heard during the period he presided over the king's bench. In the preface to the *Fift Part of the Reports* (London, 1607 [1606]), entitled "Of the Kings Ecclesiasticall Law," Coke attempted, by an introduction and by the survey of the reign of each English monarch since Edward the Confessor, to prove that the English crown and Parliament constituted a spiritual jurisdiction as well as a secular authority, independent of Rome, from their very origin. It is this preface to which Donne is referring as "his Lordships" book. As Donne notes, the Catholic side immediately took up the attack against Coke's preface. The chief Roman apologist, whom Donne calls "ordinary instrument" of the devil, was the Jesuit Robert Parsons in *An Answere to the Fifth Part of Reports* (Saint Omer, 1606), to which Donne referred later in his own preface (p. 17).

26   *inconculcated*:   to inculcate repeatedly.

Page 11.

9–26   *For since Cassander . . . in the Fathers*:   "PR" were the priest Robert Parsons' pseudonymous initials on the title page of *Treatise Tending to Mitigation towards Catholicke-Subjectes in England* [Saint Omer?] 1606. The work was an answer to the Anglican Archbishop Thomas Morton's *A Discovery of Romish Doctrine* (London, 1605) that cited the call of the Catholic Cassander of Bruges to the Emperors Maximilian and Ferdinand to reconcile Catholics and Protestants (hence

Donne's reference to Cassander). For his suggestion, Cassander was attacked by Bellarmine, and his writings were put on the Catholic *Index*. As Morton had argued that Catholic intransigence made tolerating them difficult, Parsons retorted that Calvinist writings regularly recommended the regicide of Catholics and cited the *Vindiciae contra Tyrannos* (1579) (which Donne mentions by title) of the French Protestant François Hottoman, as an example (I, 11, p. 39; V, 30, p. 164). Parsons attacks Cassander as a "grammarian" who knew little theology and should have kept to rhetoric (VI, 67, p. 239), while Donne, quoting the attacks, then argues that Hottoman's *Vindicae* supported the rule of court judgements rather than regicide to remove kings from their thrones. Parsons and Donne argue on the assumption of their contemporaries that Hottoman, who was the author of *Francogallia* (1573), a tract on state liberty in primitive pre-Roman France, was also the author of *Vindiciae*. However, in recent centuries, its author has been taken to be another French Protestant, Philippe du Plessis de Mornay, and, lately, their fellow Calvinist Johan Junius de Jonge (D. Visser, "Junius, the Author of the *Vindiciae contra Tyrannos*," *Tijdschrift voor Geschiedenis*, LXXXIV, 1971, pp. 510–511), the latter of whom wrote under the pen name of Stephanus Junius Brutus. The Cajetan involved in both Parsons' and the German Gretser's works was the Italian Dominican and cardinal, Tommasso de Via Gaetani (b. Gaeta, 1469; d. Rome, 1534), an expert — as Donne says — in Thomism, who is referred to several times in *Pseudo-Martyr*, and he must not be confused with Saint Cajetan, the founder of the Theatines also mentioned often, who was his contemporary. For the Emperor Maximilian, see Commentary for p. 45, l. 32–p. 46, l. 6.

26–30 *though in that . . . Erasmizando*: In Volume I, *Controversiam Roberto Bellarmine . . . Defensio . . . Tomus Primus de Verbo Dei. Adversus Witackerum*, Book I, Appendix 1, Col. 358 (Ingolstadt, 1607); and Volume II, *Tomus Secundus . . . . adversus Iunium; Danaeum, Sibrandum* (Ingolstadt, 1609), by the German Jesuit controversialist theologian, James Gretser (b. Marckdorf, 1562; d. Ingolstadt, 1625). The first volume, which Donne principally uses, is largely devoted to attacking the English divine, controversialist and Master of Saint John's College, Cambridge, William Whitaker (b. Burnley, Lancashire, 1548; d. Cambridge, 1595). Whitaker wrote a number of tracts against Bellarmine in *Disputatio de Sacra Scriptura . . . imprimis Robertum Bellarminum* (Cambridge, 1588), and the posthumously published *Pralectiones in quibus tractatur controversia de ecclesia contra pontificios, imprimis Robertum Bellarminum* (Cambridge, 1599), among others. In turn, Donne is taking up Whitaker's defence against Gretser, and his marginal note identifies the passage in Gretser by the opening words of its paragraph "Idem dictum." Donne employs the practice of identifying the sources of his citations by the first words of a paragraph regularly, though not exclusively, in *Pseudo-Martyr*. The second reference to Gretser's *Controversiam* is to Volume I, Book I, 7, Col. 93, "Quare inanem operam capit haereticus, cum nobis Caietanum opponit . . . . ipso étiam S. Hieronymo iubente et lubente," and the third again to Volume I, Book II, 14, Col. 718, "Quod Whittackerus obiicit, Caietanum negasse." By playing on words with the

Latin gerundives of "Hebraizando" and "Erasmizando," Donne attacks Gretser for criticizing the Catholic Cajetan (*Controversiam*, Volume I, Book I, Appendix I, Col. 359). Cajetan upheld Erasmus' interpretation of Hebrews which Protestants generally accepted but which many Catholics found dangerously Protestant.

30–4 (p. 12) *Since, when . . . upon me*: "Tractatus De Novis Haereticorum Translationibus Biblicis," a tract on new heretical translations of the Bible, added separately but as a sequence to Book II (entitled "De variis librorum Canonicorum editionibus") of Gretser's *Controversiam Roberto Bellarmini*, Vol. I, Col. 946. Donne cites the tract to show that certain Catholic arguments support the Protestant position on Biblical exegesis and style, and that these are officially condemned by Rome for their Protestant leanings. Donne's next reference is to Bellarmine's refutation of the Catholic Driedo's interpretation of Daniel, and to his description of Erasmus as "semichristianus" in Chapter 9 ("De quibusquam Capitibus Danielis") of Book I of the first general controversy "De Verbo Dei" in Volume I (Ingolstadt, 1590), Col. 34 of *De Controversiis*. The Belgian scholar, John Dridoens, or Ioannes Driedo (b. Tornhout, Brabant, n.d.; d. Louvain, 1555), author of *De Ecclesiasticis Scripturis et dogmatibus libri IV . . . Coloniae* (1543), and of *De Libertate Christiana libri tres* (Louvain, 1548), is one of Bellarmine's Catholic opponents in several of his works, including the "De Verbo Dei" and the *Responsio ad Duos Libros . . . Moguntiae*, 1606, pp. 40–41, a work to which Donne refers later in *Pseudo-Martyr* (p. 170). Bellarmine's "De Verbo Dei" was his very first controversy, "Controversia Prima," in his monumental collection of tracts against the reformers. The collection was published under the title of *Disputationes Roberto Bellarmini Politiani, Societatis Iesu, De Controversiis Christianae Fidei, adversus huius temporis haereticos*, in three volumes in Ingolstadt between 1590 and 1593.

Page 14.

9–10 *Vitruvius . . . Churches*: The first-century Roman architect and military engineer Vitruvius Polio, builder of a basilica at Fanum and author of *De Architectura . . . multis aedificiorum, Horologiorum, et Machinarum Descriptionibus* (Venice, 1567), which was one of the many available Renaissance editions.

32–34 *by Baronius . . . some scandall thereby*: *Annales Ecclesiastici auctori . . . Soxano ex congregatoratii S.R.E. Presbytero Card. Tit. SS.Nerei et Achillei*, 12 Tomes, published in 7 Vols., Cologne, 1601–1608, by the Italian Cardinal Caesar Baronius (b. Sora, Naples, 1538; d. Rome, 1607), who is one of Donne's principal adversaries in *Pseudo-Martyr*. Baronius' *Annales* purported to be a whole history of the Roman Church from the time of Christ, chronologically, through the history of practically every year of the reign of every pope. Donne's reference to *Annales* here appears to be a general one to the scandal of secular jurisdiction over the Church, supposedly caused by the control over ecclesiastical authority that Pope Urban II gave to the secular Count Roger of Sicily in 1099. Whether or not Urban did give such power to Sicily was a burning issue in late sixteenth- and early seventeenth-century Italian and Spanish circles; and, Baronius deals with the events of 1097–1099 in *Annales*, Vol. VI, Tome 11, for the year 1097, Col. 883, No. 21, and Col. 885, Nos. 28 and 29, to which Donne is referring here. Baronius was a follower of Saint Philip Neri, the founder of the Oratory. He succeeded Saint Philip as head of the order, and he was intimately connected with the struggles between the papacy and the Kingdom of Sicily and Naples because of his origins in Naples and of his support, nevertheless, for the papacy. Donne is turning Baronius' complaint about the hold of secular princes on temporal power against him. He offers it as proof that princes everywhere have been throwing off papal power.

Page 15.

1–4 *That the Cardinals . . . injure them*: In Baronius' *Responsio Apologetica Adversus Cardinalis Columnae iudicium de Siciliae Monarchia*, No. 31, pp. 221–222, with a new edition of *Tractatus de Monarchia Siciliae* in Paris 1609. The "Monarchia Sicilia" was an ecclesiastical tribunal controlled by Sicily's secular ruler who created each new council and named all its clerical members. Through this tribunal, Philip II of Spain and his son Philip III, who ruled over Sicily and Naples, also controlled the Church. In support of papal claims to regain control of the Church in Italy, Baronius wrote his *Monarchia Siciliana*. However, as the issue of these papal claims was not clear cut among Catholics themselves, another cardinal, Ascanius Colonna (b. c.1560; d. 1605), writing in behalf of Spanish power, answered Baronius with *De Monarchia Sicilia*, and Baronius subsequently answered with his *Responsio Apologetica Adversus Cardinalis Columnae*, which Donne is paraphrasing here. Cardinal Colonna was the only critic of his defence of the papacy whom Baronius answered in writing (Cyriac K. Pullabilly, *Caesar Baronius, Counter-Reformation Historian*, Notre Dame, Ind., 1975, p. 108). Donne used both Baronius' *Annales* and *Responsio* to show that the question of the position of papal power among Catholic princes is not clear either to Catholic cardinals or the Princes themselves.

9 *seposed*: set apart or reserved.

11–18 *lawes Parsons . . . for that purpose*: In Chapter 5 of his *Treatise of Mitigation* (1607), No. 41, p. 172, Parsons defends the pope's secular power and he mentions "the foresaid Authors Carerius, Bozius, Bellarmine, Sanders," and later "Penia, Baronius, Bovius, Eugenius, Nardus & others" as having supported the pope's claims against Venice. Donne's second reference is to the Swiss-born career diplomat Jacques Davy Duperron (b. Berne, 1556; d. Paris, 1618), a Calvinist converted to Catholicism about 1578, who later entered orders and became a firm friend of both Henry III and, after his assassination in 1589, of Henry IV of France. Duperron was Henry IV's chargé d'affaires in Rome and was created cardinal there in 1604. With Cardinal François de Joyeuse (b. 1562; d. 1615), Duperron was charged by the French king to negotiate the reconciliation between the state of Venice and the papacy (hence Donne's reference). Paul V sent de Joyeuse to Venice with a list of conditions for lifting the excommunication against the city, and de Joyeuse reported back with the Venetian answer, as a result of which Duperron wrote to Henry his extraordinary letter of 5 April 1607, describing, in human as well as diplomatic detail, the meeting between de Joyeuse and the Pope. Not the least of the Venetian demands, as Donne reminds Parsons, was that the Jesuits continue to be banished from their state. Duperron's letter also states that the earlier pope Clement VII's cause against Henry VIII of England, and Leo X's cause against German Protestants, were just, but perhaps delivered in a fashion to provoke the division rather than the reunification of Christianity. Duperron's letter coming as it did from a Protestant turned Catholic, was immediately held to be of profound historical importance and was published in three languages in the volume of mainly political and diplomatic addresses to kings entitled *Monita Politica* (Frankfurt, 1609, pp. 155, 158), on how to deal with the immense power of the Roman Curia, and it circulated widely throughout Europe (see Introduction, p. xxvi). Donne cites the letter to show that Paul V was kinder to the Venetians than Parsons and his authorities in *Treatise of Mitigation* are to the English. His citation, moreover, is made as well in the larger context of Duperron's already existing reputation in England. With de Joyeuse, Duperron had negotiated the conversions of both Henry III and Henry IV to Catholicism, and he had also delivered in Paris in 1587 a spectacular oration on the occasion of the death of Mary Stuart. His *Réplique à la Réponse du Roy de la grande Bretagne*, answering James I's defence of his throne, was published later, in 1620, two years after his death.

18–31 *to looke so farre backe . . . Kings in their duetie*: In the first of Donne's three examples of how temporal states attempted to reconcile themselves with papal power, Nicolo Machiavelli (b. Florence, 1469; d. 1527) recounts in his *Historie di . . . Cittadino et Secretario Fiorentino* the story of his exile from Florence in 1512 (Donne is referring his reader to the edition of 1587 published at Piacenza in North-central Italy, pp. 34–35). Machiavelli was compelled to leave Florence because he supported its government, and this government inadvertently fell with the defeat of the French who had kept it in power. The second example is that of Henry II of England (b. 1133; d. 1189), who established his Assizes to contain the power of his Barons, particularly in the North, but who also passed, with only partial success, the Constitutions of Clarendon that were meant to restrain the clergy's freedom to act outside of the jurisdiction of royal courts. The third example is that of Cardinal Colonna, courtier to the viceroy of the king of Aragon, who defended Philip III of Spain's rights over the Kingdom of Naples and Sicily in his tract against Baronius' pro-papal *De Monarchia Siciliae*. Colonna's tract was published as an appendix to Baronius' *De Monarchia*, p. 158, in the Paris edition of 1609 to which Donne's note refers his reader (see Commentary for p. 15, ll. 1–4 and p. 17, ll. 18–28).

Page 16.

9–11 *That many . . . immunities of the Clergie*: Giovanni Antonio Bovio (d. Molfetta, 1622), in his *Risposta Alla Considerationi del Padre Maestro Paolo* *de Venetia, Sopra le Censure della Santita di Papa Paolo Quinto Contra la Republica di Venetia*, published originally in Rome and Bologna in 1606, and republished in 1607 in the large, extraordinary collection of documents, tracts and letters, *Raccolta degli Scritti*, on the quarrel between Paul V and the Venetian Republic (see Introduction, p. xxvi). Bovio's *Risposta* defended Paul V's excommunication of the Venetians against the attack by the Venetian Fra Paolo Sarpi of the order of Servius in a tract entitled *Apologia per le Oppositioni Fatte Dall'Illustrisimo Signor Cardinale Bellarmino* (Venice, 1606). Bovio's work was therefore part of a quarrel among Italian Catholics themselves about the justice of the Venetian excommunication, and Donne is evidently drawing parallels between the Venetians and the condition of English Catholics to attempt to convince them to take the Oath of Allegiance. The rapidity of Bovio's reply to Sarpi bespoke the danger of his document to the papal cause. In 1607, Sarpi's work was translated into English and published in London under the title of *An Apology . . . . made by Father Paule a Venetian . . . . unto the Exceptions of Cardinall Bellarmine against the Treatises of John Gerson against certain Treatises concerning the force and validitie of Excommunication*, so that by 1610 the whole argument was familiar to Donne's English readers. Bovio was defending the pope against Sarpi; Sarpi was defending the Venetians against Bellarmine; Bellarmine was defending the pope against the French Protestant John Gerson; and Donne is defending James I by citing Bovio's "tale immunita non sia de iure divino" on p. 50 of *Risposta* in *Raccolta*. Donne's marginal notation to this passage as being on p. 196 suggests that he confused its pagination with that of his later note to *Raccolta* (p. 86).

18-6 (p. 17) *And for the Sword-men . . . expresses that Kings jealousies*: Donne uses the word "sword-men" as a general term referring to the military, and he mentions two incidents of military encounters, the first between the Spanish emperor Charles V (b. Ghent, 1500; d. Yaste, 1558) and Pope Clement VII, pope from 1523 to 1534, and the second between Charles, son of Philip II and Pope Paul IV, to describe the ferocious opposition of secular rulers to the pope's "temporal jurisdiction." In the first case, Charles de Bourbon, the French renegade dauphin of Auvergne (b. 1490; d. Rome, 1527), was commander of the Spanish forces in Italy, and he led the sack of Rome on 6 May 1527, during which he was killed. The sack of Rome was supposedly conducted by de Bourbon without Charles V's knowledge or approval, hence Donne's suggestion of connivance. However, the war of which the sack of Rome was part, was justified on the Spanish side by Charles' desire to protect his Italian domains from the attempts of Clement VII to free Italy of foreign domination. In the second case, the Duke of Alba, Fernando Alvarez de Toledo (b. 1508; d. 1582), was a successor to de Bourbon as head of the Spanish forces in Italy, under Philip II. He marched on Rome in 1557 to inflict on Pope Paul IV, who was attempting to restrain Spanish power in Italy, the same fate that de Bourbon had wrought on Clement VII. However, interim terms of peace between Philip and Paul cut short Alba's campaign (see Commentary for p. 187, ll. 20-32). Donne then refers to a third (and this time a non-military) example of a secular ruler confining the temporal jurisdiction of the papacy. He again uses the history of Philip II, but now in his relationships with a later pope, Gregory XIII, who had offered his diplomatic service in the conflict between Spain, France and Portugal over the succession to the throne of the latter country in 1580. For his information about the Portuguese incident, Donne was using a copy of the first Italian edition of the Genoese Girolamo de Franchi Conestaggio's *Dell'Unione del Regno di Portogallo Alla Corona di Castiglia* (Genoa, 1585), Books III, p. 82, and VI, p. 155. The serious pretenders to the throne of Portugal were Philip II himself, Emmanuel Philibert Duke of Savoy, Katherine Duchess of Bragance, Anthony the Prior of Crato, and the son of the Prince of Parma, Rainucius Farnese, who were all somehow descendants of Edward and Emmanuel of Portugal. Anthony of Crato was the winner, and he was named king first in Saint Arem, and then in Lisbon, but his nomination immediately led to war with Philip II, who defeated him and who was subsequently named king. The legate whom Gregory XIII sent into Spain and whose offer of mediation Philip II refused was the papal nuncio Filippo Sega. The concluding irony of Donne's passage, of which his readers were aware, was that the Duke of Alba, who had served Philip so well in Italy and also effectively invaded Portugal to press Philip's claims, was jailed by him for the extraordinary cruelty his troops inflicted on the Portuguese.

Page 17.

7–17 *the politique governement . . . to that Authoritie*: The purpose of Donne's allusions to Parsons and Baronius is to weaken the Catholic historical argument that Pope Urban II (b. c.1042; d. Rome, 1099) did not give up spiritual power over Sicily when he ceded its governmental control to the Norman Count Roger of Sicily in 1099 (see Introduction, p. xxviii). When Spain came to rule Sicily as a fief, it claimed that Urban had also yielded spiritual power over it to Roger, and that the kings of Spain had inherited it. Parsons rejected the Spanish pretensions to a "spiritual" monarchy, parallel to their "temporall" monarchy in Sicily, and to similar parallel monarchies in the hands of the English kings, in his *Answere to the Fifth Part of Reportes*, Chapter V, p. 102. As the argument of the parallel "spirituall" and "temporall monarchies" is crucial to the whole of *Pseudo-Martyr*, the passage in Parsons deserves quoting: "And yet will none of those that defend this spirituall monarchy at this day (for by that name it is called) say, that it descended by right of their Crownes, but by concession and delegation of Popes." Parsons believed that the pope had delegated the power and had the right to take it back; Baronius for the year 1097 in *Annales*, Vol. VI, Tome 11, Col. 882–884, Nos. 19, 20, 25 argued that the pope had never given up the power at all because the papacy even by granting dispensations could never divide up its prerogatives; and Donne agrees with Baronius against Parsons that the pope never gave up the power but for the very different reason that he had never possessed it exclusively. Donne's parenthetical reference to Parsons having abandoned the Church in favour of Spain must be understood in terms of the remainder of his argument and its support in Baronius' *Annales*. Baronius made it a matter of Catholic faith that the pope never ceded spiritual power to Duke Roger. Therefore, for Parsons even to state that the pope delegated power should, according to Donne, put him outside the boundaries of Catholicism. Parsons's *Answere* to Coke was a reply not to the whole of *Fift Part*, but principally to its long prefatory "De Iure Regis ecclesiastico" or "Of the Kings Ecclesiasticall Law" — hence its relevance to Donne's argument (see Introduction, p. xxxvi). The body of *Fift Part* was a collection of law cases tried in English courts, recorded in a detailed explanatory fashion for the education of student lawyers, whereas its preface touched directly on the issue of kingship and spiritual authority at the heart of *Pseudo-Martyr*. Coke argued historically, monarch by monarch, from Edward the Confessor to the present, for the existence of an independent spiritual crown in Britain founded on the country's oldest legal traditions. The existence of a primitive state pre-dating the imposition of papal authority upon it is at the centre of Donne's argument, and the argument was current in the works of a few contemporary Protestant writers whom he mentioned earlier (see Commentary for p. 11, ll. 9–26). Donne describes Baronius as a more credible authority than Parsons because he was a Neapolitan and therefore a subject of Philip III of Spain who was also king of Sicily and Naples, and therefore more qualified to speak, as he was a cardinal, an Italian and a Spanish subject.

18–28 *his brother . . . ruenta Petra*: Donne is translating from the third and fourth parts of that edition of Baronius' *Tractatus De Monarchia Siciliae* published in a single volume with Cardinal Colonna's answer to the tract in the form of an open letter, with Baronius' *Apologetica* in answer to this letter (No. 21, p. 201), and with Baronius' letter to the reigning king of Spain, Philip III (b. Madrid, 1578; d. 1621), entreating him as ruler of Sicily and Naples to submit to the authority of the pope (pp. 236–237). Donne's reference to Baronius' "his brother Cardinall Columna" is to be taken in terms of their cardinalship but it may also be playing on the very similar titles of their tracts, *Monarchia Siciliana* and *De Monarchia Sicilia*. Donne's reference to "that Booke" is to Baronius' *Annales* published three years earlier. Under the year 1097 (Vol. 6, Tome 11, Nos. 18–35, Cols. 881–887), Baronius deals with the jurisdiction of the papacy over secular rulers and he supports Urban II's right over the Emperor Henry III of Germany, and he used the same arguments to reply to Colonna's tract.

35–2 (p. 18) *For as . . . bloody Government*: The Roman rhetorician and anecdotal historian Aelianus of Praeneste (b. c.170; d. 235), in *Variae Historiae . . . Rerumpublicarum descriptiones* (Lyons, 1604), Book I, Chapter 29, p. 24.

Page 18.

15–19 *wisemen of Persia . . . conjecture*: Aelian, *Variae Historiae*, II, 17, pp. 56–57.

26–30 *that Anastatius . . . his temporal provision*: Philippe Bosquier (b. Mons, 1561; d. Avesnes, 1636), a famous preacher of the Cordeliers Order to whose predicatory talent Donne refers a few pages later, was the author of the *Monomachia Iesu-Christi, et Luciferi, Incruenta; seu Concionum XL De Tentationibus Christi In Deserto Notae*, in *Opera*, 3 Vols., Cologne, 1621. In "Concio 6" on Jesus being led into the desert to be tempted by the devil, Bosquier narrates the story of how Anastius a monk of the early church (who may be Anastius, d. c.700, abbot of the monastery of Saint Catherine, on Mount Sinai), tamed a hundred devils into constructing aqueducts and building a monastery. Bosquier had a reputation as a blood-and-thunder preacher who used vivid examples to illustrate his theological points.

Page 19.

2–4 *To let blood . . . new fashion*: The late last century B.C. and early first-century Roman historian of medicine, Aulus Cornelius Celsus, in his *De Re Medica*, Book II, Chapter 10, p. 163 (Lyons, 1592), a work which served as a leading model for Renaissance manuals of medicine. Celsus was considered the Cicero of medical writers because of the beauty of his style.

10–11 *to entrappe . . . Mandrake, whose operation*: The first-century Roman engineer and officer, Sextus Julius Frontinus, in his *Strategemata*, Book II, Chapter 5, in Richard Mowsine's translation (London, 1539), Sig. Fiiii. However, Donne has mistaken Hannibal for his lieutenant Maharbal, the son of Himilion, who did the drugging of the wine.

27–32 *yet we finde . . . meanes*: The Dutch medical historian and surgeon, Petrus Forestus (b. Alcmar, 1522; d. 1597), in *De Venenis*, Book 30 of *Observationum et Curationum Medicinalium* (Leyden, 1606), "Observatio 1," "Scholia," pp. 6–18.

Page 20.

3–5 *Fish . . . at the rocke*: Aelian, *Variae Historiae*, I, 1, p. 2.

11–13 *aunciant Physitian . . . owne violence*: The Greek physician contemporary of Socrates, Hippocrates (b. 469; d. Larissa, Thessaly, 399 B.C.), in *Aphorismi Graece et Latine* (Lyons, 1580), Part I, aphorism 22, pp. 24–25.

Page 21.

3–12 *consider the occasion . . . performe it*: Claude d'Espence (b. Châlons-sur-Marne, 1511; d. 1571) called Espencaeus, the Catholic Rector of the University of Paris, who was accused of heresy, in his commentary on Paul's epistle to Titus, *In Epistolam D. Pauli Apostoli Ad Titum Commentarius* (Paris, 1567), Chapter 1, pp. 69–70, where he records the address of 1522 before the Imperial Parliament in Rome of Pope Adrian VI (b. Utrecht, 1459; d. Rome, 1522). Adrian, who reigned for little less than a year, worked ceaselessly to reform the Roman Curia, and d'Espence records him as telling the Parliament that God had permitted the Lutheran heresy because of the sins of the Catholic clergy and the bishops.

12–19 *If you consider . . . way to this Reformation*: Florimond de Raemond (b. Agen, 1540; d. Bordeaux, 1601) a jurist who studied law at Paris and Toulouse, who contemplated becoming a Huguenot, but who from 1566 onwards became a firm defender of Catholicism and a member of the Parliament of Bordeaux. Donne is quoting form Raemond's major and posthumously published work, *L'Histoire de la Naissance, Progrez, et Décadence de l'Héresie de ce Siècle* (Paris, 1605), of which his son, François, also a jurist, wrote the sixth of the eight books, on the English schism with Rome. Donne is making two references to the projects of Francis I (b. Cognac, 1494; d. Rambouillet, 1547) of France, and of his sister Marguerite d'Angoulême, queen of Navarre (b. Angoulême, 1492; d. Odos-en-Bigorre, 1549) to create a French court at once Catholic, humanist and cultured. Francis surrounded himself with humanists versed in philosophy and language, as Raemond described in Book 7, Chapter 2, p. 149b. Some pages later in Chapter 3, 151b–152a, to which Donne also refers, Raemond narrates how the bishop of Meaux near Paris, Guillaume Brissonet or Briconnet (b. Paris, 1470; d. 1534), Marguerite's spiritual advisor, allowed "Luthero-Zwinglians" into his court to share in their ideas, skill in languages and powers of argumentation. He was later accused of heresy and recanted.

31–33 *Taxa Camerae . . . Casuists*: The *Taxa Camera* apostolic chancellory was in charge of issuing papal bulls; the summists were the creators like Aquinas of global commentaries on Catholic belief; d'Espence criticizes them in his *Commentarius* of Paul's epistle to Titus, Chapter 1, p. 67.

Page 22.

7–13 *how blinde a prognosticator . . . more advanced*: Firstly, Johann Paul Windect, the sixteenth-century Dutch controversialist and Catholic canon of Markdorf, in his forty-two reasons predicting the fall of Protestantism, in his *Prognosticon Futuri Status Ecclesiae . . . In quo duabus et quadraginta Rationibus Apodicticis demonstratur, Lutheranorum Calvinianorum, aliasque Sectas, contra Romano-Catholicam Ecclesiam* (Cologne, 1603). Secondly, Raemond, in his preface to Pope Paul V in Volume I containing the first five books of *Histoire de la Naissance*, Sig. a[iii], wrote that "l'Heresie . . . dé-ja cache, et topit en divers lieus, où elle a été n'a guières adorée;" and, finally, in the preface to the Chevalier Sillery in Volume II containing the last three books, he commented that "tant de Sectes diverses . . . marquant la ruine qui fuit de prez toutes ces confusions" (Sig. a[iii]).

16–17 *said, Nothing . . . as Errour*: In Justinian's *Corpus Iuris Civilis*, Volume I (Paris, 1590), *Digestorum*, 2, 1, No. 15, Col. 36.

30–32 *a law . . . he was commaunded*: Aelian, *Variae Historiae*, II, 37, p. 75.

Page 23.

4 *Calenture*: Burning passion, ardour, zeal.

8–9 *Preachers . . . Nette*: See Commentary for p. 18, ll. 26–30.

12–17 *Pope cannot command . . . after it is once made*: Gratian's *Decretum* (Lyons, 1584), Distinction 61, Chap. 17, Col. 310 (see Introduction, p. xxxiii). Donne is quoting from the Latin translation, *Enchiridion sive Manuale Confessionorum, et Poenitentium* of the Spanish cleric Navarrus, or, as was his real name, Martin de Azpilcuet of Navarre (b. Barasoain, 1491; d. Rome, 1586). Charles V made Navarrus head of the University of Coimbra on the publication of the first edition of his manual in Spanish in 1551. A jurist and theologian, Navarrus, to whose works Donne refers several times in *Pseudo-Martyr*, was reputed for his defence of the Spanish Friar Bartholomew of Carranza (whom Donne also cites extensively), when the latter was arraigned by the Inquisition on charges of heresy. Navarrus accompanied Carranza to Rome to defend him. The *Manuale* that Donne is here citing, Chap. 23, No. 38 (p. 553, in the Rome edition of 1588, *Opera Omnia*), was a work that dealt extensively with freedom of conscience, confession and the rights of the church in the sacrament of penance. Significantly for the presence of Navarrus in Donne's pages, in the very year of 1609 when he was writing *Pseudo-Martyr*, his printer Stansby in London published an English translation of Bellarmine's and Navarrus' tracts on differences of opinion within the Catholic Church, showing how these two Catholics themselves varied in their attitudes to these differences (*The Peace of Rome*, London, 1609).

20–21 *Pythagoras schollers . . . a Beane*: Diogenes Laertius, the third-century compiler of the lives of the ancient philosophers, in *De Vitis . . . clarum philosophorum* (Geneva, 1593), pp. 567–626.

25–26 *Scimus eos . . . to beleeve*: Donne is paraphrasing the introduction of "Praecapitulatio dicendorum" of Cardinal Baronius' martyrology (see Introduction, p. xvii): "In Anglia potissimum atque in Galiis ab haereticis passos, et in caelum (ut par est credere) inter alios Martyres aequali scimus triumphi gloria cooptatos," *Martyrologium Romanum, ad novam Kalendarii Rationem, et Ecclesiae Historiae veritatem restitutum* (Antwerp, 1589), 8, p. xxi.

27 *died of the bite . . . Lion*: Aelian, *Variae Historiae*, XIV, 4, p. 394.

Page 24.

1–2 *those men . . . in anger*: Aulus Gellius, the second-century Roman compiler of notes and anecdotes on law, history and philosophy, in his *Noctes Atticae*, Book IX, Chapter 4 (Frankfurt, 1603), p. 210.

20–22 *that vicious affectation . . . Sacerdoturientes*: In "Concio" 4 of his *Monomachia Iesu-Christi*, p. 580 of Tome I, Bosquier cites at length a passage from the late fourth- and early fifth-century monk Cassianus (b. ?Scytha, c.360; d. c.435) on the nature of the priesthood. Bosquier uses the form "sacerdoturiens" for false or "would-be priest," as opposed to "sacerdos" for a real priest. The form "sacerdoturiens" is a play on the Latin future imperfect structure of verbs.

Page 25.

6–9 *in those times . . . Bruta fulmina*: Gaius Plinius Secundus or Pliny the Elder, the first century A.D. Roman philosopher and historian, in Chapter 43 "De tonitrius et fulguribus," Book II, Col. 19, of his *Naturalis Historiae*, Venice, 1559.

Page 26.

12–20 *Physitians . . . state of health*: Also in the title of third meditation, "Decubitus sequitur tandem" and "The Patient takes his bed," in *Devotions*, p. 14. William Salmon in his *Synopsis Medicinae*, second edition (London, 1681), Book II, Chapter 1, describes the "Decumbiture" as "That moment of time . . . that the Sick is forced to take his Bed," p. 189.

33–3 (p. 27) *your owne Authors . . . to his Prince*: Stanislaus Cristanovic, in *Examen Catholicum Edicti Anglicani, Quod Contra Catholicos est latum, Auctoritate Parlamenti Angliae* (Paris, 1607), p. 32.

Page 27.

19–21 *not in their owne blood . . . them to white*: See Holy Sonnet IV, ll. 13–14.

21–23 *Chrysostome writes . . . her blood*: Saint Chrysostom, the fourth-century bishop of Constantinople and Doctor of the Church, in "In psalmum quinquagesimum, Miserere mei deus Homiliae duae," *Opera*, 5 Tomes in 4 Vols. (Paris, 1570), Tome 1, Col. 852, where he cites the incident of the repentant sinful woman in Luke 7.

35–1 (p. 28) *Romane Armies . . . non fugere*: Flavius Vegetius Renatus, the late fourth-century Roman military historian, in Book II, Chapter 17, "Commissa pugna gravem armaturum stare pro muro," p. 40, of his *De Re Militari* (Leyden, 1607).

Chap. I
Page 29.

2–7 *Depositarie . . . Proprietary*: Legal terms, a "depositary" being a trustee committed to maintaining the property of another in safe-keeping; and "proprietary," a proprietor who holds some object as his possession.

22–23 *we read . . . to kill themselves*: Gellius, *Noctes Atticae*, p. 364, who cites the story of the women of the town of Miletus described by Plutarch as rife with corruption.

COMMENTARY

Page 30.

5–8 *That nothing . . . fall upon us*: Aristotle, *Ethica Nicomachea*, trans. by W.D. Ross, Book III, No. 7, in *The Works of Aristotle* (Oxford, 1925), p. 116^a, and the sixteenth-century Burgundian law specialist and professor at the Sorbonne, Jean Matal or Ioannes Metellus, who was a student of the Spaniard Hieronymous Osorius, in his preface to Osorius' history of the Portuguese, *De Rebus Emmanuelis, Regis Lusitaniae*, in the Cologne edition of 1576, Sig. 5^v.

15–23 *The Emperors . . . and Sedition*: Justinian's *Corpus Iuris Civilis*, Vol. I: *Digestorum*, 48, 19, Law 38, Col. 1898; 49, 16, Law 6, Cols. 1939–40. The canons forbidding a complete Christian burial to those who committed suicide were passed at the provincial church council of Antisiodorens (Canon 17) in 578 during the reign of Pope Pelagius II, and the first council of Braccarens (Canon 33) in 411 during the reign of Innocent I. Finally, Petrus Gregorious or Pierre Gregoire (b. Toulouse, 1540; d. Pont à Mousson, 1597), the canonist known as Tholosanus, describes the severe Flemish judgement of treason passed on suicide, in his *Syntagmatis Iuris Universi*, 2 vols. (Lyons, 1582), Vol. II, Book 36, Chapter 22, No. 13, p. 711.

26–27 *that forme of a State . . . delineate*: Plato, in *The Laws*, Book IX, No. 873, p. 263 (London, 1934), edited by A.E. Taylor. Thomas More, *De optimo Reipu. Statu, Deque Nova Insula Utopia* (Louvain, 1548), Book II, Chapter "De Servis," p. 128.

Page 31.

22–24 *Abels sacrifice . . . Martyredome*: Chrysostom, "De Martyribus, Sermonis," *Opera*, Vol. II, Tome 3, Cols. 832–833. See Commentary for p. 27, ll. 21–23.

Page 32.

12–18 *Justinians great Officer . . . that signe*: The eighth-century Lombard Benedictine and historian, Paul the Deacon, in Book 18 of his additions to the ten books of Eutropius' *Historiae Romanae* (Lyons, 1594), pp. 179–182. The incident of the cross and the stones to which Paul Deacon refers occured in the eleventh year (i.e. 576 A.D.) of the reign of the Eastern emperor Justin or Justinian II, when Tiberius Constantine was the commandant of his imperial guard.

24–28 *That when . . . Martyres doe*: Chrysostom, "Homilia in Psalmum Nonagesimumquintum," *Opera*, Vol. I, Tome 1, Cols. 875–876; "Homilia de David et Saule," Tome 1, Col. 509.

Chap. II
Page 34.

2–17 *Orthodox Martyres . . . was called Martyriani*: A considerable amount of Renaissance information about the history of martyrdom is condensed in Donne's lines here, as well as on pp. 110–111. The first reference is to the Spanish Friar Minor of the Regular Observance of Saint Francis, Alphonsus à Castro (b. Zamora, n.d.; d. Brussels, 1558), the royal councillor to Philip II, several times in England during the period of his marriage to Mary Tudor, and author of *Adversus Haereses* (Paris, 1534). The second reference is to Gabriel du Preau or Prateolus (b. Marcossis, 1511; d. Saint Sauveur, Peronne, 1588), the French humanist and anti-Protestant author of *De Vitis, Sectis et Dogmatibus Omnium Haereticorum* (first published in Cologne in 1569). Donne is referring to the section "Martyrium" in Book X of *Adversus Haeresis* (col. 634, Tome I, *Opera Omnia*, Paris, 1578) and to Chapter 19 on the "Circuitores" in Book III of *De Vitis*, p. 129, but also to Chapter 30 on "Iudas Iscario" in Book IX, p. 237, which he does not annotate in his margin. The "circumcelliones" or "circuitores" who lived as hermits in the fields and woods and who sought martyrdom desperately, were a fanatical early fifth-century offshoot of the century-old Donatist heresy led by Petilian, the bishop of Cirtha in North Africa, and Augustine wrote against both Petilian and the Donatists in his *De Haeresibus*, Chapter 69. The name of the "circumcelliones" sprang from their habit of attacking their Catholic enemies by first encircling their houses, and du Preau or Prateolus derided their belief that Judas was a martyr. Donne's third reference is to the sixteenth-century edition of Saint Epiphanius' *Contra Octoginta Haeresis Opus Panarium*, Basel, 15[??].

23–24 *by the Canon . . . in the Romane Church*: Gratian's *Decretum*, Distinction 15, Chapter 3, cols. 55–58. The decree "Sancta Romana", one of the principal ones to which Donne refers in *Pseudo-Martyr*, was released by Pope Gelasius (elected in 492) probably in the year of his death in Rome in 496. The decree lists those biblical and Christian works, duly recorded in *Decretum*, which were apocryphal and those which were not.

29–8 (p. 35) *out of Binius . . . to execute her*: In "Notae in Concilium Eliberitanum" for the year 305 in Volume I, p. 248, col. 2 of *Concilia Generalia, et Provincialia* (Cologne, 1606) (four tomes in five volumes) by the German Counter-Reformation scholar Severinus Binius (b. Randeroth, Westphalia, 1573; d. Cologne, 1641) (see Introduction, p. xxxiii). Binius' *Concilia* was a collection of the complete acts and decrees of all the church councils since the beginning of Christianity with, as its wider polemical aim, the refutation of Protestant arguments against Catholic doctrine and church practices, and it was one of the chief works of reference that Donne used in *Pseudo-Martyr*. Relying on the authority of an outstanding contemporary controversialist scholar to support his attack on false martyrdom, Donne quotes and translates Binius' account of the wilful provocation of infidels by early Christians such as Eulalia, and of the rejection of these practices by Pope Marcellus I at the Council of Eliberitane in 305 (*Concilia*, Vol. I, p. 245, col. 1, although the *Catholic Encyclopedia*, New York, 1907–1914, 16 vols., Vol. 9, p. 640, records that Marcellus may not have become officially Pope until 308, and the exact date remains historically obscure). Donne's marginal note to the early Christian poet Prudentius (b. Calahorra, Spain, 348; d. Saragossa, Spain, ?424), originates in the passage in Binius (p. 248, col. 2), where he refers to Prudentius' "third hymn" as the source for Eulalia's story. However, Donne must have also consulted Prudentius' hymn directly, or known the story from another source as well, as he mentions two facts, that for her martyrdom she emerged from her father's house and that she was twelve years old, which are not in Binius' account (Prudentius, *Hymns for Every Day*, "The Martyrs' Crowns,", No. 3, trans. Sister M. Clement Eagen, C.C.V.I., *The Fathers of the Church Series*, Vol. 43, Washington, 1962, pp. 129–131). Binius was of such international stature as a scholar that Cardinal Baronius in Rome had him named to the prestigious canonicate of the Church of St. Cunibert in Cologne where he was already professor of history and theology at the university (Pulpilly, *Baronius*, p. 133).

Page 35.

9–12 *a Catholique Author . . . in such dying*: The treatise on demonology and on the operations of wicked spirits on Christians, *De Magorum Daemonomania Libri IV* (Basel, 1581), pp. 344–345, by the Renaissance French political philosopher, Jean Bodin (b. Angers, 1530; d. Laon, 1596), first published in French in 1580 as *Démonomanie des sorciers*. Donne's Latin title for the work suggests that he was working with the Latin translation of the following year. Donne cites Tertullian the Roman church father (b. c.155; d. c.222) as Bodin's source, and Bodin refers to Tertullian without identifying his text, but the source work is probably Tertullian's *Ad Matryres* which appeared in a French translation by Florimond de Raemond in Lyons in 1595, with the title of *Aux Martyres . . . de Q. Septim. Tertullian*. Tertullian warns his readers against false martyrs (pp. 12–13), but does not mention the edicts against the execution of Christians to which Donne refers, probably to support his argument.

22–24 *also Sampson . . . as martyres*: Donne's reference to the *Historia Ecclesiae* of Eusebius, bishop of Caesarea (b. c.260; d. c.340), considered to be the father of church history, is obscure. In Chapter 24 of Book 8, there is no mention of either Samson or virgins who drowned themselves to preserve their virginity, as Donne's marginal note suggests. In the later Chapter 26, mention is made of a virgin of Gaza who was martyred, but there is no connection with Samson. In the earlier Chapter 12 of Book 8, however, Eusebius deals at length with the story of the chaste matron of Antioch and her two virgin daughters who flung themselves into a river rather than bear the outrages of marauding enemies, *The Aunciant Ecclesiasticall Histories of the First Six Hundred Yeares after Christ* (London, 1585), pp. 151–152. The indices to Baronius' *Martyrologium Romanum*, and to its English translation in 1627, make no mention of Samson either. Donne's source may be Bellarmine's discussion of Samson in purgatory in the Sixth General Controversy, "In Purgatorio," of Volume I, *De Controversiis*, col. 1872, where however no explicit mention is made of martyrdom.

Page 36.

2–5 *it is not allowed . . . for the time past*: The Franciscan controversialist and theologian Franciscus Feuardentius (b. Coutances, 1539; d. Paris, 1610), in his treatise against the Calvinist theology of the Huguenots, *Theomachia Calvinistica* (Paris, 1604), Book VIII, Chapter 13, No. 13, p. 295, col. 2. The chapter lists his reasons for declaring that Calvinist martyrs are not real ones (see Introduction, p. xv).

21–26 *the third Canon . . . holy Communion*: See Commentary for p. 34, l. 29– p. 35, l.8.

Chap. III
Page 38.

8–13 *upon that Canon . . . the Pope exceedes a Prince*: In the "Extravagantes" of John XXII, Title 2 "De Majoritate et Obedientia," Chapter 1, "Ecclesiae Romanae," *Corpus Iuris Canonici* (Lyons, 1591), Col. 274.

14–21 *their Jesuite Clavius . . . Rescripts of Emperours*: The German Jesuit, Christopher Clavius (b. Bamberg, 1538; d. Rome, 1612), author of *In Sphaeram Ioannis De Sacro Bosco Commentarius*, of which Donne was using either a copy of the Venice edition of 1601, or of the Rome edition of 1585; and, Amandus Polanus of Polansdorf in his *Symphonia Catholica seu Consensus Catholicus et Orthodoxus* (Basel, 1607), Chapter 24, Thesis 9, which cites the examples of the contentions of the German Emperor Frederick II with Duke Otto of Bavaria and Louis IV in 1324.

Page 39.

7–24 *the subject of the Canon Law . . . part of Jurisdiction*: In "Regula II" of "De Regulis Juris" of Boniface VIII in 1298, *Liber Sextus*, V, Tit. 12, in *Decretum*. Agostino Steuco or Steuchius (b. Gubbio, 1496; d. Venice, 1549), exegete and renowned librarian, was appointed Vatican librarian by Paul III in 1538. In *De Falsa Donatione Constantini* (Lyons, 1547), No. 60, pp. 111–112, Steuchius argues that Charlemagne wrote his *Opus . . . contra Synodum, quae in partibus Graeciae, pro adorandis imaginibus* published in the *Imperialia Decreta De Cultu Imaginum* collected by Melchior Haimensfeldio and published in Frankfurt in 1608 (a copy of which Donne was using) to defend the use of images for worship against both the pseudo-Council of Constantinople of 754 that forbad their use, and the second Council of Nicaea in 794 that proposed them for unlimited veneration. Charlemagne commended his volume to the then Pope Adrian I who reigned from 772 to 795 and who presided over the council of 794. Donne is citing Paul III's librarian Steuchius' statement that no copy of Charlemagne's volume was in the Vatican Library on the Palatine, and that Paul would benefit from a copy to deal with his own problems involving images. Charlemagne had convened a special synod in Frankfurt in 794 immediately after the second Council of Nicaea had passed its decretals to support the total veneration of images, to condemn them. Donne's quotations are from Charlemagne's preface, pp. 91–92.

30–33 *Imperial Law . . . Commandement of the Prince*: *Corpus Iuris Civilis*, Vol. I, *Digestorum*, Book 11, 7, Law 8, Col. 328.

Page 40.

3–11 *And Leo the first . . . Sacerdotalem*: Leo I, pope from 440 to 461, writing first to the Roman emperor at Constantinople, Martianus (or Marcian) (b. Thrace, 390; d. 457), who ruled from 450, in a letter dated 15 April 454; and, second, to Martianus' successor Leo I, emperor from 457 to 474, in a letter dated 1 December 457, reminding both emperors at the beginning of their reigns that they were Christian rulers with responsibilities for the Church: Joannes Dominicus Mansi, *Sacrorum Conciliorum Nova et Amplissima Collectio* (1758–1798) (Paris, 1903), Vol. 6, Epistles 134 and 156, Cols. 288, 323–325.

12–20 *diligence in the Church . . . makes it false*: Pope Simplicius, who reigned from 467 to 482, writing to Zeno Augustus who was eastern emperor from 474 to 491, on 10 July 479 (*Sacrorum Conciliorum*, Vol. VII, Col. 988); and Felix III, pope from 482 to 492, in a letter in 488. The "Extravagantes de Rescriptis" of Donne's margin were compiled by Pope Alexander III, who reigned during the quarrel of Thomas à Becket with Henry II. Finally, Pope Lucius III to Ioannes Andreas in Chapter 11 "Ad audientiam," Title 3 of Book I of the "Liber Extra" or "Decretals of Gregory IX," *Corpus Iuris Canonici*, Col. 13.

21–28 *Synodicall letter . . . inclitus*: At the first Council of Aurelian, held under Pope Hormisdas I in 511, the Synodical Council wrote to the newly crowned Clodimir of France, son of Clovis I, that it was incumbent upon him to help in the care of the newly-converted Christians because of their great numbers (*Sacrorum Conciliorum*, Vol. 8, Col. 350). In "Epistola Anastasii ad Senatum verbis Romae," Vol. II, Tome 2, p. 320, Col. 2, of *Concilia*, for the year 516, in the reign of the same pope Hormisdas, Binius writes that the Emperor Anastasius Augustus used the title of "Pontifex" to describe his own secular crown "almae urbis Romae," which Donne considers to have imposed the power of the prince over the papacy. See Commentary for p. 42, l. 24–p. 43, l. 14.

29–4 (p. 41) *Gregory himselfe . . . can affoord*: First, a paraphrase in translation of the opening of Gregory I's letter to the Roman Emperor Maurice (b. 539; d. 602) in the last decade of the sixth century, on the occasion of the assumption of the title of "oecumenical patriarch" by John IV of Constantinople, IV, Epistle 32, *Sacrorum Conciliorum*, Vol. 9, Col. 1206. Gregory and Maurice differed regularly over their respective rights as rulers. Second, Gregory VII (b. Soana, Tuscany, c.1020; d. Salerno, 1085), in September of 1073 shortly after he was elected pope, in a letter to Rudolph Duke of Swabia giving him his benediction in his differences with the German Emperor Henry, I, Epistle 19, *Sacrorum Conciliorum*, Vol. 20, Cols. 75–76. The "two dignities" that Donne mentions are Gregory's "sacerdotii & imperii."

Page 41.

5–9 *from Binius . . . sui certaminis*: First, Binius' marginal note to a letter which John of Antioch sent to Cyril Patriarch of Alexandria concerning the Nestorian heresy (that Mary was only the mother of the human Christ) reads, "Imp[eratores] sacra et secula ex aequo curant." The note is contained in his account of the Council of Ephesus that condemned the heresy, for the year 431 in *Concilia*. Second, the letter of John VIII (pope from 872 to 882) in 873 to Louis II, the Stammerer, King of France (b. 846; d. Compiègne, 879), son of Charles the Bald, asking him for his help against the supporters of Carloman of Bavaria who had expelled him from Rome. Donne is paraphrasing John's "cooperatores effecti nostri certaminis" (*Sacrorum Conciliorum*, Vol. 17, Cols. 75–76).

9–20 *Balsamo saith . . . flatterie of the Emperour*: The twelfth-century Greek canonist, Theodore Balsamo, Patriarch of Antioch, in his commentary on the seventeenth canon of the Council of Chalcedon (451 A.D.), dealing with the nature of parishes and dioceses, in *Canones Sanctorum Apostolorum* (Paris, 1561), p. 184. The so-called Council of Trullo in 692 was an historical misnomer of later church historians, and both Binius and Mansi hasten to say that it was confused with the Church's sixth general synod and the third general council held in Constantinople that began in 680 (*Sacrorum Conciliorum*, Vol. 11, Col. 922; Vol. 12, Cols. 47–51). The Council of Trullo appears to have been an informal synod called by the Emperor Justinian at his palace of Trullo in Constantinople to which the real Council's canons were mistakenly attributed. Finally, Donne refers to Binius' marginal note, "Hunc canonem adulatio genuit," in his account of the last sessions of the Council of Constantinople in 692, but he is also quoting his text, "Et sufficient sicut et Antistites," *Concilia Generalia*, Vol. III, Tome 3, Part 1, p. 156, Col. 1.

27–10 (p. 42) *So Leo the first . . . his assistance*: Leo I in a letter dated 15 June 453, to the Emperor Martianus, Epistle No. 121 in *Sacrorum Conciliorum*, Vol. 6, Cols. 251–252. For John (and not the 1610 text's Leo) VIII's letter to Louis the Stammerer, the son of Charles the Bald of France, see Commentary above for lines 5–9. Charles' other son mentioned in John's letter is Carloman. Third, for Pope Leo I's letter to the Emperor Martianus, see Commentary for p. 40, ll. 3–11.

COMMENTARY

Page 42.

11–20 *though Gregorie . . . not subreptitious*: Gregory I, in a letter of April 593, to Maximin the Usurper in Salon, France, who had been consecrated on orders of the Emperor Maurice (*Sacrorum Conciliorum*, Vol. 9 Col. 1169). Gregory was not known for extending his authority over secular princes, but his reign was reputed for his consolidation of papal power over all patriarchs of the Church.

24–14 (p. 43) *Anastasius testifies . . . in our owne words*: Of Donne's three examples from the history of the early church of successful negotiations between popes and emperors in matters of church unity, the first refers to the exchange of letters between Hormisdas (b. Frusino, n.d.; d. Rome, 523), elected Pope in 514, and the Emperor Anastasius of Constantinople over the question of the Acacian heresy in the see of Constantinople. Anastasius ruled from 491 to 518, and supported the heresy. The delay in the correspondence Donne mentions was the lapse of time between the delivery of Anastasius' two letters of December 514 and January 515, to Hormisdas. The second letter, which was the less conciliatory and which simply asked for Hormisdas' intervention in the dispute, arrived first, in early April, whereas the first, more conciliatory letter, was not delivered until a whole six weeks later in mid-May (Binius, *Concilia Generalia* Volume 2, p. 315, Col. A, and p. 316, Col. B). Donne's Latin citation from Hormisdas' second letter is a collection of its ideas, and is not a literal transcription. With Athanasius' successor, Justin I, the Eastern Emperor who ruled between 518 and 527, Hormisdas' task of settling the same problem of the Acacian heresy and of the appertinence of the eastern bishoprics, was easier. The new emperor was an orthodox Christian, and Donne sees in Justin a second secular ruler in a row attempting to end a rift between the Eastern and Western Churches. The *Divinos Apices*, that is, Justin's sacred missives, are mentioned by the Emperor in his letter to Hormisdas delivered in September of 518 (Binius, p. 335, Col. B). Hormisdas reacted quickly to Justin's overtures and the rift between the Eastern and Western Churches was formally healed rapidly with a ceremony in the Cathedral of Constantinople on Holy Thursday in March of the following year. Justin's letter to Hormisdas was intended as a petition to the conciliar fathers as well as a letter to the pope, and Donne is evidently drawing a parallel between the Emperor's successful attempt at peace between the Eastern and Western Churches, and the need for an accord between seventeenth-century Rome and London. Finally, Donne's third example of the mutual solicitude of secular and spiritual authorities is that of Pope Pelagius I (b. Rome, n.d.; d. 561) and the eastern Roman Emperor Justinian I, the Great (b. Tauresium, 483; d. 565), once more over the unification of the Eastern and Western Churches. In 544 Justinian issued his decree on the "Three Chapters" against the schisms of the Eastern churches which nevertheless maintained clauses profoundly offensive to Western bishops so that a schism of a new sort was caused. Pelagius, who became pope in 556, succeeded in avoiding this schism completely in France by reassuring King Childebert I (d. Paris, 558), Clovis' fourth son who ruled a large part of the North of France, that Rome upheld the old church unity in spite of its adherence to Justinian's decree. Donne is translating from Pelagius' letter of reassurance to Childebert in 556 on the occasion of the delegation to Rome led by Childebert's envoy Ruffines. In Donne's translation, Pelagius mentions Pope Leo I, the Great, who reigned between 440 and 461. The Leontine "Confession of Faith" which Pelagius is vowing to Childebert in Donne's text was the declaration of the primacy of the Roman See over the Eastern Churches not, however, in questions of temporal authority, but in matters of Christology, about the Incarnation and the union of divine and human persons in Christ, that agitated the East. Childebert had his own problems stamping out pagan Celtic myths in France, and he desired assurance on the church's unity in the face of possible theological deviations from the Roman conception of the nature of Christ. The last three quarters of Pelagius' letter are "Fides Papae Pelagii" (Binius, Volume 2, p. 633, Col. A). Under Childebert's encouragement, the French bishops adhered to Pelagius, so that both Justinian's and the French king's dealings with the papacy ended in success. Donne's original marginal note to Childebert reads "*Pelagius I. Epist. 16. & 25. q.1*, Satagendum" (p. 24, 1610 edition). The "*& 25. q.1*" are incomprehensible as they refer to literally nothing and are removed in the present edition. Sixteen letters of Pelagius survive and the one which Donne cites is the last so that there can be no "and 25." "Satagendum" is the word in Epistle 16 that opens the passage which Donne is citing.

Page 43.

26–31 (p. 44) *Justinian the Emperour . . . Abiiciantur Episcopatibus*: The fourteen references to Justinian are to the "Codicis" of the *Corpus Iuris Civilis*, Volume II.

Page 44.

31–34 *And in the matter . . . and Jurisdiction of secular Princes*: The Spanish canonist and jurist, Didacus or Iacobus Simancas or Simancha (b. Cordova), who studied in Salamanca and later became Archbishop of Toledo. In Chapter 40 "De Confugientibus Ad Aedes Sacras" of Book VIII of his *De Republica Recte Instituenda, Conservanda et amplificanda* (Rome, 1565), Simancha described how religious shrines should be administered and visited. He established rules for large as well as small basilicas, for the punishment of those who desecrated shrines, and for the comportment of women in churches, pp. 488–491 (Cologne, 1609).

Page 45.

1–6 *when an Emperour . . . and quietnes*: Donne is translating Pope Simplicius' closing admonition, "Unde quae à vobis amore quietis sancte & religiose sunt ordinata, reprobare non possumus," in his letter of 479 to the Eastern Emperor Zeno about the latter's sacrilegious consecration of a bishop in the See of Antioch which was under the jurisdiction of Bishop Acacius of Constantinople. The decree of the first Council of Nicaea to which Donne alludes stipulated that only the pope could dispense with the approbation of the existing local bishop in the consecration of another bishop. See Commentary for p. 40, ll. 12–20, and *Sacrorum Conciliorum*, Vol. 7, Col. 989.

14–27 *an Author of great estimation . . . his Sentences*: Of Donne's three examples of Catholic thinkers pointing to the inconsistencies in the church's doctrine on the relationship between priests and the state, and to the judgements of Catholic secular rulers on ecclesiastics, the first is to d'Espence's *In Priorem D. Pauli Apostoli ad Timotheum Epistolam Commentarii* (Paris, 1561), Book I, Chapter 6, p. 275, of which edition Donne was using a copy. D'Espence points to Hildebrand or Gregory VII's decrees against lay investiture as provoking the schism in which Henry IV of Germany named an anti-pope. The second is to a passage in the *Index Expurgatorius Librorum Qui Hoc Saeculo Prodierunt*, called *The Belgian Index*, p. 15, but more generally pp. 11–18 in the Strasbourg edition of 1599 which Donne was using. The passage in the index of forbidden books relates how the Frankish monk Bertram, or Corbiensis Ratramus, appealed to King Charles II the Bald of France (b. Frankfurt, 823; d. Brios, 877) and to his council of ministers to judge the truth of the charges of heresy brought against his tract on transubstantiation *De Corpore et Sanguine Domini*. The third example is that of the fierce German anti-Lutheran controversialist Joannes Dobneck or Cochlaeus (b. Wendelstein, 1479; d. Breslau, 1552), the canon of Mayence, in the preface to his *Historia . . . De Actis et Scriptis Martini Lutheri*. Cochlaeus writes that an imperial edict issued at Worms in 1521 condemned Luther, his propositions and the whole of his theology as "seditiosa et haeretica," Sigs. U^{2v-3r}. Donne's concluding reference is to the prescriptive sense given to the power of the ecclesiastical ruler over the secular ruler in Sixtus V's official Catholic Vulgate Bible's translation of Deuteronomy 17.9 as "ex decreto," that is, by decree (Rome, 1590), p. 161, rather than by the "et" (and) or the "aut" (or) of the Protestant Latin Bibles, such as the Junius Bible (London, 1597), p. 163.

32–6 (p. 46) *Maximilian the first . . . the Emperiall Crowne*: On 16 September 1511, the Catholic Emperor Maximilian I of Germany (b. Vienna, 1459; d. Wels, Austria, 1519), wrote a letter to a Baron Paul in Liechtenstein requesting his advice on his plan to unite his crown with that of the papal tiara, thus creating a world-wide secular monarchy based on the universal spiritual power of the papacy (*Monita Politica*, pp. 33–35). The occasion of the letter to which Donne is referring was the desperate illness between 25 and 27 August of 1511 of the warrior-Pope Julius II (b. Abissola, Savona, 1443; d. Rome, 1513), the great Renaissance patron of the arts, who was elected in 1513 and who was committed to liberating not only the papal states but the whole of Italy from foreign influence, particularly that of Maximilian and Louis XII of France (b. 1462; d. 1515). During the struggle, the schismatic Council of Pisa was called to depose Julius and opened on 1 September, and Maximilian seized on the opportunity presented to him in Julius' illness of assuming the papal crown and uniting it to the German imperial crown of Holy Roman Emperor. But unknown to Maximilian, because the news was slow in reaching Pisa, by 28 August Julius had begun to recover rapidly from his near fatal illness. The "Baron" in Donne's note appears to be the Dutch astronomer Paul von Middleburg (b. Middleburg, 1455; d. Italy, 1534) who was Maximilian's political counsellor, who dedicated one of his writings to him in 1584 even before he was crowned emperor, and who represented him at the Lateran Council of 1513 called to repudiate the schismatic Council of Pisa. The importance of Maximilian as a background figure in *Pseudo-Martyr* is evidenced by his presence in the opening lines of Donne's preface.

Page 46.

7–16 *a Lay-man be elected Pope . . . holy Orders*: Donne cites three authoritative Catholic works on the ability of laymen to assume clerical functions without taking holy orders. These are, first, the *Sacrarum Cerimoniarum* on Catholic ceremonies, "De Ordinatione et Consecratione Summi Pontificis," in Section 2, p. 21, and "De Coronatione Imperatoris Absente Papa" in Section 5, p. 63 (Cologne edition of 1572 of which Donne was using a copy). Secondly, the *Thesaurus Christianae Religiones et Speculum Sacrorum Summorum Romanorum, Pontificium, Imperatorum, ac Regum, et Sanctissimorum Episcoporum* (Venice, 1559), although Donne may have been using the later Cologne edition of 1581. *Thesaurus* was a long examination of the rights, powers and duties of Christian secular and spiritual leaders written by Alphonsus Guerrero Alvarez, the Spanish adviser to Philip II of Spain in Naples and president of his council there in 1572, and Donne cites him several times in *Pseudo-Martyr*. Thirdly, the "Decretals of Gregory IX" or "Liber Extra" of 1234, Book I, Title 21 "De Digamis Non Ordinandis," Chapter 2, *Corpus Iuris Canonici*, Col. 116. The two popes to whom Donne refers are Pius V who formed the commission of the "correctores romani" in 1566 to correct the text of *Corpus*, and Gregory XIII's commission of 1582 that reinstated some of the texts that the first commission had dropped.

17–25 *The Emperour . . . the authority of a King*: On the rights of secular rulers to assume the roles normally reserved for ordained clergy: firstly, Alvarez' *Thesaurus* for Donne's information about the Roman emperor's role as a canon of the Church of Saint John Lateran, Chapter I, Nu. 40, p. 10; secondly, Barthélemy Chasseneuz or Cassanaeus (b. Issy-l'Évèque, Saône en Loire, 1480; d. Aix-en-Provence, 1541), cited briefly here to support Alvarez and who, like him, was a practical theorist on the rights of Christian secular and spiritual rulers, in his *Catalogus Gloriae Mundi* of 1529, which was republished as late as in 1603 in Cologne, but Donne was using here and elsewhere in *Pseudo-Martyr* a copy of the 1559 edition which reproduced Cassanaeus' original illustrations, Part V, pp. 221, 231; "Declarans, laudes, honorem, gloriam, et excellentias Principum secularium" (p. 203). Cassanaeus was a Parliamentary adviser and lawyer to Francis I in 1531, and was in the next year named president of the Parliament of Aix.

COMMENTARY

Page 47.

3–5 *the Clergie exceede . . . intended it*: In Book V, Chapter 6, of the third general controversy "De Summo Pontifice" of Volume I of his *De Controversiis* Col. 1063, Bellarmine developed at length the comparison of the swords of spiritual and temporal power with the body and soul of man, and went into questions of the appetites and the intellectual acts.

12–15 *their Sepulveda saith . . . the prince*: Juan-Gines de Sepulveda (b. Pozoblanco, c.1490; d. Mariano, Cordova, 1573), who entered orders after the study of theology in Alcala and Salamanca, was historiographer to the Spanish kings Charles V and Philip II, and a firm expounder of the belief that Aristotelian philosophy was wholly conformable to Christian religion; hence, Donne's use of Sepulveda's analogy between the body and soul, and the master of a household and a servant; in *De Regno et Regis Officio* (Lerida, 1571), Book I, "Anima enim in corpus herile imperium, ut domina in servum exercet, intellectus, sive ratio in appetitum, civile," but p. 72 in the 1602 Cologne edition of the *Opera* that Donne was using. See *Pseudo-Martyr*, p. 132.

21–28 *the second Nicene Councell . . . to the Church*: In Act 5 (p. 399) of the "Notae in Concilium Nicaeum II" (p. 366), promulgated in late October of 787, recorded in *Concilia Generalia*, Vol. III (Part 1), Binius cites the declaration of Bishop John of Thessalonica that the church fathers Basil and Athanasius, and the universal church generally, held that angels were not only spirits but that somehow they also had bodies. Binius, however, does not mention Methodius as being in John's list of authorities, and it is not clear to which Methodius Donne is referring, and why he included him. The second Council of Nicaea was called to settle the iconoclastic controversy over the veneration of icons in the Greek Church, and one early church father to bear the name of Methodius, the saint of Olympus and bishop of Lycia (d. c.311), wrote a treatise on the identification of the resurrected body inhabited in lifetime by the soul, and he is most likely the subject of Donne's reference.

32–33 *Spiritualis homo . . . iudicatur*: Johann Philippe Maynardus, an obscure late sixteenth- and seventeenth-century figure, the author of *De Privilegiis Ecclesiasticis Pro Defensione Censurarum, et Interdicti Sanctis. D.N. Pauli Quinti Pontificis Maximi adversus Venetos* (Ancona, 1607) which, as its title suggests, was a defence of the papacy in the crisis between it and the state of Venice. Because Maynardus defended the papacy's temporal power as the logical expression of its spiritual rights over all men, Donne suggests that he considered the pope's temporal power to be the body of the soul present in his spiritual power. However, Donne adds the word "Homo" to Maynardus' original text, which reads: "in fi. spiritualis autem iudicat omnia, et ipse a nemine iudicatur" (Part I, Article 9, p. 68).

Page 48.

17–25 *That all evill . . . scandals in every place*: The *Index Expurgatoribus* of forbidden books, more specifically the *Collatio Censurae in Glosses Iuris Canonici*, pp. 295, 306–307. The statement "That all evil proceeds from priests," is found in the gloss of Gratian's *Decretum*, Col. 243, which refers the reader for further discussion of the phrase to Cause XIV, Question III, Chapter 33, Col. 1429, later, hence Donne's third note. Pius V appointed the "Correctores Romani" to expurgate *Decretum* of its statements that contradicted Catholic teaching, and Thomas Manrique, the brother of the Palatinate order whom he (and not Sixtus V as Donne says) appointed to the Commission expurgated the phrase among his glossary corrections, and these corrections were published in 1572. Donne has mistakenly called Pius V (b. Bosco, 1504; d. Rome, 1572) by the name of Sixtus V both here and elsewhere in *Pseudo-Martyr* (see Commentary for p. 199, l. 12–p. 200, l. 3), probably because he confused him either with Sixtus Fabricius whom he mentions by family name in the very next line of his text, or with Sixtus V (b. 1521; d. Rome, 1590) who also later brought out an *Index Librorum Prohibitorum*, which was a list of proscribed titles and authors but not an analytic expurgation of *Decretum*. Gregory XIII succeeded Pius V and he named Sixtus Fabricius, who was of the same Palatinate order as Manrique to his own commission, to continue the work of the "Correctores Romani," and Fabricius brought out his corrected gloss in 1580 (as would have been indicated by the title page of Donne's copy of the *Index*), and then Gregory was succeeded as pope by Sixtus V in 1585 only five years later. It was Fabricius who put the phrase about evil originating in priests, expurgated by Manrique, back into Gratian's text. Donne's long translation from Saint Jerome is of a text that appears in the gloss of Gratian's "Distinction 50."

Page 49.

2–5 *such an influence . . . and possessed persons*: In *Praerogativa Hispaniae, Hoc est, De Dignitate et Praeeminentia Regnum Regnorum Hispaniae, et honoratiori loco ac titulo eis eorumque legatis à Conciliis, nec non Romana sede iure debito*, by the early sixteenth-century Spanish political theorist Diego Valdes, who treats of the spiritual powers of the French, English and more particularly Spanish kings (Frankfurt, 1626), pp. 323, 325, 327.

18–20 *their Missall cases . . . the dogge should*: Ioannes de Lapide, the late fifteenth-century German theologian, *Decisiones Casuum, Quis a Cerdotibus in Missarum Celebratione Contingere Solent* (Constance, 1608), p. 92.

Page 50.

1–8 *saith a Jesuite . . . Inferni, inclusive*: The Jesuit is the Spaniard Ioannes Azorius, or Juan Azor (b. Lorca, 1535; d. Rome, 1603), the author of the *Institutionum Moralium in Quibus Universae Quaestiones Ad Conscientiam Recte, aut* *prave factorum pertinentes, breviter tractantur,* a work on morals in a broad sense, examining all aspects of Renaissance life with respect to conscience, in the light of canon and civil law, published in three parts in Rome, the first two in 1600 and 1606 respectively, and the last in 1611. Donne refers to the first two parts several times in *Pseudo-Martyr,* normally with respect, even in disagreement, as Azor's *Institutionum* is a work of measured approach (see Introduction, p. xxxiv). Azor was one of the six-man committee appointed by the Superior-General of the Jesuits Claudio Aquaviva to draw up the famous "Ratio Studiorum" for Jesuit intellectual training, published in 1586. Donne's reference is to Chapter IX ("De Abdicatione, Abrogatione, Translatione, et Mutatione Imperii," p. 659) in Book X on the nature of civil power ("De his Qui Potestate et Iurisdictione civili praediti praesunt aliis," p. 636), where Azor limits secular power in the face of papal rule (p. 663). However, Donne's translation is not of Azor's text but of his quotation of the title of a bull by John XXII. The two translations that follow from the Spanish legal jurist Alvarez' *Thesaurus Christianae Religionis* touch on the legal position of the pope as head of the Church and as the secular ruler of Rome, and on the freedom of the election of the pope from both native and foreign secular political interference (Chapter 56, "De Imperio, et de Translatione Imperii ad Germanos," Nu. 12, p. 310; Chapter 16, "An Principatus Summi Romani Pontificis non solum ad spiritualia, sed etiam ad temporalia se extendat, ita quod in toto urbe iurisdictionem habeat temporalem," Nu. 15, p. 51). For his third authority for papal power over secular rulers, Donne is quoting from King Philip V (le "Long" or the "Tall") of France's charter to the Dominicans on 12 May 1317, for the foundation of a monastery in Paris. The name "Jacobins" in Donne's text was originally given to the Dominican friars in France because their first establishment in the North of country in 1218 was in the Rue St. Jacques in Paris, and Philipe le Long's charter, as recorded by the French lawyer René Choppin in his *Monasticon, seu de Iure Coenobiorum* (Paris, 1601), Book I, Title 1, nu. 15, p. 40 (Frankfurt, 1744), a century later, described the limits of their holdings. Philip was a legal reformer and, during the years of his reign, 1294–1322, he allowed citizens who lived next to the Paris gate which bounded the new monastery on one side and which was reputed as the "porta inferne" or gate of hell because of the attacks from robbers from the outside, to arm themselves in self-defence. René Choppin (b. Bailleul, 1537; d. Cachant, 1606) was a lawyer before the Parliament of Paris and the author of much French jurisprudence; his *Monasticon* on the rights of the clergy and of monasteries to which Donne refers several times was the last of his publications.

10–13 *It is the Catholique faith . . . the English Heresie:* From the question, "Quis possit excommunicari, et quis in excommunicatione non includitur," or who may and may not be excommunicated, in Navarrus' *Manuale* on confession, penance and freedom of conscience, Chapter 27, No. 13, p. 725 (see Commentary for p. 23, ll. 12–17.

15–16 *Bullam Coenae . . . many hooks:* The bull "In Coena Domini" was passed by Pius V to reassert the traditional principles of the authority of the Roman Church in general and the supremacy of the Holy See over civil power in particular, and its extraordinary importance was recognized even in its own day because it identified the kinds of excommunication that sprang from attacks on the pope's authority and that he alone or his successors could lift. For example, the English monk and theologian, Gregory Sayer compared the excommunications conducted under the title of "Bulla Coenae" with other forms of excommunication that could be rescinded simply by the retraction of the excommunicated person, to emphasize how deeply they were restricted to papal absolution ("Regula" I and II, *De Ecclesiasticis Censuris*, Venice, 1624, pp. 145–148). To justify the passing of the "Bulla Coenae" by Pius V, Sayer argued that it had been practised by Martin V in the fifteenth century well before him, and by his immediate successor Gregory XIII at the end of the sixteenth century.

20–7 (p. 51) *later Decretals . . . man without a beard*:   Donne is referring to five sixteenth-century documents bearing on the ceremonial respect due to cardinals and on the physical safety which is to be afforded them. The first is the decretal of Leo X at the seventh session (Donne's "In Septimo") of the fifth Lateran Council (1512–1517) on the relationship between secular rulers and princes of the church, *Sa. Lateranem Concilium novissimum* (Rome, 1521), p. 97^v (see Commentary for p. 80, ll. 8–12). The second document is the *Tractatus de Crimine Laese Maiestatis* of the Italian Girolamo Gigante or Hieronymus Gigas (b. Fossombrone, Urbino, late 1400s; d. ?Venice, 1560), first published in Lyons in 1570. The treatise dealt with the basis of crime against the persons and positions of the religious hierarchy, and Donne is translating from the Latin the openings of numbers 10, 2 and 6 in question 5, Rubric 4 of Book I (pp. 18 and 17 in the Speyer edition of 1598) on the guilt of emperors who permit an attack on a cardinal, even though not actively taking part in it. The third document is rather in the form of an allusion: Baronius' "abbreviator" is the Dutchman Cornelius Schulting (b. Steinwyck, Overijssel; d. 1604) who was canon of St. Andrew's in Cologne, who wrote extensively against Protestants and who brought out an abridged version of the Cardinal's *Annales Ecclesiastici* under the title of *Thesaurus Antiquitatum Ecclesiasticarum* in two volumes in Cologne in 1601. The preface to the first volume contained a "Prolegomena Ante Thesaurum" (hence Donne's marginal "Ante Librum") and two brief letters of Baronius to Schulting, both signed "V.R. uti frater" (a salutation that Donne interprets as a sign of distant confraternity between titled members of the church hierarchy); the first letter contained Baronius' approval of Schulting's abridgement, and the second his encouragement to him to continue his polemical work (Sig. ++8^v, in the edition of *Opera*, Douai, 1620). The fourth document is the *De Caeremoniis Cardinalium et Episcoporum in eorum Dioecesibus* (Rome, 1564), Chapter 42 on "De Benedictione Solemni," and Chapter 43 on "De Praeeminentiis Honorem Legato . . . in Missa praesentibus," pp. 94–96 of Book II, and also Chapter 27 on "De His Qui Intra Tribunam admitti possunt," p. 27 of Book I (Rome edition of 1580) by Paris Crassus or Grassus (b. Bologna, 14[??]; d. Rome, 1528), the master of ceremonies of Pope Leo X. The fifth document is the Catholic Church's official ceremonial guide, *Sacrarum Cerimoniarum, Sive Rituum Ecclesiasticorum Sanctae Romanae,* the chapter on "Consecratio, Benedictio, et Coronatio simul Romani Pontificis" of Book I, p. 36ᵛ.

Page 51.

10–17 *the Councell of Basil . . . that Sea of Rome*: Donne cites three sources for the history of the creation of cardinals. The first is the decree of the Council of Basel called in 1431 by Eugenius IV, at its twenty-third session in 1436, Chapter IV "De numero & qualitate Cardinalium" (*Sacrorum Conciliorum*, Vol. 29, Cols. 116–119, which limited the number of cardinals "viginti quatuor," and forbad the sons, brothers and nephews of popes and leading magistrats from becoming cardinals. Secondly, in his *Thesaurus Christianae Fidei*, Chapter 24, Nu. 15, p. 78, Alvarez states that there were thirty (and not Donne's two hundred and thirty) cardinals in the time of Pope Pontianus the Martyr who reigned from 230 to 235. Thirdly, the fourteenth-century German bishop Dietrich Theodoricus von Neim of Verden, in his history of the great Western schism of 1378 to 1417, *Pontificii Quondam de Scribae . . . Quorum tres partes de Schismate Universalii* (of which one edition appeared in Strasbourg in 1609), Book I, Chapter 12, pp. 13–14. Theodoricus narrates that Bartolomeo Pregnano (b. 1318; d. 1389), once elected as Pope Urban VI in 1378, was unable to handle power temperately, that he alienated practically the entire college of cardinals, and that he named twenty cardinals all at once to give the college a majority of Italians. Then in a war with Charles of Darazzo, king of Naples, in 1380, which resulted when the French named an anti-pope Clement VII and Charles sided with them, Urban had six cardinals imprisoned and tortured, and five (and not Donne's six) were executed (Chapter 57, pp. 63–64).

19–33 *Of which the Pope . . . good life*: Two historical examples of the exercise of papal authority, the first drawn from the Genoese Conestaggio's *Della Unione de Regno di Portogallo alla Corona di Castiglia* (Book III, p. 53) describing how the sickly aged Cardinal Henry, the former Grand Inquisitor of the Holy See, succeeded to the throne of Portugal on the death of his young nephew King Sebastian. On Henry's death, Catherine of Medici who was a poor contender for the throne, reported that the reigning Pope Gregory XIII intimated Portugal might belong to the Holy See because its last king had been a cardinal. Secondly, the quarrel between Cardinals Baronius and Colonna over the right of the papacy to excommunicate the rulers of the Venetian republic in *Tractatus De Monarchia Sicilia* (No. 31, p. 222), in which Baronius, who defended the papacy, cited Job 26.5 about the reign of giants to support the ascendancy of the princes of the Church. To demolish these two Catholic claims for clerical superiority, Donne cites two authoritative Roman documents. The first is the monumental seven-folio volume *Biblia Sacra Cum Glossis, Interlineari et Ordinaria* (Lyons, 1545), Vol. III, p. 50ᵛ, Col. 2, by the early fourteenth-century Franciscan biblical authority Nicholas de Lyra (b. Lyre, d'Evreux, 1270; d. Paris, 1340), who glosses the passage from Job as meaning that its giants (hence Baronius' Catholic princes) are monsters roaring in hell. The second authoritative Catholic document is the decree of the fifth Lateran Council's seventh session of June of 1513 and the presiding Pope Leo X's accompanying bull stipulating that cardinals should lead good lives.

Page 52.

4–14 *For these, and the Pope . . . have no kings*: Navarrus' *Manuale*, Chapter 27, No. 13, pp. 725–726, on the freedom of the pope from excommunication, which argues that it is as impossible to excommunicate a pope as a grasshopper. The authority on devils and exorcism is the Italian Friars Minor Girolamo Menghi (b. Viadana, Bologna, 1529; d. 1609), who was reputed to be the father of the art of exorcism. In his *Fustis Daemonum In Maligno Spiritus Effugandos* published several times with his *Flagellum Daemonum*, Menghi described the heretical character of the demon's appearance during the Albigensian heresy, and he explained how to excommunicate devils during exorcism (Chapters II and XVII, pp. 8 and 59 in the Venice edition of 1599). In Cause 16, Question 1, Chapter 12 on "Monachi qui sunt in civitatibus, episcopo debent esse subjecti," or "The monks in a state ought to be subjects of a bishop," Gratian's glosser explains that hermits like locusts have no king, Cols. 1095–1096.

17–19 *Thomas Becket . . . anointed*: Becket compared himself to David in his letter to Henry II in 1165, "Epistola LXIII," in *Epistolae et Vita*, 2 Vols. (Brussels, 1682), Vol. I, p. 92, and with Saul in another letter to Henry, "Epistolae LXIV," p. 98.

22–24 *Nabuchonozor . . . contumelious name*: Chrysostom, "Ad Populum Antiochum Homilia XXIII," *Opera*, Vol. IV, Tome 5, Col. 180, from Daniel 1.6.

27–16 (p. 53) *What high styles . . . A Divinitate nostra*: *Corpus Iuris Civilis*, Volume I, *Digestorum*, 31,1, Law 87, No. 4, Col. 1052, and not No. 3 as Donne's marginal "imperator" suggests; 1,4, Law 3, Col. 12; Volume II, *Codicis Domini Iustiniani*, 1,1, Law 1, the fourth-century emperor Gratian's colleagues are his half-brother Valentinian who held the title with him, and Theodosius I (b. Spain, c.346; d. Rome, 395) to whom he gave the rule of the Eastern part of the empire; 1,2, Law 10, Col. 12, passed by Theodosius and Valentinian; 1,4, Law 3, Col. 50, passed by Theodosius, Valentinian and the son of Theodosius, Arcadius, who succeeded him as emperor of the Eastern Empire; 1,17, Law 3, Col. 83, in which Justinian invokes the divine task of renovating the old laws; 1,3, Law 56, No. 3, Col. 48; 11,9, Law 2, Col. 854; 1,2, Law 8, Col. 11, the "other" emperor being Marcus Aurelius Carus (b. Narbo, 282); and finally, 1,1, Law 3, No. 4, Col. 3, in which the Emperor Theodosius II condemned the Nestorian heresy and its belief in two persons, human and divine, in the incarnate Christ.

COMMENTARY

Page 53.

16–17 *And Constantius . . . Divalia*: Irene, empress of Constantinople (b. Athens, 752; d. Lesbos, 803), wife of the emperor Leo, who, after the death of her husband in 780, was regent for her son Constantine VI and ruled with him until 790. In his *Opus . . . contra Synodum . . . pro adorandis imaginibus*, collected in the *Imperialia Decreta De Cultu Imaginum*, Book I, Chapter 3, pp. 117–118, Charlemagne objected to their use of "divalia" and "divos" to describe themselves in their correspondence with Pope Adrian I. See Commentary for p. 39, ll. 7–24.

21–30 *The highest . . . to other Princes*: Four examples of recent historical incidents in which temporal or secular rulers were accorded spiritual authority: first, Edward IV (b. 1442; d. 1483) at the creation of Thomas Grey (b. 1451; d. 1501) as the Marquis of Dorset in 1471 (Donne includes a very loose paraphrase of the description of Edward's royal power in the *Nobilitatis Politica vel Civilis. Personas scilicet Distinguendi, et ab origine inter Gentes ex Principum gratia nobilitandi Forma*, p. 75, published posthumously in London in 1608, by Robert Glover (b. Ashford, Kent, 1544; d. London, 1588), one of Britain's most noteworthy heralds and genealogists); second, Baldus de Ubaldis (b. Perugia, 1327; d. Pavia, 1406), the renowned Italian jurist whom Urban VI summoned to Rome for consultation against the anti-Pope Clement VII in 1380, and who was the author of numerous legal tracts, including the "Super Constitutione Friderici imperatoris de iure," which Donne is here citing out of the French jurist Casseneuz' *Catalogus Gloriae Mundi*, part 5, consideration 30, p. 246, col. 2; the French king in question was Philip IV, the "Fair," who was under interdiction from Pope Boniface VIII (b. Anagni, c.1234; d. Rome, 1303) in 1296 over the issue of his right to tax the clergy without papal consent, and Ubaldis' Renaissance tract supported Philip; third, the dedication to Mary Tudor, "Ad Serenissimam Catholicam, Potentissimam Augustam Mariam Reginam," in *Thesaurus*, Sig. iii^r ("esse fortissimum Christianae fidei propugnaculum"), by the Spanish jurist Alvarez, who was also her husband Philip II of Spain's vice-roy in Naples; and fourth, the contemporary monarchs who were accorded spiritual power are the living Renaissance emperors and kings (and not only the former as Donne's sentence may suggest) whom the Northern Italian noble Caesar à Branchedoro addressed as "religionis defensorum" or defenders of religion in his oration to them, *Oratio Praemonitaria ad Imperatorem, Reges, Principes & Respublicas, de Mutatione Imperii Romane & Ortu Pontificum*, in *Monita Politica*, p. 20. Donne's annotation of "in subscriptione" refers to the quotation in his text where the title of defender of religion is found.

32–10 (p. 54) *Bellarmine values . . . of making Saints Gods*: In the title of Chapter 3 of Book I of "De Verbo Dei," the first controversy in Vol. I of *De Controversiis*, Col. 7, Bellarmine addressed Saint Paul as "divi Pauli." In the retraction of his errors in *De Controversiis*, which Bellarmine entitled *Recognitio Librorum Omnium* (Ingolstadt, 1608), p. 2 (cited in Donne's marginal note), the Jesuit cardinal confessed to having mistakenly employed the word "divus" to speak of Paul because of its extensive use by non-Christians to describe their various deities. The French linguist Nicholas Serarius, Bellarmine's fellow Jesuit (b. Rambervillers, Vosges, 1555; d. Mayence, 1609), who devoted himself to the study of languages, took exception to the Cardinal's retraction of the use of "divus," in his *Litaneutici seu de Litaniis Libelli duo* (Cologne, 1609), p. 64, because of its yet further meanings of "temple" and "fortune."

Page 54.

23–26 *having undertaken . . . to the Popes*: *De Controversiis*, Volume 1, the third general controversy "De Summo Pontifice," Book II, Chapter 12 "Romanum Pontificem Petro succedere in Ecclesiastica Monarchia, probatur ex divino iure et ratione successionis," cols. 740–747.

Page 55.

9–19 *one may not appeale . . . to violate any of them*: In *De Privilegiis Ecclesiasticis*, Part III, Article 27, n. 15, Maynard writes "a sententia Papae, nec etiam ad Deum appellari potest," to support the power of the papacy. In Chapter 5 ("De Officio Diaconi in Missa") and Chapter 22 ("De Reverentiis, et Genuflexionibus omnium intra rem divinam"), Book I of his *De Caeremoniis Cardinalium et Episcoporum*, pp. 7^v and 22^r of the Rome edition of 1580, Paris Crassus writes "nomen IESU (non autem *Christi* solum) audit, detectum caput inclinat." Donne concludes that such near-deification of the popes is even supported by the passage on blasphemy against the Holy Ghost in Gratian's *Decretum*, Cause 25, Question 1, on "Violatores," Cols. 1438–39.

21 *that Princes are called . . . Dii principum*: Maynard, *De Privilegiis*, Part II, Article 14, No. 1, pp. 127–128.

24–28 *Diis non detrahes . . . Scripture of Judges*: The two Biblical passages in Exodus 22.28 and Acts 23.5, were already contentious to translators quite apart from the argument about the relative rights of popes and princes. For example, for "Diis" in Exodus 22.28, the Protestant Bishops' Bible (London, 1602) gives "judges" as the alternative translation for gods, and is therefore in accord with the fourteenth-century Franciscan biblical scholar de Lyra's and the Jesuit Sâ's translation and usage of the term. However, the Catholic Latin Vulgate treats the positions of high priest and earthly ruler in Acts 23.5 as separate, while the Bishops' and Geneva Bibles do not. Lyra's interpretation of the passage from Exodus that Donne's marginal note identifies as "in hunc locum," is found in his *Biblia Sacra*, Vol. VI, pp. 200^r, Col. 2, and 202^v, Col. 1; the Portuguese Jesuit Emmanuel Sâ's commentary on the same passage is found in his *Notationes in Totam Scripturam Sacram, Quibus omnia ferè loca difficilia, brevissimè explicantur*, first published in Antwerp in 1598, p. 401, Col. 2. Sâ (b. Villa de Code, Conde, 1530; d. Arona, 1596),

COMMENTARY 301

was professor of biblical exegesis at the Roman College and was the author of several works to which Donne refers in *Pseudo-Martyr*.

Page 56.

8–15 *For so at a Consultation . . . was Sacred*: Bald believes that the most probable explanation of the sentence is that the "Petition" was Southwell's pamphlet *Humble Supplication to her Majestie*, and that the "Consultation was a meeting of Catholic priests and laymen in the Tower of London in the last weeks of December 1591 to approve the dispatch of the document to Elizabeth" (*Life*, pp. 64–65.).

18–26 *Quirogaes expurgatorie . . . to his Majestie*: "Quiroga's expurgatorie Index" was the Spanish Inquisition's official index of forbidden books, published by the Spanish Cardinal Gaspar Quiroga in 1583, and generally referred to as the Hispanic Index. Donne was using a copy of the 1601 Salmieri edition, *Index Librorum Expurgatorum . . . D.D. Gasparis Quiroga*, which lists on p. 92^v the *De Vitis Philosophorum* of the fourth-century Alexandrian philosopher Eunapius published by the Dutch scholar of Greek, Adrian Junius, in 1568. Eunapius hoped for the triumph of paganism and despised the Christian martyrs whom he called "dirty heads." Junius' edition contained his epistle dedicatory to Elizabeth I, which was expurgated by the Index. Similarly, the Index expurgated the epistle dedicatory to Elizabeth by the French translator, Jean de Serres or Serranus (b. Bivorais, Montpellier, n.d.; d. 1597), that prefaced the first volume of his annotated Latin translation of Plato's works, and an epistle dedicatory to James VI of Scotland that prefaced the second volume (pp. 150$^{r, v}$).

31–2 (p. 57) *State businesse . . . Arcana Imperii*: The "Rationem Status," or reason of state for expurgating a volume, was given to the reader among the expurgatory instructions in the prefatory section "De Correctione Librorum," p. 18, of the *Index Librorum* passed at the Council of Trent in 1549. The *Index* was printed as an appendix at the end of several late sixteenth- and early seventeenth-century editions of the council's collected decrees, *Sacrosancti Concilia Tridentini Canones, et Decreta*, Bassani, ?1600. The "ratio status" or reason of state originated in the "ius gentium," that is, the laws of a people rather than in "ius naturalis" or natural law, and was in that sense synonymous with "dominatio" or with some legal loss of personal liberty, and could be extended to permit yet further loss of personal liberty in the name of the "arcana imperii" or security and secrecy of the empire (Schardius, *Lexicon*, Cologne, 1600, pp. 101, Col. 1; 309, Col. 1; 495, Col. 2; and 795, Col. 1). See *Devotions*, p. 52, and *LXXX Sermons* (London, 1640), 64, and V, *Sermons*, p. 299.

Page 57.

17–21 *Romane Authors . . . understand one another*: Donne's reference is to the *De Ratione Tegendi et Detergendi Secretum*, "Membri III, Quaestio III," of the Spanish theologian and confessor to the emperor Charles V, Dominic de Soto (b. Segovia, 1495; d. Salamanca, 1560) (p. 292 in the Venice edition of 1590). Soto was sent by Charles to the Council of Trent as one of his legates with another Spanish moral theologian and canonist Bartholomew Carranza (b. Miranda de Arga, Spain, 1503; d. Rome, 1576), a Dominican and Archbishop of Toledo, who was his travelling companion, and Donne quotes Carranza in his next paragraph. The passage in Soto deals with the moral nature of lying and of the circumstances of politics and fear under which a lie can be told. Donne connects this moral theology dealing with lies with the mental equivocation associated elsewhere in *Pseudo-Martyr* with the Jesuits.

18   *Intrinsecè*: correct Latin and Renaissance spelling for the adverb, *Revised Medieval Latin Word-List* (London, 1965), p. 257.

35–3 (p. 58) *Gregory the third . . . Binius hath wisely left out*: Donne is referring to the letter (c.732) about the Germans converted to Christianity, that Pope Gregory III (b. n.d.; d. Rome, 741) (elected in 731) sent to the apostle of Germany Saint Boniface (b. Crediton, Kent, 680; d. Fisia, 754), in which he gave him the right to reorganize the Frankish church. Binius' record of the letter to which Donne alludes is found in *Concilia Generalia*, Vol. I, p. 191, and its complete version from which Donne is translating is found in Carranza's *Summa Conciliorum et Pontificum à Petro usque ad collecta* (Lyons, 1600), p. 353^r. With another of Donne's often cited sources the Spanish Dominican de Soto, Carranza was sent as imperial theologian to the opening session of the Council of Trent (1545–1547) by the Emperor Charles V, and he was one of Philip II's emissaries to England to prepare his marriage to Mary Tudor in 1554, staying there until 1557. Carranza died in Rome after eight years of imprisonment on charges of heresy for which he was absolved shortly before his death, a fact that Donne surely entertained as he used Carranza's authority against Binius.

Page 58.

4–23   *in these expurgations . . . him a bull*: Donne is making six rapid references to the official *Index* of the Spanish Inquisition, and two to the so-called Belgian *Index* of forbidden sixteenth-century books. The first four references are to the Hispanic *Index*, and of these the first two are to the expurgations of the phrases "naturally admirable" in the description of Edward VI of England, and of "noteworthy" applied to one of the last, early sixteenth-century Dukes of Wittenberg, Christopher, in the *Fasti Hebraeorum, Atheniensum et Romanum* (Basel, 1556) of the Strasbourg historian Michael Beuthereus (b. 1496; d. Strasbourg, 1586), p. 148^r; the third reference is to the German precursor of the Reformation, Ulrich de Huttenus (b. Steckleberg, 1488; d. 1523), described as "Eques Germaniae doctissimus" (or Donne's "learned knight") in the sixteenth-century additions to the third-century *Chronicle* of the Christian Church of Eusebius of Caesaria (b. 265; d. 340) who never wholly abandoned Arianism (p. 93^r), and the fourth reference is to the German Greek scholar and translator of the *Iliad*, Eobanus Helius or Hessius (b. 1488; d. 1540), once more in the *Index*'s listing for Beuthereus' *Fasti* (p. 148ʳ); the fifth reference is to the listing in the Belgian *Index* of the addition of the word "sacerdotes" (and not Donne's "sacerdotem") on line 3 of p. 215 in the commentary on Aristotle's *Politics* published in Basel in 1545 by the German exegete and commentator on Aristotle, Martin Borrhaeus (b. Wurtenberg, 1499; d. 1564); while the sixth reference, once more to the Spanish *Index*, is to the expurgations in the annotations in No. 13 of the Book on Tarquinius the Superb in the edition of Livy by the sixteenth-century German scholar Ioannes Velcurio of Wittenberg, published in Strasbourg in 1545. The seventh reference, again to the Spanish *Index*, is to the expurgation of the letter "D" for doctor before Luther's name (because "quaedam contra indulgentias Papae" which Donne translates), once more in the additions to Eusebius' *Chronicle* (p. 93ʳ); and the eighth and last reference is the censure in the Belgian *Index* (pp. 153–154) of the repeated use of the capital letter "D" in the "De Iudiciis Nativitatum" in the *Opera* of the sixteenth-century mathematician and astronomer Ioannes Schonerus (b. Karlstadt, 1477; d. 1547), for reasons involving the pope and the devil which Donne is translating.

24–30 *this inhumanity of theirs . . . fellowshippe with Princes*: Thuanus was the French historian, Jacques August de Thou (b. Paris, 1553; d. Paris, 1617), a Gallican moderate Catholic, diplomat and Master of the King's Library in 1593. Donne's reference is general but he appears to be referring to de Thou's immense history of the times, *Historiarum Sui Temporis*, of which the first four parts were published before *Pseudo-Martyr* (Paris, 1604, 1606, 1607, 1608). *Historiarum* was a work that, like Baronius' *Annales* and Binius' *Concilia Generalia*, recorded history according to a strict yearly chronology, in its case beginning with the year 1543, exactly a decade before de Thou's birth. De Thou addresses his non-Catholic compeers, as Donne points out, by their recognized titles: Luther is "Augustinianus Vitembergae in Saxoniae theologiam professus," Vol. I, Book I, p. 10 (1606), and Mary Tudor, Edward Tudor, Elizabeth I, Calvin, Zwingli and Luther, are all accorded their titles some pages later (p. 20). The next point refers to Saint Francis' contemporary defender, the German Franciscan Henry Sedulius (b. Cleves, 1550; d. Salamanca, 1621), the author of *Apologeticus adversus Aicoran Franciscorum pro Libro Conformitatum* (Antwerp, 1607). Sedulius, with whom Donne takes issue numerous times in *Pseudo-Martyr*, was in the forefront of Counter-Reformation controversy in England in the first decades of the seventeenth century. His *Apologeticus* appears to have been designed to refute the republication of the second English edition of the *Alcoran of the Bare-foote Friers* which was originally published in 1550, in London in 1603, and his life of Saint Francis, *Historia Seraphica Vitae*, was published later in Antwerp in 1613. Donne attacks Sedulius for according to Saint Francis the right to address thieves, wolves and asses as his kin (*Apologeticus* I, 9, and III, 29), and yet for not according to secular princes the titles that recognize their temporal state power. See Commentary for p. 80, ll. 18–29.

33–10 (p. 59) *yet the last order . . . of our late Queene*: Francis Bozio (b. Gubbio, Umbria, 1563; d. Rome, 1643) and Antonio Gallonio (b. Rome, 1556; d. Rome, 1605) were two of the reputed minor controversialists, theologians and first members of the order of the Oratorians founded by Saint Philip Neri (b. Florence, 1515; d. Rome, 1595). The Oratory, as the new order was called, was erected into a congregation in 1575 on approval of Pope Gregory XIII, with the aim of grouping together secular priests into a community, without vows and without private means, principally to preach. The original aim of the Oratory, or the "Congregation" as it was also known, appeared to contradict what Donne considered here to be the purpose of the Jesuit order to seek worldly power, but he suggests that now Bozio's and Gallonio's new books are based on political arguments that make them akin to the Jesuits' ideals. In the opening pages of his *De Temporali Ecclesiae Monarchia et Iurisdictione . . . adversus impios Politicos, et huius temporis Hereticos* (Cologne, 1602), pp. 3–4, Bozio argued that those who did not accept the absolute supremacy of the pope as a temporal ruler were automatically excluded from salvation. For his part, in *De Sanctorum Martyrium Cruciatibus . . . . Quo portissimum instrumenta et modi quibus iidem Christi Martyres olim torquebantur* (Cologne, 1602) (first Italian edition, Rome, 1591; first Latin edition, 1594), Gallonio dealt with the instruments of torture used for the martyrdom of saints from primitive times to the present. He also attacked contemporary heretics such as Elizabeth I whom he described as the issue of the concubine Anne Boleyn, and whose persecution of Catholics he compared to that of Diocletian against early Christians (Chapter III, p. 121). Gallonio was Neri's first biographer (*Vita*, Rome, 1600), and also author of a projected multi-volume life of the saints (of which he completed the first two tomes from Saint Stephen to those who died in the year 271). Pullpilly discusses Bozio, Gallonio and Neri at length in *Caesar Baronius*, pp. 58, 157.

Page 59.

11–28 *But Baronius more then . . . imitate those tyrants*: Baronius, *Annales*, Volume VI, Tome 11, for the year 1097, Cols. 881–882, No. 18, and Cols. 885, Nu. 28, during the reign of Pope Urban II. The "great crime perpetrated" or the "Grande piaculum" of the quotation was the placing of not only papal secular authority but also of his spiritual authority into the hands of Duke Roger of Normandy and Sicily, in effect, into the hands of a secular ruler rather than of a spiritual ruler, as Baronius himself admits, says Donne ("unicum caput visibile in Ecclesia à Fidelibus . . . pro monstro et ostento caput Ecclesiae"), Col. 885, No. 29. In his account of Renaissance quarrels, Baronius criticized the Hapsburg Charles V for refusing to return the spiritual power to the pope (see Introduction, p. xxviii). Next, *Annales*, Vol. VI, Tome 11, year 1097, Col. 906, No. 87, "Praevaluit tamen ad tempus vis tyrannica, graffatio violenta, Principum latrocinium," and No. 88, "Imitantur planè atque sectantur, qui iisdem quibus illi legibus Siculam revocant atque renovant Monachiam."

COMMENTARY

Page 60.

1–12 *yet that Cardinall . . . his father and Grandfather*: From Cardinal Ascanius Colonna's answer to Baronius' tract, pp. 158–159; then from Cardinal Baronius' response to Colonna, No. 19, p. 196; and finally from Baronius' letter to Philip III of Spain, pp. 233–234, from which Donne chooses examples of the opposition of Catholic monarchs to the authority of the papacy; all three documents are appended to the 1609, Paris edition of Baronius' *Tractatus De Monarchia Sicilia*.

15–20 *the reason why . . . Primacy of the Church*: Baronius, *Annales*, Vol. VI, Tome 11, Cols. 885–886, Nos. 29 and 31, for the year 1097.

Page 61.

5–18 *for to Pope Stephen . . . Christian Rocke is abolished*: Saint Cyprian, Roman rhetorician converted to Christianity about the year 246, and elected bishop of Carthage two years later, saluted Pope Saint Stephen I (elected in 254) as "brother" (Donne's "fratri") in a letter in which he described to the pope the religious practices that he devised for his co-religionists in the face of the Novatian heresy (*Letters*, 1–81, trans. Sister Rose Bernard Donna, Washington, 1964, Vol. 51 in *The Fathers of the Church* Series, pp. 239–240). The Diocletian persecution in Donne's reference broke out in 249, and the Novatian heresy which prompted Cyprian's letter erupted among the Christians who were re-converted after the persecution ended. In a long letter to Cyprian, recorded by Binius in *Concilia Generalia*, Vol. I, Tome 1, pp. 191–194, Col. 2, which Donne paraphrases at length, Saint Firmilianus (d. 268) defended Cyprian's belief that baptism could be performed only within the confines of a church and that heretics re-converted to Christianity had to be rebaptized, against Stephen's position that perhaps they should not be allowed back into the church at all.

24–4 (p. 62) *Councell of Chalcedon . . . the Church that priviledge*: An exchange of letters between Pope Leo I, the Emperor Theodosius I, Anatole the Bishop of Constantinople, and Galla Placidia, Roman Empress and daughter of Theodosius, preceded the opening of the Council of Chalcedon in 451. The letters preface Binius' record of the council (hence Donne's "preambulatorie") in *Concilia Generalia*, Vol. II, Tome 2, Sig. *4–*6^v. Several of the letters in the exchange are entitled "sacrae litterae," and Galla Placidia herself is addressed as "Domina" (Sig. *5^5, Col. 2), and elsewhere as of "divinae memoriae" (Sigs. *5^r, Col. 2; *5^v, Col. 2). Second, Leo's first letter to the newly enthroned Emperor Leo I, dated July 11, 457, describing his missive as "this page of necessary supplication" (*Sacrorum Conciliorum*, Vol. VI, Letter 145, Col. 307), and his later letter of 1 December of the same year of which Donne quotes part of the opening sentence (Letter 156, Col. 323). Third, Felix III's letter of probably 482 to the Emperor Zeno (and not the 1610 text's marginal suggestion of 527 when both men were dead) asking that he support the eastern bishops Vitalis and Misenus in their defence of the Church (Vol. VII,

Cols. 1032–1033). Fourth and final, in about 532, the Emperor Justinian in a preface, addressed to the newly reigning pope John II, to Title 4 of his "Collatio Secunda" in the "Authenticae seu Novellae Constitutiones" which was appended to the *Codex* of what is normally the second volume of his *Codex Iuris Civilis*. In his preface which he called "Novella Constitutio IX," Justinian extended the Church's free hold on its benefices from thirty years to a hundred, and justified his constitution with the declaration that his power to do so came from ancient Rome.

Page 62.

8–34 *And Gregorie the first was . . . that Law) but also Priests*: The Emperor Maurice had passed a constitution forbidding converted pagans and infirm soldiers from entering monasteries. In a letter in 589, No. 62 in Book 2 of his "Epistolae," Pope Gregory I asked him to rescind the law (*Sacrorum Conciliorum*, Vol. 9, Cols. 1151–1152). However, Gregory did not send the letter directly to Maurice through his personal messenger, but entrusted it to Maurice's court doctor Theodoricus to whom he sent an accompanying letter (Book 2, No. 65, Col. 1155) asking for his intercession. Lines 14 to 16 of Donne's text refer first to Binius' "se haec non ut Episcopum scribere; sed iure privato loqui," in *Concilia Generalia*, Vol. II, Tome 2, p. 770, Col. 2, and secondly, to Baronius' "cum aliquam agat personam tamquam in scena," in *Annales*, Vol. IV, Tome 8, for the year 593, Col. 62, No. 18.

Page 63.

2–8 *one of his successors . . . excellentissimae Charitatis*: Saint Vitalian, pope from 655 or 657 to 672, in a letter of 6 February, probably in 656, to Vaanus the court archivist and chamberlain of the Eastern Emperor Constans II, asking his intercession for the revocation of the deposition of Bishop John of Lappa in Crete. A "cubicularius" was chamberlain, and "chartularius" was court archivist. There is some dispute among scholars about the death date of Eugene I and the beginning of Saint Vitalianus' reign, as Binius in *Concilia Generalia* suggests 655, but Mansi in *Sacrorum Conciliorum* suggests 657, Vol. 11, Cols. 17–18.

21–29 *Stephen the third . . . account with him*: With the fall of Ravenna to the invading Lombards in 752, Stephen II, sometimes called III, pope from 752 to 757, appealed for military help to the newly consecrated Pepin the Short King of the Franks, and to his brother Carloman who in 747 had given up all claims to royal power and had entered a monastery. Pepin complied, crossed the Alps and made the Lombards submit to Stephen a first time in 754, and yet a second time in 756, after they again attacked Rome.

COMMENTARY

Page 64.

17–24 *the Pope seeing then . . . in the former Epistle*: The "sons" whom Donne mentions and to whom Stephen IV, pope from 768 to 772 sent the letter, were Carloman and Charles, later Charlemagne, the children of Pepin the Short. Carloman and Charles inherited Pepin's kingdom in 768. Donne speaks of them as "sons" of the two "Princes" Pepin and his brother who also bore the name of Carloman, but the latter entered a monastery, leaving the eastern half of the Frankish kingdom to Pepin, and had no children. Of Pepin's two sons, Carloman (b. 751; d. 771) planned to marry Gerberga, and Charlemagne to marry Desiderata, both daughters of the Lombard King Desiderius. Desiderius had robbed the papacy of some of its Lombard territories, Carloman and Charlemagne had gained them back for the pope, and their political marriages to their former enemy's daughters threatened to plunge Pope Stephen IV back into territorial losses.

29–6 (p. 65) *that notorious letter of Nicholas . . . example and precedent*: Nicholas I (b. Rome, n.d.; d. Rome, 867), elected pope in 858, writing to the Eastern Roman Emperor Michael III (b. 839; d. Constantinople, 867), *Decretum*, Cause 9, Question 3, Chapter 10, Col. 876. In Book I, Chapter 4, of his *De Non Adorandis Imaginibus*, p. 121, Charlemagne objected to the Eastern Emperor Constantine VI's and his mother the Empress Irene's use of "divos" and "divilas" to describe themselves. See Commentary for p. 39, ll. 7–24, and p. 53, ll. 16–17.

Page 65.

19–33 *For so John the eight . . . his Letter to him*: John VIII in a letter of about 877 to Charles the Bald, King of France, when he sought his help against the Saracens and reminded him that he had once left his own possessions in Rome at the mercy of the imperial faction of Sergius, Constantina and Bishop Formosus of Porto and had gone to Ravenna to help him. After the death of Louis II, John supported Charles for the imperial crown and subsequently Charles received the crown from John's hands in Rome (hence Donne's quotation of "Ad Culmen Imperii") on Christmas day of 875 (*Sacrorum Conciliorum*, Letter 216, Vol. 17A–18A, Cols. 161–162). In the next letter in his *Epistolae* (No. 217, Cols. 162–163), once more addressed to Charles, John informed the king that he was sending him his nephew Farnulfus or Arnulf of Bavaria, son of Charles' late brother Carloman, to intercede for the papacy also, and in a yet later letter of 8 December (No. 230, Cols. 171–172) he urged him to act quickly on his request. But while maintaining good relationships with the western emperor in Charles, as Donne points out, John sought security for Rome from the eastern empire as well with a letter to the reigning Basil I the Macedonian (who ruled in Constantinople from 866 to 886) (Letter No. 251, dated the Ides of August, 878; Cols. 185–187).

Page 66.

13–20 *Innocent the first . . .to excommunication*: Innocent I, pope from 402 to 417, excommunicated the Eastern Emperor Arcadius (emperor from 395 to 408) for driving John Chrysostom into exile in 404, and suspected him of having taken part in the order for the forced march that resulted in John's death at Comona in 407.

21–27 *taught sufficiently . . . moved the Heavens*: In Chrysostom's interpretation of Isaiah 3:4, in "De Verbis Esaie, Vidi Dominum," Homily IIII, *Opera*, Vol. I, Tome 1, Col. 1235.

32–2 (p. 67) *Synodicall Letter . . . Adversus Regium fastigium*: The title of "supplex libellus" in *Concilia Generalia*, Vol. I, Tome 1, page 803, col. 2, as Donne's marginal note suggests, but the paraphrase joins together parts of Binius' original Latin sentences that occur on p. 804, col. 1. The Council of Ephesus took place in 430 under Celestus, pope from 423 to 432, and the Eastern Emperor to whom the synodical letter was directed was Theodosius II, who reigned from 408 to 450 (*Sacrorum Conciliorum*, Vol. 4, Cols. 1454–1455).

Page 67.

10–22 *a Bastard of Lotharius . . . his time abounds*: The bastard was Hugh, son of Lothaire II, king of Lotharingia or Lorraine, and of Waldrada. The French king with whom Hugh broke faith was Charles the Bald, and Donne's reference to "Epist." 123 was John VIII's excommunication decree of 872 (*Sacrorum Conciliorum*, Vol. 17A–18A, Col. 94). The next excommunication order to which Donne refers was against the Count of Luidtefrido and his wife who enticed the nun Garelinda out of the monastery of Angelburg (Col. 113). The next excommunication order occurs in Letter 166 to the Bishop Wibertus, and the last referred to by Donne is probably the decree John issued against Bishop Anserpus of Mediolanus (Letter 181, Cols. 122–123).

23–3 (p. 68) *And his predecessour Adrian . . . erudiendus erat*: Adrian II, pope from 867 to 872, first in a letter to Charles the Bald (*Sacrorum Conciliorum*, Vol. 15, Letter 17, Cols. 836–837), during the latter's attempted invasion of his dead nephew the emperor Lothair II's kingdom in 870; and, second, in a later letter (No. 19, Cols. 837–839) to the dead Lothair's nobles enjoining them to swear fealty to Louis the German without however taking up arms in his behalf against Lothair's son Hugo the bastard. Adrian wished to confine Louis' power to Germany and feared his invasion of Lombardy against Hugo whose ambitions in Italy he was nevertheless having to control (Letter 19, Cols. 837–838). When John VIII succeeded Adrian to the papacy, he first wrote a letter about fraud to Bishop Guaiferius of Salerno (No. 28, Vol. 17A–17B, Col. 26) and a letter later on 6 April 873 ordered Charles the Bald to make restitution (No. 42, Cols. 38–39).

COMMENTARY

Page 68.

4–11 *farther punishment . . . and confiscations*: From *Decretum*, Cause 11, Question 3, Chapter 41 "Nemo Episcoporum" and Chapter 108, "Cum aliquis vel excommunicatus," Cols. 570 and 586, but also *passim* Question 3.

12–19 *to me no evidence . . . beene his precedents*: Gregory VII, pope from 1073 to 1085; Phalaris, tyrant of Agrigente (565–549 B.C.), author of some surviving 148 letters in many of which he justified his legendary cruelty; and Marcus Junius Brutus (86–44 B.C.), Cæsar's assassin, who left letters to Cicero and Atticus.

20–12 (p. 69) *new addition of Eradication . . . of Tyrannique savagenesse*: First, Gregory VII to the bishops of France in a letter dated September 1074 about Philip I of France (b. 1052; d. 1108) who was notorious for foul morals and had been excommunicated several times (Book 2, Letter 5, Vol. 20, *Sacrorum Conciliorum*, Cols. 129–130); second, to William Earl of Poictou, dated November of the same year (2, Letter 18, Cols. 141–142), once more concerning Philip's depraved conduct that he compared to that of decadent Roman emperors; in the next year, 1075, Gregory held a synod in Rome to condemn the interference of secular rulers in ecclesiastical nominations; third, in a letter to the bishops of Germany and to the German population in general as well, in very late January of 1077, narrating how Henry IV of Germany had stripped himself of all royal attire and spent three days clad as a penitent and barefoot in the winter cold outside the gates of the castle of Canossa to obtain his pardon and to be confirmed as emperor (4, Letter 12, Cols. 218–219).

Page 69.

13–24 *And when Rodulphus . . . and of the Pope*: Rudolph (d. 1080), Duke of Swabia, brother-in-law and rival of the German Emperor Henry IV, who was elected king of Germany at a meeting of the German princes at Florschheim in 1073 after Henry was excommunicated and deposed by Gregory VII. He was crowned at Mainz in 1077 and recognized by the pope in 1080, but died some weeks later from his wounds received at the Battle of Hohenmolsen. With Rudolph dead, Henry regrouped his forces, marched into Italy in the next year, made a number of Italian alliances recognizing his power and eventually, in 1084, marched into Rome. The events are recorded in Gregory VII's two letters, both dated in 1581, first to the Abbot Hirfaugus Bishop of Padua, and second to the Faithful Universal (Letters 3 and 28, Vol. 20, *Sacrorum Conciliorum*, Cols. 342 and 360).

Page 70.

3–11 *thus delivered . . . in vinculo Anathematis*: Donne's quotation is a gathering of Gregory VII's main ideas in his excommunication of Henry IV of Germany for his refusal to implement the papal ban on the lay investiture of clerical positions in

1075 (Binius, *Concilia Generalia*, Vol. IV, Tome 3, Part 2, p. 1282, Cols. 1 and 2). See Introduction, p. xxix. The confiscation of Henry's lands was supposed to have followed his excommunication, as in the later case of Elizabeth I's excommunication.

Page 71.

1–9 *the survay of that letter . . . Kings be excepted*: The letter was written by Pope Gregory VII to Herimann Bishop of the abbatial town of Metten in Bavaria on 15 March 1080. Donne's three quotations are from Matthew 16.18, 19, and they were cited by Gregory as part of his argument to Herimann (Migne, *Patrologia*, Paris, 1853, Second Series, Vol. 148, Cols. 594–601).

12–18 *testimony of Gelasius . . . judge of the earth*: The two authorities whom Gregory VII cited were Pope Gelasius I (d. Rome, 496) who was elected in 492, in a letter to the Emperor Anastasius of Constantinople; and Julius I (d. 352) who became pope in 337, in a letter to several (and not Donne's "one") Eastern Bishops, *Epistola* I, (1), I, Migne, *Patrologia*, No. 2, Vol. 8, Col. 974. Before the claims of the Emperor Anastasius (b. 430; d. 515), Gelasius argued that the secular power of Rome sprang from the institution of the Church by Christ and not from any political preeminence that the Church might have arbitrarily held (*Patrologia*, No. 2, Vol. 59, Col. 42), whereas Julius, though not strictly defending the power of Rome, asserted the authority of eastern bishops like Saint Athanasius over the emperors.

21–2 (p. 72) *a priviledge graunted by Gregory the first . . . reads the whole sentence*: In his letter to the abbatial bishop Herimann of Metten in Bavaria who was quarrelling with the Emperor Henry over lay investiture, Gregory VII granted him the privilege of deposition against Henry. Gregory justified his act in the letter by citing the precedent of his precedessor Gregory I (b. Rome, 540; d. 604) who had accorded the very same privilege to Abbott Gerard of the Monastery of Saint Medard. Saint Medard (b. Salency, 456; d. 545) had been the bishop of Noyon in France, and the monastery bearing his name stood over his tomb at Crouy on the outskirts of Soissons. Donne argues that Gregory's letter granting the privilege to Saint Medard's Monastery was misquoted both by Gregory VII and yet much later by Bellarmine in Chapter 8 of Book V ("De Temporali Dominio et Potestate Eiusdem Pontifice"), third general controversy, Vol. I, *De Controversiis*, Col. 1070, to support the threat of excommunication against secular rulers. Gregory I's letter is in the appendix "Privilegium Monasterii" after Letter 38, Vol. 9, *Sacrorum Conciliorum*, Col. 1135.

Page 72.

12–16 *And the same Pope in erecting . . . temporall soveraignty*: Gregory I wrote his letter for the founding of the hospital to the Abbot Senator and promised him immunity even from Theodoricus the emperor (*Sacrorum Conciliorum*, Vol. 10, Book 11, Letter 10, Cols. 348–349).

COMMENTARY

17–24 *The Donation of Constantine . . . by publique bookes*: The Donation of Constantine, recorded in *Decretum*, Distinction 96, Chapter 14, Cols. 471–473, was a false document probably fabricated in the eighth century and exposed indubitably by Nicholas of Cusa in his *De Concordantia Cattolica* only in the fifteenth century, although doubts had been earlier cast upon its authenticity. The false document was supposedly a written declaration by the Emperor Constantine in which, on his conversion, he conferred on Sylvester I, pope from 314 to 335, who had baptized him a Catholic, the spiritual primacy over Antioch, Constantinople, Alexandria and Jerusalem. The document was evidently fabricated by someone to protect papal power against the power of the state, probably that exercised by Charlemagne, but the exact context remains obscure. Adrian I, pope from 772 to 795, was aware of the existence of the "Donation," as he cites it in two letters, the first to Charlemagne in 778 and the second to the Eastern Emperor Constantine VI in 785, and Leo X later also cited it in a letter to Michael Caerularius, the Patriarch of Constantinople, in 1054, but the fabrication of the document is generally thought to precede Adrian's reign.

25–7 (p. 73) *And such a Commination . . . the right hand of God*: From the record of the first church council held in Paris, listed by the Spanish Dominican theologian Carranza as having occurred in the year 553 (in his digest of the church councils, *Summa Conciliorum*, p. 243^r), but in actual fact the first Council of Paris took place much earlier, in 362 (Binius, *Concilia Generalia*, Volume I, p. 484). Carranza and therefore Donne, seem to be referring to the second Council of Paris under Pope Pelagius I but that too is uncertain because the second Council of Paris took place in 553, and Pelagius probably began his reign only in 555, although Binius records the council as being held during his papacy (*Concilia Generalia*, Volume II, p. 634). The citation of the fifth canon of 553 in Donne's marginalia is correct. His second example from the constitutions of Pope Paul I (b. Rome, n.d.; d. Rome, 767), elected in 757, is translated from Baronius' *Annales Ecclesiastici*, Volume V, Tome 9, for the year 761, Cols. 319–320, Nos. 6 and 8. Paul showed great concern for religious life in Rome and turned the paternal home into a monastery.

Page 73.

11 *ubi supra*: Baronius, *Annales Ecclesiastici*, Vol. VI, Tome 11, for the year 1097, Cols. 884–885, Nos. 25–29. See Commentary for p. 71, l. 21–p. 72, l. 2.

25–34 *His next reason . . . intolerable presumption*: Baronius referring to Gregory VII's letter of 8 September 1076 to Herimann Bishop of Metten (*Sacrorum Conciliorum*, Vol. 20, Book 4, Letter 2, Cols. 208–210).

Page 74.

1–7 *examples, of Innocent . . . consensit*: Innocent I excommunicated the eastern Emperor Arcadius for his role in the exile and death of Saint John Chrysostom in 407 (see Commentary for p. 66, ll. 13–20), and Saint Zacharias, pope from 741 to 752, confirmed the already conducted deposition of the last Merovingian king Childeric III of the Franks by Pepin III the Short in 751, *Decretum*, Cause 15, Question 6, Chapter 3, and its gloss, Cols. 1083–1084.

Page 75.

6–14   *King the Conquerour . . . you esteeme him*:   Gregory VII's letter, dated 2 April 1074, from Rome, to William the Conqueror in England; and, second, his letter to King Alphonsus of Castile, dated 1081, in *Sacrorum Conciliorum*, Vol. 20, Book 1, Letter 70, Cols. 113–114, and 9, Letter 2, Cols. 339–340.

17–26   *For this Gregorie chides . . . away from his mother*:   Gregory VII, in a letter dated 4 January 1079, to Hugo the Abbot of Cluny. However, the name of the noble admitted to the monastery is not mentioned.

30–1 (p. 76) *Gregories Dictates . . . sayes the contrarie, Lies*:   In Binius' *Concilia Generalia*, Vol. IV, Tome 3, Part 2, p. 1196, Cols. 1 and 2, a list of twenty-seven dictates, "Dictatus Papae," appended to Gregory VII's Epistle LV to the Catholic clergy. The letter touches on Gregory's interdiction of simony and incontinence at the Lenten Synod of 1074, and the appended dictates indicate the terms of power that Gregory arrogated unto himself to punish the clergy who did not obey. The supporting text for the Catholic upholders of papal power is the fourth part, "De Laude, Gloria et Ordine Ecclesiasticarum personarum interesse" of Consideration 7, *Catalogus Gloriae Mundi*, of the French court lawyer Casseneuz, pp. 168 and 176, Col. 2. Casseneuz describes the "superillustrious" character of papal power, and Donne translates from his text a quotation from the "Tractatus Solemnis de Constituto" of the Italian jurist Baldus de Ubaldis who strongly upheld a similar view.

Page 76.

2–8   *not build this supremacy . . . divers other Epistles*:   Gregory VII in the letter to Herimann Bishop of Metten: "Cum enim obedire apostolicae sedi superbe contemnunt, scelus idolatriae, teste Samuele, incurrant," *Sacrorum Conciliorum*, Vol. 20, Book 4, Letter 2, Col. 210.

11–26   *Simancha drawes into . . . came amongst them*:   *Enchiridion Iudicium Violatae Religionis, ad extirpandas haereses, theoricen & praxim summa brevitate complectens* (Antwerp, 1573), in Chapter 21 entitled "De principibus," on princes, No. 9, pp. 69–70 of the Spanish jurist and canonist Simancha. The Catholic theory of the liberation of faithful subjects from their loyalty to heretical kings and of consequent justified regicide, recurs in *Thesaurus Antiquitatum Ecclesiasticarum* (Cologne, 1606), a posthumous work of the German theologian Schulting. Donne calls Schulting an "epitomizer" because his two-volume *octavo* edition of *Thesaurus* was an abridgement of Baronius' seven-folio-volume *Annales*. His first reference is to Chapter 8, Tome I, p. 3, where Schulting discussed the Greek geographer Strabo's account of the power of the Egyptian priests in the last seventeen books of his *Geography*, and his second reference is to Chapter 243, p. 178, on the authority of the Ethiopian priests. Ergamenes was a king of Ethiopia who lived between B.C. 250 and 150, who put an end to the unlimited power of the priests of Amon at Napata by slaying them instead of killing himself as they had requested him to do by custom. The late first century B.C. Greek historian Diodorus of Sicily (b. Agyrion) records Ergamenes' life in his *Bibliotheca historicae* (IV.1).

27–2 (p. 77) *From this libertie . . . are above them*:   The marginal note to Donne's references was garbled during printing and an attempted correction was inadequate. The first reference, Chapter 30 (and not 2) "Solvitur argumentum ultimum et tractatur quaestio, An Papa haereticus deponi possit") of Book II, "De Pontifice," of the third general argument ("De Summo Pontifice") Col. 824; the second reference, "an Emperour:" Chapter 12 (and not 2) ("Cuius sit congregare Concilia") of Book I ("De Natura et Causis Concilii") of the fourth general controversy ("De Conciliis et Ecclesia"), Col. 1118; and finally, "Princes have not:" Chapter XVII ("Ad magistratum non pertinere iudicium de Religione") of Book III ("De Laicis") of the fifth general controversy ("De Membris Ecclesiae"), Col. 1748, of Bellarmine's *De Controversiis*, Volume I.

Page 77.

3–12   *a Contry-man of ours . . . to Depose also*:   The "Countryman" is the Benedictine Robert or Gregory Sayer (b. Redgrave, Suffolk, 1560) who was trained in theology in Douai, eventually became a monk at Monte Cassino, and finally a professor of theology in Venice where he died in 1602. In his *Casuum Conscientiae Sive Theologiae Moralis Thesaurus, De Censuris Ecclesiasticis*, Book I, Chapter 6 ("De variis modis quibus Iurisdictio acquiritur"), Sayer argued that there were three ways of acquiring jurisdiction: by election, by delegation of powers, and finally, by prescription, that is, through the power of the church canons, including the prescriptive jurisdiction of conducting excommunications (No. 30, p. 27). It is this latter form of prescriptive jurisdiction to which Donne objects, particularly as Sayer later in the same passage extends the jurisdiction universally. The other "great Patron of that greatnesse" of ecclesiastical power was the Spaniard José Estève or Josephus Stephanus (b. Valencia), canon of Sepulveda, professor of philosophy in Siena, and later bishop of Orihuela where he died in 1604, the author of *De Osculatione Pedum Romani Pontificis* (1579) which supported the ecclesiastical powers of the Roman Catholic Church. In Chapter XVI, "Episcopus suo iure convenire, ut omnes homines eis capita submittent, et sacras manus osculentur," pp. 121–122 of the Rome edition of 1588, Stephanus argues that contemporary ecclesiastics have reached such a height of dignity, that, contrary to the practice of the priesthood in the Old Testament, secular rulers defer to them, and Donne translates the beginning of the passage. The excommunication by Pius V to which Donne refers is Elizabeth I's in 1570.

22-28 *And of the Emperour they say . . . over his head*: Two Catholic documents on clerical precedence: Gigas' *Tractatus De Crimine Laese Maiestatis Insignis*, Question 2, No. 5; Question 4, No. 2; and Question 1, No. 6, of Rubric 4 in Book I (pp. 13, 14, and 12), describing the supremacy of the popes over secular rulers for the justification of the ceremonial rites that Gigas describes; and the Catholic Church's official volume on ceremonies, *Sacrarum Cerimoniarum*, from the chapter on "De Loco et Sedibus concilii," in the eighty-fourth section "De Concilio generali," p. 140.

Page 78.

4-7 *Bellarmine himself confesses . . . any such concurrence*: Chapter 8 ("Non accepisse Carolum Magnum a Deo immediate Imperii dignitatem") of Book I ("Romanum Imperium a Graecis ad Francos Summi Pontificis auctoritate translatum") of *De Translatione Imperii Romani a Graecis ad Francos*, published earlier but found in a second general appendix under "Index Opusculorum" in Vol. I of the Cologne edition of the *De Controversiis* in 1615, p. 407.

12-22 *That in the Pope . . . or Ecclesiastique Magistrates*: On the mediation or intercession of Christ in all human authority, both ecclesiastical and secular, in succeeding paragraphs in Col. 773 of Chapter XVII ("Idem probatur ex origine et antiquitate primatus") in Book II ("De Pontifice") of the third general controversy ("De Summo Pontifice") of Vol. I of Bellarmine's *De Controversiis*.

29-31 *the Colledge of Cardinals . . . might absolve*: For the collegial power of the cardinals over the pope, and for the origin of the power of the pope in the hands of the cardinals who elect him, the first authority is the fourteenth-century von Niem's account of the great Western schism *De Schismate Universalii*, Book III, Chapter 1, p. 141, from which Donne translates, "in Urbe propter eius temporale dominium, quod tunc integrum apud Cardinales remanserat;" the second authority is the English Benedictine Sayer's *Casuum Conscientiae*, Book II, Chapter 20 ("De Absolutione à Sententia hominis"), No. 30, p. 198. Sayer writes, "Pari ratione mortuo Papa, sede vacante, Collegium Cardinalium absolvit, quos Papa absolvere potuit," which Donne also translates.

31-2 (p. 79) *If therefore in all . . . to the Successor*: A summary of Cols. 1062 and 1063, Chapter 6 ("Papam habere temporalem potestatem indirecte"), Book V ("De Temporali Dominio et Potestate eiusdem Pontificis"), the third general controversy ("De Summo Pontifice") of Bellarmine's *De Controversiis*, Vol. I.

Page 79.

21-24 *Aquinas sayes expressely . . . upon the eldest Sonne*: Thomas Aquinas, *Summa Theologiae*, I.II. Quest. 103, Art. 3, Ottawa Institute for Medieval Studies, 10 Vols. (Ottawa, 1953), Vol. II, Col. 1313a.

COMMENTARY 315

27–29 *The Apostle did . . . the body of the Church*: A translation of the opening of the paragraph "Potest etiam" in Col. 633, Chapter 9 ("Quod Regimen Ecclesasticum esse debeat"), Book I ("De Primatu S. Petri in Ecclesia Militante"), the third general controversy ("De Summo Pontifice") of Bellarmine's *De Controversiis*, Vol. I.

31–4 (p. 80) *Councell of Paris . . . men, but from God*: A plea for the divine right of kings based on support from the records of the Sixth Council of Paris in 829 at which Pope Gregory IV had to pass judgement on the conflicting claims of the brothers Lothair and Louis the Pious, as recorded in Binius' *Concilia Generalia*, Vol. III, Tome 3, Part 1, Col. 2, Chapter 5, p. 562. In rendering judgement against Louis and in favour of Lothair, Gregory ruled that the king's secular power came from God, and that he did not only acquire it by inherited royal rights. As Lothair's main adversaries were ecclesiastical, Donne sees in his victory a canonical support for his argument that contemporary kings have rights against ecclesiastics. Donne's "Quod Regnum non ab hominibus, sed a Deo detur," is part of the title of Binius' chapter on Gregory's judgement, and his English quotation is his translation of the opening lines of the judgement.

Page 80.

8–12 *As in the Septimes . . . to Priests onely*: The "Septimes" were the collection of decretals from 1503 up to Gregory XIII's reign, and ordered included in the *Corpus Iuris Canonici* by Gregory at the end of the sixteenth century (see p. 197). In his text Donne refers to this collection as "Septimes," "Septims" or even "Septimus," but in his marginalia as "In Septimo" (i.e., pp. 101, 241, 243). However, this marginal "In Septimo" must not be confused with the identical term with which Donne refers to the seventh session of the Council of Trent (see Commentary for p. 50, l. 20–p. 51, l. 7), whose record is found in the "Septimes".

18–29 *the Dreame of Pharoes . . . King of the Jewes*: The "Booke of Conformities" to which Donne refers here and elsewhere in *Pseudo-Martyr* in relation to Sedulius' *Apologeticus* was the *Liber Aureus Inscriptus Liber Conformitatum Vitae Beati, ac Seraphici Patris Francisci Ad Vitam Iesu Christi* (1389) of the fourteenth-century Franciscan monk Bartholomeo Degli Albizzi (b. Rivano, Tuscany, n.d.; d. Pisa, 1401), also known as Bartholomaeus Pisanus. The *Liber Conformitatum*, first published in Latin in Venice, placed the life of Saint Francis in parallel with the life of Christ so closely that it almost deified him, and later editions by Franciscans, including the first Italian edition, tempered the parallels between Francis and Christ to avoid charges of heresy. As early as 1541, one of Luther's students at Wittenberg, Erasmus Alberus (b. Sprendlingen, ?1500; d. Neubrandenburg, 1553), published *The Alcoran of the Bare-foote Friers* (mentioned in Donne's marginalia) against the *Liber Conformitatum*, with a German preface by Luther himself. The Latin edition followed in 1542, the first English edition in 1550 and the second English edition, which probably provoked Sedulius' *Apologeticus*, in 1603. In the *Apologeticus*, Sedulius repeatedly makes typological interpretations of the rule and life of Saint Francis to defend Albizzi's *Liber Conformitatum* against Alberus' *Alcoran*, and Donne is attacking four such interpretations in the *Apologeticus*, the first in II.1.1, p. 66, on the dove Noah sent from the Ark in Genesis 8.8, as well as on the narration of the dream of Pharoah's officer in Genesis 40.10; the second in II.1.2, p. 67, on Luke 12.32 and Matthew 25.45, and the comparison of Francis' order to the kingdom of God; the third in III.13.4, p. 158, on the mission of the Franciscan order and the spread of God's name in Psalm 118; and the fourth, in I.18.6, p. 53, on Saint Francis as a saviour and the descriptions of Christ as king in Matthew 1.41 and 1 Timothy 2. See Commentary for p. 58, ll. 24–30.

31–3 (p. 81) *inch of the Sindon . . . be reprehended*:   Sindon, from the Latin, Christ's shroud in the tomb. Pope Julius II issued the bull "Romanus Pontifex" in 1506 establishing the liturgy and Mass of "de Sancta Sindone" to be said in the oratory where the shroud is preserved in Turin. The liturgy was described by the Archbishop of Bologna Alfonso Paleoto (b. Bologna, n.d.; d. 1610) in his *Historia Admiranda de Iesu Christi Stigmatibus Sacrae Sindoni* which was published with the commentary *Cum universa Passionis seria* by Daniel Malloni, in Douai, 1607, part I, Chapter I, No. 18, pp. 21–22.

Page 81.

4–8   *By this license they . . . call'd the Decalogue*:   In Chapter 4 "Cum inter nonnullos viros scholasticos" of Title 14 "De Verborum Significatione," in the "Extravagantes" of John XXII, *Corpus Iuris Canonici*, Col. 301. Secondly Pope Leo X in a letter dated 12 June 1514, No. 17.1 of Book VIII of his *Epistolae* in the *Codex Ambrosianus* (there were two letters numbered 17, hence Donne's marginal reference to the first), L. Pastor, *Histoire des Papes depuis la fin du Moyen Age*, 20 Vols. (Paris, 1909), Vol. 8, pp. 312–330. Thirdly, Gretser's defensive history of the Jesuit order, *Historia Societatis Iesuitarum Auctore, nomine, gradibus . . . conscripta ab Elia Hasenmillero* (Ingolstadt, 1604) ("Immane verò facinus, scilicet, patravit P. Crucius, cum regulas nostras *Decalogum nominavit*; Nescit decalogi nomen Metaphoricè omnibus illis tribui"), p. 141, which Donne is attacking in order to defend the German Elias Hasenmuller or Hasenmiller (see *Ignatius His Conclave*, pp. 75–79). An ex-Jesuit turned Lutheran, Hasenmiller finished only the first parts of his projected complete history of the Jesuit order before his death (c. 1590), and these were published as *Historia Iesuitici Ordinis* in Frankfurt in 1593 (the history was completed by Hasenmiller's friend the theologian Polycarp Leyserus and published in 1605). Gretser's *Historia* which Donne cites several times in *Pseudo-Martyr*, was an answer to the Hasenmiller version of the story of the order. For the use of metaphoric language by the Jesuit Crucius, Donne is paraphrasing Gretser's text, and Gretser gives no indication as to which of the Jesuits who bore the name of Crucius he is referring. The likeliest possibility is the German James Crucius (b. Bamberg, 1548; d. Gratz, 1617), author of *De Veritate Corporis Christi* (1599), and *De Corruptione Sacrae Sculpturae facta a Luthero* (1602), or the Portuguese

COMMENTARY

Luiz da Cruz (b. Lisbon, 1543; d. Coimbra, 1604), author of *Interpretatio poetica . . . Psalmos* (1597). The Jesuit *Constitutiones* were Ignatius Loyola's rules for the Jesuits. However, the works of both Crusius (or Crucius) and Cruz contain no direct comparison of the *Decalogue* and the *Constitutiones*.

10–18 *Sedulius his guiltie excuse . . . in every thing*: Sedulius defends Albizzi's practice in *Liber Conformitatum* of applying divine epithets to Mary the Virgin and the popes. Donne's familiarity with Sedulius' *Apologeticus* (1607) is strikingly thorough, as within the space of a few lines he cites eleven passages: Preface, No. 7, Sig.**4^r; I, 9, 1, p. 21; I, 18, 3, p. 52; I, 18, 1, p. 51 and I, 20, 8, p. 63; I, 20, 5, p. 61; I, 13, 2, p. 32; I, 15, 5, p. 43; I, 18, 2, p. 51; and II, 6, 8, p. 85.

19–21 *Nor will Serarius . . . these excesses*: From the French Jesuit linguist Serarius' book on the use of language in religious composition, *Litaneutici*, Book II, Question 13, p. 79, on the manner of treating canonical matters in suitably sacred prose. See Commentary for p. 53, l. 32–p. 54, l. 10.

23–29 *And though Bembus . . . sign'd those Letters*: Cardinal Pietro Bembo (b. Venice, 1470; d. Rome, 1547), close personal friend of Leo X whom he accompanied from Urbino to Rome. Bembo remained in Rome writing, among other things, letters in his elegant neo-Platonic style for the pope, until the latter's death in 1521. The collected letters *Petri Bembi Epistolae*, were published in Basel in 1539. The first letter in Donne's marginalia, No. 21 in Book II, is dated 30 April 1513, and the second, No. 15 in Book IV, 29 August 1513, in the *Codex Ambrosianus*. However, it is uncertain which edition of Leo's letters in Bembo's hand Donne was using, as the Basel edition of 1539 does not contain Letter No. 1.17 of Book VIII referred to a letter earlier in his text.

34–10 (p. 82) *Saint Francis commanded . . . a Capon ready rosted*: Contrary to the impression left by Donne's text, in Sedulius' *Apologeticus*, the typological misuse of the Scriptures is tempered by Francis' statement to Brother Massaeus that he should tumble like a child, but in comedy ("Ridenda videri possent, nisi Christus serio iussisset," III, 1, 3, p. 130). Again, in the story of Saint Anthony and the man who cut off his foot at the saint's behest as punishment for kicking his mother, and which the saint put back into place, Sedulius considers the literal truth of the story as only one possible interpretation of the incident (III, 13, 3, p. 158). Likewise in the case of the third incident about the frog, the chicken and Saint Anthony, Sedulius examines its comic value (III, 18, 31, p. 268).

Page 82.

16–18 *Super aspidem & Basiliscum ambulabis . . . and worthily done*: A cartoon-like woodcut which accompanies the Protestant martyrologist Foxe's description of the quarrel over temporal power between the German Emperor Frederic I Barbarossa and Pope Alexander III, may lie behind Donne's reference. The woodcut shows the pope treading on the prostrate emperor's neck to throttle him, while at the same time reciting the biblical quotation that Donne also quotes to justify himself, *Acts and Monuments* (London, 1583), p. 205. The bishop who defended the pope's subjection of Barbarossa was Stephanus or Estève, in Chapter 11 ("Olim delinquentes dum peccatorum veniam postulabant, sacerdotum ac laicorum pedes ad oscula retulisse") of *De Osculatione*, pp. 74–75.

Page 83.

4–27   *And though Bellarmine seeme to deplore . . . word of the other*:   The book that Bellarmine attacked was *Aviso Piacevole dato alla bella Italia*, and the attack was appended to Chapter II ("Ad Libros De Summo Pontifice") of later editions of *De Controversiis* (Cologne, 1615), Volume I, p. 371. Elsewhere in the same appendix, as Donne notes, Bellarmine defends the work in the sense that he supports its reliance on secular writers like Dante, Boccacio and Petrarch, to uphold the Roman Church's authority (Chapters 14–22, pp. 376–382). The "authour" with the disguised name was the ex-Lutheran Gaspar Schopp, alias Nicodemus Macer (b. Neumarck, 1576; d. Padua, 1649), who was converted to Catholicism in Rome, and who, in *Discrepatio de Parenesi* (1607), defended Baronius' pro-papal *Paranesis Ad Rempublicam Venetam* (1606) in the Venetian controversy, against two tracts *Antiparaenesis* and *Duo Vota* of late 1606 by the Venice-based native Neapolitan Franciscan Giovanni Marsilio, alias Nicholas Crassus. Donne is citing Schopp's argument in his address to the reader ("Ad Lectorem") on Socrates' authority, but also later parts of the work (pp. 3, 14, 36). In the next year, 1611, Donne renewed his attack on the Catholic usage of profane works (*Ignatius His Conclave*, p. 9). Donne's use of the phrase "furious instigation of the Pope," is not entirely clear, even if the seventeenth-century uses of the word "instigation" are admitted. The phrase suggests an attack on the pope, in the sense of goading him, as well as encouraging him. As Baronius never attacked Paul V, a line of text implicating Marsilio's tractual attacks may be missing. The reference to Pope Alexander VI (Roderick Borgia, elected in 1492) concerns his incestuous relationship with his illegitimate daughter Lucretia, and the Englishman whom Donne attacks without naming is probably Parsons in his *Answere* to Coke in 1606.

28–30   *determined to kill . . . Sacrament first*:   Henry VII of Germany (1269–1313) was purported to have been assassinated by a Dominican friar who poisoned his Mass wine, at Buonconvento, near Pisa, as he descended Italy to conquer the Kingdom of Naples to complete the re-unification of the Roman Empire. Pope Clement V and King Robert of Naples feared Henry's designs.

33–4   (p. 84) *Panegyriques, to advance . . . temporall Jurisdiction*:   Donne's biblical quotation, *Omnia Subiecisti sub pedibus eius* is from Psalm 8.6 (Geneva Bible numbering); Maynardus' use of the quotation (*De Privilegiis*, Part I, Article 2, No. 22, p. 23), is in reference to Paul's letter to the Ephesians 1.22. The term "Panegyrics" is also Donne's and not Maynardus'. After Maynardus, Donne cites the Portuguese Jesuit Sâ's commentary on Luke 22.38 in his *Scholia In Quatuor*

Evangelia (Antwerp, 1596). However Sâ's reference to the paschal type of lamb and knives occurs more specifically in his exegesis of the "literal sense" of Luke 22.39 and of his additional author's notes to both 22.38 and 22.39 on p. 386 of the Lyons edition of 1602 of *Scholia*. Finally, Boniface VIII's canon "Unam Sanctam," in Chapter 1 of Title 8 "De Majoritate et Obedientia" of the "Extravagantes Communes," *Corpus Iuris Canonici*, Col. 319–320. For the numbering of Psal. 8.6 in Donne's text, see Introduction, p. lxxiii.

Page 84.

6–13 *to warre, and devastation . . . the Alcoran*: In his speech to the consistory in Rome on 17 April 1606, Baronius urged Paul V to excommunicate the Venetians for refusing Roman spiritual authority over their secular magistracy (*De Venetorum Excommunicatione, Adversus Caesarem Baronium . . . Dissertatio. In qua vera Excommunicationis ratio, tum ex Sacra Scriptura . . . Auctore Nicolao Vignierio*, which reprinted Baronius' address, Frankfurt, 1607, Sig. A2^r). Baronius cited the "kill and eat" (*Macta et Manduca*) message of the divine voice to Peter in Acts 10.13. For Galatinus on the Talmud, see Commentary, p. 116, l. 32–p. 117, l. 3. Nicholas of Cusa wrote his treatise "De Cribratione Alchorani" in 1460.

28–15 (p. 85) *And you extend those immunities . . . subject to Temporall Jurisdiction*: Donne gives eight examples of Catholic canonical writings that extend the immunities that clerics enjoy from the jurisdiction of laymen, to certain kinds of lay people themselves. First, Gratian in Distinction 21, Chapter 1 of *Decretum*, Col. 92, argues that acolytes and sacristans work in churches and that they therefore enjoy the immunities of "clericos." Second, the French master of jurisprudence before the Parliament of Paris, Choppin, in his *Monasticon* on the rights of the clergy and of monasteries, who accorded the immunity of ordained clerics from secular law to unordained Christian hermits by reason of their sanctity (Book II, Title 2, Nu. 25, pp. 295–296). Thirdly, the French Franciscan friar Stephanus d'Alvin of Tours, who published in Paris in 1607 the *Tractatus De Potestate Episcoporum, Abbatum, Praelatorum, Praesertim Regularium, Necnon Abbatissarum*, included nuns under "regular" laity covered by minor orders, rather than under "ordinary" laity, and so granted them certain forms of ecclesiastical immunity (Chapter 3, Numbers 10–11, pp. 14^v–15^r). Fourth, again in *Decretum*, Distinction 23, Chapter 24, Col. 115, Gratian admits to the clerical character of professed nuns in spite of the fact that he refuses them the right to touch the ritual articles of the Catholic Mass. Novices were called "canonica seculares" because they were covered by the prescriptions of canon law even though they were still "secular" individuals in the sense that they had not yet taken final binding religious vows. Fifth, in Chapter 4, "De auxilio animarum" of *Regulae*, Rule 47 in the "Regulae Praepositi Domus Professae" on the governing rules of professed houses, p. 68 in the Lyons edition of 1606, Jesuits were forbidden to minister to the spiritual care of professed nuns, such as hearing their confessions. The "Ecclesiastici fori" to which Donne says the "Regular" or still not yet ordained nuns were admitted was the privilege of being tried only by an ecclesiastical court, and of not being under the jurisdiction of secular courts. The Rota was the "Rota Sacra Romana," the principal Roman Catholic court for trying ecclesiastical cases, and the Rota's decision to which Donne is referring is the multitude of reforms that Clement VIII passed in the last decade of the sixteenth century defining the roles of "regular" male and female clergy, and that d'Alvin discussed at length in *De Potestate*, Chapters IV, V, VI, pp. 17–28. Sixth, once more in *De Potestate*, Chapter III, No. 13, p. 16^r, Alvin argues that nuns do not have the power to conduct excommunications but are nevertheless ecclesiastical persons. Seventh, in his enormous volume which treats of the excesses committed by secular rulers and of their crimes and punishments, *De Syndicatu Tractatus Elegantissimus et Absolutissimus* (Pavia, 1510), the late fifteenth- and early sixteenth-century councillor to Ferdinand I and Neapolitan law scholar Paris de Puteo describes the nature of clerical immunities granted to laymen (Number 29 in the Chapter "De excessibus regnum," p. 15, in the Frankfurt edition of 1605 of which Donne was using a copy). Finally, once more from Maynardus' *De Privilegiis*, Part II, Article 17, Nos. 9 and 10, p. 147.

Page 85.

20–30 *Rome which was . . . in such a case*: In his description of how the popes acquired temporal power abusively over the centuries, Donne first cites the legal historian Gregorius, also known as Tholosanus, in his *Syntagmatis Iuris Universi*. Next he cites the passage in *De Schismate Universali*, Book I, Chapter 22, pp. 23–24, in which the historian Niem recounts how Pope Urban VI, who reigned when the Great Western Schism was provoked in 1378, quarrelled with Charles of Darazzo, king of Naples. Urban made Charles king of Naples as a reward for supporting him against the anti-pope Clement VII, but Charles soon went to war against him and melted down sacred statues and vessels of gold and silver from churches and monasteries, worth eighty thousand florins, and turned them into money to pay for his armies.

Page 86.

4–11 *And for the Persons . . . Ledesma, and Bannes*: Donne's notes are to two documents in the *Raccolta degli Scritti*, the pro-papal collection of documents relating to the excommunication of the Venetians by Pope Paul V. The first document is the *Discorso . . . . I fondamenti, e le ragioni delli SS. Veneziane*, a long tract by Fra Lelio Medici of Piacenza, the Inquisitor-General of Florence, first published in Bologna in 1606. The *Discorso* attempted to establish a middle ground for the two parties and appealed to their sense of divine providence, but nevertheless upheld the freedom of clerics and their possessions from secular interference, which constitutes the argument of the passage from which Donne is quoting (p. 196). The second document is the Carmelite theologian Bovio's *Riposta . . . Alle Considerationi del Padre*

Maestro Paolo de Venetia against the Venetian Paolo Sarpi's criticism of Paul V. In arguing in Paul's behalf (p. 50), Bovio nevertheless listed a number of Catholic writers who put restrictions on papal power, all of them Spanish, and who, more specifically, placed limits on the immunity of ecclesiastics from secular jurisdiction. Donne referred to the same passage earlier in *Pseudo-Martyr*, p. 16.

25–28 *The Students in the English Colledge . . . of the Church*: Donne's translation is a paraphrase of Baronius' text. His reference to the English College in Rome, which is not in Baronius' original Latin copy, is probably nevertheless a correct interpretation of Baronius' thinking: "aliosque nobilissimos viros Anglicanos ampliori (liceat dicere) martyrio coronatos, duplicisque tituli coronis auctos," *Martyrologium Romanum*, 29 December, Col. 1, p. 567. Donne's reference to the English College reveals how the English Protestant looked upon the college's role in the Church's attitudes towards England.

Page 87.

9–22 *In every good worke . . . deserve Heaven*: Bellarmine, on the relationship of good works and merit to salvation, in three of his tracts in *De Controversiis*: first, *De Indulgentiis* which appeared in the *Opuscula*, p. 369, of 1615; second, "De Sacramento Confirmationis," Chapter 11, in the second controversy "De Baptismo et Confirmatione," Volume II, Col. 437, and also Chapter 2, Col. 406; and finally, "De Iustificatione, qui est de Meritis Operum," Chapter 17 on "Opera bona iustorum meritoria esse ex condigno, non solum ratione pacti, sed etiam ratione operum," Col. 1299, which constitutes Book V of the second controversy "principales" called "Quae est de Iustificatione Impii," Volume III.

Page 88.

27–29 *That it is . . . vaine-glory*: Donne's translation paraphrases the title of Bellarmine's third proposition in Chapter 7, "Quatenus fiducia in meritis collocari possit, exponitur," in Book V, "De Iustificatione qui est de Meritis," in the second principal controversy "De Iustificatione impii," Vol. III, Col. 1268, of *De Controversiis*.

30–35 *a man may not be sure . . . he is certaine of it*: Aloysius Gonzaga (b. Castiglione, 1568), a still relatively obscure figure in the early seventeenth century, was the young Italian heir to the marquisate of Castiglione who, as Donne states, gave up his title in 1587 to become a Jesuit, and who died taking care of plague victims in Rome in 1591. The Italian Jesuit Virgilius Ceparius (b. Panicale, c. 1564; d. Rome, 1631), an expert in beatification and canonization procedures, and who was instrumental in Gonzaga's official beatification by Pope Gregory XV in 1621, was also his first biographer, and published the first edition of *Vitae Aloysii Gonzagae* in Italian in Rome in 1606, and then in a first edition in Latin in Cologne in 1608 a copy of which Donne was using. In his account of the boy Jesuit's life, Ceparius records

Bellarmine's testimony of him before a notary of the Vatican Apostolical Chamber, which heard the case for Gonzaga's beatification, III, 2, pp. 401–402. Bellarmine testified that Gonzaga was not only free from all taint of serious sin from the age of reason at seven years old, but also before that — the point that Donne takes up.

Page 89.

12–29 *Benius in a booke . . . is shaken therein*: Paolo Beni (b. Candia, 1552; d. Padua, 1625) was one of Italy's foremost Renaissance critics and commentators on Plato and Aristotle, the author of a book on efficient and divine grace and free will entitled *Qua tandem Ratione. dirimi possit Controversia quae inpraesens de efficaci Dei auxilio et libero arbitrio inter nonnullos Catholicos agitatur* (Padua, 1603), with an opening address to the reigning pope Clement VIII (1536–1605), pope from 1592, to which Donne is referring. Beni discussed the controversy over the respective roles of grace and good works in the salvation of the Christian as a phenomenon among Catholics without reference to Reformation disputes. Donne's quotation "by what way and meanes" is a loose translation of Beni's title, and he next cites Beni's epistolary call to Clement for moderation (Sig. preliminary leaves, 4^r) and his declaration that there is not enough distinction between "sufficient" and "efficient" graces for a controversy (Chapter 3, p. 9). Donne's two other quotations are from the following "Proemium" to Clement VIII in Chapter 1, pp. 4 and 2. The marginal note to "Fo." for p. 91 is to Beni's restatement of his position later on in his works. Donne's next reference points to Bellarmine's argument for the different kinds of grace in Chapter XI "Concedendam esse partitionem auxilii specialis in sufficiens & efficax," in Book I "De gratia in genere; id est, de nomine, definitione, & partitione gratiae," of the first principal controversy entitled "De Gratia, et libero arbitrio," in Vol. III of *De Controversiis*, Cols. 559–564.

Page 90.

11–13 *And howsoever . . . Franciscan Families*: Among the titles applied to the members of the Franciscan sodality in the directory, *Athenae Orthodoxorum Sodalitii Franciscani* (Leyden, 1598), p. 1, *passim*, by the Belgian Franciscan Henry Willot.

20–23 *in these bookes . . . perfited and accomplished*: Pius IV issued his bull "'De Indice Librorum prohibitorum'" (in Donne's margin) at the twenty-fifth session of the Council of Trent from which flowed the "Regula" for "Libris Prohibitis," in the sitting for 24 March 1564 (*Sacrorum Conciliorum*, Vol. 33, Cols. 227–228).

27–3 (p. 91) *in that Catholique booke . . . died for our salvation*: The Spanish *Index*, p. 149^r, expurgated two passages on p. 34 of the *Ordo Baptizandi, cum Modus Visitandi* (Venice 1575), dealing with the theology of Christ's death and the salvation of the individual Christian. The *Ordo* was an official church document on the preparation of the parties in a Catholic baptism and on the rules for the ritual.

COMMENTARY

Page 91.

8–14 *in his Indices, and Tables . . . Bellarmines Index*: Donne says that Bellarmine's indices in his "Index Rerum" and "Index Locorum Sacrae Scripturae" at the end of each of the three volumes of *De Controversiis*, arranged by letter and by subject, do not conform to the matter treated in the text. He singles out the case of the "Index Rerum" entry under "Martyr," which reads "Martyrium tollit peccata [Col.] 1069C," and the passage to which it refers in Chapter 9 of Book II entitled "Qui est de iustitia inhaerente," of the second principal controversy "Quae est de Iustificatione Impii" in Vol. III, Col. 1069. Paraphrasing Bellarmine, Donne takes issue with his interpretation of Saint Jerome's "Commentary on Psalm 31," and argues that his index discusses the martyr rising above sin, and his text about sin not being imputable to the martyr.

18–20 *Junius hath noted . . . to Chrysostome*: The French theologian Franciscus Junius the Elder (b. Bourges, 1545; d. 1603), in his preface "Pio, fideli, et Christiano Lectori," *Index Expurgatorius* or Belgian *Index*, Sig. A9^v, on Chrysostom's sermon on the Pentecost.

22–33 *To proceede then . . . haynousnes thereof be*: For Bellarmine, the act of martyrdom automatically instilled grace and charity into the martyr without the need for prior religious disposition such as prayer and penance: hence, the "ex opere operato" effect of martyrdom that Donne quotes from Bellarmine's *De Baptismo et Confirmatione*, I, VI, *De Controversiis*, Vol. II, Col. 306. Donne's translation of Bellarmine a few lines later is from the same general passage, Cols. 305 and 306, and later from Chapter 2, entitled "Extare thesaurum aliquem in Ecclesia, qui sit Indulgentiarum fundamentum," in *De Indulgentiis*, in the appendices of Vol. I (p. 440) of the Cologne edition of *De Controversiis* in 1615. The two Spanish theologians whom Donne mentions, the Dominican Soto, author of *Commentarii in Quartum Sententiarum* (1555–1560), the Salamanca edition of 1569 being used here, and the preaching monk Martin Ledesmius (b. Salamanca, n.d.; d. Coimbra, Portugal, 1574), author of *De Natura et Gratia* (Venice, 1594), had preceded Bellarmine on the question of martyrdom and grace with different positions than his, and Bellarmine attacked them in *De Baptismo*, Col. 305. The fact that Soto was personally chosen by the Emperor Charles V to be his imperial theologian at the Council of Trent, and that Soto also wrote his tract for the Trent fathers, would have appealed to Donne in his refutation of Bellarmine. Donne's marginal references to "Quinto" both here and on p. 92, are wrong as there is no paragraph beginning with "Quinto," and no fifth proposition either, in Chapter II of *De Indulgentiis*, and the paraphrases are from Proposition 4, the paragraph beginning with "Et tamen."

34–1 (p. 92) *as Ferus doth directly . . . other sense*: The sixteenth-century German Franciscan Johann Ferus of Mainz in his *Evangelium Secundum Matthaeum Commentario* Book III, Chapter 18, pp. 128–129 (in the Rome edition of 1577); Franciscus Sixtus of Siena (b. 1520; d. Genoa, 1569), the bibliographer and theologian, commented on Matthew 20 and on Ferus' interpretation in Annotation 99 of his *Bibliotheca Sancta . . . Ex Praecipis Catholicae Authoribus Collecta*, p. 467 in the third, Cologne edition of 1586.

Page 92.

18–26 *As Morbizan the Turke . . . useful fables*: In 1461, Pius II (b. Corsignano, 1405; d. Ancona, 1464), wrote a long letter to Morbizan the Turkish Sultan, called Mahomet II, attempting to convert him to Christianity, and explaining the need of the papacy to seek military arms against the Turks for successfully invading large parts of Europe. The letter was printed in a considerable number of editions and the one to which Donne's marginal note may refer is entitled *Pii Papae Secundi Epistola, ad Morbisanum Turcarum* (Cologne, 1532), which contained the Sultan's short reply on its unnumbered pages 97–99. However, the Sultan's courteous reply to Pius did not use the word epigrams, and Donne may be referring to the appearance of the "Epigrammata" in Binius' list of Pius' works in *Concilia Generalia*, Vol. IV, p. 511, to describe the very numerous love poems on sensuous topics that the pope wrote as a young courtier before turning to religion. Donne's use of the word "Epigrammes" to denote poetry would be an evident way of reminding his readers of the controversy that Pius II's secular verse provoked for many years after his death. Donne's second example of the rejection of papal authority is from the Swiss theologian Isaac Casaubon's *De Libertate Ecclesiastica . . . . Ad Viros Politicos Qui de Controversiam inter Paulum V Pontificem Maximum et Republicam Venetam* (1607), p. 9. In the year of the appearance of *Pseudo-Martyr*, 1610, Casaubon (b. Geneva, 1559; d. London, 1614) was to take up permanent residence in England. Donne's third example touches more directly on the misuse and on the apocryphal character of non-Christian or non-religious writings, and he refers to his arch-enemy Bellarmine's rejection of the Spanish-born fourth-century Christian poet Prudentius' "Hymno de novo lumine Paschalis Sabbathi." Bellarmine quotes from the hymn in Chapter XVIII of Book II of "De Purgatorio" in *De Controversiis*, Vol. I, Col. 1890; then, in his fifth proposition "Ad Quintum," Col. 1891, he rejects Prudentius' use of classical images to describe the existence of purgatory. In *Ignatius His Conclave*, in the next year, Donne was to repeat this argument about purgatory, though satirically (pp. 7–9).

27–13 (p. 93) *Canus expresses himselfe . . . Church hath approved*: Melchior Cano (b. Trancon, Cuena, 1509; d. Toledo, 1551), Dominican theologian, presented as bishop of the Canary Islands by Charles V in 1552, in his *De Logis Theologicis* (Louvain, 1564), Book XI, Chapter VI on "Qui sint probate fide auctores, qui contra non sint," pp. 657–658. Justus Lypsius (b. Overijse, 1547; d. Louvain, 1606), the Dutch philologist and humanist, defended Cano's theology generally but took issue with his attitude towards the historical records of miracles in his *Diva Virgo Hallensis* (Antwerp, 1604), which was included in the compendium of defences of the miraculous appearances of Our Lady, Anastasius Cochelet's *Palestrita Honoris divae Virginis Hallensis* (Antwerp, 1607), p. 1, as Donne's note indicates. See Commentary for p. 182, ll. 8–10. The conclusions of two of Donne's poems, "The Relique" and "The Funerall," attack satirically the credulity of the faithful in the miracles that he discusses here.

Page 93.

18–25 *for so S. Brigids . . . was of Swethland*: Daniel Malloni's account of the fourteenth-century Saint Bridget of Sweden's description of her visions of Christ crucified, in his prefatory epistle to the reader in Paleoto's *Historia Admiranda . . . Sacrae Sindoni*, which also contains his notes, Sig. +5. Bridget (b. 1303; d. 1373) was married at thirteen, widowed in 1344, and in 1346 received the divine revelation for the rule of the order that she founded and that bears her name. She was canonized by Boniface IX in 1391 and Martin V confirmed the rule of her order early in the next century.

25–28 *According to which superstition . . . the Divels dwell*: In a high or sung Mass, the Catholic priest was to face the east, but his deacon was to face north to read the gospel in order to drive away the evil spirits that dwelled there, as described in Paris Crassus' *De Caeremoniis*, Chapter 29 on "De Evangelio Cantando, Ubi, et qualiter, ac pro quibus Evangeliis praesamur versum," Book I, pp. 39^v–40^r. Donne is saying that Saint Brigit appears to originate from the north with the devils of Catholic superstition.

Page 94.

7–16 *if Canus weigh . . . to them for ever*: Cano, bishop of the Canary Islands, author of *De Logis Theologicis* and *De Poenitentia* (Cologne, 1605). See Commentary for p. 92, l. 27–p. 93, l. 13. Thomas More, in his dedicatory letter to Thomas Ruthall (d. 1523), bishop of Durham and secretary of first, Henry VII, and later, Henry VIII, prefaced to his edition of the Roman Lucian, in *The Complete Works of St. Thomas More*, Vol. 3, Part 1 (New Haven, 1974), p. 7.

22–2 (p. 95) *Philip Nerius . . . worke no miracles by him*: Donne refers to Neri as the "Institutor" because the saint's intention had not been to found a new order but rather an "Institute" which should group together ordained priests and clerics, who would not take vows, and who would dedicate themselves to preaching (V.J. Matthews, *St. Philip Neri, Apostle of Rome and Founder of the Congregation of the Oratory*, London, 1934, p. 86). Donne was using the Mainz, 1606, edition of Neri's first biography, *De Vita et Rebus Gestis Beati P. Philippi Nerii Florentini. Congregationis Oratorii Fundatoris*, by Gallonio, one of the first members of the Oratory. The *Vita* originally appeared in Italian in Rome in 1591, and was followed by the first Latin edition there three years later, of which the edition Donne used was a derivative. Donne is actually enlisting Neri's caution towards apparitions to support his argument against Purgatory. However, the account of Neri's attitudes towards apparitions and devils in Gallonio's *Vita* is questioned by one of the saint's modern biographers, Meriol Trevor, in *Apostle of Rome, A Life of Saint Philip Neri* (London, 1966), pp. 46, 69–70, and 206–207. Trevor suggests that Gallonio's melancholic personality exaggerated Neri's apparitions.

Page 95.

4–14 *their greatest Authors . . . God, is not Idolatry*: The three "greatest" Catholic authors on demonology are, first, the Flemish theologian and canonist Peter Binsfeldus (b. Binsfield, Flanders, 1540; d. 1598), the author of the *Tractatus De Confessionibus Maleficiorum et Sangarum Recognitus et Auctus* (Treves, 1589), Chapter XII, pp. 67–68, in the Treves edition of 1591, a copy of which Donne was using ("esse facilè, cognoscere Diabolum è manibus vel pedibus. Item non esse difficile, discernere ex membris et corporis constitutione"); secondly, the Italian canonist Menghi who, in his *Fustis Daemonum*, Chapter VIII, pp. 307 and 315, described the shapes of devils and how the possessed could vomit them by drinking holy water ("Modus Bibendi Aquam Benedictam contra taciturnitatem"); and, thirdly, the Spanish Jesuit theologian and commentator on Aristotle, Gabriel Vasquez (b. Villaecusa, 1549; d. Jesus del Monte, Alcala, 1604), who, in his *De Cultu Adorationis* (Alcala, 1594), argued for the innocence of the adorer who was deceived by the devil who inhabited an image of Christ, Book 3, Chapter 5, p. 190B. However, for the story of Friar Ruffino that Donne is using to illustrate Menghi's principle of the oral emision of the devil by the possessed, he is citing Alberus' anti-Franciscan *The Alcoran*, Sig. C^{4r}, and not the *Fustis Daemonum*. Donne refers to Vasquez as one of Catholicism's saddest divines because of the frequent opposition he met to his ideas, particularly from the controversialist Jesuit Francis Suarez, and once from Clement VIII who requested him to retract his ideas.

18–28 *Yea Serarius . . . any envie from us*: In his *Litaneutici*, Book 2, Question 20 (and not 2, as Donne's original marginal note indicates), Nos. III and IV, pp. 111–113, Serarius points to two passages, one in Baronius' *Martyrologium Romanum*, p. 326, for 25 July, and the other in the writings of the sixteenth-century Spanish Augustinian theologian Laurentius Villavincentius (b. Andalusia, n.d.), the author of *De Recte Formando Theologiae Studio* (Antwerp, 1565). Both passages question the historical validity of some stories of saints and those of religious ikons. The third of Donne's references is from Chapter 20 on "Locus S. Francisci in caelo . . . De reliquis sacri eius corporis," Book I, No. 7, p. 62, of the Franciscan Sedulius' *Apologeticus* in defence of the "booke of Conformities" mentioned by Donne, Albizzi's *Liber Conformitatum*.

31–32 *As Bellarmine sayes truly . . . upon some truth*: Donne translates "Quia mendacia super aliquid verum, ut plurimum fundari solent," in Col. 973, Chapter 8 ("De erroribus qui falso ascribuntur Romanis Pontificibus . . . qui non solum Pontifices, sed etiam Martyres fuerunt") in Book IV ("De Potestate Romani Pontificis in causis spiritualibus") of the third general controversy ("De Summo Pontifice") of Vol. I of Bellarmine's *De Controversiis*.

COMMENTARY

Page 96.

14–16 *Let us excuse . . . opposed in Disputation*: A translation of the section on the argument for indexing the *Liber Bertrami Pres. de Corp. et Sang. Domini*, of the ninth-century Frankish monk Bertram of Corbie of the Court of King Charles II the Bald, of France in the Church's Belgian *Index*, p. 12.

16–25 *Nor dare we obtrude . . . such as he sent*: A "quinquagesima" was a statutory fast usually around Lent and Easter. Pope Telesphorus who reigned from c. 127 to c. 137 imposed seven days of fast on the clergy before Easter, and he fixed Easter itself as being always on a Sunday rather than on the moveable Jewish feast of the Passover, *Decretum*, Distinction I, Chapters 4 and 5, Cols. 11–12. In Distinction 12, Chapter 11, and its gloss, Cols. 40–41, *Decretum* records the letter of Innocent I to Decentius the Bishop of Eugubinus about the extent of the power of Peter the Apostle and of succeeding popes, and the commentaries on Gratian's text. Innocent I was the first pope to make such extensive claims for the spiritual power of the papacy, and he sought to bring the Eastern Church back under the full control of the Roman see.

25–30 *We dare not correct . . . Commentarie uppon Genesis*: Earlier in the paragraph, Donne has already translated a passage from Bertram of Corbie's *De Corpore et Sanguine Domini*, and is here citing another change made to Bertram's text on the visibility or the invisibility of the presence of Christ in the Eucharist, in the Belgian *Index* of forbidden books, pp. 17–18. Donne's next two references are to the Spanish *Index* of the Inquisition, the first to the addition of the word "non," Col. 3, p. 306, in the *Commentaria in Lucae Evangelia* (Alcala, 1578), of the sixteenth-century French monk Didacus Estella (or Latin Stella) who wandered in Portugal and Navarre (p. 66^r), and the second to the similar addition of the negative "non," in Number 8, Chapter I, Book I, on the definition of the erring soul, in the *Commentariis in Genesine*, or commentary on Genesis (Basel, 1531), of the fourth-century bishop of Lyons, Eucherius or Eucharius (b. Lyons, 343), p. 92^v.

32–34 *as Bellarmine hath done . . . be admitted*: Donne concludes his rhetorical attack against certain Catholic interpretations of scriptural and other theological texts by pointing to Bellarmine's removal of the word "non" or "not" in Gratian's text, *Decretum*, Cause 27, Question 2, Col. 1513 of a letter by Pope Leo I in "De Matrimonii Sacramento" of the fifth controversy ("De Extrema Unctione, Ordine, et Matrimonio") of *De Controversiis*, Col. 1563 of Vol. II. Bellarmine altered Gratian's text of the letter, written by Leo to Saint Rusticus the Bishop of Narbonne (b. ?Marseille, n.d.; d. 461), to make it conform to what he considered to be the pope's original words.

34–5 (p. 97) *Bellarmine makes the Pope . . . Chrysostome and others*: Donne draws his examples from Bellarmine's criticism of the anti-papal "De Primatu Papae" (c. 1340) of the fourteenth-century Archbishop of Alexandria and Metropolitan of Thessalonica, Nilus Cabasilas ("De Primatu" was translated into English as early as 1560 by Thomas Gressop and published in London). Bellarmine's criticism of

Nilus occurs in Chapter 27 of Book II ("De Successione Romani Pontificis in eo primatu") of the third general controversy ("De Summo Pontifice") in Vol. I of *De Controversiis*, Col. 713. Actually, in Chapter 27 of Book II in question, Bellarmine takes issue only with four of the fathers whom Donne mentions — Honorius, Jerome, Augustine and Cyprian — and Donne's list includes numerous other fathers as well with whom Bellarmine sometimes takes issue throughout *De Controversiis*.

Page 97.

6–18 *And when Damascene cites . . . prophane and blasphemous*: The first two citations are to Cols. 1890 and 1891 of Chapter 18 of Book II ("De Circumstantiis Purgatorii") in the sixth controversy ("De Ecclesia, Quae est in Purgatorio") of *De Controversiis*, Vol. I. Bellarmine rejects as apocryphal the story of the talking skull that Saint John Damascene narrated in one of his sermons. Damascene got the story out of the history of the monks of Egypt and Palestine, *Historia Lausiaca* (c. 420) of Palladius (b. Gallatia, 368; d.c. 431) whom Donne mentions. His third citation is from Bellarmine's first controversy ("De Verbo Dei"), Chapter 10 of Book III ("De Interpretatione et vero sensu Scripturae") of *De Controversiis*, Vol. I, Col. 195, where Bellarmine argues that none of the Church Fathers is necessarily free from error. Donne juxtaposes to this text yet a fourth citation from the same volume of *De Controversiis*, Chapter 8 of Book IV ("De Potestate Romani Pontificis in causis spiritualibus") in the third controversy called "De Summo Pontifice," Col. 973. There, Bellarmine refutes the credibility of the second-century heretic Tertullian (b. Carthage, 160), who came to adhere to the sect of Montanus, and who accused the contemporary Pope Zephyrinus (pontiff from 198 to 217) himself of Montanism, that is, of rejecting the validity of the Apocalypse of Saint John and adhering rather to other prophesies of the end of the world. Donne mentions both Zephyrinus and Tertullian, and then, for a fifth time referring to the *De Controversiis*, he cites the opening paragraph of the fourth controversy entitled "De Sacramento Poenitentiae" in Vol. II, Col. 1163, where Bellarmine excludes Tertullian from the traditional body of Catholic Church Fathers: "Tertullianus, quem tamen inter Catholicos non numeramus." The "centuriatores" of Magdeburg were the Protestant authors of a Church history divided by "centuries," entitled *Historia Ecclesiae Christi* (Basel, 1559–74), which was universally recognized to be full of errors.

18–22 *So also doth Medina say . . . and Wickliffe*: In Book I, Chapter 5, of the treatise on the origins of Christian celibacy, *De Sacrorum Hominum Continentia* (Venice, 1569), pp. 5–6, of the Spanish Franciscan Miguel de Medina (b. Belalcázar, 1489; d. Toledo, 1578). Aerius was a fourth-century presbyter of Pontus who claimed that there was no distinction between the function of rank of bishops and priests, and Medina writes that a number of the church fathers and lesser known historians, as well as Wycliffe and the thirteenth-century Peter Waldo of Lyons who supposedly founded the primitivist Protestant sect of the Waldensians, agreed with him. Pimasius was the sixth-century bishop of Hadrumetum in North Africa; Theodoret,

COMMENTARY

an Antiochan fifth-century bishop of Cyrrhus; Oecumenius, the sixth-century author of the oldest known Greek commentary on Revelations; and Theophylact, the eleventh-century archbishop of Achrida (Bulgaria) and author of commentaries on both Old and New Testaments.

23–30 *But as Gratian . . . is not true*: In the gloss to Chapter 11, of Question 2, Cause 36, of *Decretum*, Col. 1884, Gratian prefers to base his arguments about the punishment due to men who assault women on Jerome's use of divine law, rather than on the decretals of the Council of Rheims. There follow in Donne's text two references to the Spanish *Index* of forbidden books, both to corrections by the Inquisition of the 1582 edition of the *Hypotyposes Theologicas ad intelligendos Sacrae Scripturae Sensus* (1565) of the sixteenth-century Spanish professor of theology at Salamanca, Martin Martinez. The first correction in the *Index* (p. 146^r) adds a marginal note to Martinez' citation of a passage on the creation from the late third- and early fourth-century Arian Christian historian Eusebius of Caesaria (Book II, Col. 275). The second correction (p. 147^r) stipulated that an addition was needed in Martinez' text on the creation on the grounds that his statements, which claimed to be founded on the writings of the second-century Saint Justin and of the fourth-century saint and biblical archaeologist Epiphanius, were nevertheless not substantiated by any expressions of faith by Adam in Genesis.

Page 98.

2–15 *Azorius subjects himselfe . . . in keeping it*: In a passage on the role of human fear in the making of vows, Chapter 14 ("De re, et materia Voto subiecta," Col. 1376), of Book 11 ("De Secundo Praecepto Decalogi, Non assumes nomen Domini Dei tui in vanum," Col. 1323), in *Institutionum Moralium*, part 1, Col. 1377, the Jesuit philosopher-theologian Azor casts doubt on the validity of Jephthah's vow in Judges 11.30 to sacrifice the first person to come out of his house if the Lord gave him victory in the field of battle. Jephthah sacrificed his only child, a daughter, and Azor cites the invalidity of such a vow. Azor then writes that "alii iuniores Catholici Rabbinos," the "Rabbines" and other Catholics to whom Donne refers, however, doubted that the daughter had really been burned, as various Bibles gave different nuances to the passage. Azor sides at first with these interpreters, including the French Hebraist theologian de Lyra, the author of a five-volume work on the Scriptures, *Postillae Perpetuae* (Rome, 1471–72), but then accepts the authority of the official Bible of the Council of Trent, the Latin Vulgate, that the child was really burned.

17–21 *take Chrysostomes libertie . . . of the persons*: Chrysostom's interpretation of Acts 19, in "Ad Populum Antiochum Homilia IIII, De Patientia, et tolerantia, et de abstentia à iuramentis," *Opera*, Volume IV, Tome 5, Col. 39, and not "De militia spirituali, Ho.4. To.5" as Donne's marginal note indicates.

30–32 *got Lypsius . . . despise our fellowes*: The Dutch humanist Lypsius in his *Diva Virgo Hallensis*, republished by the French Carmelite monk Cochelet in his compendium of a number of contemporary defences of the veneration of the miraculous virgin of Halle, in his *Palestrita Honoris*, p. 285. See Commentary for p. 92, l. 27–p. 93, l. 13.

32–19 (p. 99) *And that powerfull Indulgence . . . with most cleare reasons*: Donne refers nine times to Sedulius' *Apologeticus* to attack both the doctrine of indulgences and the existence of Purgatory, and also the doctrine that the power to bind and loose souls in Purgatory lay in the hands of the popes. Donne's examples sometimes alter the literal sense that Sedulius applied to the biblical passages in question. All of the examples are organized to link the doctrine of Purgatory to what he considers to be the pretentions of the Franciscan order, rather than to the misapplications of biblical typology to the life of Saint Francis, on which his earlier references to Sedulius' work in *Pseudo-Martyr* concentrate. The references are to the *Apologeticus* I, Chapter 16 on "Magno opere salutem hominum procurans, Indulgentias . . . Vicarius Christi adprobavit," Nos. 4 and 7, p. 46; II, Chapter 9 on "Salutariter mori in Ordine perseverantes," No. 1, p. 110, and Chapter 11 on "De fructibus Ordinis, & studiosis eiusdem," No. 4, p. 117; I, Chapter 19 on "Quae in excessu S. Francisci contigerunt. Multo liberavit è purgatorio," No. 3, p. 57, for both references; III, Chapter 21 on "Animas defunctorum in hac vita . . . è poenis purgatorii liberari," Nos. 4 and 7, pp. 220, 222; and the "Approbatio," the permission to print, by Friar Gerardus Jaceanus, the provincial for the Lower German Province, that Donne refers to as "approbation" and that he translates. The "approbatio" appears with other printed permissions in the closing pages of the *Apologeticus*.

Page 99.

19–20 *Soto might weigh . . . above tenne yeares*: Translated from Soto's *Commentarium Fratris*, Distinction 19 ("De satisfactione, et de purgatorio"), Question III, Article 2 ("Utrium poena purgatorii excedat omnem peonam temporalem huius vitae") on whether the pains of purgatory exceed all the dolors of this life (in Vol. I, p. 861, Col. 2). Soto estimates the soul's sojourn in purgatory as between ten and twenty years.

21–27 *Bellarmine sayes, that . . . often every day*: The three passages from Bellarmine are cited to contradict Soto, to put in question the length of time that souls spend in purgatory, and hence to discredit the idea of purgatory as Donne was to do once more in the following year in *Ignatius His Conclave*, p. 11. The three passages from Bellarmine are, firstly, from Chapter 9 entitled "De tempore quo durat Purgatorium" in Book II called "De Circumstantiis Purgatorii" of the sixth general controversy "De Ecclesia, quae est in Purgatoria" of Vol. I of *De Controversiis*, Cols. 1877–1878; secondly, from Chapter 2 entitled "Respondetur ad ea quae adversus Indulgentias Ioannes Calvinus obiecit" in Book II of the *De Indulgentiis*, in the appendices to the Cologne edition of 1615, Vol. I, p. 460, Col. 2; and, thirdly, in Chapter 9 entitled "Utilem esse Indulgentiam omni hominum generi," of Book I of the same work, p. 450, Col. 1. In the last of these passages, Bellarmine discusses Soto's position at length, p. 449, Col. 2.

32–4 (p. 100) *And therefore Martin . . . shoppes together*: The Jesuit, Horace Torsellino (or Tursellinus) (b. Rome, 1544; d. 1599), historian and biographer, in his history of the town of Loretto near Rome, *Lauretanae Historia* (Rome, 1607), recounts how Martin V early in the fifteenth century laid down rules for the sale of indulgences during shopping hours in the town's shrine to the Virgin Mary in order to restrain the crowds who came there, and how the rules were maintained by Julius II, Sixtus IV and Leo X.

CHAP. IV
Page 101.

5–9 *they may be content . . . determined the contrary*: The reference is to the "Observationes In Ioannem Cassianum" by an unidentified commentator, published as one of the Appendices at the end of the early fifth-century Eastern hermit Cassianus' *De Institutis Renunciantium Libri XII. Collationes Sanctorum Patrum XXIV*, Lyons, 1606, pp. 739 and 740, the edition of which Donne was using a copy as he indicates in a further note to the same passage on p. 199. However, the original numbering of the reference should read "Ex Collat. 17. cap.15," rather than "Ex Collat. 19" which is a deformation of the already existing error of "Coll. 9. cap.19" appearing in the commentator's text. The commentator cites Origen, Book 6 (and 10 probably) of his "Commentary on Saint John"; Chrysostom at the end of Book I of *De Sacerdotibus*, *Homilies* 32 and 53 on Genesis, as well as his *Epistle* to Olympia; and Saint Jerome in Chapter 2 on the *Epistle to the Gallatians*. The commentator also mentions Augustine as objecting to the justification.

10–13 *That it was then lawfull . . . in that point*: The question of the state of the soul between death and the last judgement was brought up by Bellarmine in Chapter 14 ("De Ceteris Pontificibus, quibus error in fide falso tribuitur") of Book IV ("De Potestate Romani Pontificis in Causis Spiritualibus") of the third general controversy ("De Summo Pontifice") in Vol. I, *De Controversiis*, Col. 1012. Bellarmine developed his argument to defend Pope John XXII (b. Cahors, 1249; d. Avignon, 1334), the Avignon pope elevated to the papacy in 1316, against the charge of heresy by Calvin in *Institutes*, Book IV, 7, No. 28, who said that later cardinals themselves attacked John's position on the soul's state after death. The question of the soul's state preoccupied Donne elsewhere in his works (Holy Sonnets VII and VIII) and he finds justification in Bellarmine's defence of the pope.

15–19 *Senensis, who rejects . . . is large enough*: The Senensis Donne mentions was Pope Sixtus V who initiated the project of the Catholic Vulgate Bible, which contained many errors that were corrected in its subsequent editions under the guidance of Clement VIII. Donne is referring to the controversy over one of these errors. Sixtus' edition of the Bible rejected the canonical validity of the seven books of Esther which the Council of Trent had approved only a few short years before. The Jesuit Gretser in his *Controversiam Roberto Bellarminii . . . Defensio*, Vol. I, I "Appendix prima ad librum primum contra Pappum," Col. 362, defended Sixtus for having simply committed a human error ("Humanum errorem commisit"), which drew from Donne a request for the same sort of charity to the English cause as was accorded to Sixtus. Donne's concluding citation is a rough translation of part of Gretser's text: "Nam quod Sixtus [Senensis] etiam post Tridentinum Concilium in errorem impegit; id accidit; quia . . . id ob negligentiam et incogitantiam et incircumspectionem."

23–24 *Haeresis proxima . . . Sesqui-haeretica*: In Chapter 2 ("Proponitur quaestio, Sitne certum Papae?") of Book IV ("De Potestate Romani Pontificis in causis spiritualibus") of the third general controversy ("De Summo Pontifice") of Vol. I of *De Controversiis*, Bellarmine uses the term "haeresi proxima" which Donne mistakenly quotes "Haeresi proximum." The other three phrases, "Semi-haeretica," "Hyper-haeretica," and "Sesqui-haeretica," that is, half-heretical, hyper-heretical, and heretical and a half, constitute a satiric attack by Donne on Bellarmine's four possibilities for heresy in the same passage.

25–8 (p. 102) *when by a new Decretall . . . hurt them, is made Treason*: Paul IV issued several decretals on heresies and schisms, which Donne lists, and which Gregory XIII included in his "Septimes" of the *Corpus Iuris Canonici*, Vol. II, "Liber Septimus," Cols. 187–190. See Commentary for p. 80, ll. 8–12, and p. 243, ll. 7–23.

Page 102.

12–17 *their first institution . . . and other Dignities*: With the help of Giovanni Petro Caraffa (b. Benevento, 1476; d. 1559), Saint Cajetan founded the Roman Oratory of Divine Love which was to become the new religious order of Clerks Regular called the Theatines in 1524. Caraffa was also bishop of Chieti — Theatinus in Latin — and it was his name, and not Cajetan's that was given to the order. Caraffa was also the first superior general of the order and was later to be elected pope as Paul IV on Paul III's death in 1555. The Theatines aimed at recalling the clergy to an edifying life by a vow of absolute poverty, and the laity to the practice of virtue. As head of the Theatines, Caraffa accepted Paul III's offer to sit on a committee to reform the papal court and was granted a cardinalship by him in 1536, to all of which Donne's paragraph is alluding. In his marginal note to Gretser's *Historia Ordinis*, Donne is referring his reader to a passage where the Jesuit controversialist defends the Theatines against the Protestant charge that they contradicted their order's ideal by allowing their first general Caraffa to be elected pope (Chapter II, "Sextum Mendacium"), p. 45. It is these charges that Donne is here reviving. As Paul IV, Caraffa was the pope who refused to recognize Elizabeth as queen of England on Mary Tudor's death, on the grounds of her illegitimate birth.

18–21 *Those of their Order . . . have prevailed*: Donne is referring to the abbreviated biographies of Diego Laynez (b. Almazan, Castile, 1512; d. Rome, 1565), elected second general of the Society of Jesus in 1558, and Francis Borgia, Duke of Gandie (b. Gandie, Valencia, 1510; d. Rome, 1572), who after the death of his wife entered the Jesuits in 1551 and became third superior general of the order on Laynez's death. Their abbreviated biographies appear in Pedro Ribadeneira'a *Illustrium Scriptorum Religionis Societatis Iesu Catalogus*, which was the first bibliography of the Jesuit order, originally published in Antwerp in 1602. Ribadeneira (b. Toledo, 1527; d. Madrid, 1611) was a pioneer of modern bibliographical work. His bibliography lists the name of each Jesuit alphabetically and it is followed by a brief biography and by a list of his writings in chronological order. The bibliography went through several corrections and augmented editions in the seventeenth century. Donne's copy belonged to the Lyons edition of 1609, which he cites several times in *Pseudo-Martyr*. Ribadeneira was a particularly contentious individual to the English for his record of the break wth Rome in *Historia Ecclesiastica del Scisma del Reyno de Inglaterra* (Madrid, 1588), and Donne's tone towards Ribadeneira is usually acerbic. In the biographies of Laynez and Borgia (pp. 100–102; 58–59), Ribadeneira describes their refusal of the cardinalship, and in the biography of Borgia he uses the adverb "constantissime" (p. 58), or steadfastly, that Donne quotes to describe his reaction in the face of Julius III's pressure on him to accept it. By contrast, Bellarmine, attacked for ceding in *Pseudo-Martyr*, accepted the cardinalship from Clement VIII in 1599, and Francisco Toledo (Donne's "Tolet") (b. Cordova, 1532; d. Rome, 1596), also a Jesuit and a preacher to popes and cardinals for twenty-four years, and reputed to have sought the cardinalship, was accorded the red hat by the same pope in 1593.

21–25 *Hee which gives . . . Divine Contemplation*: The giver of Rules is the hermit Cassianus, in Liber XI ("De spiritu Cenodoxiae"), Chapter 17 ("Quod monachum debet vitare mulieres et Episcopos'), *De Institutis Renunciantium* pp. 149–150. Donne's reference to the Jesuits breaking Cassianus' rule is to their regulation in their *Regulae*, No. 4, "Summarium Constitutionum," that the Jesuit must live in the world, and must not be cloistered, to save souls effectively, p. 4.

29–34 *Azorius his disputation . . . to be the Electors*: Donne translates the Jesuit moralist Azor's argument from his *Institutionum Moralium*, Vol. 2, Part 2, Chapter 5 ("De Romani Pontificis electione"), p. 258, Col. 1 ("quoniam talis formula non est iure divino constituta, sed Canonico; at ius Canonicum Papae potestati subijcitur: ergo ea formula electionis Pontificiae potest Romani Pontificis Constitutione mutari"). However, Azor does not mention that the provincials of the Jesuits may elect the pope.

Page 103.

12–18 *Laynez in the vacancy . . . if he will, refuse it*: In his bibliography of the Jesuits, *Catalogus*, Ribadeneira describes how Laynez the superior general of the Jesuits got twelve votes in the Conclave of 1559, called to elect a successor to Paul IV, even though he had refused the late pope's offer of a cardinalship, p. 101

in the 1609 Lyons edition. Bellarmine, who accepted the cardinalship in 1598, was also reputed to have received votes for the papacy in both conclaves to be held in 1605 to choose a successor first to Clement VIII and then to his successor Leo XI who died after only twenty-eight days of rule. The right of an individual to refuse his election to the papacy is described in the chapter on "De indumentis electi, et prima veneratione à Cardinalibus" in the very beginning of the first part of Book I, of the Catholic church's official *Sacrarum Cerimoniarum*, p. 18.

20–34 *as modest as the Carthusian . . . written after his death*: Donne gives four examples, one Carthusian, one Franciscan, and two Jesuit, of what he considers to be Catholics abusing typology to force biblical texts to support the power of the religious orders. The first example is that of the Carthusian ascetic and controversialist, Theodore Petrejus (b. Kempen, Overijssel, 1569; d. Cologne, 1640), in his *Bibliotheca Carthusiana, Sive Illustrium Sacri Cartusiensis Scriptorum Catalogus*, pp. 304–310, of which Donne was using a copy of the 1609 Cologne edition. Petrejus lists the members of the Carthusian order who became cardinals, archbishops and bishops. The second example is that of Sedulius who described certain prophetic figures of the Old Testament as precedents for the ideals of the Franciscans, in Chapter 11 ("De fructibus Ordinis"), No. 1, of his *Apologeticus*, p. 115, and who also pointed to contemporary doctors and popes fathered by the order. Donne's third example is that of the Jesuit Serarius in Chapter 24 ("An, Mosaica stanti Synagoga, vere haeretici Sadducaei") of Book II on the Sadducees in his *Trihaeresium Seu De Celeberimus Tribus, Apud Iudaeos, Pharisaeorum, Sadducaerium, et Essenorum Secti* (Mainz, 1604), p. 159, where he describes Herod as "Tyrannus magnus" and "Macchiavellistica." *Trihaeresium*, which Donne cites several times in *Pseudo-Martyr*, was a study of the three heresies (Pharisees, Sadducees, and Essenes) of the ancient Jews. Donne's final example is that of the noted Jesuit controversialist theologian Gregory of Valentia (b. Medina, Spain, 1550; d. Naples, 1603), who taught at the University of Ingolstadt, and who published *De Rebus Fidei Hoc Tempore controversiis libri, qui hactenus extant omnes*, containing a *De Purgatorio*, in Lyons in 1591. Donne is referring to the passage in *De Purgatorio* where Gregory, to prove Catholic docrine on purgatory, declares that Plato had a dogma on the reality of a spiritual state equal to that of Purgatory ("aliquid simile purgatorio in Platonicis scriptis reperitur"), and that Plato's proof for its existence is similar to that used by Catholics based on the Book of Macchabees (*De Rebus*, p. 904, Col. 1, Nos. C, E).

Page 104.

1–6 *the Jesuites decay . . . the family of the Franciscans*: In his *Histoire de France . . . du Regne de Henri IIII* (Paris, 1605), the French lawyer and historiographer to Henry IV, Pierre Mathieu (b. 1563; d. 1621), records that the Jesuits founded colleges for Philip II in Vienna, Prague, Munich, Halle, Innsbruck and Turnant in Hungary, but on Philip's death they were the only religious order that had served him which he completely ignored in his will (Tome I, Book I, Narration 4, p. 69ᵛ). The reference to the Franciscan anti-Christ had a more controversial history. The idea that the Franciscans would produce anti-Christ is strongly attacked by the Catholic Sedulius in his *Apologeticus*, II, 12, 8, p. 122, and Donne borrows the quotation from Sedulius. However, he does not indicate that Sedulius thought that Saint Francis' declaration about the emergence of anti-Christ in his order had to be taken figuratively.

9–15 *the Authority of the Pope . . . to receive you*: For the ability of the pope to command angels, Donne is translating the French jurist Cassaneus' passage on why the pope has precedence over all the dignitaries of the world, in *Catalogus Gloriae Mundi*, Part 4, Consideration 7, p. 176, Col. B ("Et maior authoritatis Papae, quam sanctorum"). On the other hand, for the ability of the priests to exorcise devils, Donne is paraphrasing in translation passages on the expulsion of demons in Chapter 4 and in the rite of "Exorcismus III" of the demonologist Menghi's *Flagellum Daemonum*, pp. 12 and 110.

16–20 *And though Tortus say . . . too old to bee Canoniz'd*: Matthew Tortus was Cardinal Bellarmine's pseudonym in some of his controversies and tracts. Donne is quoting Bellarmine from his "Aviso alli sudditi del Domino Venetiano . . . sopra d'una lettera de Frate Gio. Battista Palmieri sinto Romito." Bellarmine's tract was an answer to Palmieri's open letter of 1 December 1606 from the hermitage of Santa Valle, published early in 1607 and republished in *Raccolta degli Scritti* in the same year. Palmieri encouraged "all faithful" Venetians to abide by their state rulers against the excommunication order of Paul V, and he accused the Jesuits of possessing special privileges through the rules of the foundation of their order that enabled them, along with the Oratorian Cardinal Baronius, to force the pope's hand in proceeding with the excommunication (*Raccolta*, p. 116). Bellarmine replied immediately after Palmieri's letter appeared in *Raccolta*, and Donne translates from the passage dealing with the defence of the Jesuit order. Bellarmine argued that the Jesuits had sought the canonization of their founder Ignatius but had failed, so that it was untrue that they could force a pope to act (p. 126).

20–31 *two great Princes . . . neglected the Jesuites*: In his *Histoire de France*, Tome II, Book VII, Narration 4, p. 355b, Matthieu narrates that at the consistory held under Clement VIII in Rome to consider the quarrel over the nature of grace between the Spanish and French (or "Jacobin") Dominicans, the possibility of canonizing Ignatius Loyola was discussed. The name of Henry IV of France was brought up as he was the natural secular supporter to be sollicited to undertake the cause of the canonization because Ignatius was born in 1491 in the Basque province of Guipuscoa, Saragossa. The province bordered upon and was at that time ruled by Navarre, and Navarre was at present ruled by the king of France. Because he was descended from Saint Louis IX of France, Henry also considered himself, even without sollicitation, the natural supporter of Ignatius' canonization. Ignatius' companion, Francis Xavier (b. 1506; d. Sancian, China-coast, 1552), was born in the castle of Xavier, actually in Navarre. In his *Histoire*, Mathieu narrates that Philip II preferred the older Catholic religious orders like the Dominicans and the Hieronymites, and that he was generally out of sympathy with the newer orders like the Jesuits because he feared that in his day the Church was producing more religion than piety ("il estoit à craindre que le monde n'abondast plus en Religion qu'en Pieté"), Tome I, Book I, Narration 4, p. 69^v. Donne's later references to Philip's support of the canonizations of Saint Raymond of Pennafort and Fray Pedro d'Alcala or Saint Peter of Alcantara are unclear. Pennafort (b. Villafranca, c.1180; d. Barcelona, 1275), was confessor to Gregory IX and third superior general of the Dominican order, but was canonized by Clement VIII in 1601, three years after Philip's death. For his part, Alcala cannot be the Franciscan Fray Pedro de Alcala, the sixteenth-century author of the first Spanish-Arabic grammar, because he was never either beatified or canonized, and Pedro Alcantara of the Friars Minor (b. Alcantara, 1499; d. Arenas, Avila, 1562), was beatified only in 1627 by Gregory XV and canonized in 1669 by Clement IX.

32–6 (p. 105) *solicited for the Canonizing . . . testimony of the Church*: Donne is drawing his information principally from the prefatory material of the first Latin edition of Ceparius' biography of the Jesuit Saint Aloysius Gonzaga, *Vita*. The Gonzaga family sought Aloysius' canonization, and Ceparius' *Vita* contains a prefatory letter from the saint's elder brother Francis, Marquis of Castilione, to Paul V asking for the canonization (pp. 5–7). Donne alludes to this family intervention and to the illustrious cardinals in the papal senate (whom Francis described in his letter) named by the pope to investigate the cause for canonization. The *Vita* contained additional prefatory declarations by Ioannes Franciscus the Provincial of the Capucines for Brescia, and Claudius Aquaviva the superior general of the Jesuits, among others (pp. 20–29), as further testimony of Gonzaga's exemplary life, which Donne also mentions. However, Paul V conceded only to emitting the decretal for the beatification on 19 October 1606, as Donne writes, and not to either the immediate actual beatification or the canonization which would have bypassed the stage of beatification, as the family and Jesuit supporters desired. Gonzaga was actually only beatified by Gregory XV in 1621, and canonized by Benedict XIII in 1726. Donne concludes that Paul's emission of the decretal was unnecessary because tradition itself often conferred a valid legal state of saintly blessedness on holy people, as argued by the linguist Serarius in his *Litaneutici Seu de Litaniis Libelli Duo*, Question VII, "An beati omnes, etiam sancti," on whether the blessed are always saintly, pp. 65–66. Serarius lists among such holy people Albertus Magnus and Blessed Hildegard in the past, and, in the current times, no less than the Jesuits' Ignatius Loyola, Francis Xavier, Stanislas Kostka and Gonzaga himself. However, Serarius does not identify, as Donne does, the state of blessedness by tradition with beatification by Rome.

COMMENTARY

Page 105.

10–15 *your own Acosta . . . if it might be*: Joseph or José Acosta (b. Medina del Campo, 1539; d. Salamanca, 1600), was the second Provincial of the Jesuit order in Peru, and the author of *De Natura Novi Orbis . . . Et De Procuranda Indorum Salute* (Salamanca, 1589) (he was probably the brother of Christopher Acosta, one of the five Jesuit brothers martyred in the Salettes Islands whom Donne mentions elsewhere, but he was not related to the other Jesuit Simon Acosta whom he also mentions later; see Commentary for p. 119, ll. 8–14). On p. 213 of *De Natura* (Cologne edition of 1596), Acosta writes: "ac pene singulare miraculum necessarium est, mores cum Fide congruentes Hoc et abundè sufficit, et omnibus concessum est, modo velint."

21–34 *Sedulius gives new life . . . with concurse of people*: Miracles of Saint Francis mentioned in Sedulius' defence of Albizzi's *Liber Conformitatum*. Albizzi's *Liber* drew several extensive parallels between Christ's miracles and those of Saint Francis and of other Franciscans, and Donne regrets that Sedulius' defence in *Apologeticus* has made the stories of these miracles current knowledge again. Sedulius narrates the story of Saint Anthony talking to the fish in III, Chapter 13 on "De concionibus earumque fructu," No. 8, p. 160; the story of Friar Andrew ordering the roasted birds to fly again in III, Chapter 28 on "De Sanctorum dominio in creaturas ratione carentes, insensiles & sensiles," No. 30, p. 268; the story of Friar Conrad being ordered to stop performing miracles not because he was dead but because he was buried outside of monastery grounds, in III, Chapter 24 on 'Sancti miracula se facere auctore Deo fatentur," No. 25, pp. 238–239; and the story of Francis telling Friar Peter to stop arousing the people by performing miracles out of his grave, in III, 25, Nos. 26–27, p. 239. Donne repeated this latter story on p. 136.

36–2 (p. 106) *Philip Nerius . . . doe no Miracles*: Neri's biographer Gallonio narrates that Baronius was the saint's confessor in his last days, and that on one occasion Neri told the cardinal of his request to God to do no more miracles by him (the incident to which Donne refers), *Vita*, pp. 488–489. Donne refers to Neri as the founder of the "last Order" because the Oratorians had only been approved by Gregory XIII in 1575, and no later order had since been founded.

Page 106.

3–8 *nothing equall . . . exceede ten thousand yet*: Donne is satirically comparing Sedulius' description of the first Chapter General of the Franciscan order at which Saint Francis had the vision of ten thousand devils attempting to subvert the six thousand members of his order (*Apologeticus*, II, Chapter 2 on "De Ordinis excellentia," on the excellence of the order, No. 2, pp. 70–71), with the Jesuit bibliographer Ribadeneira's tabulation of the number of members in the Society of Jesus, appended to the Lyons 1609 edition of his *Catalogus* of Jesuit writings, p. 290. Counting them by province, Ribadeneira reached the figure of ten thousand, five hundred and one, and not the figure of ten thousand five hundred and eighty-one in Donne's marginal note. Donne gets his date of 1608 from the dating of the permission to publish by the Toledan Provincial Ferdinand Lucero, p. 9.

19–26 *Such renunciation . . . not made a Monke*: Cassianus describes the monk's threefold renunciation of the world in Chapters 14 to 18 of Book VII of his *De Institutis Renunciantium*, pp. 102–106. His reference to Saint Basil and the senator which Donne is citing occurs in Chapter 19 ("Sententia sancti Basilii episcopi adversus syncleticum quemdam prolata"), p. 106. Basil's dictum, which Donne is translating, was "Et senatorem . . . perdidisti, et monachum non fecisti."

30–5 (p. 107) *For this purpose . . . the Popes send forth*: The *Regulae* or *Rules* of the Society of Jesus were drafted by Ignatius Loyola and were incorporated unchanged as part of the wider *Constitutiones* two years after his death, at the society's first congregation in 1558, though chapters touching principally on congregations were added later. Ignatius' *Regulae* were practical rules for the day-to-day running of the society with the aim of assuring its spiritual ends. In Donne's first reference, the "examinator" of a Jesuit house was the man in charge of seeking out possible novices and also of screening their candidacies closely. Rule 11 of Chapter II of the "Regulae Examinatoris" states that the examiner should consider the financial background of the prospective novice's family to ensure that the monetary condition of the parents would not impede the novice's performance as a Jesuit, p. 95. A "provincialis" in the society was the head of a province, the latter consisting of a group of dispersed Jesuit houses and often equivalent to an already geographically defined territory, and the "provincialis" assisted at the congregations. In Chapter IIII on admissions to the society, "De Admittendis," Rule 36 of the *Regulae Provincialis*, p. 31, the provincial may not forego the "regulae communes" of the society and admit as a novice a person marked by "in deformitate magna," or great physical deformity. The "Rector" was a Jesuit normally in charge of an establishment constituted into a college, whereby the "superior" was the Jesuit in charge of a community of Jesuits generally stationed under the same roof. In the chapter on "Formula Scribendi" in the *Regulae*, Rule 2, p. 134, the "Superiores Domorum, et Rectores," or superiors of houses and rectors of colleges, were obliged to report "hebdomadis" or weekly to their provincial, whether they were "in Europa, in Indiis vero," in Europe or indeed in India, and, according to Rule 3, they were obliged to report on all the activities of the members of their houses and colleges, whether within or outside their walls. Finally, the "Procurator Generalis," or procurator general, of Donne's last reference to the *Regulae*, was the general overseer of the society's official papers and finances, and he coordinated in Rome (where he was stationed) all of the society's large financial projects in the construction of houses and took care of its regular business with the Vatican. In the section devoted to the procurator general in the *Regulae*, Rule 12 stipulated his responsibility for general finances, banking and credit, and Rule 13 for constituting the papal bulls and all writings relating to the order in its archives (pp. 178–179).

COMMENTARY 339

Page 107.

5–12 *And to this purpose . . . scandalous at least*: In his *Histoire de France*, Tome II, Book VII, Narration 4, p. 355, Mathieu mentions that "Un autre Jesuite publia [in Rome] une proposition qui fut trouvée bien estrange pour le peril de sa nouveauté, et de ses conséquences, Que la confession se pouvoit faire par lettre et par courrier." Several Spanish Jesuits had provoked similar protests about confession by letter, and the scandal lasted from 1602 to 1605, and the Jesuit theologian Francis Suarez was compelled to go to Rome to assure Clement VIII of the state of the church's handling of confession in Spain. The first of the Catholic authorities whom Donne considers to have supported the view of the unnamed Jesuit in Mathieu's account was the Spanish moral theologian Soto in "Membri III," "Quaestio Quarta" ("Utrum usque adeo obligemur ad secretorum fidem, ut teneamur nonnunquam mortem prius opportere, quam secretum detegere"), the fourth doubt (or "Quartum dubium" of *Pseudo-Martyr*'s marginalia) of *Relectio . . . Secretum*, pp. 349–354. This section of *Relectio* also discusses the relationship of novices to their confessors and provincials and the opinion of Soto, who was confessor to Charles V, had much weight among Catholics. In the meantime, however, Suarez, who also supported the idea of confession by letter, faced the edict issued against it by Clement in 1602 and was censured by the Holy Office in Rome in 1603. The last reference is to the Spanish theologian Melchior Zambrani's *Aureae Decisiones Casuum Conscientiae*, Chapter 4 on "De Poenitentia," Doubt or "Dubium" 2, Section 5 (Mainz, 1606), p. 197.

20–26 *Intelligencers . . . sina glossa*: Donne refers to the rules and regulations first of the Jesuits and then the Franciscans. Rule 38 in the "Regulae Communes" at the beginning of Ignatius' *Regulae*, p. 22, states that no-one within a Jesuit house may reveal, to anyone outside, the regulations by which the house is governed ("Nemo quae domi acta, vel agenda sunt, externis referat"), and adds that the superior, however, may alter the application of the order's constitutional rules under certain circumstances. The quotation about Saint Francis that follows is actually a translation not of the *Rule* of the Franciscans but of its Latin paraphrase in the anti-Franciscan *Alcoran* of Erasmus Alberus as quoted by Sedulius in his *Apologeticus*, II, 3, 2, p. 72.

27–32 *by one Bull . . . excludes all others*: The original "Hateum" and "Hatteum" in Donne's margin probably sprang from the compositor of the 1610 edition mis-reading his manuscript long "s" for a "t," and his "n" for a "u." Two of Donne's three citations are from Gretser's *Historia Ordinis Iesuitici . . . . ab Elia Hasenmillero*, which reprinted a number of Vatican bulls. Those in question here are the third bull of Pope Paul III of 1555 defending the constitution and the ministry of the Jesuit order, and more specifically for the first time allowing Jesuits to hear confession (p. 168), and the eighteenth bull issued by Gregory XIII, allowing the Jesuits to practise medicine (p. 211). One of the frequent accusations against Jesuits was their obtaining conversions to Catholicism by individuals on their death-beds

— hence Donne's reference to the Jesuits' "chiefest scenes." Donne's second citation is to the Spanish Jesuit missionary Stephanus de Avila (b. Avila, 1549; d. Lima, Peru, 1601), the author of *De Censuris Ecclesiasticis Tractatus* posthumously published at Lyons, 1608, the first edition of which Donne was using a copy. In Part II, Chapter 7, Disputation III ("De forma et modo observando in danda absolutione"), Doubt 8, p. 197, Avila argues that the papal bulls establishing the Jesuit order gave them the right to lift all forms of ecclesiastical censures against Catholics, including excommunication under certain rare circumstances, excepting only the censures reserved to the powers of the popes contained in the Bulla Coenae.

Page 108.

1–10 *To this purpose also of spying . . . impaire their strength*: In the summary of the Jesuit constitutions, "Summarium Constitutionem" No. 4, in the *Regulae*, p. 4, Ignatius states that the Jesuits must live in the world rather than cloistered away from it because they must be astute observers of the society about them ("Ratio vivendi in exterioribus iustas ob causas, maius Dei obsequium semper intuendo, communis est"), and he adds that the traditional "ordinarias penitentias" such as flagellation should not be allowed to interfere with their role in society. Later in the "Summarium Constitutiones," Rule 48 stipulates that "Corporis castigatio immoderata" or immoderate physical castigation must be confessed in the sacrament of penitence, p. 16. Rule 38 in Chapter IIII of "De literarum studiis," in the "Regulae Rectoris," requires the Rector of the Jesuits in a college to constrain them to devotions that do not impede their studies. Donne's fourth and final reference to the *Regulae* is to Rule 4 in the "Regulae Praefecti Rerum Spiritualium" or the rules for the Prefect of spiritual matters in a Jesuit house or college. In the words of the first Jesuit congregation of 1558 that approved the text, the rule states that Ignatius' *Spiritual Exercises* forbid excessive devotion that is detrimental to physical health.

10–17 *that Gonzaga . . . allow him such severity*: In Book I, Chapters 3 and 4, pp. 58 and 61, on the severity of Gonzaga's self-discipline endangering his life; Book I, Chapter 6, pp. 83–84, on his various forms of scourging; and Book I, Chapter 11, pp. 153–154, on his parents' relief that Gonzaga's joining the Society of Jesus would put an end to his scourgings, in Ceparius' *Vita* of the saint.

23–30 *And for Exemptions . . . uppon paine of Heresie*: Elias Hasenmiller, the ex-Jesuit novice turned Protestant, entered the Jesuits in 1583, soon left to become an apostate from Catholicism, and not long after made an extensive written attack on his former order entitled *Historia Jesuitici ordinis* (Frankfurt, 1593), which Gretser answered with his own *Historia Ordinis Iesuitici*. In one passage Hasenmiller attacked the bulls of the popes that regulated the establishment of the Jesuit order, and Donne is reviving Hasenmiller's attack on those of the bulls in question that were issued after the original founding decretals and that modified the order's regulations. Donne refers to six of these as recorded in Gretser's counter-attack. The first, Bull 13, issued by Pius V, gave the Jesuits "Privilege of Addition" to

COMMENTARY

increase their rights in addition to those granted by the original canon law that created them, and it allowed them more specifically the right that Catholic mendicant friars possessed, to be lodged at any monastery at any time, to which was added the condition that the right was to be exercised by a travelling Jesuit only when a Jesuit house was not available (p. 195); Bull 17, issued by Gregory XIII, gave the Jesuits full freedom of movement and communication within the church (p. 207); the third bull, No. 15, also issued by Gregory, absolved Jesuits from having to observe offices at fixed hours in chapel (p. 197); Bull 19, by the same pope, freed Jesuits from obligatory attendance at religious processions (p. 213); Bull 7 by Julius III absolved Jesuits from having to observe strict fasts (p. 186); and finally, Bull 16 by Gregory XIII, allowed them to read books on the Catholic *Index*, which as Donne points out, Pope Gregory himself in his decree in his additions called *Septimes* to *Corpus Iuris Canonici*, did not even allow to archbishops and kings without special permission from the Holy See. Donne's attack on the privileges of the Jesuits must be seen in the context of the attempted reforms of the Council of Trent. The council had worked to eliminate the abuses of the privileges of addition and of exemption that the monasteries and religious orders had enjoyed in progressively growing numbers since Pope Honorius I had instituted them in 628. Originally, the privileges had been granted by the Holy See to free monasteries from the excessive authority of bishops who were also temporal lords, but later they were extended to the members of orders, and they always made the holders directly subservient to the pope rather than to local bishops. The *Corpus Iuris Canonici* had recently listed the majority of these privileges in the "Decretales D. Gregorii Papae IX," pp. 705–707, and in the "Extravagantes Communes," pp. 878–879 of the revised *Decretalia* of Gratian and its appendices (Paris, 1587). Between the bulls by Julius III and Gregory XIII, Donne inserts the reference to Rule 84 in the "Regulae Provincialis" of Ignatius' *Regulae*, p. 42, which allowed the provincial of a Jesuit province to dispense with religious dress or habit.

31–32 *in their Constitutions they . . . Cadavera*: Rule 36 of the "Summarium Constitutionum" of the *Regulae*, p. 12, stipulates that faithful Jesuits will obey Divine Providence in the orders of their superiors "ac si cadaver essent," as if they were cadavers.

Page 109.

2–3 *Baculasenis . . . such staves*: Baculasenis, from the Latin *bacula* and *senex*, or old sticks.

5–14 *is that obedience . . . know not what it is*: Ignatius' letter entitled "De Obedientiae Virtute, Epistola," addressed to the Jesuits of Portugal from Rome on 7 April 1553, was regularly published as an appendix to the early printed editions of the *Regulae* of his order. Donne is paraphrasing in translation Ignatius' instructions in Nos. III and V of the letter, pp. 218–220. In No. 6, p. 154, in the "Catalogus Missarum, et Orationum, Quae nostris praescribuntur," describing for whom, what and how often Jesuits should say their Masses and offer prayers, the rule stipulates that a Mass must be said once a week for the superior general of the order in Rome.

27–30 *the life of Nerius . . . to worke upon*: In his life of the saint, *Vita*, p. 113, Gallonio recounts the apparition of Saint John the Evangelist to Philip Neri and his order to him to abandon ideas of apostleship in the Indies and to remain in Rome. Donne's marginalia refers the reader to Gallonio's title for the section on p. 110, rather than to the quotation in his text, which is three pages later.

32–8 (p. 110) *Caenobites who keepe . . . Mirabundus accepi*: Donne's second translation is a paraphrase by the French master of jurisprudence Choppin in his last book *Monasticon*, on the rights of the clergy and the monasteries, Book II, Title 3, nu. 9, p. 316. Choppin points out how the relatively new Society of Jesus allows the collective possession of benefits and how this departs radically from the norms of the usual monastic orders. Donne's first translation is a paraphrase of a collection of scattered comments on the kinds of monks in Choppin's *Monasticon*, for example, the discussion of hermits and coenobites on pp. 295–296 (Book II, Title 2, nu. 25).

Page 110.

10–13 *told Saint Francis . . . no more there*: From Sedulius' *Apologeticus*, II, Chapter 6 on the vow of poverty, "De voto Pauperatis," Nos. 7 and 14, pp. 85, 89.

15–18 *have Proprietie . . . in common with them*: William Watson (b. ?Durham, ?1559), and William Clark were two seminary or secular priests trained in Catholic colleges on the continent, who returned as missionary priests to England and differed strongly with the Jesuits. They were executed at Winchester on 9 December 1603 after the failure of the "Bye" plot in which they were involved with a number of other anti-Jesuit seminary priests. The aim of the "Bye" plot was to force James I to accede to their demands for toleration before he was crowned, or to choose another heir to the throne.

20–24 *Nor are they more like the Circuitores . . . all this Martyrdome*: "Circulatores" or Circuitores was the alternative name given to the "Circumcelliones," a fraternal branch of the Donatists that, in the early fifth century, were given their name because of their habit of attacking their enemies by encircling their houses (see Commentary for p. 34, ll. 2–17). Donne's three authorities are the French Protestant Lambert Daneau (b. Beaugency-sur-Loire, c.1530; d. Castres, 1595), the author of an edition with commentary of Saint Augustine of Hippo's *De Haeresibus* (Geneva, 1576), in which, in Chapter 69, Augustine attacks the Donatists and their fanatical "circulatores" branch, and in which also, pp. 195^v–196^r, Daneau explains the origin of the "circumcelliones;" secondly, Gabriel du Préau, or Prateolus, the French humanist author of the *De Vitis Sectis*, whose chapter 19 of Book III is in fact entitled "Circuitores" (which produces Donne's note of "verbo Circuitores"), p. 129, and is an attack on the suicidal desires of the sect; and thirdly, the Spanish moral theologian Castro in *Adversus Haereses*, Tome 1, who, in his sections entitled

"Ecclesia," Cols. 357–358, and "Martyrium," Cols. 633–635, narrates the history of the circumcelliones and attacks them and their parent heresy, the fourth-century Donatists.

Page 111.

32–34 *And as some diseases . . . cure the Accidents*: Salmon in his *Synopsis Medicinae*, Book I, Chapter 27, p. 39, describes the difference between the "essential" and related or "accidental" afflictions of a body, using the Aristotelian and scholastic vocabulary of the "essential" referring to being and the "accidental" referring to its particularities. The "essential" affliction demonstrated where in the body "the Root of the Disease lodges," and the "accidental" illness "shows the sympathetical affliction of other parts . . . by reason of the extremity of the Distemper which radically afflicts some other part."

Page 113.

2–9 *S. Ursulaes eleven thousand Virgines . . . to invent falshood*: In *Martyrologium Romanum*, 21 October, p. 466, Col. 2, which Donne is translating freely, Baronius retells the story of Saint Ursula and her thousand martyred colleagues, which he got out of a narration by Bishop Wilhelmus Lindanus (Guillaume Linda) (b. Dordrecht, 1525; d. Ghent, 1583). Lindanus, a famous sixteenth-century controversialist, was at first bishop of Roermond (Ruremundus) in Belgium, which Baronius mentions in the passage Donne refers to, and later of Ghent. Both Baronius and the Jesuits claimed an *A Divino* origin for the pope's power, and rejected the idea that even part of it could spring from church councils or secular princes. Donne first uses Baronius' account of the incident of Saint Ursula to turn it against the other unqualified supporters of the Papacy, the Jesuits, and then he cites another unconditional supporter of the pope, Paris de Puteo, and turns his writings against them ironically too. Donne quotes Puteo's dictum about lawyers who prepare their cases too well and end up distorting the truth (*De syndicatu*, No. 15 of the chapter on "De Excessibus Advocatorum," p. 59). See Commentary for p. 84, l. 28–p. 85, l. 15.

13–15 *Pelargus hath noted . . . a false Martyrdome*: The Lutheran and later Calvinist German theologian, Christopher Pelargus or Storch (b. Schweidniz, 1565; d. Frankfurt, 1633), in his anti-Jesuit treatise, *Novus Jesuitimus hoc est Paradoxa sive absurdissima Jesuitarum Dogmata* (Frankfurt, 1608), Chapter IX, p. 139.

Page 114.

7 *Nimietates sunt aequalitates*: None of the existing copies of *Pseudo-Martyr* (1610) contains a note for the source of this quotation in the writings of the early fifth-century hermit Cassianus, whose *De Institutis Renunciantium* and *Collationes*

Sanctorum Patrum in the collected Lyons edition of 1606, Donne refers to several times.

29–32 *And as Ribadeneira sayes . . . that he halted*: In his full-length biography of Ignatius Loyola (first published in Latin in Naples in 1572), and to be distinguished from his abbreviated biography of the saint in his *Catalogus*, Ribadeneira describes the fullness of Ignatius' recovery from the leg wound he received at the Battle of Pamplona, IV, Chapter 18, "De Statura Corporis Eius" (p. 529, in the Cologne edition of 1602). See Commentary for p. 102, ll. 12–17.

36–5 (p. 115) *That it is the greatest Argument . . . Jesuites flatter themselves*: The little tract, *Spongia Qua Absterguntur Convitia et Maledicta Equitis Poloni Contra Jesuitas* (Ingolstadt, 1591) by an anonymous Jesuit (the title page bears the "Anagramma Authoris," or the author's anagram "IHS," which was the Society of Jesus' motto) defends the Polish members of the order from charges of having sown civil disorder in their country. Donne is translating the author's boast in the question "Clamantur haec in templis," on pp. 19 and 20, that the innocence of Jesuits is automatically proven if the charges against them are made by heretics. Later in Donne's text, Xerxes, fifth-century king of Persia, inherited from his father, Darius, the task of punishing the Greeks for participating in the Ionian revolt. His ravages of Greek territory were only stopped by the Greeks under Themistocles at Salamis. In Donne's marginalia, the French humanist Marc-Antoine Muret (b. Muret, 1526; d. Rome, 1585), records the Greek oath against Xerxes in *Variorum Lectionum* (Paris, 1586), Book III, Chapter 10, p. 38.

Page 115.

13–25 *They may be as poore . . . with the head downward*: The first example, of poverty, is out of Gallonio's life of Neri, *De Vita*, pp. 491–492, in which Gallonio recounts how Neri's desire for poverty began in his adolescence and persisted until his very last days. The second example, of chastity, is drawn from the Jesuit controversialist Gretser's *Historia Ordinis Iesuitici*, in which he attacked the apostate Elias Hasenmiller's book against the order. On pp. 118–119, Gretser tells the story of the German Jesuit, John Reinhard Ziegler (b. Odenhoven, 1569; d. Mayence, 1636), who smeared his face with his own excrement to resist the charms of a lady, and hence to save his family the disgrace of having to live with the fact of his having succumbed: "ne amore inflammata clamores tolleret, totique; suae familiae perpetuam maculam inureret." The third and fourth examples originate in the hermit Cassianus' *De Institutis Renunciantium*, on the institution of the monk, Book IV, Chapter 10 ("Quanta obedientia à iunioribus étiam in naturali necessitate custodiat"), p. 38, and Chapter 24 ("De ligno putriatque, quod idem abbas Ioannes ad arbitrium senioris sui quasi adolendam rigare non destitit"), pp. 46–47. The fifth example, like the third and fourth, deals with the clerical vow of obedience and is drawn from Sedulius in his *Apologeticus*, Book 2, Chapter 5, No. 5, p. 80. Sedulius records the example that Saint Francis used, of the novice obeying the command of his abbot to plant a plant head downwards, to teach the nature of obedience, which Donne cites elsewhere. John Carey in *Life*, p. 34, has described Donne's use of such examples as symptomatic of his intellectual inability to accept the blind obedience of Catholicism.

Page 116.

16–17 *for they have a Rule . . . of conscience*: A translation of the opening phrases of Rule 56 in the section on "Regulae Provincialis" in Chapter VI, "De literarum studiis," of the Jesuit *Regulae*, p. 36.

21–25 *the Institution of a Prince . . . kill himselfe*: In his chapter on "An liceat tyrannum veneno occidere," on whether it is permitted to kill a tyrant with poison, in *De Rege et De Regis Institutione* (Toledo, 1599), pp. 80–87, the Jesuit Juan Mariani (b. Talavera, Spain, 1536; d. Toledo, 1624) discussed various recipes for poisoning tyrants who were unredeemably cruel to their subjects. Mariani also recommended at the end of his chapter that making the murder of a tyrant look like suicide was preferable to open regicide. Mariani's book, to which Donne refers as the *Institution of a Prince*, was warmly received by Philip III of Spain, to whom it was dedicated, but was banned and its copies destroyed by the Parliament of Paris on 8 June 1610, after the assassination in May of Henri IV of Navarre.

32–3 (p. 117) *And as Averroes . . . thereof was compiling it*: In Chapter 7, of his *De Confessionibus Maleficiorum et Sagarum*, p. 216, the Flemish canonist Binsfeldus narrates the story of the supposed poisoning of the Arab philosopher-mathematician Avicenna by his fellow thinker, Averroes, as an example of the devil's ability to effect his designs by indirect methods. Averroes (b. Cordova, 1128; d. Morocco, 1198) was often accused of betraying the Muslim faith by favouring the study of science and antiquity. Avicenna (b. Afshena, Bokhara, 980; d. Hamadan, 1037) was reputed to have poisoned him through the power of his migrant soul to come back from the dead into the present, and to conduct his designs, in this case, by lining the cutting edges of Averroes' book with poison. The Jewish *Targum* consisted of the Aramaic commentaries on the Old Testament composed after Hebrew ceased to be the common language of the Jews. Peter Colonna of Galatine in Otranto, Italy, a late fifteenth-century member of the Friars Minor, wrote the *De Arcanis Catholicae Veritatis* to defend the preservation of both the *Targum* and the Jewish Talmud from destruction, and cites the legend of Donne's text to refute their supposedly anti-Christian character (Frankfurt, 1602), Book I, Chapter III, Cols. 8–9.

Page 117.

7–12 *the gatherer . . . delicate paper*: The bibliographer of the Carthusian order Petrejus in his *Bibliographica Carthusiana*, p. 35. The then superior general of the Carthusians was Bruno Daffringues of Saint Omer in France.

19-24 *in the Approbation . . . of mature judgement*: The phrase "Nihil fidei contrarium" appeared often, but not invariably, on the title pages of Catholic books to indicate that they had the Church's official approval. Donne's quotation is a translation from the defense of the Jesuits' publication of books, against charges of provoking civil unrest, in *Spongia Qua Absterguntur*, p. 78, under the question "De libello contumelis et maledictis in gentem nostram pleno," p. 77.

26-1 (p. 118) *Servi papae . . . pro eo*: *Missale SS. Patrum Latinorum, Sive Liturgicon Latinum* (Cologne, 1609). The four translations and quotations from Alvares' *Thesaurus Christianae Religionis* on the legal rights of emperors and popes, are from Chapter 1 ("De Unitate Sanctae Matris Romanae Ecclesiae; & de Unitate, & Plenissima potestate sacri summi Romani Pontificis"), number 35; and Chapter 18 ("Papa non est solitus dispensare"), numbers 6 and 7. In the latter passage, Alvares cites the authority of Henri de Suse, called "Hostiensis," the Swiss canonist (b. Suse, c.1210; d. Lyons, 1271) who was cardinal bishop of Hostie and Velletri, to whom Donne refers. Suse, or Hostiensis, wrote the *Summa Super Titulis Decretalium*.

Page 118.

2-11 *So when Bellarmine . . . in the Pope*: Bellarmine's proctors whom Donne says defended him were his two fellow Jesuits the German controversialist Gretser in *Controversiam Roberti Bellarmini*, and Andreas Eudaemon-Johannes (b. Canea, Island of Candia, Aegean Sea, n.d.; d. Rome, 1625), in his *Castigatio eorum, quae adversus Roberti Cardinalis Bellarmini* (Ingolstadt, 1605). Gretser defended Bellarmine against attacks on his *De Controversiis* by the Cambridge divine Whitaker in his *Pralectiones in quibus tractatur controversia de ecclesia contra pontificios*, and in *Castigatio*, Eudaemon-Johannes defended the Jesuit cardinal principally against attacks by the Swiss Calvinist Lambert Daneau in his *De Rebus* (Geneva, 1596). Bellarmine, who had a reputation for being scholarly and for disliking open quarrels, finally took up his own defence about the same time as Gretser and Eudaemon-Johannes on his behalf, but only after a considerable number of attacks on him. The first publication in his self-defence was entitled *Responsio ad Duos Libros . . . Unum . . . Responsio ad epistolam sui amici . . . Et Alterum . . . est: Tractatus et resolutio Ioannis Gersonis* (Mainz, 1606), and appeared under his pseudonym of Matthew Tortus, but Donne was unaware that "Matthew the Turtle" was Bellarmine. However, Bellarmine did publish a second work in self-defence under his real name, entitled *Apologia . . . pro responsione sua ad librum Iacobi Magnae Britanniae Regis, cuius titulis est, Triplici nodo triplex cuneus . . . . Accedit eadem ipsa Responsio Iterum recusa quae sub nomine Mattaeo Torti* (Rome, 1609), and this is the sign of Bellarmine's "rising up" to which Donne is referring. Donne writes that Bellarmine wrote *Apologia* "unprovoked" because he ignores the fact that the Jesuit cardinal is Tortus, that Tortus' *Responsio* was one of the works that provoked James to write his anonymous *Triplici*, and that *Triplici* was therefore an answer to a disputant already long engaged pseudonymously in an old quarrel.

Moreover, Bellarmine wrote yet a third work in his defence, this time an *Epistola* or open letter addressed to the Anglican bishop George Blackwell under his real name, and he ironically published it, no less, as an appendix to the Cologne edition of *Responsio* in 1608 (p. 61), with a mock introduction under his real name to both the *Responsio* by Tortus and his signed letter, as though he and Tortus were two different people; this letter to Blackwell must also be included under Donne's reference to Bellarmine's "rising up." Late in this controversy, Eudaemon-Johannes was vivid in the contemporary English consciousness not only for his defence of Bellarmine, but more particularly for his attack in *Adversus Roberti Abbati Oxoniensis de Antichristo* (Cologne, 1609), in the very same year that Donne wrote *Pseudo-Martyr*, on the book on *Antichristi Demonstratio* (1603) by Robert Abbot of Oxford (b. 1560; d. 1617), bishop of Salisbury.

11–13 *And since that . . . when he came to be Pope*: In *Concilia Generalia*, Vol. V, Tome 4, p. 512, Col. 1, Binius records Pope Pius II's *retractum*, after he was elected pope in 1458, of his arguments in favour of conciliar power that he had made when a councillor at the Council of Basel in 1436. There, he had been in favour of the anti-pope Felix V against Pope Eugenius IV. Enea Silvio de' Piccolomini, which was Pius II's name, and which is the one that Donne uses, published in 1463 his bull containing his famous words, "Aeneam rejicite, Pium suscipite" ("drop Aeneas, uphold Pius"). The bull was his answer to criticisms by German and Bohemian secular princes who used against him his conciliar arguments which pre-dated his election to the papacy.

14–15 *a new survay and Recognition of all his workes*: The "new survey" in question is Bellarmine's *Recognitio Librorum Omnium*, a little work in which, firstly, the controversialist cardinal listed his changes of view, in the form of a glossary to his so-far published works; and secondly, in which he published a list of *errata* and alterations of phrasing in his publications.

20–24 *I said before . . . S. Thomas prevailes more with me*: Donne is translating Bellarmine's passage in *Recognitio Librorum*, p. 44, in which he explains why he now rejects his earlier view in Chapter 7, Book V (entitled "De Potestate Pontificiis Temporali") of his third general controversy, Vol. I, Col. 1067, of *De Controversiis*, that the papacy had no power against infidel princes. Bellarmine admitted to having originally followed the view of the French Dominican, Durandus of Saint-Pourçain (b. Saint-Pourçain, n.d.; d. Meaux, 1332) in his commentary, 2, Dist. 44, q.3, on the sentences of Peter Lombard, but to now having aligned himself with Aquinas' view in the *Summa Theologica* II.II. q.10, article 10, that the papacy did in fact have power over infidel princes. Donne's original marginal note to the third controversy "De Summo Pontifice" is wrongly numbered "l.4. c.8," and may represent his attempt to correct Bellarmine's own error of "Eodem quinto libro, cap. 8" in *Recognitio*, which should have read Book V, Chapter 7.

26–27 *he sayes . . . as to his Judge*: In *Recognitio*, p. 16, Bellarmine argued that the princes of the Church were ministers of Christ, that Christ was the King of kings, and that the princes of the church could therefore not be subjected to earthly kings. He thus repudiated his position in Chapter 29, Book II ("De Successione Romani Pontificis in eo primatu"), of the third general controversy, Vol. I, of *De Controversiis* (Col. 816), where the question of the power of an early Christian prince like the apostle Paul over an infidel temporal ruler like Caesar in Acts 25.10, appeared to be less clear.

27–30 *Whereas I said . . . are not approved*: In *Recognitio*, p. 52, Bellarmine retracted his statement in Chapter 16 ("De Cardinalibus") of Book I ("De Clericis") of the fifth general controversy ("De Membris Ecclesiae Militantis") of Vol. I of *De Controversiis*, Col. 1431, that in early days of the Christian world popes had been chosen by emperors. Bellarmine stated now that he had been misled by Gratian's *Decretum*, Col. 322, Part I, Chapter 22 ("Imperator ius habet eligendi pontificem"). Donne alludes to Bellarmine's discovery, which led to his retraction, that Popes Gregory VII and Leo IX in the eleventh century had interpreted the history of the early church in the opposite sense from Gratian before Gratian himself was to write on the papacy. Bellarmine now followed the belief of the early popes rather than that expressed in *Decretum*.

30–32 *And againe . . . De iure*: In Chapter 13 of Book I ("De Natura et Causis Concilii") of the fourth general controversy ("De Conciliis et Ecclesia") of Vol. I of *De Controversiis*, Col. 1125, Bellarmine expressed the view that the princes of the church were the lords of all men, but at the same time they were to obey emperors in temporal matters. As Donne points out, in *Recognitio*, p. 47, Bellarmine did not exactly retract his view but he qualified his statement to mean that the submission of church princes to emperors must be understood as not being founded on inherent imperial rights, but as current practice only: "intelligimus de facto, non de jure."

Page 119.

3–7 *their spirituall Constitutions . . . suffer for his sake*: Donne is paraphrasing Ignatius' instructions to the Jesuits in Rule 40 of the "Summarium Constitutionum" of the *Regulae*, p. 15. The biblical quotation in Donne's passage is John 12.25.

8–14 *Ribadeneira names . . . to die, then ride*: Donne is citing various incidents which befell obscure Jesuits early in the society's history, from the appendix to Ribadeneira's *Catalogus* of Jesuit writings. Some of the Jesuits concerned are spoken of only briefly in the catalogue and in some cases are not listed at all in Carlos Sommervogel's bibliography of the Jesuit order, *Bibliothèque de la Compagnie de Jésus* (Brussels, 1890–1909). Donne's first reference to the two sleeping Jesuits is probably to the Fathers Antonius and Alphonsus Mendez who were decapitated by tribesmen in the East Indies in the first official year of the order's existence in 1549 (*Catalogus*, p. 160). The next martyred Jesuit, Simon Acosta, was pitched headlong into the sea by savages, but he was not one of the five brothers assassinated in the Salettes Islands in the Indies in 1583 as Donne states, and Donne appears to be confusing him with Christopher de Acosta, brother of the Spanish Jesuit Joseph de Acosta, who was a missionary in the East Indies (see Commentary for p. 105, ll. 10–15). In his *Catalogus*, Ribadeneira records nothing under Simon Acosta's name but the circumstances of his death (p. 196) and later lists his name even without this brief information (p. 201), and in neither place does he identify him with a group of martyrs such as the five executed brothers. Nor is Simon Acosta identified as one of these five men in the Jesuit Franciscus Bincius' short epic poem to them, *Quinque Martyrum* of 1591. Rodolpho Aquaviva whom Donne next lists was, however, one of the five young Jesuits put to death, and Ribadeneira mentions him as such on p. 201, and so does Bincius, *Orationes et Carmina* (Ingolstadt, 1607), p. 364. Bincius also mentions one "Edmundus" as being among the five but nobody else. Rodolpho Aquaviva was the cousin of Claudio Aquaviva who was elected general of the order in 1581.

18–35 *the wordes of him . . . hostili ferro*: In his *Catalogus*, p. 38, Ribadeneira identified the Belgian Jesuit philosopher and rhetorician Charles Scribanus (b. Brussels, 1561; d. Antwerp, 1629), who anagrammatized his name as Clarus Bonarscius for a pseudomym, as the author of the *Amphitheatrum Honoris* (Antwerp, 1605). The *Amphitheatrum* defended the Jesuits against the attacks of the Calvinists, and describes the courage of the Jesuits in the face of suffering as superior to that of the legendary Romans, first, Gaius Mucius, called the "Scaevoles" or left-handed, who burned off his own right hand when captured in the enemy camp of Porsena to show his indifference to death with which he was being threatened; second, Cato of Utica (b. 95; d. 46 B.C.) who committed suicide when he realized that his senatorial cause in the Roman civil war was lost; and third, Portia, Cato's daughter, who deliberately wounded herself to demonstrate her solidarity with her husband Brutus' republican ideals after Caesar's death; and finally, of Cleopatra who killed herself with an asp (Chapter IV, p. 11, 2nd ed., 1606). Then, Donne's first reference to martyrdom is to the passage in *Amphitheatrum* on the Jesuit Ignatius Azevebo (b. Porto, 1528; d. 1570) martyred by Calvinists on the high seas (pp. 37–38); the second, to Edmund Campion (b. London, 1539; d. 1581) and the "Anglicana lupa" Elizabeth I (p. 41); and the third, to the other executed English Jesuit Thomas Cotham (b. Lancashire, 1549; d. Tyburn, 1582) and the "Calvinista lupa" (p. 43). For the parallel use of "Prince" as a term of celebration, see Donne's "Extasie," l. 68.

Page 120.

1–3 *Constitution of the Pope . . . publiquely there*: In *Martyrologium Romanum*, 29 December, p. 567, Cols. 1–2, Baronius writes that young Englishmen trained as Jesuits in the colleges of Rome and Rheims, are inspired to return to England to preach the faith principally by a desire to imitate the return of Saint Thomas à Becket from the continent to Canterbury, though their return is also motivated by papal decree.

3–5 *Oath Navarrus . . . into England*: It is difficult both here and on p. 123 of Donne's text to grasp what part of Navarrus' *De Regularibus* he has in mind. Donne's marginal note indicates "Consil. I" in *De Regularibus*, but all four parts of Navarrus' work are entitled "In Commentario," and none with "Consil." On p. 123, Donne is quoting the other Jesuit Azor's *Institutionum Moralium*, in which Azor during his discussion of the problems of the young expatriated English Jesuits returning home, refers to Navarrus' description of the three Jesuit clerical vows, and points to the latter's text in a marginal note as "Navar. consil. I de Regularib." However, in the "Commentarius Primus" of *De Regularibus Opera*, Vol. I of *Opera hactenus* (Lyons, 1589–1594), p. 57, Col. 2, and p. 58, Col. 1, Navarrus discusses the three vows of Jesuits that precede their entry into solemn profession, but makes no reference to young Englishmen trained in continental colleges returning to England. Donne may have made the error of believing that Azor's consideration of the young men's return was part of Navarrus' thought, and of copying Azor's marginal phrase, "Quaertit Navar. consil." (probably intending to mean, "It is to be learned from Navarrus' consideration"), as though it was a direct reference to Navarrus' text. The present edition drops the "Consil." because the word is misleading.

CHAP. V
Page 121.

19–24 *For, though Bellarmine . . . imputation*: In "De eorum reliquiis et imaginibus," Chapter 9, which forms Book II of the seventh controversy, "De Ecclesia, quae triumphat in coelis," in *De Controversiis*, Vol. I, Col. 2034 and 2038, Bellarmine discusses the condemnation of the use of images by persecuted Christians, by the Council of Eliberitane in the fourth century. He concluded, as Donne records, that the council's condemnation had been severe, given the circumstances of the persecution and the strength that Christians reaped from the images during their trials. Donne then cites Baronius and Binius as at first doubting the wisdom of the same council, and later changing their minds in its favour.

Margin 21 *Ann. 55. nu.19*: Baronius, *Annales Ecclesiastici*, Vol. I, Tome 1, for the year 55, Col. 553, No. 19, entitled, "Reliquae Sanctorum a maioribus probari solitae."

22 *changed his opinion*: Baronius, *Annales Ecclesiastici*, Vol. I, Tome 2, for the year 305, Col. 1009, No. 32, entitled, "De Fuga in persecutione."

Page 122.

26–27 *Baronius words . . . the Church*: Baronius discusses the role of the young Englishmen trained in Jesuit colleges on the continent for mission work in England, under the inscription of Thomas à Becket's name for the feast day of 29 December in *Martyrologium Romanum*, p. 567, Cols. 1 and 2.

Page 123.

2–13 *the Spanish Expeditions . . . the execution thereof*: The Catholic writers whom Donne mentions as supporting the intervention of armies in foreign countries to protect the Roman clergy are all recent religio-political commentators, but not necessily historians of the Spanish Armada's attempted invasion of England. The first is Alvarez, in *Thesaurus Christianae Religionis*, Chapter 15, Nos. 1, 2 and 3, which deal with the right of the Spanish monarchy to send troops into the Indies in the name of the papacy, and Nos. 12, 16 and 17, which demonstrate the precedents for such invasion in Christian history; and Chapter 41, No. 12, which justifies such military intervention on scriptural grounds. Donne's second authority is the Jesuit theologian Azor in his *Institutionum Moralium*, which describes the apostolic mission of the Roman Church as the origin of its right to intervene in foreign countries to protect its missionary clergy, Vol. II, Part II, Book 4, Chapter 18, pp. 286–287, and defends the right of the Church to protect its institutions from pagans, Vol. I, Part I, Book 8, Chapter 24, Col. 1025. Donne's third Catholic authority is Maynard in *De Privilegiis Ecclesiasticis*, Article 10, No. 25, p. 80, which deals with the rights of the Roman Church and justifies papal intervention in Venice.

17–19 *in many cases . . . by Martyrdome*: The Benedictine monk Hilary of Genoa in his *Commentarium In Sacrosancta IIII Evangelia*, Brescia, 1578.

29–2 (p. 124) *you enter into the Colledge . . . better performed*: Donne is translating a sentence from a passage in Azor's *Institutionum Moralium*, Vol. I, Part I, Book 11, Chapter 5 ("De Iureiurando, cui iustitia deest"), Col. 1342, dealing with the training of young Englishmen in English colleges on the continent for the English Catholic mission field. Azor discusses a text by Navarrus in *De Regularibus* on the three vows that young Jesuits take before solemn profession and disagrees with him, and he also discusses the return of young English Jesuits to the English mission field which Navarrus' own text does not deal with. Donne appears to assume that Azor's argument on the repatriation of the young men originates in Navarrus' work when it does not (see Commentary for p. 120, ll. 3–5). Azor argues that a young Jesuit does not betray his vows if he does not return to England.

Page 124.

11–13 *For a law . . . of mortall sinne*: A paraphrase of the English Benedictine Gregory Sayer's argument about sin and the disobedience of the law in *Clavis Regia Sacerdotum Casus Casuum Conscientiae Sive Theologicae Moralis Thesauri* (Venice, 1602), Book III, Chapter VII ("Quae, et Quando lex humana ad peccatum mortale obligat, et quomodo hoc cognosci possit"), No. 25, p. 163, in the Venice edition of 1615. This work which Donne also cites later on p. 263 is not the same as the *Casuum Conscientiae . . . Thesaurus, De Censuris Ecclesiasticis* (Venice, 1601) that he quotes twice earlier, pp. 77–78, but he refers to both works by the same abbreviated title of "Thesau. Cas. Consc."

20–22 *the lawes of Princes . . . in making them*: In Chapter V, "Quomodo possit cognosci legem aliquam humanam obligare ad culpem mortalem," of Book I of *De Potestate Legis Poenalis* (Salamanca, 1550), in Cols. 527 and 528 of the edition of the *Omnia Opera* of Paris, 1578, Castro discusses the nature of just laws and the evil intentions of law-makers, and their effect on the individual conscience.

33–5 (p. 125) *Lawyers teach us . . . Likely, or Possible*: Bartolus of Saxoferrato, the celebrated fourteenth-century Italian jurist, who wrote a commentary on the *Digestorum* of Justinian's *Corpus Iuris Civilis*, entitled *Interpretum Iuris Civilis*, 3 vols. (Basel, 1562), Vol. III, Digest. 46, Title 6, Law 3, p. 687, on the interpretation of the Thomistic ideas of act and potency as legal terms. Donne gives as an example a passage from Alvarez' *Thesaurus Christianae Religionis*. In Chapter 41 on the just and unjust wars, Alvarez (No. 10, p. 149) defends the right of a man to use force and to kill to protect himself from his aggressors, and he extends this approach to international encounters involving Roman interests. His second example is from Albericus Gentilis' *De Iure Belli* (London, 1588), Book I, Chapter 14.

Page 125.

8–14 *the three Emperours . . . to make that law*: The brothers Flavius Gratianus and Flavius Valentinus I, and their uncle Valens, ruled jointly as emperors over different parts of the Roman empire between 364 and 383. Though all three were Christians, they put certain legal strictures on the possessions of bishops and clerics which the Emperor Theodosius II recorded in his codex of Roman laws in the next century, *Codicis Theodosiani Libri XVI* (Lyons, 1593), Book 16, Law 20, p. 479. In his letter to Nepotianus (d. Altina, 396), friend of Gratian and Theodosius, brief years after the law was passed, Jerome attributed its passage to the general covetousness of clergymen themselves upon the rights of laymen, *Hieronymi Operum*, 5 vols., edited by Erasmus (Basel, 1524), Vol. I, *Opus Epistolarum*, pp. 16–17.

Page 126.

1–19 *a locall Interdict . . .the Merite of obedience*: In his brief of excommunication of 17 April 1606, Paul V gave the Doge and Senate of Venice three days to conform to his request for the return of property to the clergy in the litigious land claims between the Church and the state, "Breve Excommunicationis," *Controversiae Memorabilis*, p. 9. Failing the Senate's compliance with the deadline, the entire state of Venice was automatically to be placed under a "local interdict" forbidding all sacraments of the Church to be administered there. An interdict could only be decreed by a pope and was "local," as opposed to personal or general, when it forbad the performance of certain religious services like the Mass in a given, limited place. Many years earlier, in 1298, the papal decree "Alma Mater," touching on heresy and indevotion and establishing the interdict in canon law, was included by Boniface VIII in his "Liber Sextus" of Church law, Book V, Title 11, Chapter 24,

COMMENTARY

Corpus Iuris Canonici, Col. 169, to which Donne's marginalia refers the reader; and, he writes that the anonymous glosser of Gratian's *Decretum* in commenting on Boniface's decretal, expresses the opinion that a local interdict destined to punish a population for the sins of its prince and to force him to change his ideas, often dramatically produced the opposite effect to the one desired. The Tuscan canonist Bartholomeo Ugolini (b. 1540; d. 1610) supported the glosser's point of view though without specific reference to him, in the words of consolation that he addressed to the Senate of Venice in its crisis with Rome, in his *Responsiones . . . Ad Tractatum Septem Theologorum* (Mainz, 1607), Chapter I, Section 1, No. 11, p. 13.

25–27 *Law sayes . . . Securitie, Tranquilitie*: In Book 48, Title 4, Law 1, "Ad Legem Iuliam majestatis," Col. 1831, Volume I, *Corpus Iuris Civilis*.

31–33 *Queen Maries time . . . in England*: From the beginning of Mary Tudor's reign in 1553, Catholic priests were ordained in England even though the excommunication order that was issued against the entire kingdom in Henry VIII's time was still in force. The excommunication order was only lifted on 30 November 1554, but the Church nevertheless considered the ordinations valid. In the same year, Mary had Parliament re-enact Britain's statutes against heresy.

Page 127.

4–23 *Is there not a Decretall . . . is guiltie of Treason*: Donne lists four examples of Catholic pronouncements that describe heresy as a form of treason and that stipulate the need of secular punishment for a heretic's spiritual offence. The first is that of the decretal issued by Leo X at the fifth Lateran Council enjoining upon secular authorities the obligation of protecting ecclesiastics who were on journeys to assist at church councils. The decretal also condemned secular princes if they took advantage of the defencelessness of ecclesiastical princes on their travels to attack them, even though the two might be at war. The second example is that of the anonymous Jesuit author of the defence of the Jesuit order against charges of fomenting civil disorder in Poland, *Spongia Qua Absterguntur*, p. 29. The author of *Spongia* argued that charges of heresy should be brought against Vielunens Vladislaus Jagello for contesting the decrees of the General Polish Parliament of 1438. The third example is that of Pius II's letter of 1459 to Albert (b. 1414; d. 1486), Burgrave of Nuremberg and later Margrave of Brandenburg (*Sacrorum Conciliorum*, Vol. 35, Cols 111–112). The final example is drawn from the Spanish jurist and canonist Simancha's *Enchiridion*, Chapter 56, entitled "De bonis haereticorum" on the possessions of heretics, No. 5, p. 290. Donne's paraphrase adds details to Simancha's text, such as the idea of the two deaths and the corruption of kings.

37–11 (p. 128) *The Parliament of Paris . . . hee should incurre treason*: On 27 December 1594, Jean Chastell (b. Paris; d. 1594), who was then about nineteen years old, slid into the chambers of Henry IV's mistress in Paris where the king was receiving his courtiers, and attempted to stab him in the stomach, but only succeeded in hitting him in the upper lip and teeth as the king had unexpectedly bent down to help a courtier. Two days later, Chastell, who had been educated by Jesuits at the College of Clermont, confessed before the Parliament of Paris which was summoned to pass judgement on him, that he had been inspired to perpetrate the attempted regicide by Jesuits, principally by Father Jean Gueret. The Parliament of Paris passed its sentence immediately, condemning Chastell to be executed later that day, ordering the Jesuits to leave France within a few days, and holding guilty of treason any Frenchman who sent his child to a Jesuit college outside of France. Donne is translating from the parliamentary order. The order was republished in François de Verone's *Apologie Pour Iehan Chastel Parisien . . . contre l'Arrest de Parlement, donné . . . à Paris le 29. Decembre, 1594* (1605). Father Gueret was executed on the following 7 January.

Page 128.

12–18 *your Expurgatorie Index . . . preserve this sentence*: In the Spanish Inquisition's *Index Librorum Expurgatorum*, the verb "deleatur" (or the plural "deleantur") that is, "delete," was added before every phrase that was to be expurgated from the proscribed texts. For texts that had to be expurgated by the addition of a phrase or yet another text, the more common order used was "additur" or "add," but Donne's "Inseratur" or insert, could be correct (Salmuri edition of 1601). Donne is attacking the inquisition's expurgators by applying their art of deleting and adding to the injuries left on the face and teeth of King Henry IV of France by Jean Chastell's assassination attempt. The "Pyramis" was an early variant spelling of pyramid, and the "Recordes" of the Parliament of Paris were the minutes of its proceedings (see Commentary for p. 127, l. 37 to p. 128, l. 11).

14 *evert*: To turn upside down.

24 *When the Jesuits . . . from Venice*: In the conflict over land claims and the authority of secular courts over priests, Paul V absolved the Venetian clergy of its loyalty to the doge and senate of Venice. the doge and senate ordered the clergy to ignore Paul's order and, as the Jesuits refused, they were expelled.

Page 129.

14–15 *one of his owne sect . . . vitam martyr*: In his short biography of Parsons which precedes the chronological list of his works, Ribadeneira writes of him "sed per totam vitam Martyr fieret," *Catalogus*, p. 175.

CHAP. VI
Page 130.

22–31 *even in the Romane Church . . . mention of Emperour*: Donne is citing two of the most renowned Catholic jurists of international law against Baronius, the Spanish Dominican Francis à Victoria (b. Victoria, Alava, 1480; d. Salamanca,

1546), and the French courtier Cassanaeus. Victoria was the author of *Relectiones Theologicae Tredecim Partibus Per Varias Sectiones in Duos Libros Divisae*, first published in 1532 but republished in several editions, including one in Lyons in 1587, in which the Latin source of Donne's paraphrase may be found in No. 6 of the third essay on "De Potestate Civili," p. 106. Victoria's reputation was such that even early in the twentieth century he has been called "a founder of the law of Nations" (J.B. Scott, "Preface," *De Indis et De Iure Belli Relectiones*, trans. J.B. Bate, Washington, 1917, p. 5). The idea that state power springs from God through nature and not from God through the papacy ("sed tanquam a natura profectum," No. 5, p. 105), serves Donne to attack Baronius. The passage in question by Baronius, when he argues that state power is subjected to the papacy in a hierarchy of power descending from God to the pope and only then to earthly kings, occurs in his "Monarchiae nomen," the name of monarchy, in his tract supporting the papacy's jurisdiction over Spain in Naples and Sicily, *Tractatus de Monarchia Siciliae*, pp. 12–17. Donne's second illustration that kings as well as popes hold their power equally directly from God is the discussion by Cassanaeus in his *Catalogus Gloriae Mundi* of the rights, duties and prerogatives of the kings of France, Part 5, Consideration 28, p. 235, Col. 2, and p. 236, Col. 1. Donne's translations of Cassanaeus and Victoria are paraphrases rather than literal translations.

Page 131.

14–17 *a Jesuit said . . . of Regall Jurisdiction*: The Austrian Jesuit and theologian, Adam Tanner (b. Innsbruck, 1571; d. Unken, Tyrol, 1632), wrote the *Defensio Ecclesiasticae Libertatis . . . Contra Venetae Causae* (Ingolstadt, 1602) in defence of Paul V during his quarrels with the Venetian republic. Tanner taught theology for twenty-two years in Munich, was named chancellor of the University of Prague by the Emperor Ferdinand II, and was the author of a popular defence of the Jesuit presence in Bohemia and Moravia, *Apologia Pro Societate Iesu* (Vienna, 1618). In *Defensio*, II, 5, p. 252 (Ingolstadt edition of 1607), Tanner argued that God bestowed power on a pope only through his election by other men, and Donne borrows the argument to aver that God likewise bestows power on secular rulers only through the means that men choose to select them. In the immediate background of Donne's argument is the knowledge of his early seventeenth-century readers that the secular authority of the Venetian republic, which Paul was contesting, was also elective.

Page 132.

15–20 *Sepulveda, whom . . . as reason rules that*: In Sepulveda's *De Regno et Regis Officio*, Book I, p. 72: "Civile imperium intelligitur, quod in liberos homines ad ipsorum utilitatem exercetur herile aut, quod in servos ad comoditatem imperantis." See Commentary for p. 47, ll. 12–15.

Page 133.

15–26 *the governement amongst the Jewes . . . reciprocall obligations*: In *De Regno et Regis Officio*, Book II, p. 91, Sepulveda uses the biblical passages of I Samuel 8, to illustrate the right of people to choose a king, the expectations they place upon him, and the spiritual leadership they may also call upon him to exercise. Donne is drawing both on Sepulveda's authority and on that of the biblical passage to indicate that the king's power does not originate in him but is great nevertheless. The *Regna Laconica* of the Greek city states appears to refer to the Achaean League of "Free Laconians" formed in 146 B.C. by the coastal towns of Laconia in the Peloponnesus, which freed themselves from the Laconian capital of Sparta. The "Free Laconians" chose supreme officers to rule them as long as they could defend them and assure suitable internal government.

Page 134.

33–8 (p. 135) *For when a distressed Passenger . . . Abrahams worke*: The examples of excessive obedience are drawn from a single volume containing two works, entitled *De Institutis Renunciantium* and *Collationes Sanctorum Patrum*, of the fifth-century hermit Cassianus. The first example, the story of the abbot Apollo, is from Chapter 9 of *Collatio* 24, pp. 628–629; the second, from *De Institutis*, Book V, Chapter 40, pp. 83 and 84, on the story of the two young monks in Libya who starved in the desert; the third, from Book IV, Chapters 27 and 28, for the tale of Mucius the monk who obeyed his Abbot's order to throw his son into the river; and *Collatio* 4, Chapter 20, pp. 251–253, for the biblical prototype of forms of obedience.

Page 135.

9–11 *That it is . . . no body to him*: Saint John Climacus (b. Palestine, c.525; d. Sinai, 605), Byzantine theologian and ascetic, in "Gradus" or step No. 4 in the ladder of perfection of his *Scala Paradisi*.

18–28 *the late Jesuit Gonzaga . . . to read there*: In Book II, Chapter 1, of his *Vita*, Ceparius describes the incident of Gonzaga fearing that he had been uselessly flippant when he suggested to his spiritual superior that he, the superior, should go home to rest (p. 196). Again, in Book II, Chapter 4, p. 242, Ceparius describes the incident in Gonzaga's life in 1586 when he was tempted to go to Naples. Finally, a few pages later in the same chapter (p. 244), Ceparius describes Gonzaga's remorse at his quibbling over a point in Augustine.

29–7 (p. 136) *Sedulius seemes glad . . . to go preach naked*: There follow four examples of miracles and incidents in the lives of the Franciscans out of some fifty such items that Donne found in Sedulius' *Apologeticus*. Sedulius listed the miracles and incidents to support Albizzi's parallels between Saint Francis and Christ in his *Liber Conformitatum*, and Donne uses them to the opposite purpose to discredit the

COMMENTARY

manner in which the Catholic religious orders followed their rules, in this case the rule being the Franciscan rule of obedience. The examples are from *Apologeticus* III, Chapter 1 on "De simplicitate veterum Minoridarum," 2, p. 129, on Friar Ruffinus and the pig's foot; from III, 2 (on the virtue of humility, "De virtute humilitas"), No. 2, p. 131, on Ruffinus and his desire to be a smelly corpse; from III, 14, 2, p. 163 on the simplicity of Friar Juniper driving the devil away; and finally, from II, 5, 7, p. 81, on Ruffinus mistaking an order of Saint Francis and preaching naked. Donne correctly altered the derivative Spanish "Minoridarum" in Sedulius' Latin text to the current Latin "Minoritarum" when he cited the heading to Chapter 1 of Book III. The word "sodde" means to boil a bird without removing its feathers.

Page 136.

7–26 *degrees of spirituall pride . . . to say so before*: Donne makes eleven rapid references to Ceparius' *De Vita Beati Aloysii Gonzagae*, to show that some forms of humility hide what he considers to be spiritual pride: 1) Book I, Chapter 7, p. 100, Gonzaga delights in patched stockings; 2) Book II, Chapter 6, p. 306, he commemorates a saintly man by refusing to wear his discarded shoes; 3) at the end of the same chapter, p. 326, he refuses to wear gloves because the alpine cold touches everyone; 4) Book II, Chapter 3, p. 225, he declares that he has lain aside family matters so completely in becoming a priest, that he forgets how many brothers he has; 5) Book II, Chapter 1, p. 191, Gonzaga cannot remember how many brothers he has because he has strictly obeyed his religious vow of forgetting all thoughts of family on entering orders; 6) Book II, Chapter 8, p. 360, Gonzaga vows to visit the afflicted during a plague in Rome in spite of the fact that he himself is still convalescing from an illness; 7) Book II, Chapter 3, p. 220, Gonzaga fears that his scrupulousness has blinded him because he can find no trace of even a venial sin in himself; 8) Book II, Chapter 8, p. 346, Gonzaga regrets the affection that someone might give him because he fears that it is a sign of self-indulgence on his part; 9) Book II, Chapter 7, p. 335, he fears that his desire to speak in public at the Roman College is a sign of stubbornness due to his difficulty in pronouncing the letter "R"; 10) Book II, Chapter 5, p. 288, Gonzaga asked to be allowed to give a sermon in Spanish when he could not speak well, in order to be laughed at and be humbled; and, 11) Book II, Chapter 1, p. 187, he states that finally he may recite the first sentence of the Our Father with full meaning now that his father is dead, and that the first phrase of the Lord's Prayer is the only comment he can make on his father's death.

27–20 (p. 137) *Who would not . . . unmannerly quitted her*: Donne lists seven instances of what he considers to be excessive manifestations of obedience by Catholics. The first is from III, Chapter VI "De Obedientia," I, in Sedulius' *Apologeticus*, on Friar Gilles wanting to preach before Saint Clare; the second, from *The English Martyrologe* of 1608, for 16 January, which recounts the story of Saint Henry the Dane who led a severe hermit's life on the English island of Cochet and damaged one of his knees from constant praying, pp. 14–15; and the third from the sixth-century ascetic Saint Dorotheus of Gaza in his *Expositiones et Doctrinae XXIV*, p. 410, Vol. 12 of the *Bibliotheca Veterum Patrum Antiquorum Scriptorum Ecclesiasticorum*, in the Venice edition of 1778, who recounts the story of the abbot, the monk and the honey in "Doctrine VII" on the examination of personal culpability. The fourth example is the story of the Jesuit Alphonsus Bracena's or Barzana's encounter with Satan in the Indies, as told by another Jesuit Diego Torres-Bollo (b. Villalpendo, Old Castile, 1550; d. Plata, 1638) in his *Relatione Breve . . . con gli Indiani di Peru* (Venice, 1604), p. 52. Barzana (b. Cordova, 1528), who was surnamed "the Apostle of the Tucumen," learned to speak the language of the Tucumens as well as that of the Paraguays, and died in Cusco, Peru, in 1598 (pp. 52–53). The last three examples are once more from Sedulius' *Apologeticus*, from III, 24, 26, p. 239, on Saint Francis commanding the deceased Vicar General Friar Peter to stop stirring up the monks and laity by performing miracles from his tomb, an incident to which he referred earlier (see Commentary for p. 105, ll. 21–34); from III, 25, 18, p. 246, on the deceased Friar Rainaldus vacating his grave for an incoming corpse, hence testifying to the miraculous power of Franciscan relics; and, from II, 5, 8, p. 81, on Friar Gilles once more, with whom Donne began his list of examples of excessive obedience, who, during an apparition, left the Virgin Mary standing cold to answer the call of a weak, needy brother. Donne translates "infirmo fratre" by "inferior friar," and so exaggerates Friar Gilles' effrontery to the Virgin, as though he would leave her for a subaltern, but the more honest translation of "infirmus" suggests physical infirmity rather than inferiority.

Page 137.

20–25 *this Obedience is Ignatius . . . is ever excepted*: In the letter entitled "De Obedientiae Virtute" that he sent to the congregation of Portuguese Jesuits on 7 April 1553 (regularly appended to the early editions of *Regulae*), Ignatius warned against the deterioration of obedience as a virtue, No. 2, *Regulae*, p. 218. The reference to "Extra." is to Book II, "De Iureiurando" or Title IX of the "Clementines" in *Corpus Iuris Canonici*, Cols. 200–213.

31–33 *Now they are come . . . neede not worke*: Saint Benedict describes the hours of the day spent by monks, outside the periods of communal life and exercise regulated by the canonical hours, as "incompetentes" or inadequate, *Regulae*, Chapter 48 (Paris, 1609), p. 111. He also discusses the religious offices of a monastery fixed to the canonical hours and their relevance to monastic life in Chapter 65, pp. 166–167.

Page 138.

6–8 *Aquinas, who . . . Regular conversation*: *Summa Theologica*, II.II.ae. Quest. 104, Art. 5, answer to the third objection.

COMMENTARY

28–30 *An obedience . . . be no member thereof*: In *Institutionum Moralium*, Vol. 2, Part 2, Book 4, Chapter 7 ("De Romanae Potestatis Pontificiae Abrogatione"), p. 262, the canonist Azor argues that a heretic and a schismatic share one and the same faith with the Catholic; otherwise they could not be heretical and schismatic. Therefore, he continues, they continue in the faith, though separated from it by their heresy, and they continue to owe allegiance to the pope.

Page 139.

28–35 *by the vastnes . . . that opinion*: Boniface VIII's canon "Unam Sanctam" in Chapter 1 of Title 8 "De Majoritate et Obedientia" of the "Extravagantes Communes," *Corpus Iuris Canonici*, Cols. 319–320. The French bishop of Vincennes, lawyer and theologian, Pierre Bertrand (b. Annonay, 1280; d. Montaud, Avignon, 1349), argued the question of fact and faith in his tract *De Origine Jurisdictionum* (Lyons, 1549), Tome 4 of *Tractuum Ex Variis Iuris Interpretibus Collectorum*, p. 98ᵛ. The sixteenth-century Roman political philosopher and theologian Alexander Pesantius, author of the *Tractatus de Immunitate Ecclesiastica et De Potestate Romani Pontificis* (Rome, 1606), Part 2, argued for the universal power of the pope over all secular princes, "super universum orbem," in his "Disputatio Prima," pp. 44–45. The work is dedicated to Paul V.

Page 140.

1–16 *by their expunction . . . simply a temporall Jurisdiction*: Donne is enlisting a number of Catholic authorities, Victoria, Soto and Roselli, on the limitation of the power of the papacy, against the arguments of two other Catholics, Simancha and Azor, who contended that this power was absolute. Simancha and Azor held that the pope exercised his spiritual power through the practice of unlimited state power. Against this position Donne invokes first the Italian lawyer Antonio Roselli (b. Arezzo, 1380; d. Padua, 1466), whom he mentions by name, and then the two Spanish Dominican jurists Victoria, the author of *Relectiones Theologicae* on the origins, virtues and vices of temporal power, and Soto, the author of *De Ratione*, on the same subject, whom he does not cite by name here but whom he quotes often elsewhere in *Pseudo-Martyr*. Victoria and Soto are the objects of the two texts by Simancha and Azor that Donne cites. Roselli was the author of the *Tractatus de Monarchia, Sive Tractatus de Potestate Imperatoris et Papae* (Venice, 1483), and Donne is translating the expurgation order against part of Roselli's text on the limitation of papal power, in the Belgian *Index*, p. 86. Donne turns Roselli's argument against Simancha in the latter's *De Republica*, Book III, Chapter 7 on "Quam sit Venerabilis," in the section "Strabao sermone de Legibus," p. 112, where Simancha cites Strabo in the pope's cause. Donne then refers to the Spanish Jesuit Azor, but only to subvert his position with the writings of his co-religionists Victoria and Soto, whom he criticized for what Donne calls sarcastically "their modesty" in attributing only limited state power to the papacy (*Institutionum Moralium*, Vol. 2, Part 2, Book 4, Chapter 19, p. 290, Col. 2, and p. 291, Col. 1). However, Donne does not defend Victoria and Soto. Azor complained that Victoria and Soto held to the theory that the pope's spiritual power was not temporal but administered "as though temporall" ("cum temporalia administrat," p. 291), and Donne considers that Victoria's and Soto's position is as dangerous for secular monarchs as Azor's.

20–26 *Tannerus the Jesuit sayes . . . they should hinder them*: Donne is attacking the arguments of three Catholic authorities that clerics, because they fall under the jurisdiction of the popes, are therefore not under the jurisdiction of secular princes. The first authority is the Jesuit Tanner who argued against the power of the Venetian state over clerics in Chapter I, "De Origine et Authoritate Potestatis Politicae," of his *Defensionis Ecclesiasticae Libertatis*, II, p. 211. The second authority is the controversialist Maynardus who claimed universal jurisdiction for the temporal state power of the popes in Part II, Article 16, No. 2, p. 139, of his *De Privilegiis Ecclesiasticiis*. The third and final authority is Bellarmine who argued that the obedience which clerics owed to secular authorities was limited, in Chapter 28 of "De Clericis," Book I of the fifth general controversy "De Membris Ecclesiae Militantis" in *De Controversiis*, Vol. I, Cols. 1488–1491.

27–8 (p. 141) *this Universall Jurisdiction . . . nor can doe treason*: Donne cites the speculations of three Jesuit authorities on the freedom of clerics from the interference of secular rulers: first Tanner in *Defensionis Ecclesiasticae Libertatis*, II, Chapter 12 "Impium Esse Dicere, Ecclesiasticae Libertatis Observationem Temporali Statui Reipub. esse perniciosam," pp. 335–336; second, the Spaniard Juan Mariana who denies the right of the secular prince to execute a clergyman even though he deserves it, in Book I, Chapter 10, of his book on the institution of the prince, *De Rege et Regis Institutione*, p. 111; and third the Portuguese theologian Sâ in the section "Clericus" of his book of theological aphorisms, *Aphorismi Confessionarum Ex doctorum sententiis collecti*, first published in Antwerp in 1599 (on p. 67 of the Paris edition of 1600), on the relationship between clerics and secular authorities. All three authorities agreed upon the immunity of clerics from temporal state power, in the cases of Mariana and Sâ even when crime or treason are to be judged. Sâ's *Aphorismi* were put on the Church's *Index* for theological deviations in 1603.

Page 142.

4–8 *The cause why Childerique . . . was Effeminate*: *Decretum*, Cause 15, Question 6, Chapter 3, Col. 1083; Childeric III, the last Merovingian, was declared deposed by Pope Saint Zacharis in 751 (see Commentary for p. 74, ll. 1–7).

14–28 *to Syndicate Kings . . . or Excommunicate, or an Hereticke*: Donne is using the word "syndicate" in the sense of "to censure." He cites three examples of the Catholic censuring of secular rulers to demonstrate the excessive scope given by Rome to the legal terminology of "excesses" and "enormities" in the commission of civil crimes. The first is from de Puteo's chapter on the excesses of kings, "De excessibus Regnum," in *De Syndicatu*, Numbers 1, 2, 4, 13, 15 and 19, on pp. 26–29. The second reference to de Puteo is to the section entitled "Rex autem," on the tyranny of kings against their subjects, which deals with the question of civil disobedience, and forms part of the chapter of the previous reference (p. 26). Between these two references is the third, to Distinction 86, Chapter 8, of Gratian's *Decretum*, Col. 410, describing the prerequisites for the good conduct of bishops.

Page 143.

8–16   *a most learned and equall . . . in all other cases*:   Donne lists three examples of the power of secular authority over spiritual authority. The first is from Isaac Casaubon's *De Libertate Ecclesiastica* dealing with Paul V's excommunication of the Venetians (p. 46). Casaubon, a Swiss theologian, vacillated between the Roman Catholic and Calvinist positions and had not yet taken up permanent residence in Protestant London, but was to do so later in the year of *Pseudo-Martyr*'s publication. To defend Venice against the papacy, Casaubon used the example of the late eleventh-century quarrel between Gregory VII and Henry IV over the conflicting rights of their titles in the matter of lay investiture. Both Gregory and Henry claimed to have the right to name bishops for the good of the Church. Donne's second example of the conflict between the two powers is found in Azor's *Institutionum Moralium*, Vol. I, Part 1, Book 5, Chapter 14 ("quaestiones Ecclesiastica apud Iudices civiles tractari, & iudicari soleant"), Col. 524. Azor does not use the word "authority" but the phrase, "potest a Rom. Pontifice imperare privilegium," to describe the temporal ruler's authority over bishops. Finally, Donne refers to Book 2, Title 11, Chapter 1, "De Sententia et Re Iudicata," *Corpus Iuris Canonici*, Col. 214, of Clement V's "Clementines." Clement was pope from 1305.

Page 145.

7–10   *When some Priests in England . . . Contingentibus*:   At the trial of the Jesuits Henry Garnet and Edward Oldcorne early in 1606, arrested as a result of the discovery of the Gunpowder Plot. The Catholic "De fide" position of the pope's right to depose princes was upheld by Bellarmine in his controversialist writing and, after the Gunpowder Plot, he elaborated upon it in his tractual disputations in "Responsio ad librum: Triplici nodo" (1608) and "Apologia pro responsione ad librum Jacobi I" (1609) with James.

20–26   *therefore Mat. Tortus . . . is repeated*:   As Donne did not know that Matthew Tortus was Bellarmine's pseudonym, he mistakenly says that the writer of the attack on Palmieri's open letter to the Venetians to support their state officials was not a Jesuit. In "Aviso alli sudditi," to which Donne referred earlier in *Pseudo-Martyr* (p. 104), Bellarmine defended the Jesuits against Palmieri's charges that they had unduly forced Paul V's hand in issuing the excommunication against the

Venetian senate. Donne is paraphrasing in translation Bellarmine's or Tortus' claim that the Jesuits were a Roman Catholic religious order like all the others (he names several, including the Franciscans and Oratorians), with no special privileges in their dealings with the papacy (p. 105). Paul III's bull incorporating the Jesuit order in 1541 repeated the fourth vow on the Jesuit's obedience to the pope contained in Ignatius' *Regulae*.

33–17 (p. 146) *For though they bee . . . forfeit their dignities*: First, Simancha in Chapter 5, "De Schismaticis," No. 3, of his *Enchiridion*, pp. 29–30, where he argues that doubts over the methods of a pope's election do not annul the election itself; and second, the *Septimes* or collection of decretals ordered by Gregory XIII (see Commentary for p. 80, ll. 6–10). The decretal on the simoniac election of a pope was issued by Pope Julius II at the fifth Lateran Council, *Corpus Iuris Canonici*, Vol. 2, Col. 10, Book I of "Liber Septimus," Title 3, Chapter 1.

Page 147.

5–9 *amongst Lawyers . . . was formerly prohibited*: In de Puteo's *De Syndicatu*, the chapter "Arbitrium," No. 9, p. 179; the sub-chapter "Potestas," No. 8, p. 192, and No. 9, p. 193. See Commentary for p. 84, l. 28–p. 85, l. 15.

Chap. VII
Page 148.

8–21 *Consummate Martyrdome . . . who died in Prison*: Aquinas discusses the necessity of death in the making of a martyr in *Summa Theologica*, II.II. Quest. 124, Art. 4. At Troas, on his way to martyrdom in Rome, Saint Ignatius, the second-century bishop of Antioch, wrote to his fellow martyr Saint Polycarpe, bishop of Smyrna, a letter in which he addressed himself as a martyr, "Ignatius Episcopus Antiochiae, qui est martyr Iesu Christi," *Epistolae* (Oxford, 1644), p. 135.

23–25 *Chrysostome sayes . . . a Martyr*: Chrysostom, in "Adversus Iudaeos, Orationes V," Oration V, *Opera*, Vol. IV, Tome 5, Col. 971.

26–3 (p. 149) *Devotion is apt . . . Invocation ever since*: Bellarmine's brief narration of the miraculous appearance of the ghost of a dead criminal to Saint Martin of Tours (b. Sabaria, Hungary, c.316; d. Candes, Touraine, 397), which he found recorded in Martin's biography in *Vita B. Martini*, p. 17, section A, of *Liber de Passione Domini . . . Abdiae Babyloniae episcopi, et Apostolorum* (Basel, 1552), by the ecclesiastical writer Sulpicius Severus (b. Aquitaine, c.360; d. Rome, 420), who had been a follower of the saint both in Eauze and in Toulouse (*Vita*, trans. from the French of Paul Monceau by M.C. Watt, London, 1928, *Saint Martin of Tours*, pp. 1–111). In Sulpicius' account, which he wrote to honour Martin, the criminal arose from the dead to inform the saint that the population of Tours venerated him falsely as a martyr because he was damned. Donne's citation springs from the first book "De beatitudine et Canonizatione Sanctorum" of the seventh general controversy "De Ecclesia Triumphante" of Bellarmine's *De Controversiis*, Vol. I, Col. 1944, and not from the "De Purgatorio" as his marginalia of 1610 mistakenly suggests, an error which he repeated on p. 231. Donne's second reference to Pope Alexander III (b. Siena, n.d.; d. 1181), also springs from the same passage in Bellarmine, though the marginalia might be taken to suggest that it derives directly from Alexander's writings. The marginalia also repeats Bellarmine's reference to Alexander's canon, "Audivimus extra de Reliquiis et Sanctorum veneratione," in Book 3, Title 45, Chapter 1 of "Liber Extra" in *Corpus Iuris Canonici*, Col. 526, in which the pope berated his compatriots for venerating a drunkard, "hominem inebrietate occisum." Finally, Donne's third example of the unreliability of Roman martyrial standards is the removal by the Jesuit Serarius of the name of John Hyrcanus (b. 135; d. 105 B.C.), the third son of Simon Macchabee, from the litany of Catholic saints on the grounds that he was a heretic, in Chapter 28 ("An Iudaeorum Pontifices Maximi aliquando Sadducaei fuerint") of Book II on the Sadducees in his *Trihaeresium* (pp. 165-170). Serarius wrote that Hyrcanus ruled over Judea when the heresies of the Pharisees and Sadducees appeared and that he shared their ideal of power, and he expressed surprise that Albertus Magnus, or Albert the Great (b. Lauringen, Swabia, c.1206; d. Cologne, 1280), the medieval Roman father of theology, whom Donne mentions, had honoured Hyrcanus with sainthood (*Trihaeresium*, p. 166). Donne is evidently choosing his example of Serarius with care. In 1609, only one year before the publication of *Pseudo-Martyr*, Serarius issued a new litany of Roman saints, *Litaneutici*, to which Donne often refers. Donne was attacking a reputed and well-known Counter-Reformation litanist and pointed to his disagreement with Albert the Great over the standards of martyrial sanctity to sway English Catholics into accepting his arguments against martyrdom.

Page 149.

3–9   *And when Gregory the thirteenth . . . did often mistake*: In *Concilia Generalia*, Vol. I, Tome 1, Col. 1, p. 490, Binius narrates the story of the rehabilitation of the Arian anti-pope Felix II who, in 355, replaced the legitimate pope Liberius whom the Arian emperor Constantinus then banished to Thrace. Felix was deposed in turn and replaced by the same Liberius on the signing of the third formula of Sirmium. However, through the centuries, despite his Arianism Felix was popularly held as a saint, either on genuine historical grounds or through the confusion of his name with that of early martyrs who were also called Felix. Donne refers to the plans of Pope Gregory XIII in the sixteenth century to drop Felix's name from the list of those of proven sainthood definitely when, in 1582, his tomb, according to Baronius' *Martyrologium*, p. 333, was found under the altar of the Church of Saints Cosmas and Damien in Rome, along with the relics of several martyrs. Felix's name was immediately reinstated into the calendar of saints, for celebration on 29 July, because the discovery of his tomb gave credence to the legend that he had been martyred by his former Arian compatriots. Binius' biography to which Donne refers his readers is "Notae in Vitam Felicis II" that follows the record of the acts of Felix's papacy in *Concilia Generalia.* Bellarmine discusses attempts by the popes to avoid the so-called canonization of saints by popular sentiment in Chapter 7 of Book I, "De Beatitudine," of the seventh controversy "De Ecclesia Triumphante" of *De Controversiis.*

10–21 *And this medicine . . . say your Authors*: First, Bellarmine's discussion of the pronouncements on the saints by the medieval popes Leo III, Innocent II and Alexander III, in Chapter 8 of Book I "De Beatitudine" of the seventh controversy in *De Controversiis*, Col. 1945. Donne notes one Catholic point of view that the English Church had no martyrs for eight hundred years, throughout the Middle Ages, until Thomas à Becket's quarrel with Henry II under Pope Alexander III. Second, Bellarmine's discussion of the Lutheran, Calvinist and other heretics, among whom he singles out John Wycliffe for his virulence, who question the pope's infallibility in matters of canonization, in Chapter 9 "Credendum esse, Pontificem non errare in Sanctorum Canonizatione," in the same book and controversy of his work. Donne is translating and paraphrasing both the opening sentence of the chapter and its third proposition. Finally, for the canon "Extravagantes de Reliquiis," see Commentary for p. 150, ll. 8–10.

26–32 *And though not in Bellarmine . . . thing against Faith*: Donne translates loosely a number of phrases in the long opening paragraph of the section entitled "Et Primo de Inquisitione et commissione causae" at the beginning of the chapter on "De Canonizatione" of the official Roman document on Catholic ceremonials, *Sacrarum Cerimoniarum*, pp. 70^{rv}. The passage describes the pope's conduct in proceeding to a canonization to assure himself of the sanctity of the candidate and of not offending the faith of the Catholic public.

Page 150.

1–8 *Nor is this private worship . . . the cause of his gravity*: In Chapter 10, "Sanctos non canonizatos privatim posse coli, non publice," in Book I "De Beatitudine" of the seventh controversy in Volume I of *De Controversiis*, Col. 1948, where Bellarmine argues that the canons of the Church on canonization allowed the private veneration of yet uncanonized saints with images, even on their anniversaries, providing it was not made publicly and in the name of the Church.

8–10 *In the two Canons, sayes he . . . permits private*: Two canons in the veneration of the relics of saints, first, "Audivimus," discussed by Bellarmine at the end of Chapter 7 of Book I, "De Beatitudine," Col. 1944, and second, "Cum ex eo," discussed by him in Chapter 10 of Book II, "De Reliquiis Sanctis," Col. 2005, to both of which he alludes conjointly in the opening of Chapter 7 of Book I, Col. 1948, in the seventh controversy of *De Controversiis.* The canon "Audivimus" was promulgated by Alexander III, and the canon "Cum ex eo" by Innocent III, and both are recorded in Gregory IX's collection of decretals "Liber Extra" (hence Donne's annotation), and are found in Chapter 1 and 2, Title 45, Book III, in *Corpus Iuris Canonici*, Col. 526.

21–25 *Catholique Priest . . . of their History*: See Commentary for p. 162, ll. 16–21.

Page 153.

16–20 *Aquinas cites this . . . a Martyr, faith*: In *Summa Theologica*, II.II. Quest. 124, Art. 2, Part 1 and answer to the first objection.

27–32 *Leo the first . . . All, and sound*: Leo I, pope from 440 to 461, in a letter dated 18 February 449 to the Eastern Emperor Theodosius II (b. 401; d. 450), known for his *Codex Theodosianus* for public officials, recorded in *Sacrorum Conciliorum*, Vol. 5, Cols. 1241–1242. The martyrs in question were those slain during the breakout of the Nestorian heresy in the Eastern Empire, which instigated Leo's reassertion of the doctrine of two persons in Christ, one human and the other divine, that he mentions in the letter Donne quotes.

34–9 (p. 154) *expounding that place . . . Delectantur cadaveribus*: Chrysostom's interpretation of Jeremiah 7, in "In Evangelium Marci, Homilia XIII," in *Opera*, Vol. II, Tome 2, Col. 1102. Next, a reference, probably to Bellarmine's argument against the authority of secular states over the temporal power of the papacy, in *Responsio*, p. 13, or his argument on the unity of the Church in Chapter 2 "De Definitione Ecclesiae," of Book III "De Ecclesiae natura et proprietatibus" of the fourth general controversy "De Conciliis et Ecclesia" in Vol. I, Col. 1228, of *De Controversiis*.

Page 154.

28–30 *For Baronius himselfe . . . the Catholique faith*: In his *Martyrologium Romanum*, p. 567, under his inscriptions of the saints for 29 December, Baronius, in his description of the mission of young priests in England, distinguished implicitly between the faith of a Catholic and the right of the Church to make claims on it to defend its liberties: "cum non solum (ut Thomas [à Becket]) pro ecclesiastica libertate, sed pro fide Catholica tuenda, restituenda, ac conservanda nobilissimo martyrio occuberint." See Commentary for p. 122, ll. 26–27.

Page 155.

10–13 *a Corporall injurie . . . the same reason*: De Puteo, in *De Syndicatu*, the sub-chapter "Dicit constitutio," No. 15, p. 484, in the chapter "Inquisitio."

18–25 *Cassianus hath amass'd . . . a selfe-murderer*: Cassianus' second "collation" in his *Collationes* is entitled "De Discutione" and gives numerous examples of meritorious works that led to disaster due to either too great discretion or indiscretion. Donne's example of Heron and the evil spirit occurs in Chapter 5, "De morte Heronis senis," pp. 201–202. Of interest for the subject of Donne's *Biathanatos* that he completed a few years before *Pseudo-Martyr*, Cassianus' chapter ends with the phrase "ut non (inter biothanatos reputatus) etiam memoria et oblatione pausantium iudicaretur indignus."

Page 156.

6–11 *For as a man . . . hee might avoide*: Legal terms: *felo de se*: one who deliberately kills himself directly or as the result of felonous act; *fur de se*: one who absconds secretly from fulfilling due services, as opposed to one who withdraws by force of arms; and, *proditor de se*: one who betrays one's own humanity before the law of nature, as opposed to one who commits treason according to civil law.

25–31 *that History recorded . . . admit any reconciliation*: Saint Nicephorus of Antioch (b. 190; d. 248) and the priest Simplicius, whom Donne calls Sapricitius, were close friends, then quarrelled and were both condemned to death during the persecution of Valerian. Simplicius rejected Nicephorus' request for pardon for their differences a first time on principle, and then yet a second time even when he, Simplicius, was condemned to death for his Christianity. Simplicius recanted to save his life, and the recantation so touched Nicephorus that he offered himself to the sword of Simplicius' persecutors to replace him in their execution. The story is narrated in Symeon Metaphrastes' later tenth-century compilation of the legends of saints in the *Menologia* of the Byzantine Church.

Page 157.

9–17 *Is there any charitie . . . obliterated*: Between his accession to the throne in 1603 and the month of March in 1604, James I let fall almost into disuse the penal laws against recusant Catholics that were passed first with Elizabeth's Statutes of Supremacy and Uniformity in 1559 and later supported with a number of more particular laws touching the priesthood, the attendance at Catholic colleges and inherited estates. The "bloudy lawes" to which Donne refers are the "Act against Jesuits, Seminary priests and other such like disobedient persons" of 1585 which made it high treason punishable by death to be a priest or to hide one, and the "Act to retain the Queen's Majesty's subjects in their obedience" of 1581 that also made it high treason to be reconciled with or to reconcile anyone to Catholicism. The "pecuniarie lawes" in Donne's reference were the statutes, among several, by which an English-Catholic parent was fined £100 for sending a child to a Catholic school on the continent, and by which Catholics were severely fined if caught assisting at Mass. Under Puritan pressure and due to Catholic agitation James began to re-enforce the laws in 1604, and was compelled to apply them rigorously with the discovery of the "unnecessarie act" of the Gunpowder Plot (as Donne describes it) of 1605.

COMMENTARY

21–27 *Was it charitably . . . a just resolution*: George Gervase (b. Boscham, Suffolk, 1571; d. Tyburn, 1608), the underground Benedictine missionary priest in England, during his trial after his arrest when he refused to take the Oath of Allegiance, and was consequently executed.

Page 158.

3–6 *make the difference . . . distresse then before*: Paul V's two *breves* or briefs against the Protestant throne of England, of 10 October 1606 and 10 September 1607. See Introduction, pp. xxiii and xlvi.

26–3 (p. 159) *a farre better Title . . . for contempt of chastitie*: *Summa Theologica*, II.II. Quest. 124, Art. 4, principally from the answer to the second objection.

Page 159.

10–13 *Bellarmine makes . . . and the Lutherans very slacke*: In Bellarmine's "De Notis Ecclesiae," Chapter II, which forms Book IV of the fourth controversy, "Quartae Controversiae Generalis, De Conciliis et Ecclesia," *De Controversiis*, Vol. I, Cols. 1298–1299.

23–18 (p. 160) *Feuardentius the Minorite . . . charges us:* In his *Theomachia Calvinistica* (see Commentary for p. 36, ll. 2–5), Feuardentius structured his argument on a dialogue some eight hundred folio pages long between himself and a Calvinist divine with whom he supposedly came into discussion accidentally in Geneva. All of Donne's references to *Theomachia* in *Pseudo-Martyr* are to its Book VIII which deals with heaven and Paradise, and with the ability of Calvinists and Protestants to attain them, Chapter 13, Numbers 1, 3, 4, 6 and 10 (p. 292, Col. 1; p. 293, Col. 1; p. 293, Col. 2 to p. 294, Col. 1; p. 294, Col. 2 to p. 295, Col. 1). Feuardentius concludes that Calvinists and Huguenots are "Pseudomartyres" even in execution (VIII, 13, 12, p. 296, Col. 1). For the Eliberitane Council of Pope Marcellus I in 305, see Commentary for p. 34, l. 29–p. 35, l. 8, and p. 121, ll. 19–24.

Page 160.

31–4 (p. 161) *not the Recorder . . . and Intruder*: The Jesuit Parsons in *The Judgement of a Catholicke English-man, living in Banishment for his Religion: Written to his private friend in England* (1608) against James' *Triplici Nodo*. Parsons argued that in his bull of excommunication of 1570 against Elizabeth, Pius V had defended Mary Stuart's right and that of her descendants to the English throne, No. 33, pp. 90–91.

Page 161.

15–17 *the right Heire . . . Dolemans booke*: Donne appears not to have known that "R. Doleman" was the Jesuit Parsons' pseudonym when, in 1594, he published *A Conference About the Next Succession to the Crown of England*. Parsons argued for the hereditary right of Philip II of Spain, who had directed the Armada against Elizabeth, to the throne of England because he was descended from John of Gaunt's daughter, Part II, Chapter 8, p. 161.

23–32 *you seeke it against . . . humane infirmities*: For the condemnation of the useless pursuit of martyrdom by the Eliberitane Council in 305, see Commentary for p. 34, l. 29–p. 35, l. 8. For the Friar Feuardentius' accusations of vainglorious martyrdom against the Protestants, see Commentary for p. 159, l. 23–p. 160, l. 18, and his *Theomachia*, VIII, 13, No. 10, p. 294, Col. 2. For the "chamber epistles," as Donne calls Paul V's *breves* or briefs (which a pope issued in his personal name and not in a church council), see Commentary for p. 158, ll. 3–6, and Introduction, p. xxiii.

Page 162.

8–14 *Baronius his Martyrologe . . . bodies, as Martyrs*: In his introduction or "Praecapitulatio dicendorum" to Chapter II of his *Martyrologium*, p. x, Baronius discusses the authority of the writings of the apostles and of the church fathers on the reality of martyrs in the Old Testament. He includes the Acts of the Apostles, and the writings of Peter and Paul and of Saint Jerome. However, Baronius does not mention Paul's *Epistle to the Hebrews* which praises the sanctity of the prophet Enoch whom Donne held in great veneration as an Old Testament prototype of the new Protestant poet (*Essays*, p. 92; *Conclave*, p. 7). It is Enoch's exclusion from Baronius' list of writings on the martyrs that Donne criticizes.

16–21 *our Countryman amongst you . . . 25 December*: The *English Martyrologe . . . the Lives of the glorious and renowned Saintes*, published at Saint Omer in 1608, probably by the Jesuit John Wilson (see Introduction, p. xix). The martyrology celebrates Constantine (who, according to one Renaissance tradition, visited Britain) on 21 May (p. 134), and Pope Saint Gregory on 25 December (p. 351). The authorship of *Martyrologe* is unproven and this explains why Donne does not mention its author either here or on p. 150. *Martyrologe*'s title page states only that its author is a "Catholicke Priest" and its epistle is signed "I.W. Priest," and its advertisement is also signed "I.W." The same "I.W." confirms that he published an *English Martyrologe*, this time in his epistle prefaced to the first English version of Baronius' *Martyrologium* entitled *Roman Martyrology* (Saint Omer, 1627) (Sig.*[3]), according to its title page translated by yet another priest "G.K. of the Society of Jesus." Both "G.K." and "I.W." could be the same man obscuring his identity deliberately. Sommervogel, in *Bibliothèque*, Vol. IV, Col. 1028, identifies "G.K." as the Jesuit George Keynes of Somerset, and both the revised *STC* (entry 17533) and the *Dictionary of National Biography*, Vol. XI, p. 86, concur in this identification. However, Sommervogel says that Keynes was born in 1628, and the *D.N.B.* in 1630 (and that he died in 1659). If Keynes is the author of *English Martyrologe* in 1608 and of the epistle in the *Roman Martyrology* of 1627, his birth date must be moved back by some forty years for him to have authored writings so familiar to Donne in 1610. Whether the author of *English Martyrologe* is George Keynes or John Wilson, he almost certainly conceived of his work as an answer to Foxe's Protestant martyology in *Actes* (see Introduction, p. xvi). Donne writes that the author of *English Martyrologe* included close to five hundred Catholic martyrs in his calendar, which is also the approximate number of "Bishop-pseudomartyrs" whom Parsons, in his *Treatise of Three Conversions of England from Paganism to Christian Religion*, 3 Vols. (Saint Omer, 1603), Vol. 1, Sig.********v, says that Foxe included in his collection of false Protestant venerables. Parsons' calendar of martyrs in *Three Conversions* was meant to prove that the history of the English martyrs from earliest times was rooted in Roman history and not in English history as Foxe contended, and the *English Martyrologe* elaborated on Parsons' work considerably.

21–31   *And of those which did . . . errour whatsoever*:   In the first section of Part III of *Treatise of Three Conversions*, Parsons laid the groundwork for a Catholic calendar of martyrs in England rooted strictly in the history of the early popes. Later, in the second section of Part III, January to July at the end of Volume 2, and July to December in Volume 3, Parsons drew up a new English-Catholic calendar of martyrs to supplement Baronius' *Martyrologium*. In Part III, Chapter 1, No. 3, Vol. 2, p. 43, Parsons argued that Christian martyrdom originated in the history of the Roman Church and that it could not possibly have originated in England because the early history of the English Church produced no martyrs. It is to these parts of Parsons' work and to his latter argument that Donne is referring. His quotation that follows is actually a paraphrase of Parsons' argument and of his use of the authority of Canon 63 of the sixth General Council of the Roman Church on the validity of the Roman martyrology, in *Three Conversions*, Part III, No. 10, Vol. 2, p. 37.

Page 163.

2–10   *somwhat hard to beleeve . . . least note of falsitie*:   From Part III of Parsons' *Three Conversions*, Vol. 2: Tacitus, p. 33; Gregory and Bede, p. 35; Matthew of Westminster, p. 46; Nicholas Sanders (b. Aston, Surrey, ?1530; d. Dingle, Ireland, 1581), the Catholic controversialist, pp. 93, 105, 123; Matthew of Paris, p. 103; and Lawrence Surius, the hagiologist (b. Lubeck, 1522; d. Cologne, 1578), pp. 39, 123; also, the Benedictine historian, Thomas Walsingham (b. ?Norfolk; d. ?1422), and Polidor Virgil (b. Urbino, 1470; d. ?1555), the historian to Henry VIII.

12–18   *not onely the Abbesse . . . S. Hugh for a Martyr*:   In *English Martyrologe*, pp. 204–205, the anonymous author tells the story of the crucifixion of the boy-saint Hugh of Lincoln at the hands of local Jews in 1255, under 27 July, hence Donne's marginal note. The *Martyrologe*'s comparatively detailed account of Hugh's death may have been intended to refute the doubts cast on the authenticity of his history by Foxe's *Actes* (1583), Vol. I, p. 237. In both the official *Roman Martyrology*'s original Latin version of 1589 by Baronius (pp. 328–329), and its English translation by "G.K." in 1627 (pp. 236–237), no mention is made of Hugh of Lincoln. The seventh-century Abbess of Ely whose herdsman Saint Alnoth was martyred by two robbers at Weedon, was Saint Ethelreda, once queen of Northumbria. Saint Edwin (b. c.585), the first Christian king of Northumbria, was slain in a battle against Penda, the pagan king of Mercia, in 633 or 634.

Chap. VIII
Page 164.

12–13 *the fresh contemplation . . . to insert therein*: The Oath of Allegiance, passed quickly by Parliament late in 1605 and early in 1606, only weeks after the failed Gunpowder plot of early November. See Introduction, pp. xxii–xxiii.

Page 166.

5–6 *as your owne men . . . you call Ecclesiasticke*: A paraphrase of the argument on pp. 31 and 34, of *Tractatus de Vi et Potestate Legum Humanarum . . . . Duaci Catuacorum* (1608), of the late sixteenth- and early seventeenth-century French theologian and master of law, Claude Carnin.

28–34 *any of those Rules . . . rectifie that Errour*: For the "Rule" on problems of doubt and restitution of church property, see Commentary, p. 168, l. 17–p. 169, l. 4.

Page 167.

10–31 *it fals out often . . . which made those lawes*: Three examples of Catholic thinkers who agree that time and place often determine the correctness or wrongness of a point of conscience or dogma. The first is the Jesuit Azor's discussion of the grounds of sin in his *Institutionum Moralium*, Vol. I, Part 1, Book II, Chapter 12, Cols. 144–145. Azor makes a distinction between moral questions that spring from law and others that arise from opinion. The second example is Navarrus' *Relectio Cap. Novit. de Iudiciis* which was published in several editions at the end of the sixteenth century with his *De Regularibus*, and appeared in the collection of his Latin works printed in Rome in 1589. However, like Donne's marginalia for *De Regularibus* (see Commentary for p. 120, ll. 3–5, and p. 123, l. 29–p. 124, l. 2), his reference to *De Iudiciis Cap. Novit.* is unclear, and he does not identify it beyond its title. Numerous passages of the work refer to the power of the papacy (e.g., No. 2.3; and No. 3.41, 100, 107, and 109, particularly), but none of them makes a reference matching Donne's citation. Moreover, *De Iudiciis* was written by Navarrus in 1548, many years before the friction between Henri III and Henri IV of France and the papacy, to which Donne seems to refer. In Vol. I, No. 3.41, p. 144, Col. 1, Navarrus discusses the relation of the kings of France to the papacy generally in terms of its dealings with other monarchs. The third example is that of Carnin in his *De Vi et Potestate*, Part I, Chapter VI entitled "Assertio Navarri legum dissipatrix quarta, late retunditur," pp. 32 and 37, in which he takes issue with the major theologians of his day, Soto, Navarrus, Sâ and Azor, over the often prickly questions of the historical excesses of certain Catholic writings, and of the tolerant liberality of the schoolmen towards matters that contemporary men handled too rigidly.

Page 168.

9–10 *Ad pulpita Canonistarum*: Donne's Latin paraphrase, from Carnin's passage in *De Vi*, Chapter 5, pp. 19–20, on the stand of Catholic theologians on the nature of sin, and not to Chapter 6 as suggested in the original marginalia.

17–4 (p. 169) *Carbo a good Summist . . . notorious detriment*: Ludovico Carbo and Soto were moral theologians. Carbo, a late sixteenth-century master of Thomism from Costacciaro near Perugia, in Italy, was the author of a moral commentary on Aquinas' *Summa Theologica*, called *Summa Summarum Casuum Conscientiae* (Venice, 1606), and Donne is referring to the argument on the restitution of lands in Tome I, Part I, Book 5, Chapter XIII, p. 155, and on the cleric's obedience to his superior's orders in the same chapter (pp. 156–157). Donne sees an extension of Carbo's theory in the Spanish Dominican moral theologian Soto's book on revealing and withholding secrets, *De Ratione Tegendi et Detegendi Secretum*, in which Soto argues in behalf of following one's conscience. Donne is translating from the paragraph "Sed contra secundam conclusionem," of "Membri III," Question 2 ("Utrum subditus teneatur obedire praelato interrogati secretum, quotiescumque dubitat iure ne interrogetur an iniuria," of *Tegendi*, pp. 282–283.

Page 169.

25–23 (p. 170) *the Casuists are indeede . . . consent of the Fathers*: The citations are first probably from passages in Soto's *De Ratione Tegendi* or Carbo's *Summa Summarum* but not from Navarrus; and second, from Simancha's *Enchiridion Iudicium*. Neither the two folio volumes (Lyons, 1589 and 1594) of Navarrus' collected works, nor the five-volume edition of 1588 published in Rome, reveals a chapter entitled "Confraternitas," and he did not deal with issues in his works by organizing them by number and question as Donne's marginalia suggests. Navarrus talks about a "Contraternity of the Rosary" at length in *Miscellania de Psalterio* (Rome, 1588), Vol. III, pp. 23–24, without reference to Catholic confession and the restitution of goods in Donne's citation. Donne's subsequent use of the word "Confessors" is a pun intended to include, in the style of the Catholic casuists, those who hear confessions with those who confess in the sense of asserting belief in the Catholic faith.

Donne's point is that a casuistic or equivocal way of telling the truth is a perversion of the biblical metaphor of the cloud and the witness used to describe the spirit as testimony to the truth in Hebrews 12.1. The cloud is of an obscuring rather than enlightening nature. Under such obscurantism, Donne now includes the Spanish casuist Simancha and Pius IV. He attacks Simancha's description of the role of the human understanding in the scholastic three powers of memory, understanding and will in the giving of testimony, in *Enchiridion Iudicium*, Chapter 35, "De Testibus," No. 31, pp. 148–149. Pius IV issued his bull "De Forma Juramenti Professionis Fidei" (in Donne's margin) at the twenty-fifth session of the Council of Trent, in November of 1564. The bull described the oath of allegiance that was applicable to all the church's teaching (*Sacrorum Conciliorum*, Vol. 33, Cols. 220–222). See Commentary for p. 171, ll. 10–21.

Page 170.

25–27 *If you extend this Ius Divinum . . . the Law of Nature*: Donne is translating Bellarmine's "Nec solum per ius divinum intelligitur scriptura sancta, sed etiam lumen naturale, sive ratio, aut lex naturalis," in his *Responsio . . . ad duos libros*, "Propositio Quinta Authoris" (wrongly numbered "Quarta") and "Responsio" No. 6 (hence Donne's marginal note), p. 40. He repudiates Bellarmine's claim that the justification for the immunity of clerics from secular law is found in divine law, the Scriptures, human reason and natural law. Donne's subsequent charge against Bellarmine — that he took upon himself the new role of canonist — springs from the cardinal's claim a little earlier in his text (p. 39) that canonists as well as theologians supported his argument about the immanence of divine law in both human reason and natural law.

Page 171.

10–21 *Navarrus is . . . no universall consent*: First, Donne paraphrases in Latin Navarrus' discussion in *Relectio Cap. Novit. de Iudiciis*, No. 3.41, Cols. 1 and 2. Second, he cites the pro-Venetian Marsilio's reply, *Responsio . . . ad Libellum Inscriptum: Responsio Doctoris Theologi* to Bellarmine's own answer to attacks on Paul V by Venetian theologians who defended the secular power of their state. Marsilio's tract is found in *Controversiae Memorabilis*. Third, Donne's "another Catholique" is William Barclay, the Scotsman (b.c. 1546; d. Angers, France, 1608), courtier of Mary Stuart and finally professor of civil law at Angers. Barclay's work on the power of the papacy was published by his son John (b. Pont à Mousson, 1582; d. Rome, 1621) in 1609 one year after his death, under the title of *De Potestate Papae: An et quatenus et Principes seculares ius et imperium habeat: . . . Guil. Barclaii I.C. Liber Postumous*. Donne is citing the beginning of Chapter 2 where Barclay comments on Pius IV's oath of allegiance to the papacy (see Commentary for p. 169, l. 25–p. 170, l. 23).

COMMENTARY

Page 172.

20–30 *Direct or Indirect . . . the other Indirect*: In *De Potestate Papae*, pp. 235–237, Barclay discussed the nature of "direct," "indirect" and "oblique" power. See Commentary for p. 188, ll. 23–28, and p. 188, l. 28–p. 189, l. 10. According to canon law, "direct" power sprang from a code of law immediately identifiable in the canons of the Church, whereas "indirect" power sprang from God through the expression of divine law in the Scriptures and in nature as well as in the canons.

35–9 (p. 173) *of the law, That to that . . . appeared equally in either*: In his tract on the Venetian controversy, *De Iustitia et Validitate Monitorii Ac Censuram Pauli Quinti* (Bologne, 1606), Chapter III on the freedom of the church from the power of princes ("De libertate Ecclesia, an à Principe laico tolli, impedirive possit"), the Tuscan canonist Ugolini argues that the church has its power "de iure divino," that is, by divine law, and so cannot be limited by the power of princes which is only "circa secularia," p. 23. He therefore concludes, "Potestas igitur secularis immunitates Ecclesiarum tollere non potest" (p. 26), to which Donne is objecting. Pompey was Cnaeus Pompeius (b. 106; d. 48 B.C.), the Roman triumvir who was surnamed Magnus and who also became consul.

Page 173.

11–14 *Bellarmine can finde . . . serve his turne*: In the third general controversy "De Summo Pontifice" of Volume I of *De Controversiis*, Bellarmine treats of the "praerogativae" or prerogatives of the papacy. In Chapters 21 and 22 of Book I ("De Primatu S. Petri in Ecclesia Militante") to which Donne refers, he deals with the incident of Christ in John 13, washing the feet of his apostles on Holy Thursday, and later the Lord's admonition to Peter in Acts 10.13, as examples of the testimony of the Scriptures to papal authority. The appeal to Catholic controversialists of the passage in Acts was common; Baronius was to make it one of his main arguments in his support of the papal excommunication of the Venetians in his speech to the Roman consistory in 1606 in support of Paul V, which Donne has already attacked in *Pseudo-Martyr* (p. 84).

15–26 *But to turne a little back . . . Knowledge to be certaine*: Donne is citing, first, Thomas Aquinas on knowledge and conscience in *Summa Theologica*, I. Quest. 79, Art. 18, the "Conclusion" on the conscience as "act"; and second, extraordinarily, the Italian moral theologian Carbo on the same subject, to support his argument that English Catholics who declare themselves ignorant of the Oath of Allegiance cannot claim to be free from having to take it. The reference to Carbo is to his commentary on Aquinas' *Summa Summarum Casuum Conscientiae*, Tome I, Part I, Book V, Chapter XII ("An bonitas interni actus pendeat a ratione errante, sive, an conscientia erronea obliget"), p. 151. Carbo argues that "lex divina" or divine law is at the basis of what governs conscience.

Page 174.

4–21 *And if this refusall of the Oath . . . all possible industrie*: Carbo discusses the question of culpable ignorance in *Summa*, Tome II, Part I, Book IV ("De peccatorum caussis universè"), Chapter 2 ("Sit ne ignorantia caussa peccatis, et peccatum") on whether ignorance can be a cause of sin, p. 95; and the question of blind faith being responsible for ignorance in matters of conscience, in the following Chapter 3 ("Quid homini faciendum sit, ut eius ignorantia sit invincibilis, et quarum rerum dicta ignoratio esse possit"), p. 98. It is Carbo who brings up the example of the third-century converted bishop of Carthage, Saint Cyprian, and Donne's reference to Cyprian is a translation of Carbo.

Page 176.

22–24 *Integrity of Confession . . . a third person*: For the declaration of the provincial Council of Malines in 1607 on penance in Paul V's reign, *Sacrorum Conciliorum*, Vol. 34, "Titulus Quintus," Cols. 1448–1449.

28–12 (p. 177) *Comitolius (a Jesuit . . . but the Election voide*: Donne is using three examples from Catholic writers, Paul Comitolus, Simancha and Azor, to prove that Protestant Englishmen are provoked to reject the authority of Rome for the same reasons that Catholics are led to reject the legitimacy of a pope whose past is rooted in simony or fear. The first example is from the *Responsa Moralia* (Lyons, 1609) of the Jesuit moralist Comitolus (b. Perugia, 1544; d. Perugia, 1626), who was a strong defender of the papacy in its quarrel with the state of Venice. Comitolus argued in the *Responsa*, Book I ("De Sacramentis"), Question 99, pp. 212–213, that the annulment of a pope's election can only be made by a pope himself who recognizes that the vote was conducted out of motives of simony. Donne's second example is this time indirect for he points to the opposite of Comitolus' view about the destitution of popes in the Spanish canonist Simancha's *Enchiridion*, Chapter 5, "De Schismaticis" on schismatics, No. 3, pp. 29–30. Simancha argues that doubts about the pope "qui rectè non est electus," who is not well elected, do not invalidate the election itself, "nec enim ad fidem catholicam pertinet ea, quae ex facto dubio pendent." Donne's third and final example is the argument by Azor on the role of fear in the decisions of cardinals in papal elections in *Institutionum Moralium*, Vol. 2, Part 2, Book 4, Chapter 2 ("De Potestate, quam habent Cardinales in Romano Pontifice eligendo"), p. 249. Azor declares that an election founded on fear cannot be validated in any manner, and must be entirely begun over. The Council of Constance was held in 1417 under Martin V.

Page 177.

16–21 *Azorius gives this . . . they may obey it*: Azor discusses the relationship of the heretical ruler to his Christian subjects in Chapter 2 ("De creatione Regnum quae sit"), Part 2, pp. 668–669, of Vol. 2 of *Institutionum Moralium*, and describes the nature of oaths in Book 11 of Part 1, Chapters 2 to 13. Donne is citing three of the most renowned Catholic theologians and commentators on canon law, Azor, Tolet and de Puteo on the relationship of Catholic subjects to their heretical rulers to prove that English Catholics may take the Oath of Allegiance to James. Azor had been named by the superior-general of the Jesuits to the six-man committee to formulate the "Ratio Studiorum" for Jesuit training.

31–1 (p. 178) *Tolet cites Caietans . . . of their goods*: The citation of the Dominican theologian Cajetan by the Jesuit Tolet (see Commentary for p. 102, ll. 18–21) in *A True Sincere and Modest Defence of English Catholiques that suffer for their Faith both at home and abrode: against a false, seditious and slaunderous Libel intituled; The Execution of Justice in England* (Rouen, 1584), Chapter 4, pp. 86–87, by William Allen, the English cardinal and founder of the English College in Rome.

Page 178.

2–3 *per fas & nefas*: "fas" is divine law, and "nefas" something which is contrary to it: de Puteo in *De Syndicatu*, pp. 327 and 778.

Chap. IX
Page 179.

11–17 *one of their greatest Doctors . . . should make it so*: Donne appears to have misread Victoria's *Relectiones Theologicae*, III, No. 14, p. 112, which elsewhere he cites sympathetically (see Commentary for p. 130, ll. 22–31). In the passage in question, Victoria is not talking about the pope but rather, as a theoretician in international law, he is setting up a "corollary" to his own idea about the origin of state power in nature and therefore in men. Victoria advances the idea that a number of states that are already politically independent may, if they wish, constitute themselves into a larger state: "Sicut maior pars Reipublicae regem supra totem Rempub. constituere potest, aliis in iustitia pars maior Christianorum, reliquis etiam renitentibus, Monarcham unum creare iure potest, cui omnes principes et provinciae parere teneantur." Donne misreads the papacy into Victoria's lines so that they come to support for him the other Catholic disputant Bellarmine's thesis that the power of both secular governments and their princes was subject to the popes. Bellarmine argued that papal power was the only existing authority on earth that reflected Christ's intentions for mankind directly, and he cited the examples of Spain, France and Venice as proof, *Responsio . . . ad Duos Libros*, pp. 3–5. He considered that the papacy was the only spiritual power in which secular authority could claim to have roots, and he described as heretical (hence Donne's translation) the idea that the secular authority of the papacy was only one among equals with other secular powers (p. 3).

Page 180.

10–30 *this spirituall Monarchie . . . Guard and assistance*: Donne is making seven rapid references to the recently published Catholic book on the kinds and the functions of angels, *De Angelorum Custodia* (Padua, 1605), by the late sixteenth-century Italian canon regular Andrea Victorellus: p. 16ʳ, on the ministry of angels to the smallest of creatures like flies; p. 133ʳ, on the guardianship of angels of non-Christian lands as well as of Hebraic and Christian countries; p. 121ʳ, on the angel surveying the welfare of anti-Christ; p. 17ʳ, on the presence of an imperial angel overlooking the safety of hell; p. 104ᵛ, on the guardianship of the papacy by two archangels, Michael the more important, and Gabriel his assistant; p. 105ʳ, on the testimony of Canticle 1 of the romance epic writer Torquato Tasso's *Gerusalemme Liberata*, and of the precedence of Michael over Gabriel in the list of angels in the old Roman liturgy, supporting the contention that Michael is the more prestigious archangel; and p. 106ʳ,ᵛ, on the guardianship of an angel over every existing political and religious territory. Donne also obtains his vocabulary of the papacy's two kingdoms, "the spiritual Monarchie" and the earthly kingdom, from those pages: "Duplex est Rom. Pontificis imperium; alterum caeleste, seu spiritale; alterum terrenum, seu corporeum," p. 106ʳ. The tutelar angel which must guard every papal conclave would, as Donne borrows Victorellus' words, have the whole world as his diocese: "Singulae metropolitanae, singulae Episcoporum Ecclesiae singuli Religiosorum hominum ordines," pp. 106ʳ,ᵛ. The idea, this time, of not one but two angels watching over a conclave to elect a pope recurs in *Ignatius His Conclave*, p. 5.

Page 181.

1–2 *For all the Apostles . . . Vicarii Christi*: A paraphrase of Aquinas' ideas in *Summa Contra Gentiles*, Book IV, Chapter 20.

2–8 *And this name . . . Totius orbis Praeses*: As Victoria is one of Donne's Catholic authorities against the upholders of absolute papal power, he here translates part of his discussion on the limitations of the pope's power as Vicar of Christ. Victoria writes that as Vicar, the pope ministers but does not absolve from Christ's commands: "vicarius non habet quod non prohibetur, sed solum quod conceditur. Christus autem non concessit solutionem aut relaxationem mandatorum suorum, sed solum ministerium et dispensationem illorum," "Relectio III, De Potestate Papae et Concilii 1," *Relectiones*, p. 132. Cyprian, to whom Donne then refers, was the third-century bishop of Carthage, and the *Liber De Locis Hebraicis: Sive Onomasticon Urbium Sacrae Scripturae* of Eusebius Pamphilius, the early fourth-century bishop of Caesarea, was translated from the Greek into Latin by the Jesuit Jacob Bonferius (Paris, 1559).

16–27 *Pontifex Maximus . . . farre from the matter*: In Chapter 16 ("Idem probatur ex eo, quod summus Pontifex a nemine iudicatur") of Book II ("De Successione Romani Pontificis in eo primatu") of the third general controversy, Vol. I,

De Controversiis, Bellarmine discussed the inapplicability, to which Donne refers, of the title of "Romanus Pontifex" to the pope because the title had been applied through the early history of Christendom to many bishops and to the Roman emperors as well (Col. 805). Therefore Bellarmine left the rubric out of the list of fifteen titles that he applied to the papacy later in his work (Chapter 31, "Idem probatur ex nominibus, quae Romano Pontifici tribui solent"), Col. 826. The title of "papa" or pope was not reserved to the bishop of Rome as head of the Catholic Church until towards the end of the first millennium of Christianity (hence Donne's "nine hundred years"). Donne's next reference is to Jerome's letter to the late fourth-century Saint Chromatius, bishop of Aquileia, in which, however, there is nothing that resembles his citation. The reference may more probably come from Jerome's letter to Nepotianus which Donne cited earlier, *Hieronymi Operum*, Vol. I, p. 14 (see Commentary for p. 125, ll. 8–14). Then, Donne cites Azor's discussion of the development of the title of pope, principally during the reigns of Leo I (pope from 440 to 461), Gregory I (from 590 to 604), and Leo IX (from 1048 to 1054), and particularly to the quarrel over the title between Pelagius II (from 579 to 590) and the Patriarch John of Constantinople, *Institutionum Moralium*, Vol. 2, Part 2, Book 4, Chapter 4 ("De Summo Pontifice Romano"), pp. 256–257. Donne uses the term "Predicament" in its Aristotelian and Thomistic sense, particularly in logic, of asserting or "predicating" something about another thing, particularly in relation to its "essence" and "accidents," in order to distinguish it from other beings: Aquinas, *Summa* I, Q. XXVIII, Arts. 1 and 2.

29–1 (p. 182) *they having beene call'd Papists . . . upon themselves*: Donne is paraphrasing Bellarmine's concluding paragraphs in Chapter 4 of Book IV "De Notis Verae Ecclesiae" in the fourth general controversy "De Conciliis et Ecclesia" in *De Controversiis*, Vol. I, Col. 1301, rather than Chapter 4 of Book III "De Ecclesia Militante" of the same controversy (Cols. 1231 and 1233), to which the original note refers. In the passage, Bellarmine discusses the nature of the heresy created by those who profess to follow Christ but assume another name for their religion than Christian. In *Essays in Divinity*, p. 23, where his interests took him into the same field of religious denomination, Donne expressed the belief that a person's own name, rather than the name of his religious group, contributed to his holiness.

Page 182.

8–10 *Carmelite . . . in that Name*: The "late" Carmelite is the French monk Cochelet in his *Palestrita Honoris*, pp. 9 and 6, who wrote his tract on adoration and idolatry to defend Justus Lypsius' support of the veneration of Mary at Halle in Brabant in his *Diva Virgo Hellensis*. Donne refers to Cochelet as "late" not because of his death, as he died only fifteen years later, but because his defence had appeared but a few years earlier. See Commentary for p. 92, l. 27–p. 93, l. 13.

12–20 *For so that Councellour . . . not to blot it out*: The French jurist and defender of Catholicism de Raemond was a member of the Parliament of Bordeaux for a long period in the second half of the sixteenth century, a hundred years after its foundation, and he took part in the trials of Huguenots. The Parliament had been founded in 1460 and was first called by Louis XI in 1462, with other provincial parliaments, to relieve the pressure on the central Parliament of Paris from its excessive burden of judging at trials and dispensing royal justice. Donne is citing the title, as well as the sixth book of Raemond's major work, *L'Histoire de la Naissance, Progrez, et Décadence de l'Héresie de ce Siècle*. However, Donne is unaware of the fact that this sixth book, dealing with the English schism from Rome, was not written by Florimond de Raemond but by his son François who succeeded him to the Parliament. Donne was using a copy of the first edition of *Histoire*, Vol. II, IV, Chapter 3, p. 20a, which was the only edition of the work published before the appearance of *Pseudo-Martyr*, and he is translating François's text literally ("Mais encore en haine du S. Père, il fut établi que jamais on ne le nommeroit Pape: & céte loi s'observoit de telle sorte, que si on eut leu ce mot dans aucun livre sans être éfacé, on étoit condamné à mort"). François also described the execution of Catholics in England during Henry VIII's reign, listed a number of English Carthusian monks who were martyred, and for these cited as his source the English-Catholic apologist Sanders' *De Origine ac Progressu Schismatis Anglicani*, Book I on Henry VIII, pp. 94–95. Donne's reference to Ribadeneira, which gives the impression of originating in Raemond, actually springs directly from Ribadeneira's own *Historia Ecclesiastica del scisma del Reyno de Inglaterra*, which describes the martyrdom of the same Carthusians to whom Sanders refers (pp. 100[a,b]). On the first page (Sig. A) of his preface "Al Christiano piadoso Letor," Ribadeneira recognizes his debt for his work to Sanders' *De Origine*, which came out only three years before his *Historia*.

23–33 *that great Prince . . . the same Expositor*: The "great Prince" is the king of Ethiopia whose title of "Praestegiani" or "Prestigianus" is discussed by Caesar à Branchedoro in his oration to kings, emperors and princes, *Oratio Praemonitaria*, in *Monita Politica*, p. 18. However, the origin of the term is obscure. "Prestigianus" in any of its variant spellings in Donne or Branchedoro is not Latin or Italian. The word is not found in the three seventeenth-century Latin-Ethiopian lexicons, Ludolphus' *Lexicon Aethiopico-Latinum* (London, 1661), Wemmers' *Lexicon Aethiopicum* (Rome, 1638), or the second edition of Ludolphus' *Lexicon* (Frankfurt, 1699) which, however, adds the word "praesulatus" meaning "good prelate" or "bishop" (Col. 133), that Donne uses a few pages later in *Pseudo-Martyr*, p. 187. The hyphenation of the word in Branchedoro's text, broken by the end of a line, may have misled Donne into thinking the word was always hyphenated. The word may also come from the Latin *praestringere*. As Donne's text continues, he takes issue with the interpretation of Isaiah 9.6 by the biblical scholar de Lyra in his scriptural gloss *Biblia Sacra*, Vol. 4, p. 25[r], Cols. I and II, the passages reading: "Et factus est principatus super humerum eius. Crucem sibe baiulando, ut dicit Joh. xix," and "Princeps pacis. sciliter triplicis, quia dat pacem conscientiae internam." Donne attacks Lyra's interpretation of Isaiah because it binds contemporary

COMMENTARY 379

English Catholics to submitting to martyrdom for the definition of one of Christ's titles.

Page 183.

7–13 *The Pope represents . . . no Regall power*: Donne has completed his rebuttal of Catholic arguments that support the supremacy of the pope over secular princes on the basis of his titles, and now begins his refutation of those arguments that support it on the legal grounds of his "ordinary" and "extraordinary" jurisdiction. Donne cites four of Bellarmine's examples which uphold the claim that the pope's authority was not "ordinarie": "Superest nunc . . ." (Col. 1057), "Sed iam explicanda . . ." (Col. 1060), and "Ceterum hoc . . ." (Col. 1057) of Chapter 4 ("Papam non habere ullam temporalem iurisdictionem directe"), and "Gregorius lib.2. epist.61. ad Mauritium" (Col. 1056) of Chapter 3 ("Papam non esse Dominium totius orbis Christiani"), in Book V ("De Temporali Dominio et Potestate eiusdem Pontificis") of the third general controversy ("De Summo Pontifice") of *De Controversiis*, Vol. I.

17–25 *That as Christ . . . any Apostolique Tradition*: Bellarmine denied at length that the pope had direct or "ordinary" jurisdiction over secular princes in order to prove that his power over them was "extraordinary" and beyond the range of their "ordinary" power. Donne's citation is from the paragraph "Ut igitur, et probetur hoc principium," Col. 1057, Chapter 4, Book V, of *De Controversiis*, Vol. I. Donne argues that Bellarmine is in fact claiming both "ordinary" and "extraordinary" power for the popes, and cites his paragraph "Iam vero" (Col. 1055) in Chapter 3 ("Papam non esse Dominium totius orbis Christiani") in Book V of *De Controversiis*, Vol. I.

Page 184.

6–16 *Ordinary Jurisdiction . . . limited to that*: The terms "ordinary" and "extraordinary" were used in canon law as opposed to civil and British common law. In his *Lexicon Iuridicium*, Schardius explained that "ordinary" law (that of the secular prince, in Bellarmine's argument) adhered to the case to be heard rather than to the judge, and that "extraordinary" law (that of the pope, again in Bellarmine's argument) sprang from an underlying religious rite or observance (p. 658, Col. 2; p. 357, Col. 1). It was this latter association of "extraordinary" law with papal power in Bellarmine's two passages of Chapter 4, Book V of the third controversy of *De Controversiis*, Vol. I, Cols. 1059, 1057, that Donne attacked.

18–22 *Bellarmine argued . . . Pope to follow*: Donne is treating his paraphrase translation of Bellarmine's paragraph, "Gregorius lib.2. Epist. 61. ad Mauritium" (Col. 1056) of *De Controversiis*, Vol. I, as though it were a plaintiff's legal "declaration." In his legal dictionary *The Interpreter: or Booke Containing the Signification of Words* (Cambridge, 1607), Sig.X⁴ʳ, Donne' contemporary John Cowell, and also in *An Exposition of Certaine Difficult and Obscure Words, and Terms of* *the Law* (London, 1609; first edition in Latin, 1523), p. 56ᵛ, the early sixteenth-century barrister John Rastell described a "declaration" as a statement which a defendant deposited in court in a personal case, and it was to be distinguished from the "count" which was the court statement that a defendant deposited in a "reall" or public case. Donne is handling Bellarmine's defence of the "declaration" of the papacy as though it were a personal and private case rather than a public matter pertinent to the whole of Christendom. His reference to "Consequence" is also legal. "Consequence" was the legal issue of a case that sprang from one of its parts rather than from its whole (Schardius, *Lexicon*, p. 242, Cols. 1–2). As Donne points out in his next paragraph, such a "consequence" was inconclusive if it did not settle the litigation.

23–29 *that the Pope hath no power . . . Simon Magus*: The first part of Donne's paraphrase, "*that the Pope hath no power, but such as Christ exercised*," is actually the title question of Maynardus' "Argumentum" for the twenty-sixth number of Article 8 in *De Privilegiis Ecclesiasticis*, p. 63, except that he has changed the word "Peter" for "Pope." The rest of Donne's paragraph is from Part I, Article 7, Nos. 5, 6 and 7, pp. 57–58, as indicated in the marginal note, and in Article 8, Nos. 3 and 4, pp. 65–66.

30–1 (p. 185) *S. Paul appealed . . . he had before*: Donne's second discussion in *Pseudo-Martyr* of Bellarmine's retraction in *Recognitio*, pp. 16–17, of his position in *De Controversiis*, Chapter 29, Book II, Third General Controversy, Vol. I, Col. 816, that in Acts 25.10 Paul accepted *de iure* his submission to an earthly ruler (see Commentary for p. 118, ll. 26–27). Donne pointed out a few lines later that Bellarmine made a similar retraction elsewhere in *Recognitio* (see Commentary for p. 118, ll. 30–32).

Page 185.

13–21 *Bellarmine argues . . . to those ends*: Donne's argument about the happy Christian commonwealth and his recourse for support to Bellarmine's *De Controversiis* (Chapter 7, Book V of the third general controversy, Vol. I, Col. 1065), must be placed in context. By the time of Donne's composition of *Pseudo-Martyr* in 1609, the argument about the happy Christian commonwealth finding its purpose in its unsullied primitive origins, had also already been advanced by Protestants such as Hotoman in Chapter I of his *Francogallia* (Geneva, 1573) and once more either by Hotoman or by Philippe du Plessis Mornay in *Vindicia Contra Tyrannos* (Basel, 1579). See Commentary for p. 11, ll. 9–26.

Page 186.

2–4 *this supreme authority . . . not as Pope*: Donne's translation of the second sentence of the opening paragraph of Chapter 6, Book V, third general controversy ("De Summo Pontifice"), Vol. I, Col. 1063, of *De Controversiis*.

COMMENTARY

14–15 *Bellarmine sayes . . . Ecclesiastique Princes*: In the concluding paragraph of Chapter 15 ("Proponitur quaestio, An summus Pontifex habeat iurisdictionem verè coactivam, ita ut possit leges condere, quae obliget in conscientia, et iudicare ac punire transgressores"), Book IV ("De Potestate Romani Pontificis in causis spiritualibus"), of the third general controversy ("De Summo Pontifice"), *De Controversiis*, Vol. I, Col. 1018.

29–1 (p. 187) *Though the Pope . . . the holy Ghost*: The concluding paragraph of Chapter 18 ("Episcopos in Conciliis non Consiliarios, sed Iudices esse"), Book I ("De Natura et Causis Conciliis"), fourth general controversy ("De Conciliis et Ecclesia"), *De Controversiis*, Vol. I, Col. 1140. Book I deals with the origins, causes and nature of church councils and of papal authority over them.

Page 187.

20–32 *For it is strange . . . to distinguish them*: Philip II of Spain assumed the crown of Sicily and Naples on the abdication of his father Charles V in 1555, and was immediately plunged into a war with Pope Paul IV and Henry II of France over Spanish rights in Italy. The leader of the Spanish forces in Italy was, as Donne mentions, Philip's Neapolitan viceroy, the duke of Alba, Fernando Alvarez de Toledo, who defeated the French forces under the duke of Guise at Civiletta. Philip's fury against both the French and Paul IV was increased by the fact that Paul belonged to one of Naples' oldest ruling families, the Caraffa, which was known for its hatred of Spanish rule, and that as a Neapolitan Paul was a subject of the kings of Spain. On Philip's orders Alba proceeded to take Rome, but the Venetians successfully restrained Philip from having the city sacked and they urged him to seek peace with the pope. Donne gets his account of the event from Lelio Medici's long tract, "Discorso . . . . I fondamenti e le ragioni delli SS. Veneziani," in *Raccolta degli Scritti* (p. 194), which tried to establish a middle ground in the later conflict between Rome and Venice and used the Neapolitan event as an example. Philip had submitted that it was difficult to separate the man, Pietro Caraffa, from his position, Paul IV, and for this reason out of respect for the papacy had given up the idea of sacking Rome to punish Caraffa. Medici's tract tried to use the same argument to convince the Venetians to soften their attitude towards Paul V in their conflict with him in 1605, and Donne in his turn is using both events to encourage the papacy to soften its stand against England.

Page 188.

7–10 *though I confesse . . . all other Nations*: A number of sometimes related controversialist works lie behind Donne's phrase. The first are the Catholic apologist Sanders' *De Visibili Monarchia Ecclesiae Libri VIII* (Louvain, 1571), and the *De Origine ac Progressu Schismatis Anglicani* to which Donne has already referred in *Pseudo-Martyr* (see Commentary for p. 163, ll. 2–10, and p. 182, ll. 12–20). Both speak of the nature of the pope's powers and differentiate them from his person in many places. Of the other Catholic controversialists, Thomas Stapleton (b. Henfield, Sussex, 1535; d. Louvain, 1598), wrote *A Fortresse of the Faith first planted amonge us englishmen, and continued hitherto in the universall Church of Christ* (Louvain, 1565), which related directly to Donne's general arguments about the origins of English Christianity.

17–18 *new Order of the Congregation . . . both they are*: The Oratorians, founded by Saint Philip Neri in 1575, were known as a "Congregation" rather than strictly as an order, which Neri had no intention of founding, because they were meant to group clerics already ordained in various orders who should not take yet more vows, but who should simply dedicate their lives to preaching and to hearing confessions. Baronius and Bozio were among the first members of the Oratory. See Commentary for p. 58, l. 33–p. 59, l. 10; also, Matthews, *St. Philip Neri*, p. 86.

23–28 *his Direct and Ordinarie power . . . as Christs Vicar*: The Oratorians Baronius and Bozio maintained that papal power sprang in significant measure from an objective code of law and was therefore "direct" and "ordinary," as described by canon law, rather than *ex iure divino* or from divine law and therefore extraordinary, as argued currently (according to Donne) by Jesuits like Bellarmine. Alexander Carrerius was the Paduan theologian, the author first of the "De sponsalibus matrimonio" published with Gregory XIII's *Tractatus Universii Juris* in 1584 and, some fifteen years later, of *De Potestate Romani Pontificis, Adversus Impios Politicos, et Huius temporis Hereticos* (Padua, 1599). Donne picks up the phrase "Impious Politician" against Bellarmine from Carrerius' title; hence, his marginalia's "Titulo libri." In 1602, Bozio also borrowed the phrase and included it in the title of his tract, *De Temporali Ecclesiae Monarchia et Iurisdictione*, to support Carrerius' stand. Donne is paraphrasing in translation Carrerius' argument that the pope's authority springs from his position as a prince rather than from his function as vicar of Christ, *De Potestate*, Book II, Chapter 8, p. 124 (Cologne edition of 1601).

28–10 (p. 189) *But Bozius [Barclay] also calls . . . themselves, have tolde mee*: The references are to the general arguments on the origins of papal power in Chapter 11 of Book II and Chapter 18 of Book V of Bozio's *De Temporali Ecclesiae Monarchia et Iurisdictione*. However, Donne does not appear to be quoting Bozio directly, but citing him rather from William Barclay's *De Potestate Papae*, to which his marginalia immediately refers. Moreover, it is not Bozio, but Barclay, who speaks of the "novos Theologos," and it is Barclay's marginal references to Bozio's "Lib.2, cap.11," and "Lib.5, cap ult." which also appear in Donne's margin. The present edition does not drop Bozio's name in Donne's text as this would require re-writing two of his sentences, but Barclay's name is included in square brackets after Bozio's. Donne paraphrases in translation a passage in Chapter I, p. 5 of Barclay's *De Potestate*, where he takes issue with two unnamed Catholic writers, "Duplex Catholicorum" (p. 4). Donne interprets these Catholics to be Bellarmine and Baronius. His later references are to Chapters 3 and 40 of *De Potestate*.

COMMENTARY 383

Page 189.

19–28 *Doctor Franciscus . . . authority upon them*: Donne is using the writings of the two Catholic jurists, Victoria and Alvarez, who held that the pope had only "indirect authority" over secular princes, against the arguments of other Catholic jurists that this authority was "direct." In *Relectiones*, "Relectio I, De potestate Ecclesiae prior," Section VI, Nos. 4, 2 and 3, pp. 37–39, Victoria allowed the pope only indirect authority, and, Donne is here suggesting that Victoria's arguments to limit the pope's direct authority, should also be used to limit his indirect authority. Donne's next illustration of a legal precedent that supports his case, is the story of the ironic intervention of an angel in canonical hours that he found in Alvarez' *Thesaurus*, Chapter 33, No. 4, p. 101, that Alvarez himself indicates he got from the Benedictine canonist Nicolo de Tudeschi (b. Sicily, 1386; d. Palermo, 1445), the cardinal of Palermo known as "Panormitanus," and that he says moreover Panormitanus got from yet another canonist Giovanni Andrea (b. Mugello, 1275; d. Bologna, 1348). The use of a legal illustration known to be employed regularly but ironically by jurists and canonists, was made even more attractive to Donne by the fact that Alvarez was jurist in the Spanish Neapolitan kingdom already sensitive to its rights against the papacy, and that Panormitanus had at first supported Pope Eugenius IV, then sided with the conciliar movement against him, and finally supported the antipope Felix V. Panormitanus' *Tractatus de Concilio Basiliensis* upheld the authority of a general church council over the pope.

CHAP. X
Page 190.

24–28 *the name . . . offered under that name*: The bishops Ursacius of Singidunum and Valens of Mursa supported the Arian doctrine of the non-divinity of Christ, but did not attend the Council of Nicaea which condemned the doctrine in 325, as Carranza seems to suggest in his *Summa Conciliorum et Pontificorum*, pp. 91^v–92^v, which Donne cites. Rather, as Binius writes in his *Concilia Generalia*, Vol. I, pp. 460, 470, much later in 353 Ursacius and Valens more correctly attended the Council of Arles which they manipulated and where, to the dismay of Pope Liberius, who reigned between 352 and 366 and who called it, the assembly failed to condemn Arianism as had the Council of Nicaea.

30–31 *Canon law . . . auncient Councels*: See Introduction, p. xxxiii.

Page 191.

13–17 *And had the Bishops . . . doe at that time*: Donne's marginal note refers to Title 1 "De Summa Trinitate, et Fide Catholica, et ut Nemo de ea publice contendere audeat," "Lex" or Law 1 promulgated variously by the emperors Gratian, Valentine and Theodosius, at the very opening of the *Codicis* section, Vol. II, of Justinian's *Codex Iuris Civilis*.

Page 192.

2–8 (p. 193) *Archbishop Augustinus . . . thousand yeeres past*: Donne is using Augustinus' *De Emendatione Gratiani* (the edition here, Paris, 1607), to attack the Catholic system of decretals. Augustinus (b. Saragossa, 1517; d. Tarragona, 1586), an ardent Dominican reformer, served as jurist and theologian for three years at the Council of Trent and, as his chief work of reform, set out to correct the written legal sources of Catholic authority, particularly Gratian's twelfth-century *Decretum* which had become textually corrupted. Augustinus' crowning achievement was his publication of *De Emendatione* of the *Decretum* at Tarragona in 1587. The other two sixteenth-century attempts to correct *Decretum*, to which Donne refers, were Pius V's commission or "Correctores Romani" named in 1566 to prepare a new edition of *Corpus Iuris Canonici*, particularly of that part of it containing *Decretum* and its gloss; and secondly, the further textual corrections and, more importantly, the index that Gregory XIII ordered to be compiled for *Decretum* in the new *Corpus* published in Rome in 1582. Donne cites Augustinus' *De Emendatione* thirteen times, mainly to show that using *Decretum* as a textual source for theological rules is an uncertain enterprise, and he interlaces these references to *De Emendatione* with citations from *Decretum* itself. The references to *De Emendatione* are: 1) Book I, Dialogue 1, p. 1, and 2) p. 6; Donne points out that though doubt has been cast on it, *Decretum* is still used as the basis of canon law, and that yet further laws were based on *Decretum* and promulgated after it, including the "Extravagantes" of John XXII, and of other popes who preceded John but which were compiled under his guidance and were called "Extravagantes communes." 3) Book II, Dialogue 8, p. 225. 4) Book I, Dialogue 4, p. 24. 5) Book I, 19, p. 159, and 6) I, 16, p. 137, where Augustinus criticizes the lack of reference to source material in *Decretum*. 7) I, 3, pp. 16–17, and 8) pp. 18–19, where Augustinus points out errors in Gratian's lists of popes and councils, for example that a "Nicholas," rather than Nicasius of Culusitanus, convened the first Council of Carthage in the third century, when there was no Pope Nicholas until the ninth century (so that Donne's text records inaccurately the death of Pope Nicholas before a Council of Carthage), *Decretum* II, Causa 21, Q. 3, Chapters 1 and 2, Col. 1236, and I, Distinction 20, Chapter 1, Cols. 88–89. The seventh and eighth references also mention Augustinus' revised corrected chronologies (hence Donne's use of the word) of popes and councils from the apostle Peter to the present, that Gregory XIII had prefaced to certain editions of *Corpus Iuris Canonici* (Sigs. a^{iiiv}–b^{ir}), Paris, 1587. 9) I, 3, p. 20, and 10) 4, p. 25, refer to Gratian's transcription errors — Jerome for Jeremy, the emperor Henry in Ephesus rather than in the German town of Erphesfurd, and the "heretical" Archbishop of Ravenna rather than Henry Archbishop of Ravenna. 11) I, 5, p. 34, refers to Augustinus' argument that Gratian mistook a quotation from Saint Paul in

1 Tim. 6, for a passage from 2 Peter 2, and Donne writes that the marginal gloss to the passage in *Decretum*, Distinction 54, Chapter 12, Col. 280, compounded the error by lengthening the quotation beyond its text in the Bible. 12) I, 4, p. 28, where Augustinus corrects a passage in *Decretum*, "De Consecratione," I, Chapter 56, Col. 1906, that stated that a Pope Macharius, who never existed, held a council in Geneva, which never took place, to read correctly that a Pope Zacharius held synods in Rome in 743 and 745; the "Palea" to which Donne refers were the notes that sometimes followed some of Gratian's chapters, and that are not to be confused with the glossary (see Commentary for p. 209, ll. 22–28). Finally, 13) I, 8, p. 224, where Augustinus cites the passage on ignorance from Saint Paul. Donne concludes his list of errors that Augustinus found in *Decretum* with two suggested corrections of his own, both of interpretation rather than of fact. The first, Donne writes, was the misreading of "sedem" (or "seat") for "fidem" (or "faith") in *Decretum*, "De Poenitentiae," Distinction I, Chapter 52, of Ambrose's *De Poenitentiae*, Book I, Chapter 6. The translation of Ambrose's text was a subject of discussion among Renaissance translators even outside the arguments of the Reformers and Counter-Reformers. Gregory XIII's corrected *Decretum* (Lyons, 1584), Col. 1687, and his corrected *Corpus Iuris Canonici* (Paris, 1587), Col. 364, as well as, incidentally, *Patrologia*, Series I, Vol. 16, Col. 476, No. 33, also read "sedem," but the 1529, Paris Catholic edition of the works of St. Ambrose (p. 48) containing Erasmus' "preface to the Reader" and, no less, the 1583 editon of the *Opera Omnia* prepared by Donne's opponent in *Pseudo-Martyr*, Caesar Baronius (Vol. 2, p. 185, in the Cologne edition of 1616) which is addressed by Baronius to Gregory XIII himself, agrees with Donne's reading of "fidem." Donne's second example of Gratian's misinterpretation of history is his reference to the list of the decrees of the Council of Agathensis under Pope Sixtus III who reigned from 432 to 440, in *Decretum* II, Cause 21, Q. 1, Chapters 26–27, Cols. 904–905, supporting papal power over secular states.

Page 193.

8–14 *Clericum nullus . . . to the world therein*: In Binius, *Concilia Generalia*, Vol. II, Tome 2, Col. 1, p. 306, n. 32 and margin, the text reads "Clericus nec quenquam praesumat," whereas the marginal note reads "I.q.1. Clericum nullus praesumat." Donne points to an apparent inconsistency between the text and its suggested source in Gratian. The council of the Church to which he refers is that of Pope Symmachus (d. 514) held in Rome in 506.

14–18 *Bellarmine hath delt herein . . . in these words*: Donne's note to Chapter 28, Book I ("De Clericis") of the fifth general controversy "De Membris Ecclesiae Militantes" of Bellarmine's *De Controversiis*, Vol. I, Col. 1490, is not to a citation of a church canon but a reference to a series of decrees by three popes, Caius and Marcellinus at the end of the third century, and Gregory I in the sixth century. Bellarmine's citations of the church canons, No. 9 at Chalcedon, No. 32 at Agathensis, and No. 9 at Carthage III, which concern clerical submission to church authority, occur higher in Col. 1490, in the paragraph "Probatur Primo ex Conciliis" of his text.

25–31 *Baronius is forced . . . called Capitularia*: In Baronius' *Annales Ecclesiastici*, Vol. V, Tome 9, Col. 409, No. 13, for the year 774, and Col. 622, No. 12, for the year 801. Donne's marginal notes copy Baronius' notes and reproduce this error of "Distinction 65" instead of the correct "63." Bellarmine caught the error later and corrected it in his *Recognitiones*, p. 17. Donne's next marginal note is to Baronius' text, "To.9, Anno 801. fo.622," and to its marginal note in *Decretum*, 11.q.1. "Volumnus," more precisely to Chapter 37. The latter passage by Gratian discussed the nature of Charlemagne's "capitulaire" or "capitularia" laws that were passed at his great synodal assemblies in the last decade of the eighth century and in the first decade of the ninth. The "Capitularia," as Donne calls them, were decided upon by the emperor following his deliberations with the ecclesiastical and lay nobles whom he summoned to huge assemblies, often in an impromptu manner. The "Capitularia" came to form part of the body of both legislative and civil law, and often passed into the body of French common law.

32–23 (p. 195) *With like danger to the Romane Sea . . . which wee noted before*: Donne makes sixteen rapid references to Gratian's *Decretum*. Not only do the references point out errors of text, as is Donne's usual practice for citing Gratian, but they often are made to bring up questions of faith and dogma that contradict certain papal decrees. The first reference is to *Decretum* I, Distinction 31, Chapter 13, Col. 153, on the celibacy of priests, a passage with which Augustinus of Tarragona, whom Donne cites, also took issue in *De Emendatione*, Book I, Dialogue 8, p. 67. The Greek council to which Donne refers was the sixth ecumenical and third General Council of Constantinople which Pope Agatho (b. Sicily, 577; d. Rome, 681) summoned in 680, but Agatho, who was already over a hundred years old, died before the decrees promulgated in Constantinople reached Rome, and it is one of the decrees of this council on celibacy of which Gratian failed to note the eastern, rather than Roman character. The second and third references are jointly, first, to *Decretum* I, Distinction 13, Chapters 1 and 2, Cols. 48–49, in which Gratian, citing the eighth Council of Toledo, under Pope Martin I who reigned from 649 to 655, discusses the problem of the morality of necessary evil; and, second, to the related problem of the obligatory character of confession of sins in "De Poenitentia," Distinction I, Chapters 88 and 89, Cols. 1715–1718, where Gratian makes a survey of Catholic opinion on the subject and concludes that because of the occasional uncertain reality of sin, the obligatory character of confession must somehow, sometimes, be left to the judgment of the reader ("Cui autem harem potius adhaerendum sit lectoris iudicio reservatur," Col. 1717). The fourth, fifth and sixth references are to the voluminous gloss of *Decretum*, which surrounds on three sides practically each page of Gratian in most later editions, that Donne says are comically out of character with the main text; of these, the first passage is from Distinction 50, Chapter 16, Cols. 243–244, in which Gratian describes the union between God and the sinner by comparing it typologically with the Biblical story of the shepherd who left ninety-nine sheep safe in the wilderness to look for one lost sheep. Donne says the gloss identifies "wilderness" (*deserto*) derisively as the "heaven" which Satan abandoned with the fall (*quod Diabolus per casum deseruit*), but he himself corrupts the quotation by changing *casum* to *pecatum* or "sin"; and the second and third references to the laughable character of the gloss are to *Decretum* II, Cause 24, Question 2, Chapter 6, Col. 1414, where Donne finds discordant the gloss's correction to "Constantinople" of Gratian's error of "Rome" in the description of the Patriarchate of Dioscorum of Constantinople in 444 as a "papacy." The seventh to twelfth references are to attempts in the gloss of *Decretum* to make the meaning of the text support current interpretations of Catholic faith; of these, the first two references are to Distinction 21, Chapter 9, Col. 99, and Cause 24, Q.2, Chapter 6, where Gratian discusses the Patriarch Dioscorus of Alexandria's difficult relationship with the Roman pontiffs; the third reference is to Distinction 15, Cols. 53–54, where Gratian describes as not a fundamental error of faith Dioscorus' defence of his fifth-century contemporary, the heretic Eutyches, who believed that the risen Christ had only one divine nature and no longer a human nature as well (and Donne believes that the gloss for "Defensorum" in Distinction 15 covers up a heresy in Gratian himself); the fourth reference bringing up discordances between the text and the gloss and thus creating errors in Catholic dogma is to Distinction 31, Chapter 2, Cols. 149–150, where Gratian writes on clerical celibacy using Bede's *Commentaries on Luke*, and is contradicted by the gloss, according to Donne, and the fifth reference is to Distinction 32, Chapter 16, Col. 163, where Gratian discusses the interdiction against the presence of women in the houses of bishops, supported by the decrees of the second Council of Nicaea in 787; however, the gloss adds that the wives of the bishop's men may be allowed in, contradicting (to Donne) the decree of the council; and, finally, the sixth reference in the series of dogmatic errors, once more on celibacy but introducing an element of lust into the discussion, is to Distinction 34, Chapter 1, Cols. 167–168, dealing with the hunt-loving ninth-century Archbishop Lanfred of Germany who, in addition to having his hunting activities limited by decretal, was also reprimanded for his public sexual advances to his daughter by Pope Nicholas I, and the gloss adds details of Lanfred's conduct that, to Donne, once more contradict the spirit of the Church's decrees described in the main text. The thirteenth reference in the overall current series to the *Decretum* raises the hypothetical figure of 23,000 men that a woman must have befriended to merit the title of prostitute, Distinction 34, Chapter 116, Col. 173. The figure was of the hypothetical speculative nature in the scholastic consideration of moral and philosophical problems, such as how many angels can dance on the head of a pin. Before undertaking the fourteenth reference, Donne points to the fact that *Decretum* never received official Roman recognition as a church document, even with the corrections made in it in the sixteenth century on orders of Pius V and Gregory XIII, and therefore he asks how the decretals recorded in *Decretum* can be held to bind Protestant England. The fourteenth reference is to the inherent disdain that Donne perceives to be contained in the gloss of Distinction 68, Col. 342; Gratian's consideration of the reconsecration of those who have already been consecrated, says the gloss, is a task fit for a schoolteacher. Both this reference, and the fifteenth reference to the *Decretum* dealing with the anger toward's Gratian's errors expressed in the gloss, are to pp. 22 and 23, Chapter 2, of the *De Libris Iuris Canonici, Disputationes tres* (Hanover, 1605), of the Italian Oxford Regius professor of law Albericus Gentilis (b. Sanginesio, Ancona, 1551; d. Oxford, 1611). Gentilis, who shared the Protestant ideas of his father and was forced to leave Italy, takes issue with numerous passages in Gratian. However, Gentilis' notes are not reliable, and Donne's own note to Distinction 68 of the *Decretum* does not repeat Gentilis' error that the "magister" quotation comes from Chapter 2 when it originates in Chapter 1. Nor does Donne's fifteenth reference to *Decretum*, "Fateor plane," repeat Gentilis' error that the quotation comes from Cause VII, Question 3, because he knew that there is no third question in the cause concerned, but he does not identify the source other than citing Gentilis. Finally, Donne's sixteenth reference to *Decretum* deals once more with Gratian's pronouncement on necessary evil in Distinction 13, Chapter 1, Col. 48, but now raises the question of scholastic "perplexities" to which the gloss refers: "Videamus ergo quis iuris sit de perplexitate. Dicunt quidam, quod aliquis potest esse perplexus inter duo mortalia" (Col. 47). As a term in moral theology, the perplexities were questions dealing with contradictions in human affairs, such as might exist in the conflict between a human conscience and a completed act.

Page 195.

25–34 *Bellarmine sayes . . . recants them*: Bellarmine called Gratian's authoritativeness into doubt in Chapter 12 ("An sit maior auctoritas Concilii quam Scripturae"), Book II of the fourth general controversy ("De Conciliis et Ecclesia"), in Vol. I of *De Controversiis*, Col. 1203. In Distinction 19 of *Decretum*, Col. 1, Gratian misapprehended Augustine's reference "to the Scriptures of Catholic churches" in Chapter 8, Book II, of *De Doctrina Christiana*, for the "decretalls" of the Roman pontiffs, and his editors corrected the error in their gloss, and Donne is raising the question of Bellarmine's reference to this correction. But then he also raises the question that elsewhere Bellarmine retained an error out of Gratian, the accusative "Clericum" instead of the nominative "Clericus," in his citation of the decree of the Council of Agathensis (see Commentary for p. 193, ll. 14–18), in his "De Clericis," Book I, Chapter 28, of the fifth general controversy in *De Controversiis* (see Commentary for p. 193, ll. 8–14). Donne chastises Bellarmine for not recanting the error in his *Recognitio*, where he nevertheless admits having been misled by Gratian elsewhere (pp. 17–18).

Page 196.

3–10 *Decretum . . . Hereticos versus*: In a curious theological tract, *Pro Sacerdotum Barbis* (Rome, 1531), the Italian scholar Giovanni Pietro Valeriano Bolzani

(b. Venice, c.1477; d. Padua, 1558) tells the story about Adrian VI. Adrian, the last "barbarian" pope, so-called because of his birth in Utrecht in 1522, inadvertently came to consider as heretical the "Carmen Paschale" of the fifth-century Christian poet Sedulius because of an error in his copy of *Decretum*. Valeriano, or Pierius as Donne refers to him in his marginal note, narrates (Paris edition, 1558, pp. 24–25) that Adrian even as late as in the sixteenth century was using a defective edition of *Decretum* that substituted the word "hereticis" for "heroicis" (or perhaps even for "eruditis," as Migne's *Patrologia Latina*, Vol. 59, Cols. 173–174, also lists that word as a possibility), in its reference to Sedulius' *Carmen* in the decree "Sancta Maria Romana" (Distinction 15, Cols. 55–58) issued by Pope Gelasius in 496. Gelasius' decree listed those biblical and Christian works which were apocryphal and those which were not. It praised Sedulius' *Carmen Pascale*, which was a summary of the Old and New Testaments in five books, as the work of a great Christian writer. See Commentary for p. 34, ll. 23–24.

12–16 *as the Canonists . . . Fictione Canonica*: *Decretum*, Distinction 75, Chapter 4, Col. 362, the gloss for "Sabbati."

16–20 *English Priest . . . pontificatus faeminei*: The English Jesuit controversialist John Gibbons (b. Wells, 1544; d. Himmelbrode, 1589), or the Catholic-convert controversialist John Bridgewater (b. Yorkshire, ?1532; d. ?Treves, ?1596) who signed some of his anti-Protestant works "Aquapontus," as it is uncertain which of the two was the author of *Responsio ad Georgio Sohnio . . . De Antichristo Romano* (1589), Thesis 15, p. 10.

24–4 (p. 197) *The next limme in this great body . . . Decretalium*: For the collections of decretals that constituted the *Corpus Iuris Canonici*, see Introduction, p. xxxiii.

Page 197.

17–27 *Bellarmines confession . . . the word Radant*: A paraphrase of Bellarmine's argument on "De fide" in the second "Respondeo" of Chapter 14 ("De ceteris Pontificibus, quibus error in fide falso tribuitur") of Book IV of the third general argument, Vol. I, of his *De Controversiis*, Col. 1009. The Catholic writer in question is Valeriano or Pierius (hence Donne's note), who discusses "ad fidem" the wearing of clerical beards and who describes the accidental dropping of the word "radant" at the end of the decree No. XLIV "Clerici neque comam nutriant neque Barbam Radant," of the fourth Council of Carthage in 525, in his *Pro Sacerdotum Barbis*, pp. 19–21. The mistaken transcription of the decree led to the tradition against the wearing of beards by clerics in the western Church, enforced among others by Alexander III who recommended prison for clerics who wore beards.

Page 198.

10–22 *therefore the Canons . . . from secular Judges*: *Decretum*, Distinction 15, Chapter 3, Col. 55, the decree "Sancta Romana" of Pope Gelasius (see Commentary for p. 34, ll. 23–24), and Cause 25, Question 1, Chapter 5, Col. 1438, of which Donne is translating the title. Donne's first translation is from Bellarmine's "Objectiones" section in "Defensio Secundae," Chapter 4 of his *Responsio . . . Ad Libellum Inscriptum: Responsio Doctoris Theologi*, p. 294, in the *Controversiae Memorabilis* (Rome, 1607) that also republished the documents of Giovanni Marsilius, the anonymous letter writer "Doctor Theologi," and Baronius on the Venetian controversy. The second translation is from Marsilius' "Errata XI" in Chapter 5, pp. 300–301, in which he cites the canons of the emperors Constantine and Theodosius out of Gratian's *Decretum*.

24–31 *Gratian . . . auribus Canones*: In his *Treatise Tending to Mitigation*, Chapter 7, Nos. 42, 43 and 45, pp. 302–303, 305, Parsons claimed that, in all, five questions dealt with in Cause 22, Part II of *Decretum*, supported his argument that several popes had introduced strong regulations against prevarication into canon law. Peter de Vineis (b. Capua, n.d.) was the early thirteenth-century councillor to the Emperor Frederic II of Germany. His correspondence with the emperor while the latter was in Italy defending his right to the Kingdom of Sicily against an interdiction of Innocent III, was later published as a political document entitled *Epistolarum* (Amberg, 1609), Book I, Letter 4, p. 98.

Page 199.

1–5 *for so sayes he . . . the Pope hath decreed it*: The unidentified compiler of the *Observationes* of the early church hermit Cassianus' *De Institutis Renunciantium* and *Collationes*, pp. 739–740, cites Plato's opinion in Book III of *The Republic*, that wise men should perhaps be allowed to lie, mentions that Origen, Chrysostom and Saint Jerome (the "other Fathers" of Donne's text) appear to support Plato's declaration, but adds that Augustine of Hippo disapproved of all forms of official approbation for not telling the truth. The commentator does not mention the Pope's approval either, but refers rather to "official practice." See Commentary for p. 101, ll. 5–9.

12–3 (p. 200) *though Sixtus 4 . . . Doctrine from beeing Hereticall*: Sixtus IV (b. Abisola, 1414; d. Rome, 1484), elected pope in 1471, issued the decree *Cum Praeexcelsa* on 28 February 1476, and later a second decree entitled *Grave Nimis* on 4 September 1483, proclaiming the Immaculate Conception of Mary ("Extravagantium Communium," Book III, Title 12, Chapter 1 and 2, *Corpus Iuris Canonici*, Cols. 373–374). The two decrees resulted from a quarrel among Italian theologians about the place of Mary in Catholic belief, with each side accusing the other of heresy. The Catholic authority whom Donne is using to contradict Sixtus IV's second decree on the freedom of Mary from original sin at her conception is Victorellus in his *De Angelorum Custodia*, p. 99ᵛ. Victorellus writes that it is not heretical to say either that Mary was conceived with original sin or that her body or soul was not assumed into heaven. Then, Donne summons the authority of the "Correctores Romani," formed first by Pius V (and not Sixtus V, as Donne's printed text mistakenly indicates; see Commentary for p. 48, ll. 17–25) in 1566 and later sanctioned by Gregory XIII in 1582 to expurgate Gratian's errors and produce a correct text of *Corpus Iuris Canonici*. Donne's marginalia refers the reader to the supplement "De Consecratione," Distinction III, Chapter 1, Col. 1965, of Gregory's Lyons edition of 1584 that supports Victorellus. The unidentified Jesuit to whom Donne says he has already referred is the same anonymous individual of Mathieu's *Histoire de France*, Tome II, Book VII, Narration 4, p. 355, which he cited earlier (see Commentary for p. 107, ll. 5–12). A current of Catholic thinking supported as valid the sacramental character of written confession, but the official Church rejected it. At a meeting of the inquisition in the Palace of the Quirinal in Rome on 20 June 1602, Pope Clement VIII issued his severe interdict against written confession, which Donne is translating from Comitolus' *Responsa Moralia*, Book I ("De Sacramentis"), Question 16, pp. 26–27. Comitolus named several scriptural and patristic sources to suggest the possibility that written confession was acceptable (p. 27).

Page 200.

9–17 *Which way . . . then Canons*: Maynardus, *De Privilegiis*, Part I, Article 11, Nos. 8, 9, p. 88. This passage concerns the authority of the pope to use laws and canons in the condemnation of heretics and to alter the laws of secular princes in the name of correcting them.

30–8 (p. 201) *Canons doe never binde . . . is not receaved*: *Decretum*, Distinction 4, Chapter 3, Col. 11, the gloss on the decree of Pope Telesphorus, early in the second century; and, a millennium later, in the mid-twelfth century, Alexander III's decree on abstinence in armies. Second, in Navarrus' *Manuale* on confession, penitence and freedom of conscience, Chapter XIII, No. 1, p. 198 (1588), which deals with the observance of the Sabbath (see Commentary for p. 23, ll. 12–17). Third, the "canonist" is the Tuscan theologian Ugolini, and "this Pope" is the reigning Pope Paul V to whom Ugolini addressed his tract on the Venetian controversy, *Responsiones . . . Ad Tractatum Septem Theologorum*. In Chapter I, Section 1, Number 9, p. 10, Ugolini argues, like Navarrus, that in certain circumstances, such as those of unpublished papal or council decrees, the decrees can have no binding effect on Catholics.

Page 201.

22–23 *as acceptation . . . abrogate it*: In Azor's *Institutionum Moralium*, Vol. 2, Part 2, Book 7, Chapter 3 ("De Assidua Praesentia, qua Beneficiarii in suis Ecclesis commorari, & ut dici solet, residere debent"), p. 494, Cols. 1–2, and Ugolini's *Responsiones*, I, 1, 9, p. 10.

Page 202.

21–29 *one Catholique Author . . . libertie of the empire*: Alberico de Rosate (b. Rosate, n.d.; d. Bergamo, 1354), the practical jurist of Bergamo, in his dictionary of legal terminology, *Dictionarium Iuris, tam Civilis, quam Canonici* (Venice, 1601), p. 92 A, Col. 2, under "Electio."

30–17 (p. 203) *The first is a letter . . . confirmed Otho*: In May 1202, Innocent III sent the letter "Venerabilem" to the German duke Berthold V of Carinthia and Zahringen who, with the leader of the Guelphs Otto IV of Germany and the leader of the Ghibellines Philip, duke of Swabia, the brother of the dead emperor Henry VI, was a contender for Henry's throne on his death in 1197, "Decretals of Gregory IX" or "Liber Extra," Book I, Title 6 "De Electione," Chapter 34, *Corpus Iuris Canonici*, Cols. 59–62. Berthold's, Otto's and Philip's rivalry for the throne sprang from Frederick I Barbarossa's gift thirty years earlier of the duchy of Swabia first to his son Henry who became Henry VI and later to his younger son Philip who now sought his brother's vacant throne. But the succession was complicated by the fact that in 1196, only one year before his death, Henry had all the German princes convened at Frankfurt sign a promise that his infant son would succeed him as emperor. As his son was only three years old, the Guelphs had Otto IV crowned emperor at Aachen in 1198, the Ghibellines had Philip crowned emperor at Mainz in the same year, Henry's widow Constance had Innocent crown her infant son Frederick king of Sicily, Innocent supported Otto as Emperor and the latter, after murdering Philip, reigned as emperor until his deposition in 1215, and Frederick II became emperor. The letter "Venerabilem" to the duke of Carinthia was written at the height of the struggle for the imperial throne that filled the immediate years after Henry's death. Donne's reference to King John of England and Innocent III is to their quarrel, at the very same time as the German struggle, over the nomination of the papal candidate Stephen Langton to the archbishopric of Canterbury in 1208, when Innocent placed England under an interdict and, in 1213, John placed his country into the hands of the pope as a fief.

Page 203.

26–3 (p. 204) *thus abridged . . . as Emperour*: Donne lists the five chief points of Innocent's letter "Venerabilem."

Page 204.

27–31 *given by Pipin . . . striving for both swords*: Clement V, in Book II, Chapter 1 of Title 9 "De Iureiurando," in the "Clementines," *Corpus Iuris Canonici*,

Cols. 210–213, passed at the Council of Vienna in 1311. Pepin III (d. 768) son of Charles Martel and sole ruler of his father's empire from 747, received considerable legal endowments that gave him control over the church in France from Pope Stephen II for helping him subdue his Arab and Lombard enemies in Italy, and for subsequently helping him consolidate the papal states.

Page 205.

5–8 *made to his brother . . . confirming another Emperour*: Henry VI's brother, Philip of Swabia, was present at the meeting of the German princes in Frankfurt in 1196 at which the princes swore that they would elect Henry's son Frederick as emperor on his death. By supporting another candidate, Innocent III's letter "Venerabilem" appeared to absolve the princes of this oath.

26–2 (p. 206) *Of whose profit . . . their Suites and Causes*: The *Ursperger Chronicle* or *Urspergensis Coenobii, Ordinis Praemonstratens. Ad Midulam, In Augustana Diocesi Abbatis . . . Chronicon*, pp. 243–244 in the Strasbourg edition of 1609, a history of the world from the reign of the Assyrian king Ninus to the year 1229, once attributed to Conrad of Liechtenaw, but now considered the work of Burchard of Biberach, born in the late twelfth century, provost of the Monastery of Ursperg, where he died in 1230.

Page 206.

3–27 *second Canon . . . calamity and miserie*: For de Rosate, see Commentary for p. 202, ll. 21–29; and for the canon "De Sententia et De Re Iudicata" in Clement V's "Liber Sextus," see Commentary for p. 207, ll. 20–24. Frederick II was threatened with excommunication by Honorius III in 1225, and was actually excommunicated twice by Gregory IX, pope from 1227 to 1241, on 29 September 1227 and 20 March 1239, and once by Innocent IV, pope from 1243 to 1254, at a general Council of Lyons in June of 1245, to which Innocent had fled to escape Frederick, and where he called the council especially to excommunicate him. Frederick had promised Innocent III to go on a crusade in return for his help in securing the imperial crown, but in order to consolidate his power in Italy, including Rome, and to unite the kingdom of Sicily with the German Empire, he repeatedly put off the crusade under the succeeding popes, Honorius III, Gregory IX, Celestine IV and Innocent IV. The latter lost patience with Frederick, both for delaying the crusade and for his expansionist aims, fell into open conflict with him and was defeated, and, feeling that the moment was not right for his martyrdom, fled Rome by night in disguise, pursued by Frederick's soldiers. As narrated by Binius in his *Concilia Generalia*, Vol. IV, Tome 3, Part 2, pp. 1480–1481 (in Donne's marginal note), Innocent had refused Frederick's proposals for peace over the estates surrounding Rome, and, once safely in Lyons, overruled the protests of Frederick's justiciar Thaddeus of Suessa, excommunicated and deposed Frederick, and ordered the German princes to elect another emperor. Nevertheless Thaddeus continued to represent Frederick's interests before the council and offered guarantees for the emperor's good conduct from Henry III of England and Louis IX of France. But Innocent refused them on the grounds that he would be drawn into conflict with the English and French kings if hostilities with Frederick resumed. Donne obtains his information about the intervenion of the English ambassadors from Binius' *Concilia* (p. 1483, Col. 2), and when he refers to Frederick II as the "son" of Frederick I Barbarossa he must mean his descendant as the younger Frederick was the older's grandson.

34–37 *Pius the fift . . . called a Canon*: See Commentary for p. 160, ll. 31–p. 161, l. 4, and p. 217, l. 35–p. 218, l. 1.

Page 207.

20–24 *third of these foure principall Rescripts . . . their obedience*: The third of the rescripts is the "Pastoralis" forming Chapter 2 of Title 11 or "De Sententia et Re Iudicata" in the "Clementines," *Corpus Iuris Canonici*, Col. 217, of 1306. Henry VII intended to complete the re-unification of the Roman Empire with the reconquest of the kingdom of Naples, but was resisted by both Robert of Sicily and Clement V. Robert was never king of Sicily, although he tried to conquer it repeatedly from the Aragonese, and Donne is ascribing the kingship to him because of the eventual re-unification of Naples and Sicily under the Spaniards. As Robert's overlord, Henry deposed him, but Clement, as the overlord of both Robert and Henry, declared valid the oath of allegiance of Robert's subjects to him. See Commentary for p. 253, l. 36–p. 254, l. 7, and p. 259, l. 20–p. 260, l. 7.

Page 208.

28–4 (p. 209) *The fourth Canon . . . Oathes, as such*: For de Rosate and the "De Iureiurando" of the "Clementines," see p. 202, lines 21–29, and the corresponding Commentary. Clement V tried to preserve peace between Henry VII of Germany and Robert of Naples and issued his edict to that end at the Council of Vienna in 1311, in the "unicum" or only chapter of Title 9 "De Iureiurando" of the "Clementines," *Corpus Iuris Canonici*, Cols. 211–213. When Henry VII died, John XXII, who had succeeded Clement, issued his own edict claiming authority over both Louis of Bavaria and Frederick of Austria to prevent them from warring over the dead emperor's crown. See Commentary for p. 221, ll. 5–22.

Page 209.

7–17 *the first being a Constitution . . . Empire upon him*: *Decretum*, Distinction 63, Chapter 33, Col. 330; and, a paraphrase of Bellarmine's argument in Chapter 8 of Book V of the third general controversy ("De Summo Pontifice"),

COMMENTARY 395

Vol. I, *De Controversiis*, Col. 1071, in which the origins of imperial power and its relationship to papal authority are discussed.

22–28   *The first whereof . . . credit of Canon law*: For the Donation of Constantine recorded in Distinction 96 of *Decretum*, see Commentary, p. 72, ll. 17–24. The "Palea" or "Palaea" originated in the name of "Paucapalea" who was supposedly the principal commentator or "glosser" to add marginal commentaries to Gratian's work (see Commentary for p. 192, l. 2–p. 193, l. 8).

Page 210.

6–8   *Azorius tells us . . . no such title*:   In Azor's *Institutionum Moralium*, Vol. 2, Part 2, Book 4, Chapters 19 ("De Potestate Romani Pontificis in rerum temporalium administratione"), and 20 ("De iis, quae iure Canonico, & Divino, sunt Romano Pontifici reservata").

16–22   *to keepe this Order . . . of all Creatures*: *Decretum*, Distinction 16, Chapter 2, Col. 23, on Augustine, *Confessions*, Book 3, Chapter 8.

31–1   (p. 211) *the tenth Distinction . . . their jurisdiction*:   *Decretum*, Distinction 10, Chapter 1, Cols. 30–31, Nicholas I, in the mid-ninth century, citing Gregory I and Innocent I, writes to his bishops in council.

Page 211.

7–13   *A Pope writing . . . in this world*: *Decretum*, Distinction 22, Chapter 1, Cols. 99–100, Nicholas II, pope from 1058 to 1061, writing to Archbishop Guido of Milan about his simoniacal and married clergy.

22–27   *Gelasius writes . . . upon Theodosius*: *Decretum*, Distinction 96, Chapter 10, Col. 468, records Gelasius II, pope from 1118 to 1119, writing to Anastasius VIII, the eastern emperor. For Ambrose and Theodosius, see Commentary for p. 246, ll. 18–25.

32–5   (p. 212) *follow Gratian . . . or murderer*: *Decretum*, Cause II, Question 7, Cols. 702–703, with reference to Nathan, the prophet who reproved David for his adultery with Bathsheba in 2 Samuel 12.1–16.

Page 212.

6–15   *second Question . . . by Angels*:   *Decretum*, Distinction 9, Question 2, Chapter 7, and its gloss, for the epistle of Gelasius II to the bishops of France; then, the canon "Fratres" of Pope Sixtus II, pope from 257 to 258, to the bishops of Spain; finally, Nicholas I, in his letter to Michael the Emperor, *Decretum*, Cause 9, Question 3, Chapter 10, Col. 876.

19–33   *The Canon Alius . . . places it appeares*:   Gelasius II writing to the eastern emperor Anastasius, *Decretum*, Cause 15, Question 6, Chapter 3, Cols. 1083–1084 (see Commentary for p. 73, ll. 25–34); Cause 7, Question 1, Chapter 14, Col. 824, for the letter of Pope Gregory I to the Bishop of Etherium, and Chapter 17, Col. 827, for the letter of Pope Zacharias to the Archbishop Boniface of Mainz.

Page 213.

5–7 *a Canon or two . . . from Oathes*: *Decretum*, Cause 15, Question 6, Chapter 2, Cols. 1082–1083, Pope Nicholas II writing to the bishops of France.

18–14 (p. 214) *famous Canon of Gregory . . . damage of the subject*: *Decretum*, Cause 15, Question 6, Chapter 4, Col. 1084, which Gregory VII issued against Henry IV of Germany; and Cause 11, Question 3, Chapter 103, Cols. 958 and 959, with the glossary annotations for "Quoniam" and "Temperamus." The great man in Donne's passage is the Spanish Jesuit Avila. In his *De Censuris*, Part II, Chapter 6, Disputation 11 ("De casibus in quibus licitum est communicare cum excommunicato"), Doubt 9, p. 166, Avila qualifies the application of Gregory VII's canon "Nos sanctorum," by stressing that Catholics who are strong believers do not necessarily disobey the Church if they enter into contact with excommunicated Catholics under special circumstances. The word "innovation" in Donne's text refers to religious practices that are not modelled on scriptural prototypes or precedents but only on human invention (as in *Conclave* the following year, pp. 11–15).

Page 214.

15–26 *his Successor . . . Henry in Germany*: Gregory VII was succeeded by Pope Victor III (1086 to 1087), and Victor was succeeded by Urban II. The "man" to whom Donne is referring is Urban, elevated to the cardinalate by Gregory in 1078, who served as papal legate in Germany. While in Germany, Urban called the synod of Quedlinburg to anathematize the anti-pope Guibert of Ravenna (Clement III), and to excommunicate the German Emperor Henry IV who supported him and who refused to implement Gregory's decrees against lay investiture. Binius, *Concilia Generalia*, Vol. IV, Tome 3, Part 2, pp. 1092–1093, and *Decretum*, Cause 15, Question 6, Chapter 5, Col. 1084, narrate the conflict.

27–34 *In the 25 Cause . . . other examples*: *Decretum*, Cause 25, Question 1, Chapter 11, Cols. 1440–1441. The monastery built over the tomb of the sixth-century saint Medardus at the gates of the city of Soissons, was awarded a privilege of deposition by Gregory I (see Commentary for p. 71, l. 21–p. 72, l. 2). In his *Tractatus De Rebus Ecclesiae* (Bologne, 1606), Part II, Book III, Chapter 5, No. 17, p. 564, the sixth-century Benedictine monk of the Monastery of Saint Severinus in Naples, Alphonso Villagut, lists Alexis I Comnenus (b. 1048; d. 1118), emperor of the east in Constantinople, and Basil II (b. c.958; d. 1025), who was likewise eastern Roman emperor, as having granted similar privileges to monasteries.

COMMENTARY

Page 215.

7–12 *To prove the Popes . . . a Matrimoniall cause*: To the bishops of Exeter and Winchester and to the abbot of Hereford Abbey in Chapter 4, and to the bishops of London and Worcester in Chapter 7 of Title 17 "Qui sunt Filii Legitimi," of Book 4; to the bishop of Oxford and again to the bishop of Worcester and abbot of Hereford in Chapter 17 of Title 29 "De Officio et Potestate Iudicis Delegati" of Book I, of the "Liber Extra" or "Decretals of Gregory IX," in *Corpus Iuris Canonici*, Cols. 580–582, and 131.

27–30 *Another Canon, not much . . . matters extended*: A letter of Innocent III addressed in May 1202 to the duke of Zahringen (see Commentary for p. 202, l. 30–p. 203, l. 17), Chapter 13 "Per Venerabilem," Title 17, Book 4, "Liber Extra," *Corpus Iuris Canonici*, Col. 583. Innocent's canon does not identify the King of France in question, who was Philip II Augustus.

Page 216.

29–31 *Translation . . . transgressour of the sentence*: The argument from Deuteronomy is actually one used by Innocent III in his canon "Per Venerabilem," Col. 585 of *Corpus Iuris Canonici*, "Liber Extra," Book 4, Title 17, Chapter 13.

Page 217.

15–17 *Victoria frame . . . Temporall matters*: The Dominican jurist Victoria comments on the limitations of Innocent III's power over temporal affairs in *Relectiones*, "Relectio I, De potestate Ecclesiae prior," Section VI, No. 2, p. 38. The canon to which Donne is referring is Innocent's bull "Per Venerabilem" of 1202 (see Commentary for p. 202, l. 30–p. 203, l. 17). Ten years later, in 1212, Innocent excommunicated John Lackland for refusing to accept his choice of Stephen Langton as Archbishop of Canterbury, and ordered Philip Augustus of France to carry out the deposition and excommunication orders. John capitulated to the pope and on 13 May 1213, surrendered England as a fief to the papacy.

18–27 *Another Canon of the same Pope . . . directed him*: Innocent III, in the canon "Novit ille," about King Philip II of France, Chapter 13, Title 1 "De Iudiciis," "Liber Extra" of Gregory IX, Book 2, Cols. 194–195.

35–1 (p. 218) *Parsons say true . . . by reason of a Statute*: Parsons discussed Elizabeth as holding onto her title of queen of England by statute of Parliament rather than by what he considered to be genuine hereditary right, in *The Judgement of A Catholic English-man* against the Oath of Allegiance in 1608, pp. 35, 90–91, and *passim*; in *An Answere to . . . Syr Edward Coke* of 1606, Chapter 3, p. 55 and Chapter 15, pp. 365–366; and finally in his pseudonymously published tract *Elizabethae Reginae Angliae Edictum . . . Ad Idem Edictum Responsio*, p. 6 and pp. 66–68 (1594 edition), where he signed himself Andrea Philopatrus.

Page 218.

4–6 *In the title . . . one particular place*: In the "Decretals of Gregory IX" or the "Liber Extra," Book V, Title 39 "De Sententia Excommunicationis," Chapter 49 on the canon of Honorius III, pope from 1216 to 1227, "Noverit fraternitas tua" in 1224, and Chapter 53 on his canon "Gravem venerabilis," in 1225, in *Corpus Iuris Canonici*, Cols. 738–740.

15–7 (p. 219) *That the Canons . . . from the Emperour*: In Innocent III's canons in his dealings principally with Henry VI of Germany, recorded in Chapter 20 "Quoniam Omne" of Title 26 "De Praescriptionibus" of the "Liber Extra" or "Decretals of Gregory IX," *Corpus Iuris Canonici*, Col. 314, which Bellarmine interprets in Chapter 6, Book V of the third general controversy of *De Controversiis*, Vol. I, Col. 1064. The "Nota quod" and "Tam canonica" in Donne's marginalia derive from the wording of the canon.

Page 219.

10–25 *also by a Canon . . . lawes in that point*: Emerich King of Hungary from 1196 to 1205, son of Bela III, was repeatedly contested by his brother Andrew II (b. 1175; d. 1235). Emerich accepted Innocent III's authority to consolidate his power over his own throne, but was repeatedly in conflict with the pope over crusades, and lost part of his kingdom in the Fourth Crusade. He was succeeded by his young son, Ladislaw III, who reigned only a few months before dying at the age of five, leaving the throne finally to Andrew who reigned till his death in 1235. In Chapter 6 or "Licet" of Title 34 "De Voto, et Voti Redemptione," in Book III of "Liber Extra," *Corpus Iuris Canonici*, Cols. 474–475.

26–4 (p. 220) *The Canon Solitae . . . veritatis*: Issued by Innocent III to the eastern emperor, Chapter 6 "Solitae benignitatis" of Title 33 "De Majoritate et Obedientia," Book I of the "Liber Extra," *Corpus Iuris Canonici*, Cols. 159–162. The "Tanquam" later in Donne's margin is in the wording of the canon.

Page 220.

16–22 *In the Canon Gravem . . . remained Excommunicate*: See Commentary for p. 218, ll. 4–6. To the bishops of Pisa and Siena in 1225.

27–29 *next volume of the law . . . this point*: The "Sextus Liber Decretalium" of Boniface VIII (see Introduction, p. xxxiii). The canon is "Grandi non immerito" of Innocent IV in Chapter 2, Title 6 "De Supplenda Negligentia Praelatorum," Book 1 of "Liber Sextus," *Corpus Iuris Canonici*, Cols. 38–39. It was addressed to the barons and other nobles of Portugal, in 1245, during Innocent's quarrel with Sanches II of Portugal over his marriage and the rule of his kingdom.

COMMENTARY 399

Page 221.

5–22 *Extravagants of Pope John . . . bound to them*: John XXII, in an edict of 13 March 1317, during a quarrel between Louis of Bavaria and Frederick of Austria over Henry VII's throne, in which Louis took the upper hand, declared that all imperial jurisdiction ultimately rested with the papacy. On 23 March 1324, John excommunicated Louis who, in 1328, marched upon and entered Rome and was crowned emperor by Sciarra Colonna. Colonna then had John declared a heretic in Louis' name and had him replaced on 22 May by the anti-pope Nicholas V. Nicholas was eventually set aside, and Louis later recognized John. The canon "Si fratrum" in Chapter 1 of Title 5 "De religiosis domibus" in John's "Extravagantes," *Corpus Iuris Canonici*, Cols. 279–280.

31–8 (p. 222) *unam Sanctam . . . prove that Conclusion*: "Unam Sanctam" was the bull which Pope Boniface VIII issued against Philip the Fair of France on 18 November 1302. Philip had first attacked papal power on the grounds that he had at will the right to tax ecclesiastical property and later the right to arrest clerics and bring them to secular trial. Boniface first replied with the bull "Ausculta Fili" and a year later with "Unam Sanctam." Donne is using the words "essential" and "formal" in their Thomistic and Aristotelian sense, "essential" referring to substance or content, and "formal" to shape as a principle of being. In Chapter I "Unam Sanctam," of Title 8 "De Majoritate et Obedientia," Book I, "Extravagantes Communes," *Corpus Iuris Canonici*, Cols. 319–320. See Introduction, p. xxxiii.

Page 222.

14–7 (p. 223) *That he cannot be saved . . . Tis well, Tis enough*: Three passages in Sâ's *Scholia in Quatuor Evangelia*, p. 487 for the "literal sense" of John 10.16, and pp. 388 and 389 for the two references to Luke 22.38 (the third reference at the end of Donne's paragraph appears to be to Luke 2.35 but is also to Luke 22.38). The arguments of the native of Euboea and eleventh-century Byzantine exegete Theophilact, and of the three church fathers Saints Chrysostom, Ambrose and Basil about the same passages in John and Luke, which Donne mentions, are quoted in Sâ's commentaries on pp. 487, 388, 389.

Page 223.

8–11 *Bellarmine is our warrant . . . this place*: Donne is paraphrasing Bellarmine in Chapter 5, Book V ("De temporali dominio et potestate eiusdem Pontificis") of the third general controversy, Vol. I, *De Controversiis*, Col. 1061. In addition to Boniface VIII, Bellarmine also mentions Bernard of Clairvaux (b. Fontaines, Dijon, 1090; d. Clairvaux, 1153) as a mystical, rather than a literal interpreter of the scriptural passage on the two swords, Luke 22.38.

35–37   *made another Decree . . . making of that Decree*:   Clement V's canon "Meruit charissimi" concerning Philip of France and Boniface VIII, in Chapter 2 of Title 7 "De Privilegiis," Book 5, "Extravagantes Communes," *Corpus Iuris Canonici*, Col. 391.

Page 224.

15–21   *the last Volume . . . as matter of faith*:   In Book I of "Liber Septimus," in Title 2 "De Rescriptis, et Mandatis Apostolicis," Chapter II (which begins with the "Licet felic." of Donne's marginalia) recording Leo X's canon "Statua et ordinationes" of March 1518; and Chapter III recording Clement VII's canon "Personae excommunicantur" of January 1533, *Corpus Iuris Canonici*, Vol. II, Cols. 5–8.

Page 225.

6–7   *Droict du Canon . . . against him*:   The Constable of France was Anne, duke of Montmorency (b. Chantilly, 1493; d. Paris, 1567), Henry II's general who defended Provence against Charles V, was defeated at the battle of St. Quentin, and won but was mortally wounded at the battle of St. Denis.

Chap. XI
Page 226.

1   *to there*:   The twin columns of faults and corrections in Donne's list of *errata* mistakenly invert "this" and "there." They list as correct the "this" which already appears in both "The Table" and the chapter heading, and as faulty the "there" (for the modern "their") which was meant to replace it. In copy L^3, an anonymous contemporary hand has altered the supposedly correct "this" in the chapter heading to "there."

9   *lay more*:   The text's original phrase reads: "challendge more obedience, and lay a more obligation" (quarto p. 322). The present text drops the indefinite article "a" to give the sentence grammatical and internal sense. The "more" cannot be the substantive adjective "more," normally spelled "mair," which was already archaic in Donne's day, but which would have made sense of the "a."

22–27   *For they say their Buls . . . too little*:   Augustinus in *De Emendatione*, Book II, Dialogue 2, p. 190 ("a Latine bulla pro tumore . . . aut cum in vestibus auream bullam"); and Gregorius in *Syntagma Iuris Universi* (Frankfurt, 1591), Book XV, Chapter 42, No. 10, p. 192 ("anulo piscatoris . . . unde et brevia dicuntur apostolica"). See Commentary for p. 30, ll. 15–23.

COMMENTARY 401

Page 227.

5-21 *For Navarrus testifies . . . to transgresse them is sin*: First, the section, "Quae lex humana obligat ad mortale," on the binding power of human law on the individual conscience, in Chapter 23, No. 48, of Navarrus' *Manuale*, p. 555, hence Donne's use of the phrase "ad mortale"; the Dominican Thomist Cajetan died in 1534 well before the opening of the Council of Trent in 1545, so that Donne is referring to his widely-known hope about the power of civil law over the consciences of men as described by Navarrus, rather than to an actual intervention by Cajetan at Trent; Navarrus cites Cajetan's *Commentaria*, 2.2.q.186, Art. 9, Col. 4, on Aquinas' *Summa*, an argument on the binding power of the law of princes which Cajetan proposed before the fifth Lateran Council in 1512 (and not at Trent). Second, the French moral theologian-lawyer Carnin on the failure of civil laws to bind consciences absolutely all the time in Part I, Chapter 8, p. 45 of *De Vi*; on the human character of civil laws in I, Chapter 1 ("Exodium ab usu et necessitate legum in Republica"), p. 4; and on the equally binding powers of divine and human laws in Chapter 3, pp. 10–11. The Catholic adversary who opposed Carnin's ideas was Bellarmine in Chapter II of *Controversiae De Laicis*, but the latter work appeared many years before Carnin's *De Vi*.

Page 228.

29-13 (p. 229) *Alexander the third . . . a Bishop sonne*: In Chapter 2, "Ex parte Conventrensis," and Chapter 5, "Si quando aliqua," of Title 3 "De Rescriptis" of Book I of the "Liber Extra," *Corpus Iuris Canonici*, Cols. 10–11. Also, for Pope Lucius III, pope from 1181 to 1185, Chapter 11 "Ad audientiam nostram," Col. 13.

Page 229.

22-6 (p. 230) *Eugenius the fourth . . . of the beginning thereof*: Eugenius IV (b. Venice, c.1383; d. Rome, 1447), pope from 1431, dissolved the Council of Basel on 18 December 1431, and intended to move it to Bologna, but at the second session on 15 February 1432, the council fathers refused to disperse. Eugenius issued a number of other bulls against the fathers but, because of the force of the conciliar movement and of his own inflexibility, he was soon compelled, on 15 December 1433, to withdraw his dissolution with the bull "Dudum sacrum."

Page 230.

19-25 *So Stephen the sixth . . . cast it into Tiber*: In *Summa Conciliorum*, p. 414^v, Carranza records this incident: in January of 897, Stephen the VI or VII (there being two numberings for the popes called Stephen as Stephen II in 752 died four days after his election without being consecrated), pope from 896 to 897, ordered, under imperial instigation, the exhumation of the body of his predecessor,

Pope Formosus (b. 816; d. 896). During his reign from 891, Formosus showed considerable intransigeance towards the eastern Church and refused to accept the validity of the ordination of priests by Patriarch Photius of Constantinople (b. c.810; d. 895), thus provoking the hate of the eastern emperors who were attempting to consolidate their authority over Rome. At the exhumation of Formosus' body, as Binius records in *Concilia Generalia*, Vol. 3, Part 2, p. 1047, Col. 1, and at the end of a revolting trial in the presence of the corpse, the three fingers which Formosus had used in the consecration of priests were cut off, his body was some days later thrown into the Tiber, and all priests whom he had ordained were compelled to be re-consecrated. A monk withdrew the body from the river and re-interred it, and it was yet re-buried in St. Peter's with full honour in 897 by Stephen's successor Pope Romanus (b. Gallese, Civita Castellana, n.d.; d. Rome, 897). Romanus also abrogated all the acts against Formosus. However, Sergius III (b. Rome, n.d.; d. 911), who was consecrated pope in 904, immediately rescinded Romanus' abrogation and declared anew all of Formosus' ordinations of priests invalid. Formosus' body was once more exhumed and what was left of it was this time decapitated (Carranza, p. 415^r).

Page 231.

3–10 *the common opinion . . . are in Gratian*: Pope Eugenius III (b. Pisa, n.d.; d. Tivoli, 1153), elected pope in 1145, encouraged Gratian's work on the *Decretum* at the Council of Treves in 1148. The "learned bishop" is Augustinus of Tarragona writing in "Dialogus III" of Book II of his *De Emendatione*, p. 196, on Eugenius' support of Gratian's work.

12–23 *Bellarmines fashion . . . Paleotus they have done*: The first book "De Beatitudine et Canonizatione Sanctorum" of the seventh general controversy of Bellarmine's *De Controversiis* follows the "De Purgatorio," and Donne mistakenly called the former work by the title of the latter in his marginal note as he did also on p. 148, but quoted its book and chapter numbers correctly. Donne is paraphrasing the passage in Bellarmine's Chapter 9 of "De Beatitudine" entitled "Credendum esse, Pontificem non errare in Sanctorum canonizatione" (Col. 1946), which deals with the power of the pope to bind the faith of Catholics in the celebration of canonized saints, and at the same time to leave them free in conscience to believe in their miracles. The passage is immediately followed by a discussion on faith in the church's declarations and on the power of the pope to require it in cases of recognized martyrs, with reference to Eugenius and Gregory (Col. 1947). For Boniface IX, Martin V, Saint Brigid and Paleotus, see Commentary for p. 93, ll. 18–25.

34–21 (p. 232) *the Jesuite Tannerus . . . to the practise thereof*: Donne is paraphrasing both Tanner and his quotations from Aquinas, in his *Defensionis Ecclesiasticae Libertatis*, II, Chapter 9 "Deteguntur Breviter Alii . . . errores circa Potestatem Ecclesiasticam summi Pontificis," pp. 300–301, on the means available to the papacy to avoid error. Donne mentions that Tanner is citing "schoolmen," but except for a closing reference to Saint Bernard, Tanner's quotations are all from Aquinas' *Summa* II.II. Question I, 10.

Page 232.

26–30 *It is good Doctrine . . . recourse to the Superiour*: In Part I, Chapter 10, pp. 55–56, of Carnin's *De Vi*.

Page 233.

4–14 *Their immediate Superiours . . . complaint against the first*: The appellants' controversy involving a number of secular priests in England and the archpriest George Blackwell and the Jesuits broke out in 1597 when the question of naming a head to the English-Catholic organization became urgent as its church hierarchy had died out. A number of secular priests, headed by William Bishop and Robert Charnock, were refused a hearing by the acting head, Robert Parsons, as the struggle spread out from among secular priests in liberty and reached into the ranks of those imprisoned in Wisbeck. Bishop and Charnock went to Rome to plead their case and to protest the nomination of Blackwell who in 1602 published a document forbidding all appeal from his decisions. The first papal brief to which Donne refers was that of 6 April 1599 confirming the naming of the archpriest, and the second was that of 5 October 1602 which limited the power of the archpriest but which did not concede to the demand of the appellant priests that Catholics be forbidden to plot against the crown. "Subreption" meant the concealing of facts to obtain some preferment or concession.

30–35 *Navarrus upon good grounds . . . the truth*: In the section on the vaingloriousness of the disobedience of subjects to their superiors, entitled "De Inobedientia filia vanaegloria," in Chapter 23, No. 38, of Navarrus' *Manuale*, p. 552, but also in No. 37, which Donne does not annotate (see Commentary for p. 23, ll. 12–17).

Page 234.

18–21 *Might he not . . . so great inconveniences*: The reference to the eleventh-century Archbishop of Canterbury Saint Anselm is an unannotated citation from the fourteenth-century Niem's little volume on the oaths of cardinals in the conclaves of papal elections entitled *Nemoris Unionis*, Tract IV, on the powers of popes and church councils, Chapter IX, p. 345: "Et sicut minimum inconveniens Deo est impossibile, secundum Anshelmum." The origin of the quotation is the *Tractatus De Concordia . . . Cum Libero Arbitrio*, Question I, Chapter 2, No. 123 and Col. 509 in Vol. 158, Series 2, of the Migne *Patrologia, Opera* of St. Anselm.

31–6 (p. 235) *That generall Rescript . . . locall interdict*: For the canon of Clement VII, see Commentary for p. 224, ll. 15–21; and for Pius V's "Bulla Coenae," p. 50, ll. 10–13.

Page 235.

22–24 *It was whilst Nero . . . it was not so*: The *Annales* of the Roman historian Tacitus (b. c.56; d. c.120).

30–1 (p. 236) *Dante, and Bocace, and Petrarche . . . Court of Rome*: In Chapter 12 of the "Appendix ad Libros De Summo Pontifice" of the *Opuscula* of *De Controversiis*, Bellarmine responded in detail to the "trium auctorum . . . Dantis, Petrarchae, atque Bocacij," who had attacked the papacy and the court of Rome, but who had nevertheless remained Catholic thinkers. The response runs from Chapter 12 to the very end of the last chapter, 24, of the "Appendix." It cites at length passages from Dante's *Inferno* (Cant. 1, 3, 11, 19, 22), *Purgatorio* (2, 11, 13, 18, 19, 20, 26) and *Paradiso* (Cant. 1, 3, 5, 6, 11, 12, 13, 18, 24, 25, 29, 30, 32); from Petrarch's *De Vita Solitaria* (Book II) and *De Otio Religiosum* (Book I); and from Boccaccio's *Decameron* (for example, the first fable). Petrarch (b. Arezzo, 1304; d. Arqua, 1374), spent the last years of his life in monastic seclusion at Padua, and the two works which Bellarmine quotes date from his years of inner struggle leading to this seclusion, and so they praise Catholicism. The work comparing Rome to Babylon, which Donne mentions, is the canzona *Rerum Vulgarium Fragmenta* No. 138, and dates to Petrarch's early life. The first quatrain of this canzona reads: "scola d'errori et templo d'eresia, / già Roma, or Babilonia falsa et ria," ll. 2–3, *Canzoniere*, intro. G. Contini (Turin, 1964), p. 193.

Page 236.

6–17 *Pope Stephen and Cyprian . . . the purest times*: In a section dealing with the errors of the popes, in Chapter 7 of Book IV ("De potestate Romani Pontificis in causis spiritualibus") of the third general argument of Vol. I of *De Controversiis*, Cols. 967–968, Bellarmine treated of the third-century dispute between Pope Stephen I (b. Rome, n.d.; d. Rome, 257), and the Bishop of Carthage Saint Cyprian (d. Carthage, 258). The dispute between Stephen and Cyprian centered on the re-baptism principally of the followers of the anti-pope Novatian, but also of Christians born of lapsed Catholics during the Decian persecution in Carthage. Cyprian, who was a convert to Christianity, was probably baptised when he was already in middle age, about the year 246, and he held rigorously to the view that all heretics, no matter what their provenance, had to be baptised anew on their entry or re-entry into the Church. His position was strongly endorsed by two synods of African bishops in Carthage in the spring and in September of 256. Stephen immediately retorted with a decree stating that re-baptism was not necessary and that the Roman practice of laying of the hands on the repentant baptised heretic was sufficient for his reinstatement in the Church. Donne's description of Cyprian "amongst the blessed Saints" in spite of his defiance of Stephen is a reference to the presence of his name, due to his martyrdom by pagan Roman decree, both in the canon of the then new Mass of the Council of Trent and in the principal current Roman martyrologies, including the ninth-century *Martyrologium* of Saint Ado of Vienna (Migne, *Patrologia Latina*,

Vol. 123, Col. 170, and Vol. 124, Cols. 467–468), the new Renaissance *Martyrologium Romanum* of Baronius, pp. 407–408, and its translation by "G.K." as *The Roman Martyrologe*, p. 303, under 14 September.

19–10 (p. 237) *not denied by Baronius . . . sanctitie of this reverent man*: Donne's second example of an excommunicated bishop who nevertheless became a Catholic saint is that of Saint Ignatius Patriarch of Constantinople (b. c.799; d. 877). In *Annales*, Vol. 5, Tome X, No. 42, p. 623, Baronius records his history briefly in his account of the reign of John VIII from which Donne gets the story. Among ninth-century popes, John had remarkably good relations with the Slavs and sought to bring the Bulgarian church back under the direct jurisdiction of Rome, as it had fallen under the rule of the Patriarchs of Constantinople, but Ignatius continued the policy of retaining the Bulgarian church under the eastern see, which had already merited him to be deposed for nine years in 867. The period of conflict between him and John came at the end of his otherwise relatively peaceful life, as the papacy tried to keep the Church free of the conflict among the warring factions of the eastern emperors. As Donne mentions, John cited Leo IV who in 854 refused to confirm Ignatius' deposition of Gregory bishop of Syracuse because he had acted without his prior consent. John thought the deposition correct but the methods by which it was effected were incorrect because they lacked initial papal approval.

Page 237.

11–16 *Dioscorus the Bishop . . . hath observed*: Dioscorus (d. 454), Patriarch of Alexandria, was deposed and excommunicated at the third session of the Council of Chalcedon in 451 for supporting the Christological doctrines of the heretic Eutyches, and he retaliated by excommunicating the pope Saint Leo I: *Decretum*, Distinction 21, Chapter 9 "In tantum hac," Col. 99, and Cause 24, Question 2, Chapter 6, Cols. 1413–1414. The "late Neophite" was the ex-Protestant Theophilus Higgons (b. Chilton, ?1578; d. Maidstone, 1659) who turned Catholic and became a controversialist with his tracts explaining his adherence to Rome, in his "Try Before You Trust," appended to his *The First Motive* (Douai, 1609), Part I, Chapter I, No. 3, p. 32, refuting his Protestant adversaries' use of Bishop Grosseteste of Lincoln's difficulties with the papacy in 1251 to support their cause.

19–28 *when Bartholinus . . . confiscated their estates*: Bartholinus of Placentia in Northern Spain argued in the Curia of Pope Urban VI during the crisis of the Great Western Schism which began in 1378, that a strongly deficient pope might be put under the tutorial of a curator. The event is recorded by the fourteenth-century historian of the schism, von Niem, in his *De Schismate*, Book I, Chapter 42, pp. 46–47. As the listening cardinals, among them the most influential of the Curia, tended to agree with Bartholinus, Urban, whose capacities were being put in doubt flew into a rage, "Unde statim Papa furore accensus," and he threw six of the leading cardinals into prison and confiscated their property.

29–33 *But if . . . the Popes Breves*: Donne is citing the section on the excommunications conducted under the "Clementines" of Pope Clement V, as discussed in Navarrus' *Manuale* on penance and penitence. Donne's marginal note cites *Manuale*'s sub-heading in No. 147 of Chapter 27 (and not 21, as his original text states), p. 793, over the section dealing with the Popes John XXII and Nicholas III, and the excommunication of Saint Anthony. Sylvester Mazolinus Prieras, the early sixteenth-century anti-Lutheran, was the author of *In Presumptuosas Martini Lutheri Conclusiones de potestate papae Dialogus* (Wittenburg, 1518), a short tract dealing with the power of the papacy, Sig. Biii^v.

Page 238.

12–32 *their great Victoria complaines justly . . . as they list*: Donne's four references are to Victoria's *Relectiones*, "Relectio IIII, De Potestate Papae et Concilii." In No. 6, p. 139, Victoria complains that dispensations from the Roman Curia are causing scandal. In No. 12, pp. 148–149, Victoria cites Gregory I as an example of a holy pope capable of being deceived as much as any other man (and Donne agrees with Victoria), because Gregory was profoundly respected universally for his humility. It was Gregory who began the conversion of England by sending Saint Augustine to evangelize it. Then, in No. 12, p. 149, Victoria writes that Catholics coming to Rome for dispensations may claim them by law and need not expect to have to obtain them from the Roman Curia by extortion ("et oporteat adhibere magnas machinas ad extorquendam unam dispensationem, et non sint Romae expectantes, an quis velit petere dispensationem omnium quae legibus sanctia sunt"). Finally, in the last reference, No. 12, p. 151, the "87" in Donne's marginalia may be the page number in the edition he used, but which edition is unclear. The three popes, Linus, Clement I and Sylvester I, to whom both Victoria and Donne refer, date to the very earliest years of the Roman Church. Linus is historically accepted as the Apostle Peter's immediate successor, and so was the second pope, ruling from ?64 to ?79. In his reign, of course, church councils did not exist, and Linus' rule was a direct apostolic pontificate. Linus may have been immediately succeeded by Saint Clement I, who is ascertained to have ruled in the very early years of the church, and who was the author of an epistle to the Corinthians. Clement restored order in the Corinthian church during its rebellion against its rulers, by urging obedience to the presbyters whom the letter appears to identify with bishops. The third pope is probably Sylvester I, in the era of Constantine the Great. Sylvester reigned during the first Council of Nicaea, in 325, but it is not certain that Constantine actually arranged beforehand with Sylvester the calling of the council. Sylvester did, however, send delegates to the Council.

Page 239.

2–6 *Naturall Reason . . . would never receive it*: Azor's *Institutionum Moralium*, Vol. 2, Part 2, Book 4, Chapter 5 ("De Romani Pontificis electione"), p. 258, Cols. 1–2.

10–29 *Fran. à Victoria . . . or outward things*: Donne cites four Catholic authorities on the limitations of the powers of the papacy. The first is Victoria, in his *Relectiones*, "Relectio IIII," "De Potestate Papae et Concilii," No. 17, p. 155, who argues that an unjust command from a pope may be disobeyed, "non teneretur parere." The second Catholic authority is the Jesuit Avila whose major work, *De Censuris Ecclesiasticis*, on the church's powers to censure Christians, had only just been published. In Part II, Chapter 6, Disputation 11, Doubt 9, p. 156, Avila limits the powers of Gregory VII's bull "Nos Sanctorum" that was intended to prevent Catholics in good standing with the Church from associating with excommunicated Catholics (see p. 214 for the same reference). The third authority is yet another moral theologian, Castro, who, in his tract on the power of punitive laws, *De Potestate Legis Poenalis*, Book I, Chapter V, Document 1, writes, "cum id sine scandalo fieri poterit, optimè fiet," Col. 527. The fourth authority is the Jesuit Comitolus, in *Responsa Moralia*. Donne calls him the "late unentangler" because of the very recent appearance of his book on moral theology that sought to resolve the unanswered moral question on the powers of the papacy in the works of other writers like Navarrus in *Manuale*, which was published in English translation by Donne's printer Stansby in 1609, and which therefore was already known to Donne's readers. Navarrus' *Manuale* dealt particularly with problems of conscience, without necessarily offering solutions for practical everyday life, whereas Comitolus' work proposed immediate day-to-day solutions, such as in the question of assistance at the rites of the Greek orthodox church which Donne singles out, Book I, Chapter 47, Col. 2.

Page 240.

21–22 *Court of Rome . . . Cyprian, Ignatius*: See Commentary for p. 236, l. 19– p. 237, l. 10.

Chap. XII

Page 241.

7 *Communis sponsio*: From Book I, Title 3, Law 1, in Justinian's *Corpus Iuris Civilis, Digestorum*, on the definition of law.

22–31 *a Lawyer sayes . . . interpretative perjury*: De Puteo in *De Syndicatu*, p. 481, No. 4 in the sub-chapter "Dicit constitutio" of the chapter "Inquisitio"; and, Marcellus Donatus, the Count of Ponzan, in his commentary on Chapter 16 of Suetonius Tranquillus' *In Galba*, in his *Scolia Sive Dilucidationes Erudissimae . . . Historiae Romanae Scriptores* (Venice, 1604), p. 527.

Page 242.

11–16 *There is no warre . . . one of them*: A paraphrase of Gretser in *Apologeticus . . . Societatis Iesu Theologi* (Ingolstadt, 1600), Chapter 5, p. 176.

19–34 *The Jesuites . . . swallowed and digested*: The Jesuit who professes to avoid useless oaths more than perjury is the anonymous author of the short tract, *Spongia*, pp. 79–80, which defends the Jesuits against causing civil unrest in Poland ("quod quis inter eos dixerit, iureiurando fortius habent, iusiurandum verò, periurio deterius vitant"). Donne's next authority for this attribute of Jesuits towards oaths is Serarius in Article 34, Chapter 4 of Book 3 on the heresy of the Essenes in *Trihaeresium*. Serarius describes how the Essenes refused to take oaths on the grounds that their word was their honour (p. 216), and, in Article 37, he also lists the Essenes' twelve exceptions to this rule; the fifth exception to which Donne refers states the Essenes' promise never to inflict harm on their civil magistrate (p. 218). Then, Donne cites two Catholic authorities, de Puteo and Gigas, in such a way as to attack the Jesuits and support the Oath of Allegiance. De Puteo's quotation is from *De Syndicatu*, pp. 989–990, No. 18 "An stetur" in the chapter "Tortura." Gigas' statement on the presence of the venom of the fathers in their sons is from No. 2 of Question 5, Rubric 1 of Book III of his *Tractatus de Crimine Laesae Majestatis*, p. 358.

Page 243.

7–23 *When Paulus 4. . . . & fide Catholica*: The oath referred to in Donne's text is that recorded in the canons of the Council of Trent, Session 7, Chapter 1, and elaborated upon in Session 14, Canon 1, and Session 21, Chapter 1, as mentioned in Azor's *Institutionum Moralium*, Vol. 1, Part 1, Book 2, Chapter 9, Col. 133. The oath was expanded upon by Paul IV in his decretal included in Gregory XIII's collection and published in the *Corpus Iuris Canonici* in 1582, and thus became an integral part of canon law, as Donne notes. Azor mentions texts by the Scottish Catholic turned Lutheran theologian, Alexander Alesius (b. Edinburgh, 1500; d. Leipzig, 1565), and Saint Bonaventure (b. Bagnorea, 1221; d. Lyons, 1274), which do not follow the Council of Trent's view of the sacrament of Confirmation; by the German medieval theologian Hugo of Saint Victor (b. Hartingham, Saxony, c.1096; d. Paris, 1141) and again by Bonaventure that diverge from the Tridentine view of the sacrament of Extreme Unction; and, finally, by the canonist Henri de Suse, the Bishop of Hostie, and Durandus of Saint Pourçain, the Dominican scholastic, that did not concord with Trent's description of marriage as a sacrament. Azor lists Bonaventure and not Peter Lombard with Hugh of Saint Victor on Extreme Unction as Donne's original text mistakenly mentions. Donne may have momentarily confused Lombard and Bonaventure, as both Bonaventure and Durandus wrote commentaries on Lombard's *Sentences*.

COMMENTARY

24–28 *that oath . . . upon his body*: Baronius' *Responsio Apologetica Adversus Cardinalis Columnae* was intended to counter the pro-Spanish Cardinal Colonna's attack on his *De Monarchia Siciliae*. Baronius took the opportunity of expressing his distraught feelings over the considerable number of disputes between the papacy and secular rulers being brought before the Roman Court, and he reminded Colonna that it was the duty of a cardinal to honour rigorously his oath of allegiance to the pope in spite of the emotional strains it put upon clerics like themselves.

29–5 (p. 244) *oathes framed . . . bound to any other*: The approved Catholic statement on the oaths of emperors was contained in the chapter on the coronation of emperors ("De coronatione Imperatores") in the ceremonial book *Sacrarum Cerimoniarum*, pp. 63^v and 64^r. The same volume contained the description of the oaths made by a duke at his creation, to which Donne also refers at the end of his paragraph (in the chapter "Ordo Servandus in Creatione novis Ducis a Paulus II institutus," which is the opening part of the sixth section of the work, entitled "De Pluribus Benedictionibus," pp. 75^v and 76^r). The Catholic oaths were designed to protect the Church's clerical hierarchy at the same time as they bound Catholic secular rulers to one another.

Page 244.

6–9 *Gregory the seventh . . . Alleageance to the Pope*: Richard the Norman prince of Aversa captured and became prince of the fortress town and region of Capua in the see of Campania near Naples in 1058, and Capua's history was thereafter linked to that of the kingdom of the two Sicilies and also to the see of Rome. In his oath of allegiance to Pope Gregory VII on 7 October 1073, only months after the latter became pope, Richard swore fealty not only to Gregory but to any emperor whom Gregory and his successors would ask him to obey. Gregory exacted this oath of Richard of Capua and other Italian princes to consolidate his power against the German emperors and their anti-popes. Centuries later Capua was one of the bishoprics assigned to Bellarmine.

10–15 *the Emperour . . . Oath of Alleageance*: Henry VII was elected German emperor in 1309 with the support of Pope Clement V who, as Binius relates in *Concilia Generalia*, feared the extension of French power if Charles of Valois became king of Germany, Vol. IV, Tome 3, Part 2, pp. 1509–1510. Henry, who had himself crowned in Rome in an attempt to consolidate his power, abjured his oath to Clement in reaction to his decretals in his "Liber Clementinarum."

17–26 *they had not given . . . obnoxious matters*: Berenger of Tours (b. Tours, c.999; d. St. Cosme, 1088), theologian of the school of Chartres, who in the ninth-century controversy about the real presence of the body of Christ in the Eucharist denied the transubstantiation. His recantation is recorded in Distinction 2 of "De Consecratione" in *Decretum*. The Czech theologian Jerome of Prague, (d. Constance, 1416), was condemned to death at the nineteenth session of the Council of

Constance in 1415 for defending John Huss, and was burned at the stake in 1416 after he went back on his recantation.

27–1 (p. 245) *though Castrensis say . . . this Absolution*: Castrensis is Alphonsus à Castro, whom Donne elsewhere refers to by his Spanish name. In Chapter 3, "De differentia inter propositionem haereticam, et erronem, et temerariam, et scandalosam," of Book I, of *De Iusta Haereticorum Punitione* (Salamanca, 1557), Cols. 19 to 25 in the 1578 Paris edition of the *Opera Omnia*, Castro argues out the questions of the number of heresies for which a heretic can be tried by the inquisition, and whether he must renounce all heresy or only the actual heresy for which he stands accused.

Page 245.

21–30 *clause of the Oath . . . the imminent dangers*: In Justinian's *Digestorum*, Book XII, Title 2 "De Iureiurando," Cols. 348–349, of Vol. I, *Corpus Iuris Civilis*, for the discussions of the various terms and conditions of oaths. The "Leagues" would also have connotations with the union of the Catholic parties against the Huguenots in sixteenth-century France.

Page 246.

18–25 *Though the Metropolitane . . . Bishop in his Diocesse*: The Jesuits whom Donne has in mind are Bellarmine and the lesser known Avila whose *De Censuris* defended the right of popes and bishops to excommunicate members of the church and secular rulers. To support his argument, Donne uses Avila's illustration of the excommunication of the Emperor Theodosius I by Saint Ambrose of Milan for having ordered the slaughter of seven thousand Thessalonians in 390 to avenge the murder of Roman officials. The passage in Bellarmine's *De Controversiis*, Chapter 3, Book V, third general argument, Vol. I, Col. 1055, uses Ambrose's pronouncements on excommunication but does not specify the incident with Theodosius. Power wielded "Iure divino" was exercised by divine right, and power wielded "Iure commune" was exercised by civil law (Schardius, *Lexicon*, p. 494).

27–29 *Bishop Excommunicate . . . their jurisdiction*: The Council of Trent, Session XXIV, Chapter 6, in *Sacrosancti Concilii Tredentini Canones, et Decreta . . . Bassani*, 1600, p. 165, imposed restrictions on the right of bishops to conduct certain forms of excommunication and absolution. Donne is drawing a distinction between natural law, which is of divine origin and may not be changed, and positive law, which is man-made and may be waived, as in the case of the excommunicated ruler whose subjects have nevertheless the obligation to defend him.

Page 247.

36–1 (p. 248) *suspition and doubt . . . relation to the Pope*: Albericus Gentilis, in *Disputationes tres: I. De libris Iuris Canonici. II. De libris Iuris Civilis. III. De Latinate veteris Bibliorum.*

Page 249.

31–32 *Bellarmine . . . lacked strength*: Chapter 7, Book V ("De temporali dominio et potestate eiusdem Pontificis"), third general controversy of *De Controversiis*, Vol. I, Col. 1067.

Page 251.

23–32 *wee will joine . . . disturbed thereby*: In Azor's *Institutionum Moralium*, Vol. 2, Part 2, Book 4, Chapter 5 ("De Romani Pontificis electione"), p. 258. Donne's translations of "law of nature" and "Christian Commonwealth" are renditions of Azor's terms, "ius naturalis" (natural law) and "Reipublica Christiana" (Christian Republic), while "natural reason" is a literal translation of his "ratio naturalis."

Page 252.

20–22 *Bellarmine and Baronius . . . faith in England*: Bellarmine denies the pope's direct power in temporal affairs in Chapter 4 ("Papam non habere ullam temporalem iurisdictionem directe"), but affirms indirect power for him in Chapter 6 ("Papam habere temporalem potestatem indirecte"), Cols. 1057–1060, 1062–1065, of Book 5, of "De Summo Pontifice" in Vol. I, *De Controversiis*, whereas Baronius everywhere affirms the papacy's right at direct intervention in the field of secular power, *De Monarchia Siciliae*, pp. 34–35, *passim*; and in his address to the Roman consistory on 17 April 1606, in *De Venetorum Excommunicatione*, Sig. A^{2r,v}. The reference to Sergius and Mohamet is obscure. There were many Turkish sultans called Mohamet, as well as the Islamic prophet himself, and the only record of a Sergius having contact with Islam, but not in the context of a heresy, is Pope Sergius II (b. Rome; d. Rome, 847), elected in 844, who witnessed the Saracen sack of the territory surrounding Rome in 846. However, if Sergius is an error and should read Sylvius, the reference becomes immediately clear, and points back to Donne's earlier reference in *Pseudo-Martyr* to the contest of jurisdiction between Mohamet II, otherwise known as Morbizan the Turk, and Pius II, whose pre-election name of Aeneas Sylvius, Donne has also otherwise cited in the work. (See Commentary for p. 92, ll. 18–26, and p. 118, ll. 11–13). Sylvius, or Pius II, sent Mohamet a letter requiring him to accept his jurisdiction, and Mohamet sent him one back informing him he had no jurisdiction over him at all, *Epistola ad Morbisanum*, pp. 97–99.

25–15 (p. 253) *Dubium speculativum . . . he doubt of the cause*: Two prominent Catholic moral theologians: first, Carbo in his *Summa Summarum*, Tome I, Part I,

Book V, Chapter XIV ("An contra conscientiam dubiam, et propriam opinionem agere liceat"), pp. 154–155; Donne's quotation "That where one part is certain," is a translation of Carbo's dictum on the examination of speculative doubt; second, Victoria in *Relectiones*, "Relectio VI," "De iure belli," No. 25 "Tertia propositio" and No. 27 "Tertium Dubium," on the royal secrecy necessary for the just conduct of war.

Page 253.

36–7 (p. 254) *these Absolutions . . . Subjects of the Church*: See Commentary for p. 207, ll. 20–24, and p. 259, l. 20–p. 260, l. 7. The canon "Pastoralis cura" issued by Clement V at the Council of Vienna, in Chapter 2 of Title 11 "De Sententia et Re Iudicata" in Book II of the "Clementines," *Corpus Iuris Canonici*, Cols. 214–215.

Page 254.

8–11 *Emperours . . . his oath*: *Corpus Iuris Civilis*, Vol. I, *Digestorum*, 50 "Ad Municipalem et de incolis," 1, Law 38. Marcus Aurelius and Lucius Verus were co-emperors of the Roman empire from 161 until the latter's death in 169.

13–14 *your Canons . . . absolving an oath*: *Decretum*, Cause 15, Question 6, Chapter 2, Cols. 1082–1083.

Page 255.

14–20 *for Castrensis . . . properly concerning faith*: Donne attacks the argument, in two Catholic works, that the power of the pope and of dogma rest upon tradition as well as upon the Bible, first in *Adversus Haereses*, Book I, Chapter 5, Col. 24, *Opera Omnia*, where Castro claims that some heretical tenets may be refuted on the grounds of church tradition only and not of the Scriptures; and, second, *Defensionis Ecclesiasticae Libertatis* (1602), II, Chapter 9, pp. 298–299, where Tanner argues that one of Paul V's adversaries in the Venetian controversy made the mistake of believing that the Pope was infallible in all things and not only "in rebus fidei.' But, Tanner quickly adds (hence Donne's paraphrases) that "nihil proprie circa fidem statuitur, sed mores conformantur," or, that customs of the church govern some things even if papal infallibility does not.

26–33 *Which faith wee beleeve . . . Resurrection of Christ*: Donne's numbering of Leo I's and Augustine's letters is of uncertain origin. Leo's letter No. 95 dated 20 July 451, "Ad Pulcheriam Augustam," appears to be his source. Augustine's letter (also usually numbered 52) touching on the significance of the word "Catholic" in the description of the Church, was written to his cousin Severinus in about the year 399.

COMMENTARY

Page 256.

8–10   *Bellarmine ... fidei*:   From Chapter VIII of Book III "De Veritate Corporis Domini in Eucharistia," of the fourth general controversy "De Eucharistia" of *De Controversiis*, Vol. II, Col. 702: "Quod si illa est haeresis, contraria erit veritas fidei, proinde veritas a Deo revelata."

13–30   *Castrensis foresaw . . . Priest had consecrated*:   Of Donne's three Catholic authorities who recommended restraint in the declaration of heresies, the first is Castro at the beginning of Chapter 7, Book I, of his *Adversus Omnes Haereses*, *Opera Omnia*, Col. 37; the second is the Bolognese Alphonsus Bovosius, a canon regular of the Holy Saviour, the author of the widespread *Disputationes Catholicae* (Bologne, 1607) on the heretical character of certain Greek Orthodox beliefs, with reference (cited by Donne) to the rigorousness of the Greek Orthodox Church towards the use of bread in the Communion, Book II "De Ritu Romanae Ecclesiae Consecrandi in Azimo Disputatio," pp. 58–61; the third is Azor in Chapter 15 ("Quo tempore, et qua ratione Graecorum Ecclesia a Romani Pontificis potestate, et Jurisdictione se subtraxerit"), Book IV, Part 2 of *Institutionum Moralium*, Vol. 2, p. 282, on two of the points disputed by the Roman and Greek Churches, Holy Communion, which Donne mentions, and baptism. Azor cites the judgment of Innocent III, elevated to the papacy in 1198, at the fourth Lateran Council in 1215 (Chapter 4) that the members of the Greek Church were free to use the species of bread or wine or both for communion, provided that they respected the practice of Roman rites on their altars as well. The reference to Eugenius IV is to his statute at the Council of Florence in 1438, *Corpus Iuris Canonici*, "Liber Septimus," Book 1, Title 1, Chap. 2, Cols. 2–3.

Page 257.

15–19   *Leo the tenth . . . many Heresies*:   The fifth Lateran Council between 1512 and 1517, first under Julius II at the seventh session which began on 17 June 1515, second under Leo X, Giovanni di Medici (b. Florence, 1475; d. Rome, 1521), who was elected pope on Julius' death in 1513. The conflicting passages in Bellarmine's writings are, first, Chapter 8 of Book III of the third general controversy ("De Sacramento Eucharistiae"), Vol. II, of *De Controversiis*, Col. 702, and, second, Chapter 3 of Book IV of the third general controversy, Vol. I, Cols. 960–961. In the latter chapter, Bellarmine names four major heretics, Pelagius, Priscillianus, Jovianius and Vigilantius, who were condemned by popes Innocent I (in 417), Damasius (c. 381) and Siricius (392), and by Saint Jerome (c. 406), respectively.

20–27   *this liberty . . . had determined*:   In his dedication in *De Vitis*, Sig. A⁵ᵛ, the French theologian Prateolus or du Preau supported the pope's power to condemn heretics, by citing the fourth-century bishop of Salamis Saint Epiphanius' *Panarion*, and several works by Augustine of Hippo. In *Adversus Omnes Haereses*, Book I, Chapter 7, Col. 40, Castro talks of the pope's freedom to issue decrees without conciliar approval. Conrad of Schlusselberg in Westphalia was a Protestant theologian and author of a commentary on Calvin's theology, *Theologiae Calvinistorum* (in one edition, Frankfurt, 1592), and of a treatise on the anti-trinitarians, the Manicheans and the sacraments, *Haereticorum Catalogus* (Frankfurt, 1597). Du Preau's *De Vitis* was prefixed by a catalogue of heretics and heresies indexed century by century since the beginning of the Christian era, and, with Schlusselberg's *Catalogus*, lies behind Donne's phrase of the "catalogues of heretics." Danaeus was the French Protestant commentator on Augustine's *De Haeresibus* (Geneva, 1576).

27–31 *Parliament of Paris . . . Hereticall*: In its order for the execution of Jean Chastell for the attempted assassination of Henry IV, the Parliament of Paris declared that his statement that the king was a false Catholic, which he had supposedly learned from the Jesuits, was "scandaleux" and "seditieux." The Parliament ordered to be condemned as "heretiques" all Frenchmen who repeated it, Sig. A-2, *Apologie Pour Iehan Chastel*. (See Commentary for p. 127, l. 37–p. 128, l. 11.)

Page 258.

9–14 *men still doubt . . . of this Sacrament*: The passage from the Jesuit Francis Suarez (b. Granada, 1548; d. Lisbon, 1617) originates in Alvin of Tours' *Tractatus De Potestate Episcoporum*, Chapter 23, Number 5, p. 136^v. However, the passage is not a quotation but a paraphrase of Suarez' argument in Numbers 3, 4 and 5 of Section 4, of Disputation 28 in his *Disputationes Theologica*, on *De Poenitentia Sacramento*, in Volume 22 of *Opera Omnia*, ed. Charles Breton (Paris, 1856), p. 587. The section deals with the church's delegation of the power to hear confession and to ordain clerics.

21–32 *the other obstacle . . . proceede against Heretiques*: The fourth Lateran Council of 1215 presided over by Pope Innocent III, recorded in Chapter 13 of Title 7 "De Haereticis" of Book 5 of the "Liber Sextus" of Gregory IX, *Corpus Iuris Canonici*, Cols. 642–644, and the German emperor in question was Frederic II. Also, the *Decreta et Constitutiones Summorum Pontificum Ad S. Inquisitionis Officium penitentia*, Florence, 16[??].

Page 259.

1–8 *If a temporall Lord . . . furtherance thereunto*: *Corpus Iuris Civilis*, Volume II: *Codicis Iustiniani*, 1, 5, Law 4, Col. 62.

20–7 (p. 260) *solemne Clementine Pastoralis . . . so large a power*: The canon "Pastoralis cura" of Clement V in Chapter 2 of Title 11 "De Sententia et Re Iudicata," Book II of the "Clementines," *Corpus Iuris Canonici*, Cols. 210–213.

COMMENTARY 415

Page 260.

19–21 *Iure Divino . . . him therewith*: In "De Iure Canonico," Title 2 on "De Iure Divino," *Corpus Iuris Canonici*, Cols. 1–2.

Page 261.

6–17 *the Romans dealing . . . Drusius is Heresie*: In *Institutionum Moralium*, Vol. 2, Part 2, Book 4, Chapter 15, p. 283, dealing with the reasons for the schism of the Greek Church from the Roman Church, Azor recounts the story of the short-lived union of the two churches negotiated by the east Roman Emperor John VIII (sometimes VI or VII), surnamed Palaeologus (b. 1390; d. 1448), at the Council of Florence in 1439. John, who ruled from 1423, had subsequently to receive the complaints of the Greek Church against the Roman Church during their brief unhappy union. Donne is citing Azor's distinction betweeen errors "a Fide & religione," or between "Orthodoxall truths" and "matter of faith," that John used to try to keep peace between the two churches. Serarius took the Protestant theologian, John Drusius (van den Driesche) the Elder (b. Oudenarde, Flanders, 1550; d. Franeker, Friesland, 1616) to task on the same point of orthodoxy and faith in the last chapter of *Trihaeresium* ("An haereticus Io. Drusius?"), p. 326, and questioned Drusius' use of the argument on the basis of faith. Donne was familiar with the protracted quarrel between Serarius and Drusius, but he may be mistaking the moment of Drusius' self-defence. Drusius wrote the commentary on the Scriptures *De Hasidaeis Libellus* and Serarius attacked him in the *Trihaeresium* which Donne is here quoting (pp. 329–330). Only then did Drusius issue his first self-defence, in his *Responsio ad Serarum de Tribus Sectis* in the next year, 1605. A few months later in the same year, Serarius answered Drusius with *Minerval divinis Hollandiae*, and Drusius then issued his second self-defence with *Ad Minerval Responsio* in 1606. Both defences by Drusius followed, and neither preceded the publication of the Jesuit's *Trihaeresium*.

20–21 *Bellarmine designes Heresie . . . in the world*: Book III, Chapter 8 of "De Sacramento Eucharistiae," *De Controversiis*, Vol. II, Col. 702.

25–29 *for sometimes but fifteene . . . Imperiall Clergy*: Venericus Bishop of Vercelli, in *De Unitate Ecclesiae Conservanda, et Schismate, Quod Fuit Inter Henricum IIII Imp. Rom. et Gregorium VII. Pont. Max.*, in Schardius, *De Jurisdictione* (Basel, 1566), pp. 63–64, *passim*.

Page 262.

6–7 *Bellarmine . . . manie Heresies*: Bellarmine's treatment of the four possible kinds of heresy in Chapter II of Book IV of the third general controversy, Vol. I, *De Controversiis*, which Donne satirized earlier, p. 101.

15–17 *Augustine . . . new opinions*: From Augustine's *De Utilitate Credendi*, Chapter XIV, No. 31, but the paraphrase also suggests perhaps more exactly the closing passage of No. 32.

25–6 (p. 263) *The Imperiall Law . . . your Simancha*: The "Imperial Law" described by the emperors Theodosius I and Valentinian in *Corpus Iuris Civilis*, Vol. II, *Codicis Iustiniani*, 1, 14, Law 5, Col. 80. To attenuate the Roman use of the word heresy against the Oath of Allegiance and its acceptability to English Catholics, Donne cites the writings of his Catholic foe, the canonist Simancha, as an ally for the first time in *Pseudo-Martyr*. In Chapter 24, "De propositionum qualitate," on the quality of a proposition in a theological debate, No. 20, of *Enchiridion Iudicium*, p. 90, Simancha writes that a proposition may sometimes contain several ambiguous or contradictory significations, so that experts disagree on its pertinence to heresy, and the word heresy itself is subject to various meanings.

Page 263.

9–12 *Bartholus . . . opinione*: Bartolus of Saxoferrato, the fourteenth-century jurist, in his commentary on Justinian's *Digestorum*, *Interpretum Iuris Civilis*, Vol. III, "Ad Lib. XXXIX Digest.," II, No. 18, p. 71. However, in *Corpus Iuris Civilis*, Vol. II, *Digestorum*, 39, Title 2 "De Damno Infecto," Law 13, Col. 1380, the number within the law entry is 14 and not 18.

15–23 *Councell of Constantinople . . . to sinne*: The second Council of Constantinople called in 553 by the Emperor Justinian to condemn the pro-Nestorian "Three Chapters" on the presence of two persons, human and divine, in Christ. The council promulgated a list of fourteen "Anathemas" of which the thirteenth contains a list of declared heretics, and the name of the third-century biblical exegete Origen concludes the list. Then, a reference to the "De Peccatione Originale," No. 5 of the fifth session of the Council of Trent which began on 17 June 1546, *Sacrorum Conciliorum*, Vol. 33, Cols. 28–29.

24–34 *A great Casuist . . . unjust matter*: The great "Casuist" and "Countreyman" is the contemporary Suffolk Benedictine Sayer who became a monk at Monte Cassino. In Book III, Chapter 8, ("De lege poenali, eiusque institutione, et interpretatione"), Nos. 6 and 7, pp. 169–170 in the Venice edition of 1615 of his *Casuum Conscientiae*, Sayer argues that law must at once possess the clear sense given to it by the law-maker to avoid personal interpretation and ambiguity ("Nam, si verba legis unam solum significationem habeant, illa tunc sequenda erit, nec pro libito interpretari licebit"), but that it must also be adaptable to different places and customs while maintaining its integrity.

Page 264.

9–15 *Sayrs rule . . . common sense*: A free translation of the opening of No. 7, Chapter 8, Book III, p. 170, *Casuum Conscientiae*: "una verò sit propria significatio, altera vero inpropria, tunc interpretatio legis faciè da erit iuxta illam significationem, in qua constat ex aliqua verisimili ratione legislatorum voluisse verba intelligi."

18–20 *when S. Paul sayes . . . left out the wordes*: The official Latin vulgate edition of the Bible omitted the words "in vobis" after "haereses," and reads for 1 Corinthians 11.18 (in the 1590 Roman edition, and 11.19 in the derivative 1605 Antwerp edition): "Nam oportet & haereses esse." The Protestant German Latin edition, prepared principally by the Reformer Francis Junius, includes the phrase but replaces the reference to heresy with the weaker word "contention": "Oportet ut etiam contentiones sint inter vos." In "Defendentur Loca ex prima Epistola ad Corinthos," in *De Controversiis*, Vol. I, II, 14, Col. 748, Bellarmine upheld the vulgate translation, and Gretser defended Bellarmine's position in *Defensio* II, 14.

29–32 *Leo 10., in a formall Decree . . . had erred*: In the "Bulla Apostolica . . . contra errores Martini Lutheri" of the Medici pope Leo X in 1520, in Binius' *Concilia Generalia*, Vol. V, Tome IV, p. 654.

Page 265.

1–9 *the Canons in the law . . . be an heretique*: *Decretum*, Distinction 12, Chapter 6 "Consuetudinem laudamus," Col. 39, in a canon of Pius I; "De Consecratione," Distinction 4, Chapter 72 "Si non sanctificatur," Col. 2004; and "In septimo," in Gregory XIII's corrected "Correctores Romani" in *Corpus Iuris Canonici*.

11–18 *From which sense . . . to heresie*: Tertullian, the second- and early third-century African church father, in *Adversus Marcionem*, Book II, Chapter 2 (Oxford, 1972), Vol. I, p. 91; and in *De Oratione et De Virginibus Velandis*, Chapter 1 (Antwerp, 1956), pp. 39–40; and Castro in *Adversus Haereses*, Book I, Chapter 9, in Col. 54 of the *Opera Omnia*.

19–26 *the Jesuits themselves . . . and haeresi proximae*: Two examples of "proximate heresy" by Jesuits that would allow English Catholics to take the Oath of Allegiance without having to fear that they would become "actual" or "proper" heretics: 1) Bellarmine's distinction between "propriè haeretica" and "haeresi proxima," from the concluding paragraph listing the four possible kinds of heresy of Chapter II of Book IV, third general controversy of Volume I, Col. 153, *De Controversiis*; and 2) Gretser's defence of this distinction in "Appendix Prima ad librum contra Pappam," *Controversiam Roberti Bellarmini . . . Defensio*, Vol. I, Book I on "De Libris Canonicis, éorumque numéro," Col. 366, in a passage dealing with the validity of the decretals of the church. Unlike "proper heresy," "proximate heresy" was tolerated by the church because its ideas had never been formally condemned by a pope or a church council. Donne's original marginal notation of "Interim" points to the wrong paragraph in Gretser's text, and is altered here to "Haec" which it should read. Gretser's text also refers to Saint Augustine, and Donne had this passage in mind in his immediately preceding citation and annotation to the controversialist Castro, with references to Saint Augustine on heresy.

27–11 (p. 266) *the Schoolemen somtimes . . . have committed*: In the *Summa Theologica*, II.II. Quest. 2, answer to objection 2, Aquinas refers to Jerome's Commentaries on the Epistle to the Galatians, Chapter 5. Jerome argues that it is heretical to give a different interpretation to the Scriptures than that sanctioned by the Holy Spirit. Next, four Catholic commentaries that support this position: 1) the fourth-century Palestinian bishop of Salarnis Saint Epiphanius' *Contra Octoaginta Haereses Opus, Panarium* (Basel, 1560), which describes several Gentile heresies such as the Platonists, Pythagoreans, Stoics and Epicureans, and Jewish heresies like the Pharisees, Scribes, Sadducees and Samaritans (pp. 5–6, 13–15). 2) The author-theologian Bernard of Luxembourg's *Catalogus Haereticorum* (Cologne, 1522), as cited by Castro in his *Adversus Haereses*, Book I, Chapter 9 ("Quis sit dicendus haereticus"), Col. 54, *Opera*; Bernard (b. Strassen, n.d.; d. 1535), listed the Arab philosopher mathematicians Averroes and Avicenna as heretics for promulgating false gods, *Catalogus* (Cologne edition of 1523), Sig. E^{3v}, E^{4r}. 3) The *Chronica Majora* of Britain by Matthew of Paris, the monk of St. Albans (b.c. 1200; d. St. Albans, 1259), whose chronicle spanned the history of England from creation to 1259. Paris recounts the story of the death of the Bishop of Lincoln, Robert Grosseteste, to whom Donne is referring, in 1253 (pp. 400–401 in the 1872 London edition, Vol. II, ed. H.R. Luard). As Grosseteste lay dying, he derided the heretical conduct of his colleagues to John of Saint Giles, and Donne's quotations are a translation from Paris' Latin rendition of this death scene. 4) Venericus Bishop of Vercelli's *De Unitate Ecclesiae Conservanda*, which tells the story of Gregory VII's struggle with the Emperor Henry IV.

Page 266.

32–34 *as when men . . . can beleeve them*: Pope Leo I in a letter dated 12 August 447, to Turribo Bishop of Asturicens, *Sacrorum Conciliorum*, Vol. 5, the letter beginning in Col. 1188, but the reference being to its concluding Chapter 17 in Col. 1201.

FINDING LIST

The Finding List that follows is intended primarily to be used for information by readers of *Pseudo-Martyr*. It refers them to the page and line numbers of the text in the notes in the Commentary, for one and sometimes for two references to each item. Its purpose is not to serve as an exhaustive index or a complete or select bibliography. The list notes the titles of publications and documents (such as papal decrees) and the names of the principal authors and historical figures that are often pivotal to understanding the meaning of Donne's lines.

Acacius, Bishop of Constantinople; p. 45, ll. 1–6.
Acosta, Christopher; p. 105, ll. 10–15.
Acosta, Joseph or **José;** p. 105, ll. 10–15.
Alvarez, Alphonse Guerrero; p. 46, ll. 7–16.
Arcadius, emperor; p. 52, l. 27–p. 53, l. 16.
Adrian I, pope; p. 39, ll. 7–24.
Adrian II, pope; p. 67, l. 23–p. 68, l. 3.
Adrian VI, pope; p. 21, ll. 3–12.
Aelianus. *Variae Historiae;* p. 17, l. 35–p. 18, l. 2.
Agatho, pope; p. 193, l. 32–p. 195, l. 23.
Albert the Great; p. 148, l. 26–p. 149, l. 3.
Alberus, Erasmus. *The Alcoran of the Bare-foot Friers;* p. 80, ll. 18–29.
Albizzi, Bartholomaeo Degli. *Liber Conformitatum;* p. 80, ll. 18–29.
Alexander III, pope; p. 82, ll. 16–18; p. 148, l. 26–p. 149, l. 3.
Allen, William, cardinal; p. 177, l. 31–p. 178, l. 1.
Alesius, Alexander; p. 243, ll. 7–23.
Alma Mater, decree; p. 126, ll. 1–19.
Alvin, Stephanus de, of Tours; p. 84, l. 28–p. 85, l. 15.
Anastasius Augustus of Constantinople, emperor, p. 40, ll. 21–28; p. 42, l. 24–p. 43, l. 15.
Anastasius VIII, emperor; p. 211, ll. 22–27.
Appellants' Controversy; p. 233, ll. 4–14.
Aquaviva, Claudio; p. 50, ll. 1–8.
Aristotle; p. 30, ll. 5–8.
Audivimus, decree; see *De Reliquiis.*
Augustine of Hippo; p. 262, ll. 15–17.
Antonius Augustinus. *De Emendatione Gratiani;* p. 192, ll. 2–8.

Avila, Stephanus de; see Stephanus de Avila.
Aviso Piacevole; p. 83, ll. 4–15.
Azorius, Johann. *Institutionum Moralium;* p. 50, ll. 1–8.
Azpilcueto, Martin de, Navarrus. *Relectiones Theologicae and De Regularibus in Opera,* p. 120, ll. 3–5; *Relectio Capit Novit de Iudiciis,* p. 167, ll. 10–31; *Enchiridion sive Manuale Confessionorum,* p. 23, ll. 12–17.

Balsamo, Theodore, Patriarch of Antioch; p. 41, ll. 9–20.
Barclay, William. *De Potestate Papae;* p. 171, ll. 10–21.
Baronius, Caesar. *Annales Ecclesiastici,* p. 14, ll. 32–34; *De Venetorium Excommunicatione,* address to the Roman consistory, p. 84, ll. 6–8; *Martyrologium Romanum,* p. 23, ll. 25–26, and see Introduction, p. xvi; *Responsio Apologetica . . . Columnae and Tractatus de Monarchia Siciliae,* p. 15, ll. 1–4, and p. 60, ll. 1–12.
Bartolus of Saxoferrato; p. 124, l. 33–p. 125, l. 5.
Basil I, the Macedonian; p. 65, ll. 19–33.
Becket, Thomas. *Epistolae et Vitae,* 2 Vols.; p. 52, ll. 17–19.
Bede; p. 193, l. 32–p. 195, l. 23.
Belgian Index; see *Index Expurgatorius Librorum.*
Bellarmine, Robert; "Aviso . . . Palmieri sinto Romito," p. 104, ll. 16–20; *De Controversiis and De Verbo Dei,* p. 11, l. 30–p. 12,, l. 4; "Letter to the Arch-Priest," in English Translation, second edition of *Triplici Nodo,* p. 3,

ll. 15–16, and p. 118, ll. 2–11; *Opuscula*, p. 78, ll. 4–7, and Introduction, p. xxxiii; *Recognitio Librorum*, p. 53, l. 32–p. 54, l. 10; *Responsio . . . ad duos libros* and *Responsio ad Matthai Torti*, p. 118, ll. 2–11.

Bembo, Pietro; p. 81, ll. 23–29.

Benedict, Saint; p. 137, ll. 31–33.

Beni, Paulo; p. 89, ll. 12–29.

Berenger of Tours; p. 244, ll. 17–26.

Bernardus of Luxemberg; p. 265, l. 27–p. 266, l. 11.

Berthold V of Carinthia; p. 202, l. 30–p. 203, l. 17.

Bertram or **Bertramus**; see Ratramus.

Bertrand, Pierre. *Tractatus De Origine Iurisdictionum*; p. 139, ll. 28–35.

Beuthereus, Michael. *Fasti Hebraeorum*, p. 58, ll. 4–23.

Bibliotheca Veterum Patrum Antiquorum; p. 136, l. 27–p. 137, l. 20.

Binius, Severinus. *Concilia Generalia et Provincialia, quaecunque reperire potuerunt; item epistolae decretales, Et Romanor. Pontific. Vitae. Omnia Studio et Industria*; p. 34, l. 29–p. 35, l. 8.

Binsfeldus, Petrus. *Tractatus*; p. 95, ll. 4–14.

Blackwell, George; p. 118, ll. 2–11.

Boccacio; p. 235, l. 30–p. 236, l. 1.

Bodin, Jean. *De Magorum Daemonomania*; p. 35, ll. 9–12.

Bonaventure, Saint; p. 243, ll. 7–23.

Boniface VIII, pope; p. 53, ll. 21–30.

Boniface, Saint; p. 57, l. 35–p. 58, l. 3.

Borgia, Francis; p. 102, ll. 18–21.

Borrhaeus, Martin; p. 58, ll. 4–23.

Bosquier, Philippe. *Monomachia*; p. 18, ll. 26–30.

Bovio, Giovanni Antonio; p. 16, ll. 9–11.

Bovosius, Alphonsus. *Disputationes Catholicae In quibus praecipue Graecorum quorundam opiniones orthodoxae fidei adversae reijciuntur*; p. 256, ll. 13–30.

Bozio, Francis; p. 58, l. 33–p. 59, l. 10.

Bracena, Alphonsus; p. 136, l. 27–p. 137, l. 20.

Branchedoro, Caesar à; p. 53, ll. 21–30.

Bridgewater, John; p. 196, ll. 16–20.

Brigid, Saint; p. 93, ll. 18–25.

Brutus, Stephanus Junius; see Jonge, Johan de.

Bulla Coenae; p. 50, ll. 12–13.

Burchard of Biberach; see Ursperger Chronicle.

Cabasilas, Nilus. *A Briefe Treatise, Conteynynge a playne and fruitfull declaration of the Popes usurped Primacye*, trans. Thomas Gressop, London, 1650; p. 96, l. 34–p. 97, l. 5.

Cajetan, Saint; p. 102, ll. 12–17.

Cajetan; Tommasso de Via Gaetani; p. 11, ll. 9–26.

Campion, Edmund; p. 119, ll. 18–35.

Cano, Melchior. *De Locis Theologicis*; p. 92, l. 27–p. 93, l. 13.

Caraffa; see Paul IV, pope.

Carbone à Costacciaro, Ludovico. *Summa Summarum Casuum Conscientiae sive Totius Theologiae Practicae*; p. 168, l. 17–p. 169, l. 4.

Carloman, brother of Pepin the Short; p. 63, ll. 21–29.

Carloman, son of Pepin the Short; p. 64, ll. 17–24.

Carnin, Claude; p. 166, ll. 5–6.

Carranza, Bartolomé. *Summa Conciliorum et Pontificum*; p. 23, ll. 12–17; p. 57, ll. 17–21, and l. 35–p. 58, l. 3.

Carrerius, Alexander; p. 188, ll. 23–28.

Casaubon, Isaac; p. 92, ll. 18–26.

Cassanaeus, Bartholomew. *Catalogus Gloriae Mundi . . . In quo doctissime simul et copiosissime de Dignitatibus, Honoribus, Praerogativis, Et Excellentia Spiritum, Hominum, Animantum, rerumque caetarum omnium, quae Caelo Mari, Terra Infernoque continentur*, 1529; 1559 edition, p. 46, ll. 17–25.

Casseneuz; see Cassanaeus.

Cassianus, Johannes; p. 24, ll. 20–22; p. 101, ll. 5–9.

Castro, Alphonsus. *Adversus Omnes Haereses*, first edition Paris 1534, later edition Cologne 1539; *Opera Omnia*: 1. *Adversus Haereses*, with Appendix; 2. *De Justa Haereticorum Punitione*; 3. *De potestate legis poenalis*; 4. *Homiliae vingtiquatuor habitae ad populum Salmanticae*; 5. *Homiliae vigintiquinque in Psalmo 50*; Paris, 1578; p. 34, ll. 2–17; p. 124, ll. 20–22; p. 244, l. 27–p. 245, l. 1.

Celestine I, pope; p. 66, l. 32–p. 67, l. 2.

Celestine IV, pope; p. 206, ll. 3–27.

Celsus, Aulus Cornelius; p. 19, ll. 2–4.

Ceparius, Virgilius. *Vita B. Aloysii Gonzagae*; p. 88, ll. 30–35, and Introduction, p. xxi.

Charlemagne. *Opus . . . contra Synodum*, and *Imperialia Decreta De Cultu Imaginum*; p. 39, ll. 7–24; p. 64, ll. 17–24.

Charles II the Bald; p. 41, ll. 5–9, p. 45, ll. 14–27.
Charles V, emperor; p. 16, l. 18–p. 17, l. 6; p. 59, ll. 11–28.
Charles de Bourbon; p. 16, l. 18–p. 17, l. 6.
Chastell, Jean; p. 127, l. 37–p. 128, l. 11.
Childebert I, king of France; p. 42, l. 24–p. 43, l. 15.
Childeric III, king of France; p. 142, ll. 4–8.
Choppin, René. *Monasticon*; p. 49, l. 32–p. 50, l. 5.
Chrysostom, St. *Homiliae* and *Sermones in Opera*; p. 27, ll. 21–23.
Clark, William; p. 110, ll. 15–18.
Clavius, Christopher; p. 38, ll. 14–21.
Clement I, pope; p. 238, ll. 12–32.
Clement III, pope; p. 214, ll. 15–26.
Clement V, pope; p. 143, ll. 8–16.
Clement VII, anti-pope; p. 85, ll. 20–30.
Clement VII, pope; p. 16, l. 18–p. 17, l. 6.
Clement VIII, pope; p. 84, l. 28–p. 85, l. 15; p. 89, ll. 12–29.
Clementines; p. 143, ll. 8–16; see Clement V, pope.
Clovis I, king of France; p. 40, ll. 21–28.
Cochelet, Anastasius. *Palaestrita Honoris*; p. 92, l. 27–p. 93, l. 13.
Cochlaeus (or Dobneck), Joannes; p. 45, ll. 14–27.
Codex Justiniani, part 2 of *Corpus Iuris Civilis*; see Justinian the Great, emperor.
Codex Theodosianus; see Theodosius II, emperor.
Coke, Sir Edward. *The Fift Part of the Reports*, containing the prefatory "Of the Kings Ecclesiastical Law"; p. 9, ll. 14–26.
Colleges, English; p. 86, ll. 25–28; p. 120, ll. 3–5; p. 123, l. 29–p. 124, l. 2.
Colonna, Ascanius; p. 15, ll. 1–4, and ll. 18–31.
Colonna, Peter; p. 116, l. 32–p. 117, l. 3.
Comitolus, Paulus. *Responsa Moralia in VII Libros*; p. 176, l. 28–p. 177, l. 12.
Connestaggio, Girolamo de Franchi; p. 16, l. 18–p. 17, l. 6.
Constantine, the Great, emperor; p. 72, ll. 17–24.
Constantine VI, emperor; p. 53, ll. 16–17.
Constantinus, emperor; p. 149, ll. 3–9.
Correctores Romani; p. 48, ll. 17–25; p. 192, ll. 2–8.
Council of Agathensis; p. 192, ll. 2–8.
Council of Arles; p. 190, ll. 24–28.
Council of Aurelian, First; p. 40, ll. 21–28.

Council of Basel; p. 51, ll. 10–17; p. 229, l. 22–p. 230, l. 6.
Council of Carthage; p. 192, ll. 2–8.
Council of Chalcedon; p. 41, ll. 9–20; p. 61, l. 24–p. 62, l. 4.
Council of Constantinople, Second General; p. 263, ll. 15–23.
Council of Constantinople, Third General; p. 41, ll. 9–20.
Council of Constantinople, pseudo-; p. 39, ll. 7–24.
Council of Eliberitane; p. 34, l. 29–p. 35, l. 8; p. 121, ll. 19–24.
Council of Ephesus; p. 66, l. 32–p. 67, l. 2.
Council of Florence; p. 256, ll. 13–30.
Council of Lateran, Fourth; p. 256, ll. 13–30.
Council of Lateran, Fifth; p. 45, l. 32–p. 46, l. 6; p. 50, l. 20–p. 51, l. 7.
Council of Nicaea, First; p. 44, l. 32–p. 45, l. 6.
Council of Nicaea, Second; p. 39, ll. 7–24.
Council of Paris, First; p. 72, l. 25–p. 73, l. 7.
Council of Pisa; p. 45, l. 32–p. 46, l. 6.
Council of Toledo, Eighth; p. 193, l. 32–p. 195, l. 23.
Council of Trent; p. 90, ll. 20–23; p. 243, ll. 7–23; p. 246, ll. 27–29; p. 263, ll. 15–23.
Council of Trullo; p. 41, ll. 9–20.
Council of Vienna; p. 204, ll. 27–31.
Cowell, John; p. 184, ll. 18–22.
Crassus, Nicholas; see Giovanni Marsilio.
Cristanovic, Stanislaus. *Examen Catholicum Edicti*, Paris, 1607; p. 26, l. 33–p. 27, l. 3.
Crassus, Paris; see Grassis.
Cum ex eo, decree; p. 150, ll. 8–10.
Cyprian, Saint, Bishop of Carthage; p. 61, ll. 5–18; p. 236, ll. 6–17.
Cyril, Patriarch of Alexandria; p. 41, ll. 5–9.

Damascene, Saint John; p. 97, ll. 6–18.
Daneau, Lambert. *D. Aurelii Augustini . . . De Haeresibus*; p. 110, ll. 20–24; *De Rebus*, p. 118, ll. 2–11.
Dante; p. 235, l. 30–p. 236, l. 1.
De Digamis Non Ordinandis; p. 46, ll. 7–16.
De Iureiurando, decree; p. 137, ll. 20–25; see also Clement V.
De Majoritate et Obedientia; p. 38, ll. 8–13.
De Re Iudicata; see *De Sententia*.
De Reliquiis, Audivimus extra, decree; p. 148, l. 26–p. 149, l. 3.

De Sententia et Re Iudicata; p. 207, ll. 20-24.
D'Espence, Claude; p. 21, ll. 3-12; p. 45, ll. 14-27.
Digestorum, part 2 of *Corpus Iuris Civilis*; see Justinian the Great, emperor.
Diogenes Laertius; p. 23, ll. 20-21.
Dioscorus, Patriarch of Alexandria; p. 237, ll. 11-16.
Doleman, R.; see Parsons, Robert.
Donation of Constantine; see Constantine the Great.
Donatus, Marcellus; p. 241, ll. 22-31.
Dorotheus of Gaza, Saint; p. 136, l. 27-p. 137, l. 20.
Driedo or Driodoens, Ioannes; p. 11, l. 30-p. 12, l. 4.
Drusius the Elder, Joannes; p. 261, ll. 6-17.
Duperron, Jacques Davy. *Letter to Henri IV de Navarre* and *Réplique à la réponse du Roy de la grande Bretagne*; p. 15, ll. 11-18.

Edward IV, King of England; p. 53, ll. 21-30.
The English Martyrologe; p. 136, l. 27-p. 137, l. 20; p. 162, ll. 16-21.
Epiphanius, Saint; p. 97, ll. 23-30; p. 265, l. 27-p. 266, l. 11.
Espencaeus; see Claude d'Espence.
Estella; see Stella.
Eucherius of Lyons; p. 96, ll. 25-30.
Eudaemon-Johannes, Andreas; p. 118, ll. 2-11.
Eugenius I, pope; p. 63, ll. 2-8.
Eugenius, III, pope; p. 231, ll. 3-10.
Eugenius IV, pope; p. 51, ll. 10-17; p. 229, l. 22-p. 230, l. 6.
Eunapius; p. 56, ll. 18-26.
Eusebius Pamphilius; p. 181, ll. 2-8.
Eusebius, Bishop of Caesarea. *The Auncient Ecclesiasticall Histories*; p. 35, ll. 22-24.
Extra De Reliquiis; see *De Reliquiis*.
Extravagantes, canons; p. 192, ll. 2-8.
Extravagantes Communes; p. 192, ll. 2-8.
Extravagantes de Rescriptis; p. 40, ll. 12-20.

Fabricius, Sixtus; p. 48, ll. 17-25.
Felix II, pope; p. 149, ll. 3-9.
Felix III, pope; p. 40, ll. 12-20.
Felix V, pope; p. 118, ll. 11-13.
Ferus, Johannes; p. 91, l. 34-p. 92, l. 1.

Feuardentius, Franciscus. *Theomachia Calvinistica, sedecim Libris Profligata Quibus Mille et Quadringenti Huius Sectae novissimae errores . . . In iis Confession fidei Hugnostica, et Catechismus Calvinianus*; p. 36, ll. 2-5.
Firmilianus, Saint; p. 61, ll. 5-18.
Forestus, Petrus; p. 19, ll. 27-32.
Formosus, pope and bishop; p. 230, ll. 19-25.
Foxe, John. *Actes and Monuments*; Introduction, p. xvi.
Francis of Assisi, Saint; p. 81, l. 34-p. 82, l. 10.
Francis Xavier, Saint; p. 104, ll. 20-31.
Frederick I Barbarossa; p. 82, ll. 16-18.
Frederick II, of Germany; p. 206, ll. 3-27.
Frontinus, Sextus Julius. *Strategemata, the Stratagemes, sleyghtes, and policies of warre . . . translated into English by Richard Mowsine*; p. 19, ll. 10-11.

Galatinus, Petrus; see Colonna Peter.
Galla Placidia; p. 61, l. 24-p. 62, l. 4.
Gallonio, Antonio. *De Sanctorum Martyrium Cruciatibus*, and *De Vita . . . Nerii*; p. 58, l. 33-p. 59, l. 10; p. 94, l. 22-p. 95, l. 2.
Garnet, Henry; p. 145, ll 7-10.
Gelasius I, pope; p. 71, ll. 12-18.
Gelasius II, pope; p. 211, ll. 22-27.
Gellius, Aulus; p. 24, ll. 1-2.
Gentilis, Albericus. *Disputationes tres: I. De libris Iuris Canonici. II. De libris Iuris Civilis. III. De Latinatate veteris Bibliorum*. Hanover, 1605; p. 193, l. 32-p. 195, l. 23.
Gerson, Jean; p. 16, ll. 9-11.
Gibbons, John; p. 196, ll. 16-20.
Gigante; see Gigas.
Gigas, Hieronymus; p. 50, l. 20-p. 51, l. 7.
Glover, Robert; p. 53, ll. 21-30.
Gonzaga, Aloysius; p. 88, ll. 30-35; p. 104, l. 32-p. 105, l. 6.
Grassis, Paris; p. 50, l. 20-p. 51, l. 7.
Gratian, emperor; p. 52, l. 27-p. 53, l. 16.
Gratian, Joannes. *Decretum*; an edition containing Gregory XIII's glossary; p. 23, ll. 12-17.
Gravem Venerabilis, canon; p. 218, ll. 4-6.
Gregorius, Petrus. *Syntagmis Iuris Universi, Atque Legum Pene Omnium Gentium et Rerum Publicarum Praecipuarum*; p. 30, ll. 15-23.

FINDING LIST

Gregory I. *Epistolae*, Appendix IV, in *Patrologiae*, no. 2, Vol. 77; p. 40, l. 29–p. 41, l. 4; p. 71, l. 21–p. 72, l. 2.
Gregory III, pope; p. 57, l. 35–p. 58, l. 3.
Gregory IV, pope; p. 79, l. 31–p. 80, l. 4.
Gregory VII, pope; p. 40, l. 29–p. 41, l. 4.
Gregory IX, pope; p. 40, ll. 12–20; p. 206, ll. 3–27.
Gregory XIII, pope; p. 16, l. 18–p. 17, l. 6; p. 48, ll. 17–25.
Gregory of Valentia; p. 103, ll. 20–34.
Gretser, James. *Apologeticus*, p. 242, ll. 11–16; *Historia Ordinis Iesuitici*, p. 107, ll. 27–32; *Controversiam Roberti Bellarmini . . . Defensio*, with *Tractatus De Novis Haereticorum*, p. 11, ll. 26–30.

Haimensfeldio, Melchior. *Imperiala Decreta*; p. 39, ll. 7–24.
Hasenmiller, Elias; p. 108, ll. 23–30.
Helius, Eobanus; p. 58, ll. 4–23.
Henry II, of England; p. 149, ll. 10–21.
Henry IV, of Navarre; p. 15, ll. 11–18; p. 127, l. 37–p. 128, l. 11.
Henry, king of Portugal; p. 51, ll. 19–33.
Henry VI, of Germany; p. 202, l. 30–p. 203, l. 17.
Henry VII, of Germany; p. 83, ll. 28–30.
Herimann or Herriman, Bishop of Metten; p. 73, ll. 25–34.
Hessius; see Helius.
Higgons, Theophilus; p. 237, ll. 11–16.
Hilary of Genoa; p. 123, ll. 17–19.
Hippocrates; p. 20, ll. 11–13.
Honorius III, pope; p. 206, ll. 3–27; p. 218, ll. 4–6.
Hormisdas I, pope; p. 40, ll. 21–28.
Hotoman, or Hottoman, or Hotman; p. 11, ll. 9–26.
Hugh of St. Victor; p. 243, ll. 7–23.
Hugo the Bastard; p. 67, l. 23–p. 68, l. 3.
Huttenus, Ulrich de; p. 58, ll. 4–23.

Ignatius, Patriarch of Constantinople; p. 236, l. 19–p. 237, l. 10.
Ignatius of Antioch. *Epistolae*; p. 148, ll. 8–21.
Ignatius Loyola; p. 104, ll. 20–31; the Letter "De Obedientiae Virtute," p. 109, ll. 5–14.
Index Expurgatorius Librorum; p. 45, ll. 14–27; p. 56, l. 31–p. 57, l. 2.
Index, Spanish or Hispanic, or Quiroga's *Index*; see Quiroga.
Innocent I, pope; p. 66, ll. 13–20; p. 74, ll. 1–7.

Innocent II, pope; p. 149, ll. 10–21.
Innocent III, pope; p. 202, l. 30–p. 203, l. 17; p. 256, ll. 13–30.
Innocent IV, pope; p. 206, ll. 3–27.
Interdict, Catholic; p. 126, ll. 1–19.
Irene, empress; p. 53, ll. 16–17.
James I. "To all Christian Monarches, free Princes, and States"; *Triplici Nodo*, second English edition, p. 3, ll. 15–16, and Introduction, p. xxxvi.
Jerome, Saint. *Operum*, edited by Erasmus, Basel, 1524; p. 91, ll. 8–14; p. 125, ll. 8–14.
John IV, emperor; p. 40, l. 29–p. 41, l. 4.
John VIII, emperor; p. 261, ll. 6–17.
John II, pope; p. 61, l. 24–p. 62, l. 4.
John VIII, pope; p. 41, ll. 5–9; p. 65, ll. 19–33.
John XXII, pope; p. 38, ll. 8–13; p. 101, ll. 10–13.
John of Antioch, Patriarch; p. 41, ll. 5–9.
John Lackland; p. 217, ll. 15–17.
John of Constantinople, Patriarch; p. 181, ll. 16–27.
Jonge, Johan Junius de; p. 11, ll. 9–26.
Joyeuse, François de; p. 15, ll. 11–18.
Julius I, pope; p. 71, ll. 12–18.
Julius II, pope, Giuliano della Rovere; p. 45, l. 32–p. 46, l. 6.
Junius, Adrian; p. 56, ll. 18–26.
Junius, Franciscus; p. 91, ll. 18–20.
Justin I, emperor; p. 42, l. 24–p. 43, l. 15.
Justinian the Great, emperor. *Corpus Iuris Civilis*, 2 vols., Vol. I *Digestorum*, Vol. II *Codicis Justiniani*; p. 22, ll. 16–17; p. 42, l. 24–p. 43, l. 15.

Lapide, Joannes de; p. 49, ll. 18–20.
Languet, Hubert; see Stephanus Junius Brutus.
Laynez, Diego; p. 102, ll. 18–21.
Ledesmius, Martin; p. 91, ll. 22–33.
Leo I, emperor; p. 40, ll. 3–11.
Leo I, pope; p. 40, ll. 3–11; p. 42, l. 24–p. 43, l. 15.
Leo III, pope; p. 149, ll. 10–21.
Leo IX, pope; p. 181, ll. 16–27.
Leo X, pope; p. 50, l. 20–p. 51, l. 7; p. 257, ll. 15–19.
Liber Extra, canons; p. 46, ll. 7–16.
Liber Septimus; see *Septimes* and Gregory XIII.
Liber Sextus; p. 126, ll. 1–19.
Liberius, pope; p. 149, ll. 3–9; p. 190, ll. 24–28.
Lindanus, Wilhelm; p. 113, ll. 2–9.
Linus, pope; p. 238, ll. 12–32.

Lothario II, or Lothaire; p. 67, ll. 10-22.
Louis of Bavaria; p. 208, l. 28-p. 209, l. 4.
Louis XII, king of France; p. 45, l. 32-p. 46, l. 6.
Louis the Stammerer; p. 41, ll. 5-9.
Lucius III, pope; p. 40, ll. 12-20; p. 228, l. 29-p. 229, l. 13.
Lypsius, Justus. *Diva Virgo Hallensis Beneficia eius et Miracula fide atque ordine descripta*; p. 92, l. 27-p. 93, l. 13.
Lyra, Nicholas de; p. 51, ll. 19-33.

Machiavelli, Nicolo; p. 15, ll. 18-31.
Macrus, Nicodemus; p. 83, ll. 4-15.
Malloni, Daniel; p. 93, ll. 18-25.
Manrique, Thomas; p. 48, ll. 17-25.
Mansi, Joannes Dominicus. *Sacrorum Conciliorum*; p. 40, ll. 3-11.
Marcellus I, pope; p. 34, l. 29-p. 35, l. 8.
Mariani, Juan; p. 116, ll. 21-25.
Marsilio, Giovanni; p. 83, ll. 4-15.
Martianus, emperor; p. 40, ll. 3-11.
Martin of Tours, Saint; p. 148, l. 26-p. 149, l. 3.
Martinez, Martin; p. 97, ll. 23-30.
Mary Tudor; p. 53, ll. 21-30.
Matal, Jean; see Metellus.
Matthews, V.J. *St. Philip Neri*; p. 94, l. 22, p. 95, l. 2.
Matthew of Paris; p. 265, l. 27-p. 266, l. 11.
Matthew of Westminster; p. 163, ll. 2-10.
Mathieu, Pierre; p. 104, ll. 1-6.
Maurice, emperor; p. 40, l. 29-p. 41, l. 4.
Maximilian I, German emperor; p. 45, l. 32-p. 46, l. 6.
Maynard, John Philip. *De Privilegiis Ecclesiasticus*; p. 47, ll. 32-33.
Mazolinus, Sylvester; see Prieras.
Medard, Saint; p. 71, l. 21-p. 72, l. 2.
Medici, Lelio; p. 86, ll. 4-11.
Medina, Miguel de. *De Sanctorum Hominum Continentia . . .in quibus sacri et Ecclesiastici caelibatus origo*; p. 97, ll. 18-22.
Menghi, Girolamo. *Flagellum Daemonum*, and *Fustis Daemonum*; p. 52, ll. 4-14.
Metellus, or Matalius, Joannes; p. 30, ll. 5-8.
Methodius, Saint; p. 47, ll. 21-28.
Michael III, emperor; p. 64, l. 29-p. 65, l. 6.
Migne, J.P.; see *Patrologia*.
Monceaux, Paul; p. 148, l. 26-p. 149, l. 3.
Monita Politica; Introduction, p. xxvii, and p. 15, ll. 11-18.

Morbizan the Turk; p. 92, ll. 18-26.
More, Thomas. *De optimo Reipu*; p. 30, ll. 26-27; *Lucian*, p. 94, ll. 7-16.
Morton, Thomas; p. 11, ll. 9-26.
Muret, Marc-Antoine; p. 114, l. 36-p. 115, l. 5.

Navarrus; see Azpilcueta.
Neri, Philip, Saint; p. 58, l. 33-p. 59, l. 10.
Nicephorus, Saint; p. 156, ll. 25-31.
Nicholas of Cusa; p. 72, ll. 17-24.
Nicholas I, pope; p. 64, l. 29-p. 65, l. 6.
Nicholas II, pope; p. 211, ll. 7-13.
Nicholas V, pope; p. 221, ll. 5-22.
Niem, Theodoricus von; p. 51, ll. 10-17.
Nos Sanctorum, canon; p. 213, l. 18-p. 214, l. 14.

Oldcorne, Edward; p. 145, ll. 7-10.
Oratory, The; p. 58, l. 33-p. 59, l. 10; p. 105, l. 36-p. 106, l. 2.
Otto IV, of Germany; p. 202, l. 30-p. 203, l. 17.

Palea; p. 209, ll. 22-28.
Paleoto, Alphonso. *Historia Admiranda*; p. 80, l. 31-p. 81, l. 3.
Palladius; p. 97, ll. 6-18.
Palmieri, Giovanni Battista; p. 104, ll. 16-20.
Panormitanus; see Tudeschi.
Parliament of Bordeaux; p. 182, ll. 12-20.
Parliament of Paris; p. 127, l. 37-p. 128, l. 11.
Parsons, Robert. *An Answere to the Fifth Part of Reportes Lately set forth by Syr Edward Cooke Knight, the Kinges Attorney generall concerning The ancient and moderne Municipall lawes of England, which do apperteyne to Spirituall Power & Jurisdiction*; p. 9, ll. 14-26; *A Conference About the Next Succession To the Crown of England*, by R. Doleman, pseudon., p. 161, ll. 15-17; *Elizabethae Reginae*, by Andrea Philopatri, pseudon., p. 217, l. 35-p. 218, l. 1; *The Judgement of a Catholicke English-man*, p. 160, l. 31-p. 161, l. 4; *A Treatise of Three Conversions*, p. 162, ll. 16-21, and Introduction, p. xviii; *A Treatise of Mitigation*, p. 11, ll. 9-26.
Pastoralis Cura, canon; p. 253, l. 36-p. 254, l. 7.
Patrologia Latina et Graeca; p. 40, l. 29-p. 41, l. 4.
Paul I, pope; p. 72, l. 24-p. 73, l. 7.

Paul III, pope; p. 39, ll. 7–24 ; p. 102, ll. 12–17.
Paul IV, pope; p. 102, ll. 12–17.
Paul V. "Breves" or "briefs" of 1605 and 1606, English translation, second English edition of *Triplici Nodo*; p. 84, ll. 6–8; see Introduction, p. xxxv.
Paul Deacon. *Utropii Historiae Romanae Liber X His Additi Paulli Diaconi Liber LIX*; p. 32, ll. 12–18.
Pelagius I, pope; p. 42, l. 24–p. 43, l. 15.
Pelagius II, pope; p. 181, ll. 16–27.
Pelargus or Storch, Christopher; p. 113, ll. 13–15.
Penal laws; p. 157, ll. 9–17.
Pepin III the Short, king of France; p. 63, ll. 21–29.
Pesantius, Alexander; p. 139, ll. 28–35.
Peter, Friar; p. 136, l. 27–p. 137, l. 20.
Petrarch; p. 235, l. 30–p. 236, l. 1.
Petrejus, Theodore. *Bibliotheca Carthusiana*; p. 103, ll. 20–34.
Philip I, of France; p. 68, l. 20–p. 69, l. 12.
Philip II, Augustus, of France; p. 215, ll. 27–30.
Philip IV the Fair, king of France; p. 53, ll. 21–30.
Philip V "le long," king of France; p. 50, ll. 1–8.
Philip II, king of Spain; p. 16, l. 18–p. 17, l. 6; p. 187, ll. 20–32.
Philip III, king of Spain; p. 17, ll. 18–28.
Philip of Swabia; p. 202, l. 30–p. 203, l. 17.
Photius, Patriarch; p. 230, ll. 19–25.
Pierius; see Valeriano.
Pius II, pope. *Epistola ad Morbisanum Turcarum*, with Morbizan's (or Mahomet II's) reply; and *Epigrammata*; p. 92, ll. 18–26; p. 118, ll. 11–13.
Pius IV, pope; p. 169, l. 25–p. 170, l. 23.
Pius V, pope; p. 48, ll. 17–25.
Plato; p. 30, ll. 26–27.
Plessis du Mornay, Philippe du; p. 11, ll. 9–26.
Pliny the Elder; p. 25, ll. 6–9.
Polanus, Amandus; p. 38, ll. 14–21.
Polycarpe, Saint; p. 148, ll. 8–21.
Pontianus, pope; p. 51, ll. 10–17.
Prateolus; see Gabriel du Préau.
Préau, Gabriel du; p. 34, ll. 2–17.
Prierias, Sylvester; p. 237, ll. 29–33.
Prudentius, The Poems of; p. 34, l. 29–p. 35, l. 8.
Pulpilly, Cyriac K. *Caesar Baronius*; p. 15, ll. 1–4; Introduction, p. xxvii.
Puteo, Paris de; p. 84, l. 28–p. 85, l. 15.

Quiroga, Gaspar; p. 56, ll. 18–26.

Raccolta degli Scritti; p. 16, ll. 9–11; p. 104, ll. 16–20; Introduction, p. xxv.
Raemond, Florimond de; p. 21, ll. 12–19.
Rastell, John. *An Exposition of Certaine Difficult and Obscure words, and terms of the laws of this realm. Newly amended and augmented, both in French and English*; p. 184, ll. 18–22.
Ratio Studiorum; p. 50, ll. 1–8.
Ratramus, Bertram. *De Corpore Sanguine*, Geneva, 1541; p. 45, ll. 14–27; p. 96, ll. 14–16.
Regulae Societatis Iesu; p. 84, l. 28–p. 85, l. 15; p. 106, l. 30–p. 107, l. 5.
Ribadeneira, Pedro de. *Historia Ecclesiastica*, p. 102, ll. 18–21; *Illustrium Scriptorum*, p. 102, ll. 18–21; *Vita Ignatii Loiolae . . . Jacobi Laynis . . . Francisci Borgiae*, Introduction, pp. xix, xx–xxii.
Robert of Sicily; p. 207, ll. 20–24.
Roger of Normandy; p. 59, ll. 11–28.
Roger of Sicily; p. 17, ll. 7–17.
Romanus, pope; p. 230, ll. 19–25.
Romito; see Palmieri.
Rosate, Alberico de; p. 202, ll. 21–29.
Rosselli, Antonio; p. 140, ll. 1–16.
Rudolf, Duke of Swabia; p. 40, l. 29–p. 41, l. 4; p. 69, ll. 13–24.

Sâ, Emmanuel. *Aphorismi Confessionarum*, p. 140, l. 27–p. 141, l. 8; *Notationes in Totam Scripturam*, p. 55, ll. 24–28; *Scholia in Quatuor Evangelia*, p. 83, l. 33–p. 84, l. 4.
Sacrarum Cerimoniarum, sive Rituum Ecclesiasticorum Sanctae Romanae Ecclesiae; p. 46, ll. 5–14.
Sacrorum Conciliorum Nova et Amplissima Collectio. See Mansi.
Salmon, William. *Synopsis Medicinae. A Compendium of Physick, Chirurgey, and Anatomy*; p. 26, ll. 12–20.
Sancta Romana, decree; p. 34, ll. 23–24.
Sanders, Nicholas. *De Origine ac Progressu*, p. 182, ll. 12–20; *De Visibili Monarchia*, p. 188, ll. 7–10.
Sarpi, Paolo; p. 16, ll. 9–11.
Sayer, Gregory or Robert. *Casuum Conscientiae*, p. 263, ll. 24–34; *Clavis Regia*, p. 124, ll. 11–13; *De Censuris Ecclesiasticis*, p. 50, ll. 15–16.
Schardius, Simone. *Lexicon Iuridicium*, p. 56, l. 31–p. 57, l. 2; *De Iurisdictione, Auctoritate, et Praeeminentia Imperiali, ac Potestate Ecclesiastica*, Basel, 1566; p. 261, ll. 25–29.

Schlusselburg, Conrad; p. 257, ll. 20–27.
Scribanus, Charles; p. 119, ll. 18–35.
Schultingius, Cornelius. *Thesaurus Antiquitatem Ecclesiasticarum Ex Septem Prioribus Tomis Annalium Ecclesiasticorum Cardinales Caesaris Baronii*; p. 50, l. 20–p. 51, l. 7.
Sedulius, Henricus. *Apologeticus . . .libri tres*; p. 58, ll. 24–30; Introduction, p. xxii.
Senensis; see Franciscus Sixtus.
Septimes; p. 145, l. 33–p. 146, l. 17.
Sepulveda, Joannes Genesius; p. 47, ll. 12–15.
Serarius, Nicholas. *Litaneutici*, p. 53, l. 32–p. 54, l. 10; *Minerval divinis Hollandiae*, p. 261, ll. 6–17; *Trihaeresium*, p. 103, ll. 20–34.
Sergius II, pope; p. 252, ll. 20–22.
Sergius III, pope; p. 230, ll. 19–25.
Serrarius; see Serarius.
Serres, Jean de; p. 56, ll. 18–26.
Serranus; see Serres, Jean de.
Severus, Sulpitius; p. 148, l. 26–p. 149, l. 3.
Si Fratrem, canon; p. 221, ll. 5–22.
Silvius, Aenius; p. 118, ll. 11–13; see Pius II, pope.
Simancha, Iacobus. *De Republica*, and *Enchiridion Iudicium*; p. 44, ll. 31–34; p. 76, ll. 11–26.
Simplicius, pope; p. 40, ll. 12–20.
Sixtus II, pope; p. 212, ll. 6–15.
Sixtus III, pope; p. 192, ll. 2–8.
Sixtus IV, pope; p. 199, l. 12–p. 200, l. 3.
Sixtus V, pope; p. 45, ll. 14–27; p. 48, ll. 17–25.
Sommervogel, Carlos. *Bibliothèque de la Compagnie de Jésus*; p. 119, ll. 8–14.
Soto, Dominic de. *Commentariorum Fratris Dominici . . . in Quatrum Sententiarum*, p. 91, ll. 22–33; *Relectio . . . De Ratione Tegendi*, p. 57, ll. 17–21.
Southwell, Robert; p. 56, ll. 8–15.
Spongia Qua Absterguntur Convitia et Maledicta; p. 114, l. 36–p. 115, l. 5.
Stapleton, Thomas; p. 188, ll. 7–10.
Stella, Didacus; p. 96, ll. 25–30.
Stephanus de Avila, José Estève. *De Censuris Ecclesiasticis*, p. 107, ll. 27–32; *De Osculatione Pedum*, p. 77, l. 3–12.
Stephen I, pope; p. 61, ll. 5–18; p. 236, ll. 6–17.
Stephen II, pope; p. 63, ll. 21–29.
Stephen IV, pope; p. 64, ll. 17–24.
Stephen VI, pope; p. 230, ll. 19–25.

Steuchius, Augustine. *De Falsa Donatione Constantini*, Lyons, 1547; p. 39, ll. 7–24.
Storch; see Pelargus.
Strabo the Geographer; p. 76, ll. 11–26.
Suarez, Francis; p. 258, ll. 9–14.
Suse, Henri de; p. 117, l. 26–p. 118, l. 1.
Sylvester I, pope; p. 72, ll. 17–24.

Tacitus; p. 235, ll. 22–24.
Tanner, Adam; p. 131, ll. 14–17.
Telesphorus, pope; p. 96, ll. 16–25.
Tertullian; p. 265, ll. 11–18; *Aux Martyrs* in *Erreur Populaire de la Papesse Jane*, Lyons, 1595; p. 35, ll. 9–12.
Thaddeus of Suessa; p. 206, ll. 3–27.
Theatines; p. 102, ll. 12–17.
Theodoricus, doctor; p. 62, ll. 8–34.
Theodosius I, emperor; p. 52, l. 27–p. 53, l. 16.
Theodosius II, emperor. *Codicis Theodosiani*; p. 125, ll. 8–14.
Tholosanus; see Gregorius Petrus.
Thou, Jacques-Auguste de; p. 58, ll. 24–30.
Toledo, Francisco; p. 102, ll. 18–21.
Tolet, or **Toletus**, or **Toletanus**; see Toledo.
Torrez-Bullo, Diego. *Breve Relatione . . . Circa il frutto che si raccolie con gli Indiani di quel Regno*; p. 136, l. 27–p. 137, l. 20.
Torsellini, Horace; p. 99, l. 32–p. 100, l. 4.
Tortus, Matthew; p. 104, ll. 16–20; see Bellarmine, Robert.
Tudeschi, Nicolo de; p. 189, ll. 19–28.
Tursellinus; see Torsellino. in

Ubaldis, Baldus de; p. 53, ll. 21–30.
Ugolini, Bartolomeo. *De Justitia et Validitate Monitorii*, p. 172, l. 35–p. 173, l. 9; *Responsiones*, p. 126, ll. 1–19.
Unam Sanctam; p. 83, l. 33–p. 84, l. 4.
Urban II, pope; p. 17, ll. 7–17.
Urban VI, pope; p. 51, ll. 10–17.
Ursperger Chronicle; p. 205, l. 26–p. 206, l. 2.

Vaanus; p. 63, ll. 2–8.
Valdesio, Diego. *Praerogativa Hispaniae*; p. 49, ll. 2–5.
Valens, emperor; p. 125, ll. 8–14.
Valentinian, emperor; p. 52, l. 27–p. 53, l. 16.
Valeriano, Giovanni Pietro, also **Pierius**; p. 196, ll. 3–10.
Vasquez, Gabriel; p. 95, ll. 4–14.

Vegetius Renatus, Flavius. *De Re Militari*, Leyden, 1607; p. 27, l. 35–p. 28, l. 1.
Venerabilem, papal letter; p. 202, l. 30–p. 203, l. 17.
Venericus, bishop of Vercellus; p. 261, ll. 25–29.
Venice, State of; p. 126, ll. 1–19; p. 128, l. 24.
Verone, François de; p. 127, l. 37–p. 128, l. 11.
Victor III, pope; p. 214, ll. 15–26.
Victorellus, Andrea. *De Angelorum Custodia Lib. II In Quorum Altero Angelorum ministeria, ex Sacris Litteris rescentur*; p. 180, ll. 10–30.
Victoria, Francis à; p. 130, ll. 22–31.
Villagut, Alphonsus; p. 214, ll. 27–34.
Villavincentius, Laurentius; p. 95, ll. 18–28.
Vineis, Petrus de. *Friderici II. Imp. Rom. Epistolarum libri VI*; p. 198, ll. 24–31.

Visser, D.; p. 11, ll. 9–26.
Vitalian, pope; p. 63, ll. 2–8.
Vitruvius Pollionus or Polio; p. 14, ll. 9–10.
Vulgate Catholic Bible; p. 45, ll. 14–27; p. 101, ll. 15–19.

Watson, William; p. 110, ll. 15–18.
Whitaker, William. *Disputatio de Sacra Scriptura*, and *Praelectiones*; p. 11, ll. 26–30; p. 118, ll. 2–11.
Willot, Henry. *Athenae Orthodoxorum*; p. 90, ll. 11–13.
Windect, Johann Paul; p. 22, ll. 7–13.

Zacharias, pope; p. 74, ll. 1–7.
Zambrani, Melchior. *Aurea Decisiones*; p. 107, ll. 5–12.
Zeno, emperor; p. 40, ll. 12–20.
Zephyrinus, pope; p. 97, ll. 6–18.

GENERAL THEOLOGICAL SEMINARY
NEW YORK